Autobiographical Memories
by George Christopher Turner

CONTENTS

September 10th 1929 to August 31st 1

MY LIFE STORY

I

Autobiographical Memories of my Life
By George Christopher Turner

Growing up at home and school.

Chapter 1 My background - brief history of parents etc.

I was born at home on September 10th 1929 in what was then known as a slum area of Birmingham at 88 Mansfield Road, in the Parish of Lozells, Aston, (as my Dad once told me - between a Chemical Works and a Pickle Factory with Ansell's Brewery nearby!) in a two up, two down house. Apparently the houses were all joined together in a long row. Each one had a front doorstep that had to be holystoned regularly in order to keep it clean. According to my mother that was where most of the local gossip was passed around as the ladies formed part of a large but very close community - something of which they were very proud.

At that time my Father, George Frederick Turner, was living and working in the Parish of Lozells. He had one sister, Dorothy, born March 11th 1898, who emigrated to New Zealand and married Norman Bell of Balclutha, South Island, after the First World War. They lived at Palmerston on the South Island and had 4 children, Joan, Dorothy, George and Kathleen. My Father, born on August 2nd 1901, became a Church Army Captain and had been for around 10 years when I was born.

Father was educated at King's School, the Peterborough Cathedral School where he was a chorister. One amusing story about his schooldays is worth repeating. He did not enjoy running so when he was sent out for a school run he decided to nip through a wood and take a shortcut. Unfortunately he rejoined the race - near the end of course - too soon and came in 7th. As the first 8 runners home were nominated for the School running team he had to take part in the next Interschool race. He came in a very exhausted last and was soundly rated for his poor performance!

Father left School at 13 and went to train as an engineer at Brotherhoods - an Engineering Works in Peterborough. He spent 5 years there. Unfortunately at the age of 15 he suffered a horrific industrial accident. He lost the thumb and first finger of his left hand so he became a draughtsman.

In 1919 he felt that he had a calling to become an evangelist and so he joined the Church Army. He had a beautiful singing voice that he used to good effect all his life. He went twice to America and Canada in the 1920s, helping to set up the first Church Army Training College in Rhode Island, USA. He returned home and got married to my mother Rose Hannah on September 5th 1928 at Westerham in Kent where he worked for a spell before being sent to Birmingham. He had already taken part in several Church Army 'route marches' both in Canada and the US as well as around the UK, preaching and teaching - in the open air mainly, often on beaches at various seaside towns and villages. In 1930 he went to study for his General Ordination Exam at Lincoln Theological College. His Precentor at the college was the Reverend Arthur Ramsey who later became Archbishop of Canterbury. In December 1932 he was ordained, first as a Deacon and then, in December 1933, as a Priest, at the Parish of St James, Northampton. His Vicar there was the Reverend Norman Millard who later became my benefactor when I moved to Oakham School in 1943. Prior to that I had been a chorister at Magdalen College and a pupil at Magdalen College School, Oxford from April 1939 - more of that later.

In February 1936 my father became Chaplain to Camp Hill Borstal Institution on the Isle of Wight. When the Second World War began in 1939 the Borstal closed. Most of the inmates joined the armed forces and went to France in the British Expeditionary Force. Father subsequently became a Chaplain at what then became part of Parkhurst Prison. Many men, murderers amongst them, serving life sentences in prisons around Britain were transferred to Parkhurst - quite a gathering! In March 1941 the family moved to Northampton where he became Vicar of the Parish of St Mary, Far Cotton, in the Diocese of Peterborough. While there he was appointed as a non-residentiary Canon of Peterborough Cathedral. The family moved to Rothwell in Northamptonshire in November 1951 where father became Vicar of Holy Trinity Church, Rothwell and also of Orton Church, in the village nearby. He was appointed as Rural Dean in September 1954. He was there until September 1962. During his ministry at Rothwell his love of music was combined with a church that was noted for having the most perfect acoustics in Britain. He brought this to the attention of the management who looked after the interests of the London Philharmonic Orchestra. Concerts were arranged each year, most being conducted by Sir Adrian Boult. The Church could seat upwards of 1000 people and attracted people from many parts of the country. Canon George Turner, as he was known, had a great interest in Education and served for many years as Chairman of Kettering Divisional Education Committee and Chairman of the Governors of Kettering Grammar School.

Next my Father took up his ministry at Cranford with Grafton Underwood, on the Duke of Buccleuch's estate. Both villages were near Kettering. He retired in 1972 and went to live at Warkton, another village on the Duke's estate. His 'grace and favour' cottage, once a bakery just down the road from Warkton Church, dates back to 1623. As well as his ministry in the Church of England he served as a trustee on the board of Wicksteed Park, Kettering, for many years until his death in 1980. His ashes are buried in the graveyard of the Church of St John at Cranford. The gravestone for Mother and Father is near the Church door. There is a plaque to Father's memory on the north wall of the Church.

My Mother, Rose Hannah Tullett, was born on January 26th 1897 and lived her early life at West Wickham in Kent. The house where she spent those early days is shown in a painting by a family friend, Mr F.Fautley. As the youngest member of the family this original painting was left to her and is a valuable family heirloom. There are six other smaller copies of that picture and they were given to the 3 other brothers and 3 sisters. Mother worked as a secretary at Shell House on the north bank of the River Thames in London, not too far from the Houses of Parliament, during and after the First World War. Her sister Helena, known to everyone as Nell, who was married to William Cosgrove, had a sweet shop by the Green at Westerham in Kent. My mother often visited them. She met my father there when he was working as a Church Army Captain at the Parish Church of St Mary the Virgin, Westerham. They married at that Church on September 5th 1928.

As a matter of interest there are two statues on the Green at Westerham now. They are dedicated to General James Wolfe and Sir Winston Churchill. One of my earliest recollections was when I stayed at Westerham as a very small boy. My Aunt Nell was well known during the 1930s for making ice cream and people would come from miles around to sample her wares. Three girls, Sarah, Diana and Mary, used to serve sometimes in the shop and I was always the lucky recipient of free ice cream whenever we stayed there, hence my love of ice cream! The three 'shop assistants' were actually the daughters of Sir Winston Churchill who became Prime Minister during the Second World War. He lived at Chartwell, his home near Westerham. My cousins Bill and Molly Cosgrove were living at the shop in the early 30s too. My mother devoted her life to supporting my father in his Christian Ministry and spent much of her time furthering the cause of the Mothers' Union. She had a series of heart attacks starting in 1958 and was a virtual invalid until her death on August 1st 1968. She died and is buried with my Father at Cranford. Prior to her marriage she had a serious mastoid operation that left her paralysed on one side of her face. She had a loving and generous personality and was a strong influence during my early days. Unsurprisingly she did not have many photos taken, but there are one or two amongst our collection of family photographs. Her ashes are in the family grave.

My Mother's family were as follows:

Her Father - William Tullett was born at Handcross in Sussex on Oct 10th 1850. He died at The Green, Westerham, Kent on May 25th 1931.

Her Mother - Hannah Tullett (nee Willis) was born at Isham, Northamptonshire on April 1st 1851. She died at The Green, Westerham, Kent on April 8th 1935. They were married at St Andrew's Church, Burnsbury, on April 30th 1883. Their children were all born at West Wickham, Kent.

James Edward Tullett - born on August 4th 1884. He emigrated to New Zealand and married Kate Smith at St Paul's Church, Wellington on November 27th 1916.
He died at Wellington on September 29th 1965. They had one daughter – Kathleen, who married Derry Pointon. They lived at Raumati, North Island, New Zealand.

Annie Louisa Tullett – born on November 20th 1885. She became companion to a descendent of royalty - Miss Russell. She died at Beckley in Kent on April 1st 1955.

Arthur Victor Tullett was born on May 25 1887. He married Ella M. Fusselle on April 16th 1912. They had 3 children – Victor, Eric (Tom) & Daphne Rose.

He died in a motorcycle accident on Jan 12th at West Wickham, Kent.

Harry Tullett was born on May 20th 1889. He married Eleanor Collier on June 30th 1914. He died on May 19th 1943. Eleanor died in the flu' epidemic of 1918. They had 1 son - Gilbert. Harry later had a partner named Steppie. They had two children - Jimmy and Yvonne.

Mary Helena Tullett was born on February 27th 1891.
She married William Cosgrove on December 26th 1912.
She died on July 19th 1978. They had two children - William James and Mollie.

Grace Hackney Tullett was born on August 30th 1892. She became a Nun in 1927, joining the Society of the Sisters Of Bethany. She died on May 13th 1977.

Minnie Eliza Tullett was born on December 23rd 1894. She died on January 7th 1895.

Chapter 2 Early Days

What I know about my earliest days stems mainly from what I was told by my parents. I was born with a severe heart murmur, which necessitated constant medical monitoring. At 18 months, while Mother and I were staying with my Aunt at Westerham, I contracted pneumonia, apparently due to travelling in an open sidecar in foggy wet weather. My Father was a keen motorcyclist so that was our mode of transport. By the time the pneumonia developed Father had gone back to his College at Lincoln where he was studying to enter the Church Ministry. Apparently I got worse despite medical attention and my Father was sent for. The story goes that once he got to see me I started to get better, but I gather that it was a close call!

My earliest personal memories go back to early 1933. My Father had been made a Deacon in 1932. Our home was now at 4, Althorpe Road, St James, Northampton where my father started his Church of England ministry. The house was small, and backed on to a cobbled alleyway at the end of the yard. My first real memory as a three year old was very painful - I had been given an old pedal car and I managed somehow to open the back gate. Unfortunately I did not allow for the fact that there was quite a drop down to the cobbles. I went headfirst out of the car onto my head and finished up being picked up and carted back into the house with bumps and bruises but very little sympathy!

One man I shall always remember was Mr Alf Smith, who was our local butcher and a family friend. Every time I went with my parents to visit he would say to me, 'When you can wiggle your ears one at a time I will give you the biggest red rosy apple I have got in my store'. He would then wiggle each ear separately for my benefit! I spent literally hours and hours trying to do his bidding until one day the miracle happened and I was able to claim that apple! It is something which I have never seen done by anybody else, but I utilised that skill so often that I was able to show others as a child, and later in life I used it to very good effect when I became a teacher - for some reason children were - and still are - fascinated by seeing my ears waggling one at a time! I would often tell the younger children at School (and elsewhere) stories and say that if someone talked while I was telling a story my right ear would start to wiggle. I think they were more fascinated by watching than listening! The left one wiggled if they had behaved so luckily that ear got more practice!

One lady in particular, again, I shall never forget. Her name was Mrs 'Flo' Robinson and she was a member of St James's Churchhe often used to 'babysit' at our house. When I got a bit older but still at preschool age, I was taken to her house at number 24 Symington Street, a short walk from home. Again, one thing stands out even today in my mind. The toilet was at the end of the garden and the so-called 'loo' roll was torn up bits of newspaper. This was explained by telling me that one could first read the news before using it for other purposes! That was ok in summer but winter was not good as the water froze and that caused chaos! I spent many happy hours with her and as I grew up, although we had left Northampton, we always went to see her and Ted, her husband. He had died fairly young, having been badly gassed in the trenches during the first World War and he had difficulty in breathing. But he was a kindly man whom I grew fond of too. There are many stories I could tell about them and their son Charles, but one springs readily to mind. 'Auntie Flo' always fed me on sausages. That is where I gained my love of eating them - something I have enjoyed all my life. Habits die hard! On one occasion I was offered sausages for dinner as usual, but I knew that I was really supposed to go home early. So I just said, "Yes please, I would like some". She bought some from Alf Smith's, the butcher, and took me to her house. When we arrived I then told her I had to go straight home and could not stay for lunch. Instead I took the sausages home. Very resourceful I thought but no one else agreed and I was in trouble!

I was something of an embarrassment to my parents on several occasions, as I fear I was no saint as a small boy. One day, when father was doing his rounds, calling on parishioners, he arranged to call at a house containing two elderly unmarried sisters. Their family name was Butcher and they were well known in the parish as the Miss Butchers. My Father and Mother both told me, 'When one of the Miss Butchers ask you to take your hat off, politely say no thank you. We shall tell them that we cannot stay to tea as your Father has a meeting'. Unfortunately I had heard my Father say to Mum, 'I do not want to stop at the Miss Butchers - we shall never get away. We will tell Christopher what to say'. They did, but I embellished it considerably when asked to take my hat off. I replied, 'No thank you. My daddy does not want to stay as he thinks you talk too much and he will never get away'. There was complete consternation all round and father had some explaining to do. I gather that tact was not my greatest asset as a small child! On another occasion I decided that I wanted to cut some paper up but I was not allowed to use scissors. However I found the scissors when my mother went out a bit later and I proceeded to 'cut' my hair. As a punishment I was made to walk up the street with no hat on. Looking back I don't suppose anyone noticed but at the age of only three and a half I didn't realise that and I yelled blue murder the whole time we were out! My great Aunt Annie Sewell - I always called her

Great Aunt Sewell – never Annie, although I cannot imagine why - used to come over from Peterborough to stay with us from time to time and would volunteer to baby-sit. She had been a Headmistress and she must have decided that it was time for me to go to bed. I was unwilling to go and she got cross. I duly kicked her, unfortunately just as my parents returned. Needless to say my Father was very cross and so I finished up with an extremely tender posterior! However she must have forgiven me as she was kind to me in one particular way. She used to make the most scrumptious fruit cake and whenever we went over to see my Grandad at   number 392 Lincoln Road, Peterborough, she would always give me a big cake to take home. My Great Aunt Annie Sewell lived with my Grandfather for several years - I think to look after him after my Grandma died. Sadly I do not remember her as she died soon after I was born.

Another story of note concerned a present that I was given for Christmas 1933. The present was a clockwork train that my Father's Vicar, the Rev. E.N.Millard, had bought as a special treat. We had gone to spend Christmas Day with him. As soon as it was put together I was ready to play - but, oh no – I was made to sit inside the oval track and watch all afternoon while two grown men played with a clockwork train. Every time I tried to join in I was told to sit quietly and watch as I should only break everything. That was probably true too but I was not too impressed at the time!

Chapter 3 Education - My Early Schooldays

At the age of four I went to St James CE School that was situated behind our house. The headmistress was a severe lady named Miss Bradley. She ruled the place with a firm hand and it certainly did not pay to step out of line. Naturally I did and caused more problems for my parents. In my early days at school I could somehow never master the art of standing still and in the right line, waiting to go to my classroom. Inevitably I finished up in the wrong room on several occasions and so when registers were taken I was to be found outside Miss Bradley's office looking and feeling completely lost. However I must have improved as I managed to get the job of milk monitor. That only lasted a few days as I helped myself both before and after I had given the bottles out - the trouble was I liked milk! My final fall from grace came one day when I was learning to write. All went well at first, but then I was shown how to make a full stop. I liked the dot but it seemed too small so I embellished it into a blot. That apparently wasn't the object of the exercise and once again I finished up in Miss Bradley's office. The problem was that whenever my Father came into St James's School he was regaled with stories about his wayward son so I got into trouble again when I got home!

So much for St James C.E. School - I survived my initiation into the world of Education and, more importantly, the School managed to put up with me despite my ability to get into scrapes. This was an ominous sign for the future according to my final report, so my Mother told me. However in 1936 my Father moved to the Isle of Wight when he was appointed Chaplain of Camp Hill Borstal Institution. I was enrolled at a School for the sons and daughters of Gentlefolk - in Newport, the Capital town of the Island. That was a right laugh for a start! I arrived and was taken to a classroom where, as I recall, the 'desk' was a long sloping wooden affair, rather like a trestle table. There were about 8 children sitting side by side. Each child had an inkwell in front of his or her section of the desk and a sort of open drawer where books were kept. The secretary would take the roll call each morning. The teacher had taken registration at my previous school and we had to say 'present' or someone else would say 'absent' if we were missing. But the words used to announce one's presence at this new School meant absolutely nothing to me. 'Abest' or 'Adsum' - my ignorance was profound and I just used to guess. Sometimes I said one, at other times I mouthed the other. At the end of the second week, according to the register, I had been away for more days than I had been ticked present! Needless to say this did not go down too well with the Headmistress. When my parents were asked why I had missed so many days they were mystified as they had delivered me at the School gate every morning. I found out the hard way – 'Adsum' is latin for 'I am here'. 'Abest' is the latin for 'He (or She) is away'.

The other children had started to learn latin a year or two before - I hadn't! This was not a good start and I fear that things went from bad to worse. After only one term I was summarily removed across the road to a Preparatory School for boys at Newport Grammar School and I guess at last I was able to settle down. Naughty boys were common enough so I did not stand out any more. But I had one cross to bear. Having been born with a pronounced heart murmur, this prevented me from playing games so my lunchtime was spent resting - against my will, naturally - in the Headmaster's study. In those days lunch break was two hours. However, that apart, I enjoyed my time there. My chief recollection was seeing teachers wearing gowns - a common practice in those days as most of the teachers must have been to University and so were entitled to dress that way. At least we knew who the teachers were.

My School reports started to improve quite considerably. My Father, a very talented singer, noted that I too had that in common with him. During games lessons and sometimes after School I attended singing classes with a certain Mr Hare. Actually he was as bald as a coot and I found this highly amusing at the time as the spelling did not matter. But he was a lovely person who understood children and who could get the best from them. I worked hard to improve my one talent. I had the ability to pitch notes unaided and apparently this gave me an edge over other would be singers. He recommended that I should be given a voice test with a choir. I was accepted as a local Church choirboy in 1938 but almost immediately I was entered for two professional choirs - Winchester Cathedral and Magdalen College, Oxford.

I went with my Father to Magdalen College, Oxford first, for the voice test. There were about twenty five boys being tested that day and two were required to join what was then considered to be one of the three top choirs in the country - St George's Chapel, Windsor and King's College, Cambridge were the others. The test was comprehensive indeed. Initially I was asked to sing one of two prepared pieces from the Messiah. The first was called 'How beautiful are the feet of them that preach the Gospel of Peace'. This I duly did while standing at the front of the music room. I was then called to stand by the piano and was asked to sing a note - middle C. I waited, thinking that I would be given the note first, but no - I had to pitch it myself. Luckily, as I had what is called in musical parlance 'perfect pitch', it was easy.

Following that test various other notes were then requested and I picked them out satisfactorily. I then had to 'read' a piece of music and sing the relevant notes and again that went well. Finally I was requested to sing my second piece from the Messiah - 'Come unto him, all ye that labour and I will give you rest'. I then had to sit and wait while Dr McKie decided whom he wanted. The outcome was that I was one of only two boys starting in the summer term of 1939. It meant that at 9 years old I would be away at School. As all School fees were paid by the College that apparently made me a professional singer. Naturally my Father was delighted at this success and we boarded the train back to Southampton in order to catch the passenger ferry back across the Solent to Ryde on The Isle of Wight. At Ryde there is a pier about a quarter of a mile long and the passengers had to disembark at the pier head. A train carried the passengers off the pier but we walked instead. Mother was waiting at the other end for our return and I remember running up to her saying, 'I did it! I did it! I won!' I guess she was pleased too although she told me later that the thought of me being away from home at the tender age of nine appalled her.

Chapter 4 Magdalen College School, Oxford - leaving home

My boarding school career started in late April 1939. My Father had recently become the proud owner of a 1928 Morris Cowley car, bought for the princely sum of £10 - a lot of money in those days. It had two seats at the front under a canvas roof and a 'dicky' seat behind which was folded down when not in use. We set off from the Isle of Wight and crossed the Solent on the car ferry from Cowes to Portsmouth in the early hours, then drove to Oxford where I was taken into Magdalen College School boarding house and introduced to a severe looking lady known only as matron.   My cases were left and then we went out to the car and stopped on Magdalen Bridge. This was the moment I had been dreading and the tears were not far away. My Mother gave me a big hug and the 'waters' broke for both of us. Father said rather gruffly, "Come on Mother. Time to go. We have a boat to catch". I naturally wanted to go too but the moment of truth had arrived. I stood very forlornly on the Bridge - a homesick little boy of 9 - while my parents drove away. I returned to the School and the Matron sympathetically took me into her room until I was ready to go and meet other boys in the Choir. Once that happened things brightened up considerably. There were only 16 of us altogether. We had to report at School a week before the rest of the boys as we had to practise the music that is sung by the choir on May Day every year from the top of Magdalen College Tower. We attended the School as Choir Scholarship boys and, as I found out a week later, our School days were very different from those of other boarders and dayboys. Each morning of that first week we dressed in white shirts with eton collars, black trousers and black Marlborough coats. Next we put on our gowns and mortarboards and walked across Magdalen Bridge to the College where we had a choir practice room. Each day we practised the music selected for the singing on top of the tower and we also went through the Church music that was to be sung at evensong. This took place every evening in the College Chapel. There were 7 choir men who made up our numbers. They of course sang the alto, tenor and bass lines of our music. Being 'plunged in at the deep end' so to speak was very hard at first but I soon adapted as I loved the singing that we did above all else. The music was beautiful to hear and to be part of those making it was for me a great experience – but more of that later.

Chapter 5 First experiences

May 1st 1939 was the May Day permanently etched on my memory. It was my first big musical event. We got up at about half past four in the morning and after a drink and a biscuit set off in gowns and mortarboards to walk across Magdalen Bridge to the College choir practice room. There we put on our Choir robes - black cassocks and white surplices - before proceeding in a column of twos around the cloisters and thence to the tower entrance. Here I got my first shock. We had to climb wooden steps before settling off up a spiral staircase leading to the roof on the tower. It seemed to me to go up for ever but at last we reached the top - puffed out. Then our Choirmaster, Dr Willam McKie, indicated where he wished us to stand. We lined up adjacent to the microphones that would broadcast our singing on the radio and also to the crowds of people down below. The roof, which was wet from what I can only assume was morning dew, was sloping up to an apex. I slipped and slid down to the edge of the tower where my feet actually finished against one of the tower portals and for a terrifying second or two I could see straight below to the ground 144 feet below. I have suffered from vertigo ever since! I scrambled shakily back to my place and we sang the music which must have sounded beautiful to all those below - some in punts on the river, others on the bridge or street nearby, and yet more in the college grounds. Eventually we retraced our steps down to ground level and were rewarded with a substantial breakfast. Then we were taken out to the College boat landing stage and got into two punts. Choirs are normally divided into two sides in chapels and cathedrals. On the south side, looking towards the altar, are known as 'Decani' and on the north side are termed 'Cantoris'.

The words 'Decani' and 'Cantoris' are Latin. The former means literally 'singers on the side where the Dean sits' and the latter means 'leaders of singing'. Used in the choir sense where tunes were written as duets on the treble lines of music the boys on 'Decani' sang the top treble notes and 'Cantoris' sang the lower treble notes. Naturally there is always great rivalry between the two sides whenever competition can be found and punting was no exception. We boys had a paddle each and knelt down ready to propel the punt. University singing students usually augmented the choir each year so two of them would invariably volunteer to use the punt poles to push and steer in the respective punts. I vividly recall on that occasion seeing the 'Decani' punt way out in front of us when the unfortunate student steering that punt got his pole stuck in the river bed and performed a gentle parabola into the water! Needless to say we quickly caught up and passed the hapless student and then the rudderless 'Decani' punt to cheers from the river bank and shouts of glee from us! All in all that was quite an introduction to my earliest days as a professional chorister.

There were several perks too for the choir. We would give concerts, sing at weddings and various other public functions and every time we were given money - perhaps a shilling (5p) or even half a crown (12.5p) to spend. Those amounts sound very small now but in those days a shilling could buy a lot of things that these days would probably cost several pounds, so we did quite well. For me it was virtually my only pocket money apart from, initially, a penny a week. This eventually went up, after three or four years, to 6d (2.5p). Wages in those days were often measured in shillings per week for the man in the street and families had to be brought up on that. I recall with great clarity the pleasure and excitement that we felt when the opportunity to set off from our boarding house with what to me was true riches – money that we had earned by singing at weddings and concerts. I cannot remember any of the names of the shops from where we made purchases. However I do recall one of the toys we all bought on one occasion. Once the war had begun on September 3rd 1939 it was inevitable that model aeroplanes soon came top of the list. These models were made of lead and cost one shilling (5p) for a 'Hurricane' or a 'Spitfire'. These were the Royal Air Force fighters that fought for Britain against the German aeroplanes. Later on there were other planes too of course, but they were more expensive as they were bombers such as the two engined 'Wellington'. We used to play a bombing game with very sharp pencil compasses dropped from a great height, standing on a chair – quite skilful - but also dangerous!

Chapter 6 Boarding routines at School

The weekly routine began when the other pupils returned to the school boarding house. We were roused at 7.30am by a prefect who was in charge of the dormitory. Washrooms were outside the dormitory and there was always a rush to get in first. There were a few basins and three or four baths so competition was fierce! Baths were used only in the evenings and there was a strict rota. Water had to be shared as there were lots of us and only a few baths. I can remember the fun we had at bath time. There was a game we called 'flicks'. This could be played by any number of us. The idea was to undress ready for your turn in the bath and, while waiting, 'flick' your fellow bathers with your towel without getting 'flicked' yourself. When towel ends got wet it could be very painful and there were many red marks left on one's skin by the time we were finished. There was only one rule - no 'flicking' at anyone in a bath. Officially it was frowned on of course, and if we were caught there was often the added pain of a cane across one's backside afterwards! But invariably, if you were involved you owned up. Sneaking was just not done. But woe betide either a sneak or someone who did not own up - you could not win! In fact 'telling' on one's fellow pupils was seriously frowned on whatever the reason and retribution was swift if that happened. Boys could be very cruel to other boys!

We choirboys had to wear our school caps, white shirts with eton collars, black Marlborough coats and pinstripe trousers, while the other boys wore white shirts with soft collars, grey jackets and trousers. In the boarding house we were supposed to wear plimsolls in order to try and keep floors clean and change our shoes when we went out. We each had a shoe locker and these, by common consent, were never touched. On the whole, as juniors, we all got on well enough as we were more or less united by the fact that we had to act as 'fags' for the prefects and senior boys. This meant that any odd jobs such as cleaning shoes, tidying rooms and running errands etc. had to be done whenever required. It was something of a lottery really. If you 'fagged' for a good senior prefect that was fine, but sadly there were some senior boys who took great delight in making life difficult for us. Bullying was rife, with some of us often on the wrong end of trouble. Prefects ran the house and saw to everyday routines. They also had the responsibility to see that discipline was maintained and any minor infraction of rules was quickly punished by having to write lines, copy Latin (very hard) and sometimes learn English or Latin Verses (even harder!). More serious misdemeanours were punished by strokes of a cane on the backside and 'sergeant's stripes' were commonplace. Often we were given a choice - 100 lines or '6 of the best'. I always chose the latter as it was over more quickly and I hated writing lines or learning latin verses!

Our 'studies' were fairly spacious and there were usually 5 or 6 of us to each room. We had our own 'tuck box' in which our worldly goods were stored and these boxes also doubled as chairs for much of the time. There was a communal table in each room where we supposed to do our homework. There was little other furniture apart from four chairs so we took turns to use them. Invariably anyone given lines to write as punishment got precedence. This worked well except when we all got into trouble for making too much noise or fooling around! We had 'prep' to do in the evenings and it was hard for we choristers as, after evensong in the College Chapel, we had to walk about half a mile back to school and then start work. But one soon got used to the routine and the boarding house staff were decent enough - not that we saw them that often. I remember two of the various head prefects' names. One was Chavasse and another, after him, was Rees. They reported to higher authority, usually to the second master, Mr Stannier, when necessary.

But in fact our real nemesis was the Headmaster, Mr R. Kennard-Davis. He was the ultimate 'ruler' of our world and woe betide those who crossed his path! Only genuinely serious misdemeanours were reported to him by Mr Stannier. The Head's dwelling was opposite the boarding house so he was never too far away, but he rarely visited us except when we had our evening meals, and then he sat on the top table with the duty housemaster, staff and the prefects.

On my first arrival at school the meals were quite reasonable as there were no great shortages, but after the war had been going for a while rationing was introduced and food became difficult to come by. But we just ate whatever was there - one could not afford to be choosy and we were taught to eat up everything put on our plates. I recall that when potatoes were in short supply we had rice instead. There was little fruit and luxuries were non-existent. Meat dishes became an occasional treat. There was something loosely termed as 'powdered egg'. It really was revolting but hunger soon put a stop to worrying about taste! There was also powdered milk (Klim) for when real milk was scarce. Porridge was our staple diet at breakfast as oatmeal was in plentiful supply. We had to queue for that. Occasionally the cooks got it wrong and the porridge was burnt - but we still ate it. The bread we had varied considerably and often came in what we called 'doorsteps'. This simply meant that slices were very thick and so filled us up. Butter was a luxury we seldom had - a sort of margarine was doled out and served the purpose well enough. Again, jam or marmalade on Sundays was a great treat for us.

Unsurprisingly we were constantly made aware, and rightly so, that sailors were risking their lives to get ships laden with edible goods, including fish, from abroad. Merchant ships were regularly being sunk by German 'U' boats and food shortages were serious. America had not entered the war then and so was a neutral country although much of our food was obtained from the US under normal trading agreements. Sweets were virtually unobtainable and we used to buy some sort of glucose tablets that, fortunately, were harmless. With rationing being so strict only absolute essentials were imported. One seldom, if ever, saw anyone who was fat, but paradoxically we were fit enough as luxury goods such as ice creams, soft drinks and sweets virtually disappeared. Inevitably there was an economy known as 'the black market' where extra food and meat could be obtained unofficially if grown-ups had the money. Some boys mysteriously received extras such as jam and cakes from home. Wisely they shared them around! It also paid to be friendly with a farmer or two according to common belief as they produced milk, meat and certain other goods in the first place. One early slogan that became a by-word was DIG FOR VICTORY. Allotments and gardens were mainly used to grow vegetables and thus families could supplement their meagre rations. I suppose everyone who could do so joined in. Posters were on hoardings everywhere and warned us of the dangers of being overheard and thus giving away secrets. Three examples were:- 'CARELESS TALK COSTS LIVES', 'DIG FOR VICTORY' and 'BE LIKE DAD - KEEP MUM'. It took me a while to work that one out! Each poster was made up as a cartoon in order to catch the eye, but they all carried a serious message.

Chapter 7 Life as a Choirboy

There were several perks too for the choir. We would give concerts, sing at weddings and various other public functions and every time we were given money - perhaps a shilling (5p) or even half a crown (12.5p) to spend. Those amounts sound very small now but in those days a shilling could buy a lot of things, which these days would probably cost several pounds, so we did quite well. For me it was virtually my only pocket money apart from, initially, a penny a week. After three or four years this eventually went up to 6d (2.5p). Wages in those days were often measured in shillings per week for the man in the street. Families had to be brought up on that.

Our days were very busy, particularly as choristers. Each morning we went to the College for choir practice under the watchful eye of Dr William McKie - later to become Sir William McKie. We knew him as 'Daddy Mac' - but not to his face of course. He was a kind and considerate man whom we grew to love and respect. He was a superb musician and set very high standards. He had a profound influence on me and was a fine example to us all. He continued with our voice training and I eventually became a regular soloist in the choir. It was a sad day indeed when he told us he had joined the Royal Australian Air Force to serve in the war. In his place a man by the name of Dr Hylton Campbell Stewart came out of retirement and took over once again. He had been Choirmaster until 1938. He was another delightful person for whom we had great love and respect. As well as evensong each day we would frequently give concerts at the college - usually on the grass area within the cloisters or in the College grounds. These were always well attended and must have given great pleasure to many, particularly to those servicemen who were on leave. I recall Dr Stewart once telling us that we 'represented a modicum of sanity in a war torn world' and he explained just what he meant by saying we 'brought a glimpse of peace to people in wartime'. I never forgot that and we understood better then why we sang so often to audiences at college and also to those who listened on the radio as most concerts were broadcast. From then on I felt that singing solos was an added privilege for me and I felt great pride and satisfaction because I could give pleasure to others with my voice, although, sadly, I never heard myself singing as records were a rarity then. When I went home for holidays, although he often got me to sing solos at his church services, my father would never have my voice recorded as he felt I might get too bigheaded! That was a great shame and something he also regretted in later life.

There are several events that took place during my singing career at Magdalen that stand out in my mind. On one occasion we broadcast a combined concert at Oxford with the Choir of Saint George's Chapel, Windsor. This was considered to be a major highlight in the annals of both Choirs and attracted a vast audience in the hall where we performed and also on the radio. Regrettably I cannot recall the music that we sang but I remember that we performed both as individual choirs and also sang certain pieces together too. All this was very well received and the applause was deafening! But my main memory concerns our clothes. We wore Marlborough jackets and choristers from St George's Chapel wore short Eton jackets. This provided us with much verbal ammunition and there were comments in both directions. But it was a unique occasion because travelling anywhere excited comment. Petrol was only allowed for essential services and we were very envious as they had come by train! In those days going anywhere was a real treat.

Another memory concerns a concert sung one Christmas Eve. We had to stay on at school after everyone else had gone home and we were not too pleased. However, we duly performed the concert before many distinguished guests including the Master of the King's Music, Sir Geoffrey Parratt, and Sir Sydney Nicholson, a famous composer and musician of the day. The Dean of Magdalen College, the Reverend Adam Fox, was also present, together with many Senior Members of the various other Colleges - and their families - that make up Oxford University.

If we were up to no good we always posted a 'watchman' whose job was to warn us of unwelcome 'visitors'. Prefects would also check that we were doing whatever prep work had been set. If a prefect shouted 'fag' we all rushed to get to him first on the grounds that he who was last got the unwanted job. Then the rest of us could return to our rooms. In my first term, just prior to the Second World War against Germany, I became a 'personal fag' for a kindly prefect. His name was Kirby and he treated me well - especially if I made him a decent cup of tea and toast done on an open fire in winter. Sadly, when war was declared on September 3rd 1939 he had just left school. He went with the British Expeditionary Force to France and tragically was killed in the early days of the war. His name was read out in School assembly one morning and his name is one of the first on the School Memorial list dedicated to those who gave their lives in the Second World War. Furthermore many of the teachers were called up to join the forces and inevitably a number of ex-teachers were brought out of retirement and dragooned into taking the places of those young men on the staff. I suspect that discipline suffered and life must have been hard for those in charge. Prefects had greater responsibilities thrust upon them and boarding house rules were stringently adhered to. But I fear that my ability to get into trouble was undiminished and I reckon that most weeks in each term I managed to upset prefects as I saw the wrong end of the cane with monotonous regularity. The misdemeanours were not always bad although I must admit to doing certain things deliberately from time to time. We had to run baths for the prefects and were expected to see that the temperature of the water was right. I invariably made baths too hot or too cold - often with malice aforethought! I got on well with my study-mates but my peers were much less enthusiastic about me and I soon learned a few tricks - like hiding in cupboards when being required to answer for my so-called sins! There was a certain irony too which failed to endear me to older pupils. Because of my heart murmur I was not allowed to play games – football, rugby, cricket or hockey. But I could run and had some talent at table tennis.

There was one older boy with the surname of Mertz - a 16 year old Austrian whose family had fled from their home country. They were Jews and had been persecuted by the Nazis. He was an excellent table tennis player and he taught me everything he knew about the game. After the war he and his family were probably able to return to their home. He apparently won a championship in England first although I cannot vouch for this as it was years later that by chance I saw a sports list in a national newspaper and his name appeared. I learned quickly and within a year as a ten year old I was winning games against older boys. We had a house team and so I was tolerated as Mertz and I won virtually every time we competed. But I never beat him even once. However things came to a head in the house competition. I got through to the semi-final and at the age of 11 found that I was playing another Jewish boy of 18 named Neumann whose family had escaped from Germany. He and Mertz did not get on as there was little love lost between the Germans and the Austrians at the school so my table tennis 'teacher', who had already qualified for the final gave me his backing. I won fairly comfortably but to be beaten by an 11 year old was more than Neumann could stand. He was a bully - doubtless as a result of being ill treated by the Hitler youth in Germany - and the result was that I was beaten up and kicked by him and a pal or two and was bruised quite badly. Mertz and his cronies joined in the fray on my behalf and honour was satisfied. Sneaking about things like that was not popular so I made up some excuse or other to the matron and that was that. I expect she realised perfectly well what had happened as fights were frequent in those days.

In the final I lost to Mertz. We remained friends until I left the school in 1943. In fact I reached the finals twice more but he always finished up the winner. I won several times at Oakham School and in 1967 I went to Vichy, France, as a senior student of 37 and won a tournament there at the University. I had not played for several years but the skills soon came back with practice. I also reached the semi-final of a competition at the Argentat Campsite when we were on holiday there some years later. But to return to MCS - our real coup-de-gras turned out to be when a fellow pupil returned from his home in Purley, London. There had been regular air raids on London during 1940 and German planes dropped thousands of bombs. One of these had landed on his house and had penetrated the roof but failed to go off. He had found it in his room and secretly brought it back to school hidden in his case! As I recall it was not too heavy. We kept it in the study for several days and, as boys would do, played with it. Inevitably our 'trophy' was discovered and the six of us involved were summoned to see Mr Davis, the Headmaster. To our horror he first called the police and then an army bomb disposal soldier arrived and removed the bomb. We were given six strokes of the cane each on our backsides by Mr Kennard Davis, the Headmaster, because we were deemed to have put other lives in danger as well as our own. Later, when we were summoned back to the Head's study, the soldier had returned to say that the bomb had been live and it had been detonated. We were then warned of the dangers of playing with unexploded bombs and other suspicious objects as well - a bit late! That was the end of the affair. However that same day I was in trouble for some other misdemeanour and this time was given the choice - write 100 lines or be caned. As usual I chose the caning as the pain was already there! This brought the total of strokes administered to twelve for the day – an unenviable record!

Being brought up in this environment inevitably had much to do with the formation of my character and one lesson I learned came about one day when I was playing with a friend called Michael Revell. He was not strong and had been the butt of bullies from time to time. On this occasion a Jewish boy with the surname of Paiba, who was about a year older than I, started hitting Michael. I tried to stop him so he turned on me. All the hurt and resentment of bullies that I felt surfaced and I just ignored the pain and kept fighting to such effect that I really hurt him and he ran away crying to his two elder brothers who were in the boarding house. He was taken to the school sanatorium after treatment. I had chased him up to the house and the two brothers grabbed me and asked what had happened. I told them, frightened that they would hit me. Amazingly the older boy said, "Good. He needed a lesson". He then told me of the terrible time they had all had in Germany as Jews - of the burning of their parents' shop by Nazis and of the beatings they had received from Hitler Youth bullies. This had led the youngest to believe that fighting was the only normal way that he should behave so, after he had escaped to England just

17

before the war, he had turned to bullying to get what he wanted. He was really too young to differentiate between his treatment in Germany and here in Oxford and his brothers wanted him to learn. I was very upset and went to say sorry. At first he turned his back to me but then we spoke a few words. That was it. There was no problem with the Housemaster who understood. We did not become close friends but he gave up bullying and I resolved never again to really lose my temper to the point where I did not care what happened. After all, I had been hurt too. But I learned a lesson for life that day myself!

Chapter 8 School procedures at MCS

The first thing I clearly recall on being put into Class Junior 1 was that we split into three different groups. There were Dayboys, Choirboys and House boarders and this caused a bit of a problem at first. But these divisions soon disappeared as we got to know each other better. When the bell was rung we all lined up and trooped off to our classrooms. Different teachers taught the various subjects so there was a constant change of face at the front of the class. Class registers were taken by one's so called class teacher. He was the master who was ultimately responsible for us if there were any problems – good or bad! I did not start too well I fear. One teacher's name was Mr Johns who had the nickname of 'Botty' as he had an ample backside I think. I had only heard the name 'Botty' from one of my classmates as I had been away when he had come in to teach the first lesson. The next time he came he asked who I was and I replied 'Turner, Mr Botty.' He was NOT impressed and I had to write his correct name 40 times as a punishment! For we choirboys work was something of a lottery. We had a choir practice every morning of the week in the practice room at Magdalen College. It took us a while to walk to and from the College and we practised for an hour. So we missed a lot of schooling – usually Maths and Latin - so in the afternoons when the rest were doing English and Art we had to make up our Maths and Latin work before rejoining for the less arduous subjects like English Literature. No wonder I have never been good at art over the years!

When the war started on September 3rd 1939 the younger staff went off to join the forces and older teachers were brought out of retirement to take over. It must have been hard for them but they were very much pre-war veterans who ruled with firm hands! Mr Davis, the Headmaster, was much in evidence too if there was trouble – so was his cane. In fact all the staff had canes in those days and it did us little harm other than to toughen us up. It was accepted practice and no one worried about it. Caning was the option offered if one did not want to do lines. I always opted for the cane when pressed – it was over quicker and did not affect my after school activities, whatever they were.

Before school commenced, at playtimes and at dinner times there was plenty of fun and games going on. The School had quite a lot of 'shinty' sticks and several red hard rubber balls. A shinty stick was shaped like an inverted walking stick with the equivalent of the walking stick handle being flat. This part was about 8 inches long and the game of shinty was like hockey. At least it was the way we played it. For some reason this was a very popular game and the playground enabled those wanting to play to do so. The actual playing area was marked out and if one was lucky enough to get a shinty stick one was picked by a captain to play for one side or the other. Those not playing used the areas around the pitch and between the classrooms.

Sporting activities had a high priority and there was a Training Corps for boys who fancied joining the forces after they left School. Of course once the war started there was no longer a choice as every able-bodied male was called up either to fight or to take their part in what was considered an essential occupation such as manufacturing munitions, working in factories and so on. Men were sometimes sent into mining. They were known as Bevin Boys after the Cabinet Minister, Ernie Bevin, who was responsible for that side of things. There was also a troop of cubs and Scouts for the younger pupils.

Various activities took place closely connected with School studies. I remember when there was an outdoor production of a Shakespeare play 'The Tempest' that was performed by the School cast on the far end of the playing field. The 'ship' that foundered in the storm was actually built on the floating wooden raft, or platform, where boats were normally brought in after rowing. This was superbly designed and the idea was that it floated down the river, landing on the riverbank adjacent to where the play was taking place. Everything went perfectly for the first two days. The weather was fine and there was no wind. However on the third occasion the wind got up and, instead of the ship 'docking' near the stage setting, the wind caught it and it sailed past with people frantically heaving on ropes to try to stop its progress. Alas there was a real foundering as the raft floated on and eventually got stuck further down stream! We choirboys provided some of the music for the play but were so amused that our singing deteriorated into laughter that was echoed by most people there, actors and audience alike. However the Producer was not amused!

I recall the army carrying out an exercise where one side invaded Oxford and the other side tried to repel them. We were kept indoors while it all happened and we watched from the windows. At one point live hand grenades were thrown into the river to simulate the attack. Next morning the surface of the river was awash with dead fish!

Work-wise I was a fairly undistinguished pupil. I managed to cope fairly easily with whatever had to be done and homework kept us busy in the evenings. There was really very little time during the week for getting into serious mischief. At weekends we were able to go into Oxford itself and spend what money we had. As choirboys we used to look forward to doing some extra singing engagements, at concerts and weddings because we got paid and so had a chance to buy sweets, model planes - in fact more or less anything we wanted. It was such a treat to be able to get out of school that we were careful not to get into too much trouble as being 'gated' meant we were not allowed to leave the premises. But I fear that my antics got me 'gated' quite a few times! I suppose I found the biggest chore at School was being made to study latin as a subject. Quite a lot of our religious music, including some anthems in the College Chapel, was sung in latin. We sang lustily in the language but most of us hadn't a clue what the words meant. Later on we did find out and I must say that as I grew older it was interesting to find out just what I had been singing about. Sometimes it was quite a shock! By the age of 12 I was considered a singer with a mature and well-modulated voice and became a chief soloist in the choir. We broadcast quite often on radio, singing into a large microphone. As a soloist I had my own 'mike' on the table near me too and that was special. Nowadays recordings are common but in those days there were no recorders of any kind apart from ordinary gramophone records so I never actually heard myself sing. At home, alas, my Father would never have a record cut of me singing. He thought it might make me big headed to hear myself. How things have changed!

In 1943 my voice eventually broke and I had to leave the choir. It was decided by my parents that I would have to leave Oxford as the scholarship I had won at 8 years old ran out when my voice was no longer of the treble variety. Magdalen College School was founded in 1480. The School motto, on the School Crest, was in Latin - 'Sicut Lilium' – 'Like the Lily'. I never really understood just how it applied to schoolboys! Of all the things that I experienced at Magdalen College School singing in the College Choir as a professional was the thing I really enjoyed most.

I would also have loved to continue as the cox of a school rowing 'four', but sadly that was not allowed. My skill as a table tennis player, even at the age of 10, only caused jealousy although I used it with much pleasure as I grew up. Looking back on my time there I suppose I gained a reasonable grounding for my future but I cannot say that I enjoyed it all very much. Still, the fact that I had a beautiful singing voice enabled me to go to Oxford. That was wonderful and compensated for the less enjoyable times, of which there were many. I missed my parents and the independence I inevitably acquired led to frequent disagreements when I went home for holidays. My Father found this hard to accept as he was a strong character with firm ideas of family discipline. Naturally I had accepted the necessarily firm discipline at school as there was no alternative. It was a question of either conforming or being punished. But at home I was not prepared simply to do as I was told without being given a reason. The words 'Because I say so' did not go down at all well! But as I matured no doubt I learned many things from my Dad's example. I saw how other people, boys, girls and adults all liked and respected him, not just because he was a parson but rather because he understood them and had endless time for them. He was a leader and gained respect – quite a lesson for me. Growing up is quite hard and you certainly have to work at it!

Chapter 9 Holidays

Before I continue further with my schooldays there is one thing that I have not mentioned. Prior to my going away to school I had a happy childhood. I have already mentioned my early days in Northampton where I was well looked after and treated with much loving kindness by my parents. Inevitably my Father spent much of his time doing pastoral work. He would regularly go visiting parishioners during the day and occasionally he would take me with him. When we moved to Camp Hill Borstal on the Isle of Wight I loved it. We had a very spacious residence – the Chaplain's House as it was called – with a large garden. The Borstal boys used to do the gardening and they were always very kind to me. They built me a large swing in one section of the garden and used to play cricket with me when their dinnertime break allowed. Only the 'trusties' were permitted to stay where they were working during break times and if it rained they could shelter in the garage. In 1937 my Father bought a car for the princely sum of £10 – probably the equivalent of £500 or more these days – and it was left in the garage. One wet day we were aroused by the sound of a motor being turned over, which then faded and stopped. Then Father quickly went outside and there was one of the trusties sitting in the car. He had managed to find the starter but did not know that it was necessary to pull out the choke in order to keep the engine running! He was trying to escape, although he could not have got off the Island. Poor lad, he lost his privileges and his status as a 'trusty' too. I think my father had left the key in the ignition!

I duly went off to Oxford and so holidays, when they came, were special. My first one in July, August and September 1939 was rather fraught, as the threat of war loomed ever closer. I remember that on September 3rd 1939 we sat in the drawing room and listened as the Prime Minister, Neville Chamberlain, announced that England was at war with Germany. I was due to go back to school and we were all afraid that bombing would commence at once. Actually it didn't but the fear was there. I was taken back to school and I know that a lot of Jewish refugees had arrived from Germany. Several of them came to Magdalen College School and the tales they told of ill treatment were frightening. But for quite a while nothing seemed to be happening in England although all the boys at the Borstal left to join the army as an alternative to finishing their sentences. The Borstal became another part of Parkhurst Prison, which was just down the hill. Prisoners in jail for serious offences were sent to the Camp Hill section of the Prison. Next to the Prison was an Army Barracks and there was a section of open ground between them and the Camp Hill Prison site. This was requisitioned for allotments. The road was at the edge, running along by the Prison wall opposite.

When I returned for the Christmas holidays I found these changes and life was very different. An air raid shelter had been built inside the Camp Hill Prison walls ready for trouble. I do not recall much of what happened apart from us having to practise getting to the shelter quickly. By this time we had also been issued with gasmasks and I remember playing billiards with my mother and wearing them for practice – very noisy, amusing, but unpleasant. The warning that gasmasks must be put on was given to us by means of a wooden 'rattle' which could be swung round so that it made a loud and ear-splitting noise. In peacetime rattles were used by spectators at football matches for encouraging their team. We had to practise from time to time and we soon became expert at putting on our gasmasks. One night during a particularly heavy raid we had to run to the shelter as incendiary bombs were being dropped nearby. My mother was carrying a set of draughts in a wooden box and as she ran it rattled loudly. On arriving at the shelter we were staggered to find everyone wearing gasmasks. They thought they had heard a gas attack warning. Actually as my mother ran towards the shelter the draughts set that she was carrying - so we could play during the bombing - had sounded just like a rattle. We were not popular that night!

By the summer holiday things were bad and there were regular raids. We used to go into the shelter about 8pm and emerge again in the morning. I remember this being frightening for many bombs were dropped nearby although the main raids were on Portsmouth and Southampton. On one particular evening, after phosphorous bombs had been dropped in and around the prison itself, some warders who were acting as Air Raid Wardens picked up the tails of 19 of the bombs and brought them into the shelter. There were 19 children so we were given one each as a souvenir. I kept mine for years. We also had small pieces of shot down German aeroplanes. I recall going to Newport and seeing a shot down Messerschmidt 109 on show with a large caption in front of it which read 'MADE IN GERMANY. FINISHED IN THE ISLE OF WIGHT! We were allowed to sit in the plane and examine it. There were bullet holes everywhere. Even the pilot's bloodied flying jacket was on show. He had been wounded when he was shot down. It was good for our morale. War made one feel that we should have revenge one way or another – sad, but very true at this time in our lives.

I had become friendly with John Williams who was the son of the other Prison Chaplain. I was invited to go to his house one afternoon. He lived at the bottom of the hill, near the main Parkhurst Prison building, about half a mile away. I set off to go to see him. As I got level with the allotments on the open ground near the Prison wall a German fighter plane an ME 109, flew straight towards the prison wall, its guns firing. I was petrified and recall seeing only the briefest glimpse of the plane and its pilot as it tore overhead, very low. After that I remembered no more until I was found crying - curled up in a ball near the prison wall - by some prison officers. I told them what had happened and I would not go past the allotments again. I was hysterical apparently. My Father was called. He was angry – he thought I was making up a story to explain how my best clothes had got filthy! But one of the warders went to the prison wall and picked up several flattened bullets. He showed them to my Father. On closer examination it was then found that I had two holes in my clothes – one through a sleeve and the other in my trousers. How the bullets missed is an absolute miracle. But that influenced my parents who were very upset. Once I was taken back to school I never returned to the Island again. Local children were evacuated to the mainland because of the dangers of a possible invasion of the Isle of Wight. My Father was offered another 5-year contract with the Prison Service but he had also been offered the chance to become the Vicar of the Parish of St Mary's, Far Cotton, Northampton and he was persuaded to move there by the Bishop of Peterborough. I quickly made new friends during my holidays at Far Cotton and whenever I was home I used to sing solos in Church at evensong.

Our dog, a black Labrador called Jumbo, never got over hearing the bombs. Whenever he heard any loud bang or thunderclap he would hide under the table. Soldiers were billeted at the Vicarage with us. Sadly several of them were later killed in action. I still have stamps in an album that came off letters they sent to us from various parts of the world.

Chapter 10 Oakham School, Rutland

Because we, as a family, were living at Far Cotton in Northampton where my Father
was Vicar of St Mary's Parish, the thought of moving away from School at Oxford came as something of a pleasure. I was to move on to Oakham School in Rutland. I was quite unaware at the time that the fact that I was going away again was fortuitous for me. The cost of boarding at any School was considerably greater than being at home of course. I had a benefactor, The Reverend Norman Millard. He had been my Father's first 'boss', having been Vicar of the Parish of St James in Northampton when Dad had been ordained curate of that Parish. They were probably more or less from same era and had become close friends. I had known the Vicar only as 'Vicky' – the name by which I knew him throughout his life. He had always been someone I had looked up to, and luckily for me he had taken a genuine interest in my time at Oxford. He became my benefactor and paid for my education at Oakham. I left Magdalen in July 1943 and in September I moved on to Oakham School in the capital town of Oakham in Rutland. The School was founded in 1584.

What a difference I found! Once again I was a young pupil in the Senior School age wise. I had just celebrated my 13th birthday. When I arrived the matron of the House to which I was assigned warmly greeted me. The House was, and still is, called 'Wharflands'. Some of my fellow new boys had never been away from home before and found it all a bit of a wrench to be left by their parents – just as I had in 1939 on Magdalen Bridge, Oxford.

I was able to reassure them that things would improve and thus I got to know them fairly quickly. Our 'studies' were in a wooden building that was formerly an Army Hut. This was at the back of the main Wharflands building where the older boys were housed. In our Hut were 6 studies. These were simply partitioned areas separated by wooden walls about 6 feet high. The studies took up half of the hut, the rest was a communal area where we did evening prep, read books or just sat and mixed with each other. One boy was Head of the Hut and shared his study with the Deputy Head of the Hut. There were probably about 20 of us altogether – 8 new boys in two more of the studies and the other 8 in the 3 studies left. They had entered the House at some stage during the previous year. The hut was heated only in the open area by a large enclosed stove with a metal chimney up through the roof. It gave out a lot of heat, but the studies were not very warm and much time was spent in winter near the stove. We kept our personal belongings in a 'tuckbox'.

Wharflands, in terms of accommodation, was effectively split into three parts – the Hut, the Back of the House and the Front of the House. Seniors and prefects had studies at the front. The 3rd years and some 2nd years had studies in the Back of the House and the rest of the 2nd and 1st Years were lodged in the Hut. Meals were taken in a large communal room in the main building. There were 4 dormitories in the main building. These were known as Upper 10 and Lower 10, Upper 12 and Lower 12. Each dormitory had a prefect to sleep in it and keep order. Our first Housemaster at Wharflands from 1943 to 1945 was also the Headmaster of the School – a man by the name of Mr G. Talbot Griffiths. He was firm but fair and was generally much respected. There were also two other masters in the house at that time – Mr Mostyn Robinson and Mr 'Bushey' Watts, plus a matron and ancillary staff. Mostyn Robinson enjoyed producing plays and I once took part in a play called 'THE HOUSEMASTER' – great fun. As the name implies it was based on life at a school. I well remember one line in particular. It was supposedly written by the 'Housemaster' in a report about one of the characters in the play and said, "Despite his natural levity he habitually gravitates to the bottom". It would probably have fitted me well enough, although fortunately I managed to avoid that unenviable position!

Once again, soon after our arrival as new boys, we went through the traditional 'fagging' process – very different from my previous experience, but the main task of filling baths was still to be done. Things were less onerous although the so-called 'tradition' of making life difficult for new arrivals continued. It was fairly harmless – being pummelled with cushions by the older boys in the Hut and generally being made to 'show respect' for their authority. It was stupid nonsense and a daft 'tradition' so beloved of former authoritarians of yesteryear. It was something that happened just once and was supposed to toughen one up. Having suffered many worse things elsewhere at my previous school my reaction was somewhat different from what was expected. I fought back vigorously when this so called toughening up process happened to me and was promptly left alone! However the prefects, who were much older and had responsibility for running the house properly – were fair for the most part and did not indulge in idiotic traditions of that kind, but more of that later.

Chapter 11 The Daily School Routine.

The School itself had several 'campuses'. That is to say that we often had to move from one area of the school to another and that involved a walk of about ten minutes. School House, situated in the centre of Oakham Town, had most of the classrooms and the School Chapel. Every morning all pupils attended Chapel for morning prayers and Assembly prior to lessons. So there was the usual rush to get up in the mornings and have breakfast before going to the Chapel. Almost invariably we had porridge and toast for breakfast. Cooked breakfasts were usually at the weekends when there was a bit more time to eat properly! The porridge was served from a very large bowl and dolloped into our bowls with a large spoon. It varied from very hot - if one was in the queue early – down to cold for those at the back of the queue. It was an excellent way of making sure that we all rushed to get up. I soon learned to lay my clothes out in such a way that I could dress very quickly!

After breakfast we grabbed our schoolbags, jammed our caps on our heads – wearing caps in the street was a school rule - and started the day. Morning lessons – from 9.15 to 12.45 - consisted mainly of the basics - Maths, English Language and Latin or Science. Lunch was around 1.00. Sport took up afternoons from 2.00 to 4.00 and everybody was expected to take part in one way or another unless illness prevented this. School restarted at 4.15 and continued to 6.15. Lessons were usually in the categories of History, Geography, Scripture, English Literature, French, Drama, Art and the like. After the end of lessons bell we returned to our respective houses to have supper. 'Prep' was officially done from 7.30 to 8.30 in our studies and the younger pupils went to bed at 9.00. Older pupils stayed up later and went to bed around 9.30, while seniors and prefects had more latitude and retired around 10.00 to 10.30. There was certainly method in this timetable – it left very little time for getting into serious mischief during the day. Sunday afternoons were looked forward to as we were free to do as we pleased – go out into the town or the countryside if we wished and generally enjoy ourselves.

Chapter 12 Sporting activities

On Saturdays the School Sports teams always had matches arranged. In summer either the 1st XI or the 2nd XI would play at home and pupils not engaged in other activities would be expected to spend the afternoon watching. Occasionally games took place in mid-week and that meant missing lessons for the players involved so competition for places in the team was fierce. Every sport had expert coaches and standards were high, particularly in Rugby, Hockey and Cricket. I recall being coached by a former professional cricketer named John Haywood as well as by the master in charge of cricket, John Moore, known as 'JM'. John Haywood must have been well into his 60s but his enthusiasm was undiminished. John Moore was an excellent cricketer too so we were well served. He played for Leicestershire Gents, a well-known Midlands side, whenever he could, and Oakham Town on Sundays. Quite often I was asked by him to turn out for the Oakham Town 1st XI. They were a top local side and competition was fierce to play with them. One story appertaining to my playing for the Town involved my vain attempts to learn Greek. I was hopeless compared with my fellow pupil, Brian Simpson, who later became a Don at Oxford. He would be given great chunks of Greek to translate and if he made any mistakes he was soundly told off. I, on the other hand, was given a few lines of the bible, written in Greek, to translate. I could of course look up my translation so it was easy for me. One day I had a section which, when translated, said, "Consider the lilies, how they grow. They toil not, neither do they spin. Yet I say unto you, even Solomon in all his glory was not arrayed like one of these". As usual I had looked up the answer and trotted it out. JM grinned at me and said, "Spinner (my nickname), which word is lilies?" I managed that one ok but then he continued, "and which word is arrayed?" I hadn't a clue and guessed wrong, as usual. He laughed at me and said, "Spinner, you'll never make a Greek scholar, but if you agree to turn out for Oakham Town Cricket Club with me on Sundays from now on you can do that instead of weekend homework". I did not need a second invitation and we shared more than one batting partnership together on a Sunday afternoon. JM was, in my book, a great teacher. He was a strong influence in my life and set a fine example, although NOT by trying to teach me Greek! Wisely he kept that for his star language pupil – Brian Simpson!

I actually managed quite an interesting cricket career at school. At the age of thirteen I was suddenly allowed to play outdoor sports officially for the first time in my life as my heart condition had greatly improved and the doctors involved considered it safe for me to do so. I threw myself into everything with great enthusiasm and I spent one year in the Under 14 side before being promoted to the 2nd XI the following year. I did quite well in that season and I got into the 1st XI by the end of the summer term and stayed there until I left 3 years later. I won the 1st X1 Batting Cup one year and headed the bowling averages as well. I even feature in 'Wisden' in the 1947 and 1948 editions under Oakham School. I had trials for Northants on leaving Oakham but no contract was forthcoming. I also decided that I should find playing three day matches boring so it was no great loss as I quickly dropped the idea of trying to become a full time cricketer.

In winter pupils not representing the School at rugby or hockey at weekends were again required to turn out and support the 1st or 2nd teams depending on which one was playing at home. Rugby was played from September to December, and Hockey from January until March. I played both games and represented the School at both sports. I only played rugby because I had to – I played hockey because I wanted to! But in summer cricket was my major passion at school and I spent countless hours in the summer practising with fellow enthusiasts from Wharflands. We had good house teams at all major sports and the hardest fought games were always inter-house matches. Of course there were other important sports to take part in – Athletics and Swimming featured large in the sporting calendar although we did not at that time compete against other schools. We had an outdoor pool about half a mile from Wharflands and swimming lessons took place in the afternoons in summer. Again, it was a sport I enjoyed, particularly when diving and plunging was taking place. In fact I learned how to breathe properly as a result of swimming and plunging. Plunging involved a flat dive and then seeing how far one could reach up the baths without making a stroke. It was necessary to hold one's breath as long as possible. I managed to win several plunging competitions and breaststroke races. I took part in various forms of athletics but never managed to achieve any records worthy of the name. When there was no other form of sport to play we were sent out on a run around the countryside. This was not my favourite pastime! I fear that, like my father before me, I looked for short cuts or stopped for a secret smoke. However, unlike him I never got caught or put into running teams by taking short cuts and returning to school too soon! For some reason football never featured on the sporting timetable so we just played amongst ourselves. On the 'minor sports' side there was one game that intrigued me although I never had much time to really improve my skills. It was a game called 'Fives' and we had several courts. The idea seemed to be to hit the small ball as hard as possible with one's hand. We wore a glove on our hitting hand to prevent damage. Opponents returned the ball – above a certain marked height – and points were gained by preventing your opponent from returning the ball correctly. Table tennis was also played but that was mainly in one's house although there were a few school competitions. I won several of those and was considered a good player although we never played against outside opposition.

Chapter 13 Forces training

One afternoon a week was dedicated to Army and Air Force training. With the war as a constant reminder of the dangerous times we lived in we were taught how to fight. Initially there was just an OTC - Officers' Training Corps. We all had to take part, being issued with uniforms as worn by army privates. We trained with rifles and also had an army band, which I joined as a drummer. We marched around the field with rifles on our shoulders and there were seemingly endless drill to learn. I was taught to map read, drive a van and ride a motorcycle. There was a shooting range and we practised regularly with 0.22 bullets but I was never very proficient in that department.

An Air Training Corps was also set up for those who thought that the RAF would be a better bet. I joined that and had a lot of fun training. Morse code had to be learned amongst other things. We used to go off to local Aerodromes - RAF Wittering and RAF Luffenham. These were used as both training and operational stations during the war with Lancaster bombers mainly at Luffenham and a combination of fighters and bombers at Wittering. They were stations where bomber crews were made up together for training and I flew several times with a Lancaster bomber crew. Had I been called up I should have opted for either the RAF or the Navy but fortunately for me the war ended in 1945 so I never had to fight. We got experience of 'hands on flying' in Link trainers. These never actually left the ground – they had simulated flying controls and we were given the impression that we were flying. It was quite scary but very exciting. Many years later it came in very handy when I got the chance to fly a Cessna both from what is now Leeds/Bradford Airport and from the local airstrip at Rotorua in New Zealand. That was quite hairy as we flew to the top of Mount Tarawara which is a volcano and when the pilot took off we literally flew over the edge of the mountain and dived a bit to get up to speed. I got my chance after that so the other two passengers must have been relieved to get back to Rotorua in one piece!

I thoroughly enjoyed the opportunities we got to fly at school, thanks to John Moore, the master who was in charge. Usually I was in the company of my good friend "Tot" Treanor with whom I had more than one hilarious experience, particularly when, while at R.A.F. Wittering, he inadvertently picked up his parachute by the wrong 'handle' and it flew open. As we were approaching a Lancaster bomber from behind for a flight at the time - the engines were already running - the parachute billowed out and after the flight there was a fine of two shillings and six pence to pay for this misdemeanour - a lot of money to us in those days. On another occasion we flew from R.A.F. Luffenham in an old Anson. The pilot - a certain Flight Lieutenant Barrie - allowed J.M. to take the controls for a spell, during which time we got lost in cloud. After several anxious moments we spotted the spire of Oakham Church - too close for comfort, I might add - and managed to follow the railway line back to base, landing half an hour after our E.T.A. (estimated time of arrival) apparently having used up virtually all the reserve supply of fuel in the process. The engines stopped immediately we had landed and the plane had to be towed away by tractor – rather humiliating for the pilot and altogether quite an experience for us!

It is an interesting fact that unofficially several of us learned to make homemade bombs. These we put together with cordite taken from bullets, together with rags stuffed inside glass bottles. Sometimes we buried them and laid a fuse. They exploded with quite a satisfying bang! Others we lit and threw. These burst all over the place and were lethal – like Molotov cocktails, which are still in use today I fear. There was a virtually endless supply of cordite extracted from bullets given to us by American servicemen stationed nearby - they were being trained for the coming invasion – so it was not too surprising that warlike activities were at a premium. But if England had been invaded we should probably have tried to use quite a few Molotov cocktails!

When the war finished the ATC was disbanded and we all had to go back to army training. I found that somewhat onerous, but I became a lance corporal and managed to get a job teaching other boys to ride the motorbikes. I enjoyed that but inevitably it got me - and a couple of others - into trouble. We eventually got fed up with just riding around the school field and a large quadrangle, so one day we headed off for a drive around the country. It was great fun but unfortunately we were delayed when the bike I was on virtually ran out of petrol! We got caught on our return and were severely punished – painful, but on this occasion fully justified – 6 strokes of the cane - ouch! After all, we had no insurance, no helmets and very little petrol. That was the root cause as the bike I was on stopped. What little petrol that was left went to the rear of the tank and it had to be 'persuaded' to reach the reserve tap by tipping the bike – not easy. However it bred in me a love of riding motorcycles and I only gave up when I reached 70. I used to buy old bikes, do them up and maintain them myself. There was an amusing and somewhat embarrassing sequel to the above escapade. At the end of the school year there was an amusing tradition that any commonly known 'deeds' that had happened during the previous 12 months were written up and made into a song. This also included infringements of school rules. I was 'immortalised' in one verse of a song entitled 'Have you ever heard such a funny thing before?' Other pupils were also mentioned in other verses for their exploits. The only trouble was – most of them had done good things. Still, at least it caused much laughter!

Two further clangers that upset the Army hierarchy attached to the School took place during an official inspection by General Sir John Hackett, who had been a prisoner of war in Colditz Castle for a time. When marching and carrying a rifle one is supposed to salute by slapping the butt of the rifle. I was marching my section past the General and somehow managed to salute by putting my hand to my head instead of the correct way. Luckily he was merely amused – but the School's accompanying Army Officers weren't! I then had this mistake embellished within a few minutes. My section was supposed to be demonstrating how to ride the two motorbikes around in a circle. The first boys to do so got on fine but unfortunately one poor fellow tried a bit too hard when his turn came. He lost control and sped off straight into a nearby hedge where he finished up in a dithering, but fortunately uninjured, heap. By the time he had been extricated from the hedge the General had moved on, but I guess his remark would not have been too favourable! Naturally I was verbally 'disciplined' afterwards and threatened with loss of rank. I saluted – correctly this time – when I marched away!

The other thing we were expected to do was shoot. We used small-bore rifles that fired 0.22 bullets. I managed to hit targets reasonably well and gained a 2nd class badge for my pains. We were checked every term. Alas I was eventually downgraded to a 3rd class shot on one occasion when I failed to hit the target sufficiently close to the bull's-eye. I had to wait another term before managing to regain my badge. Somehow, I do not think I should have made a good soldier. Fortunately I was never put to the test!

There were, of course, many other escapades in which I joined. A summer favourite was to sneak out of Upper 12 dormitory down the fire escape and go for a midnight swim. Surprisingly enough no one was ever caught. Inevitably smoking was another forbidden fruit that attracted many, including me. The height of amusement on one occasion came when I had retired up a tree on the far side of Doncaster Close (the School field) and had lit up. Who should come along but a young master by the name of Cyril Hiscocks with - wonder of wonders - a lady in tow! I will not comment further except to say that I was trapped up the tree as they sat beneath it. If they had even looked up once I might well have been doomed, but lady luck smiled on me (and on them too!) and I was merely late - extremely late - for prep.

On another occasion one of our dormitory boys foolishly got into debt. In order to pay this off a rather novel way of payment was decided upon. The boy in question had to go down the fire escape after lights out and run right round the cricket field. Dangerous if one was caught but not an impossible task. The only difficulty for him was that he had to do it virtually unclothed. To his credit he managed it after a few hairy moments such as having to hide behind a hedge as a member of staff happened to pass nearby. Eventually he returned pretty exhausted. His debts were eventually cancelled but one or two boys involved initially objected as he still had his socks on! Boys can be very cruel!

Chapter 14 School discipline

Eventually the Headmaster, Mr Talbot Griffith relinquished his 'extra' duties as Housemaster of Wharflands when Major 'Bertie' Bowes returned from the war. From then on Wharflands seemed to be a run by nothing more than a series of rotas. There were army-style rotas for everything from getting up to going to bed - and I fear that this style of 'command' left me somewhat cold. School lists - do's and dont's - I could understand but I'm afraid that the so-called military logic of "Obey without question, however useless it appears", didn't appeal, and I fell foul of Major Bowes on several occasions. These often ended somewhat painfully at the wrong end of a cane and I gained the equivalent of sergeant's stripes quite regularly. Thus I found that standing was infinitely preferable to sitting down! However his wife Jane took my part more than once and secretly expressed her sympathy - on one occasion with a glass of his excellent sherry that I gratefully quaffed - standing up!

Pubs were out of bounds and woe betide anyone caught breaking rules. In addition it was a heinous offence to be seen talking to the local girls. During my time at Oakham a factory wall served as a boundary to the school playing field. I do not recall just what business was carried on there but it certainly involved young ladies who used to watch us through the windows. Inevitably, suitably encouraged by us, they would open the windows and chat. These factory girls would offer to see us at weekends. I recall going off one day with a friend, David Hill, and walking a couple of miles from Oakham to meet a couple of them, sisters, outside their home. It sounds dull by today's standards but we enjoyed it – mainly because we were breaking rules and having fun. On that occasion all was well, but one day I was apparently seen by a master standing beneath a factory window chatting to on of the female workers. She threw out a magazine called 'A Basin full of Fun' for us to read. It had suggestive pictures in and a few jokes that were a bit near the nail. I was completely unaware that I had been seen. I went off to play cricket at an away match so was excused Chapel. To my horror, on my return I was informed that my name had been read out with the notices after the service. I had apparently been warned in front of all the Senior School that a repeat of the offence would result in my being sent home – expelled permanently. The Headmaster was not aware that I had missed Chapel so I was never spoken to officially. But wisdom prevailed and I kept a very low profile for a week or two. Fortunately my parents never got to know about that little episode!

But while the above stories reflected one side of life there was another in which I became involved that affected my life at the time, and my whole outlook later on when I grew up. After I had been in the Hut for a year in 1943/4 - initially as a new boy and then as just another pupil - I had seen and experienced at first hand certain idiotic traditions, apparently designed to make life difficult for those who had just left home for the first time. It often made them homesick. I had been through all that at Oxford and I coped with this sort of tradition without much difficulty. This fact had not escaped the Headmaster apparently for he knew what had, by tradition, been going on for many years and he intended to change things. He took me on one side at the end of my first year and asked me about my feelings where these things were concerned. At first I would not say anything so he simply said straight out, 'Christopher I want you to remain as head boy of the Hut. I want you to try to ensure that no more 'traditional treatment' is carried out this next term. You can do it. Your reputation for rebelling and refusing to be overawed has been noted by me and I think you are strong enough to stop the bullying, for that is what it is'. I agreed to try. That term was very hard as the older boys who had 'gone through the mill' tried to make me carry out these traditions. I refused and more than once became involved in fights. But in the end they left me alone and that type of bullying stopped. Fortunately the senior boy, a renowned bully who wanted the tradition to continue, was also the Captain of the School Cricket 1st XI and I think he felt that if he tried to take his irritation out on me I would not do my best for him on the cricket field – some mentality he had! Anyway it had the desired effect from my point of view. I immediately moved into the 'back of the house'. However when the former Housemaster, Major Bowes, returned from the war, as I said earlier, I found his regime was not to my liking. He and the Head did not get on too well initially I gathered, as many of the old Wharflands House 'traditions' had gone by the board. I suppose he must have held me partly responsible for the changes and he virtually ignored me whenever he could. Furthermore although he could not stop me from become head senior he deliberately refused to make me a prefect. I further upset him when I found a young new boy from Rothwell, Northants, had come to the School and was unhappy. He was being bullied so I took him under my wing but, sadly, without success. He eventually ran away and would not return.

The interesting point of all that happened to me was that the other masters - including Ronnie Henton, a junior housemaster in Wharflands – who were responsible for my education, both academic and sporting, knew what was happening and did their best to ensure that I was able to get on normally in school. In later years Ronnie Henton became a good friend. I was popular and I stood up for myself. Bowes could not stand that! Typical of the way he would treat me was shown when I was captaining the Cricket 1st XI in an away match. We won the game – something our team had not managed for a long time as it happened. After we had returned, at supper he asked the players how we had got on and upon hearing the result he was very pleased – until he asked who had captained the side. But as soon as he was informed, by the other players, that it was me he just turned on his heel and went! The players all laughed and, of course, so did I. They all knew the score and always saw that I did not miss out on anything. But again it was a lesson learned. I tried never to treat anyone like that and the thought has stayed with me throughout my life – both in school and out.

There was something else that I learned during my last year at Oakham. The Headmaster periodically used to invite prefects to his house for an evening meal. I was also included each time there was an invitation – as he later told me, he was fully aware of the problem Bowes had with me, and vice versa – and we were always well entertained. I shall never forget the amazement we all felt the first time when, after an excellent meal and a glass of wine with him and his wife, he passed round the port and offered us cigarettes. His comment was proof positive that he knew exactly what was going on. He said, "I know you boys all smoke, so have one here. However if I catch you smoking anywhere else in school I shall punish you, but if you want one at any time come here to my house". Needless to say I do not think anyone took up the offer but it proved to be a wonderful lesson in the psychological understanding of his job. He was a fine example to me and I admired the way he did an extremely difficult job during wartime.

Chapter 15 A brief synopsis

In the long run I guess that the school inculcated good habits when they mattered. It was certainly character-forming. I made many good friends amongst staff and pupils alike, and some of those have stayed with me all my life. I learned the meaning of truth, loyalty and honesty – things that I have always tried to pass on to pupils who over the years have been in my care. In the long run, in my opinion, there were just a few unhelpful traditions which sprang up amongst all the good things that the School offered in the way of an all round education. Such schools by their very nature can breed a type of arrogance that comes quite often with so-called privilege, and that is inevitable. It depends on the individual. I learned to show outward confidence however I felt inside and I developed an ability to cope with most normal life situations. There are so many good traditions – courtesy, friendship, helpfulness, honesty, unselfishness, truth – to name but a few. The list can be whatever you want to make it. But that is what I gained from the first eighteen years of my life. My early experiences at Magdalen College School taught me the futility of hate and bitter resentment, although some of my time away from my parents turned out to be unhappy. But at the same time it taught me self-reliance above all. I soon realised that jealousy and envy were poor companions too. It is the quickest way to lose friends. Everyone I met at school (and since come to that) had a talent of some kind and the sensible ones used those talents to make their way in life. A talent for singing helped me, thanks to my father, who saw a way to give me an education that I could build on. The bonus of being taught to sing properly also enabled me to enunciate clearly and I won the school prizes for reading with meaning and interest as well as for public speaking every year of my time at Oakham School. I must say that my early experiences gave me the feeling that by going away so young I lost the close relationship with my parents that I now see as so important. At the same time this left the way clear to making a few long lasting friendships from among all those who, like me, were spending much of their youth away at school. Three names come to mind, all associated with Oakham School - Steve Taylor, Oliver Adams and Peter Hall. Peter and I shared a study together when I first arrived at Oakham and Oliver was my study mate a year or two later. Steve and I travelled by train to and from school at each term's start and end. We played cricket together and we ignored the personal rivalry that existed between members of different School Houses. We also spent much time together during school holidays. Steve was in 'School House' while I was in 'Wharflands'. Oliver became, like his father, a farmer. Peter became a business rep. in the leather trade and Steve took over his father's business. We have kept in close touch throughout our lives and, as well as visiting each others homes over the years, sometimes used to meet, for good measure, at Oakham on Old Boys' Day. But I think that life has changed so much these days. I have managed to recall long forgotten experiences from my schooldays over 60 years ago that indicate how we were brought up and what it was that made me something of a rebel. It has been a good lesson in humility although I must have been quite an irritant to one or two of those who lived the lives of conformists. I always believed that the 'do as I say' and 'because I say so' attitude was the easy way out and that there should be reasons for actions. What irony then that I should have become a Headmaster and a so-called pillar of society!

Oakham School was founded in 1584. The school motto is written in Latin, on the School Crest.

Et quasi cursors vitae lampada tradunt

(And like runners they carry the torch of life)

Moving into Adulthood

Chapter 1 Shaping the future

After I left Oakham in July 1947 the thought that I would no longer be hidebound by the rules, regulations and traditions that had inevitably surrounded and conditioned virtually everything I was expected to do both excited me and set a challenge that I just literally could not wait to begin. Traditionally we went away on holiday to Folkestone. This was because my father suffered from what later turned out to be a gastric ulcer and he had to have a special diet at all times. The boarding house where we stayed catered for his every need so year after year we returned there. I was somewhat reluctant to go at first but that soon changed as my interest in meeting girls (stifled at Oakham!) quickly resurfaced. Furthermore my school friend, Steve Taylor came with us. Steve and I had become close friends at Oakham and we spent much of our school holidays together at either his parents' house at Newport Pagnell or our home at the Vicarage of St Mary's Church, Far Cotton, Northampton. He left school a year before me. His scholastic achievements were not considered by his parents to be a firm basis for his future. So instead he worked for a time at his Father's firm, bottling fizzy drinks and making mustard. The business was good in those days. I also used to work there in my holidays to earn extra pocket money. Steve had to learn about running the place too as it would eventually come to him when his father retired. Later on his father sent him to work at a firm in Derby where he learned more about running a 'pop' business.

There was a dance hall adjacent to the pier at Folkestone called the Leas Cliff Hall. Holidaymakers went there, particularly when the weather was inclement, as there was an Amusements Hall containing attractions such as one-armed bandits and a variety of gaming machines for children as well as adults. There was also another Amusements Hall down near the beach and Steve and I had become very proficient on certain gaming machines – so good in fact that we were able to make a healthy profit. Sadly that did not last as we were banned by the management – for a small financial consideration of course! Needless to say we did even better at the one in the Leas Cliff Hall and made quite sure that we did not get caught. It was all above board and subsidised our pocket money. There were other attractions too. Young ladies frequented the dance hall in the evenings. The resident band was good and we enjoyed socialising, dancing - and romancing!

After the holiday was over we both came down with a bump. I had to report to a medical centre along with dozens of other 17/18 year olds in order to see if we were fit for National Service in the forces. This was statutory and everyone had to attend. Two years National Service was the minimum time that had to be served – in the army, navy or air force. The training was tough and those involved learned what real discipline meant!

I reported in August 1947, keen to join the navy or the air force, but sadly it was not to be. Although initially I was passed as A1 (fully fit) I was called back to see the heart specialist again as the Senior Medical Officer in charge knew both me and my medical history and as I was being issued with the requisite pass to show my state of health he intervened. The heart specialist was admonished and told to check again. This time he detected the heart murmur with which I had been born and so I was downgraded to C3 (not fully fit) and that was that! I went home much deflated, as I had been looking forward to joining up with my friends. But the war had been over for two years and only the fully fit were conscripted. Their duties took them to many parts of the world where, amongst other jobs, they oversaw the rebuilding of war torn cities and kept order, preventing everyday occurrences such as looting, fighting and theft. National Service was continued for 9 years after the Second World War, until 1954. It had several advantages for the country both at home and overseas. Discipline – both enforced and personal - became second nature to most young men and continued in later life for the vast majority.

I well recall returning home afterwards. My father had not been idle – once again he wanted to map out my future! He offered to make 'openings' available for me and mentioned a variety of jobs for which I could train – as a cleric in the Church of England, banking, civil service, office management and a host more. Inevitably I refused them all as I had no wish to be dragooned into something I did not want. At that point University beckoned as I had passed an exam at school that would enable me to go to Keble College, Oxford later in the year. While at Oakham it had been assumed – incorrectly as it turned out – that I would follow my Father into the Church. At the time I had made no decision, but in those days it was often the norm to go into a career that was similar to one's parent. At 16 years old I had even gone to an

34

office in Dean's Yard, Westminster in London to be interviewed at C.A.C.T.M. (Central Advisory Committee on Training for the Ministry) to assess my suitability to take Holy Orders). At a later stage in early 1947 I requested the opportunity of making a second visit to Westminster to find out more about entering the Ministry. I have to admit that the idea of having a further couple of days off School really appealed to me too and I took full advantage! And thereby follows a quite remarkable tale:-

After I had been interviewed at C.A.C.T.M. again I was walking back along the pavement in Dean's Yard, when I saw an official Army car pull up outside a building entrance about 20 yards away. Curiosity got the better of me and I stood and watched. To my utter amazement William McKie, my Choirmaster of Oxford days, came out of the entrance behind his guest who was the legendary wartime leader, Field Marshall Bernard Montgomery. I learned later that they had had lunch together. Montgomery was at the height of his fame. He had been the General who had led the British Army through Europe and was instrumental in planning the eventual defeat of Germany in the Second World War. I was unable to walk on until the car drove away as an armed soldier had taken up a position by the door of the vehicle. When I eventually did move Dr William McKie (better known to me as 'Daddy Mac' from when I was a young choirboy) walked towards me. I did not speak and I had actually got past him when I heard a voice say "George?" (He had always called me that, as he preferred it to Christopher). I replied in the affirmative. He shook my hand firmly and then said, "Please come with me. I am going to choir practice with my choristers at Westminster Abbey. I want to introduce you to the choir as the first boy I ever chose to join Magdalen College Choir when I came to England in the autumn of 1938." With that we walked along to the Song School. He then told me that he was having trouble getting the boys to sing a particularly difficult piece of Church music correctly. He said that I should know the music and would I try to explain the problem to them? Fortunately, as it turned out, I was able to point out where the difficulty lay so all was well. The boys were somewhat in awe of this 17 year old who knew what they were singing! I stayed and listened to them practising for evensong – a truly wonderful experience that I could fully understand as I had done just that a few years earlier in the Choir Practice room at Magdalen College.

Dr William McKie, an Australian from Melbourne, was later knighted and became known as Sir William McKie after the Coronation of our new Queen – Elizabeth 2nd. He trained the choir for the Coronation Service, wrote some of the music and played the organ himself. He was a truly wonderful man for whom I had the greatest love and admiration. He certainly knew how to get the best out of the boys in his choir. He was firm but kind and was greatly respected by all who knew him. His influence on me was profound and I have always tried to emulate the openness and honesty that was so much part of his character. Many years later, while working in Hackney, painting a house in 1986, I completed the cycle of his life. I took time off and went to Westminster Abbey and spoke to the assistant organist who told me that Sir William had died in 1984. He then showed me a plaque commemorating his life and recording his death. It is in the Abbey Cloisters. His ashes are interred there together with those of his wife.

Continuing the theme of helping me select a job for the future, my father pointed out that if I went up to Keble College as planned I would be taking a degree in Religious Studies. At that time I suddenly realised that, if I qualified, I would be expected to become a parson. Teachers at Oakham School had taught me to think things through and I had come to realise that life as a Minister in the Church of England was not for me. My unquestioning belief in God was no longer automatic. I felt that I could not follow that direction in my future career. In fact I became something of an agnostic. So I spoke of this at length with my father. To his eternal credit he listened and accepted that my mind was made up. I decide to look towards the teaching profession. At the time I assumed – wrongly as it turned out – that I could still go up to Keble College and study English. We contacted the College to ask for the change of subject and I was informed that I would have to take another exam and be interviewed by the English Department. I duly attended only to find that there were over 300 applications and only 36 places available. I was not accepted so I lost my chance to go to Oxford as a student. The irony of all that only became apparent later on when I found out that, had I gone up to Keble at the start of the University year without contacting the College about my change of heart I could have changed my 'school' and would probably have been accepted without demur! My father had not been to University and had not realised this – neither had I. That was a hard lesson!

Chapter 2 Starting work

When the autumn term of 1947 started in Northampton I went voluntarily to Highfield School for a few weeks to see if teaching was for me. I was not paid but soon realised that this was what I wanted to do. I cycled every morning – about 5 miles – to the school and met up with other teachers on the way - also cycling. I thoroughly enjoyed myself and so I applied for a paid permanent post as an unqualified teacher. I was accepted and spent 9 months on supply working at the Northamptonshire village school of Blisworth. This was quite an experience. The toilets, as I recall, were outside earth closets for the children as the only water supply and sewerage system was within the school building itself - quite a change from what I had been used to! There was one staff toilet within the building as well. Joe Cole, the Headmaster, was recovering from a nervous breakdown and it was hardly surprising I suppose, as the conditions had not really attracted experienced staff to the school. I arrived on the first morning to find that I was to be put in joint charge of a class of 12 year olds. My fellow teacher was also unqualified and was waiting to go off to College in a year's time. We managed somehow – he was only slightly more experienced than I in that he had been at the school since the start of the term. He had started in September - I arrived in mid October. Fortunately we got on well and coped all right.

But one makes mistakes in the early days without training and I was no exception. One day I was sent to take over the top class. These were 15 year olds. I started to tick the register of the children's names and initially all went well, although I suspected that a trick might be played on me somewhere along the way. There were about 40 children and they were only 3 years younger than I was. I got through the boys' list of names all right – then I asked the first girl's name. She did not immediately answer and a boy sitting in the row behind spoke up – "Joe Crow, Sir," he said. Like an idiot, expecting trouble, I said, "Pull the other one." Immediately the girl burst into tears and there was silence. Eventually the girl sitting next to her spoke up. "It's right Sir", she said. Fortunately I was able to apologise by saying I had not heard her answer for herself and it was passed off without too much difficulty. But I never made that mistake again. To this day I shall never understand why no one laughed! Fortunately the rest of the lesson passed off all right as I had already set a maths test that had to be finished before the end of the lesson. My first pay packet for the month was about 12 guineas (£12.60) – working out before tax at the princely sum of £180 a year!

One of the main things that I offered at Blisworth School was centred around sport. My reputation as a sportsman helped and I took great delight in organising football, netball, cricket and anything else required in the sporting line. After 9 months – in September 1948 - I was moved on to another village school at Walgrave, not far from Kettering and about 11 miles from our home at St Mary's Vicarage, Far Cotton, Northampton. I acquired an old autocycle for £25 and I travelled to Walgrave All Age School on that for a month or so, but I rode it too hard and the engine kept seizing up! One day I returned home and my Father, who enjoyed playing tricks, sent me out to the garden. There was a brand new autocycle – with two gears. Grumpily I commented that he had bought it for himself to go around the parish. He laughed and eventually said it was for me to use. I soon changed my tune! After a few months of driving it too hard to work I decided that a motorcycle would suit me much better and, without saying anything at home, I traded in the autocycle for a 350cc ex War Department Royal Enfield for a total cost of £65. Father was not amused. There were words exchanged but as he too had been a rider – a fact that I duly pointed out – he had little choice but to accept what was already 'fait accompli'!

Again, the experiences I gained at that school were invaluable and the Headmaster, Mr Corby, was a helpful and sympathetic man. This time I finished up in charge of a class of 11 year olds. In that group of children were, incredibly, two sets of identical twins. I never encountered that anywhere again. The girls' names I have forgotten but the boys – who were great jokers – were called Brian and Terry Morrell and more than once they surreptitiously changed seats and the pullovers I insisted they wore for me to distinguish them. Even their parents admitted that it was a problem for them occasionally – hence the different clothing. They were extremely good-natured lads and were very popular. Another member of that class was a lad named Glyn Gross. He loved creatures, particularly birds, and he kept pets. One thing happened during a period of time that concerned him. In the classroom several children had brightly coloured articles. I had a silver pen and pencil. These things started to disappear. Then the headlamp rim on my motorbike was scratched and other marks were found on highly coloured articles – too big to carry. We checked everyone in the class, convinced that there was a thief in our midst. This lasted about a week and even the Headmaster became involved. Then, one day, an embarrassed Glyn turned up at school with all the stolen articles. He had previously acquired a pet jackdaw. The bird had found a way into school and taken everything! The caretaker found out that there was a hole in the eaves that led into my classroom. It turned out that the jackdaw was also responsible for the scratches on my bike and on several cars as well – some thief!

I ran the football team during my time at the Walgrave School. We had a fair side and the locals used to come and watch on a Saturday morning when school matches were in progress. I used to referee. Occasionally I would turn out for Walgrave FC league side if I was not playing elsewhere. I well recall the time when I was asked to play in a Cup match one evening. Being left footed was quite useful and left wing was my position. However the ball never seemed to be coming my way so at half time I moved into the centre and scored a couple of goals. The second was virtually scored from the last shot of the match and was the winner, so my standing from then on was high at Walgrave! I turned out for them occasionally at cricket as well and as I was playing at a high standard in Northampton at the County Ground there were runs aplenty and wickets too. I also played in a Town League side at Far Cotton and was drafted in to the Wayfarers 1st team - a side consisting of local teachers. We did not have a home ground as such and so played all our fixtures away. There were some delightful grounds around the County. We only played evening fixtures during the week as on Saturdays we turned out for various league sides in Northampton. Little did I realise at the time that two of the players I met, when I first played for the Wayfarers at 18, would have a profound influence on my career in future years. One was the 1948 Captain, Stan Hutchins, and the second was the wicket keeper, Corin Judge. These two became Headmaster and Deputy Headmaster respectively of Kings Heath School in Northampton in the early 50s. After I had qualified at Durham I returned in 1953 to play for Rothwell CC in the Northamptonshire County League. My Father had become Vicar of Rothwell in 1952. I went off to work in Nottingham for a couple of years in 1956/7. When I decided to return to Northampton I applied for a job to the Education Department. I was sent to Kings Heath Junior School to look round as there was a vacancy to be filled on the staff.

When I arrived, to my surprise and pleasure, I was interviewed by Stan Hutchins and Corin Judge showed me round the School beforehand. Needless to say I did not need to be asked twice about joining the staff! I remained there until 1964 and played countless times for the Wayfarers XI. We were able to field a very good side when required in local cricket competitions, but most of the games were friendlies played at various venues around the County in mid-week. It was a very happy period as I also played County League matches at weekends - initially for Rothwell Cricket Club, then later for Vallence Cricket Club in Northampton after getting married in 1959 and moving back to live in the Spinney Hill district of the town.

During this transitional period in my life – leaving school and going off to Durham three years later – I was growing up with cricket featuring large in my agenda. I had at one time felt that maybe I had sufficient talent in that direction to consider becoming a professional cricketer. In 1947 I was offered the opportunity to play in 'trial' matches at Northamptonshire County Cricket Club by Captain RHD Bolton. He was a Senior Officer in the Northamptonshire Constabulary and had considerable knowledge and influence in the cricketing world in those days, particularly where schools were concerned. School leavers who had excelled at cricket amongst their school peers were of particular interest to him as we were featured in the cricketers' 'bible' ie Wisden. This only happened if our performances over the season merited a mention and as I had achieved this in 1946 & 47 (shown in the following years' copies of Wisden) he would have taken due note I expect. I won the School Batting Cup in 1946 and in 1947 I had a good bowling season. I played in several matches for Northants at 'Club and Ground' level but I never aspired to the 1st XI County side and I realised that my career would have to take another path. Cricket would be a major sport for me but would not be classed as a living!

Being an enthusiastic cricketer I attended County matches whenever I could. There I met a host of other young people who enjoyed watching. We used to meet in an area we called the 'Scratching Shed' and there was always someone to chat to. Several girls came to watch and so inevitably we had girl friends. I met up with Mary Dixon, as she was named then, and we spent a lot of time together.

She knew my parents and they thoroughly approved. In fact it turned out that Mary's mother had lived in St James' Parish prior to her marriage and when my father was curate there. As both my mother and Mary used to come and watch me playing cricket on Saturdays they became good friends and I think my parents secretly hoped that we might one day make a permanent match of our friendship but that did not happen. Mary loved to come motorcycling and we spent many happy hours driving around the country. On one occasion we even drove down to Folkestone to stay with my parents on their annual holiday. During the journey the weather was awful, heavy rain and a violent thunderstorm. We got soaked and frozen, at one point being reduced to sitting in a wayside café drinking cocoa while trying to thaw out. Two bedraggled creatures arrived in Folkestone that evening! Those teenage years were happy ones and we formed a close personal friendship that still exists. We used to go dancing and partnered each other at many functions often connected with our respective churches. Mary attended St Michael's Church in Northampton. I had a party at home for my 21st birthday just prior to going off to College. I was able to invite Mary and several of those friends whom I had first met in the 'Scratching Shed' at Wantage Road, the name of Northamptonshire's Cricket Ground.

Mary was also due to train as a teacher and when I went to Durham in 1950 she went to Coventry Teachers' Training College. We remained friendly although our paths inevitably went in different directions and we both made new friends at College. Our close relationship ended but the friendship has continued. She married Bernard Butler, another friend of mine. In fact I became Godfather to the youngest of their three daughters. Her name is Kathryn. The older two are Jane and Anne. Bernard was actually the curate at

St Michael's Church in Northampton and later moved on to a parish in Luton. Sadly he died quite young – of a brain tumour.

Chapter 3 College life

Now to return to my career - I applied to UCCA – the University Central Colleges Application Department in 1947. I had already obtained the required exam results in my School Certificate and so had exemption from the Matriculation exam needed for consideration for a place at University. But there was a real shortage of places due to the fact that men who had served in the war were, rightly, given priority. I had to wait for nearly three years before my application was dealt with. Durham was my first choice, London my second. I was offered a place at Bede College, Durham and went there in September 1950. I had been given a choice at my interview – my qualifications were good enough. Either I could wait a further year until 1951 and take a degree course or I could take the two-year Teacher Training Certificate then on offer at the College. I was fed up with waiting so I decided to start straight away at Bede College and qualify as soon as possible. My arrival by train left a lasting picture in my mind when I first went up for interview in early 1950. Durham is one of those beautiful cities that combined the old with what was then the new. Towering above everywhere else stands the ancient Cathedral. The closer one gets the more impressive it becomes. There is a large green leading up to the entrance. On three sides are Colleges and lecture areas. Castle, Hatfield and St John's Colleges give a strong impression of the true seat of learning, but there are many other colleges situated in the city and each one has its own individuality. I left the station and found a bus stop. While I stood there a bus, travelling in the opposite direction had the name 'PITY ME' on its destination board. It was a while before I discovered that it was actually the name of a village in the countryside!

In September 1950 I arrived by train laden with luggage. I duly reported to the College of the Venerable Bede (invariably known as Bede College) and found out that my digs were a short walk away at 44, Claypath – the cobbled road that went up past the College. New intake students went into digs outside the College for the first year. I was listed to share a room with a certain Bryan Stubbs and our landlady was Mrs Nelson. What a wonderful welcome I received from the Nelson family and when I met Bryan I knew that I was really going to enjoy myself. He was possessed of a dry Geordie sense of humour and his 'off the cuff one liners' were hilarious! We retired to the local pub – The Pig and Whistle' as it was then, almost opposite our digs - on the first evening to get to know each other. A firm friendship started that evening and has remained as close as ever after over 50 years. We have shared a lot of wonderful times together including holidays, first as students and then as friends and confidants when occasions have deemed it necessary. His parents, who lived in Shildon, County Durham, always made me most welcome and I regularly went for Sunday lunch - once I had gone home to Far Cotton, Northampton, to fetch my motorcycle during the first half term break. It was an ideal situation – Bryan got a lift home and I was treated to delicious roast beef and Yorkshire puddings! Several other students lived in or near Shildon so we would often meet up in the Shildon Working Men's Club on

Sundays for a pre-lunch pint. It was a ritual that Bryan's Dad insisted upon as he enjoyed his ale!

Breakfast was served every morning in the main dining hall at College from 7.30am until 9.00am. Almost invariably we just managed to arrive in time for a bite before going off to lectures. During the first year the Courses offered covered a wide range of general subjects – Maths, English, Geography, History, PE etc. so there was a full timetable. The full basic Teaching Certificate work had to be completed in 2 years at that time. Later an extra year was added to cover the same work and eventually the whole Course was extended to 4 years and became known as a Batchelor of Education Degree. This qualification could apparently be claimed when Teaching Certificate students all became part of Durham University in the 70s. I fear that I never bothered to make the claim – to me it was something of a farce as the work covered was virtually still the same.

One thing I particularly enjoyed during my time at Bede was reading out loud. It was something I was good at. I sometimes read the lessons during weekday services in the chapel. It was a beautiful place where one could go and sit quietly and think things through, particularly when work became stressful. We were given a tremendous amount to cover as time was at a premium. There was a considerable amount of work to be completed during the holidays too.

I well remember returning to an English lecture after one vacation. We were given the task of writing an immediate essay. We were apparently supposed to have read an educational book of one kind or another but I had not done so. I asked Bryan for an author's name. He said 'Basil Henriques'. I made up a totally imaginary quote from his book that read as follows: 'A Magistrate must be firm, kind, and infinitely far seeing'. I let my imagination run riot – e.g. travelling on trains without a ticket, standing outside the loo door imitating a ticket collector, asking for a ticket to be passed out through the door and then showing it to the real inspector before returning to the loo and handing the ticket back to an unsuspecting owner! There were several other experiences – both real and made up – that I wrote about. Several of the stories harked back to what I had gleaned when we lived on the Isle of Wight and my Father was at first Chaplain at the Borstal and later Chaplain of Parkhurst Prison - attempted escapes etc. One particular story was absolutely true – I remember it happening when I was about 8 years old. A 'Trusty' (ie a Borstal boy nearing the end of his sentence) used to work unsupervised in our large garden. When it rained, instead of having to return to the Borstal, he was allowed to shelter in the garage. He worked out how to start the car – a 1928 Morris Cowley that father had bought for £ – and one day decided to try and drive away and catch the ferry to the main land. He got the car out of the garage all right but then the engine stopped as he did not realise that it needed the choke to be pulled out to keep the engine going until it got warm. Poor lad – he lost his remission. Another story concerned a borstal boy who caught the eye of our 15 year old maid. She used to bake him cakes – amongst other things. He also wanted to get away but she let him down at the crucial moment. She had secreted something in a cake and a warder found it – bad luck. But the net result of facts both real and imaginary written down in my essay was excellent - I got an A+! At least it taught me that I could write what in all honesty was mainly fiction in an interesting way. I remember afterwards being roundly accused in jest of having had a mis-spent youth - by Bryan and the rest of the lads - as my essay was quoted by the tutor, Jack Carrick, as being the best. Obviously he had never read any books by Basil Henriques!

There were many other tasks to be completed during our vacations – plenty of reading to do and several theses to write. Having a Father who had been in the prison service was most useful as he had several books that were ideal for references. But I unwittingly went too far on one occasion. I borrowed a 'classified' book – one kept on the 'most secret' list – explaining in detail how to deal with problems that arose in both Borstals and Prisons. It also laid down the rules and regulations appertaining to these Institutions. We had to state from where we had obtained our information for each thesis. I put down the names of the various documents used, stating that they were from a copy of HMPR (His Majesty's Penal Regulations) etc. The thesis was over ,000 words and told of the inner workings and general organisation of Borstals and Prisons. As it happened all my work was sent in as examples of the type of Course work being done by every student. I got good marks, but when I asked for all my Course work to be returned the thesis on Borstals and Prisons had been summarily removed and apparently sent to the Home Office. Emboldened by my tutor's encouragement I had intended to publish it. Instead it had been destroyed and I received a warning, sent via the College Principal at the request of the Home Office, that any other copy of that work must also be destroyed as it was full of classified information. My tutor thought it a great joke, but I was less impressed! The rest of the work was returned eventually.

We were sent out to schools in County Durham for 4 teaching practices during our two years. I really enjoyed these as I had had 3 years experience prior to coming to college. But there were some tough schools in the mining areas and certain experiences were quite hilarious for the most part. I remember once teaching in a Junior School in Stockton, down by the docks. One day most of the children did not immediately return after dinner. There had been a murder committed in dockland and they had gone to watch a body being fished out of the water. When they returned not a word was said. The place was a bit like a cauldron waiting to boil over and the Head knew how to deal with the problem – a wise man!

On another occasion at that school I was telling the story of how Jesus was taken to the hill of Calvary carrying his cross. I waxed eloquent on the subject and one little lad was getting quite agitated and muttering to himself. I then built up to the climax of the nails being hammered into Jesus' hands and this lad suddenly jumped up and shouted out, "The bastards!" No one laughed (apart from the class teacher) and I completed the story. Quite an experience! The standard of intelligence over all at that school was not high but the kids were very streetwise and always had interesting stories to tell when invited – nicking things, cheeking the police, telling about fights at home and in the streets, and 1 other tales – their education was not conventional – but very thorough! Bryan and I were together on that practice. We loved that school. I guess I have always had a lot of sympathy for the underdog throughout my life – teaching or otherwise.

I did one practice at a Secondary Modern School at Birtley. The kids were great and responded to my interests, particularly in sport. But the Head was less enthusiastic about students and we were, to him, nuisances. He put us in a separate room from the staff and so at first we were not privy to much that went on. However the teachers to whom we were assigned soon put that right and told us that the Head was newly appointed. I heard later that he had not stayed long at the School. I wasn't surprised! I refereed a number of the school's football matches and was invited back several times after my practice was completed there. Newcastle United had a great team in those days and as I went to watch them whenever I could the boys hung on every word. My other two practices were in primary schools and at the end of the final teaching practice, when assessments were made, I was one of 6 students picked out to be watched by outside assessors. We knew that three were at the lower end of the scale and three were at the upper end but we did not know who was which. However all went very well and I finished up as one of only four students awarded a distinction in teaching, thank goodness, out of 52 of us. As I had completed all my written work too it was sent in for a level to be used for assessment. I was told about that when I had to go home early because of my Father's illness, so I knew I had passed. The distinction in teaching turned out to be invaluable as I was successful in getting the first job that I applied for.

Lectures were hard work. In the first year of general subject studies there were always plenty of us to take notes and swap them too. However we specialised in the second year. I studied PE and History. Most of the PE was of the practical variety so that cut down much of the paper work. However History was a different matter. Our tutor, Wilfie Hart, was a dapper little man who loved his liquor. He had been a commissioned officer in the Navy during the war and 'pink gins' often entered any conversation. But he had a different slant on the imparting of history – he would always be telling us of the illicit affairs had by the royalty of the day – "on the wrong side of the sheets", as he would say - and he always seemed to know who were the illegitimate children as well as the luckier ones. He would often have us in stitches – a popular tutor with a real sense of humour. My particular specialism was that of Romano-British history and I developed a genuine interest in the way in which they lived during the 300+ years of 'occupation'. There are many sites dotted around the country and I was able to see quite a few, mainly in the North of England. I also enjoyed the PE syllabus and I went out voluntarily to teach at both Bede Grammar School in Sunderland and at Bishop Auckland Grammar School once a week. As I had had a heart murmur that had prevented me from doing National Service I felt I had something to prove. What I did not know was that, thanks to the medical report I had been given and which was subsequently passed on to the College and PE Department, I was being secretly monitored with the object of assessing my suitability to go on to the top PE College at Carnegie in Leeds. We were always doing exercise tests and it was noted how I performed. I only learned about all this when I applied for a place at Carnegie. Fortunately the rest of the PE students were unaware as to why there were so many tests – if they had known that I was the reason for them my name would have been mud! Sadly, in the end, I could not take the proffered PE place as I had to leave Bede College immediately exams were finished in order to help with family problems, something expected of sons and daughters in those days. This unfortunately also meant missing out on a College cricket tour to the South of England.

My Father was desperately ill and in June 1952 had to go to the Prince of Wales Hospital in Tottenham for an operation to have a gastric ulcer removed. I travelled by motorcycle to our new home at the Vicarage, Rothwell, in Northamptonshire, where Father had previously been instituted as Vicar of Holy Trinity Church, to look after my Mother and also to carry out certain speaking commitments for my Father. I also had to drive mother up to London to see Father who was on the danger list for a longish spell. In addition to that I had just landed myself a teaching post at an All Age School at Broughton, near Kettering. It was an incredibly difficult time, but I certainly learned the art of public speaking the hard way!

But to return to college days – these were some of the happiest days of my life. I took part in a variety of sports at senior level, representing College at Cricket, Football, Hockey and Rugby. I swam for College and was a fairly undistinguished member of the Athletics team. I also did well at the minor sport of table tennis.

Doing a PE Course kept us extremely fit and on several occasions I played football in the morning and hockey in the afternoon. I even took part in swimming matches on occasion, after having played rugby, but that was not the best preparation to win breaststroke races! I went dancing in Durham most Saturday evenings – first to the 'Waterloo', in Old Elvet, until .30 pm and then across the road to the 'Three Tuns' that stayed open till midnight. My favourite tipple was the local brown ale - very popular! I also sang with a college band from time to time and earned a bob or two. I remember on one occasion, when we were camping out on the moors near Stanley in Co. Durham, a group of us went into the Working Men's Club in the village of Stanley. We were all short of money so I was deputed to sing at what nowadays would be called karaoke. We all got free beer for the evening! But I got my own back by making the others stand up and try to sing 'Swing low sweet chariot'. They were dreadful!

My trips up to Durham by motorcycle were lengthy and sometimes a College friend John Myson, who lived in London, would get a lift to Northampton and then we would travel back on my bike together. However on one occasion when I was on my own I fell foul of the police at a halt sign near Oxley, Nottinghamshire, and was eventually issued with a summons that was headed REX v TURNER. It was delivered to me at college by a local policeman. He was actually more interested in my motorcycle than anything else. On that night King George VI died. A day or two later the same policeman turned up with another summons. He said that as the King had died the first summons was invalid. I could not, by law, be summonsed by a deceased King. However the heading was now changed to REGINA v TURNER and I still had to pay a 30 shilling (now £1.50) fine!

There were many interesting escapades that took place during my time at Bede. I frequently went to Sunderland, to Roker Park, to watch Sunderland FC play. Afterwards

I went dancing at Seaburn Hall until all hours, then rode back to college on my motorbike and surreptitiously coasted silently down to an old air raid shelter in the college grounds where I housed it. I then had to cross over to the PE block where my room was during my 2nd year, knock up the guy who had the room nearest the outer stairs, and he would let me in. On the floor below our history tutor, Wilfie Hart, had his room. He knew what went on I expect, but invariably he had quaffed plenty of spirits and always slept soundly! As I stated earlier, he was an ex naval officer, having served during the war. We found him quite a character and he had an excellent rapport with his students, sometimes offering us a drink while carrying out tutorials! His finest hour came on the night before we were due to sit our History exam. I was passing his room about .30pm, having been doing some last minute revision with another student. He came out and said, "Mr Turner, fetch all history students to my room immediately please" – and promptly shut the door! I gathered everyone together and we went to his room, not knowing what to expect. He looked very serious for a second, then said, "Open that cupboard", and pointed to one on the wall. It was duly opened and then he said, with a broad grin, "Help yourselves". It was full of beer and spirits! We had a party until about midnight. Before ushering us out he commented, "Fortunately for you the history papers are marked internally". The next morning we assembled in the exam room. Wilfie walked in looking ghastly, put his head in his hands and murmured, "I am glad you are doing this exam and not me". The upshot was that I do not think anyone actually failed – a tribute to Wilfie's hangover!

But apart from the above story the work was hard graft and I gather that several students had to return the next year to take exam resits, particularly in the Maths and Science Departments. To this day I have never managed to discover why Wilfie Hart was permitted to mark his own students' papers. Maybe it was because he was a senior lecturer in the University's History Department.

The building next to Bede College was Saint Hild's College for ladies. We were sometimes invited there for dances and unsurprisingly we got to know some of the students well. They also shared an occasional lecture with us when course work coincided. (Nowadays the two Colleges are combined, as part of Durham University, under the name of the College of St Hild and St Bede) The Principal, Miss Angel Lawrence, was a tartar for discipline and, according to the girls, used to carry out amongst other things, regular fire drills. Mischievously a group of us decided to help out in this direction by setting off the fire alarm at an unscheduled time in the early hours of the morning. Several of our students, including me, were going out with some of the girls from the College and one of them arranged for a downstairs window catch to be left undone when required. I was 'commissioned' to make a fitting that would screw on to the fire alarm to break the glass. So I wangled myself an invitation into Hild's and measured up the fire alarm casing. I then made a fitting with a central screw which, when turned, set off the alarm, the idea being that once the alarm sounded the fitting would be removed on the way out. It worked perfectly. One snowy night in the winter of 1951, just before the Christmas holiday we drew lots and four lads, dressed in dark tracksuits, went into the building and rolled out toilet rolls on the lower corridors. They then removed the ordinary light bulbs and thus the rolls looked like fire prevention hosepipes in the emergency exit lighting in the corridors. They set off the alarm and got out quickly. The rest of us watched from a safe distance and saw the girls streaming out in their night attire while the alarm rang. It was harmless enough but Miss Lawrence was not impressed! Inevitably there were some repercussions when it was all over and only the timely intervention of someone on the staff smoothed the troubled waters and prevented anyone involved being sent down. An apology was forthcoming so, as Miss Lawrence later admitted, it showed that in an emergency the fire drill worked well. But we were warned not to try any other tricks!

Quite apart from the studying that we were expected to do – the course itself was very intense and kept us very busy – I think that the chance to mix with so many other students who were at the University was of paramount importance. I gained a tremendous lot from rubbing shoulders with people with so many diverse talents, particularly in the field of sport. Many young men and women went on to represent their local areas in politics, public service and sport as well as in the field of Education. There were any number of societies one could join and the opportunity to take part in games of all kinds was virtually unlimited. Add to that the fact that, because we were studying Physical Education at advanced level, there was always a gymnasium available whenever we required to use one. Fitness levels were very high and I used to run a course for several students who wanted to get fit. I also attended an extended course to study the art of remedial exercises and massage. This stood me in very good stead in later years when I was running various sporting events and teams – pulled muscles often featured large on the agenda! In fact this 'extra curricular' study turned out to be probably the most useful acquisition of anything I studied as I have used those skills whenever there have been minor sporting injuries to be dealt with on the spot. It is equally useful for treating muscular back pain that affects so many people, particularly in later life.

A story that comes to mind that illustrates this very well. I met a student - who was later to become one of my closest friends - when playing cricket at Durham. During the summer of 1951 I played cricket for Bede College and sometimes for the combined Colleges XI. Early in the season I started very badly, failing to score any runs at all in the first three matches and taking only an occasional wicket. For the only time in my cricketing career I was dropped from a side and in the next match was only picked as 12th man (reserve). I was very disappointed as I had spent a lot of time practising in the nets after my early failures. Luckily for me, unluckily for my replacement, he injured himself just prior to the match, which was away from Durham, so I was required after all. I was really fired up and for the only time in my cricketing career I batting right through an innings, having opened. We were all out for

84 runs on a difficult pitch. But lady luck was on my side. I scored 61 runs not out. I then opened the bowling after tea, took 7 wickets for 32 runs and we won fairly easily - by about 12 runs. The next day, a Sunday, I went for a net practice. The ball looked as big as football and I hit everything cleanly until the coach, an ex-Yorkshire cricketer named Alec Coxon, came down the net and said to me in broad Yorkshire dialect, "Tha' can't 'it every ball out of t' ground, lad". "No, Mr Coxon," I replied and then proceeded to hit the next ball he sent down straight back over his head. There was a tall lanky man standing by the nets watching. "Ey, Frank, cum an' bowl at this bugger," said Alec. The guy took off his jacket and tie and disappeared down the ground – so far that I thought he had gone to fetch the ball I had just hit. How wrong I was! He ran in like an express train and bowled so fast I never saw anything much of the ball till it reared up off a good length. I went one way, my cap went the other. He went back to repeat the dose and as he ran in I backed away. The ball hit the stumps – and broke one! I walked down the net and muttered, "I'm not facing him again. He'll kill me if he hits me!" As I passed Alec Coxon he grinned at me, poked me in the chest and said, "I told thee tha' couldn't hit every ball out of t' ground!" Then he introduced me to Frank Tyson who was a student at Hatfield, a College bordering Cathedral Close and virtually in the shadow of Durham Cathedral – a truly magnificent building. Just two years later Frank was picked to go to Australia with the England team. He became known as 'Typhoon Tyson' because he was recognised as the fastest bowler ever to play cricket and was instrumental in helping England to win the Ashes in the 1953/4 tour. His finest hour was at the MCG (Melbourne Cricket Ground) when he took 7 wickets for 27 runs in the match that clinched the series. Strangely enough when we walked together across to the pavilion – for me to change after my net batting stint and for him to change into cricket gear ready for his net bowling practice under the watchful eye of Alec Coxon - we talked of things other than cricket and as time progressed we became very close friends. We have kept that up all our lives. He married a lovely Australian lady – then Ursula Myers – in 1958 and they moved to Australia in 1963. I saw a lot of him when he came to play for Northamptonshire in 1953 after he finished at Durham. He stayed with my family on occasions and often visited us in the early days of his career at Northants. He had a close rapport with my father over the years too. We spent much time together whenever circumstances permitted and frequented the dance hall at Franklin's Gardens (where the Northampton 'Saints' Rugby team played) on many a Saturday evening! However, the import of this story is that we became friends, not just because of sport but for a much deeper reason. Friendship often can come from sport but as one grows older that becomes less important. The true friendship lasts long after the ability to play sport wanes with age. One outcome of our friendship has been that I have, over many years acted as a sort of unofficial agent for the Tysons in England. Frank has done the same for me in Australia. Through our mutual friendship and trust we have managed to do a variety of interesting and useful things both in education and elsewhere. In later life, after the development of cancer in the form of a malignant melanoma forced early retirement upon me at 55, I arranged a variety of speaking engagements to Cricket Clubs around the country for him, chauffeuring him to most of those events, and so we have been able to enjoy precious times shared together. I organised an Under 16 Boys' cricket tour of

England in 1991 for him when he was teaching at Ivanhoe Grammar School, Kew, a suburb of Melbourne. In return I have spent many months in Australia with him and with George Tribe, another famous Australian Test cricketer who played for eight seasons for Northants. But more of that will be mentioned later in this autobiography.

Chapter 4 My Student days - a summary

Being at - to give it the full title - the College of the Venerable Bede, Durham, greatly widened my worldly horizons. Above all I learned that people living in various parts of Britain often had different approaches to life. While Southerners were fairly restrained towards each other – keeping themselves to themselves, so to speak, Northerners had a very open and friendly approach to their peers - and to strangers as well - and I gained much benefit. I settled in quickly and sensed that the welcome that I received from my fellow students, ninety five per cent of whom actually lived in pit villages quite close by, was truly genuine. Yet one thing did amuse me – if serious decisions had to be made amongst any group of students we southerners did not get a look in. This even extended to which pub we were going for a drink after lectures! Mind you understanding the Geordie dialect with all its attendant local colloquialisms was an education in itself and it took me 6 weeks before I could 'translate' much that was being said. I well remember, on being asked by a Geordie student and friend, Sam Davis, what I was doing at the first half term holiday, I replied that I was going home to fetch my motorbike. "Wor man," said Sam, "tha's ganin yem do'n so'th! Gerawa' Chris!" I practically needed a translator – apart from the last word!

The tutors were a mixed bunch of individuals. They varied from those with a sense of humour that came out during lectures in particular, to others who found it difficult to communicate what they had to impart to us in a way that was interesting. Consequently there were considerable diversities in the results obtained. For instance the Maths tutor's lecture was dry, and completely devoid of anything appertaining to a good laugh. We really dreaded spending two-hour sessions with him and the tests he set did not produce good results. We found him difficult to understand and he seemed to be unable to explain what he was supposed to teach us. On the other hand our English tutor would often have us chuckling away when explaining Shakespearian colloquialisms and the like. But Chaucer was his favourite subject and I learned to appreciate the true richness of the language and the stories that he 'translated' for our benefit. He had the ability to 'paint' verbal pictures – a skill that in later life I tried hard to emulate. In fact his lectures often lasted longer than the officially designated times. These experiences certainly showed me the true importance of making lessons interesting. One of the finest exponent's of this skill I found to be an authoress of children's books – Elizabeth Clarke. She came to Bede College and gave a general lecture to any students who wished to attend. The place was packed as her reputation had preceded her. She had us all emulating young children and she used the technique of repetition to gain our interest. It certainly worked and I used it throughout my career. Lecturers were expected to give the occasional 'demonstration' lesson. These lessons were supposed to show us how teaching should be done. Most of them were dreadful! But our PE lecturers brought out the best in us. The practical bias meant that we were expected to perform to a high standard and to this end we were required to give displays. It meant that we had to rely on each other for support – literally. Performing handsprings, headsprings, back flips, bar work etc. could all be extremely dangerous and we learned to rely implicitly on each other. We must have done something right as I do not recall many serious injuries being sustained by anybody – despite one student who was quite useless as a performer and should never have been let anywhere near apparatus. Needless to say, he failed his practical exam at the end of his first year and was directed to safer fields of education. However, in fairness to him, he was one of those capable of taking adequate PE lessons with young children. I must say that, whenever he got near equipment it was left to tutors to give him support when there was anything even remotely dangerous to learn. But it was all absolutely invaluable training, as we in turn had to give that physical support to others, first at College and later in Schools. I opted to go out to two Grammar Schools during each week, one in Sunderland and the other in Bishop Auckland. The members of staff at those Schools were great and at one point I could have had a full time job either teaching Physical Education at Bede Grammar School, Sunderland, or at Bishop Auckland Grammar School. But I declined to stay in County Durham after I had qualified as I wished to return to my home county of Northamptonshire - despite the fact that the authority did not hand out any student grants apart from basic fees. It was not so easy to become a college student as standards were at that time set by University Boards and Entrance exams had to be sat in addition to taking School Certificate grades and the Matriculation exam into consideration. Any failure of first year exams meant being excluded the following year.

Above all, I know that I learned the true value of comradeship while at Durham. I still had friends at home, but being able to mix with people who, in some respects, represented what amounts to a different way of living – almost an alternative culture if you like – opened my eyes in ways I would never have suspected. Working in pit villages, meeting parents who had a much harder time making ends meet financially than I had come across before, and learning to try and understand what made them tick, was an experience I have never forgotten. I vividly recall once going to a School for blind children in Blaydon, Newcastle. One -year-old boy led me round the school so confidently that it was incredible. He also turned out to be a brilliant musician and he asked to play for me. Then, at one point, he suddenly had a tantrum. A member of staff was quickly on the scene to try and calm him down. Eventually he resumed playing and later the member of staff explained that he had a 'perfect ear'. The piece of music that he had played had a 'rogue' chord in it and the boy could not accept it. I never forgot that and I often wondered if, in later years, he had grown into a concert pianist. Over the years I have worked with blind people and it is amazing how the loss of sight - one of the five senses – is so adequately compensated for by the other 4 remaining senses. It was that little boy who in effect inspired me to take an interest in the welfare and development of people who are blind. I have read articles for a 'Talking Magazine for the Blind' for over 40 years and have spent many hours since retirement helping those who were unfortunate enough to lose their sight. One of these was a teacher who wrote articles and stories. He was 17 when he gradually lost virtually all his vision and he initially found it hard to readjust. Much of the work involved reading his writings back to him and also enabling him to mark children's essays and other written work. I also helped a lecturer in the field of politics who, amongst other things, was writing a book in conjunction with a former fellow student from St Andrew's University in Scotland. Again, I learned so much from reading the letters appertaining to his political career – quite fascinating. I also gained a far greater understanding of the way in which intellectuals studied political aspects of life as they related to countries other than our own. For a spell, as a student, he had embraced Communism as the fairest form of living, with all men supposedly being equal – until he visited Russia. He had flirted with different parties throughout his life and to be privileged to follow his ultimate thoughts about the world as a whole was fascinating. Sadly he died before the book was completed, but I have no doubt that his fellow author produced a political insight into the basics thinking behind so many different ways of running our world!

Part 3 Gaining Experience in Life

Chapter 1 Settling in

I left Bede College in June 1952, immediately after finishing my finals. My Father had recently moved from Northampton, having been appointed to the living of Rothwell with Orton as Vicar. Unfortunately he had, over the years, suffered from what was thought to have been a duodenal ulcer and had been treated for that but had not made progress towards recovery. On further examination it was found that actually he was suffering from a gastric ulcer and it had become necessary for him to have an operation as his condition was deteriorating rapidly. He was sent to the Prince of Wales Hospital in Tottenham where Mr Dixon Wright, a well-known surgeon who specialised in the operation required, worked. I arrived home from College and within a short space of time Father went off to have this life saving operation. Although I could drive a car I had not passed my test and had to take a qualified driver with me when I drove Mother to the Hospital. He was advanced in years and on the occasions that we went to see Father he would sleep for most of the journeys - which was probably just as well. On our first hospital visit Father was still on the danger list and we sat outside the ward. After a couple of hours the doctor who was on duty suggested that we go out for an hour or two as there was nothing we could do while father was in intensive care. This we did as I needed to go to a shop in Oxford Street in Central London to have an electric razor mended. Unfortunately the trip proved an absolute disaster. We travelled there by tube train. While Mother and I were on the underground platform at Leicester Square waiting to return to Tottenham and the hospital, a man committed suicide when he threw himself in front of the tube train as it came into the station. There were only 4 people on the platform altogether – two others at the far end and us. The alarm sounded and at the same moment my Mother collapsed. Eventually, after being given first aid, she recovered. I offered my name and address as a witness and was told to give details to the ticket collector at the station exit. I spoke to him but he refused to take any details and told us to read the evening edition of the paper. When we did so it was reported in the stop press that a man had been swept off a crowded platform! We learned later that suicides were quite common, particularly amongst refugees, and this poor man had been a forty nine year old refugee from Hungary. This was how the situations were usually dealt with. It was a very nasty experience indeed. We returned to the hospital by tube train – this time as a very nervous couple! But things do not go singly. What with Father being on the danger list, then having the ghastly tube station experience, it seemed inevitable that something else would happen. Next day it did. I went back to fetch the razor – this time by bus – and it was involved in a traffic accident! Thank goodness that was the end of our London Transport experiences. Father slowly improved but was away from Rothwell for several months recuperating in a rest home. He had lost several stones in weight and it took time for him to recover.

The point of the story I have just written was that, prior to his sudden departure to hospital my Father had arranged to speak at several functions and I found out that I was expected to stand in for him. At 23 years old I certainly learned how to deliver speeches the hard way! In the end the experiences I had during the six months of his convalescence stood me in good stead but as I was holding down a full time teaching job at the same time it proved difficult. I coped quite well until his return but unfortunately the suicide I had seen at Leicester Square Station preyed on my mind and I dreamed about it night after night. Eventually I had a nervous breakdown myself. At the time it felt awful but I found out that by getting back to teaching as soon as I could things were bearable. Mind you I picked a good day to start – Coronation Day, June 3rd 1953! Sport also helped me to recover. I played cricket throughout the summer for Rothwell and also rejoined the Schoolteachers' cricket team, the 'Wayfarers' at Northampton. As autumn came I turned to hockey, playing for Kettering Town, and I even had a few County trial games. Golf also featured on the list. The fact that I was aware of the cause of the problem helped too and eventually I put it behind me, but it took quite a while to fully recover – about 18 months.

I recommenced my post college teaching career at an All Age School in the village of Broughton, near Kettering, Northants, in September 1952. The Head Teacher, Mr Richard Waterfield, was an excellent boss. The School was well organised and he had got together a happy staff.

My first class were 11 year olds and I also taught PE throughout the School. We had plenty of equipment and a spacious hall that was used for other activities as well. There was a large field adjacent to the building. I ran the football team in winter and cricket in summer. Athletics also featured large and I organised Sports Days each year. In addition to this I started a Boys' Club - and this was affiliated to the National Association of Boys' Clubs (NABC) - with the help of another male teacher, Mr Hill, and two or three parents, one of whom was the local policeman. Saturday mornings were almost invariably spent either refereeing school football or umpiring school cricket matches. In fact, I was given licence to introduce any activities –

sporting and practical - that the Head felt would be beneficial to the school. Although the school numbers were comparatively small – around 160 pupils in all - we were able to give an adequate account of ourselves in sporting activities and in music festivals. One advantage of being in the countryside was that it enabled the senior boys to go out cross-country running as a change from a PE lesson or two. It certainly kept me fit! Our team competed in local competitions against a variety of opponents from larger schools and we did well in the District Sports Days. We also had a PE display team that performed for parents and visitors on Open Days. The experiences I gained at Broughton were invaluable later in my career, particularly on the organisational side of school life. One thing of great importance to me was that the Head Teacher allowed me to use my initiative, particularly where the Boys' Club was concerned. He agreed to be President but initially 'sat on the fence' – doubtless waiting to see if the ideas I had would inspire the village lads to come and join the club. Fortunately for me they did and I laid down fairly strict rules to enable the School building to be used and not abused. I did have to 'remove' three boys who threatened the continued running of the club, but that was where recruiting the local policeman to act as a helper came in. He soon sorted them out!

Music featured quite large in the curriculum and the School had the opportunity to take part in various Festivals. I conducted and my namesake, Miss Turner, provided the musical accompaniment on piano. It was enjoyable and gave the school a chance to travel to other parts of the county to perform. It was time consuming as much of the practising took place out of school hours but it was very rewarding and great fun too!

Apart from anything else the pupils involved really appreciated what we were trying to achieve and they joined in whole-heartedly. They were drawn from most year groups - apart from the infants who were deemed too young to travel. Although we sang 'away' at other venues much of the time we were able to entertain parents on Open Evenings and also make some money for local charities. Sadly, when the Education Authority decided a form of reorganisation was deemed necessary and the older children had to go to complete their secondary education at schools in Kettering, it became apparent that the 'heart' of village life began to change. Eventually it virtually disappeared as Senior School loyalties moved farther afield.

However there are several amusing stories that I recall while I was teaching at Broughton. There was one particular boy who, whenever there was a sports lesson outside always 'forgot' his kit. On one occasion I was taking the class he was in out on the field. "Please Sir, what about me?" he said. "Oh, go and whitewash the last post!" was my reply. "Yes Sir. Please Sir, where shall I get the whitewash from?" said the lad. "Ask Miss Collins," I commented, thinking that she would send him into the room next to the Head's study to do some extra school work. The Headmaster, Mr Waterfield, was a strict disciplinarian and would 'keep a close eye' on anyone who was sent to that room near his office. This was the normal practice and quite effective as a punishment or deterrent. The boy disappeared back into School and I thought no more about it. Work was always left for dodgers to do to keep them out of mischief.

However, unbeknown to me Mr Waterfield had gone out to a meeting. When he returned he found the boy whitewashing a post at the end of the school drive and making a mess of it. I was duly summoned after the lad had told the Head I had given him the job to do and once I had explained we had a good laugh about it. Worse, poor Miss Collins got her leg pulled and never lived it down! On another occasion, when the posts of Deputy Heads were first introduced into All Age Schools in the County, my name sake, Miss Turner, was appointed as she was the senior member of staff at the time. For several mornings afterwards the poor woman was met by the rest of the teachers who all saluted her each time they saw her! It was all in fun of course. Broughton was a very happy school and we had a lovely staff. I spent four truly enjoyable years there. Sadly, it did not last as circumstances changed radically for me one evening. As I've already mentioned, I ran a Boys' Club at the school for all the lads in the village as well as those at Broughton School. I organised a strict timetable for the sessions and invited sportsmen to come and coach various games such as football and cricket for a variety of groups. We also did a variety of other activities such as woodwork – an extension of the school curriculum – and social activities involving older people. It was very much a community club in the heart of the village. On one particular evening I had approached an American serviceman who had a child at school during his period of 'overseas' posting to England. He used to teach the boys baseball. On one particular evening we organised a game with the adults versus the Youth Club boys. I scored a 'homer' and ran round the diamond, sliding in at last base. Unfortunately I did not get up and, to cut a long story short, I was found to have two chipped vertebrae in my back – the result of a rugby accident I had sustained when playing in a practice match at college 5 years before. I was paralysed for a while – a frightening experience. Many years later I wrote a poem in blank verse about it that was published in St Margaret's school magazine around 1974 that summed it all up. I called it 'Jerked back to reality'. It went as follows:-

JERKED BACK TO REALITY

A sudden jerk - that's all it takes,
A stab of pain across one's back.
Bent double, groaning,
An insidious fear - is this the time?
When will I walk again?

WILL I EVER WALK AGAIN?

Once immobilised - one never forgets,
However many years pass by.
Lying flat upon a board,
Eyes open - and yet not seeing,
Musing on the past - daydreams.

A young man in his prime,
No doubt with thoughts of next week's rugby match in mind,
Makes bold to clinch his place,

Running with grim determination,
Holding the ball - swerving to avoid a tackle - once - twice,
The line is there, a dive - a try!

But fate has run its course. A late tackle, a loud crack,
Then - silence.
A stretcher, an ambulance, pale faces, shaking heads,
A dazed feeling, a soothing voice,
A sudden pricking sensation in the arm,
Oblivion.

Later, much later, distant voices... drowsiness... lie still.
LIE STILL? I CAN'T MOVE!
Patience, patience, patience.

The hours slowly pass - no feeling,
Just fear and nagging doubts.
At last! A slight sensation - a pricking, stabbing in my legs, my back.
MY BACK? - PAIN!

Thank God, at least I feel SOMETHING!
It hurts. Good - success, no more paralysis!

I never thought that pain would bring relief - but it did.
And then rest - and more rest - and time.
Patience, patience... PATIENCE!
Finally, walking again.
A reminiscence? More than twenty years have passed.
Frequent reminders - knowing what to do and how to live with it.
But pain is only transitory and we know
That all goes on around us just the same. That's life.
So much to do, to look forward to.
IT'S GOOD TO BE ALIVE!

The sad outcome of all this was that I had to give up teaching PE as my major contribution to Broughton School. Although I also had a class to teach as well I could no longer offer the practical expertise in Physical Education for which I was originally appointed. I was advised never to give any further practical demonstrations of activities such as headsprings, handsprings, back flips and all the other movements appertaining to the teaching of PE. I was also advised that I should never play sport of any kind again but I was determined to ignore that piece of advice. I was prepared to put up with the consequences – a problem that has affected me throughout the greater part of my sporting life and for which I have had several operations to enable me to keep mobile. I have had to accept that but it has been part of my life and I have always been determined to do every activity to the best of my ability. It has been part of my character and paradoxically it strengthened my determination to remain positive whatever the odds. While all this was happening things became difficult for my parents too. My mother suffered the first of several heart attacks early in 1956. She eventually became an invalid and needed to be looked after during the last few years of her life. As well as me living at home in the old Vicarage at Rothwell from 1952 an acquaintance of mine from College days was teaching in Kettering and we welcomed him to live with us. His name was Ivor Welch. He was a Yorkshire man who had been brought up in York and was at one time a choirboy at York Minster. He was at Bede College at the same time as I was and we became close friends. He obtained his degree in French and became a teacher of French at a Secondary School in Kettering. We met again by chance in the summer of 1953 at a Sports Day held for all schools in the area. The event took place yearly at Wicksteed Park, Kettering. My Father was a trustee of the Wicksteed Park Trust for many years – until his death in 1980. It was an enjoyable time and the experiences I had when setting up and organising the Boys' Club held me in very good stead for what was to come later. Apart from evenings at school doing various activities – woodwork, sports training and meetings (the general idea was for the Club to become self sufficient so that it would be continued when I left) there were regular outings and charity work in the community. But once my mother was incapacitated it was quite impossible for Ivor to stay and I also decided to move away too as it had become necessary to change direction in my teaching career due to my inability to continue as a PE specialist.

Chapter 2   Moving on to Bosworth Road Junior and Infant School, Nottingham

I applied for a teaching post to Nottingham Education Department in February 1956. The only post available at that time was at Bosworth Road Junior School in the Meadows area of the city and I was sent there for the Summer Term, the intention being to move me to a Secondary School in the September. The Meadows had a reputation for being a tough place – it was a slum area adjacent to a large slagheap near a Nottinghamshire coalmine. The Headmaster was a delightful man by the name Ron Gent. He was a true gentleman by name and nature. We became good friends as well as colleagues – a friendship that was maintained until his death in the 1990s. There was a certain irony in being sent to Bosworth Road – I had become, by nature, something of a rebel and so I relished the challenge. After all, I was in effect returning to my roots and I found that I had much sympathy for youngsters who were being brought up in a deprived area. The outcome of all this was that, when I was interviewed again by the Nottingham Education Staffing Dept. with a view to being moved to another school – a well known place named the 'John Player Senior School', I offered to stay at Bosworth Road. As it was practically impossible to get staff o teach there for any length of time the Staffing Officer was delighted! I found that the next class I had was fairly formidable in that there were 43 pupils in it, almost half of whom came from other countries. There were several West Indians. Others came from Poland, Lithuania, Rumania, Italy and India. The rest were British! But I loved it and the great thing was that one felt that here were children who, in many cases just responded to me as a person while others really needed the stability of being cared for. I shall never forget a note from one girl when I left that, after thanking me for teaching her, said, 'Please don't forget me – no one else cares'. After reading that I nearly rescinded my resignation! But, again, there were several interesting and sometimes moving stories to relate, but more of those later.

I obtained digs in West Bridgford – a nice part of the City on the south side of the river Trent and not too far from the Meadows, which was on the north side. It was a most enjoyable cycle ride over a footbridge and along the north bank of the river. There were two other lodgers – a rather neurotic lady in her 50's and a workman who was skilled in building and painting. His surname was Clark. Inevitably he was nicknamed 'Nobby' and he was real character with a terrific sense of humour. He was a Cockney and came from London. He travelled home at weekends, hitching lifts as money was tight. While at Nottingham I had acquired another motorcycle. It had a 197cc 2 stroke James engine and the make of bike was a 'Sun'. It was the sort used for dirt track riding and hill climbing. It was not overly comfortable – but it certainly went! On one occasion I was giving Nobby a lift on his way home when he was taken short and we stopped near a loo in Melton Mowbray. He rushed in but came out almost as quickly, chased by an irate lady – he had gone into the wrong entrance! Much to my amusement she was waiting to berate him further when he eventually came out of the Gents side, but he ran past her and we beat a hasty retreat with a host of swear words ringing in our ears. Soon after that I bought an old 1934 Vauxhall 12. It needed painting and I was no expert. Nobby was. He bought some cheap blue paint for the bodywork and some black paint for the mudguards for me – from Woolworths. By the time he had finished it looked brand new. He could use a paintbrush to such good effect that it looked as though the car had been sprayed – a great guy.

Bosworth Road School was certainly tough. On my second day, as I walked into school I was spat at by a mum who shouted, "Bloody teachers!" Fortunately she missed me. I sarcastically said, "Good morning," and hastily disappeared through the school entrance! I learned more about how to discipline children there than at any other educational establishment I ever worked in. The use of a 'tawse' for corporal punishment was standard practice. A tawse was a thin leather strap with three long 'fingers' at the end. A smack on the hand from that stung a bit. One male member of staff was expected to carry out this form of chastisement if a child was sent to him and fill in a 'punishment book' stating the reason for the punishment. When the member of staff responsible for what I considered an utterly barbaric practice left the Headmaster gave me the job. I got the impression that this sort of punishment had been carried out regularly for years and that the Head guessed that I would change things. He obviously wanted it phased out quietly! I immediately decided that I had absolutely no intention of following my predecessor's example anyway. Some ladies on the staff who, in my opinion, often used this form of punishment as an easy option when things went awry, eventually realised what was happening and tried to make life difficult for me – after all, sending them to someone else was an easy option anyway - until I threatened to suggest to the Head that they should attempt to carry out corporal punishment themselves. This would certainly have 'put the cat amongst the pigeons!' Some of the older children would simply have lashed out at them without a second's thought. I was quite prepared to speak sternly each time an errant pupil was sent to me for punishment if I thought it was justified and I found that it worked perfectly well. Anyhow the punishment book remained empty. I think this was probably because I was normally very friendly and was prepared to listen to children's troubles if they wished to confide in me – a form of pastoral care that was well received. Many of them knew little else but being knocked about at home or fighting in the streets and sympathy was a rare commodity although I got on well with parents. I quickly realised that swearing and hitting children in that area was just a way of life and it was not unusual for a child, when asked to write about anything they wanted to, would tell stories of brutality at home – mothers and fathers having a go at each other as well as at them. Drink had a lot to answer for and swearing was the normal language that many children used. I recall that there were times when I would ask a child what the swear words they used actually meant. They never knew although it was simply their normal speech. I tried explanations but it proved to be a losing battle!

Sports of any kind appealed to the children – netball and rounders for the girls, football and cricket for the boys proved the most popular. These games took place in the large playground when practising and football matches were played on a recreation ground on Saturday mornings. We had quite a good team – not too much skill but plenty of rough and ready determination! Refereeing called for skills outside the standard rules and it was not unknown to have to stop fights when tempers boiled over. But sending off players was very rare – had it been otherwise sides would have finished up with only 5 or 6 players a side! Most of our matches were against schools with backgrounds similar to Bosworth Road School – they had to be. However on one occasion Bosworth Road was involved in a Cup match with a school from out of the district. Our team had 4 players sent off and, unsurprisingly, lost. Cricket was played in the school playground. The wickets were two narrow dustbins. Bats and a hard rubber ball were used but there were no pads or gloves. All in all it was the survival of the fittest!

There was also a sort of evening session for older youngsters to come to the school if they wished. It was organised by the Nottingham Education Authority and I volunteered to take part. There was some hourly extra payment to be earned and that was a useful addition to my salary. We played all kinds of games in the school playground, which was really large, and I grew to enjoy it all immensely. I became quite well known in the area and I certainly learned a lot – particularly about human nature! Some of the Dads and Mums came and joined in too and I reckon that the time I spent at Bosworth Road School was one of the most satisfying times of my life. I was able to build up the sort of rapport with parents as well as children that paid dividends and the support I got when there was serious trouble was remarkable. The use of knives and firearms was quite common and the police spent a lot of time in the area dealing with vicious gang fights and disputes between families. Occasionally there were fatalities but these never happened at the evening sessions fortunately. All this had its downside as well of course and I found myself in tricky situations more than once. The following experience was typical of what did happen.

On November 5th 1956 the children in my class asked me to go along to their bonfire. At the time I rode a motorcycle so I put on my kit as it was cold and went to the area near the school. There were no fields nearby but, despite a rule forbidding fires to be lit in the street, the bonfire was situated at the end of cul de sac. I stopped just short of the fire and sat astride my bike watching the fun. Some of the children saw me and called out as they went past. Most were with Mums and Dads. But there was also a group of four lads who I later found out were not from the area and they were intent on causing trouble. They suddenly moved across the road towards me and they had sparklers in their hands plus a firework or two. They started to pull me off my bike and at the same time tried to remove the petrol cap from the tank. Their obvious intention was to set fire to the bike. Some of the kids nearby saw what was happening and quickly called their Dads. In no time the four were given a severe beating up and they eventually limped away. Then one of the Dad's said to me – and I quote – "We all knows what ya do for uz kids, Mr Turner. If any other buggers ever try to git you jus' tell 'ar kid and we'll sort them bastards a't". I was very grateful to them all but I had a good laugh afterwards. The Dad who said that had a son who was nicknamed 'Dwarf' – he was the smallest boy in the class – about 3ft 6ins tall – my imagination ran riot! But his Dad was certainly a real tough!

On another occasion in winter a crisis sprang up on my duty day. A staff meeting was arranged for the dinner break, after lunch. The meeting started on time but due to the number of items to be dealt with - some of which were quite controversial - the discussions continued for longer than expected. The children were allowed some extra playtime. However it was a very cold day and after a short while I decided to leave the meeting and fetch them in. I went into the playground and instead of the normal 300 or so pupils there were only 6 out there. I asked where the others were and was told they were on the slagheap outside the School premises, keeping warm in the heat coming out of the slag. I quickly ran to the base of the slagheap and there, ranged out upon the heap itself, were all the children. They were obviously fired up and the situation was truly ugly. Several of them picked up pieces of the slag. The boys nearest to me looked threatening, holding their slag pieces ready to throw them. I did the only thing I could and stood back, at the same time targeting the two or three nearest to me and telling them quietly not to silly and put their slag lumps down. The impasse must have lasted about 20 seconds before the boy in front of the rest dropped his piece and walked past me back towards the playground. Several more followed his lead. To those who were still belligerent I shouted that the 'rozzers' (police) would be called if any child was still standing outside the School gate in 2 minutes. Fortunately that did it. Not another word was spoken. Once they were all in I went back to the meeting and strongly advised everyone to get straight to classrooms but to say absolutely nothing about what had happened. The Head Teacher accepted this and walked round the school as pupils came in after I had lined them up. The atmosphere inside School was quite electric for a while but by afternoon break things were back to normal. But it proved that those children were used to a routine and to change it could produce real trouble. It never happened again during my time on the Staff. I often wondered what would have happened if even one boy had thrown his missile. I think a lot more would have followed suit and that would have caused a riot. It would not have been too healthy for me either. I have always been a stickler for punctuality and it was a lesson learned that stood me in good stead in future years.

I'm afraid that other even less savoury things happened to some staff from to time, but fortunately not to me. On one occasion sand was poured into a petrol tank and ruined the engine of one unfortunate member of staff's car. On another occasion sugar was put into the tank of a staff member's motor scooter. That had to be cleaned out before it would go again. There were several other incidents of a similar nature – paint being used on car bodywork, tyres slashed and windows broken. All I had was a bicycle with a small motor that could be lowered onto the back wheel. I never used it for anything other than to travel to and from school. By using a footbridge to cross over the River Trent I cut the journey by a third. I could also lock the bike away in the school caretaker's store for safety!

One amusing story came from a home visit I made (these visits were not normally recommended in this area but I wished to see a parent in order to help a bright girl in my class to enter for an exam that she wished to take in order to get into a grammar school the following year). I duly arrived at the girl's house and found a curtain across the doorway. Thinking it covered the door I tried to knock – but there was no door. I pulled back the curtain, called out, and attracted the attention of the girl's mother. When I asked her where the door was she replied, "We cut it up for firewood as we 'ad no coal left - but we're got our coal pile now". Her husband was a miner who was allowed a free load of coal every two months. I went in, had a cup of tea (in a cracked cup!) and I managed to persuade the mother to let the girl sit the exam. During the conversation there was an intermittent grunting noise to be heard nearby. By now I was fully convinced that I was in a house of ill repute (it was in a red light district). The woman then told me that the council had recently fitted a bath in the house. Then she ushered me into the corridor. I was distinctly uncomfortable – was I being offered a free 'lady of the night' or what? She opened the door and pointed proudly at the bath. It was half full of coal and in the other half was a goat! This was the grunting I had heard! Very relieved but still inquisitive, I ventured to ask what the goat was doing in the bath. She replied, "We pinched it so we could 'av some milk, but don't tell no one will ya!" I left quickly, having learned far more than I had expected or needed to hear. I often wonder if the family ever replaced the front door or returned the goat to its rightful owner!

Working at Bosworth Road Primary School was indeed a remarkable experience. The people were tough, rough and ready to say the least, but they were also kindly people, most of whom, once their trust was earned, were pleased to support anything we did at the School. The Head Teacher, Ron Gent, with whom I often played golf, was great to work for and I spent many happy times there. He was indeed a gentleman by both name and nature. Having been born in a slum area of Birmingham myself, I seemed able to empathise with both children and parents. When I decide to move on it was quite a wrench to leave, but I felt that I wanted to get back nearer to home as I was still playing cricket for Rothwell in the Northants League. Having to travel home each week to do so was both time-consuming and expensive. Working in Nottingham meant that I could not practise with the team and this did not go down well. I also wanted to return to Northampton to start playing cricket again for the teachers' side - known as the Wayfarers – during the summer evenings. While at Nottingham I played for Ruddington – a village club side. They were a great set of lads and made me very welcome. I made a couple of close friends there, one of whom, Derek Hellawell, I worked with at Bosworth Road. I enjoyed it but the standard left something to be desired and I felt I needed a harder challenge if I was to maintain the standard I knew I could achieve. I was a competent hockey player too – I'd played for Kettering Town and once had harboured an ambition to represent Northants. I was actually chosen to play for the County in 1954 but unfortunately continuing serious back trouble eventually put an end to my hopes of becoming a regular County player. As I mentioned earlier, I had suffered a nasty back injury while at college. It finally caught up with me and I was advised not to play any more. It was a great disappointment but at least I had been able to enjoy the challenge for a while.

Chapter 3 Teaching in Northampton

Having decide that I could further my sporting interests back in Northamptonshire I applied for a post in Northampton – the town where I had first decided that teaching was to be my chosen career. I had also spent my teenage years there and so it felt like coming home. Mr Skerrett, the Chief Education Officer, sent me for an interview at Kings' Heath Junior School. On arrival I was conducted to the Head Teacher's study to meet Mr Hutchins, the Head. He turned out to be the man who had been captain of the Wayfarers cricket team way back in 1948. I had actually played several games under his captaincy but he did not immediately recognise me. As he told me afterwards, Mr Skerrett had told him I was the son of the former Vicar of Far Cotton, Canon George Turner. His reply was succinct and to the point. "I don't give a damn who he is or what he has done. I want a good teacher and if he's no good I don't want him". I applauded that at the time. My Father had always wanted to stick his nose in and I had absolutely no wish for him to do so. As it happened the interview went well and I was offered the job. He then took me to meet the Deputy Head. Incredibly it was Corin Judge – another man I had played cricket for and against nearly 10 years before. He greeted me profusely and then told Stan Hutchins who I was. Sport had featured large in the interview and my expertise as a former PE specialist had got me the job. I was told that my first task would be to set up a PE department and help out teachers who found Physical Education a difficult subject to tackle. This was meat and drink to me and by good fortune I had landed in the ideal place to pursue my interests in sport and I never had cause to regret it. The School had only opened a couple of years before so ideas were still new and there was a great opportunity to fit in with a blend of experienced teachers and some straight from college. Stan turned out to be a great boss – hard as nails but with a heart of gold too. He was both liked and very well respected. I was a qualified referee and took part as both a coach and referee in our School matches and in interschool Cup games. Refereeing a School

Cup final in front of a very partisan crowd was one of was my greatest achievements. I was lucky to get away after the match in one piece! We had an excellent school side for several years. Most of the male staff helped out with the football matches on Saturday mornings, including the Headmaster, Stan Hutchins. He was the most vociferous of the lot at school matches! Corin Judge, Derek Buswell and I coached the team. Frank Groome and Colin Dunn provided some refreshments and saw that all visiting teams were well looked after. Our facilities were very good and the school playing field was frequently used for 'neutral' matches by schools in the town. Cricket, Netball and Athletics took place during the Summer Term. There was an excellent lady teacher by the name of Peggy Ward who ran the netball side and organised Sports Day each year. Corin Judge and I coached the cricket team and organised an Athletics team to represent the School.

On the academic side the 11+ Examination featured large during the summer term. Each year group had 3 classes and these were streamed. The majority of the children in the 'A' stream class were considered likely to go to an academically biased schools such as the local Grammar and High School – in this case Northampton Grammar School or Northampton Trinity High School. These children would be placed according to IQ results. Potential Grammar School pupils would have the highest IQs – usually from around 120 plus. IQ scores from 112 upwards would automatically be placed in one of the two Schools. Those below that IQ score were considered to require a more practical education and would move on to the various Secondary Modern Schools in the town. There was a system of interviewing 'borderline' children by specialists from the Education Department. These were pupils whom teachers felt might still benefit from an academic education despite their IQ scores. As in all testing some children were nervous and did not always do themselves justice. On the whole this worked satisfactorily as teachers were well aware of those children with nervous dispositions. Children who were in the 'B' class and 'C' class streams were, naturally, also considered more likely to benefit from a practical education although they sat the 11+ exam just the same. The original concept of the 11+ exam was not to pass or fail. The idea was that children could continue their education by following a course of learning that would best fit them for life after leaving school. It had great merit as a system for making placements but, aided by press interpretations and comments, parents came to view the results in terms of pass or fail – a 'pass' meant a place was available for a course with an academic bias at a Grammar or High School. What was erroneously termed 'failure' meant moving on to a Secondary School. In fact there was much of a practical nature to be studied and worked at in a Secondary School – Cooking, Needlework, Housecraft, Woodwork, Metalwork, Art of various kinds and a host of sporting activities for both girls and boys.

I spent six happy years at the School, during which time I built up a close bond of friendship with 3 male members of staff that has lasted for the rest of our lives. They were:- Corin Judge, Frank Groome and Colin Dunn. All three, like me, went on to become Head Teachers – quite a tribute to Stan Hutchins.

Stan also saw that School trips took place every year for the top year children and we would usually go by train to London and visit various well-known places. We were organised into 5 groups of 10 or so with two teachers to each group. were strictly timetabled when to move on to each new venue. The Tower of London, the Science Museum, the Planetarium, Madame Tussauds and the Houses of Parliament were the regular centres of interest. Once we had arrived all was well, but sometimes things did not go according to plan and there were several hiccups on the way. Travelling first by train from Northampton to London was fine as we all set off together, but on arrival it was the responsibility of staff members to direct their children to the tube station and thence to whatever venue was first on the list. I recall with much amusement watching two lady members of staff directing their groups on to the tube train. When the doors shut that was the last we saw of them for nearly two hours as they had not got off at the right station for the Planetarium. Eventually, as my group passed on a bus, an exhausted group of our children were seen walking along the Thames Embankment towards the Houses of Parliament! What was more, only one member of staff was with them – a lady by the name of Peggy Ward. The other member of staff had disappeared. The upshot was that the children had stopped off for a toilet stop and then set off again, assuming that the second member of staff with them was bringing up the rear. Unfortunately for her she had turned the wrong way on exit. When the rest of the children arrived exhausted at the Houses of Parliament a taxi drew up and out stepped the other very embarrassed lady member of staff – there were no mobile phones then. But they were good trips and the children were able to experience the excitement of visiting places that we had described in detail as class topics beforehand. The children must have been tough as the only people I ever saw feeling off colour by the end of the day were certain members of staff!

Frank Groome and I always took a group of children to Wembley to watch Schoolboy International Football matches. This was, for me, the trip of the year and we never missed a Wembley trip. I once saw Jimmy Greaves playing as a schoolboy against Scotland. England won by 8 goals to 2. Greaves scored 6! However, although we went by bus and thus arrived together, with so many thousands of children and staffs milling about outside the ground it was pretty chaotic to say the least. There was nearly always one child who contrived to get lost on the trip and had to be 'found'. On one occasion we had real fun and this lad led us a merry dance. He was a lad by the name of Richard Ritchie. He was real dreamer who often appeared to live in a world of his own. We all arrived at our designated entrance gate and the boys lined up to be checked in. Ritchie was given directions like everyone else. We showed our tickets and went to our seats. Who was missing? Richard Ritchie! Looking over the wall at the top of the stadium we spotted him still standing by the entrance gate! He just had not gone through the turnstile in spite of being pushed firmly in that direction. I rushed down to the entrance. Fortunately he still had not moved and I was able to attract his attention. After an argument with the ticket man I got hold of Ritchie and literally tied him to my coat with his mackintosh belt. He stayed firmly tied there until after the match and until I got him back on the bus. It became something of a joke afterwards as the boys, whenever they got things wrong referred to it as 'doing a Ritchie!'

Discipline at the school was firm – it needed to be. 'A' and 'B' classes had between 40 and 50 children in them. 'C' classes were smaller and pupils who needed extra help in certain areas of the syllabus could be, to a certain extent, catered for. Teaching methods of the time allowed for large class numbers although marking was often something of a nightmare. Every morning I would have a task already set for the class to do when they came into the classroom. This varied from dictionary work to arithmetical processes – sometimes both – and it was expected that pupils would complete the work set in the time allowed. If not, then it was the child's responsibility to find time to finish off during the day. This work was marked at the end of the day's teaching and competition was fierce. With the 11+ coming up during the summer term most of the early morning work was geared towards using 'short' methods to find results. In point of fact, I learned a lot too and it was often hard to complete tests before the children – in time to mark them together. As a form of discipline it worked very well and, provided that the questions were graded so that for the marginally less able pupils there were still targets to attain, I never came across anything better. The fact that, whether a pupil was actually being taught by me or not, the discipline was still a valid option as, at the end of the day, he or she was answerable to me for his or her behaviour. Thus staff backed each other up. Bullying was summarily dealt with – segregation at playtimes and dinnertimes being the major factor and suitable work was set out for pupils to be completed. A teacher took responsibility for overseeing those to be punished each day – more serious cases of misdemeanours were taken to the Head Teacher – not recommended as Stan Hutchins brooked no nonsense and parents were both informed and invited up to School to discuss the problems involved. As the system of having work ready for children to commence immediately they entered the classroom started with the youngest pupils in the school it became accepted as part of the day's timetable. It had the added advantage that for those who were late without good reason the work was still there to be done before going home! The ultimate punishment could be administered with a cane but those cases were very few – virtually non-existent at Kings Heath despite the rough area. Outside school hours were very much the province of the police, and policemen made their presence obvious as they often walked around the area. They also liaised with the School. Most children knew the 'local bobbies' as they were called, and respected them – begrudgingly sometimes no doubt, but they represented and enforced the law. On the whole children catered for themselves and made up games galore to play outside when the weather allowed. After the war plans were made for children to join organisations – for example the NABC – the National Association of Boys' Clubs – was just one of many. There was an equivalent club for Girls as well. Brownies and Girl Guides and Cubs and Scouts were popular too. It enabled children to get together socially away from the confines of the classroom. TV did not play a major part in the bringing up of young people. The number of programmes for children was limited and any form of violence was not normally shown until late evening and initially this only consisted of old films. In later years TV programmes were introduced for use in schools and were a great asset to teachers both as a basis for discussion and also for imparting knowledge backed up with visual work, particularly in history and geography. The TV programmes were timetabled for schools well in advance and copious notes were included in order that we, as teachers, could give background to the programmes being shown. It was, at the time, a great help and as a result programmes were made to include Science and Maths. The programmes were scheduled for all ages and represented a big step forward in the world of visual education. Teachers were invited to send in 'feed back' so that producers could improve their service. The element of competition for viewers was not at this stage present.

There is no doubt that at Kings Heath I saw the start of the changes that have since affected the world of Education to such a large degree. We were able to experiment with new media. With the assistance of Schools Inspectors, who arranged courses for teachers both in and out of school, we were advised as to the various ways we could use the media and adapt our teaching techniques accordingly. It was very much a partnership and the opportunities to introduce new teaching skills and methods were welcomed by those of us who would accept the fact that the integration of the new ideas being put forward, combined with tried and tested methods, could only be for good. Obviously not everything worked for all teachers. It was a question of going through what was on offer, picking out what suited both the schools at which we worked, using our own teaching techniques, and putting it all to good use. Staff meetings were often, to say the least, lively! In the end the rewriting of the school syllabuses depended in large measure upon the strengths of the staff 'in situ' and thus it was possible to ascertain where the over all strengths and weaknesses lay. Consequently this gave new direction to Head Teachers when looking for staff replacements. There were no shortages of teachers willing to adapt to whatever was required and colleges had to try to ensure that modern ideas were given plenty of credence when presented to their students. Post war ideas of teaching gradually took shape as the perceived needs of the communities in the country changed.

Chapter 4 More about my personal life

Upon leaving school in July 1947 the first thing I wanted to do was to have some regular form of reliable transport. Inevitably, during my school holidays I rode a bicycle and as I had no money to spare I had to make do with that. However I had learned to ride a motorcycle at Oakham School. I aimed to make enough money to buy something with a motor as soon as I could. Once I had started to earn money as an unqualified teacher on supply there was enough to save a little and initially I supplemented this by doing odd jobs for anyone who required them. But first of all I worked on a farm in August 1947 for a spell, haymaking, and potato picking. Unfortunately that ended in near tragedy when a friend, Arthur Ley, who was also haymaking, stuck a pitchfork into my leg when attempting to pick up a bale of hay. I fainted with pain, was unable to continue, and ended up in hospital. By the time I had recovered haymaking was over. However I guess I was lucky - an inch or two higher and I could have been injured for life - some friend! My first paid teaching post was on supply at Blisworth village, about 4 miles from Far Cotton, Northampton. I used my bike when the weather allowed, but 1947 turned out to be the coldest winter for years and the ice and snow caused absolute chaos on the roads – even buses were unable to get me to Blisworth on several occasions. I actually walked there once but the weather was so inclement that it was something I did NOT repeat!

After working for 9 months at Blisworth I was moved to Walgrave, a village not far from Kettering. This journey was about 11 miles as I recall, and I decided to buy an old autocycle. This was really a glorified bicycle with a motor and only one gear. Top speed was about 25 miles an hour and one had to help things along by pedalling up hills. This was not ideal, and one day I returned home after work a bit fed up. The autocycle had broken down. My Father said, "Go into the garden". Then he disappeared into the house. I duly did as I was told and standing there was a brand new two-geared autocycle. I jumped to the wrong conclusion and went to berate my Dad for buying one for himself to ride round the parish when I was struggling with my old one. Fortunately, before I could say anything he said, "Do you like it?" I somewhat grudgingly said I did and asked if I could have a ride. "Of course you can", he said. "It's yours". That changed my tune in a flash and off I went. It was marvellous after my old one! That had been put in as a part exchange. "Thanks very much Dad!" was my first remark on returning home. As a matter of interest, I paid £25 for the old autocycle – the new one cost £49. That, by today's standards of finance would be a lot of money. My first year's salary in 1947 was just £180 gross. Tax brought that down to £144 a year. I used that auto cycle for several months, going to Walgrave to work and also to enjoy travelling around the county. But it was not what I really wanted and so, after about a year I went to Spokes' Garage in Northampton where the two auto cycles had been purchased and, after prolonged negotiations with Percy Spokes, I bought my first motor cycle – a 350cc ex war department Royal Enfield for £65. As the auto cycle was put in part exchange I only had to find £25. It had originally been used as an army dispatch rider's machine. The only problem I had to overcome was telling my Father what I had done. He was not too pleased, but as the deal had already been done with Percy Spokes it was rather a case of 'fait accompli'. Anyhow as a former rider of motorcycles himself he soon accepted the situation and gave me some advice concerning riding the machine safely. I had to take a motor cycle driving test and managed to pass the second time. I had that bike for three years, only changing it for a 1939 Norton 350cc after a year at Durham. The Norton was fast – top speed around 90 miles per hour. I used to motorcycle to College and used it regularly there. On Saturdays I would take a friend, usually Bryan Stubbs, or a supporter of whichever team was playing in a football match at Sunderland or Newcastle. If there was no home match at either place we would ride over to Middlesbrough. There were some famous footballers of the time for us to go and watch at all of those grounds – Jackie Milburn (Newcastle), Len Shackleton (Sunderland), and Wilf Mannion (Middlesbrough) to name but three. Opposing sides had top players too of course.

I bought my third motorcycle – a 'Sun' with a James Villiers 197cc 2 stroke engine – while teaching at Bosworth Road, Nottingham in 1956.

Looking back over the post war years at this period in my existence I came to realise that I had matured considerably in my general outlook. Going to Durham in 1950 gave me a different perception on life. Having been away as a child in two boarding schools I had accepted the confines necessary to ensure the furthering of my personal education. Every day was timetabled to make certain that as pupils we were kept busy and there was little time to make decisions about when work was to be done, only that it had to be fitted into the times set aside for lessons and prep. There was no choice about attending classes. Everything was clearly laid down and we had to conform to strict standards and a code of good behaviour or be expelled. College experiences changed all that. I had choices to make and my exam results depended entirely upon my own decisions – either work hard or fail to gain the best results I needed to further my career in teaching. It was simple, but still an entirely free choice. I also found that ways of living in Durham County and its environs were very different from that which I had been used to. It was an area strong in the traditions of coalmining. In the many pit villages abounding in the county sons of coalminers were more or less expected to follow their fathers down the pit. It had been a tradition ever since mining became a large industry and in the early days families spent their entire lives living and working in the pits for wealthy industrialists. Many of those men were dedicated to increasing their wealth and the miners needed to earn a wage sufficient to keep their families from starving. Thus they were forced to work down the pits as there were no other jobs available to them. Some mine owners were philanthropists and looked after their respective work forces well, providing them with both reasonable living and working conditions. Others were only concerned with lining their pockets and spent little money ensuring the safety of their work forces. Years later I wrote a poem about one child whose story I had come across during my studies. This is what I wrote:-

Conditions in a mining village circa 1830 - 40

A day in the life of a child

The bell strikes three - I turn and groan, for now I start my day,
A hasty bite, a mug of tea, I must be on my way.
For there's no pay if I am late - I only get the cane,
T'will mark my back, for that's my fate. I'll work my shift in pain.

Outside it's dark. My God it's cold, it feels like hell all round.
The wind doth howl right through the trees and makes a fearful sound,
And I am scared. I have not seen - for weeks - the light of day,
For work begins while it is dark. The mineshaft's far away.

I run and stumble through the night towards the bleak pithead,
Where chains go slowly up and down - hooks swing and these I dread,
For they can tear your arms and legs and make you sore indeed.
No help is near and you go down and bleed - and work - and bleed.
But if you're lucky and all's well you simply reach the floor
Of our old pit - a living hell for me - someone who's poor.

I walk through tunnels dank and black - all grimy - from coal dust
That fills my lungs and makes me choke and cough - nigh fit to bust.

I catch my shins, my legs get sore, I stumble to my place,
A tiny cleft within the rock close to the tunnel's face.
And now I'm waiting for the chance to show that I am here,
Just rats around, I hear them squeak and cower back in fear.

At last! a flicker in the dark, a putter on his way.
The candle casts a gloomy light. For me it is like day.
I open up the wooden trap to let the putter past
And as he goes a gust of air revives me at long last.

But when he's gone the dark is back and I am scared once more
For fear of falling on the track when opening my door.
Boys come, boys go, but few can speak, their heavy loads too much
For them to spare a kindly word or slow their truck a touch.

But then, like magic, comes the word for which we all await.
"Loose! loose!" the cry and everyone moves down to freedom's gate.
Up through the gloom I slowly move. At last the top is here.
The air strikes cold, but then - who cares? I only want to cheer!

With many stifled yawns I go to reach my waiting bed,
To have a bath and eat some food, then rest my weary head.
Alas tomorrow soon will come - sun, wind, frost, snow or rain.
To me it will not matter much - I go to work again!

Even children younger than 10 worked down the pit for many hours at a time
and barely saw the light of day in winter. I was very interested in the history of
mining and was appalled to find that even babies were taken into the pits and
left in terrible conditions while their mothers carried coal to the pit face – a
truly awful existence.

During my course at College I wrote a lengthy treatise about the Coalmining
Industry. Durham was the perfect place to make an in depth study of the
subject and I worked in the Durham Advertiser's Newspaper Office. There I
had access to copies of the newspaper reports going back to the 1830s and
the more I read the more fascinated I became. As well as reports of actual
speeches made by Lord Salisbury and others in the House of Commons I
came upon a book made by Mines' Inspectors about working conditions in the
mines. Much of it was made up of drawings – some of the inspectors
preferred visual pictures to writing - and the sight of the terrible ways in which
women as well as men were forced to work aroused my interest to such an
extent that I studied the Mines Act of 1842 just to see how things changed
after the Act was eventually passed. Children still worked in the pits, but 10
hours a day was the new maximum working time permitted by law - what a
life! There was no such thing as a Social Security System where those who
were sick could 'sign on' and be given money by the State to buy food and

clothing. People were turned out of their homes and sent to the workhouse if they could not earn sufficient to feed and clothe their families so children were forced to go to work in the pits as soon as they could earn money that would go towards the family budget.

Chapter 5 Motorcycles and Cars - My Hobby

In 1953 I bought my first car. It was a 1932 Austin 7. I quickly began to learn what to do when things went wrong. The first major job I had was to replace a burnt out valve on the engine. It played up while Steve Taylor and I were on holiday near Minehead. By chance we met a holidaymaker who worked on aeroplane engines. He offered to show me how to replace the problem valve. We literally stripped the engine down then went to a garage and bought a set of 8 valves for the car - 4 inlet valves and 4 exhaust valves. Then he showed me how to grind a valve in to fit the engine. Instead of just replacing the one burnt out valve, between us we replaced the lot! I think I manage to do just two – he did the other six! Thanks to him the holiday was a great success, the car ran beautifully and I was hooked into learning how to work on both motorcycle and car engines and do repairs – something that has saved me a lot of money. My second car, bought in 1955 was a 1936 'Singer' costing £50, followed by a 1934 Vauxhall 12 costing £45 in 1957. This was a real luxury car with lots of extras such as soft leather seats, a rear window blind, and small pullout tables for rear seat passengers. I worked on each car, learning all the time about engine part replacement and maintenance. I also smartened them up and sold every one at a small profit. Next I moved upmarket and purchased a Ford Prefect in 1958. This was a disaster as it developed a problem with both the steering gear and the engine, but I managed to get it replaced free of charge by the garage I had bought it from in the first place and I took a new Ford Prefect van in exchange. I kept that until after I was married. In later years, when we moved to Leeds, doing my own repairs and maintenance enabled us to run two cars – a decent one and a 'banger'. The 'banger' was for me of course! I maintained whatever old car I managed to get hold of. Molly bought me my first 'banger' in 1967 – a 1952 Austin A30 for £50. As we now taught in different parts of Leeds we were both able to have transport to get to our respective schools - but more of those times later. The first thing I did was to replace all valves and change some worn piston rings. I also worked on the chassis, replacing rusty panels with tin made from old oilcans. These I fixed with screws so that if necessary the panels could easily be changed. One could not do that nowadays! I even used chicken wire and papier-mache to mend the rusted sills. By the time I had finished one could not tell the difference and it passed three tests in successive years. Over the next 15 years in the banger range I had a Triumph, a Ford Anglia, A Wolsley Hornet (that was really a glorified mini) and a 12 year old Saab. I enjoyed doing them up – it was a hobby really. All of the cars were very cheap apart from the Saab – nothing above £125. By this time, in the 1970s car prices were in the thousands so I was indulging in very cheap motoring! I also had a succession of two-wheeled vehicles that I bought cheaply and did up. I always sold at a small profit too – in order to purchase the next machine. I once even bought a motor scooter for £5 and sold it for £20. It was French and called a

'Concorde' but did not exactly go very fast! I suppose my finest deal came in the mid 1970s when I bought a 1961 Triumph £350cc twin cylinder machine for £30. Not many were built as the 650cc Triumph Speed Twin model was more popular. I spent a lot on time doing it up, ran it for about 3 years and then, after severe illness, I was forced to stop riding for a while. I happened to mention to a friend who was interested in vintage motorcycles, that I had an unusual 'vintage' Triumph. He offered to pass on the information to anyone who might be interested. The next thing I knew a gentleman called at the house, asked to see the bike, and promptly offered £200 for it. Mind you, it nearly broke my heart to let it go but I sold it and put the money away until I was fit enough to buy another machine. I guess that I had never grown up when it came to riding motorcycles! But I had learned plenty about riding on roads over the years and I never indulged in the ridiculous business of overtaking at high speed so I never had any dangerous excesses of speed to concern myself with. My next purchase came in 1986. I decided, after two cancer operations, that I might as well indulge myself by finding a trail bike. This is a machine that can be used over the moors and in what are normally inaccessible places. I found one in Sunbury on Thames when staying with my cousin Daphne and her husband Frank. It was exactly what I was looking for. It was a 250cc 2 stroke Honda – a specialist's bike – one that I could use to ride cross-country and out on the moors. Although at this point I still was not well enough to ride a machine, I decided to buy it anyway. One of the many trips I made was to deliver carpets for a friend in the trade. After making my deliveries to Courts Stores in Kent and Surrey, I called at the motorcycle owner's house in Sunbury on Thames and put the Honda in the delivery van. I got it home and was able to put the finishing touches to perfecting the bike for use when I was able to ride again. Once I was fit enough to venture out I had a series of interesting and quite hair-raising rides across the moors, the most memorable one being at Middlesmoor. I intended to take the bike over what looked like a low concrete wall. As I approached I realised that it was much higher than anticipated. I laid the bike down – literally – having crashed through the gears to prevent hitting the obstacle. I succeeded in stopping and sliding off the bike without injuring myself – something I had been taught to do years before by a wartime dispatch rider. I got up and lifted the bike up. It appeared undamaged but when I set off I realised I had broken off all the splines (cog-wheel pegs) on the main drive and the bike would only go on the flat or downhill! Eventually I reached the police station (now defunct) at Ramsgill where I eventually got the AA to get me home with the bike. I purchased new parts for the engine and had it repaired. Then, sadly, fate took a turn. I went to the Leeds General Infirmary for a check up to see if my cancer operations had been successful and parked in a motorcycle area at the rear of the Hospital. When I came out to go home the bike had been stolen and that was the last I saw of it. The Insurance Company eventually paid out £250 and I purchased a standard road bike – a Honda Superdream. The bike was good for riding on roads but useless for cross-country so that put a stop to my forays onto the moors. After 3 years I purchased another Honda Superdream and rode that until I was 70 years old. Then finally I had to give up motorcycles as I was having trouble with my hips and back and riding became too painful a business to continue.

But returning to the cars that I used over the years – car number 2 was a 1934 Vauxhall 12. It had belonged to a stonemason who never drove it quickly as he towed a trailer that usually had gravestones, headstones or something heavy to transport. Inside it was quite luxurious. Driving it was a bit like driving a tank. It went well but only had cable brakes and they were unable to stop the car very quickly. That was ok until one day a dog ran out into the road in front of the car and I only missed it more by luck than judgement. So I sold that for a £10 profit and proceeded to borrow some money from a local man of means who enabled me to buy, as mentioned previously, a Ford Prefect for around £390. I ran this for a short while but a problem developed with the steering mechanism and I quickly returned it to the garage from where I had made the purchase. In place of it I chose a new Ford Van of similar design and cost. There was no car tax to pay on vans in those days. That saw me through until we moved to Yorkshire as a family in 1964 – more of that later. From then on I purchased several decent cars over the years, more or less in tandem with the numerous 'bangers' that I bought – and in one case in 1980, inherited - that was my late Father's Ford Cortina Mark 3 Automatic. A lovely little car, a Morris 1000cc came next in 1964, followed by a Ford Cortina Mark 1 a few years later. My worst purchase was a Skoda, NOT a good buy! But then, from around 1970, when we bought a new Sprite 'Musketeer' Caravan to replace of the previous one owned by my in laws, I bought higher-powered vehicles – a Vauxhall Victor 1800cc, a Triumph 2000cc. and an Austin Princess 2200cc. My last towing vehicle was big Ford. The decent vehicles were used by Molly to travel to work in – I used either a banger or two wheels. When I no longer needed to run two cars I bought a Triumph Acclaim followed by a standard Renault 11. This was followed by one very fast one – a Renault 11 turbo. I have stuck to Renaults – six all told so far with one being an automatic - ever since, apart from a spell driving a Nissan automatic. But I soon returned to a Renault with a standard 5 speed gearbox that I could control myself with a gear lever. My reason for having Renaults was simple – 2 years after severe illness in the form of cancer forced me to retire from teaching. I worked for a year in Horsforth delivering cars around the country – great fun, as I have always enjoyed driving. The garage looked after my interests when I decided to change cars from time to time. But perhaps the greatest achievement took place while I was still recuperating from my illness in 1985 after my return from a six months holiday in New Zealand. In order to give myself something that I had never achieved before I decided to try and virtually rebuild a Fiat 128 Sports car. I bought it from a former colleague and friend, Alan Willey. He had intended to have it rebuilt professionally but his plans went awry and he decided to get rid of the car. I offered him £95 for the body chassis and the engine parts. They were stored in boxes. Putting this together would be the greatest challenge I could take on. I had a friend by the name of Joe Adams. He was the father of Sheila Scatchard, a friend and former colleague. Joe was 78 years old at the time and had been, amongst other things, a lorry driver and later a chauffeur. He had also worked for the local Council and had kept the council vehicles serviced and in good nick. What he did not know about car engines was not worth knowing! He agreed to help and so I managed to get the body/chassis back home and into the garage. Over a period of about a year we completely rebuilt the Fiat's engine. There was also some welding to be done and I took that to an expert welder. When the day came to try the engine for the first time the whoop of delight I gave when, at the second try, the engine fired, must have been heard all over Cookridge! That car gave me a lot of pleasure – it reached over 100 miles an hour more than once and the sporty performance was well worth the experience! I lent it to several people who visited from Australia - Frank and Ursula Tyson, his son Philip, George Tribe and his partner Bon Carmody. It also did the rounds in the family and my son Philip certainly enjoyed driving it! Sadly it ended its days in a road accident on the M1 after I had lent it to Sarah Sharman's boy friend Graeme. It was not his fault – a lorry ran into the back of it when it was stationary. The insurance that was eventually paid out after a year of waiting - £429 – was not bad for an original £95 purchase. At least it was some recompense for the countless hours of work put in to rebuild the car in the first place!

Summing up, I think that motoring was more pleasurable in the 50s, 60s, and early 70s, when there were fewer cars on the roads. Motorways were built to allow drivers to reach their destinations more quickly and at the same time more families could afford to get their own forms of transport – cars, vans, lorries, and the like. But inevitably the roads are becoming ever more crowded, with goods being transported by road rather than on the railways and seemingly endless queues cause frustrations. So the joys of motoring are diminishing I fear. However, my hobby has lasted a lifetime and I still get pleasure from seeing the tremendous advances in engineering, that have been made during my life time, mainly since the second World War. I suppose the main difference is now that engines are so complicated that a complete amateur like me no longer dares to try and mend faults – doubtless computers do it all much better.

Part 4 The Middle Years

Chapter 1 Social and family life

At this point I shall return briefly to the time I spent at home before going to Durham. Inevitably after I left school I lost touch with most of my former fellow pupils. However I remained close to Steve Taylor and Oliver Adams who became a farmer. Oliver's father had a farm at Watford, near Long Buckby. The Adams family own a lot of land in the area and Oliver, after he got married, went to live on part on the farm known as Thrupp Grounds near Daventry. When his father retired Oliver took over the business and now his family are closely involved and in their turn have taken over the bulk of the responsibility for the land. They even have a farm now on the North Island of New Zealand – at Taihape – a lovely area.

Two friends from my boyhood days at Far Cotton were Bernard Cross and Jack Green. Jack got on well with Steve Taylor as well and so he sometimes joined us at Newport Pagnell. On occasions we went out to local pubs and Jack came to parties with us too. There was a special celebration on Jack's 21st birthday. That afternoon Steve and I fetched him from BTH Rugby, where he was training as an apprentice. I remember that we had imbibed fairly copiously at a various hostelries on the way back to Newport Pagnell before returning to 'The Limes' – the Taylors' residence - unbeknown to Mr and Mrs Taylor. The whisky bottle came out on our return and we talked until about midnight. Steve and I refrained from too many further drinks after a couple of small whiskies. However Jack continued to quaff a few more until quite suddenly in mid sentence he sank slowly onto the settee, spilled what was left of his drink and proceeded to remain there, fast asleep. Steve and I went to our respective beds and slept until about nine o'clock. Suddenly there was a foot on the stairs and Mrs Taylor appeared – quite concerned to say the least. She had found Jack still out to the world on the settee and, as she had no idea who he was, wanted an explanation. Luckily Mr Taylor had not yet got up, otherwise I guess that all hell would have been let loose! Eventually, after explanations we got Jack to his feet, gave him a bite to eat and I drove him home before Steve's father appeared – but it was a close run thing! Mrs Taylor, with masterly understatement, had the last word. "Steve, if this happens again your father will be told. In case by any chance he does find out, I suggest that your friend Jack does not return here for a while for his own good!" We duly took the hint and nothing was said – otherwise I dread to think what might have happened to us both as well! Actually Jack did come again – officially this time, much to Mrs Taylor's amusement. – Our main concern was that she might have told her husband of the incident. She had us over a barrel but she was a good sort and Mr Taylor was never informed. She was very aware that he ruled with a firm hand and we knew it too!

Jack and I travelled many times on my motorcycle – an ex WD 350cc Royal Enfield. On one occasion we went to Stratford on Avon for the day and in the afternoon met up with a couple of girls near the Shakespeare Memorial Theatre. After a bit of banter we all went for a drink and afterwards wandered back towards our respective vehicles. They had an old Austin 7 and it was parked alongside the wall that bordered the grassed area at the rear of the Theatre. My motorbike was parked only a short distance beyond their car. As we left them they went off to the toilet before setting off for their respective homes. For a joke we quickly removed the bonnet of their car, put it over the wall, got over ourselves and hid nearby. We also stuffed a wad of grass up the exhaust pipe. In a couple of minutes they returned and when they saw what had happened there was consternation. But they soon spotted the bonnet so we reappeared and put it back on. When the driver started the engine there was a loud bang and the grass blew out of the exhaust pipe! More panic, but it was quite harmless and they took it in good part and off they went – quite a good day out!

On another occasion we went to Silverstone to watch some motorcycle racing one summer's afternoon. When it was over we were caught up in a traffic jam near some traffic lights at Weedon. Jack stood up to stretch his legs just as the lights changed and the traffic started to move again and I set off, completely unaware that he was not properly seated on the back. Fortunately he managed to attract my attention before I had gone any distance and I stopped. He was unhurt and we had a good laugh about it afterwards!

There were a variety of other things of interest around that time between my leaving school and going to College. I have already mentioned several earlier in this diatribe, but a couple of further things come to mind that would indicate the trends that were apparent during my later teenage years. Firstly I had met up again with my lovely cousin Daphne – now 16 - after about 12 years or so. At that time she was living with her brother 'Tom' Tullett (not his real name - that was Eric - but he preferred Tom) and his wife Diffy. They had a flat in Albany Mansions near Albany Bridge, Battersea, on the south side of the river Thames in London. She came to stay with us several times then and we became very close friends as well as being relatives. She was orphaned at the age of 9 and I know my father would have liked her to come to live with us but her brother Tom would not agree. He looked after her in London. Daphne has remained in my life ever since then – like a slightly older sister really. She has always been there for me and I for her. I also looked up to Tom who was a real character. He served with distinction in the forces during the war. After demob he joined the Metropolitan Police Force and became a member of the CID. After that he branched out further and became a crime reporter. He worked his way up and became notorious in the world of journalism. Eventually he became a chief crime reporter and as such met many top criminals of his day. Probably the most notable was Christie – a multi murderer who was hanged for his misdeeds. There were many others too and I was always much in awe of him. He was always very kind to me – he even took me out with him on the odd occasion when I was staying at the flat. In fact he apparently procured the flat after having been there during a murder investigation. The owner was found guilty and so would never return to the flat. I asked him once about it when I was staying there. He took me and showed me a small hole in the wall. He would never fill it in he told me. It was where the fatal bullet had finished up. As he then remarked, "Well, the former owner had no further use for the place!" He had a remarkable career and was consulted by Scotland Yard on several occasions I believe. His intimate understanding of the criminal mind was invaluable and he wrote several books on crime under the name of Tom Tullett. The first one I read was called 'Strictly Murder' - spine chilling! On the few occasions that I met him later on in life we invariably got on well and he would always find time to chat to me – a great man.

Daphne married Frank Sharman whose home was in Battersea. He became a good friend since they got together and again he is a wonderful guy. But more of Frank later – he inhabits the sporting world I have always loved.

The second thing that comes to mind is my involvement with other young people in the Parish of St Mary's Far Cotton. There was a Church Youth Group and they did a lot together in terms of Christmas Pantomimes, dances and plays. I never actually played any particular character in any of these affairs as I was away at School, but I helped with things like scenery and a variety of props when I was at home. After I had left School I took part in several choral concerts. But I remember a few classic errors that were very amusing for almost everybody at the time. The first happened during one Christmas production. It was in a Nativity play and one of the three Kings was carrying a lamp with a lit candle inside. He was swinging it gently as he entered the stage. He was looking for the star of Bethlehem that was over the stable where Jesus had been born. The 'star' was a covered up torch. He was supposed to spot it and shout out, "Light! I see light!" He certainly shouted out his line but then unfortunately swung his lamp much too enthusiastically and tripped up at the same time. I was holding the 'star' aloft right opposite him but was of course behind the scenery. His lamp came off the ring he was holding in his hand and hit the scenery. He also came flying across into the scenery and I was left in full view holding the torch. Naturally the audience were in stitches and the atmosphere was ruined. We were all helpless with laughter too - apart from the poor old King who stalked off the stage in complete disarray. Eventually we restarted and completed the play, but it was without doubt the most hilarious Nativity play I have ever helped with!

A second occasion was in a Pantomime. I was standing inside a tall but rather wobbly column that was supposed to be one side of a grand entrance. All went well until the girl playing 'Widow Twanky' leaned against the pillar. It fell over with me inside it. Fortunately with great presence of mind Widow Twanky shouted out,   "How's that for brute strength!" and carried on - with me still inside the column. I must have shouted out as I hit the floor and she declaimed, "It's not every day we have talking pillars – what a laugh!" She deserved an Oscar for that one!

Another time also concerned a light but fortunately not a candle. I had gone to great pains to make a 'sun' that was supposed to come up gradually from the east and shine brightly over a clump of trees. I was out of sight on the floor holding the trees in place and another props man had the task of pushing the sun up. Everything was going well until I signalled to him to push up the sun. He did it exactly as he had been shown but the higher it went the louder the laughter became. Unfortunately he had the whole thing the wrong way round! Luckily it did not ruin everything when he turned it round the right way but it added to the amusement and he got his leg well and truly pulled. There were others too but those were, I think, the most amusing experiences.

I suppose that the most difficult time for my parents came during my teenage years while I was on holiday from Oakham School. I decided that I wanted to dress rather differently. The idea behind that was that would be entrepreneurs wanted to establish themselves in some way by wearing clothing that was a bit different. Thus they coined the name 'wide boys'. I got hold of a bright green shirt and a yellow tie from somewhere, grey pinstripe trousers, a pair of yellow socks that I won on a tombola stall, and thick brown soled shoes that we used to call brothel creepers. I even had some sort of hat - like a trilby. It was a bit like the Clyde outfit of 'Bonny and Clyde' fame. I must have looked a right twit but I got away with it for a time as others wore similar garb. At least I did until the day my father found out. Someone must have seen me in town I suppose. That was that. The clothes disappeared very quickly and that was the end of that bit of individual rebellion. But I could not complain really as I had thoroughly enjoyed 'taking the mickey'!

Time passed quickly once I had left school and settled down to work. In no time it seemed College loomed on the horizon and I could not wait to get away. Once October 1950 arrived I entered a new and exciting world at Durham. I grew up quickly too. Inevitably at College one's social life revolved around fellow students. Dances, parties, boozy nights out, getting up to mischief – in fact anything that young people enjoyed was taken for granted. But once we all returned to our respective homes it was inevitable that those days were past and it was necessary to make new acquaintances and friends. When I returned home to live in Vicarage at Rothwell, Northants, my parents' new home, I soon met several people – they were known as 'Rowellians' - who lived in and were born and brought up there. Like me some had been to college and were used to socialising with fellow students. We were a mixed bunch, Brian Austin, an architect, Roy Summerley, a doctor, Paul Rowlett and myself, teachers. There were others too and most belonged to the Church Youth Club that I ran in the town. We became close friends for a time and many of the local girls – I remember in particular Gwen Johnson and her friends Molly Burditt and Iris - were also members. Social events also brought us together and inevitably friendships sprang up. Brian married Gwen and Paul married Iris. Molly married Norman Barker, another member of the teaching profession. I was friendly with them all and went out with them quite often – particularly when Youth Club events were arranged. Several members had cars and it was quite usual for us to go to theatres, cinemas and dances in Kettering, Bedford, Northampton or Peterborough. We also arranged a variety of activities including concerts to raise money for charity. But everybody worked during the week and I played hockey for Kettering Town at weekends in winter and cricket for Rothwell Town in the summer. I also played golf when time allowed so in fact life was never dull – there was too much going on. I well recall one countryside hunting sport in which we occasionally indulged, ably taught by the local printer Eric Jones. He had picked up the skill during the war when food was very scarce. We went out in cars, looking for hares and rabbits running about in the fields at night. Once we spotted one we would stop the cars, shine headlights towards them, run round behind them and shine powerful torches at them. They would become confused and actually stay quite still while someone crept up and touched them. It was simply an adaptation of one of the things we had learned as youngsters about the art of survival in wartime. During the war, apart from laying traps, it was a trick used to supplement the meagre rations - although the catchers could not use any form of illumination of course. Then any light outside a blacked out building was strictly forbidden as it could easily be seen from the air. At dusk catchers would simply stalk the hare or rabbit from all sides to confuse it. Jugged hare was actually a very tasty dish in those days of strict food rationing and so was rabbit. Our normal meat ration was very small. However in peacetime we could use torches and were only touching them for sport - it was really a test of countrymen's skills - so we let them go.

On Saturday evenings I would frequently meet up with Steve Taylor and we would go to farms where parties were held. The various farmers around the County of   Northamptonshire were often sportsmen – usually rugby players, several of whom played for Northampton Saints Rugby Union Club - hard players and equally heavy drinkers afterwards. So they would throw a barn or two open and - provided one took a bottle or two of wine or beer – everyone was welcome. They were certainly lively events and great fun. Driving home afterwards could be a problem so in most parties one person would not imbibe too heavily and would drive the rest home. As a different person was nominated each week it worked quite well, although on several occasions minor mishaps occurred and it was not unknown for vehicles to be abandoned until the following day!

There were parties in Rothwell too – it was a place where many quite wealthy families lived. At the time I lived there the shoe making business was thriving both in Northampton and in other towns in the shire. Kettering, Rushden and Rothwell in particular all had factories producing boots and shoes. For example 'Avenue' Shoes, amongst other makes, were made in Rothwell. There were several small local businesses that produced various different parts of the shoes, for instance heels, soles, uppers and toecaps, and passed them on to the main factory to be hand stitched or machine sewn together, depending on the quality required. It was a lucrative trade so there was a lot of money to be made. There were other places in Britain where the leather trade thrived. Leicester was famous for supplying leather in our area and there were shoe factories as well – the most famous being 'Lotus'. But in those days Northamptonshire was recognised as being the major source of footwear supplies in Britain. Top names such as 'Manfields' came from Northampton. A lot of the trade exported their leather wares abroad too. But gradually, with the advent of cheaper moulded shoes being made by the 1960s and distributed in bulk throughout Britain, top quality leather products suffered. But that was in the future and during the 1950s the leather shoe market flourished. As is inevitable in small towns business families knew each other, and in those days of plenty would help an ailing firm out if it became necessary. Naturally there was fair modicum of rivalry too but there was sufficient business available for everyone and over the years members of the various families had intermarried. So the party rounds were quite frequent and although anyone nor born in Rothwell was termed as an 'Incomer' there were plenty of invitations for me even after I had gone to work in Nottingham. I was single and unattached – always a useful situation to be in! The only problem was that I had to mind my p's and q's a bit as my father was the Vicar of the Parish of Holy Trinity Church, Rothwell. I guess it cramped my style somewhat. But I well remember one autumn night after a party – well, the early hours of the morning – when I was spotted by the local bobby returning home with a chamber pot on my head, around 4am. I did it for a bet. I thought I knew him well enough for that tale not to get home but the rotten so and so reported it and that was that. He did not live in Rothwell and was not a universally popular figure in the town with the local residents. So with the help of friends I got my own back when I reported a problem to him that meant he had to turn out on a Sunday afternoon – one of his rest days. He was always telling us all to report anything we saw – so I did. I told him that we had seen smoke coming from a nearby farm - quite true. He went off to investigate and simply found smoke billowing up from the hot ashes of a fire out in a paddock. It was the remains of a bonfire party that had taken place the night before – but deliberately stoked up again by several of us at lunchtime the next day, with piles of wet grass and lawn cuttings. He spoke to the farmer who was in on the affair but obviously he said nothing. We all knew as we had been at the party! Having made the report I drove off back to work at Nottingham. The 'guardian of the law' certainly realised that he had been 'had' but could not prove it. I bet he did not report THAT incident to either my parents or his superiors. Honour was satisfied - although I was careful not to cross his path too closely when I was home at weekends!

I suppose that, being the son of the Vicar and having been away, first to school and then to College, I was viewed as someone who could mix easily with people. This in its turn meant that there were plenty of opportunities for me to spread my wings in places other than Rothwell. I still had friends in Northampton, Kettering and Wellingborough and my association with Steve Taylor opened up other avenues further afield in both the social and working world. His parents treated me as a   member of their family and I spent a lot of my leisure time at 'The Limes' - their home in Newport Pagnell. Inevitably, as they were a well to do family and Mr Taylor was a wealthy businessman there were times when I could not afford to entertain on the lavish scale that was normal for them. We would often go out to hotels or pubs to meet up with his business acquaintances and sometimes our friends too. But I never went short on those occasions. Mr Taylor would simply put a £5 note in my hand and say to me 'Chris, you buy the first round of drinks'. Invariably I did this and from then on the problem was solved. He was a very generous man who saw to it that both Steve and I were always very much on an equal footing both financially and socially. In order to put spending money in my pocket I worked in the business. The normal weekly working time was 40 hours a week. I would work only 39 hours and was therefore classed as 'casual labour' and this avoided paying tax as I was never officially on the payroll. There were three business ventures on the go. The first was a Chemist's shop in Newport Pagnell High Street. Qualified chemists ran that. Then there was a factory, where I mainly worked, turning out mineral waters and cordial products. Finally there was a lucrative mustard-producing firm. This did so well that it probably brought in more than anything else and ensured that considerable profits were made overall. Mr Taylor once told me that the production of mustard paid for his whole business. '"The rest is profit", he explained. He certainly was shrewd! He also had his own petrol pump in the yard so that he was able to purchase in bulk and of course it was cheaper. Whenever I went to stay he would always ensure that the tank of my motorbike or car was full when I returned home. The family name was extremely well known around the counties of Buckinghamshire, Bedfordshire and Northamptonshire – posters advertising Taylor's Mustard graced many shops and pubs. It was great fun whenever I had deliveries to make. I would be sent out with a list of places to visit. At Mr Taylor's instigation I would represent the firm dressed smartly in grey trousers, blazer and tie on those occasions and invariably at the pubs a drink would be offered on arrival. It was quite a problem remaining sober! Fortunately as I was delivering a few crates of mineral waters as well as mustard I could legitimately ensure that I either quaffed a straight tonic water or a shandy. The main deliveries went out by lorry and that was fun too. I would put on old clothes then and as deliverymen we were always offered a pint in the back bar. If I was not driving that was OK, although humping crates was hard graft. But even there the family did well. Steve had an older brother and sister. His sister Ann married and went to live in London. Unfortunately Steve's elder brother Jim had only a mental age of about ten as he had had a problem at birth. But Jim was incredibly strong – a sort of compensation I suppose. He could literally lift crates straight up on to the delivery lorries with no trouble at all so he did all the loading. He would then come out with a driver and myself. I dealt with the financial side – Jim unloaded the crates! He was a lovely lad and I guess my experience with young children when teaching was a real bonus. He would do anything to help both Steve and I, but woe betide anyone who crossed our paths – we had sometimes to persuade him not to take action on our behalf if there was an altercation and he felt we were being mistreated. Fortunately he normally listened to both of us. However I did once see him use his extraordinary strength at home. He had been to the local pub called the 'Pig and Whistle'. It was the only one his parents permitted him to enter. It was very close to home. The landlord knew him and had firm instructions from Mr Taylor as to what Jim was allowed to drink– only 1 pint of cider. But on this occasion the landlord had gone out and his temporary replacement had not been informed. Jim was crafty and had several drinks. When he came home Steve remonstrated with him. Jim just picked Steve up and THREW him onto the settee! Fortunately his mother came in at that point and sorted things out, but it showed just how strong he was. Needless to say, I made sure I never had occasion to cross him!

Steve and I spent several holidays together, but only once, in 1953, did we venture abroad. We booked a week's holiday in France with Co-op Society Travel. Our programme was simple – we intended to stay and sightsee in Paris for 4 days and then move on to Le Touquet by train. On the Friday before we were due to leave a general strike due to last at least a week was called in France for the Sunday and all transport was halted from Sunday morning. We tried to cancel our trip but no one from the Co-op Travel Agency was answering calls, so on the Saturday we took our cases and drove to London in my 1932 Austin 7 in an attempt to call a halt to our journey there. But again the Agency was inconveniently shut so we had no alternative but to catch the train to Dover or lose our money – no insurance against strikes in those days. We left the car in an underground car park near Waterloo station and set off by train, still hoping to get a cancellation somehow. The ferry was still running to Calais and so we decided to go anyway. From Calais the train took us to Paris and a Co-op Travel rep. met us and took us to our Hotel in Monmartre. The supreme irony was that the Hotel was named 'Hotel Parfait'. It was anything but perfect! When we arrived we found out that all monies due to be sent from English Travel Agents to France had been stopped so we were not popular. However, luckily for us, the 'Patron' - or Manager as we call them - had been a freedom fighter in the Paris secret resistance force. He had been captured and tortured by the Nazis when Paris was under German occupation during the war. His toenails and fingernails had been torn out – he showed us – and he had only escaped death because he had been rescued from Fresnes - an infamous Gestapo Prison in Paris - by a resistance group organised by a British secret agent. Not surprisingly he was very pro British. He let us stay anyway. We went out on the Sunday, intending to walk up the Champs Elysee to see the sights. We certainly did that, getting caught up in a student riot by accident and having to run away from the French Police. Sadly a student was shot and killed nearby in the ensuing melee. We got away ok but it was quite an experience. The next day a trip had been arranged for us by private bus although all other transport, apart from essential vehicles, was at a standstill. Our bus was then pelted with bricks and several French road workers tried to stop us going anywhere by using large hammers and pickaxes. Unfortunately for us they were still at work as were the refuse collectors and one or two more of the necessary services such as hospitals and food shops remained open. However the bus driver managed to drive us away and we visited the Palais de Versailles. Next day we went to 'L'Eglise de Sacre Coeur', a famous Roman Catholic Church in Paris, then to the Louvre, and finally on to the Opera House. With our kindly hotel manager doing his best to help us we tried to hitch a lift to Le Touquet. But it was hopeless as all motorists risked instant arrest if they were found to have picked up any hitchhikers. So we decided to cut our losses and went to find an airline office. Ironically the only one open was 'Air France' and they took us for all the French money we had. We obtained tickets to catch a plane to Heath Row on the Wednesday. It was a BOAC (British Overseas Air Corporation) flight that was calling in at the Airport en route from elsewhere. The plane left in the late afternoon so we returned to our hotel where our travel rep. was due to pick us up in a taxi at 3pm. He arrived on time but when we set off again the street was blocked at both ends − by refuse lorries − the dustbin men had been called out on strike at exactly 3 o'clock! After protracted negotiations and a lot of swearing in French by our rep. and the taxi driver, we got out by driving on the pavement. We were taken to a centre from where we could get to the Airport. The only trouble was we had no money left to pay off the taxi and give our rep. a tip. Things looked a bit dodgy as they still had our bags, but our luck was well and truly in at last. A guy named David Hill, who had been at School with us at Oakham until he left in 1946, was actually in the waiting area and came over to speak to us. We hastily explained our predicament. He kindly lent us some French francs and we were able to pay off the taxi, retrieve our luggage and give the rep a well earned tip. I managed to pay back our debt to David several years later when we met up again at an Old Boys' Day at Oakham School. I shall never forget him!

But that was not quite the end of the story. We walked out to the Airport and there was not a customs officer, or indeed an official of any kind, to stop us. Incredibly, we watched as the plane − an Elizabethan - flew in. When it had landed we ran out to the steps where one or two passengers were alighting and explained who we were to a startled airhostess by the name of Miss Whitehead. She was brilliant and arranged for us to fly out with them although they had no prior knowledge that anybody was to be picked up. Doubtless the clerk at the Air France office had pocketed our money after issuing so called air tickets and two on board luncheon tickets for good measure. There were no proper seats and we were squeezed in at the back of the plane on a seat reserved for airhostesses. What a fabulous, and at the same time hairy, experience we had had during our holiday - and thank goodness for the commonsense of the aircrew!

When we landed after that flight we were able to retrieve my old Austin 7, but only after I had managed to get some money out of my Post Office savings book. The only problem was that actually there was no money in the book!

We went to a local Post Office near Heath Row and as luck would have it the lady behind the counter was very busy and did not notice that our 'funds' were nil. She duly gave us £3 in cash. We boarded an underground train back to Waterloo Station. We then got the car back after paying a small parking charge and drove straight to Newport Pagnell. Next we went to the Post Office there and deposited £10 back in the book so all was well - but it was a close call. In those days £10 was a lot of money. As always the Taylors lent us some more money so we were able to drive down to near Minehead where my parents were staying for their summer vacation. It was here that I met the man who helped replace the valves on my old car – a story I have already referred to earlier. We then continued up on our way via Porlock hill, a very steep climb, and drove down to Land's End before returning to Newquay. We met up with a couple of medical students while there and thoroughly enjoyed several nights in some of the many pubs in the area adjacent to where we were staying. Only one further problem arose when we wanted to set off for home. We had a flat battery! Again, lady luck was on our side and a friendly mechanic at a Newquay garage recharged our battery. He then reckoned that we could get about 300 miles before the battery went flat again. The problem was that the battery charging system on the car – the dynamo -had given up the ghost. By the time we left Newquay it was obvious that we would have to complete our journey at night, in the dark. The battery would not serve the lights and the engine for long so, as it was a moonlight night I drove without lights except when other vehicles came into sight. We got away with it, but only just. We got back to Newport Pagnell at about one o'clock in the morning, stopped the car – and that was that! The battery had run flat again after about 280 miles. Still, the next morning after a recharge I got home and managed to get friends to help me replace the dynamo. In those days a dynamo provided the electric current required to keep the car running and use the lights too. There were no alternators in those days.

On other holidays Mr Taylor lent us his old 1936 Lanchester – a lovely comfortable car. We visited several seaside places for our holidays over the years until one winter's evening the car came to a sticky end. Steve had been staying at Rothwell with us and it started to snow. He insisted on setting off for home but it was very cold and ice had formed on the roads. Grit was not put on roads very often in those days. He was driving towards Wellingborough, skidded on ice as he was crossing a bridge, and went through the railings. Literally the car hung over the edge and it was a miracle that it did not go into the water below. Steve struggled out through the back door. He managed to get to a telephone and we fetched him back to Rothwell, shaken but unhurt. Eventually the car was retrieved but shortly afterwards the engine was ruined when a piston went through the engine block and that was that. The replacement car was a brand new Rover 60. What a car that was!

For me there was an interesting story attached to the new car. Some three years before it was purchased I had driven the Lanchester from Newport Pagnell on holiday with Steve in the passenger seat. Unfortunately Mr Taylor was not impressed when he saw me driving as I had not got his permission. He informed me on our return from holiday that I should not drive his vehicles again. I took that to mean – wrongly as it turned out, that I should not drive the works van either – a bright yellow machine advertising mustard. So I never did, until one day he wanted me to drive to Nottingham for a delivery and to take a cricket bat to Gunn and Moore's – a factory famed for making cricket bats. I was going in my Austin 7 and was filling it with petrol out in the factory yard when Mr Taylor shouted from the office window, "Don't take that thing – take the Rover. Come up to my office and fetch the key". I did not need a second invitation and off I went. What a great day I had! From then on I was allowed to use the car whenever it was available. After I got back from that trip he asked me why I had never driven the various vehicles appertaining to Taylor's Mustard etc. When I told him he roared with laughter and said, "Good God Chris – I didn't mean it!" - so typical of the man!

I thoroughly enjoyed working at 'T. & F.J. Taylors', but as time went on the demands of teaching inevitably made visits fewer in number. As we matured thoughts turned towards settling down and Steve started what proved at first to be a very close - and later permanent - relationship with a young lady by the name of Susan Harrison. Susan was the daughter of Cyril Harrison and his wife. They lived at the Manor House at Flore, near Weedon, when I first got to know them. Cyril Harrison was the Senior Partner of a well-known firm of Solicitors – Shoesmith and Harrison - in Northampton's Market Square. We became friends and I was often invited to join Susan and Steve at many functions connected with the family. Indeed when Susan and Steve had differences of opinion from time to time Susan would ring me up. Off we'd go to a pub and we would have a good old chinwag about the rights and wrongs of everything. I became a sort of unofficial confidante to them when they were courting and was made privy to many private matters appertaining to them both. Privileged they were then and privileged they have remained to this day. Nevertheless there were occasional times when things did not always go exactly to plan.

Susan was training to work on the land, farming, at Moulton Agricultural College during the mid 50s. Her transport was an old Hillman soft top. The front doors of the car opened forwards as opposed to the modern car where they open to the rear. The Hillman was nicknamed 'Fay' but I never found out why. It went quite quickly too. On one occasion I duly had a call to go out for a pint and she called to pick me up. It must have been the result of a row of some kind for she was hopping mad about something. We set off and she put her foot down. I clung on for dear life – no seat belts in those days! With a sharpish right hand bend coming up I closed my eyes and grabbed a handle of some kind on the dashboard. It was just as well. As we slide round the bend virtually on two wheels the front door swung open – and disappeared! I finished up with both legs OUT of the doorway and had to cling on until we stopped. That certainly worked off her anger! Somewhat shaken, but still in one piece I got back on my feet and we turned round, setting off more sedately to try and find the door. It took ages but eventually it turned up over a hedge and part way across a field. So – back to my place we went. I got some tools out and after a struggle we managed to put the door back on. I knocked out a tell tale dent and that was that, but it was too close a call for comfort!

With modern cars fixing a door back on to bodywork would certainly not be an option.

I suppose that in the 50s our lives followed a fairly conventional pattern for much of the time. We all seemed to work hard and inevitably played hard too. Until 1954 food was rationed, clothes were purchased only if one had the requisite coupons, and austerity was the order of the day. We still had petrol coupons although it was easy enough to get extra if you knew someone who owned his own pump – and we did – Taylor's factory had one. Farmers got petrol for tractors. When it was introduced during the war the farmers' petrol had something added to colour it red, and woe betide anyone caught using it in cars! However controls were relaxed by the early 50s and more or less anything went. There was a freeze on money too. When one travelled abroad there was a limit of around £50 per person – it may have been even less but it certainly was not more. Britain was in a mess financially due the debts run up during the 2nd World War. America introduced the 'Marshall Plan" where they lent us money to get the economy back on an even keel, but it had to be paid back by our Government. So money was tight and goods had to be imported or made in this country. Housing was cheap, but wages were poor. In 1947 I was paid £144 in my first year after tax amounting to £36. In 1953, after I had qualified as a teacher, I was paid the princely sum of £325 after tax of £81 for a year's work! – just less than £7 per week after tax. Of course that bought a lot more for the money than nowadays with petrol being only a shilling or two a gallon. As the country gradually became economically stronger more goods appeared in the shops and television sets came on the market. The pictures were grainy and black and white only. The screen had 405 lines - as opposed to today's set that have so many more - and colour too! Only better off families even considered buying TV sets so we went out and made our own pleasures.

There were many other friends with whom I spent happy times. I have mentioned some already, but playing sports introduced me to a world far removed from the mundane. Being friendly with cricketers and being a reasonably good performer I could hold my own among potential County players as well as at Club level. But I did not have the temperament or the inclination to play cricket day after day. I knew that it would be a case of the survival of the fittest and that meant constant repetition. I loved playing, but I soon saw that too many games, played almost every day, would begin to pall. In addition there were others who I knew were better than I was temperament-wise and so I only turned out once or, at most, twice a week. That way I never got fed up and I was able to mix with a greater variety of people who had interests outside the world of sport too. Frank Tyson was a County player who shot to fame one golden summer 'down under' in Australia and New Zealand in 1953/54. Prior to him going on the tour he was unknown and we could go anywhere together with no danger of recognition anywhere but among local cricketing fans in Northants. But by the time of his return so great an effect had he had during his time on tour when England won back the Ashes that he became a national hero – one of many in that touring party – and fame quickly caught up. With fame came problems too. Initially he enjoyed being recognised and did not mind signing autographs. But this soon palled and it all became something of an embarrassment. Everywhere we went in the country he was more or less forced to wear dark spectacles and a hat or cap of some kind to try to avoid recognition. At times this developed into farce. Then came the downside. Frank was injured during the 1954 summer and was not picked to play for England. In fact he only ever played in four test matches in England – the rest were abroad. I fear that I did not always help because there were always those who 'smarmed' round him and instead of politely declining invitations for drinks etc. he got taken for a ride on several occasions. One evening we had been playing at Rothwell on opposite sides in a benefit match for one of the County cricketers. After the match we were invited to a social club in Rothwell and Frank allowed himself to be 'taken over' by a certain cricketer named Jack Stanyon. Locally he was known as a 'pain in the backside' and because I knew it was going to happen I warned him and suggested that he sign a few autographs and we could then withdraw but he ignored this so I left him to it. He eventually got back to Northampton a bit the worse for wear! The summer season was in full swing so I did not see him again for a while. I went up to Lords to see one day of a Test Match. Frank was not picked for England but was at the match. We met up and went off for a drink in the Lord's Tavern. We were sitting at the bar when there was something of a commotion. Ian Carmichael, the actor, came in followed by a few so-called fans. In the ensuing crush he bumped into me, spilling my drink. He was full of apologies and bought me another, standing and chatting to us for a while. That was an education – what an unusual man! But he was pleasant and after he left us it was interesting to see how he coped with hangers on very effectively. I think Frank learned from him that day – Ian Carmichael was masterly! We enjoyed quite a few evenings out at pubs in the County. The 'Cherry Tree' at Great Houghton, a village just outside Northampton, was one and there were others where the cricketers collected after a match. I first met George Tribe socially at that pub and many years later we met up again and became close friends when I was visiting Australia in 1984.

Life continued happily enough for a while and friends at Rothwell were getting married. I attended the various weddings. Paul Rowlatt married Iris. Brian Austin and Gwen married too. Next Molly Burditt married Norman Barker, a Yorkshireman who had come to teach in Kettering. Brian Summerley moved away from Rothwell and he also got married. Then I was best man for Eleanor Gamble and Geoff. Wells. My Father took the ceremony. I think he was getting concerned that I had shown little sign of settling down – but I simply told him that I had not met the right person and that was that.

Then came the day that was to irrevocably change my life.

Chapter 2 Settling down

Among the various friends I had made while at Oakham was John Tozer, who lived at Burton Latimer, near Kettering. We frequently met up when time allowed and he asked me to act as an usher at his wedding around Easter 1958. I was smartly clothed in morning dress on the day of the wedding but my car, a 1934 Vauxhall 12, would not start. I had the bonnet up and was trying to correct the fault when my mother brought a young lady to the door. She had been to a confirmation class I think and was on her way out. I noticed that she had a fur coat on so she must have caught my eye! My mother introduced her – Molly Holroyd. We chatted briefly and that was that. I managed to get the car started then and I went into the house to wash my hands prior to leaving. Incredible as it seems now I said to my mother, "I would like to marry that girl one day Mum". Then I went off to do my ushering at John's wedding. My parents told me that she was a teacher at Rothwell Secondary School. My Father, who was Chairman of the Governors at Rothwell Secondary School, had apparently interviewed her for the post and was very impressed by her interview and the qualifications she had. She gained her degree at Manchester. He did not tell me what her qualifications were.

Some weeks later Molly and I met up again. She was out with a girl friend who was a resident of Rothwell. She was an acquaintance of mine. I had just bought another car – a Ford Popular - and I offered them a lift. I recall that her friend got into the front seat and chattered incessantly while Molly sat quietly in the back of the car. When I had dropped her friend off at her house we decided to go for a drink. She told me that she came from Drighlington in Yorkshire. Things gradually moved on from there and I asked her out for a date or two but as I was still living in Northampton we did not meet that often. I do recall making a fool of myself on the first of those dates in the early days. I sat down at a piano and played some simple melody or other – probably to try and impress her I expect. She said nothing but when I had finished strumming she sat at the piano and played so beautifully that I never played in front of her again. It was then that I discovered that she had a degree from Manchester College of Music and that Drama was another part of the course!

One weekend I was at home and as usual I was due to read the lessons at evensong in Rothwell Church. Molly sang some solos, probably on that same evening, in a concert. As a singer myself I appreciated a good voice when I heard one. But her singing was truly exceptional and I guess it was then that I started to fall head over heels in love with Molly – and her singing voice. From then on my one wish was to spend what time I could with her.

At that time I had only ever stayed once in the Oakwood area of Leeds - with Al Deighton and his wife. Al was a former teaching colleague at Walgrave School, Northants. He had moved to Leeds in 1950 to run a Boys' Club Centre in Oakwood and he invited me down from College in Durham in 1951.

I had never been to Drighlington, near Leeds, but on one occasion I decided to drive up to Durham in my Ford Popular car and on the way back call at Newton Aycliffe to see my former room mate, Bryan Stubbs and his wife Joan, whom I had never met. They had started a family and had twins. Naturally I was keen to see them too so I stopped off for a couple of hours. My next port of call was at Drighlington in order to see Molly, who had gone home for the school holidays, and to meet her parents. However as I was approaching Drighlington the car started to wander a bit on the road and I realised that there was a problem with the steering. I arrived safely but had to take the car in to be examined at a local Ford Garage. They managed to fix things, told me that I had been lucky not to have an accident as the steering nut had worked loose. They warned me to take it straight back to the garage where I had bought it as it was not safe. They also wrote a note to the garage about the bad state of the steering. We returned to Rothwell and I returned the car. The firm accepted responsibility and as a replacement I got a new Ford Popular Van. In those days one did not have to pay tax on the purchase of vans.

I was later invited by Molly and her parents to go to Drighlington for the Christmas period. There was a large party at which friends and family attended. It probably happened each year and this was no exception. I met other members of Molly's family including her Aunt Hilda and her Uncle Clarence, her cousin Malcolm and his then girl friend Nesta. It was something of an ordeal really – I felt a bit like a 'prize pig at the fair'. I suppose that, not being a Yorkshireman, I was not used to the way things were done at Christmas. I recall seeing lumps of coal being brought in during the evening – a northern tradition that I had not come across before. Neither had I eaten Christmas cake together with a slice of cheese before. Nevertheless it was all very good-natured though and I got to know a lot of people during that Christmas holiday as there were other parties to which we were invited. Malcolm took me to see my first Rugby League match at Headingley too. I found that the grey stone of house, factories, public buildings and walls was something new and struck me as dour at the time. I remember being told that it had much to do with the factory smoke that was prevalent then. Another theory was that when the stone was quarried it was light grey but turned darker on contact with the air. Molly's parents were shareholders in the large brickworks opposite their house in Drighlington. The brick

buildings were in stark contrast to the stone ones. It was all very different from my home and a good experience to have had.

Meanwhile Susan Harrison and my close friend Steve were seeing plenty of each other and not long after Molly and I started to go out regularly they got engaged. We were invited to the engagement party at Newport. It was quite an affair and it was the first time that Susan and Molly had met.

Their wedding was to be held later in the year – 1958 - at the Church at Flore and I was invited to be best man. As this was to be what we would term a 'society' wedding there was a lot to do prior to the actual day. First the service was to be conducted by my Father – he knew both bride and groom well. Next I met all the ushers and we worked out the various jobs that needed to be covered both at the Church and afterwards at the reception. There was to be a large Marquee on the lawn at Flore Manor and Cyril Harrison was in his element overseeing what we had organised. Food was to be provided for all the guests – there must have been getting on for 100 I should imagine. I remember at one point Susan got so fed up with it all that she almost decided that it would be easier to elope! However she was persuaded that this would not be a good thing and so everything was scheduled to go ahead. But I was asked to accept one proviso by Susan and Steve. Officially they would be going off in the Taylor's Rover 60 car – but as they guessed that some of the guests would 'fix' the car I was press-ganged into secretly getting 'Fay' – the old Hillman – hidden nearby so they could change and get away in that. Fortunately the plan worked but I was almost thrown into the garden pond when the ploy was discovered! There were a lot of well-oiled guests who had to be placated by that time. The final job I had as best man was to organise a dinner and dance for all involved in the wedding arrangements at the 'Cornhill' – a hotel nearby – after the festivities had concluded. This turned out to be a great success, aided as it was by Cyril Harrison. He took me on one side after the wedding and revealed a box holding a dozen bottles of champagne. These were given to us all as a 'thank you' present for our efforts in making Susan's and Steve's wedding a day to remember. Having had the champagne poured out towards the end of the dinner the first 'toast' I gave was 'to absent friends!' Sue and Steve loved that when they were told about it on their return! Needless to say there were other toasts too and the champagne rapidly disappeared.

On the actual day of the wedding the weather was fine. Steve and I arrived a few minutes prior to the start of the ceremony. The church was packed and the service, conducted by my Father, was lovely. Pictures were taken, first of the bride and groom and their families and then of many leaving church. Other photos had been taken as guests arrived before the service too. We all repaired to the Marquee at Flore Manor for the reception. Food was eaten, speeches were made and wine was plentiful. During my 'best man' speech one gentleman – a solicitor by the name of Andrew Marchant - had imbibed well but not too wisely. He made a few loud comments and I had to shut him up in no uncertain terms – I quite enjoyed that impromptu bit of the speech! Cyril Harrison heartily approved of how I had dealt with the situation and a week later invited me to his office in Northampton. He offered me the opportunity to join his firm of Solicitors - as he said, "to work in the courts". I gave it serious thought and Cyril even offered to forgo the money required for me to become articled as a solicitor in his firm of Shoesmith and Harrison. Nevertheless I decided against making the change after I had discussed the offer with Molly. She was not keen as for one reason or another she was not overly fond of Susan. As it happened I was already qualified as a teacher anyway, working in a school I liked, and it would have meant quite an upheaval in my life.

After the reception the bridesmaids, the ushers and their respective partners repaired to the 'Cornhill' and we partied until the early hours. It had been quite a day! There was however one rather unfortunate happening as Mrs Taylor was due to drive the Rover home. Someone had swapped the plug leads over and instead of Susan and Steve being inconvenienced when the car refused to go she got the shock of her life when the car backfired several times! Fortunately someone was able to put things right but she was not amused!

Chapter 3 Getting Married

As things were going well with Molly I decided to return to live at home for a while and travel each day to King's Heath School, Northampton – a journey of about 16 miles each way. We duly got engaged at Easter in 1959. We immediately drove up to Drighlington to see Molly's Mum and Dad. The day after our arrival we drove into Leeds to put the announcement of our engagement in the papers. I think Sally was a bit perturbed about things – I guess I probably did not come up to her expectations as a future husband for her daughter as I was several years older than Molly. When we arrived back she asked where the receipt for the money paid to put the announcement in the Yorkshire Post was. Neither of us could find it and we were not concerned until Molly asked her why she wanted it. The reply shook me – "So you can sue him for breach of promise if he changes his mind". Afterwards Sally always swore that it was a joke whenever it was mentioned – no comment required! However she need not have worried. It was a very happy time for us.

More importantly from my point of view was the almost instant affinity I felt for Molly's dad, Willie, my future father in law. He told me of the awful problem he had during the war when he was thrown off a fire engine as it was answering a call to a fire. He was more or less given to understand that the damage done to his back was so bad that he would never walk again. But he was determined to prove the medics wrong and he forced himself to walk short distances, "Initially", as he said quite casually one day, "using telegraph posts to lean on every 22 yards or so". Listening to what he had done was a great source of inspiration for me. I had suffered a serious rugby accident at College that was misdiagnosed at the time. The outcome was that early in 1956 I was paralysed for a spell and taken to hospital. I had two chipped vertebrae in my lower back but an operation to put things right could have had serious consequences. If it failed I could have been an invalid for the rest of my life. My parents and I decided against my taking that risk. Instead I was fitted with a boned corset. It was very painful and eventually I stopped wearing it once the worst of the pain had gone. I was advised not to play any sport but I ignored that and continued to play cricket, at first wearing the corset when I batted, for several years. Periodically I would have to lie flat on my back for a day or two as I was virtually unable to move my legs. It took that long for the recurring, but fortunately temporary, paralysis to ease sufficiently for me to get about. I then had to 'learn to walk properly' again – in other words get my back and legs mobile enough to return to normal. This could take about a fortnight – sometimes more. Eventually I learned how to avoid the worst excesses of the problem and as I grew older. I gave up hockey and rugby however. Eventually there was sufficient improvement and I was able to dispense with the corset but I suffered a lot of pain. Eventually things got so bad that at the age of 46 I stopped playing cricket altogether. Cricket gave me up rather than the other way around and it was two or three years before I could go and watch matches without feeling that I wanted to be playing. I was able to continue playing golf though. Throughout his active life Willie always encouraged me to walk as much as possible. He took great delight in being able to walk quickly and he often left me trailing, particularly when we went to watch Huddersfield Town play football. He used to park his car a fair way from the ground. In the end he dropped me off while he parked up but after the game I had to try to keep up – not easy! But he was a source of help that I truly appreciated.

We decided that it would be a good idea if we got married in the summer holiday. With this in mind we went to Northampton and decided that the Spinney Hill area would be a pleasant spot to live. New houses were being built at Spinney Hill so we put down a deposit of £50 on one – number 58, Spinney Hill Road as it turned out. It was a three-bedroom semi–detached, just the sort of place that suited us. With the summer holiday being around 6 weeks long we reasoned that we could have a lengthy honeymoon – part of which was to be at a seaside bungalow belonging to Molly's Aunt and Uncle, Hilda and Clarence Best on the cliff top at Skipsea. Unfortunately a date early in August was not convenient for Molly's Aunt Hilda's family due to the running of the family business at Rimmington's Chemist Shop in the centre of Bradford. Pauline Hurst, Hilda's daughter, was to be Maid of Honour. Her husband Bill was to be an usher. So in order to suit them a decision was made that we would have our wedding later in the month - on Saturday, August 29th. This meant that as part of our originally intended honeymoon at Skipsea was arranged for the second week of August we would still go but as a shared holiday week with Molly's Mum and Dad. So the date was duly fixed and arrangements for the wedding to be held at St Paul's Church, Drighlington duly went ahead. We spent the week at Skipsea being chaperoned – not at all in the way we had originally planned. It was quite a frustrating few days for us. I then returned home to Rothwell until the wedding was due to take place.

The night prior to our wedding I stayed with Hilda and Clarence Best in Bradford. It was lovely weather for our wedding day, blue skies and pleasantly warm. Steve Taylor, who was my best man, and I joined forces and travelled to St Paul's Church in Drighlington. When we arrived the ushers, dressed in top hats and tails, were seeing the congregation into their seats. There were 4 of them – Frank Sharman (my cousin Daphne's husband), Chris King (a friend from Northampton), Malcolm Overend (Molly's cousin), and Bill Hirst (Hilda's son in law). Pauline Hirst was Molly's Matron of Honour. Elizabeth Hirst was the youngest bridesmaid and David Hirst was the pageboy. There were four other bridesmaids in the Bridal Party.

My father, Canon George Turner, conducted the ceremony. Molly, being given away by her Father, looked absolutely beautiful. It was a lovely service – very moving. We duly signed the register and went outside for the wedding photos to be taken. In those days photos were in black and white. The photos were later made up into a wedding album. Everyone then went to the Hotel Metropole, close to Leeds City Centre, where the wedding reception was held. Eventually we left in our Ford 'popular' van to drive to a hotel in Uttoxeter where we spent our first night together. The next day we drove on to the Golden Hind Hotel at Moreton in the Marsh. Unfortunately, because the wedding had taken place so late in August, after a couple of days of sightseeing we then had to make our way back home to our new house at 58, Spinney Hill Road, Northampton to get ready to start a new term on September 3rd. Molly had obtained a teaching post at Moulton Secondary School, just outside Northampton. It was quite a challenge for her to have to start a new job so soon after we had returned home.

Chapter 4 Setting up home

We soon made friends locally. Chief amongst them were Jeanette and David Freeman. David worked with Molly at Moulton. Like me David had trained as a teacher with Physical Education as one of his major studies. I too had PE and History as my two major subjects and we both taught PE throughout our respective schools in the early stages of our careers. We had a lot in common and our friendship has survived throughout the rest of our lives. At one stage in early 1964, when circumstances were such that we decided to move to Leeds to live, I had to find myself a teaching job. There was a post advertised - with PE as the main subject to be taught - at a Residential National Children's Home Education Department near Bramhope. I applied for the post and was called for interview. Molly was also involved as of course it would have meant that we should have had to live on site. We drove up to the School and were taken round the School. It was fine for me but Molly preferred to live elsewhere rather than on the premises. She found it all rather claustrophobic. In the end I turned down the job as it would have not suited us both as a family unit. The job would have been ok but then other considerations dictated that it was not to be. When we returned to Northampton we mentioned the vacant post to David. He immediately applied and was appointed so both we and our good friends were to move up north to live and work. I later got another post in Leeds – more of that later.

Returning to our family life in Spinney Hill – we settled into a routine with teaching being our major source of income. Even with our combined salaries it was difficult to put money by. Still, at least we had obtained some furniture, chairs etc. that were passed on to us by relatives. Initially carpeting the house was a priority and naturally, in order to save money, we fitted whatever we could ourselves. Several things come to mind when I recall our efforts in that direction. The first was when we were laying a carpet in the dining room cum lounge. It was a through room, and quite a large area. We had done quite well but, although there was no actual wall to divide the two areas there was a section which jutted out a couple of feet from the central wall and fitting the carpet round it presented us with a problem. My mother and father turned up while we were putting the carpet down and we were deciding the best way of getting carpet round the protrusion when they arrived. My mother, wanting to help, picked the scissors we had been using to cut the carpet carefully to shape. Before we could stop her she had cut out a section of carpet, gauging it by eye instead of measuring it. She put it down and unfortunately she had removed too much and the edges were not straight! We said little at the time but after they had left we had to 'fudge' it as best we could. Molly did a great job cutting a piece to fit and it looked fine, but it meant twice as much work had to be done and we decided there and then that no further 'help' was required! On another occasion when we were up in Leeds we went to a local warehouse to buy another carpet. Leeds and Bradford were great places to buy goods as competition was fierce, particularly among the Jewish population who had settled in Leeds after the war and had set up various businesses. These were mainly in clothing, floor coverings and furniture, and bargains abounded. They always tried to give customers value for money. We picked the carpet we required – it cost £10, a lot of money for us in those days. When Molly was asked where we living she replied "Rothwell" and we exchanged surreptitious glances. She was well versed in the arts of bargaining! The offer to deliver to our door came immediately. When she gave our full address of course Northampton was mentioned. This caused consternation, but the offer had been made and to their eternal credit the goods were delivered – in Northampton! I gathered that the lorry was making bulk deliveries of orders to outlets in the area so he dropped our carpet off en route. That would not happen today I think. I learned a lot from Molly and her mother Sally, about making purchases in this part of the country, and it has stood me in very good stead over the years. I recall that, on one occasion when we had gone to Drighlington for our summer holiday I went to purchase a set of cups and saucers. I made such a fuss when I noticed that the colours of the set were not a perfect match that when I eventually returned to Drighlington Sally reckoned that I had learned the ability to barter for exactly what I wanted to perfection. She was a great one for bargaining!

Life followed a standard pattern for a while. Our garden soil was rather heavy so, to break it up, we planted potatoes and some runner beans. Our first year's potato crop was a good one and the soil had broken up sufficiently to allow us to lay some grass too. We entertained a few friends occasionally. We eventually bought a 14 inch television for £4 10 s 0d (£4.50). The picture was in black and white and rather grainy but that was pretty standard. The picture quality depended to a large extent on the signal we were able to receive on the roof aerial. It was tall and in high winds tended to move around. As I recall winters were quite harsh and pipes tended to freeze. In fact there was quite a bit of trouble because the builders had not put the water pipes deep enough on our estate. The drains were shallow too, and one evening we saw what we thought were some cats near where the drain ran. It turned out that they were large rats – the sewer pipe had cracked! That caused chaos and the builders came and filled the fractured pipe with concrete. They then had to return and sort out the drains again. One winter the weather was so cold that the pipes froze up completely and in order to have water we had to get supplies from Jeanette and David Freeman as fortunately their supplies were unaffected. We kept our water in the bath. We could not empty that either as the exit pipe was frozen. Even the toilet pipe had to have hot water bottles put on in order to get water into the cistern. It was a bad time! Still, we coped and Molly performed miracles with her cooking. I do not know how she managed but she did and we ate well. Things have moved on considerably these days, thank goodness! We even had problems with the open fire in the lounge. It was a 'Baxi' and relied on a strong draught keeping the fire burning from underneath. But for some reason it did not work very well and eventually a pipe was put through to the outside wall of the house and a few bricks were taken out to give draughts some access.

Chapter 5 Early holiday times

My mother suffered several heart attacks during her latter years of life and we visited her whenever we could. Sally and Willie paid us visits from time to time and we spent most of our holidays in Drighlington. I often went out with Willie when he was working. He was the Chief Milk Recorder for Yorkshire – a responsible job that took him to all parts of Yorkshire. Sometimes we would drive around 200 miles in a day, calling at farms and dairies. He was well liked and he would often return home with farm products that he had collected on his travels. But I remember the first time he took me to a dairy outlet at Gargrave. He told me that I should find it interesting but did not tell me why. He always had a twinkle in his eye when there was anything a bit different from the normal run of things. When we arrived we were met by half a dozen ladies working in the cheese department and they greeted Willie effusively. I thought I had heard strong language before but it was absolutely nothing compared to those girls who worked there! But he was used to them and made his own jokes at their expense – and he never swore once. But it certainly added to my education that day – I had never heard so many expletives used in such a short space of time in my life!

Another side to his character emerged on more than one occasion. He never passed anyone who was in trouble and would stop if a car had broken down. I remember the day we stopped for lunch near a children's playground in Barrow in Furness. A child fell off a slide and hurt herself. He immediately went across to offer to take mother and child to hospital although it would have made us late. As it happened things were not as bad as they had appeared and the child soon recovered, but that was so typical of him. He used to carry sweets and give them to children. But sadly, as things changed and people became suspicious of strangers, he had an experience that upset him greatly. I had already mentioned that it was no longer a wise thing to do as police were instructing children not to speak to strangers and we, as teachers, were asked to reinforce the message to children at school. But he had always given sweets away and was reluctant to change a habit. He could see nothing wrong – it was to him simply a kind and friendly way to act. One day he spoke to a young child who was walking hand in hand with her mother in the street. He went to offer the child a sweet, perfectly innocently, but the mother swore at him and called him some sort of pervert. I tried to explain to her that he was genuine but she screamed out that she would fetch the police and we had to beat a hasty retreat. He did not say a word for about half an hour. It was a hard lesson and was one of the few times that I ever saw him completely nonplussed. He never did it again to my knowledge but he did say to me that he thought the country was 'going to the dogs' when he could not even give sweets away without being sworn at – poor Willie!

To the best of my knowledge he never drank alcohol. He once told me that he had worked in a pub for a time in Drighlington and had seen the results of over imbibing. He was generous almost to a fault and was completely honest in his dealings. He was responsible for organising schedules for people employed by the Milk Marketing Board to go out to farms and bring in milk samples from all dairy herds. After 1964, when we moved to Leeds, I worked for the MMB as a part time milk samples' collector. I used to go out to 10 farms a month to take milk content samples during the evening milking of dairy cattle, and then return in the early hours of the morning to take further samples at the morning milking. These samples were taken to the Milk Marketing Board Centre in Harrogate for analysis to work out the butterfat contents of the various herds.

On one occasion when we were on holiday at Drighlington he ask me if I would go out delivering milk for one of his farmers who had a farm off Bolton Road, on the outskirts of Bradford. He told me that I should be paid, but he left it to the farmer, a certain Mr Greenwood, to give me what he thought best. He decided to offer me £9 a week. It was an interesting delivery route, mainly on or near Manningham Lane. I drove the farmer's diesel Landrover. As it was early morning when I started each day I did not see that many customers except on Fridays when I collected their payments for the week's milk. Obviously I had no idea who anyone was but they were quite friendly. Most houses had one or two pints a day, apart from Bradford Grammar School and a couple of businesses en route. But there was one large house where they always had 14 pints a day – except on Fridays when the delivery was only one pint. The house was set back from Manningham Lane in a cul-de-sac. Several people would offer me cups of tea during the morning rounds. Each Friday the lady of this particular establishment, always came to the door in her dressing gown with a cup of tea for the milkman when I went to collect the milk money. She was surprised on the first occasion that I went and I told her that the regular milkman was ill. She seemed quite concerned but I thought no more about it at the time. One Friday morning while drinking the tea I asked her why she only bought one pint on a Friday. "Well love", she said, "I 'ave to 'ave a day off like everyone else in this business". It turned out that it was a high-class brothel and she was the 'Madame'. The farmer's regular milkman certainly had some interesting clients to supply milk to on his round and I strongly suspect that he had more than just a cup of tea on a Friday. It was certainly interesting to see how the 'other half' lived!

While we spent our vacations in Yorkshire I was able to continue my interest in sports – rugby league in winter and cricket in summer. I even turned out on the odd occasion for Adwalton Cricket Club. That way I met some of the locals. Much of my summer holidays were spent either at Headingley or Park Avenue, Bradford, watching Yorkshire when they had County fixtures while on other occasions I watched teams in the Yorkshire Cricket League. I was able to have a look round the cities of Leeds and Bradford too and spent time in the markets of both places – honing up my bargaining skills! Both markets had great appeal to a variety of people and there were some real characters – down and outs as well as the day-to-day shoppers. I enjoyed talking to several of the ones who were down on their luck and I bought them cups of tea and the occasional titbit to eat. I never mentioned this at Drighlington as I suspect my mother in law would not have been impressed. It would not have been her scene! After all, some of them were, I suspect, pinching things from the stalls. One could often tell. Having sat and chatted to one old lady around dinnertime I noticed that she wore a long rather baggy dress. She was quite thin, looked down and out, so I bought her some lunch. Later that afternoon I happened to see her again and hardly recognised her. She looked, to say the least, considerably more portly! The dress must have secreted several items - including tins of food no doubt – all filched surreptitiously from various stalls. I often wondered if she ever got caught! There was another person that I once met in Leeds market who told me that he was from St George's. At the time I did not know just what St George's was – a temporary hostel for people who slept rough in those days, I found out later. He smoked like a chimney and probably drank a lot too. He specialised in 'finding' cigarettes. I saw him pick up the odd fag end that had been thrown away and I also saw him later outside the market transferring cigarette packets from the wide sleeves and inner lining of a 'throw over' coat – no pockets apparently, just a couple of cut out slits below his armpits where no doubt he secreted what he had pinched! He even produced a bottle of whisky from the inner lining. Needless to say I made sure that I had disappeared again when he turned to walk away! But it gave me a further insight into the various ways that people existed. Having taught in the slums in Nottingham I had seen at first hand many of the illicit dealings that took place on the quiet. Certainly I made sure that life was never dull, and it gave Molly time that she could spend with her mother on her own at home. Of course we went around the county too and she showed me interesting places in Yorkshire, many of which I have visited frequently since. My education was certainly enhanced both by what I learned from my wife and her parents and from my solo trips into Bradford and Leeds. Indeed I saw both sides of the equation!

We found some difficulty in making ends meet financially, particularly in our early days, so in order to boost our income I took a second job - at a National Children's Home on the outskirts of Northampton. There were some pretty tough lads and lasses there who had had raw deals in their early lives. Several had been rejected by their parents or had been taken into care for a variety of misdemeanours that had put them into juvenile courts. They were sentenced to varying periods of detention depending on the offence. Parents were permitted to see their offspring but, sadly, few bothered to visit and some of the youngsters became very bitter. I remember one lad called Glyn who always dressed up every Saturday, convinced that his mother would turn up. But she never did even once during the two years I was at the Home. I felt so sorry for him and I took him out when I could. Working with deprived children appealed to me and I spent two or three evenings a week at the Home. There were various projects that were arranged by Mr Deaton, the superintendent of the Home. His wife acted as the matron. I am sure that he meant well where the young people in his care were concerned but he lacked the experience to run the home as well as it should have been and inevitably in some cases certain of the teenage residents took liberties. I think the main problem arose from the fact that the wages on offer did not attract the sort of senior people who were experienced in the ways of dealing with wayward and under privileged youngsters.

In my early years, from the age of 6 onwards, I had seen my father at work with the convicted inmates of Camp Hill Borstal Institution. Although I was only a child at the time I got to know several of the Borstal boys quite well. I was considered as something of a mascot by them, and on Sports Days I used to sit near the track and they would speak to me. I wished them good luck in return. One or two of them even touched me as they walked by as a sort of good luck charm! They were very kind to me and I got to like several of them. They often worked either in the garden of our home - the Chaplain's House - or in nearby Parkhurst Forest, the trees of which literally bordered our garden fence. In fact our house, known as the Chaplain's house, had been built on land reclaimed from the forest. So there were tree roots still being removed by the boys long after we had arrived in 1936. Inevitably when I was playing in the garden I chatted to them – and probably got in the way at the same time! The Warders, who were in charge of the boys at work, kept a close eye on what had to be done - and on me too I expect. It was only a small community at Camp Hill itself so everybody knew each other well. Warders' children often came to our house so I was never short of friends to play with. The Borstal boys built us a swing in the garden and cleared a lawn for us to play on. It was a large area – space was no problem at that house. We even had frames put up for us to climb on, all made out of branches from the trees that were being cleared in the forest. As a direct result of those early experiences, in later life I resolved to work with lads down on their luck. After all, I too had been born in a slum in Birmingham so my modest roots also must have had an influence on my future thinking as I grew up. At one stage I even considered working at a Northamptonshire School for juvenile offenders and wanted to apply for a job there. But I was not qualified at the time and I had to go to College first. I would then have had to do a further period of study to qualify to become a member of staff but this was not an option as I needed to earn money to help pay my way while living at home. I was expected to make a contribution to the family finances once I started work.

As a teacher myself I was not prepared to accept any rude or unbecoming behaviour at the National Children's home and I made that quite clear. After a short while the youngsters recognised that I meant exactly what I said and I had no problem. At Kings Heath School I was considered a firm disciplinarian with a voice to match. However Mr Deaton, head of the NCH resorted to physical punishment and as I was not in any position to gainsay this my only recourse at the time was to say that I was not prepared to have any part in that sort of chastisement. To me it was tantamount to bullying – my pet aversion. I had suffered at school myself and knew only too well the misery it could cause to children away from their own homes. However, once I had made my position clear, any punishments that were apparently meted out were administered when I was not on the premises. I only found out about the punitive measures by accident - at second hand. One thing that they all needed was kindness, consideration and genuine concern for their welfare. On Saturdays in the winter I would sometimes take over for the day while the Mr Deaton and his wife went out. I also worked during my school holidays. The Home was supposedly inspected every so often by a certain Mrs Drake. She was in over all charge of the various National Children's Homes that were in our part of the Midlands. But she was the sort of 'overseer' who wanted no trouble and she metaphorically closed her eyes to what was going on at the Home where I was working. However I learned later that some official who had paid an unannounced visit to the place had made a strong complaint about the way in which the Home was being run. My name was mentioned as a part time member of staff to whom the children deferred and with whom they felt that they were being well looked after whenever I was in charge. Apparently the children had told the official this.

My work at the Home brought in a bit of much needed extra money. After just over a couple of years of marriage we decided that we would like to start our family. Early in April 1962 it was confirmed that Molly was pregnant. We were thrilled and our respective families were delighted too. We tried to budget for the time when Molly would have to give up teaching. With the extra cash coming in from the NCH work things were not too bad and we were able to 'see the wood for the trees' – or so we thought. In fact I was asked to take over the running of the National Children's Home during the school summer holidays in 1962. I was to be paid full salary during that time. This suited us very well as the extra cash would be very useful. But once I was left in sole charge and was sleeping at the school I realised the full extent of what was going on. Something had to be done. I asked Molly to come to visit while I was working there and I showed her what I had found. She was very helpful and we discussed some new ideas. The intention was to try and introduce a few changes in such a way that they could improve the lot of the children without usurping Mr Deaton's authority. Then fate took an unforeseen hand. The police contacted me late one evening to ask if I would take in a 16 year old girl who had run away from home in Newcastle and had 'hitched' her way towards London on a lorry. The driver had stopped at a roadside eating-place called Annie's Café, often frequented by lorry drivers on the A1 in Northamptonshire. The police had found her there and taken her into custody for her own safety. They then brought her to stay overnight. This necessitated me contacting Miss Drake's office in order to see if we could help the girl financially to return to Newcastle. I spoke to the girl at some length and persuaded her that I would ensure that she would be able to return home to her mother in safety. The mother's boyfriend had forced the girl out of her family home, ill treating her in the process. In turn the mother had now got rid of the boyfriend courtesy of the Newcastle Police who arrested him for assaulting the daughter and making threats to her mother - quite a chain of events! The police were very helpful and sent a plainclothes female officer to travel on the train and keep an eye on her from a distance to make sure that the girl actually went home. Fortunately she did, so that was a good bit of social cooperation between NCH and the police.

But there were repercussions arising from the unscheduled visit by an NCH official once Mr Deaton returned after his month away. An inquiry into how he was carrying out his duties at the Home was started and I was roped in to make a verbal report on my findings to Miss Drake. At the time I probably did not condemn what he had been doing strongly enough and later on he was permitted to continue under close supervision – a mistake made by the insipid Miss Drake I felt afterwards. However I was approached again shortly afterwards by someone at a higher level and once I had repeated my report Miss Drake was apparently directed to take proper action and have him removed for the sake of the youngsters involved at the Home. I resigned at the end of my period of running the Home as I was no longer prepared to work with Mr Deaton. I remember coming home and telling Molly. She had resigned from Moulton School at the end of the summer term and was upset, as the money had proved a considerable help, but she understood I think. I recall looking at my teacher's monthly pay slip at the time. It was just over £48 net – we owed £54! However we managed to get round that all right in the end and always kept out of debt – just. I have often wondered what we should have done if there had been credit cards available in those days, But there weren't – only bank loans, and they were expensive.

In September I really upset the family applecart. My left knee gave way coming down the stairs one day and it turned out that I needed a cartilage removing. Fast bowling had caught up with me and I must have twisted my knee once too often. In October I had an operation for the cartilage to be removed at the Manfield Hospital. Fortunately the hospital was just at the end of Spinney Hill Road so Molly was able to visit me although it was hard work for her walking to the hospital with a baby on the way!

The operation was carried out by an Indian surgeon named Mr Gupta – a most caring man. He visited me several times during my time in hospital and oversaw my rehabilitation. One incident I recall – when I went going down to the operating theatre news had just been released that some Russian ships were on their way to Cuba to land rockets with atomic heads that could be trained on specific targets in America. USA President John Kennedy had threatened to take the strongest action if Nikita Kruschev, the Russian President, did not send out an order to the ships to turn round and go back to Russia. When I came round after the operation apparently I was told that the very first thing I had asked of the male nurse who was looking after me was, "Have the Russian ships turned around?" "Yes", he replied. I then went straight back to sleep!

Molly went into the Barratt Hospital in Northampton to have our baby. She told me that it was not an easy birth. The nurses had been somewhat lax in their care. She took my family gold watch to the hospital to time her contractions I think and this became a treasured possession - together with a silver one that went with it. She still has them. I was able to go into the ward and see her around dinnertime on December 12th – probably the most emotionally happy time of my life. I remember fitting baby Philip onto the palm of my left hand and wondering just how he would grow up – now I know! We were so delighted that all was well and it made me realise what a wonderful gift nature offers when a baby is born. The love I felt for mother and baby that day was so incredibly special – it is something I would never regret whatever else happened in our lives. Our parents were all delighted of course. Sally and Willie came down from Drighlington to help out and be with Molly while she recovered. I certainly found it a happy time – it was exhausting too for both of us, particularly after feeding during the night. We took Philip to see my parents regularly because by now my Mother was unable to travel. She had a companion, Mary, who looked after her at Cranford Rectory. We would often go for a walk while there – it is a beautiful part of the country. Philip was baptised at St Matthew's Parish Church, Northampton on April 21st 1963. Molly's cousin Malcolm Overend and my cousin Daphne Sharman became his Godparents.

With Molly at home and Sally a frequent visitor life went on normally for me in my teaching career at Kings Heath Junior School. Luckily Philip was unhurt when he rolled over while lying on the table and fell off. I came home one day to find that this had happened but that there was no damage done. Still, it was certainly a shock at the time. On another occasion he was thought to have swallowed something dangerous and had to have a stomach pump used to ensure he was ok.

We decided to add to our family as soon as possible and Molly once again became pregnant. But sadly this time things went very wrong. She suffered internal haemorrhaging and had to be rushed to the Barratt Hospital. She lost the baby and again the aftercare she received was not as good as it should have been. This affected her seriously and in the end she suffered a breakdown. She went home to Drighlington to recover, taking Philip with her. Her mother looked after her. She could not face going back to a hospital and she had treatment from a friend of her Uncle Clarence - a certain Mr Woodcock who was a semi retired osteopath working part time in the Bradford area. He performed wonders and helped her cope with the worst. I drove up to Drighlington at weekends and holidays when I could, but sadly I soon learned that Sally blamed me for what had happened. Willie realised exactly what she thought. He took me to one side and told me to take no notice – he called it a 'bee in her bonnet' - but it was not easy. Eventually Molly returned to Northampton but was very unhappy and so a decision was made to move up to Yorkshire so she could be near her family and continue the treatment if necessary. At the time I had been applying for a deputy headships in Northampton and then for a headship or two in village schools somewhere in the County. Fortunately, as it turned out, I had not been successful up to that point so this was no barrier to a move. It was a necessary career upheaval and so I applied for two jobs – the first one was at Upper Poppleton near York. The second was for the Deputy Headship of Holy Trinity Church of England School, Cookridge. Prior to the application at Upper Poppleton we called in at the School. We met the Head Teacher and liked what we saw in the School itself. I was called up for interview there soon afterwards. The interview went well but the Chairperson – a somewhat 'uppercrust' lady who obviously wanted to stamp her authority on any candidate involved – informed me that several people had been interviewed but no one came up to the standard required. Apparently I fitted the bill but she then proceeded to tell me loftily that as she had not seen my references she could not possibly offer me the job without 'checking my credentials as they might be fake!' I returned home to Northampton somewhat irritated by her attitude and heard nothing for three weeks. During that three-week period I was called up for interview at Holy Trinity C of E School. There were 4 candidates, all of whom were experienced teachers. Apparently it was a difficult choice for the Managers as we all interviewed well. I did not get the Deputy's post – that went to Dennis Knowles - but was called back by the Managers immediately and offered a job on the staff. I rather expected this result as they were already aware I needed a post quickly and I guess they thought that they might get two teachers out of it all. In fact they got three as they also offered a post to another candidate – Mrs Smith. As it happened I gave her a lift into Leeds after the interviews and she mentioned that she too had been approached and was considering moving to the school. I returned home having not yet replied to the letter from Upper Poppleton School offering me the post there. As I had had to wait for over three weeks before the Managers had written to me – I wrote back after a further delay – refusing the offer. I pointed out that due to the unnecessary time wasted before contacting me I had been called up for interview for another post and I had accepted. I also made the point that their delay in making contact necessitated my taking this step as, after all, the Chairperson had only to telephone me and she had my number. She had been made fully aware why I needed the job to be confirmed quickly if it was to be offered at all. My request had been totally ignored and I was not prepared to be kept waiting. I later rang the Headteacher of Upper Poppleton School who had particularly wanted me to join his staff. He needed someone to organise PE throughout the School and I offered exactly what he was looking for, as I would have been a full time class teacher as well. I apologised for not accepting the post and mentioned the reasons again. After my interview was over and I had left he had apparently been very annoyed by the Chairperson's high-handed attitude and had said so in no uncertain terms. He had seen the letter I had sent to the Managers in reply to the belated offer they had made. He fully understood how I had felt. He told me that he had said at the time that it was obvious that my qualifications were exactly what the School wanted and had pressed for contact to be made immediately. But the arrogant lady had ignored his wish and had decided upon the delay. After that I felt that I had had a fortunate escape!

So now the dye was cast and we needed a house. I came up to Drighlington the next weekend while Molly was still at home and we were driven around Leeds looking for a place that would suit. None of them appealed to me. Sally was in a state – she wanted things settled - to her own satisfaction I expect. The next morning I went down to breakfast early and was subjected to such a tirade from Sally. That only confirmed what I had suspected she had felt from the start, and I was disgusted. Molly was concerned too when I told her what had happened. She had been resting but got up straight away. We went out immediately after breakfast and drove over to Cookridge. We saw exactly what we felt we wanted and could afford, having been shown round the completed house next door by the owners – the Savilles. It was ideal and not far from Holy Trinity School. With that settled we paid a £50 deposit for the plot and returned to Drighlington. After a late lunch I immediately drove back to Northampton, relieved that we had sorted things out for ourselves. Willie took me quietly on one side before I left and said we had done the right thing. He realised the difficulties and made a joke about the older ladies of Yorkshire sometimes being 'pushy!' He even said that he agreed to do things when told to - for peace! We laughed and that was the end of the matter so far as I was concerned. But I had realised by then that I did not think the same way as many Yorkshire folk and I was certainly not prepared to be ignored and pushed around just to suit other people. This is certainly not confined to Yorkshire. It happens in most areas in different ways. I found that the Geordies that I was with at College had differing priorities, while in Nottingham and many places further south there were other ways of looking at life! But maybe the most irritating seem to come from the Southern Counties. I remember on one occasion sometime after we had moved to Cookridge Molly and I went to a party in Sunbury on Thames. One other guest asked us where we lived. When we told her that we lived in Leeds the comment was –'Oh you poor things!' We politely put her right and suggested that she should actually visit the north and sample both the wonderful hospitality and the beautiful scenery before being so critical. It turned out she had hardly ever been north of Watford Gap although she went abroad regularly for holidays. I suppose she thought that ignorance was bliss and that anyone living north of Watford Gap was practically residing in a foreign land - what an idiotic way to look at things!

From then on things moved quickly. With my resignation from the staff at Kings Heath accepted I was free to move on. I had enjoyed working at that School and it was a big step for me at the time. This was mainly because I had moved from place to place so often in my early life – Birmingham, Isle of Wight, Oxford, Northampton, Oakham, Northampton for a second time, Durham, Rothwell and Northampton once more - and until I got married had not really settled down to, as I thought, a period of stability – living in one place. But now that was changed and yet again I was on the move to Leeds. Life had not been easy for either of us and the move gave us the chance to start afresh. I had hated living in Northampton on my own while Molly was recuperating at Drighlington and I missed Philip very much too. But once we all got together again we were so busy getting ready for the move that there was little time to think of much else.

Chapter 6 Starting life in Leeds

We left 58 Spinney Hill Road, Northampton, and drove up to our new home in Leeds - 53 Kirkwood Way, Cookridge - on August 4th 1964. After settling in we went off on holiday in Sally and Willie's caravan and that was the start of a way of life that we enjoyed `for many years. It is difficult to recall just how many places we visited in the early days but I remember vividly discovering the delights of the tiny seaside village of Portpatrick. Throughout my life Portpatrick has been special. The Golf Club, at which I was later invited to become a member, was the course that had special meaning. Both Philip and my godson Stephen learned to play the game there, first on the small course and then on the full 18 hole course.

On our arrival at Kirkwood Way we soon found that we had excellent neighbours and friends in the cul-de-sac. The Thompsons lived at no. 55 - in the other section of our three bedroom semi-detached house while the Savilles were in the next semi at no. 51. Opposite were the Bells and the Loves. Roy and Barbara Thompson were teachers so we had much in common. At last we could put that sad period of our family lives, spent in Northampton, to one side and in effect start again. As other families in the cul-de-sac were moving into the newly built estate there was a great atmosphere of goodwill and it was common to see people helping each other, wheeling barrow loads of soil into gardens, laying concrete and paving slabs for paths and drives.

Furthermore when the first bonfire night came round on November 5th 1964 a joint party was held in the area behind our house and the Thompsons' house. Virtually all the street came! We had a tree trunk that we set alight at the base of the massive bonfire. Pies and mushy peas were provided by Mavis Saville. There was plenty of wine, spirits and beer to ensure that a truly convivial time was had by all, including the children. Fireworks were let off - and fortunately without incident. This party idea became a regular feature for several years – that tree trunk lasted for 3 years as the base of each bonfire! It was stored at the rear of our garden. But inevitably as time went by and gardens were laid with grass etc. it proved more difficult to find anywhere to build a large bonfire. However the firework parties continued for quite a while and more than one lawn suffered from the effects of the fires afterwards. There were parties held at various other times of the year too so it was a good time. But after a while families moved away and new neighbours arrived. Children were growing up and games took place out in the street at the end of the cul-de-sac. This caused friction in some places as footballs and tennis balls finished up in the nearby gardens and some residents objected. One man in particular, by the name of Derek Holmes - nicknamed 'Big Red' by others both in the police force and outside it - was not cooperative in the least. He was a senior policeman, the Superintendent in charge of Chapeltown Police Station. He lived in the house on the south side of the snicket that gave access to Tinshill Road. On occasion he even punctured footballs before returning them and was generally extremely unpopular with both children and many adults. I recall going to his house to fetch a ball that Philip had kicked into his garden. We had a difference of opinion as to the merits of football being played in the street and I well remember his comment, "I keep myself to myself Mister, and don't you forget it!" However we got our ball back on that occasion. But there were advantages in having him in the street too. Policemen lived in 3 of the 4 semis at the end of the cul-de-sac. Crime was unheard of in our street in those days. Sadly that changed after they all moved on.

As Philip started to grow up he soon made friends with other children. I became Godfather to Ann and Clive Bell's son Stephen and Betty Love became Godmother when Stephen was baptised. He later had a sister named Andrea, affectionately nicknamed 'Aggie'. I was known then as 'Uncle Chris' – at least that was the eventual name, but Aggie got it out as 'Uncle Crisps' for a while much to everyone's amusement – and she did eat crisps too!

My father in law, Willie Holroyd, was the Chief Milk Recorder for West Yorkshire. It was a very responsible job and he travelled to many farms. I had been out with him on several occasions before, as I have already mentioned. I had thoroughly enjoyed the outings and when he approached me to see if I would like to work part time for the Milk Marketing Board I did not need a second invitation. He required me to go to 10 farms near Leeds each month. On 4 of the farms I would be required to take milk samples at both morning and evening milkings. On the others the farmers did their own sampling and I would collect the samples each week and take them to the MMB Headquarters in Harrogate. This simply meant one round trip a week to collect from the respective farms. The job was ideal as it took place well before and well after a day at School so there was no clash of interests. Milking on the farms where I collected samples started on average around 6 am – enough time to get the work done and return to School. The major difficulty was that I did not ever have time to go home and change out of the old smelly clothes I wore when in the milking sheds. So I kept clean clothes in the men's cloakroom at school and would change there. I could get into the building past the caretaker's house, cross the hall and disappear into the men's cloakroom without passing through the children's playground. This was fine. I got my leg pulled quite a lot at first by the staff but they soon got used to me arriving just in time. In fact I was never once late in the two years that I did the job. The only problem came one morning when I had inadvertently got behind a cow as it disgorged the contents of its bowels. I got back to school, stinking of cow dung! However I followed my usual routine and got changed, thinking I had got away with it. But oh no, not that time! The aroma was too strong and something had to be done quickly. The caretaker and I wrapped up the offending clothing in an old sheet and he proceeded to creep out the back way and stick the 'parcel' under my car. Of course, it rained and when I went out to move it I had to put it in the boot. Driving home afterwards to get some more old clothes to wear I have never smelt anything so horrible! I tried to get rid of the smell but without success – then I had to drive back for the evening milking. I made it with every window wide open – I shudder to think what any poor motorist would have thought when he or she was stationary behind my car! So that was the end of those clothes – I dumped them at the farm when I got there – in the rubbish tip. No one ever said anything afterwards at the farm – I guess they did not even notice. But when I went into the byre I made quite sure I never got behind a cow again!

There was another side to the job too. The samples were taken regularly and I had to ensure that they matched up with each correct cow. This meant putting plastic tags into one ear of each beast – not a simple task to carry out if the particular cows were feeling a bit frisky. But fortunately I learned quickly – I had to. Willie showed me how to 'catch' a cow by one ear and carry out the task asap – ie before the poor creature had time to object. Fortunately there is no feeling in a cow's ear so it felt nothing. But it was still quite an art, having to persuade the cow to move where I wanted it to. I also made sure I was nowhere too near a wall, fence or hedge as cows have a knack of rubbing up against projections of any kind. I reckon they must have itched quite a lot one way or another! I guess the most useful – and the most difficult thing for me - was deciphering just what was being said. Most of the farmers and their workers spoke in a broad Yorkshire dialect and sometimes used colloquial terms which initially meant nothing to me. But I soon cottoned on. They were great characters and I made friends with one or two which have lasted for years. In fact I went to Dave Marshall's farm at Bramhope until he retired. The start of our friendship came when we were discussing how he was paid for his milk. He told me that on a scale of 1 to 5 the highest payout per beast was when they reached 4 in terms of the butterfat content of the milk produced. I studied carefully just what feed was given to the cows producing the richest milk and Dave took the risk of completely changing the feed. Luckily it worked and the magic number 4 was reached. It helped swell his financial coffers quite a bit and he was delighted!

Chapter 7 Teaching in Leeds

I started teaching at Holy Trinity CE School in September 1964. At around the same time, while Molly was at home looking after Philip, she took on the roll of pianist for the 'Monday School' for the young children. The Vicar – a delightful man by the name of Maurice Chant – was a popular priest, polite, caring and modest. He was the sort of kindly man whom the children at school and in the Parish both respected and liked. I became a member of the Holy Trinity Parish Church Council at the first election after we arrived. I had already served on the PCC at Rothwell, Northants, for a time and after we were married I served for 4 years on the PCC at Saint Matthew's Parish Church, Northampton.

Maurice Chant was a regular visitor in School. As Chairman of the Managers he took his role seriously and took a weekly morning service at Assemblies. Mr Norman Green, the newly appointed Head Teacher, was fortunate to have got such an experienced staff to open the school. I initially took responsibility for PE and Sports plus the first year junior class. I also set up the School Library. The school quickly filled up with pupils and I was offered and accepted the first post of 'extra responsibilities' to become available - in January 1966. As it happened another Church School was being completed at Whinmoor. I applied for the Deputy Head's post and was appointed in March, much to Norman's chagrin - more of that later.

One of the pleasures associated with starting in a brand new school is that there are opportunities to help map out the future conduct appertaining to the daily life of the School – standards of discipline, standards of work, subject schemes, timetables and a whole host of other ideals that go to make up a happy and efficient place. This meant staff meetings – both official and unofficial. Norman Green, Dennis Knowles and I got on well together from the start. We would often go to the 'Fox and Hounds' pub at Bramhope and, with the aid of a pint or two of beer, discuss ideas and ways of implementing good practices within the structure of the various School policies. One that particularly appealed was swimming and I opted to go with classes. Our aim was to try to ensure that every child could swim before they left the School. Another was getting a Parent Teacher Association started. That served a useful purpose in getting parents together and before long events were arranged to help swell the coffers of the School Fund. The response was tremendous and it set a good standard of mutual trust between parents and teachers. Open evenings became standard practice each term. Children were encouraged to be competitive and were put into 4 houses – Red, Green, Blue, Yellow. They had house names too but I cannot recall them. I learned a lot from the informal discussions at the 'Fox and Hounds' that held me in very good stead when I was later interviewed for the Deputy Headship of Whinmoor Church of England Primary School in 1966. Although my appointment at the school did not officially commence until September the new Head Teacher, Gordon Towse, and I met up frequently during the summer to sort out future policies. Gordon was an excellent boss to work for and both the mutual respect and friendship we developed then has lasted ever since.

To return to Holy Trinity - a Nativity play was produced for Christmas and we had a Carol Service too, in Church. Then an ambitious production of 'The Nutcracker Suite' was put on in the summer under the general direction of Mrs Davidson. We all chipped in as she needed a lot of help. The ladies made costumes and scenery amongst other things. My offering was the Arab dance – based entirely on PE activities and finished off with a series of handsprings across the Hall - set to music for good measure. The star of that was Jackie Smith who lived near in our cul-de-sac. She used to practise her handsprings at home and occasionally on our front lawn. She was very good at all PE activities and 'brought the house' down when performing in the school production. A lot of time was put in after school had finished for the day. Several staff members, myself included, formed clubs – Dancing and Drama, Gymnastics and Badminton. Norman Green had been a top class Badminton player. I also weighed in with Table Tennis. Art and Chess groups were formed too and created a lot of interest.

The sporting side – football and netball was in full swing almost immediately as part of the curriculum. The first major event I organised was the initial Sports Day in the summer of 1965. It was based on competitive athletics events between the houses – something I had already done while at previous schools. Luckily the day was fine and there was a good turnout of parents. Every child got the opportunity to compete. Maurice Chant presented the Sports Cup to the winning team at the end.

Thus the standards for Holy Trinity CE School were set out. I stayed at the school for only two years as promotion had quickly come my way. As it turned out this was a prelude to further steps up the ladder in the course of my career in teaching. The experiences that I had enjoyed as a founder member of the Staff, together with being in the fortunate position of helping to open a newly built school, held me in good stead. In 1966, as already mentioned, I was appointed Deputy Head of the new Church School on the Whinmoor Estate. I felt sure my experiences at Holy Trinity would help with the challenge and so it proved.

Chapter 8 Senior Management

I moved to Whinmoor in September 1966. I gave up my part time job with the Milk Marketing Board as the time taken travelling to and from my new job each day made it impossible to continue. Still, the money had come in handy!

Whinmoor was a School with a difference. The Head Teacher, Gordon Towse, was the ideal man to run the place. He was a committed Churchman and the good reputation that was built up at the School from almost the time we opened in September 1966 was down in large measure to his forward planning. He had an outgoing personality and it was a real pleasure to be able to work with someone like him. We always got together for a chat about the way things were going at least three times a week, more usually every day after school finished and clubs were completed. He stood no nonsense but the rules and regulations we set down as necessary to provide a good ethos for the School were well thought out and, most importantly, implemented in a firm but kindly way. All members of staff were committed to the principles set down. Whinmoor School was built as a Community School and, as there was no Church nearby, it became the focal point for worship with services being held in the School Hall every Sunday. Whinmoor itself was part of a much larger Church Community that included Seacroft and the surrounding area. In all there were five priests ministering as a team, ably led by the Reverend Norman Thomas. Our representative on the team was the Rev. Terry Short. His spirit was very willing but his ability to come into school at the times mutually agreed for assemblies left something to be desired! To combat this Gordon decided that he should join us at dinnertimes instead. That way he could both chat with the children and at the same time have a good meal. After that he was seldom late and we also had him in School after lunch – good psychology!

I took charge of much of the day to day running of the School. I taught full time, starting with the third year junior Class. I also took responsibility for all PE and sporting activities in the School plus anything else that as a Deputy I could do. I shared my office with the School Secretary and that worked well. It was kept tidy! We had a caretaker by the name of Mr Evans who was a real rogue. He had a house bordering the School, not too far from the main building. He did his job well enough but he was up to all sorts of tricks, using pieces of equipment such as cleaning materials and the like at home as well as in school. I remember Gordon going in to school unexpectedly one evening and almost falling over a long electric cable. When
he traced it from the plug onwards it stretched across the grass into the caretaker's house. It was amazing how the school electricity bills went down after this was discovered! Occasionally a TV set would be on in the School when we arrived in the morning – mistakenly left on by his children who had been into School to watch in the evenings! Eventually these things were ironed out, although he still got the sack in the end. The school was a riot of colour on the walls of the corridors as well as inside classrooms. Children's work was displayed everywhere and was changed regularly. There was an art class as one of the many after school club activities and it was remarkable to see the standard of work displayed in the corridors by those youngsters too. The accent on good manners was of major importance and quickly became the norm. The behavioural pattern stemmed from this and firm discipline did the rest. There were times, of course, where disciplinary measures were needed – the determination to 'make the punishment fit the crime' often sufficed and on other occasions parental involvement was effective. It was not always well received by any means but after a while most parents cooperated and those who did not were invited up to school to sort things out. If this failed or parents just did not turn up the 'board' man from the Education Department was asked to call and we had a good man who worked willingly on the School's behalf. Gordon was always polite but firm and always gave the staff full backing whenever difficulties occurred. So again, I learned a lot and that held me in good stead when further opportunities for promotion came my way.

Molly went back to work at Ryecroft Primary School when Philip became a pupil at Holy Trinity School in 1967. As we were working on opposite sides of the city she used our decent car while I either went in an old ' banger' – an A30 costing £50 that she bought me for a present - or on a scooter. The scooter was a French make and was aptly named 'Concorde'. I loved working on machines of any kind so I derived a lot of pleasure from ensuring that these vehicles went properly and I collected a whole range of useful tools for the job. My garage at one time must have been quite a treasure trove for a mechanic! The Concorde, purchased for £5, was a real challenge. It only had one variable gear so that when the throttle was opened it just increased speed and vice versa. At least, that was the theory. I eventually managed to work out how to make it go – probably the most rewarding job I ever did as I had to make a couple of engine parts for it. I used that during the summer of 1967.

While I was on the staff at Whinmoor decided to go on a course to improve my French I duly applied and was accepted. By chance Dennis Knowles from Holy Trinity had attended the course the previous year and he had enjoyed it. On this occasion I was in the company of two Leeds' Headteachers, Norman Green and John Reynolds. The course was held in Vichy, France. We all travelled together and were billeted at the same hotel. The course proved rewarding over all but there were several things to keep us on our toes. The whole course was conducted entirely in French – quite rightly – but I had something of a problem as I could not understand half of what was being said! I did request that the tutor speak more slowly. "Doucement s'il vous plait, Monsieur", I requested. He smiled – pityingly I think – and complied for about two sentences, then went back to express speed! A fair number of the students were French anyway and so I re-read the course details. I had missed an all-important word when I applied for the course – it was the word 'accent'. This turned out to be hilarious because, on the second day we were given set pieces to listen to on tape. We then repeated what we had heard onto another tape for assessment. This was great for me. I love copying sounds and this was a real winner. Out of the 90 or so students in attendance I came top! However, then came the downside. We were given a series of questions to answer by the tutor. We recorded our replies onto tape and – guess what? I came out almost at the bottom of the list! That night at the local bar I managed two gaffs. The first one was when I tried to order a French delicacy for the tutor who had been lecturing us that day - a canapé, which is fried bread with things like anchovies, apparently much loved by the French - and the word I had used sounded like the French word for settee! The waiter and the tutor just fell about laughing but then softened the blow with the words, "Monsieur, you speak French like a Frenchman. You have come top of the exercise set for accent". I tried to thank him but he continued remorselessly, "but you understand French like an Englishman!" He then told me I was near the bottom of the group for that! The second was when I suggested that perhaps he spoke English like a Frenchman as he had only spoken French to us all day. He promptly replied in flawless English! So everybody had a good laugh at my expense, including me – he was a great guy and he did spend time helping me in that first week. I found that after a time I no longer tried to translate. Instead I started to think in French and by the end of the course I had done quite well. I even got good marks when, at the end of the course, we carried out a similar exercise to the one I had done so badly the first time, and I got good marks. We had a further meeting in the bar before we went home and this time I got things right so he then treated me – but not to anchovies!

There was one other embarrassing moment when Norman, John and I visited a French Primary School to see how English was taught. We sat at the back of the class for 20 minutes or so listening to the teacher who was doing very well. The children were answering and copying phrases – then replying. These were simple basics like names of people and articles in the classroom such as books, pens and pencils – in fact things in everyday use. Suddenly, to our horror, John Reynolds got up, walked to the front of the classroom and just took over! To her credit the teacher stood back and we hastily assured her that he had not meant to be rude. In fact he was very rude. However he got his come-uppance in no uncertain manner. He continued doing more or less what the teacher had been doing but the children just looked at him blankly. They could not understand a word he was saying! At the end of the lesson Norman and I left with the teacher and John had to fend for himself – his own arrogance had made him look foolish. It served him right! What's more, neither Norman nor I went into another School with him again. He was too much of a liability!

Unfortunately there was a less savoury side to the course. At the end of the second week a large group of German students joined. Many of the French girls who had paired up with younger students from other countries, England included, went off with the German boys and this caused disharmony and a few fights when the drink flowed too freely. Things came to a head when a couple of German lads who got drunk tried to break in to the room of an English girl. Fortunately there were several male students around who sorted them out in no uncertain terms. After that whenever groups finished up eating in the same restaurants there was a lot of agro and mockery. As we were all given food vouchers for use only in certain restaurants it was inevitable and proved a source of contention among the younger students.

But I became involved in something quite different while in Vichy. When I first arrived I went for a swim each evening after lectures. After couple of days or so five or six of the French students came and asked me to teach then to swim as one of our lot had mentioned that I was a swimming teacher. They were all from one college in Lille. I duly obliged and we had a teaching session each evening. They were grateful and took me out with them to the local hostelries. This was very useful as my French still wasn't that good and they were all studying English at their college in Lille. I also played their national game of table tennis – a sport that, as a youngster, I had excelled in. There was a competition for all students who wanted to take part at the College in Vichy. Unbeknown to me these French students put my name down and then made such a fuss that I played, thinking that I would be beaten very quickly. However one of the French lads was keen and we practised a lot in our spare time. I got through several rounds and began to take the competition seriously. In the semis was an Egyptian whom I thought could beat me, a German, an Italian and myself. Luckily for me the Italian beat the Egyptian and I beat the German. Much to my delight I won the final quite easily. The irony of it all was not lost on me. In the final the large English contingent supported me and incredible as it may seem, so did the Germans. They hated the Italians more than the British! Afterwards I tried to speak to the young German whom I'd beaten in the semis but although he winked as I passed him he did not speak. It really was quite alarming to see that the young people of the various nationalities were so antagonistic towards each other. The supreme irony was that those of us over about 35 felt no animosity towards each other whatsoever wherever we came from – rather the reverse in fact – and we were all more concerned about the future outcome of the European countries eventually getting together for mutual trade agreements.

One further thing happened. On the course was a girl of about 19. She wanted to go to Paris one weekend and went off without telling the hotel management. At the same time a thief got into a room in the hotel and stole money. No one at the time knew who had done the thieving and when the girl returned to her hotel she was cautioned by two Gendarmes and told to report to the Gendarmerie first thing in the morning. She was friendly with a young English teacher whom I knew and he had introduced me. She was very frightened and begged me to go with her and the boy friend to the Gendarmerie. We did and I saw for the first time just what the French police could be like. They arrested her when she arrived. They were also quite ruthless with us, and when I attempted to go inside with the girl to make sure she received a fair hearing I was ejected quite forcefully and warned that I too would be arrested if I did not leave. I had to work that bit out in French, but it was quite obvious what was meant! We waited outside for about an hour and a half until eventually she came out crying. She had protested her innocence and had told them where she had been. She was in a state, but she was 'escorted' out of the Gendarmerie in such a bullying manner that it left no doubt as to what they thought. Fortunately as it turned out some students had seen a Belgian lad hanging about at one point. They knew he had gone to the station and, as it turned out, he had boarded the same train as the girl. He was eventually caught, but not before the girl was re-arrested and taken into the Gendarmerie again. I went down there once more and asked to see the girl. Luckily her innocence had been proved but there was no apology. The Belgian had been arrested crossing the border into Belgium. But I could now understand why 'Les Flics' - as the Gendarmes are called - are so unpopular. In Vichy they always went out in twos for safety as well as carried guns. In contrast the ordinary gendarme only carried a white baton – used for directing traffic.

Talking of traffic reminds me of what turned out to be a serious accident in which a lot of us were hurt or suffered whiplash. We were on our way up into the mountains for a scenic tour around the area. We arrived at a place called Riom and the bus in which I was travelling had to stop on a downhill slope. Suddenly there was a loot hoot and we saw that the bus behind ours was rolling down the hill, unable to stop. The brakes had failed! There was a loud bang at the rear of the bus and we were pushed forward. Several students sitting in the rear of our bus were badly shaken and several were injured. In the bus behind people were thrown about and some were bruised, others were hurt quite badly and were taken to a local hospital. Eventually more transport was fetched so that the rest of us could continue our journey. I thought I was all right but actually suffered quite painfully from whiplash.
The lady sitting in front of me was badly hurt and knocked unconscious. She had been turning round to speak to me over the back of her seat. She was in her early 60s and the wife of a Newcastle solicitor. As luck would have it he had insured his wife against accident for £20,000 – a lot in those days. She

was taken to a private hospital in Vichy. I went along to see how she was immediately I returned after the journey. When I arrived she had just regained consciousness and was in pain and rather distressed. The doctor was on his way, but before he arrived she asked me to make quite sure that she did not sign anything. Her husband had told her she must not do so. Actually the doctor was very sympathetic and his bedside manners were impeccable. There was no question of her signing anything and I was asked to go back again the next day to act as a witness. I did that and she was flown home later that day. When she eventually recovered, and we had returned home, she rang to thank me. I heard later that she had a serious neck injury that would eventually turn to a severe form of arthritis. Her husband must have known his stuff – she was awarded £17,000 in compensation.

Altogether it was a pretty eventful trip. On our return journey the timetable we had been given for catching a train to Paris, crossing Paris on the metro, and getting another train to Dover was a poor one so we did our own thing and sorted ourselves out. Even so when we arrived back home we were ready for a break but unfortunately it was only a couple of days before the start of the summer term. I had been taking a French Course one evening a week at the Leeds Language Centre for a few months prior to going to Vichy so when I got back I was asked to give a talk to the rest of the students in French. Surprisingly it was quite easy to speak French for several weeks after the trip and the talk went well. But eventually, despite going once a week to the course throughout the summer I eventually lost the ability to think in French. Having said that my grasp of the language was much better and helped a lot whenever we went to France in our caravan for our summer holiday.

Teaching at Whinmoor was a delightful experience thanks in large measure to the forward planning that was always being discussed and implemented. It was with enthusiasm that we all worked towards making the School a happy and industrious place. Staff meetings were lively – suggestions were welcomed and so all members felt themselves to be an important part of the team. The policy really was a form of benevolent despotism – everyone contributed but in the end what Gordon said always went – and rightly so. I've always believed that too many chiefs and not enough Indians makes for sloppy presentation and that was never a problem in the eighteen months that I was on the staff. I am sure that in all the years that Gordon Towse was Head Teacher the ethos of the school remained constant – due in large measure to the man himself. I learned a lot from him and again it was probably reflected in the way I intended to run things when the time came. That time crept up more quickly than I had expected. One Tuesday morning I arrived, as usual, around 8 o'clock. Gordon had just arrived too and in his hand he held a paper. "Have you seen that there is a job going at Kirkstall St Stephen's?" he said, "You should consider applying, but don't be long. The closing day for applications is Thursday". I muttered something about not being sure I had had sufficient experience but he put that one to rest quickly. At break time I pulled his leg, suggesting that he wanted to get rid of me. "Of course!" he laughed and he knew that I was hooked. I filled in the forms and on Thursday evening I went to the Vicarage at Kirkstall and handed in my application form. I met the Vicar but did not recognise him and he did not recognise me either at the time. It was not until I had been appointed that he mentioned that he too had been at St John's College, Durham. And there the matter rested for a while. I still had no idea that we had met. I also received two excellent pieces of advice – the first from an older friend and ex-colleague who had become a Head some years before. It was simple and direct. "Do not change anything for at least six months. It gives the staff time to get used to you and get them on your side." The second – from Mr Roy Tunnard - who was Chief Advisor for Leeds Education Department – was equally useful. He said, "You are going into a small school with around 160 children. Make your mistakes there rather than when you move on to a larger school." There was more of course but my subsequent experiences proved them both absolutely right! This next chapter encapsulates my time at Kirkstall St Stephens School. It is the reproduction of an article I wrote for a magazine after I retired.

Chapter 9 Some recollections of St. Stephen's CE School

My introduction to St. Stephen's was, to say the least, somewhat less than conventional. The Reverend Raymond Ward, at the time the resident incumbent, invited me to a Parish Meeting prior to my taking up office as Head Teacher in April 1968. Expecting, in my innocence, merely to be introduced to the assembled gathering in normal fashion, I was completely unprepared for the Vicar's words of welcome. I regret that the passage of time does not allow me to pen a precise quote, but the gist of the 'welcome' went something like: "I first encountered Mr Turner on the rugby field at Durham in the early 50s, during a 'knock out' match - an appropriate phrase - between my own College of St. John's, and Bede College. We met somewhat painfully, virtually head to head so to speak. He was intent on scoring a try while I was equally determined that he should not do so. After the match I vowed that I would get my hands on him again - well, now I've done so!" I do not recall now the eventual outcome of the match - it is of no importance - but suffice it to say, we quickly teamed up on the same side and formed a fruitful partnership - both as colleagues and friends.

The early days of any job are taken up with getting to know the ropes and I was lucky enough to acquire from my predecessor Jim Hogg, an excellent Deputy in Ron Perry, plus an equally accomplished and dedicated Staff originally consisting of Mrs. Allen, Mrs. Rutter, Mrs. Ward and Mr. Bishop. They helped me to smooth the way. This gave me an insight into the close working relationship that existed within the school on the academic side. My secretary was an absolute gem - Mrs. Dorothy Howard - affectionately known to all as Dot. She certainly lived up to her name - dotting the i's and crossing the t's. Her knowledge of the office was, to say the least, comprehensive; the mysteries of everything from sorting out dinner money problems, arranging medical appointments, dealing with stock, ordering books and ministering to the sick and injured were all made to look very easy and I benefited greatly from her expertise and tolerance. There was the occasional unfortunate mishap, particularly when the older children indulged in a form of 'playground rugby' that put almost everyone in jeopardy. Mind you - I must say that, although this game was officially banned during school hours, I am quietly convinced that the skilful dexterity with which the various members of the school rugby league side almost always managed to avoid other children was due in no small measure to the fact that, if a child was knocked over, then the perpetrator of this 'heinous' crime was immediately made to stand by the school wall for several play times in order to 'repent'. I strongly suspect that being forced to watch his fellow players improving their sidestepping techniques was the real punishment!

Inevitably, as a sports' player myself I was keen for the children to develop their sporting interests. The Rugby League sides of 68/69 and 69/70 were, thanks in large measure to the untiring efforts of the Deputy, Ron Perry, among the best junior sides I ever saw. They created a record in that they were proud winners of both the Small Schools' Knock out Cup - known as the Headingley Trophy - and the Schools' League Cup for two years running, and in the 69/70 season they won every match they played. One lad by the name of Tony Binder actually scored 166 points himself in one season. He was the best player I ever saw for his age. He later went on to sign for Leeds Rugby League Club. One thing I recall with a somewhat wry smile. We used to practise a lot after school and one of the things any boy had to achieve, if Ron felt that his tackling was not up to the mark, was to tackle me before going home. Some days I went home black and blue, never mind the boys. I reckon Ron, – a great class teacher and very popular was just getting his own back! It was all great fun and I still look with pleasure at the team photos of the day.

No less keen were the girls who developed their basketball skills in equally determined fashion. Playtimes, dinnertimes and after school sessions abounded thanks to the enthusiasm of Miss Forrester, Mrs. Emery, Miss Yeadon, Mrs. Conner, Miss Aspinall and others, including a variety of students on teaching practice. After-school matches attracted plenty of spectators. The girls had one great advantage - playing at home meant in the school yard. The boys had to traipse up to Kirkstall Rec!

The reference to Kirkstall Recreation Ground brings to mind a 'never to be forgotten' story for those involved. Sports Days became quite a major event in the yearly calendar. In those days it was sometimes difficult to get hold of the gang from the Parks Dept. whose job it was to mark out running tracks during the summer term. So, on one occasion, yours truly and a band of willing helpers - there were always volunteers in abundance as it meant missing 'double Maths' and 'English on that particular morning - set off to mark out. 'Sir' had an old A 30 car, affectionately known as 'Buttercup' as it boasted a yellow roof, and this was used to carry the required materials. There is an access tunnel under the railway to the Rec. and we duly carried our equipment through. The track was marked out and it looked great, but dark clouds had gathered and before we could do more than get to the car the storm broke so everyone piled inside. Then things got out of hand - it was the worst cloud burst I have ever seen - so I drove the car into the tunnel entrance for cover. The water started to cascade through the tunnel, eventually reaching the sills, and we had visions of floating away. However the storm passed, the waters receded and we went to view the track. Alas, nothing was left - just one of the joys of Sports Days!

One thing about St. Stephen's - one always kept fit - staff very much included. Gymnastics and apparatus work became a part of the PE syllabus and produced several excellent gymnasts. Some went to the Jack Lane Centre. One girl, Janette Swift, represented Yorkshire on several occasions. But dwarfing that was the walking which had to be done. We walked everywhere. We walked to the Zion Hall, nicknamed the dungeon, for lunch each day. Later we transferred to the Church Hall, but that was nearly as far. We walked up to the Kirkstall Rec. for most sporting activities - we walked up to Carnegie College for swimming lessons - and with regular trips to Kirkstall Abbey Museum on the 'menu', we walked there too. This was great except when it rained. Then we just walked in the rain between the drops!

But I digress. In case you should imagine that life was one long round of sporting activity I assure that it was not so at all. One thing that many school staffs possess is a multiplicity of talents - (not all of them academic!) - and St. Stephen's was no exception. The first thing which comes to mind was the development of reading skills, something which my predecessor Mr. Hogg set in motion by introducing the ITA (Initial Teaching Alphabet) system. There are 'pros' and 'cons' but as a starter it worked for a time. The Infant staff built on this initiative for a while, later reverting to the more traditional approach. At the upper end of the school, in addition to the normal curriculum, spoken French was successfully introduced. There were several very talented musicians on the staff - Pat Bishop in particular and then Roger Taylor in the latter years of my stewardship. I recall passing one classroom and stopping to listen to the delightful sounds of Lynne Yeadon both singing and playing a well-known song on her guitar, to the obvious enjoyment of her pupils. That is but one of so many examples I could quote. Art and Craft was another of the activities that abounded and at various times in the year exhibitions of children's work were held. School concerts, Nativity plays in Church and Christmas parties - the list is endless. My abiding memories of the latter are watching Ron Perry entertaining children and staff alike with 'magic' tricks and with his puppets too, and Pat Bishop, whose dramatic talents were truly great. In addition to his music he produced plays. He had his own brand of mimicry, immortalised in certain irreverent utterances that added immeasurably to the fun of working at St. Stephen's.

Within the framework of the school routine there were, of course, many others who formed an integral part of the daily round. The kitchen staff who made sure that we were adequately 'fed and watered' at dinner times. The dinner ladies who looked after the children in the playgrounds during dinner breaks, and the crossing man, Mr Oxley, who had the unenviable task of halting the traffic outside the school gate on Morris Lane during the rush hour, at dinner times and after school had finished for the day - for the children, at any rate. Again, the mention of food strikes a further chord in the memory. In September 1972 the school was lucky to acquire a Nursery Class Assistant by the name of Mrs. Emily Slight who quickly became affectionately known to us all as 'Em'. Really her title of N.C.A. was a complete misnomer - it should have been G.F., General Factotum - for she had to turn her hand to almost anything that required attention. Fortunately she was both willing and able to do so without too much difficulty. The children loved her for her caring and motherly approach, both inside and outside the classroom. She was a willing volunteer whenever school functions were scheduled to take place and often she became the arranger and provider of the 'eats and drinks' side of so many events. I recall with much amusement the day on which it was arranged that Em should show some children how to bake bread cakes. With her usual enthusiasm she had volunteered to bring a large bread bowl from home for the occasion, but in the morning - tragedy of tragedies - she had forgotten it. Thoroughly distraught, she approached the secretary, and asked if I was likely to allow her to go home and fetch this essential piece of equipment as it was vital to the success of the bread cake-making venture. (She had but recently arrived at the school and was still 'hedging her bets' by sounding out others before 'bearding me in my den' so to speak!). Dot reassured her and, thus encouraged, she broached the subject with me. Ever mindful of the fact that I was in abysmal ignorance of the intricacies of bread cake baking I offered to run her home to fetch the requisite mixing bowl. The only minor problem was that

I omitted to tell her that I had come on my motorcycle that day. However, when she found out, dedicated to the last, Em decided to risk all and 'lift off' was scheduled for dinnertime. The staff got to know - quite fatal – and at the moment of departure, with Em looking resplendent in my spare crash helmet, which was much too large, they all appeared at the gate to wave us on our way. Em climbed on to the pillion amid much ribald laughter. She had never ventured on a motorbike before so she shut her eyes and put her arms around my fairly corpulent middle. With the staff making suitably encouraging remarks - modesty forbids repetition of the comments - we set off. Immediately I was seized in a vice-like grip that gradually relaxed as Em's confidence grew and I could breathe again. We arrived at her house safely, the bowl was quickly fetched and we set off on the return journey. All went well until we were driving up Abbey Walk past Abbey House Museum. Then the Vicar's car appeared, going in the opposite direction. I hooted and Em proffered one extremely brief wave of the hand - a wise precaution as the bowl was in grave danger of slipping from her grasp, balanced as it was 'twixt her knee and my back - then the vice-like grip returned and remained in place until we arrived back at St. Stephen's in one piece, so to speak. Em entered the staff room, legs still trembling, to loud cheers and much applause. It all proved well worthwhile, for the children made some beautiful bread cakes, one of which they gave me to taste. The story became school folklore and Em, bless her, never lived it down!

The fact that the building was in such a parlous state engenders another story. There was one skill that was unique to Ken Burnell, the caretaker. We had, at that time, an extremely ancient coke-fired central heating boiler. Ken was a past master at keeping the boiler fired up by dint of feeding coke into it in such a way that no fumes escaped up into the Infant Hall or classroom above. He also exercised consummate expertise in ensuring that there was virtually no smoke to be seen outside the premises - no doubt necessary as we were in a designated smokeless zone. However, on one of the rare occasions when Ken was ill, a 'temporary' caretaker was sent from the

Education Department to take over. Poor man, he was doubtless extremely conscientious, but, alas, was no match for our recalcitrant heating system. He duly stoked up the boiler as instructed and went about his other duties. A few moments later I received an urgent telephone call from a distracted parent - she had rung the fire brigade, convinced that the school was on fire! I rushed outside and, sure enough, white smoke was billowing skywards from the wall adjacent to the boiler chimney. In fact the pointing in many parts of the school building was in dire need of repair and this section was no exception. When the fire brigade arrived I had the greatest difficulty in persuading them not to put the hoses to work! However the fire evacuation system was put to the test just in case and in no time at all the school was emptied – at least the fire-drill worked. I strongly suspect that the majority of the epithets muttered afterwards by both firemen and staff would not have been found in the Oxford Dictionary. The fumes emanating through the floor left much to be desired but fortunately it was Friday. By the time Monday came the noxious smells had subsided, Ken was restored to health and, more importantly, to work. At least, life was never dull!

One could, I suppose, continue to reminisce 'ad infinitum', but there is a side of St. Stephen's which, for me, showed the true meaning of the fine community spirit which abounded at the school: the work which so many parents, staff and friends helped to put in. It would be invidious to name names but the variety of activities which went on week after week, often under the auspices of the Parent Teacher Association, bore testimony to those who gave of their time and talents. I recall all the school lighting being changed to fluorescent tubes - a mammoth task carried out by those who understood how it was done - obtaining selotex for display purposes - the donation of the large 'Wendy' house for the reception class - there were 101 things needed. Money was raised for school and for charity - jumble sales in the basement beneath the Infant Hall – Christmas and Summer Fairs - I can see dear old Mr. Oxley now with his vintage car, a 1929 Jowett - his pride and joy - proudly displayed in the school playground while he asked people to guess how many miles the car had travelled. He was a real character. He doubled as the crossing patrol warden and our Father Christmas for many years. There were whist drive nights for anybody who wanted to come. There were well supported campaigns for improving conditions etc. and once even a double page spread in the Yorkshire Evening Post about the condition of the school roof. After that it was quickly put to rights. Mind you, during the re-roofing saga various 'artefacts' were discovered which had found their way into the roof underlay and which had been preserved by the stone dust which had collected over the years - several TONS of it! Also, I have a feeling that at some time a Head Teacher may have incurred the wrath of an erstwhile pupil, for, when the roof was finally opened up over my office, a large stone was poised right above my desk - an omen perhaps? - but not, I think, a coincidence!

Another area so often overlooked in the euphoria of reminiscence is the 'behind the scenes' work of the School Managers. The Chairman was the Vicar, Raymond Ward (I cannot bring myself to call him the Chair, as in modern parlance, for it would give me the vision of JRW with four legs!), ably supported by the ever-present Edmund Butler. For several generations the name of Butler has been synonymous with Kirkstall - the Kirkstall Forge and the School in particular - and I found that, in company with his fellow managers, he had a clear understanding of the whole ethos of the place and was able to communicate this to others. At one time St. Stephen's School provided many workmen for the Forge. It was traditional I suppose.

But perhaps the greatest event for me was, ironically, one in which, because of illness, I was to play a comparatively small part in the preparations and arrangements. On July 17th 1972 the 150th anniversary of the foundation of the School was celebrated. It was at this point that the traditions of genuine greatness really came to the fore. Names from the past - still to be seen in the visitors' book - Lord Cardigan, a famous member of the Brudenell family who resided at Deene Hall in Northants, and Lord and Lady Manners are but three who come immediately to mind, and there are many others. Lists of pupils from bygone days - sadly these records did not start at the opening of the School in 1822 - are there on record for posterity once the system of registration was introduced. There are clues to the conditions under which children studied. I vividly recall the two monitorial desks - one had an ancient timetable stuck to the inside of the desk lid. The styles of teaching - the types of punishment - the climate - the conditions - it's all there. I well remember the service of celebration and thanksgiving so beautifully conducted by Raymond Ward. The Bishop of Knaresborough gave the address, Pat Bishop played the organ and I was privileged to read the lesson. All the parents and their children, together with the many visitors, managers and staff, all shared in this historic event. This was followed by a reception and the ceremonial cutting of the cake that had been beautifully decorated for the occasion.

Now, like everything mentioned in this article which I wrote after illness forced me to retire from the teaching profession in 1984, we are part of the history of Kirkstall St. Stephen's School. There are some names that come to mind of pupils, parents and staff who were connected with the school during my tenure of office, but sadly the memory is no computer and many more have faces but no names. Inevitably there were staff changes as staff moved on and Ron Perry left to take up another Deputy's job at Beecroft Street School towards the end of my tenure. He had been a rock. In his place I was lucky enough to have a friend and former fellow cricketer as a temporary replacement as Deputy Head. His name was Jack Edmondson who was a member of Leeds Supply Teachers' Division. The staff took to him straight away and the happy atmosphere in the School continued unabated. Thus we all rubbed shoulders and each one of us contributed something of himself or herself to others.

Kirkstall St. Stephen's School has housed us all one way or another. The School has a wonderful tradition that has so far lasted well over 150 years. There are several logbooks in the city archives, written by successive Head Teachers over the years, to illustrate just that. Personally I was very proud to have been an integral part of the life and history of this wonderful old school. The friends I made and the happy memories I had have always remained very close to my heart.

Chapter 10 Home life and holidays

Once Philip had gone to Holy Trinity School and Molly had gone back to work our lives seemed even busier. Being again in a position to pick up the threads of her career in teaching must have widened her horizons considerably as she was able to once more mix with new colleagues and make friends amongst the staff at Ryecroft School. I met several of her colleagues and in particular the Head Teacher, Robin French. We became good friends over the years. Each year Molly put on some excellent musical productions at the school and on occasion Roy Thompson, our next door neighbour who became the Head Teacher of Hough Side Comprehensive School, went with me to see them. One show in particular sticks in the mind. It was called 'RUBBISH' and was a musical about the muck and filth that contaminated towns and cities. She had composed all the songs and written the script. She was an excellent pianist and accompanied the children as they sang. The whole production was outstanding and would have graced any professional stage. There were concerts too and I was always made welcome by the staff whenever I visited. I tried not to bring too many problems home after school although it was difficult not to, but Molly did not wish to talk about work in the evenings. Instead I spent time chatting with Roy about things that sometimes went amiss at School. He did the same with me and it helped us both a lot. It was a good way to work out what could be done to tackle problems that arose from time to time.

Initially our leisure times were often spent in the company of Betty and Derek Love, Clive and Anne Bell and, more often than not, with Barbara and Roy Thompson, particularly during the summer months. We would sit outside with the Thompsons on what passed for a patio in the evenings and have a drink or two. Roy had built a wall to level up his back garden and it was just the right height to sit on. We also planted a hedge at the front between our respective front gardens and put in small bushes and trees between the lawns that we had laid at both the front and the rear of the houses. We even played a form of badminton across the back lawns using the planted border as the net. Naturally first of all the 'workers' required refreshment and later the badminton players got thirsty too so the Thompson wall was put to good use both to sit on and put our drinks on. We also had coke bunkers at the back and Roy and I would bowl underarm to Philip with a tennis ball to try and interest him in cricket. He actually did very well and Roy was convinced that he would take the game up later. But it was not to be and we were soon kicking a football about instead. There were several boys living in the street and before long football took precedence for a while in the autumn. Over the years there was opposition from some neighbours who had laid out their gardens and did not want boys trampling on the gardens to fetch the ball, in particular from Derek Holmes at number 57. I have mentioned him already so will not repeat the story. Another favourite game was rounders and the girls seemed more adept at that. Mind you, there were still balls to be fetched out of gardens. There was also some sort of passing game played with a football or netball. I never managed to discover just how that worked! In the summer cricket – with the lamppost as the wicket – took place and the so over all the children were able to both entertain and enjoy themselves. Paul Whitehead, who lived at number 49, and Nigel Cryer were Philip's closest friends and they spent a lot of time together. I remember one early evening Philip coming back from Nigel's garden in a real state. He and Nigel had been hitting some plastic golf balls around. The plastic ones had holes in and they could be hit as hard as possible and, because the holes acted as a brake, they did no damage and did not go too far. However on this occasion Philip decided to hit a proper golf ball out of Nigel's garden in order to show his prowess. When he ran home to tell me what had happened he tearfully told me that he was only demonstrating a chip shot! Well, it must have been a good shot as the ball sailed over the hedge - and straight through a narrow window in the house at the back of Nigel's garden! The trouble was, the window was closed and the noise of breaking glass frightened the boys – and me too when I heard what had occurred. The owner of the house was a tough guy - an ex commando who was reputed to have killed several enemy soldiers during the Second World War. As it happened he was out, but the son was literally baby-sitting and when I went round was upset and a quite aggressive until I calmed him down. The baby was in a cot in the room where the ball came to rest. We quickly cleared up the shards of broken glass and luckily the baby was unhurt and even slept through all the excitement. Fortunately I knew the owner and when he came home I went round and explained what had happened. He was a cool customer and took it all in his stride. With his experiences of life this was small fry! I also said my son would pay for the window but he was well insured and so we left it at that. But had he wanted paying Philip's pocket money would have had to cover the cost. Nigel's Dad and I used to play golf together when time allowed and we had already said that we would take the boys to play at Roundhay Park when they were old enough to go. Maybe that eventually helped to persuade us that taking Nigel and Philip to play on an official course was a safer bet!

Television was not too invasive then and computers did not even exist so the incentive for children to get out with their mates was strong. Some chasing games featured too although only those gardens where children playing actually lived were used. Then, as they got older, some would make their way to the cricket field or to some other open spaces. Surprisingly enough most of the children had homework to do first and it was a good incentive to get it finished and then go out to play for an hour or two before bedtime. Parents quietly arranged to see that the children were made to come in at the same time after there were the inevitable squabbles. The children must have kept pretty fit judging from all the running around that was done!

The friendships, particularly with the three families already mentioned, became close. We often visited each other and had impromptu parties from time to time. It became a regular pastime on Sunday evenings to go round to the Bells' house and play canasta. Any prize money was put towards an evening out when there was sufficient in the kitty. Playing cards was never really my forte but I managed to win my share of money although I often had to be reminded of the rules of the game. A healthy amount soon built up in the kitty and it was a good excuse to have an evening out at a restaurant from time to time.

Before long we met up on holidays and, as three of the families had caravans, we would also go away to Caravan Sites at weekends and enjoy the company. The children loved it too and were able to spend many happy times playing together. Barbara and Roy Thompson had two girls, Susan and Dinah, Betty and Derek Love had Margaret and Gordon, Anne and Clive Bell had Stephen and Andrea. At one stage the Bells move to Chelmsford for a spell when Clive's job as a Customs Officer took him there, but they returned after a year or two and came to live in the next road so we were all together again.

As the years passed we started to travel farther afield during the school summer holidays. Our summer mid-term holidays lasted for a fortnight and were spent mainly at Portpatrick on the west coast of Galloway. Initially Clive and I played golf together at Portpatrick Golf Club. Then, as they grew up, Philip and Stephen spent many happy hours playing golf, first learning the rudiments of the game from us on the small course and then playing with us on the main course. We bought weekly tickets from the club and that enabled us to go at any time during our stay. The boys quickly improved so those holidays were always very popular. I remember on one occasion Philip broke all records by getting round the course in 77 shots! That was a remarkable achievement and neither Clive nor I ever managed to beat or even equal that score - what a round! There was a clubhouse where we could all meet up as families, have a meal and down a pint or two for good measure. Another 'adventure' Philip and I shared was when we were looking for a ball that had been hit into a field near the course. An errant shot by one of us had made the search necessary. What we did not immediately notice was a number of heifers taking an unhealthy interest in what we were doing. Suddenly they started charging towards us, no doubt bent on mischief. We both turned and quickly scarpered and I have never managed to get over a fence so quickly again in my life! Portpatrick was never dull!

Caravan holidays were a fairly cheap way of enjoying ourselves. Apart from playing golf there were good beaches near Portpatrick. Our favourite beach was at Killintringan, near the Black Head Lighthouse. We spent many happy hours on the sands there but it was too cold to swim. Yet on the Luce Bay side of the Peninsular the water was almost tepid. The warm waters of the Gulf Stream came round the Mull of Galloway and warmed the waters at Sandhead. It is quite a remarkable phenomenon. We sometimes went there to have a swim.

Sally and Willie owned the first caravan we used. They kindly lent it to us, together with their large car for towing. So we took them to Switzerland for an adventure holiday. That was quite a trip as they had not been abroad before. Willie drove the caravan to Hull and the five of us boarded a ship to sail across to Amsterdam overnight. It took 13 hours in all to cross the channel. We had a joint cabin for the night with bunk beds. Sally was very nervous and was up and down several times after we had turned in so sleep did not come easily. It turned out that she was worried that water might come up through the plughole in the washbasin and flood the cabin or even sink the ship! Willie and Molly eventually explained it away and we settled down. In the morning we disembarked and set off through Amsterdam. We travelled through Holland into Germany and stayed on a site in Koblenz overnight. Plenty of excitement there the next morning – a tent near our caravan caught fire. There were several cars in close proximity but luckily no petrol tank exploded although paintwork was blistered on at least one of the cars. The tent was completely burnt out. We beat a hasty retreat as soon as possible. The site was hopelessly overcrowded – something we had not previously realised as we had arrived late the previous evening. We drove towards the Swiss border via the Black Forest. At one point the car started to boil when we were negotiating a steep hill and we had to stop. Willie got out and tried to take the radiator cap off. As he loosened it the released pressure shot it away somewhere. We searched everywhere for ages without any luck. Fortunately a German lorry was driving up the hill and he stopped too. He came across and we explained as best we could – he looked down below the radiator and incredibly found the cap wedged near the drive shaft cover. It must have bounced back off the inside of the bonnet. So we were able to continue on our journey. We crossed the border at Donauschingen - and I purchased a 'green' insurance card as Willie had forgotten to get one from his Insurance Company before leaving. Sally was convinced I would be arrested because of this oversight and we would not be allowed into Switzerland. I guess that she was not really enjoying being abroad as things were very different from her native Yorkshire. Still all was well and we continued our journey. Eventually we decide to stay on a lovely site just outside Interlaken for a week. It was strange in two respects. First, in the nearby forest there were no birds at all. So then at night the crickets – normally food for birds - made an unceasingly loud noise. There were myriads of them in that forest.

Each morning Willie and I walked into Interlaken for a paper and anything else we required. It was a beautiful walk – near a river of clear blue water and with delightful dark beamed houses near the banks that had the most exquisitely lovely window boxes. We visited the surrounding countryside by car and Interlaken itself was a lively place with attractively set out shops. Wooden artefacts, watches, clocks of various kinds with cuckoo clocks in particular were on show, plus a host of other goods to tempt the traveller. Unfortunately in the 60s we were only permitted by law to take £50 per head each out of England to cover the cost of our holiday so purchases were very limited. This was because our economy was still in a mess at home. Thun, situated just around the lake, was a delightful place to visit – flowers abounded in window boxes and borders - and we went also up into the mountains one day. The views were quite breathtaking. Another favourite place was Grindelwald. Everywhere was incredibly clean and again the houses were all bedecked with brightly coloured flowers.

The journey home was incident free except that we found that the wayside stops left a lot to be desired. In fact we stopped near a field on one occasion in Germany and made calls of nature there. This caused more worry for Sally who was petrified that we would be arrested for trespassing. It got a bit fraught at times although as I was driving I was too busy to take in much of the conversation on the subject – just as well! Our boat crossing back to Hull was without incident and the only unfortunate happening was that as Willie turned into his drive – he had driven back from Hull – a piece of metal sticking out from the gate or wall took a strip of metal about a foot long out of the caravan side. No one said a word. Later we put a sheet of aluminium over it, sealed the edges and that was that. But I think that a second family trip abroad was not on the cards – once was enough – for everyone! I must admit that I thoroughly enjoyed the driving and, apart from a rear light on the van needing attention just before we found the campsite at Koblenz at the end of our first day on the continent, all was well - although I did get on the wrong side of the road for a few seconds when I set off again and a German motorist coming the other way kindly stopped and waited while I corrected the mistake – he was very understanding - and patient too!

For a while we used Willie's caravan and car but then we purchased our own. Molly paid for that and I bought a large car for towing purposes. When her Mum and Dad moved to live at Knaresbrough the caravan was kept in the drive at their house. Our summer holidays were usually spent abroad. We would set off and visit places that took our fancy. On our various trips we visited cities, towns and many well-known beauty spots in France, Belgium, Holland, Germany Austria, Spain and Italy. I remember one holiday in particular where we took Susan and Dinah with us to Venice. Barbara joined us when we got as far as Verona. Unfortunately Roy could not come due to the illness of his mother. We had a lovely walk around Verona itself and took in the sights. One amusing incident happened during that walk. Susan, who was dressed in a rather fetching yellow outfit, was walking along one street when she suddenly let out a cry – a young Italian soldier must have taken a brief fancy to her and had pinched her bottom as she went past him! We had to reassure her quickly that it happened quite often to young ladies in Italy and that it was a compliment. After that I think she was rather hoping for a repeat performance! We were actually looking at the large Roman Amphitheatre at the time. There were big crowds there as a concert was due to take place that evening. The atmosphere was electric was still warm after the heat of the day. We should have loved to have attended the concert but sadly it was not possible. This was actually during our second visit to Verona.

On the first occasion that we went to Verona, when we pulled into the caravan site it was so hot that Philip and I shot straight off into the swimming pool to cool down. I remember that when we returned to the caravan it was still so warm that we had to seek the shade of nearby trees. The pool was closed for the siesta time, but as soon as it reopened we were back. The evenings were lovely – balmy and pleasant. Of all the pleasures that caravanning on the Continent offered, sitting outside on warm summer evenings enjoying a glass or two of wine was one of the most enjoyable. I personally found the day temperatures were quite often too hot for comfort. If the car stood out in the sun too long the bodywork would be too hot to touch. As we travelled a lot during daylight the windows were always wide open to cool us down.

On both our visits we stayed on a site by the sea at Cavallino. It was close to Lido de Jesolo, another well-known resort for holidaymakers. To get to Venice itself we had to make our way to a point on the road about 3 kilometres distant. Boats went across the water to a quayside close to St Mark's Square.

We went into Venice on several occasions. There is no traffic there as there are no roads, but people travel by boat on the many canals or walk along the narrow streets. Again, Venice has its own uniquely romantic atmosphere and thousands of people visit St Mark's Church and the Doge's Palace. Walking along the quayside too is an experience and, seeing the 'Bridge of Sighs' where in bygone days prisoners were taken from the Palace to the dungeons, reminds one of a time when people were not always so welcome! With Gondoliers plying their trade, their gondolas carry visitors gently around the network of canals. One amusing interlude that Philip and I shared, much to my consternation and his amusement, was when we needed to find a loo – not easy in Venice. Eventually we did discover one and we had to pay to enter. I tendered a coin for both us – there should have been change. But instead the lady in charge handed us about 10 sweets. When I questioned this she said, "No money change! No money change!" Philip ate most of the sweets! Most things were cheap in Italy, but not when one sat outside a café in St Mark's Square. It cost us a fortune to get a drink there. We only did that once! Maybe the hardest thing to get used to in Venice was to see the rich and poor side by side. I recall, while crossing the Rialto Bridge, being asked for money for a 'bambino' that was supposedly sick. I was about to give the lady something when we realised that the baby was simply painted with red spots. I heard a few good Italian swear words that day!

On another occasion we drove down the Rhine in Germany, past the Lorelei Rock where maidens were reputed to entice unsuspecting sailors to their doom. Rudesheim, a town by the river, was remarkable in that it had one particular street where there were a whole series of restaurants and cafes, one beside the other, all the way up the street. Each place was trying to tempt customers to enter and the noise from the various bands playing in most of the restaurants had to be heard to be believed – talk about a cacophony of sound! But it was a fascinating place and quite an experience to walk up that street.

Nuremberg had something different to offer. The 'Old Town', where houses from the past abounded despite the privations of war, was quite different. In complete contrast the massive stadium where Hitler addressed his troops from a high concrete platform was not far away, and the courtroom where the Nazis, who had ruled Germany from 1933 to the end of the Second World War in 1945, were tried, was also in the city. We stayed on a campsite nearby. We met a delightful Dutch family there who spoke English and spent two or three evenings sitting outside chatting and enjoying a few glasses of wine with them. Philip and their son became firm friends despite the fact that neither could speak the other's language. As parents we were all intrigued because they understood each other perfectly in no time at all!

I also remember on that same trip I had to call out ADAC - the German equivalent of the AA - and I tried to explain that we had an intermittent problem with the radiator of our Vauxhall car. I said to the ADAC official," Mein Herr, der radiator ist cooken", and he fell about laughing – I had apparently told him I had 'cooked' the radiator! Anyhow I pointed to the word in the dictionary and he sorted out the problem. As it happened he spoke some

English anyway so all was well but it gave everyone a good laugh, including me. Even when one looks for a word in a dictionary the meaning is not always what it seems!

As time went by we also travelled or met up with friends at various camps. On one journey the Bells, Aubyn and Betty Sparkes and their two teenage sons and their daughter, Malcolm, Paul and Ann, met up with us at a campsite near the French town of Argentat in the Dordogne. It was a large site close to a river. Clive had a flat-bottomed boat that sported a sail and could also be rowed. On these trips I was responsible for trying to put things right with cars if they went wrong. They hardly ever did, fortunately, but this occasion was different. Aubyn also had a boat with an engine. The boat, which could be inflated to about 7 feet long, was packed away together with the engine. But he had a can of petrol in his car as well. I was out in the middle of the river in Clive's boat when I was hailed from the shore. By the time I got there things were more or less under control – Aubyn's car had caught fire when a wire had melted in the 110% heat and caused a short. Luckily the petrol was rescued in time but it was a close shave. All the electrics were out of action but as it happened he had a Peugeot, a French car. We contacted a garage and at eight o'clock at night a garage owner/mechanic turned up. He fixed the car so that we could start it by touching a wire to the metal of the starter motor. He told us to drive into Argentat in the morning so he could fix it. Incredibly this Heath Robinson starting system worked and we took the car into his garage. Two days later he had replaced the entire wiring system. It turned out that in France each garage specialises in one thing. The owner of this garage specialised in wiring cars – lucky indeed! With Aubyn's car fixed we motored across France to Biscarosse, a lakeside village with a large campsite. On the first night there was a tremendous storm and we had to tie the vans down. Others were less fortunate. The next day Aubyn decided that he needed a break to get over the trauma of his car catching fire. We inflated the boat and decided to go out on the lake. After all the problems he had encountered Aubyn needed to cool down and get back into holiday mood so we decided to take three bottles of red wine with us and went out into the middle of the lake with the intention of having a swim. Two bottles later we both went over the side and all was well - until we wanted to get back into the boat. We found that we couldn't just climb back! The rubber tubes that passed around the entire boat were so high that in our somewhat happy state getting in was almost insurmountable. We clung on and drifted around for several minutes until finally we made on last effort. I lifted one side up by swimming underneath – and Aubyn flopped in, laughing fit to bust. He then hauled me in and eventually, after finishing bottle number three, we returned to the shore. No one had even missed us! I know we both slept well that night! Malcolm and Paul made good use of the boat too and we all went out in it at some point. It was voted a great holiday, full of incident. That was the first of several holidays where we met up for the last week or more and getting together like that always went down well with everyone. We all realised that being in a caravan in close proximity as separate families for too long was sometimes counterproductive and I think we all enjoyed getting together anyhow.

Lacanau, higher up the Atlantic coast was another favourite. This was by a lake in one direction and near the sea as well. Walking to the beach was hard work as we always went away from the village and found a less crowded spot but it was worthwhile. People were much less inhibited than in England, probably because it was much warmer and bathing in the nude was the norm on that part of the beach.

No one was embarrassed so far as I knew although I remember Roy Thompson once saying, after he had seen a naked man in all his glory striding along the beach with only his pack on his back, "I'll never go nude again after seeing him!" In fact I don't think he ever stripped on that beach after that!

The sea was unpredictable on the coast – the Atlantic was sometimes flat calm and at other times the waves rolled in and it was ideal for board and body surfing – great fun, but NOT in the nude – it could be painful! We had so many good times together and all the young people of the families enjoyed themselves immensely. No doubt when they met up afterwards there were tales to tell – I expect there still are. I would imagine that all had happy childhood memories of holidays abroad. I think that, as adults, we also got close to all the children and even now whenever I see any of them there are always amusing stories to recall and reminisce about.

There could be dangers too. Clive always led the way energetically across the dunes, particularly outside Lacanau, and so when we got to our part of the beach there was plenty of space for us to put up windbreaks and umbrellas for shade, but no Lacanau beach lifeguards were around to keep an eye out for swimmers in trouble. Paul Sparkes was very fortunate on one occasion in particular in the early days. One morning he had been swimming off the beach on his own and as it happened we arrived after he had come out of the water. I wanted a swim and Paul insisted on coming with me. The tide was coming in quickly and the sandbank I was swimming to was, of course, much further away than it had been earlier when Paul had swum to it. Luckily Malcolm called out that he would come too and he followed on behind. I reached the sandbank first and looked back just in time to see Paul's arms go up in the air as he started to go under. He had run out of breath and could not make any more progress. I swam back as fast as I could and managed to grab him as he went down. But he was in a panic and tried to clutch me around my neck. Luckily I had been trained in the rudiments of lifesaving. I pushed him underwater again to break his hold and by this time Malcolm had reached me. Between us we stopped his struggles and I turned him on his back and swam with him to the sandbank. Eventually we got him onto it but by this time it was virtually underwater. We followed the sand bank until it led us back on the beach. We had all recovered by then and we eventually got back to the group. Luckily Aubyn was asleep so he was unaware of what had happened, otherwise he would have been concerned - and probably angry too. He only found out much later and as it was mentioned casually he didn't react at the time. But Betty had seen it all and was very relieved. It was one of the few times I'd seen Paul really subdued but he soon recovered. It is something that none of those involved have ever forgotten!

On another occasion we were driving along a motorway towards Aachen on the German border when storm clouds appeared in front of us. Other motorists immediately left the motorway so we followed them. There was a lay by along the road but it was full and we were forced to drive on. Then suddenly the rain started and it was impossible to see. Even the wipers would not clear the window. So we stopped on the side of the road and waited. The water level rose quickly and just as it was getting to crisis point up to the bottom of the doors the rain stopped as if a tap had been turned off. Within a few minutes the waters had subsided and we were able to continue our journey. I reckon that the shouts and sighs of relief coming from our car must have been heard for miles!

During another holiday we were in the Maritime Alps in France, staying at a village called Super Bess, high up in the mountains. On this occasion Betty and Derek had also driven up the narrow mountain road with their car and caravan and so had the Bells. I recall that it was a very steep climb. Our intention was to walk on a mountain path after using the chairlift up to the actual mountain slopes. We set off in the chairlift which suddenly stopped and we remained suspended a couple of hundred feet above the ground for about thirty minutes – not a pleasant experience when there was no means of communication! The walk was quite hairy too. There were several places that had little protection on the path. It was quite a drop at the edge and I have always suffered from vertigo so I kept well over the safer side of the path. On our return to Super Bess Anne Bell found a large denomination franc note – worth quite a lot of money in those days. We took it to the local gendarmerie and thought no more about it at the time. The next day a young couple and their son appeared at our site to thank us and offer us a reward of 10%. They were extremely grateful and polite too. Apparently this reward system was the normal French way. Of course we did not take the money but suggested that instead they buy their son a present with it. I thought that was a good custom. But the most amusing thing of all was when the sun shone and the site just got hotter. We, the Brits, were sitting in the shade inside our vans getting uncomfortably hot. All the other continental caravanners were sitting outside their vans when suddenly a rainstorm blew up – literally in seconds. Everybody who had been sitting in the sunshine rushed into their vans but we all ran outside in our shorts and stood in the pouring rain jumping up and down, laughing and joking. It was quite hilarious and all the other people on the site thought we were all quite mad!

We also saw the dangers that a sudden storm in the mountains could produce. We had left our caravan at Super Bess and had made our way back down the lower part of the mountain to the actual village of Bess itself. Fortunately we were able to park on a fairly flat area just off the main road through the village. We had noticed that the actual pavements were much higher than the road itself when we had first driven through towing our caravan – something that drivers had to watch out for. The sun had been shining all morning, but as we entered a shop the clouds rolled up incredibly quickly and there was a clap of thunder, so loud that it seemed to be almost outside the shop. At this point the local inhabitants immediately started to run into the shops, the nearest places of refuge under cover, and the once busy street was suddenly deserted. Then the rains came. In no time at all the streets were awash, despite the fact that the road outside the shop was quite a steep slope. The rain was torrential and the street became a rapidly flowing river. It was an awesome sight and it must have been frightening for any unwary motorist who happened to be coming up the hill! In fact we found out afterwards that vans had been washed away in places, although not on this occasion thank goodness. Then the storm passed over and the rain ceased as quickly as it had begun. Within a few minutes everything was back to normal. The locals went on their respective ways and we were able to return to our car. It had come through unscathed. That was certainly a sobering experience and one not easily forgotten!

We had another holiday in Switzerland several years later. In the meantime Philip had been on a school trip to Megeve, a ski resort not far from Chamonix, in the Mont Blanc Massif section of the Alps in France and had learned to ski. Our travels eventually took us to a site in the Lauterbrunnen Valley where we were joined by the Bells. The Valley site was superb with mountains all around – the Eiger, the Monck, and the Jungfrau. Also the Schilthorn was further along the Valley. On one trip we decided to go up to the top of the Eiger in a train that ran literally through a steep tunnel up to the top of the mountain. We caught one train from Lauterbrunnen up to the Scheidegg Plateau and then boarded the other train – the Jungfraubahne cog railway train - at Kleine Scheidegg station. Incredible as it seemed at the time, the train stopped and we were able to literally view the north face of the Eiger through a glass window. It seemed unreal to think that mountaineers had died trying to climb to the top of the Eiger via the north face. It was so steep and the rock surfaces looked so treacherous. After a second stop to view the 'Sea of Ice' (Eismeer) we then went on to the top and got out at the Jungfraujoch Railway Station. This is the highest station in Europe. We had proper climbing boots on for safety. We then went up some ice steps as high as we could on foot, with everyone clinging on for dear life to a safety rail. I found the experience ok - until I glanced downwards. That was probably the most frightening time of my life as my legs just seemed to go to jelly! My fear of heights – illogical perhaps, but at the time very real – did not help at all although once I had got down again safely I had a tremendous feeling of achievement as well as relief and over the years the fear has decreased somewhat, probably due to that experience. Anne Bell and Philip went along to the mountain ski slope. The air was much rarer up there and because of the effort required to ski Philip had to stop well before an hour was up due to the difficulty of breathing at the height of over 10,000 feet or 3000 metres. But it was great to see him using his newly acquired skill and Anne Bell, who was an experienced skier, had a wonderful time, the rarified atmosphere seeming to suit her. Eventually we made our way down on the train and breathing became easier the lower we got. There were walks to experience in the valley and a picturesquely high waterfall called the Trummelbach that we could actually walk under. Finally, one day we all went, on a series of cablecars, up to the top of the Schilthorn Mountain and sat in the Piz Gloria – the first moving restaurant ever built on the top of a mountain. It gained considerable fame courtesy of a James Bond film, 'On Her Majesty's Secret Service', with Roger Moore as the star. As the restaurant revolved one could see the Eiger, The Jungfrau and the Monck mountains – what a wonderful experience that was! That was, for me, one of the most exciting holidays I had ever experienced while caravanning.

Two more trips up mountains come to mind. On the first occasion our aim was to see something of Austria. Towing our caravan we initially drove to the beautiful Austrian city of Salzburg where the highlight of our visit was seeing the HohenSalzburg Fortress, the Castle where Emperor Franz Joseph 1st spent some time during his reign from 1848 to 1916. We also spent time soaking up the atmosphere of the city. I remember thinking how friendly and welcoming the people seemed to be – happy and smiling a lot. We also bought bratwursts in the market place – that was the first one I had ever tasted and I have enjoyed them ever since!

Next we motored on to Werfen, a village situated at the base of the Hochkogel Mountain in the Austrian Alps. Our goal was to visit the largest Ice Cave in the world - at the top of the Mountain. We decided to drive up the mountain road rather than take a local taxi as the road looked ok. But it became quite an undertaking as we found out when the road deteriorated higher up the mountain. There were several other cars on the road a long way ahead of us. We came to a red light and stopped for about five minutes. Then three Austrian VW 7 seater taxis came past, completely ignoring the red light, and continued up the road. Assuming then that the light must be there for some other reason I unwisely followed the taxis. However they were travelling much more quickly than us and had long since disappeared from view. Then suddenly a line of traffic came into sight coming down the road! Luckily there was a small area that I could back into but it was dangerously close to the edge of the mountain and we were loudly cursed – probably mainly in Austrian and German – by a succession of irritated drivers! Eventually we got to the top and parked up and I was certainly sweating. We set off up the narrow path to the Ice Cave entrance. I remember that I shook from sheer fright for a few minutes when I considered what I had done. Also at the edge of the path there was a sheer drop that did not help at all! However, the visit into the Cave was superb. We were given a thick blanket coat to wear for warmth and there were a lot of steps to negotiate as we walked round. By dint of concealed lighting one could see how vast the cave was. It took about an hour and a half in all and was well worth the effort. The drive back down the mountain was without incident but it had been quite a day over all! From what we saw on our travels in Austria it is a truly picturesque country.

The other mountain that we trekked up was in the Pyrenees in 1978. The Bells were caravanning with us and we had had quite a drive around the Paris Perifique. This road took us round the outskirts of Paris. At the time the traffic was heavy but French drivers have always had a reputation for driving quickly there and this was no exception. I thoroughly enjoyed myself but Clive, who was trying to follow us, was less enthusiastic. We had asked a Frenchman which road we wanted to look for in order to head towards Poitiers. He shouted 'assis' – at least that was what it sounded like. This foxed us at first until Molly suddenly pointed – 'Get across to the outside lane and go off at the next exit' – she had suddenly realised just in time that he had shouted A6 – in French. Clive eventually managed to thread his car and van through the traffic after us but then we had a stop for lunch. As he said forcibly at the time - towing a caravan around Paris following us was not his favourite pastime! We judiciously forbore to point out that he had been leading us towards Paris until he got lost trying to find the Perifique and we had taken over the lead - at his request. We continued without further incident through central France and down to the Basses Pyrenees and crossed over the border to northern Spain via the Roncesvalles Pass. We found a decent campsite and made that our base for a few nights. I recall that everyone near us at the site was very friendly – and noisy too!

We decided to climb one of the mountains nearby and set off fairly early to avoid having to walk during the heat of the day. At first Philip, Stephen and Andrea led the way along the mountain path, but it was hard uphill work and eventually we walked more or less together with Clive in the lead. His particular forte was walking (he had already done the Three Peaks walk – Pen-y-Ghent, Whernside and Ingleborough – back at home in Yorkshire well within the 24 hours necessary to obtain a certificate recording the feat). Eventually we all arrived, in dribs and drabs, at the top. The last section was really steep but the top was something of a flat plateau in the centre of which was a cairn. A lot of people must have completed the journey to the top before us as there was a large pile of stones and pieces of rock built up by them. We all added a stone each to the pile and then sat down to rest with our backs against the cairn. I recall that we had carried our lunch in four haversacks - sandwiches and crisps in two and the drinks in the other two. We had drunk much of the pop by the time we got to the top and we quickly polished off the rest with lunch. All was well until I looked down over the edge. Cars looked like tiny dinky toys and people were just dots. I quickly retuned to the cairn and remained there till it was time to leave. I had this totally illogical feeling that the edges of the plateau that we were on had sheer drops beyond so I more or less crawled until I got top the edge and to my relief the ground only sloped away! The walk back to our cars was ok but we were all very tired. However by the time we had returned to our respective caravans we were ready for another drink. This time the adults shared a bottle – or rather four bottles of the local red and white wines. Nothing had ever tasted so good!

On the next day we went to look for a pool where we could swim and cool down. Lady luck looked kindly upon us and we found the most idyllic place where a mountain stream ran into a large rock pool. There was even a large rock overhanging the pool – ideal for diving. Of all the places we ever visited I think that was the one I enjoyed the most. It was very warm and dusty in Spain and keeping cool was a problem. Even at night the temperatures made it difficult to sleep comfortably and we all slept on, rather than in, our sleeping bags. We did not see any other English people on the site. I do remember that there was a family of Basques in a caravan nearby. They seemed happy-go-lucky, but the other Spanish people did not mix with them and it made me realise that, even in those days, there was a lot of antipathy towards people from the Basque region of northern Spain. As we were driving back into France we stopped for lunch and I remember Clive picking up something that was lying on the ground near a river. I took no notice at the time but it later turned out to be a ram's horn. On my 50th birthday the Bells gave me a walking stick with that horn as the handle. I still have it. There was also a poem written on behalf of the Thompsons, the Bells and the Loves as a commemoration.

The stories I have related of our holidays are really the shared ones that stand out in my mind. There were many other enjoyable memories that were part of those holidays too when we travelled for part of the time on our own – spending time at Versailles, in Paris, Tours, Poitiers, Rheims, in the Dordogne, Bordeaux, Clermont Ferrand, Lyon and many other cities and towns of interest in France alone. Outstanding for me was the Church built on the rock at Le Puy.

We visited places of interest such as Troglodyte Caves where drawings done by people from the Stone Age still exist. We explored Castles and Chateaux, particularly when we drove through the Loire Valley and followed the course of the Loire River. Some names come to mind:- Villandry, Blois, Amboise, Saumur, Chenonceaux. I remember standing in the centre of the bridge at Saumur at midnight looking up at the magnificent Chateau, brilliantly lit up for all to see – an unforgettable sight. The Chateau at Chenonceaux - with part of the building standing on the arches that span the river Cher – was superb. The Gardens at Villandry were so symmetrical and well looked after. I remember visiting the factory where the famous pottery is produced at Limoges.

Then there were places of great interest in Belgium – the port of Ostend, Bruges with its cobbled square and the Carillon with its 47 bells, Antwerp, Brussels, Liege. In Germany we visited Cologne Cathedral, travelled down the Rhine Valley, drove along the Romantische Strasse, stopping at Wurzberg, Rothenburg and finally Augsburg – a beautiful place. We were once driving through the outskirts of Munich three weeks before the Olympic Games were held there. In fact we were caught in very heavy traffic and had to pull off in what looked like a square as the radiator boiled over. It turned out to be an industrial estate of sorts. We were helped by a friendly German shopkeeper who owned a business in the area. He saw the plight we were in, kindly opened up his premises and gave us food and drinks. He even went home and fetched us enough vegetables and fruit to last us for the rest of our holiday. It turned out that he was an old German soldier who had been badly injured during fighting on the Russian front during World War Two. The English had been kind to him at the end of the War when he was a prisoner, and so he always welcomed English people whenever he could. It was a lucky break for us. I vividly remember driving along the Munich to Stuttgart autobahn the next day and being loudly hooted at when I moved into the fast lane to pass a slow motorist. Apparently I must have been holding up a driver who was travelling at well over 100 miles an hour and he was not impressed! There was no speed limit on German autobahns but I had not remembered that until he hooted. Having shot past us he disappeared in seconds so I did not try to overtake anything else again. I found that driving in German cities was fine unless one got into the wrong lane at traffic lights. There was no way that anyone would give way and one had to go with the flow and work out how to get back on track afterwards – not so easy in a strange city.

Driving in Italy left a lot to be desired. There was a sort of reckless streak amongst many Italian motorists and one never knew what would happen next. Rules of the road were of limited use to some and we saw more accidents in Italy than in the rest of our journeyings abroad. The incredible thing was to hear the motorists shouting at each other. People would stop and watch and before you could say Jack Robinson they joined in the arguments too. It was quite incredible. Then the police would arrive and suddenly everyone disappeared and there were then no witnesses for the police to question! On one occasion we were crossing the border into Italy from Austria, having been staying near Innsbruck. There was some sort of a flap on and as we parked between the white lines a policeman came to us and made us move by the simple and frightening expedient of pointing a gun at me when I asked what was wrong. I moved very quickly! Molly and Philip set off to change our Austrian money into Italian lira, but as I stayed to lock the car up prior to joining them I was again threatened at gunpoint by a different policeman and made to return to the very parking place from which I had been moved in the first place – crazy! They were certainly volatile that day to say the least. We never found out what the problem was, we were just glad to get away in one piece!

Summing up our many experiences of travelling abroad - altogether we enjoyed many good holidays and shared a lot of happy and exciting times with friends. We met all sorts of interesting people, visited so many places and enjoyed the freedom that caravanning can give. But being in close contact in a confined space had its drawbacks too and caused arguments when things went wrong – like punctures and breakdowns, putting up and taking down awnings that were difficult to manipulate, getting used to different customs - and it was fortunate that there were others who were happy to meet up with us, and vice versa for part of the time, for the sake of the children as well as the adults. Maybe the hardest custom to accept was the length of time that the French people like to take over eating meals. As we were used to getting through meals fairly quickly in England the French tradition of making a meal last two to three hours when eating out caused difficulties – boredom and being kept waiting were the biggest problems. French children were used to the custom and took their time - like their parents. We were all much less patient and this caused dissention so nobody really enjoyed dining out at restaurants. But we found that the 'Relais Routier' – a sort of wayside café – catered for all tastes. I think this was mainly because French lorry drivers often used 'Les Routiers' and were more pressed for time. We soon learned. We ate out in those places in the daytime and avoided going out in the evenings – problem solved!

There is no doubt that travelling in Europe certainly broadened one's concept of the different ways in which we all try to live our lives – both as individuals from our own points of view and as visitors who were able to learn about other countries and the ways and traditions that appertained to those who lived and worked there. I am sure that if more people travelled in Europe - and indeed around the rest of the world come to that – they would have a much greater understanding of how difficult it so often is to reach mutual agreements about the many issues affecting us all. Then maybe there would be greater incentive to trust each other in order that we could live in a safer and better world.

Part 5 Time at the Top

Chapter 1 The Final Move

I thoroughly enjoyed the six years that I spent of Kirkstall St Stephens CE School as Head Teacher. I am sure I must have made many mistakes there but I was able to follow up the work started by my predecessor, Jim Hogg. When he first took over at the School he had felt that both children and staff needed a wake up call, to put it politely, and he had introduced certain changes that had necessitated the spending of almost all the capital available to him for the School year 1967/8. He had introduced the Initial Teaching Alphabet (ITA) as the introduction to reading in the early years – a scheme in itself requiring a host of new books and other expensive materials. Children were expected to wear short trousers at School whatever the weather and he expected the staff to conform to a certain style of discipline. There were various other measures too – the keeping of comprehensive weekly records of work done by the children had been paramount in his philosophy and the books written up by staff showing detailed forecasts of work to be taught. This must have improved standards considerably but he did not stay long enough at the School to see it all through. So the legacy Mr Hogg left was neither a happy one nor particularly in line with my own ideas. However sorting out what worked and what didn't gave me a chance to gain the experience I needed to look towards an eventual move to a large School.

In addition to teaching in school I had the opportunity to work with students at Carnegie College who were training to enter the teaching profession. I gave a series of lectures about both the Teaching of English and the Application of Discipline in Schools, particularly relating to School Practice periods. Apparently the latter were much appreciated by the students, and Alan Carter, Head of the Education Department in the College, sounded me out and invited me to give that particular series of lectures on several occasions. As the senior lecturer responsible for the overseeing of all Teaching Practice periods Alan had made a study of the methods being suggested to students by lecturers in the various departments. Head Teachers who had students doing teaching practices in Schools all over the city were not too happy with these instructions being put forward by lecturers – particularly in the teaching of Maths and English. In fact it became obvious that there should be serious discussions with all departments concerning the ideas being put forward for students to carry out during their teaching practices. Heads knew exactly what was required from the students. Their first task was to follow the curriculum as laid down by the Head Teacher in whichever school students went out to. This often clashed with the instructions given by individual Departments at Carnegie. Many lecturers were entrenched in their own little worlds when it came to teaching methods. I offered lecturers the opportunity to come into Kirkstall St Stephens and actually teach classes. Several were good but the less able sidestepped the chance to prove their worth and buried their heads in the sand. Eventually a meeting was arranged at which all Departments were invited to attend. Half a dozen heads also attended. They were people who lectured at Carnegie with the permission of the Education Authority. Each Department made a case to explain what they were doing – most had their own pet agenda that was fine in theory but useless in practice. After listening for over an hour to what was being put forward it became quite obvious that while internal academic standards being demanded were fine, on the practical side in the classroom, what was being peddled as good practice was absolute rubbish. We were asked to comment and I spoke for the Heads involved. I stood up – offering just two words to sum up exactly what we felt about what we had heard as it related to actual class teaching. They were good old-fashioned words - 'Balderdash' and 'Poppycock!' I then sat down again. This set the cat well and truly amongst the pigeons! Alan Carter was delighted. When asked to explain what I meant (the maths department lecturers walked out first!) I pointed out what was required 'at the sharp end' as I put it. Other Heads also had their say - more vociferously than I - and it became very obvious that changes were needed for the good of the students apart from anything else. Alan saw to it and things did improve. But none of the heads that had attended that meeting were invited back to lecture on subject matter again! However I was asked to continue my series on 'Discipline in Schools' for a bit longer. I then moved on to a bigger establishment and so could no longer spare the time to be out of my new school. It was an interesting fact that one of my referees for that post was Alan Carter. Later on he thanked us all, for what he said had caused the biggest shake up in practical teaching advice given to the respective Departments in years – he felt they certainly needed it.

My decision to move on from Kirkstall was engendered by the fact that Middle Schools were being introduced into the city and this meant that at Kirkstall I would have been left with a First School ie in charge of children up to the age of only nine as opposed to eleven. I preferred educating older children. I was never an enthusiastic disciple of the Three Tier System of Education and as it was only applied to Leeds and not to the West Riding Education Authority I applied for the Headship of Horsforth St Margaret's C of E School in September 1973 where the status quo remained as before at Primary level. If I had stayed on in Leeds I should have wanted to move to a Middle School with age levels from 10 to 13 years of age and there was no guarantee that this would be possible. I was called up for interview at the Education Department at Wakefield. There were four candidates and we introduced ourselves and stated where we had come from. When I mentioned Leeds there was a somewhat uncomfortable silence. I was then informed that no Head Teacher from the Leeds Education Authority had been appointed in the West Riding Authority for ten years – quite a start! However I was appointed - much to the surprise of the other candidates as well as to myself. I was then entertained to lunch by one of the interviewing panel. He even introduced himself as Mr Horsforth when I asked him his name and followed up with the comment, "I'm a Liberal Councillor. Everyone knows me in the area". I pointed out that I lived in Cookridge but had never heard of him – not an ideal start as it turned out that he was on the management board of St Margaret's School! During lunch he even made derogatory comments about Kirkstall St Stephens so I invited him to School for a day with the comment, "I'll take you out to dinner when you come, but not on interview expenses!" To give him credit he came and he got his lunch, but it was not the ideal introduction to my new job!

I took up my post as Head Teacher in January 1974. I had met several of the staff in the previous term when I had invited them to St Stephens. My predecessor, Mr Prince, had resigned in frustration at the inability of the West Riding Authority to do building work at the School. As soon as I was appointed I went to the new Metropolitan Authority prior to my taking up my new post to see if anything could be done about more building. It could and – after considerable discussion and argument - it was. I had just a term to settle in before work commenced on a new Hall and a corridor - with a wider area at one point - that linked three main buildings. The wide part of the corridor became the school library. As well as being joined together there was to be a staffroom and toilets, an office for me as Head, another for my Secretary, Joyce Williamson, a storeroom for the Caretaker, Ted Clark, and a stockroom. Until the work was completed the following year my Secretary and I shared a small office. I was given the chance to offer an input into the planning and carrying out of the building work and I attended every meeting held on site. Organising a way for the children to get around the school building itself was quite a job and the builders put in two temporary paths to facilitate matters. By the time building commenced there were over 460 children on roll but we managed and on the completion of the building project we had a joint party with the both the firms of Architects and Builders!

The School itself was a real challenge. I had the task of revamping the Schemes of Work in every department and bringing them up to date over a period of about three years. I involved specialist teachers wherever possible and the multiplicity of talents among the staff helped. I also taught as much as possible and this allowed staff some non-contact time each week. It also meant that I saw every child in the school at least once a week. I put two and sometimes three infant classes together for the last period each day and either read to them or told them stories. Holding their attention was fun – I can actually 'wiggle my ears' individually and before each story time I would remind them to watch my ears. I would tell them that if they saw the left one wiggle all was well, but if the right one started to wiggle then someone was not paying attention or was whispering and fidgeting and they should quietly put their hand up so that the naughty girl or boy knew that they were spoiling the story. Incredibly it never failed. I think they were convinced that this all happened automatically and that my ears allowed me to hear more than they all could! I probably suggested that anyway and it caused much amusement amongst the Infant staff as it certainly was an original way of keeping the children quiet. I often wonder just how much of the stories they took in and how much time was actually spent instead watching for my ears to wiggle!

The first major challenge I faced when I first arrived was based on the fact that my predecessor, for reasons known only to him, had not used up all the posts of extra responsibility. I decided that I would reallocate certain posts in order to ensure that the organisation of, and the responsibility for, the various areas of the curriculum were covered by teachers best suited to their specific interests and skills – Music, Maths, English, Art, Physical Education, History, Geography, Science and so on. On my arrival there were two clearly defined departments – Infants and Juniors. Mrs Audrey Jones, Head of the Infants Department, was an experienced teacher who was able to organise the department effectively and standards were good, particularly the basics of literacy and numeracy. But there were major divisions between the two Departments. My eventual aim was to run the school with less specific areas of education in order that there would no longer be a sudden transition from one to the other but rather a gradual development so that in an ideal world the trauma of change from so called Infants to Juniors would virtually disappear. This principle was not as difficult as it might appear because the School was actually on two sites when I took over. The Infant Department was housed in the main buildings while 5 classes of the 7 in the Junior Department were situated on a temporary site adjacent to the Comprehensive School, about a quarter of a mile away. David Thomas, the Deputy Head, was on site there and was responsible for those classes. They were housed in the 'Huts', or temporary buildings. Two junior classes were based at the Main School. This had certain advantages, as those older children were encouraged to mix with the infants and help in the development of social skills. They were particularly helpful when young children had to move round from one part of the school to another in order to accommodate the building workers. In fact the older girls tended to 'mother' the younger children and this meant that they both felt the need to set a good example and see that the young ones were happy and toed the line. All in all it was a very hectic period. Initially even some staff meetings were held separately and for a spell I went along with this although I had everyone together when outlining my ideas and asking for comments. Some of these were quite lively too – at times I felt a bit like an Aunt Sally - but at least Staff felt they had a say in the overall input and it showed. After a time most staff would come and chat with me about things appertaining to their teaching and that was good. I always made a point of never giving advice unless it was asked for. Occasionally there would be injudicious comments made when staff 'fell out' and that was a bit of a problem but at least I knew what to expect and could sometimes nip things in the bud. But not always – the Deputy and the Head of Infants rarely saw eye to eye and this made life difficult. In fact more than once I was in a quandary as to how to deal with their differences. While they were on separate sites there was no problem. It was only after everybody eventually had moved to the Main School that differences surfaced – not too surprising really as both had in effect been in charge of their own sites. Things did come to a head on one occasion and I had decided that enough was enough. I was about to lay the law down in no uncertain terms one Monday morning after being 'consulted' during the weekend by phone. I had even gone to see Audrey Jones on the Sunday to find out what had occurred. David had apparently overstepped the mark according to her – more by the way he had said things rather than by what he had said. Just as I was about to say what I thought - very firmly – there was a knock on my door and I was told sorted things out. However I still had my say to both separately – but much more quietly than I had intended.

As already stated, I inherited a school containing over 460 pupils. The buildings left much to be desired and class sizes were way above the norm. It was eventually decided that some children would be moved into a new School being built in Horsforth – Westbrook. By the time the building work was completed at St Margaret's Westbrook was almost ready for the first intake and one teacher agreed to join the staff there. This had the great advantage for those children who lived near the new School and were scheduled to go there. There was a familiar face amongst the newly formed staff. Around 50 children took advantage of the chance to move.

This helped considerably with class numbers and with two less classrooms to find made things more manageable. My next move was to try and get all the children together on one site. When I first arrived at the School the problem of taking children from the Main Site up to the temporary accommodation involved no more than crossing one road immediately opposite the front of the school and proceeding the short distance up to the temporary classrooms. At that time there was not a lot traffic on that particular road and there was little danger. However, no sooner had the building work been completed in school than it was decided that a new road linking the Leeds Ring Road through to the north side of Horsforth should be built to facilitate the ever increasing amount of traffic. The work was eventually finished and, unknown to either the police or to me, a date was set that should have coincided with the start of the summer holidays in 1975. It was done in good faith I was told afterwards, but unfortunately the date set for opening was the day BEFORE the holidays started. When I arrived at School about 7.45am there was traffic using the new road. Fortunately no children had actually appeared. I rang the local police station and informed them of the situation. The bollards that had been across the road the day before were still stacked up at the side of the road awaiting collection so Dave Thomas and I immediately went out, stopped the traffic and put the bollards back up. Eventually a policeman arrived in a patrol car – not easy as we had blocked off the traffic in both directions – and took over. I have never been called so many names or sworn at so often in my life while I was waiting for them to come! The old diversions were replaced for another day and I was then informed by phone – by a highly amused Sergeant Abbott - that as the person responsible I had broken the law by setting up road barriers again after they had officially been taken down. Still, at least nobody was injured and no child was put at risk. That for me was the first priority, law or no law. When I received an official reprimand from the Police Authority I contacted them to discuss the matter, then followed it up by stating that if it happened again, or indeed any lives were put at risk by inefficient beaurocratic planning I should act in exactly the same manner. Needless to say the inevitable situation occurred several times as parents and children needed to be able to cross the new main through road in safety. Sometimes no crossing warden was available to   conduct people across at the official crossing point - more of that later.

The subsequent opening of this 'through road' posed a serious problem for us from the start of the winter term in September 1975 as most Junior Department children had to cross this road in order to reach their classrooms after morning assembly. They then returned at midday and went back after lunch in the main building. Getting a crossing warden was difficult enough, but that only covered the time before school commenced in the morning and after school finished in the afternoon. It meant that there always had to be a minimum of two staff with each class when they crossed the road. There were PE lessons in the new Hall in the main building and a new library-cum-class teaching area that we had set up in the new corridor for teaching use. As a staff we spent a long time literally teaching the children how to cross the road safely as a group or class. I had already got the backing of the School Managers to fight for all the children to be housed on one campus. Incredibly I could not even have a zebra crossing put across this busy road despite being informed of the official criteria required for council consideration. It was something in the region of 5000 crossings being made in a week by people. We duly wrote down our numbers that exceeded this – there were over 170 children on the Horsforth Comprehensive School site and they crossed at least twice a day each way during school time alone. Add on the children and parents crossing before and after school plus members of the public and the large number of children who attended the Comprehensive School there was no question but that the criteria was reached – and exceeded.

A meeting was called and two Leeds City Council representatives were present together with local councillors, managers and myself. The figures were shown, together with road traffic figures. Then the bombshell fell. The representatives smugly informed us that CHILDREN DID NOT COUNT in the numbers required. There was uproar! Local Councillors protested strongly as they had helped in the whole project and a campaign was started to get the decision reversed but it did not happen at the time. We had a crossing patrol and that was all that was to be permitted. Thank goodness no one ever got hurt during school hours – a tribute to the care shown by staff and the good training given to the youngsters who were involved.

It occasionally had a funny side too. Whenever the Crossing Warden was absent from duty before and after School – this happened quite frequently as the lady appointed had an ongoing illness that could strike at any time – I rang the Police Station and requested that a policeman be sent to control the crossing area. If, as often happened, no police officer was available I always went out myself as I felt it was my responsibility to try to ensure the safety of both pupils and parents before and after official school hours. There were times when stopping traffic was positively dangerous. There were also moments that proved quite amusing, particularly when I used the crossing lady's 'lollipop stick' as we called it. I used on several occasions until one day, just after I had been 'on duty' I received a call from the local police station. Sergeant Abbott, the policeman in charge of sorting out crossing patrols, asked me if I had been using the crossing patrol pole. When I replied in the affirmative he pointed out that I was not officially trained and therefore technically I was committing another road offence! He was, once again, highly amused and we had a good chuckle about it. I actually offered to go to court to be charged in order that I could then put my case publicly for a reserve-crossing patrolman to be appointed at the same time but he decided otherwise, much to my regret. I had the ear of one press reporter in particular who would willingly have reported the case in the Yorkshire Post. However we did eventually manage to come to a serious arrangement as the volume of traffic was quite considerable and was growing more by the week. But in the meantime, being barred from using the official crossing pole, I was reduced to using an umbrella instead! Unofficially this was later seen by the good sergeant and myself as both significant and at the same time highly droll. One morning an indignant motorist kept edging forward. I think he presumed I would give way. However I turned towards him and after calling on him to stop I held my umbrella out in front of me. He swore loudly, then drove on and the ferule on the end of the brolly accidentally went into his radiator – at least that was my story. I took his number and rang Sergeant Abbott. He in turn sent a message out to his police drivers who were out on patrol to stop and detain the driver of the vehicle. They found him all right – half way along Bayton Lane, the road that goes past Horsforth Golf Club towards Rawdon. His radiator was steaming and he was unable to move as the water had all leaked out. The ferule had done its work well! He was fined and warned as to his future conduct. Funnily enough, although I must have spoken to the sergeant on dozens of occasions, I never actually met him until some considerable time later. He was one of the old school of 'Bobbies' who commanded instant respect from potential law-breakers– what a character!

On another occasion a lady member of staff, Cynthia Nichols, was abused by a passing motorist and it really upset her. I had already suggested to the staff that they always tried to get the registration number if this happened, or at least try to note some identifying feature – colour of car etc. On this occasion she had seen the name on the side of the van – a white one. I reported it, looked up the telephone number and contacted the firm. The manager was furious and later that afternoon rang me up. He explained his company's policy regarding the advertising on all the vehicles sent out. It was supposed to promote business!   Then he explained that he had fired the driver immediately on his return and he also sent a personal apology. As the police had also become involved I guess the driver in question would think twice next time anything like that happened again.

It took something like four years before I managed to persuade the Education Authority to have temporary classrooms set up on the main campus. So in effect I had spent a lot of time getting all the children together in one place, but it was worth it in the end, if only to ensure their safety.

Once I had the whole School on one campus it was possible to look at one of my ultimate goals – that of making the transfer from what was termed the Infant Department to the Junior Department as smooth as possible. This went against the ingrained ideas among some of the staff of running the departments completely separately. It soon became obvious that the best way to achieve my aim was not to change the system but to adapt it in such a way that working practices became a continuous series of progressive educational teaching methods so that by the time children entered the Junior Department there was a certain understanding of a more formal approach to literacy and numeracy. Thus the transitional period between the end of Year 3 and the start of Year 4 was put in the hands of teachers sympathetic to my ideas. It took time but I had the ideal teachers to make it work. The aim of the Infant staff was to have every child capable of reading with understanding by the end of Year 3 and this was largely achieved by combined efforts of an experienced set of Infant staff ably led by Mrs Jones. Mrs Sylvia Crewdson, who later became a Head Teacher herself, had the transitional class with its attendant responsibilities and enabled the ideas put forward to be carried out in practice. In fact in 1982 St Margaret's was one of a few schools used for a pilot scheme that was set up by the Leeds Authority to target those children with special needs. We had a good cross section of children from various backgrounds and so were able to pass on the benefits of our experience. In fact we had been using the ideas that were put forward for some time anyway. I put Mrs Crewdson in charge and gave her the status – a Scale3 post - required to ensure that staff took note of what she was doing. She and I attended courses together after school on a regular basis with the Advisors who were responsible to the Authority. The beauty of it all was that the staff as a whole were persuaded of the value of the scheme and helped to set the standard for schools in the Leeds Metropolitan Borough in conjunction with other schools carrying out the pilot scheme.

There was an emphasis placed on participation in physical activities as well as academic ones. Once again I was fortunate to have a highly competent PE Specialist, David Rushworth, on the staff. He had trained at Exeter PE College. I had also had a PE background from Bede College, Durham, so inevitably I put a high priority on PE in School once the new Hall was completed. We purchased the latest equipment for use and David used his expertise to good effect, teaching PE throughout the junior department. In the summer we held Junior and Infant Sports Days and everyone could take part. The girls had good grounding in netball, courtesy of Jean Lamb, who later became Head Teacher of Westbrook Primary School. David Rushworth coached football and David Thomas or I sometimes refereed. I also helped out with the coaching side when time permitted. David Thomas came into his own in the summer term and both he and I coached cricket. There were only three schools in Horsforth where cricket was played so we went further afield whenever we could to give the boys a game. There were plenty of opponents for both netball and football teams. Swimming also had a high priority and we aimed to see that every child could swim by the time they left St Margaret's. I was able to take part in all the sporting activities that went on in the school and frequently went to Guiseley Baths to help with the teaching of swimming. There were several clubs run on a voluntary basis and an array of after school activities took place including Drama, Music, Art and various sporting activities including table tennis. Inevitably staff moved on. David Rushworth became a Head Teacher in Wetherby and I was fortunate to find another PE specialist, Alan Wiley, to take his place. Alan had had trials with Sunderland FC and was an excellent footballer. He kept himself very fit and went out running. As well as continuing all the sporting events already on the curriculum Alan concentrated on cross-country running for the school. There were already area Sports days and also a cross-country running competition in which we took part. Alan took any children who wished to go running out in the countryside nearby and very quickly a boys' running team was formed. They were so well trained that in all the time I was Head at St Margaret's we always won the Cross Country Junior Boys Championship. 10 boys formed each team and the combined total of eight runners made up the final scores. It happened on one occasion the team came in the first 9 places and the other boy was berated by his teammates because he had been on holiday for a fortnight and had not been able to train during that time. Poor lad, he came in 12th!

Music also had a high priority under the able guidance of Alison Hill and she put on some excellent shows in combination with Drama. Under her guidance a lot of children enjoyed playing instruments and singing, and her 'after school' music group, or club, was a winner. There were other members of staff who also took music and at one point I had the luxury of being able to timetable a member of staff to take music classes wherever needed. The lady in question, Mrs Lawson, also helped out in other departments and did not have a class of her own. Unfortunately when the Authority decided to save money this post could not be filled again once the teacher had retired.

In terms of responsibility I was eventually able to arrange my staff exactly as I originally envisaged when I was first appointed. I had a Deputy Head and a Head of the Infant Department. There were four teachers with Scale 3 posts of responsibility during my years as Head – these covered Music, PE, Sports, Drama, Children with Special Needs, organising the Library, Pastoral Care, plus functions organised in connection with the School such as School visits, Church Services etc. There were a further four scale 2 posts with special responsibility for Art and Craft, Infant Welfare, Infant Music and various other general responsibilities. On the staff were also part time teachers who offered further specialised help. There was a Non Teaching Assistant, Mrs Bailey, who helped out in the Infant Department. She also took responsibility for keeping stock records, as she was very good with figures. The School Secretary, Mrs Joyce Williamson, saw to the day to day running of the office and the Caretaker, Ted Clarke, and 3 cleaning ladies kept the school clean. There were four kitchen staff and four dinner ladies. I have always been a believer in delegating responsibility where possible as it enabled heads of departments to organise their own initiatives. Inevitably staff members gained promotion to other schools at times but I was fortunate to have, or to be able to appoint, teachers who provided continuity throughout the curriculum.

As a staff we encouraged initiative among the children. The everyday values we tried to inculcate followed a normal pattern – unselfishness, honesty, thought for others, politeness, self discipline, and a host more ideals calculated to make the school a happy place to come to and enjoy. Children were encouraged to think for themselves. Underlying this approach was a code of discipline that discouraged theft, bullying, swearing, cheating and the telling of lies. Any serious infringement of these rules and the child involved was sent to me. I was never a believer in corporal punishment although the children were aware that if necessary it was there as a last resort. I never felt the need to use physical punishment and I strongly discouraged staff from doing so. But equally I was aware that for many children there were double standards. They conformed at school but sadly it was a different ball game away from the school environment. I suppose this was inevitable and for many it was the language of life. Teachers encouraged good work with the awarding of red stars in books. Three red stars in a book and a child received a silver star. Three silver stars and the reward was a gold star. Art work was displayed on walls and I put a few outstanding pictures up in my office for visitors to admire. The aim was to award effort as well as actual attainment and it worked well.

On the parental side mutual cooperation was, on the whole, very good. The Parent Teacher Association was strong and we organised a series of events every year. This helped to raise funds that in turn were used to the school's advantage, enabling us, amongst other things, to purchase items not covered by the Leeds Authority and there were plenty of those. It also engendered a community spirit that allowed for parents to enter into dialogue with staff, particularly when evening attendances were arranged each term in order for parents to see work and discuss the progress being made by their offspring. I was always happy to see parents on any matters that they wished to bring to my attention and to this end my secretary was able to arrange appointments to suit during the school day. In addition I normally stayed at school most evenings until 5.45 pm and was available to see them during that time as well. Sometimes parents would offer to attend school to help teachers in classrooms. Again, this was encouraged, particularly at the younger end where basics such as listening to children read or joining in the various teaching activities with the pupils was a real boon. Parents helped with school trips and various sporting activities too. Where there was financial hardship involved some of the money raised by parents was used to help defray the costs for pupils who otherwise would be unable to take part in outings organised by staff. The PTA raised upwards of £3000 per year through a variety of fund-raising efforts varying from Summer Fairs, Christmas Fairs, Dances, Competitions, Outings, Sporting Activities – in fact virtually any way that enabled us to swell the coffers and at the same time thoroughly enjoy ourselves. Inevitably there were highlights that come to mind. The first was a Dance organised by the PTA at the Astoria Ballroom during my first year as Head. It was a fabulous event and the place was packed. It was quite a 'cultural' shock really as I had never before come across an event of that scale in connection with a Primary School. Expectations were high and with such a diverse cross section of the community in the area it was a chance to involve parents from all social stratas in the work of the School. With so much building taking place at the main part of the school there were limitations as to what could be achieved on the actual premises but Summer and Winter Fairs took place in the Old Hall and the adjacent classrooms and it gave parents the chance to see the work that was being carried out both inside and outside the School.

There were also opportunities to take part in festivities arranged by local dignitaries. I particularly remember the excellent work that took place during the Horsforth Gala Day in 1977 – the Queen's Jubilee Celebrations' Year. A competition for the best arrayed float was organised by the Gala committee. St Margaret's School entered a 'float' and we all paraded through the streets on lorries, cars and horses and carts, all festooned in red, white and blue. Shire horses pulling a Brewery Dray made a brave sight too. A large 'crown' was made to put on our school float. It must have been around 5 feet high, made of chicken wire and covered with red, white and blue papier-mache, plus hundreds of similarly coloured flower-shaped tissue paper wads. Red, white and blue ribbons stretched out to the sides and four corners of the lorry. The lorry itself was also decorated to suit the wonderful occasion. The children were heavily involved and the finished article was surrounded by cardboard 'walls' to simulate the Tower of London. Some children, dressed as 'Beefeaters', lined the walls on the float - guarding the Crown and the Crown Jewels. Others were clad in gaily-coloured dresses with a variety of hats to match. All had Union Jacks to wave to the large crowds. I also dressed up as a Beefeater and travelled with the children on the float. The crowning glory came when the School float was declared the overall winner of the Gala Competition and we were presented with a cup to mark the occasion. The stalls on Horsforth Park were decorated in red, white and blue and many of the large crowd dressed up for the day's festivities. It was a truly magnificent sight and the weather was perfect – a very special day! The press were there in some force so the publicity was considerable. There was even someone writing an article and taking pictures for a German newspaper and I was pictured in my Beefeater costume while walking across the park after the Gala Queen had presented the Cup. In the same year I went with a party of senior children to Elland Road Football Ground to see the Queen and the Duke of Edinburgh who were visiting Leeds. Luckily I knew the official who organised the seating for schools and we were situated very close to where the Royal party were seated to watch the festivities organised in the Queen's honour. It was a truly memorable day for all of us. Over all 1977 was a highly successful year in terms of getting parents, staff and children closer together - each child being given a commemorative Cup - and this was really the starting point of what, during my stewardship as Head Teacher, I wanted to achieve in terms of mutual trust and cooperation 'twixt home and school. I felt that the staff had come to understand and accept my vision for a close working relationship with the community as a whole, although the extra time and work entailed was by no means always suited to everybody's taste. However I continued to encourage staff to put forward their ideas and, despite sometimes feeling rather like an Aunt Sally at the initial staff meetings, the input eventually won over the doubters.

1980 is the year that stands out most in my memory. It was a year dedicated to the Bicentennial Anniversary of the founding of St Margaret's Church of England School. As St Margaret's was the oldest foundation school in Yorkshire this was a real 'first'. The idea was to hold an event every month from January to June, and this the PTA duly arranged. The programme included the usual money-raising events but with the accent upon the achievements of the School over 200 years. In February Miss Sally Smith, at that time the Secretary of St Margaret's PCC, presented the school with a cheque for £250 to help with the year's expenses – a very generous gift.

David Thomas, the Deputy Head, wrote a truly remarkable historical book encapsulating everything known about the School right from the early days covering the history of St Margaret's School. It also contained fascinating contributions written by former pupils. A special plate was designed and just 200 were struck to sell as mementoes of this most famous occasion. There were also a large number of commemorative cups made with a picture motif of the School shown. Every pupil was given a commemorative cup. David's book was printed and all copies were sold. The plates and extra commemorative cups were also sold, first to cover initial expenses and then to help with other school activities. In the days prior to June 28th children rehearsed a variety of performances with which to entertain visitors to the School. There had already been articles published in the local press during previous weeks to publicise the forthcoming celebrations. Communications were received from former pupils all round the world. It was truly wonderful! But the most remarkable letters received – on the same day – came from twin brothers who were both serving as Captains of giant oil tankers several thousand miles apart. The wording was virtually identical and, as we discovered later, at the time neither brother knew that the other had written to the School! In all my years I think that must have been the most incredible coincidence I have ever come across – almost unbelievable! After the celebrations were completed I was presented with a lovely blue plate with the names of all the staff on by Mrs Audrey Jones, Head of the Infant Department, as a personal memento of events. She had designed and painted it herself and I have treasured it ever since. Surprises like that are one of the things that make everything we do so worthwhile.

An incident of note happened in November 1979. As part of the forthcoming celebration plans the following June, we decided to renovate the School Bell. We took down the old bell that had hung over the entrance to the original school building. It had not been rung for many years and disconnecting it from the rusty fittings seemed virtually impossible. However in a PTA there is nearly always someone who knows how to solve any problem and this time was no exception. When the bell fittings were eventually loosened and it was being lowered to the ground it proved to be heavier than expected. It was more by luck than judgement that we managed to prevent it actually dropping onto the step below. It nearly decapitated the unfortunate parent who was in the act of taking it down from the wall of the building! Much to our delight it was discovered that the bell was not even cracked. One of the parents took it for renovation and it was replaced just in time for a ceremony that must go down in the annals of St Margaret's history. After several fruitless enquiries we managed to track down the oldest former pupil still living. We invited him to come along to take part in the ceremony. Sadly, at the last minute he fell ill, but we then were fortunate to find an excellent replacement. He was a genuine Yorkshireman with a great sense of humour to match.

Prior to the ceremony of 'ringing in' the renovated bell there had been quite a build up to the celebrations that took place on June 28th 1980. This was also day of the Horsforth Gala and the school had prepared a float depicting 200 years of Education at St Margaret's, or as it is otherwise still known, the National School. This was to take part in the parade through the streets of Horsforth in the afternoon.

One of the parents who had a scrap metal business had got hold of a horse and a two-seater dray. He spent hours cleaning it up for the Bicentenary Celebrations. To commence festivities Mrs Knight, who was in charge of the School kitchen staff, dressed up as an early Victorian lady of fashion. I dressed as a Headmaster of that period, and together, at around 9.30am, we were taken round the local streets. We went along Kerry Street, across Horsforth High Street, and thence to the front entrance to the School – ably led by the daughter of the dray's owner and an older friend (to make sure the horse did not bolt!). There were quite a few people about in the streets - locals were invited to join in the festivities if they wished to do so. On arrival at the school gate we were met by a large crowd of children and parents, many of whom had dressed up in Victorian Costumes. Awaiting us was a pupil dressed in a truly resplendent uniform as an Army Officer in Victorian times. Later in the morning it was his job to present a ceremonial sword to me in order that Mrs Knight and I could use it to cut the Bicentennial Cake. There were a variety of entertainments for everyone to enjoy, one in particular being our own School Morris Dancers. There was a costume parade, music in the main Hall, stalls, games and plenty of refreshments too. At 11.45 am everybody assembled outside the original School building, built in 1780. After making a brief welcoming speech I introduced our guest of honour for this particular ceremony – the tolling of the renovated School Bell with its brand new bell rope. He was the second oldest living ex-pupil of St Margaret's and he had been at the school at the start of the 20th century. What a character he was! He entertained us with stories of what life at school was like in his day, with a rare turn of wit! Then he proceeded to ring the bell, together with the youngest child from each of the twelve classes, starting at exactly midday. All went well until the final bell pull. The youngest child in the whole school got so excited that she pulled too hard and too quickly for our octogenarian guest..... and the bell tolled twice! So thus history was made - with a difference. I recorded in the School log book that the bell had rung thirteen times at midday, on Saturday June 28th 1980 so it is there for posterity. This caused much laughter! There was a cheer too and some loud clapping. The ceremony was a great success.

Our next move was to the front entrance of the School where the second ceremony – the cutting of the Bicentennial Cake – took place. First of all the sword was duly officially and very proudly presented to me by the smartly uniformed 'Victorian Officer'. Then Mrs Knight and I jointly made a cut with the sword into the cake. It was taken away, expertly cut up, and pieces distributed to everyone. It certainly was a massive cake. It looked too good to eat!

There is no doubt in my mind that most of those people connected in any way with the School, pupils, parents, staff and friends, both past and present, will always remember with pleasure and pride, the events such as witnessed on June 28th 1980. It was, after all, the first Bicentenary to be celebrated in the area at a Primary School in the Metropolitan area of Leeds.

With most of the festivities completed at School I joined a number of children on the float. This represented '200 years of Education' and had been made by children and staff. In fact all the Staff, together with several parents, had done a wonderful job in every way possible. The costumes that the children wore to the celebration were picturesque in the extreme and, although we did not win a prize with our particular float, the crowds who had come to school went on to the Gala and added greatly to the colourful scene. In School we had been preparing for a long time. We even had a day in the week leading up to the Celebrations when children were encouraged to come to School in costumes of a bygone age. The Staff came in old fashioned costumes to give the children an idea of how things were at various stages over the previous 200 years. During that week I set the trend by turning up at school dressed as a

Headmaster from the Victorian era. We even taught the children for a day using the monitorial system – teaching by rote - with groups of children repeating things like tables and poems. It was great fun and the historical significance was certainly not lost on any of us! I remember at the end of the Gala that day walking back through the park very tired but highly exhilarated. It was certainly one of the major highlights of my career in education.

I have really just highlighted a few events that stand out in my memory. There were so many other things – not least of which was the production of a school magazine for a period. This was entirely the work of a few parents, ably led by the secretary of the PTA, Mrs Hughes, who collected articles written by children as well as adults. It involved a lot of putting together and sadly in the end proved impossible to maintain when children moved to the Comprehensive Schools at eleven and the parents originally involved had other loyalties to consider.

To sum up, I think that I managed to achieve my main aim – to dispel to a certain degree the 'Us and Them' situation where the school was simply a place of Education and parents had little input. I suppose that really it was the forerunner of the attempts to involve parents more closely with what goes on in school – for example helping children with reading - in fact in general numeracy and literacy. Inevitably we still did not reach everyone – that was something too much to hope for – but at least parents came into school to air their views and that way there was useful communication. I found that often I was faced with problems appertaining to family difficulties, to stressful situations where children suffered when parents fell out or split up. I remember one mother coming into school one day after her husband had literally beaten her up and then cleared off. Although she had been hurt she came to see that her children were all right and to ask that staff might be told in case the children misbehaved or acted out of character – not to complain about her harsh treatment.

I found that the Community Constable was a great help too. I recall one particular problem that I encountered – as a direct result of making myself available to children if they wanted to tell me anything. Four girls had decided to go on a stealing spree. They had been into Morrison's Supermarket in the High Street and had come out with a load of sweets and other goodies. They then got cold feet, thought they might be caught, and the next morning they came to tell me what they had done, in the hope that I could put things right. It struck me at the time that there had to be some official involvement despite the fact that normally minor incidents could be dealt with internally. But this one was too serious and had to be sorted officially. I called the parents in where I could and explained what had happened. They were obviously very concerned as the girls were not really the types to go on this sort of a rampage again. They had frightened themselves! I pointed out that official action would be taken but that if they were prepared to leave it to me I would decide what should be done. I contacted the Community Constable whom I knew well as he had also helped out when I was at Kirkstall where petty theft was a way of life to several families, and the children sometimes became involved. He could really lay the law down and put the fear of God into any reprobates when he felt it necessary. Families may not have liked him but they certainly respected him in that area! We decided that he would give the girls a strong telling off and would call at their houses too after school just to show he meant business. I warned the parents what was happening and they realised that it was the best way to keep things out of court. It solved the problem, but there was one mother who was far more concerned as to what the neighbours might think when a policeman came to her door. Obviously her daughter was only of secondary concern although she had actually been the ringleader. My comment to her was short and very much to the point!

But that was not the end of it. The stolen property had to be returned so we went to Morrison's store. The manager was in a cleft stick. He was always supposed to prosecute. Fortunately I had had words with some of his employees the previous Sunday morning. I had been to school and noticed a football match taking place on the School playing field – in those days strictly illegal. When I questioned the players it turned out that they were a team of employees from Morrison's. I too was supposed to make an official complaint about the unofficial use of the school field. So I bartered with the Manager. I agreed to drop my complaint provided that he did not pursue the prosecution. The store got most of the goods returned and I did not make an official complaint – problem solved!

I suppose that I would have to say that having to end my teaching career prematurely in 1984 was the saddest decision that I had ever been forced to make. Despite the seriousness of my illness, which necessitated an immediate operation once the diagnosis of malignant cancer had been made, I had always hoped that I would eventually be able to return to my post as Head Teacher, but sadly it was not to be.

Initially I saw the specialist on September 12th 1983. He gave me just three school days – the rest of the week - to sort out the running of St Margaret's School for the foreseeable future. I then had to go into hospital on the following Monday and the operation took place the next morning. That first operation was only partially successful and I required a further operation three weeks later. I had to have a malignant melanoma removed from my right calf, just below the knee joint. I was in hospital for about six weeks, much of the time with my right leg in plaster. I soon mastered the art of using a wheelchair in the ward and thus managed to get about and chat to other patients. More about that comes later.

At this point I must record that the school staff were fantastic. When I was preparing to get myself to the hospital I received a phone call from Mrs Williamson, my secretary, telling me that Mrs Crewdson was on the way by car to take me to the LGI. On my arrival there she insisted on seeing which ward I was to be in and she stayed and chatted with me until it was time for some paperwork and tests to be carried out. Every evening that I spent in the hospital two members of the school staff always came to see me. I also had countless people to visit – my son Philip, my estranged wife Molly, and other relatives, parents and friends - during the afternoons as well – so I was never on my own. It was truly uplifting to feel that so many people cared. I even had one from my staffing officer, Mrs Wemyss, from the Education Office! My lovely cousin Daphne caught a bus up here from Sunbury on Thames to spend an afternoon with me. Susan and Steve Taylor drove up from Northamptonshire to visit and caused chaos by producing some wine during the afternoon and evening. Then they refused to leave immediately visiting time was up! But it was all very good humoured. The nursing staff joined in unofficially and even had a small taster or two! Psychologically the warmth of feeling that emanated from all those who took time to come and encourage me to get better was inestimable.

The great day came when the plaster was removed again after the second operation and I was encouraged to try and stand up. I have never experienced such pain in my life and it took me the best part of a day to keep my foot on the floor and learn to stand up again. At first when walking I was supported by a couple of nurses. After a day or two more I was able to get about with the aid of a stick. I had an incentive. I could not go home until I could walk a bit. I swore to myself that I would WALK out of the ward and not be taken out in a wheelchair. On the Saturday morning that Philip came to fetch me the nurses and the sister came into the ward to see whether I would be able to carry out my plan. He brought the car as close to the front exit as possible and I managed to get along the corridor and made it unaided.

Inevitably on my return home I was in for a long period of convalescence, although I threw a party the day after coming out of hospital. I invited everybody who had been to see me in hospital, friends and neighbours alike. It lasted from midday until about 9.30pm and was a great success! Then the slow process of recovery began. There were weekly visits to the hospital. I remember one day that Jimmy Saville was making an advert outside the hospital entrance, leaning on the bonnet of a Jaguar XK120. When I arrived he stopped the filming and came across to help me out of the taxi. I have never forgotten that. Recovery was probably quite quick but I was not a good patient and every time I went to see my doctor at the Croft Surgery I asked if I could return to work. Eventually the surgeon, Mr Browning, and my local practitioner, Dr Lawson, both tried to persuade me that the possibility of my actual survival and recovery depended upon freedom from the inevitable stresses of my work. I was reluctant to accept this at first but came around to it in the end. However I refused to retire as a disabled person and submitted my resignation in the normal way, asking for early retirement and the financial offer that was being proffered at the time. Unfortunately that affected the amount of my pension a bit but psychologically it was the right thing to do so far as I was concerned. I was absolutely determined to get better despite the difficulty I had in walking far. The only time I was close to breaking was when I had to go into School and tell the staff that I had to retire. I was allowed back in June 1984 just to clear up. Just prior to my illness David Thomas had got a Headship so a new Deputy was to be appointed. In the meantime Alison Hill had taken over as temporary Head. During my enforced absence she had done a wonderful job of keeping the school ticking over smoothly and I hoped that she would get the post of Head Teacher on a permanent basis. But sadly it was not to be and I was not in any position to influence the eventual decision. I left at the end of the Summer Term 1984.

Chapter 2 Home life

Obtaining the Headship at St Margaret's in 1974 had given me an increase in salary that was very welcome. Although we still had a mortgage to pay it was not large by standards so there was a bit more money to aid the family finances. Philip was still at Holy Trinity as it had now become a Middle School under the recent changes in education made in Leeds - to the three tier System. He was able to remain there until he transferred at 13 to Holt Park Comprehensive School. Molly was still at Ryecroft Middle School and became the Deputy Head there. We still ran two cars and as we had a caravan we needed one to be a large and powerful car for towing. She used this to go to work. I upgraded from a 'banger' to something more reliable.

Life followed a steady pattern and we still had a close liaison with Betty and Derek Love, Barbara and Roy Thompson, Anne and Clive Bell, and latterly Betty and Aubyn Sparkes. Roy and Barbara had moved to the Weetwood Park area near Lawnswood School and we were frequent visitors there when time allowed. Anne and Clive had moved to Colchester for a spell. Clive's job as a Customs Officer took him there but he had then transferred back to a house in the next street to work at the Leeds/Bradford Airport. Roy Thompson became Head of the Teachers' Centre in Headingley and Barbara became a Headmistress at Brighouse Girls' High School. Derek was still at Maeson's Clothing Factory as the firm's accountant. He later moved to Sheffield when the Leeds branch was eventually closed.

We continued to share parts of our holidays together and the summer mid term break was invariably spent on a Caravan site at the former railway station in Portpatrick with the Bell family. The Thompsons also came on occasion. A morning game of golf for the male members of the party was the regular pattern and in the afternoons we sometimes went to a beach. One of our favourite beaches was at Killantringan, a couple of miles north. It was reached by driving along a narrow track about a mile from the road towards Killantringan lighthouse. Nearby was a small car park of sorts. It was quite a scramble among the rocks down to the sands and there were seldom many people there. The beach itself stretched a long way. It was safe
enough so that the children could play and when the sun was bright there were shady spots near the rocky cliffs. Clive was a great one for beachcombing and building fires out of driftwood. But we seldom went swimming there, as the water was so cold. In the evenings, if the weather was kind, there were magnificent sunsets to be seen from the car park too. The best place to swim was off the beach near Sandhead on the other side of the peninsula. The water was always quite warm because the Gulf Stream touched that part of Luce Bay. We spent many happy holidays on the Rhinns of Galloway, as the peninsula was called. Sometimes we went further afield up the coast to Stranraer and on towards Oban, or down to Drummore and on to the Mull of Galloway lighthouse where one could see the coasts of England, Ireland, Wales and Scotland on a clear day! There was a truly picturesque harbour at Portpatrick with a bowling green and a putting course

that proved quite a challenge for everyone! The coastal walk up to and beyond the Coastguard's lookout was certainly spectacular.

Summer holidays were still spent abroad. Sometimes we went off caravanning to separate countries and then met up on a Caravan site – usually somewhere like Biscarosse or Lacanau on the Atlantic Coast in France. On other occasions we went in convoy, usually in France, to campsites in places like Argentat. There was usually water nearby as Aubyn had a motorboat and Clive had a small sailing boat. After we had returned home Roy and I would drive up to Portpatrick for a few days. We would stay in the house where the campsite manager lived and spend almost our entire time playing golf. In later years I became a member of the Dunskey Golf Club at Portpatrick and used to motor up two or three times a year. Philip came with me occasionally. I had twelve free rounds to use as I wished each year and golfing friends, one way or another usually took these up.

When we were at home we would often have dinner parties at one house or another. These were enjoyable affairs as the meals were imaginative and there was plenty of liquid refreshment too. The same applied at Christmas times – in fact any excuse for spending time together was exercised.

We often used to go to see Molly's parents at Knaresbrough after they moved there from Drighlington. I would regularly motor down to Cranford near Kettering to see my father. Philip was heavily into sport at school on Saturday mornings – mainly football – so I went on my own. Occasionally we went as a family and stayed overnight – usually on our way to catch a boat across to France at the start of our summer holiday. My father had a good life as he had many friends in the Kettering and Northampton areas. He was also a Mason and thus he had companionship in that quarter as well. I really came to appreciate what a good man he was in later years and was lucky to be able to share quite a bit of time with him during the last five years of his life. We talked a lot and I took him out whenever I visited – virtually every fortnight. He was Chairman of the Kettering Divisional Education Board for several years and I was often able to help to steer him through difficult situations that sometimes arose, particularly where there were disputes between teachers and the Authority. I guess that I had inherited his gift for public speaking and his very real sense of right and wrong so I could understand just where he was coming from when it came to making decisions that affected the careers of those in education. In hindsight it was a pity that he was not able to see much of us as a family but he was too far away to visit us very often. When he did come to stay he liked nothing better than to travel around Yorkshire and see the beautiful countryside. He also loved to go to the Railway Museum at York.

On the first occasion that we went to the Railway Museum he stood on a long balcony inside the building. Suddenly he grabbed my arm and pointed at an engine that was on show below where we were standing. In a voice shaking with emotion he told me that there was the actual engine that his Grandfather, George Sewell, used to drive. He then gave me some of the history appertaining to it. This intrigued me and I contacted the Curator of the

Museum and we met up with him on his next visit and went onto the footplate. By this time I had researched what I could about the engine and it turned out to be the first one ever built by Patrick Stirling. It was famously known as the 'Stirling Single No. 1'. George Sewell was the first engine driver in charge of it. It was the forerunner of the 'Flying Scotsman' and travelled regularly from London to York. It was unique in that it was built with a massive driving wheel just over 8 feet across. My father had last seen it running in 1938. It was due for renovation – I saw it in 1980 - and he was invited to be there when it was to run again for engine enthusiasts. Sadly father died in May 1980 and so I rang up the organisers of the event and they invited me in his place - in July 1980 – to Rothley in Leicestershire. The interest was so great that I could not actually get through the large crowd on the platform to the organisers of the event. However I travelled on the train anyway and later rang to let them know I had been there. The organisers were actually based at Peterborough and I was invited to see them when I was in the area. George Sewell lived in Peterborough. My Grandfather and later my father were brought up in Peterborough.

In 1979 I realised that I was not in the best of health. I suffered minor stomach pains from time to time but did not realise that this might be some form of serious medical problem. There were pressures at work and, sadly, at home too from time to time. I knew that Molly and I were drifting apart but could not pin the reason down at the time. I assumed that work had a lot to do with it - I had found that I was prone to feeling very tired for much of the time and I recall that we were no longer doing things together. We still saw Anne and Clive regularly and on Sunday evenings we went round to their house to play canasta. It was also obvious that Anne and Clive were having their own problems but when we were all together things appeared all right. As the year went on I began to feel more and more isolated and the feeling that there was something wrong healthwise became a cause for concern. After work was over for the day I found that I was bringing my problems home and worrying about them. I put it down to the fact that we were both getting older, Philip was growing up and so we were no longer concentrating on our family life in the same way. It was also obvious that our personal lives appeared to be very humdrum. I had been to see Dr Lawson on a couple of occasions. He put my discomfort down to overwork and stress. However, one Sunday evening we had gone round to play canasta as usual but I had returned home early as I felt both unwell and desperately tired. I had just got home when I had the most devastating pain that I had ever suffered. It was if someone was stabbing me time and again in the stomach. It got even worse so I rang for Molly to come home. By the time she did I was doubled up in chronic agony on the floor. This went on for a while, then it began to ease and I was able to get to bed. I went to the Croft Surgery the next morning. Dr Lawson was away on holiday but another doctor dealt with me and arranged for me to be admitted to Otley Hospital. I had gallstones present and an operation was performed to remove my gall bladder. I was very ill for several days and for an apparently unknown reason I was not recovering as I should have done. Eventually, after nine days, the specialist who had carried out the operation examined me and immediately had a tube, that had been inserted by him after my operation, removed by a nurse. The moment that it was taken out the pain stopped. Apparently I had somehow managed to push the tube into my body – probably when I rolled over in bed - until it was pressing against my diaphragm and this was the problem. I was soon on the road to recovery although a sister who had been giving me sleeping pills wrongly accused me one evening of being a drug addict! Molly was furious when she heard and pointed out in no uncertain terms that our house was full of painkillers that I refused to take. At least I got the right backing on that occasion! I remained in hospital for a few more days and was soon up and walking about. But it took several weeks before I was anything like fit again and I did not return to St Margaret's that summer. My father came up to see me and we managed to get out and about. I was able to drive again by then.

After my father's death on May 8th 1980 Molly, Clive and I drove down to Warkton near Kettering to sort out his belongings. I was very grateful at the time to have some help and I assumed that this was simply part of the friendship we had enjoyed. His wife Anne told me otherwise but I had accepted the help in good faith and nothing more was said about it. However I learned later from a neighbour that Clive had been a regular visitor to my house when I was out and I must say that I was glad at the time that I was in total ignorance of that. I simply accepted that they were friends. But our relationship at home deteriorated considerably throughout 1981.

When we went to Portpatrick for our usual half term summer caravan and golfing holiday in 1982 Molly suddenly told me that she intended to leave me. Even at that stage I had not realised that she and Clive were more than casual friends – that came later and Anne confirmed it. Apparently our friends had seen it happening. Then came the supreme irony. For virtually the only time in my life I did not know how to cope with this situation, as I had no wish for us to split up. Very reluctantly I first went to try and find somewhere else to live. However Molly then decided that she was going to move in July. She had found a flat some weeks earlier but it turned out to have wet rot and needed a new roof, so I agreed to let her stay until it was put right. That was a very hard and sad nine months for both of us, but by the time she eventually left on April 7th 1983 I had started to come to terms with things. We sorted the separation details out ourselves and only involved solicitors where absolutely necessary. I agreed to purchase her half of the property and took out a second mortgage of £14,000 to cover the cost. The day before she left I went to stay with my friends Susan and Steve Taylor for a couple of days. They were very kind and helpful just when I needed it. I dreaded coming home to an empty house but my wonderful son Philip was there to see that I was ok. I shall never forget that.

Once again, I had been feeling unwell for quite a while and two years previously I had grown a beard to cover lines that were appearing on my face. At the time I put this down to the matrimonial situation that I had become aware that we were in but as it turned out it was a forerunner to something very much more serious health-wise. Again I had seen the doctor and he put it down, quite rightly, to stress. But he assumed it was work related, as I had not led him to think otherwise. During the previous summer holiday in 1981 I had gone on my own to Canada to see my second cousin Ann and her husband

Murray. For the first and only time I broke down when asked why Molly had not come with me to visit them. I had to tell them about the deteriorating situation at home and their instant understanding and sympathy was too much. I had quaffed a few drinks too so I guess that helped. Strangely enough I felt much better from then on and thoroughly enjoyed my holiday. As a lawyer Murray knew just how to advise me and I coped well until I returned home. I spent a delightful month with the Neilson family. Even the flight from Heath Row was fun. I had never travelled on a Jumbo 747 Jet before. Once I had settled in my seat, which was near the stairway to the upper flight deck, we took off and were immediately served with a meal. After that I decided to go to the upper flight deck to see what was there. To my surprise I found a small bar – serving free drinks to four other passengers. I joined them and we spent a hilarious four hours enjoying the delights of British Airways hospitality. It was a chance not to be missed! I returned to my seat prior to landing at Toronto Airport. On arrival there were the usual formalities – passports were duly checked and passengers went to collect their luggage. Mine appeared late in the proceedings but then I was met by my second cousin Ann and her mother Vera (Viv) at the exit. We drove to London, Ontario, arriving in time for supper. After a good night's sleep I was raring to go. Ann took me on a tour around London and I was able to get my bearings okay. We visited an old time museum village that showed the buildings of yesteryear. It was fascinating to see how the former settlers had lived and the farm implements that were on show – similar to those used in the past in England. There were a variety of carts for carrying harvested crops plus anything else that required. In the houses were also relics of past days, cooking utensils, open ranges for cooking and heating, spinning wheels, tables and chairs and a host of other examples of a bygone age such as printing machines and even an organ that was pumped with air by foot pedals. But most interesting to me were the vehicles. These were old-fashioned open coaches of all sizes mounted on skis for winter and were pulled by horses. There were also larger closed coaches, open landaus, and gigs for warmer weather. Many of these were highly decorated and no doubt reflected the wealth of the owners. That evening I went with Ann and Murray to meet their friends at a party across the street.

Close friends of the Neilsons were Jim and June Morant who lived across the road. Jim, who worked on the railway, was the number one engine driver in the area. When we arrived at the party I was introduced to him and I mentioned our family connection with the 'Stirling Single' engine that my great grandfather, George Sewell, also the number one engine driver of his day, had driven in the 1870s on the railway line that ran from London to York. Jim was most intrigued. He promptly offered to show me the recently delivered high-speed train that was to due to go into service between London and Toronto. This train was to be the Canadian Railway's 'flagship' and Jim was to be the first driver. I was delighted to go with him - particularly as my ancestral family had worked on the railways in England for so many years – virtually since steam trains had become such a major part of transport in Britain as a whole. Prior to that of course, few people travelled far from the towns or villages where they had been born. Those who could afford to do had to go on horseback or by coach and so faced a variety of dangers – not least from highwaymen who robbed at gun point and sometimes even killing passengers, guards and drivers.

There was to be a handing over ceremony the next morning so I went with Jim. An official photo was taken with him in front of the train at the ceremony. However, unknown to us, we were also photographed by a London Press photographer while looking at the train and the picture appeared in the local newspapers. I remember the fuss when we arrived home that evening! I recall one remark made to me by my cousin. "We've been here for several years and never got a mention. You arrive and are emblazoned on the front page two days after you get here!" Family jealousies abounded in no time!

The sequel to this story is that Jim actually took me with him to Toronto on a train he was driving and we spent an enjoyable lunchtime at the York Hotel where engine drivers were permitted to stay. I stayed on for a couple of days sightseeing at a small hotel nearby. There was so much to see and I visited the famous CN Tower, the Eaton Square Shopping Mall and the Science Museum. Chief amongst the many   exhibits was an American Space Capsule. There was a variety of old cars and even the framework of an old aeroplane, together with various hands-on gadgets for young and old alike to experiment with – great fun! I also walked through Toronto's Chinatown, first visiting the market and then passing through what turned out to be the 'Red Light' district. It was not a place to tarry, as there were some shady looking and aggressive characters around. At one point a guy whose eyes were like pinpoints spoke me to. He was obviously a drug taker and, as he attempted to keep my attention, another man tried to move in close behind me. I noticed this. Fortunately I saw a man in uniform nearby and ran quickly towards him. I did not stop! The two druggies disappeared quickly – and so did I, straight back into the main shopping area – not an experience to be repeated! I later met up with Jim again at the York Hotel. While I was waiting in the railwaymen's rest room at the Hotel I experienced at first hand quite a remarkable insight into human nature. We had heard on the radio before we left London for Toronto that there was to be a three-day lightning strike of air traffic controllers in America. It had started on the day that I was due to travel back with Jim to London on the train.   Inevitably there were many holidaymakers from the States who were staying in or passing through Toronto As this was the main Airport through which people into and out of the state of Ontario, there were a lot of extremely frustrated passengers who could not fly to destinations in America. I heard something of a commotion in the main hall as I came down the stairs. The reception desk was absolutely besieged by people that I presume must have been fairly rich – one does not stay at the York Hotel otherwise – it is very upmarket and rooms are expensive. They were Americans and the way in which they behaved had to be seen to be believed – pushing each other out of the way in their attempts to get to speak to the receptionist who had already had to summon some assistance to try and cope. It was entirely the women who were doing the shouting and a lot of them were fat to say the least! The henpecked husbands seemed to be somewhat smaller in girth than their spouses and were laden with luggage. There were too few porters on duty to cope. Eventually the police were called and the arguments started again with them but they soon calmed things down and eventually the lucky ones got rooms for the night. Whatever happened to the poor beggars who had to look elsewhere I do not know but I had only heard that Americans tended to be brash – now I knew for sure that some certainly were! Eventually Jim arrived so we left for the station and returned to London. That was quite a trip!

Murray had arranged to take a fortnight's holiday while I was with them. First we played a couple of rounds of golf at the local 'Twin Streams' Golf Club on the outskirts of the city. Then the whole family and I motored through the rolling plains of wheat and barley – other crops too – to a cottage at Point Clarke, situated in a wood near the shores of Lake Huron, first passing through several one street settlements. These seemed to consist of a Main Store and a Pub, plus a few buildings where the inhabitants lived. We saw a factory of sorts in one place where the locals must have eked out a living. I guess everyone else must have worked on the land for there appeared to be little else anywhere apart from the occasional garage with an eating-place nearby. It was all very remote too. There was very little traffic and I remember thinking that if there was a breakdown it could be a while before anybody appeared to help! We spent an idyllic 10 days playing golf at the Goderich Golf Club, fishing, having family fun together, swimming and sunbathing on the beach. We even saw fish caught in a net that was physically trawled by locals off the shore and out in to the Lake. It was extraordinary to see how many fish were caught in this fashion. I fished from off the shore but bites were few and far between. It did not matter in the least. I met a delightful couple on the beach one day. They were going round the Lake in a canoe. They said that this would apparently take them a very long time – about a month! Everything was so laid back that I was able to relax and unwind completely and was only sorry when it was time to return to their home.

My next port of call was to stay with my cousin Gilbert and Vera - known as Gil and Viv to everyone - at their house. They had come to live in Canada in 1975 and had stayed on permanently. There was so much to talk about and we had a lot of catching up to do. While I was staying with them I was able to meet their son Anthony. He was considering joining the Canadian Army. He is 23 years younger than his sister Ann. She was born in January 1942 at Parkstone, Dorset. Anthony was born at Bovingdon, Dorset in December 1965. Bovingdon is where tank drivers were trained before, during and after the Second World War. Gilbert was in charge of security there until 1975. Prior to that he had joined the War Department Police in 1946 and had served in Cyprus. Then he joined the Corps of Commissionaires when he arrived in Canada and later worked as Courthouse Security in the local Court in London. Ann took us all to see Niagara Falls, which is on the border between Canada and the United States. This was a truly magnificent sight, very impressive from the Canadian side. How anybody is supposed to have survived in a barrel I shall never know – the cascade of water was absolutely awesome. Even seeing boats going out to the base of the Falls seemed to me fraught with danger but obviously it appealed to the braver souls – a wet business though!

I returned to Ann's for a couple of days before setting off for home. I went by minibus to Toronto Airport and saw the dawn come up while flying back to Heath Row and home to Leeds – a magnificent sight. I arranged to go for a trip to France in the August school holiday with a female colleague, Mary Nevill, Head Teacher at Rodley Primary School. I had known her for several years. She had never been to the continent. It seemed a good opportunity for me to have a holiday and, at the same time it would prevent me from brooding about what had happened at home during the past few months. As I've already mentioned it transpired Molly could not move out in July because of a problem with her flat – it required roof repairs. No doubt thinking that she would have moved out, she had already made her own holiday arrangements without reference to me.

Mary owned a British Leyland 'Mini' and we decide to use that for the holiday in France. We shared the driving to Dover and crossed by ferry to Calais. We motored along the coast for a while through Boulogne, Abbeville and Dieppe, staying at small hotels for three days. Dieppe was particularly interesting. On the beach were ornate tents hired by the owners of many of the boats there. There was even waiter service. I have never seen drinks served like that on a beach before – or since! As Mary spoke no French I sorted out everything that we required and I also drove most of the time as of course driving had to be done on the opposite side of the road from England. She did try once but found it taxing and elected not to continue. We turned inland after a while, visiting Rouen, before turning westwards again to Harfleur, where the rich and famous have their yachts and other seagoing vessels in the beautiful harbour. We then proceeded along the east coast, where the D Day landings took place in 1944. One could still see traces of the conflict and there were memorials in many French villages. We continued on to my cousin Daphne's cottage, in the Cherbourg Peninsular. The cottage is situated near the east coast, about 10 kilometres south east of Cartaret, using that as our base for the next three days. Cartaret is the main port where crossings are made from France to the Channel Islands. One day we drove to Mont St Michel – a truly remarkable place set in the sea with just one road to link up with the mainland. The main feature is the famous Monastery that towers above the rest of the buildings. We also went for a short flight over the area – very picturesque. We also visited Carentan and Bayeux. We saw the famous Bayeux Tapestry. Our journey home was from Cherbourg. Unfortunately Mary did not enjoy that much as she found out the hard way that she is not a good sailor! However it was an enjoyable trip and we saw plenty of the Normandy coast as well as the Cherbourg Peninsular. On my return home we started what was a very sad period for both Molly and myself. However we survived it and I did everything I could to try and persuade her to change her mind. But, as I said earlier, she had made her decision and she left on April 7th 1983.

I got the Staff together at St Margaret's and told them what had happened. I asked them not to talk to me about it. They respected that but nevertheless several of the ladies came up with cooking tips for me! It is a strange fact, but because I had been brought up to believe that marriage was entered into for life, I felt ashamed about what had happened and took much of the blame myself. I even seriously considered resigning as I reasoned that if I could not run my own life successfully how could I expect to set an example to young people? But a chance meeting of several parents who had attended a party and had spoken to someone who knew of our coming break up had a significant effect on my thinking. As I had told no one but the staff I was completely unprepared for what happened. A parent, who was a senior Police Inspector and a member of the PTA Committee, called in before school started, on his way to work. He told me what he had heard at a party and in the same breath said that under no circumstances should I even consider resigning. He obviously understood me better than I did myself! He told me that friends who were there had discussed it and they had decided that I might think that offering my resignation would be the correct thing to do in the circumstances. Apparently by chance among those present was a married couple that I had helped at some point - he refused to say who they were - when they themselves were in a particularly difficult situation appertaining to their own marriage and they felt that my experience had actually enabled me to give them the right advice. The Vicar also refused to hear of resignation either. At least I felt that I had some sound advice worth listening to and so that was that.

The thing that amazed me most after I had come to terms with what had happened was that a number of friends seemed to come 'out of the woodwork'. I received several invitations to go out for meals and to visit people and this certainly boosted my self-confidence. I remember one occasion, when Philip was learning to drive, that he drove me up to the top of Sutton Bank in my old Saab in mid April and we stopped to see the view. We saw Sheila Scatchard, a head teacher colleague, and her husband John. They were taking a party of schoolchildren along to the aerodrome on the hilltop to see the gliders flying. They invited me to a meal the following week. I duly went and we became friends. I was also invited out to make up foursomes at dinner parties on several occasions and all these events helped me to begin life as a single person and feel less lonely. It made me realise that there were so many other people in similar situations to mine. I was once taken along to an evening with people who had joined 'NEXUS' – a club that catered for men and women who were separated and living on their own. It was interesting but not really my cup of tea.

I immersed myself in work during the rest of that summer term, but I knew that my health was deteriorating. One day in early June I was invited by Mary Nevill to a fancy dress party. I do not recall just who I was meant to be but it so happened that I wore shorts for the occasion. During the afternoon Mary, amongst others, happened to notice that my right leg was bleeding and mentioned it to me. I noticed that it appeared to be a mole that was bleeding. I was advised to see a doctor to have it checked out but I was very busy at work and did not do so immediately. Mary rang me several times and eventually I fixed an appointment. Dr Lawson asked for an appointment to be made at the LGI but there was the inevitable delay and I heard nothing until August 1st. By this time I had been invited by Barbara and Roy Thompson to join them for a fortnight's holiday at a couple of 'gites' in France – the second 'gite' being in the Dordogne. I was also due to drive from there to a small seaside village in Brittany to meet up with a large party of friends including

Mary – a long trip. Literally twenty minutes before I left home the appointment had been delivered through my letterbox. I immediately called the hospital and asked for another appointment to be made later on as I could not keep that one. Barbara and Roy had left for France two days previously and I was due to meet them at the 'gite'. There was no way to contact them – mobiles weren't an option then – so I felt I had to go. A crossing was booked from Dover to Calais and, having made all the arrangements, I set off. I had a great time with Barbara and Roy, then drove through the night up into the Brittany area. I had to stop around 5am as there was some early morning fog. I slept in the car until around 8am and then drove on into a small village. The thought of a warm croissant and a large cup of french coffee spurred me on. I stopped at the French equivalent of a café-cum-bar, having first purchased a croissant and the 'patron' served me with a delicious cup of coffee. In the place there were two men drinking French beer. As I finished my coffee another cup mysteriously appeared and the two men smiled. They had sent it over to me. I replied with a couple of beers for them and before long I had joined them for what turned out to be a hilarious hour – at least it was until I mentioned something about French people. One immediately said that he was Spanish and the other stated unequivocally that he was a Breton, not French. He did not even like the French! Eventually I asked them the way to the village of PLUINEC that I thought was close by. That was a big mistake as they thought I was looking for a large French seaside resort called PLUHINEC - a name similar to the place I was due to go to. I guess my pronunciation gave the wrong impression! There was only one letter different in the name. They directed me some 70 kilometres up the coast before I found out that I had arrived at the wrong place! Luckily I eventually found someone who knew of the village I wanted and he sent me back to within 5 kilometres of the place where I had had my coffee and croissant. I stayed for three days with the party. The highlight of my stay was when all 14 of us went to a 'bistro' and partook of a lovely French meal and several bottles of wine. Driving back to our 'billets' was somewhat erratic but fortunately without incident! I intended to drive back through France to Calais, as my passage was booked on the ferry there. Mary reminded me that she was a bad sailor and so wanted to take the shortest possible crossing back to England. Her friends suggested she should return via Calais with me. One of her sons agreed to drive her car back home via St Malo – the port through which the party had entered France. I was happy to agree to the idea. We spent several days on the journey and on the way through the Loire valley called in to see four superb chateaux - Saumur, Villandry, Amboise and Chenonceau - talk about seeing how the 'other half' lived!

However, before we left the patron of the holiday 'billets' where we had all been staying invited us to share a bottle of wine with him. He turned out to be a fascinating character! He was short in stature but a giant in deeds. He was a member of the wartime resistance group in his area. He told us, amongst other stories, how during 1944, a large German Army group that had been based in Brittany for a while had been ordered back to the Cherburg area where the D Day landings had taken place. He was part of the secret resistance army that had been organised to fight when the time came, and it was decided that this was the time to mobilise and try to stop troop movements across a river that ran across much of Brittany. The way he told his story was hilarious! He had been ordered at a moment's notice in the early hours of the morning to go to a pre-arranged spot on the riverbank where all the other resistance fighters were gathering. As he said, he took his croissant, a loaf of bread, a flask of coffee – and his rifle. When he arrived he was sent to watch out for signs of enemy troops at a spot where the river narrowed and a crossing could be attempted. No sooner had he started to eat his breakfast than they came to the riverbank opposite, with inflatable craft, ready to cross the river. Thoroughly intrigued, I asked him what he did and his reply was the perfect understatement of all time. "We shot wiss our rifles", he said in his anglicised, heavily accented way, "and after a while zee enemy run". "What happened then?" I inquired, utterly absorbed by this lovely man. "Monsieur", he smiled, "I sit down 'encore', open my flask, drink my 'café' and finish 'mon repas'. I was 'ungry!'" It was so incredibly understated that we were both highly impressed and at the same time equally amused! He showed us his old rifle, then he produced a sort of French flute, a bit like a school recorder, and he played the most beautiful and haunting melodies for us for about half an hour. It was such a wonderful experience to meet such a true and, at the same time, such a modest hero. Apparently the German army was held up for several hours during which time the Allied Armies landed along the coast around Cherbourg. The action he and his comrades took that day must have saved many lives. It was with great reluctance that we eventually left him and set off on our journey to Calais.

On returning home I went, as usual, with Roy Thompson up to Portpatrick at the end of August for four days golf prior to the commencement of the Autumn Term. This was an arrangement that we had carried out regularly for several years.

During the first week back at School I received a further appointment through the post for September 12th to see a Surgeon by the name of Mr Browning. Dr Lawson indicated to me that he would remove what I assumed was simply a troublesome wart on my right calf. By now it was quite a dark colour and had spread somewhat. Nevertheless I was completely unprepared for his diagnosis. He examined the wart carefully, made a simple test, removing a small section for analysis. He then told me that it was a melanoma and that it was malignant. It was imperative that it be removed immediately and he also asked why I had not got to him earlier. I told him of the circumstances leading to the cancellation of my initial appointment – arranged holiday etc. He then asked me if I had any objection to students being brought in to see the melanoma on the following day, in which case would I return the next morning? I replied in the affirmative. He warned me that it would possibly be some time before I would be able to return to my post as Head Teacher and advised me to arrange for someone to take over in my stead after I had seen him again the following day. I was quite shocked to realise that I had a form of malignant cancer, but he led me to understand that it could be removed. I arrived the following morning and went straight to a ward where the students were due to appear. When they all arrived Mr Browning, who was conducting some form of lecture, completely ignored me after saying good morning. He the proceeded to show the students the melanoma, saying – and I quote –

"This is the perfect example of a fully grown melanoma. Now in order to remove it we must operate as soon as possible". He then looked at me and continued, "You are a Headmaster. You have three days left this week to sort out your school and get someone in charge for at least three months. Then get yourself to this hospital next Monday morning. If no beds are available and you are told to go home, refuse outright. Use your Headmaster's voice and refer them to me. It is essential that I operate at the earliest possible moment. That will be next Tuesday morning, September 19th". Without further ado he ushered the students out. Then he nipped back into the ward and reassured me that come hell or high water he would operate. He further told me that not much was yet known about melanomas in this country but that he was in over all charge of the research being carried out and that people might be calling in from time to time to talk to me as part of their research. There would also be more students so I should now recall what it was like to be quizzed when I was a boy! He laughed about it and from then on I knew that at least I was in capable hands, but I was badly shaken.

As soon as I got back to St Margaret's I started sorting things out. First of all I refused to have anyone from outside the School to take over. This caused the Education Department concerned to break sweat but I was determined to have one of my own staff that I could trust to carry on running the place the way I required. After two days wrangling I got my way and Mrs Hill, my Acting Temporary Deputy Head, was given permission to take over as Acting Head. So that was that. I had one other function to fulfil over the weekend and that was to attend a running match against another school. I was not feeling too well when I went and one of the mother's came up to me and offered to fetch a cup of tea. This was very significant as it happened. One of her sons had been taken to hospital in the same week and had also been diagnosed with a form of cancer. I broke my own resolve to say nothing to anyone about what had happened. I told her that I would be away for a while and told her why. She was the same lady that I had helped not long before when she came into school after she had been knocked about by her husband who had subsequently left her. For years after I had retired I still enquired as to the boy's health. He never made a full recovery I'm afraid, but I never forgot about him.

Chapter 3 Dark days

I arrived on Monday morning, as I have already said elsewhere, courtesy of the staff.The operation was duly performed and I was ensconced in bed while post operative treatment was carried out.

One morning, about three days after my operation, Mr Browning came to see me once more. As my leg was encased in plaster he simply asked if I was ok. After a brief chat about how things would be during my recovery period he suddenly said, "I want more help with the students. I am bringing them round shortly and I want to try a different approach. You are a teacher and ideal for the job so I have brought some questions I want you to study and then ask the students". "Fine", I replied, "but I shan't know the answers". "Doesn't matter", he stated. "I will just listen to what they say to you. Look wise, and then I will discuss their answers with them. It will depend on how confident you appear to be as to whether this will be a success". This was interesting! I duly studied what I was required to ask. I hadn't a clue what some words meant, but afterwards he reckoned that was the most useful part. "You did not know and they did not know either", he laughed. "So you could not explain and they had to think for themselves". The man was a psychologist as well as a surgeon, I reckon! Anyway I soon learned just what was required and as the various sets of students appeared I was able to trot out the questions on queue. The aftermath was quite surprising. Some of the students would look in as they were passing and so I got even more visitors. It was great psychology on Mr Browning's part and good fun for me as well. It certainly stopped me getting bored!

As I mentioned previously I had to have a second operation 3 weeks later. Something had gone seriously wrong and it was decided that the plaster had been put on incorrectly as well – it was much too tight. In fact, when I had had the first operation the two staff nurses who normally specialised in carrying out plaster cast work for Mr Browning after he had operated both happened to be on leave. I knew one of them, and when they returned to work both came to see me. During the conversation I was asked if I was in any pain. Not surprisingly I answered that I was and showed them the plaster as they requested. They were concerned and immediately fetched a plaster cutting implement to slit the plaster. Incredibly the pain then virtually stopped. It was decided that the wound should simply be treated each day and bandaged firmly in the hope that the first skin graft would take. Unfortunately it didn't and the decision was made to carry out a further skin graft. Mr Browning was not pleased, and apologised, at the same time explaining what needed to be done. The second graft operation was harder to take than the first as this time I knew just what I would have to put up with. On my return to the ward the inevitable drain tubes and temporary wiring to monitor my heartbeat etc. were being fitted by the nurses when I became a nuisance by 'coming round' from the anaesthetic too soon. I was about to be injected again but I objected to that, saying I would prefer to put up with any pain that I might consequently feel. I asked if I could simply listen to what I thought would be music on the radio through earphones instead. So that's what happened. But there was no music. Instead a rugby league match was being broadcast at the time. I listened on and off as I was still feeling quite woozy, but I got the name of the broadcaster, **John Herbert**, into my head. I vowed to find him after I'd recovered in order to thank him. He had done me a fantastic service without knowing it and I was most grateful. I did track him down some time later after I came out of hospital and we had a pint or two together. We also became friends – a real bonus. That was how I first heard about the Hospital Relay Broadcasting Service. I felt that I might be able to help and as soon as I was fit enough I joined the cricket commentary team, courtesy of another ex Headmaster, John Rex. I soon realised that I had some talent for describing in reasonable detail the game that I had enjoyed playing for so long, and I have been commentating from Headingley Grandstand on all kinds of cricket matches ever since.

But recovery after such a serious operation was a slow, painstaking business. I had seen the wound several times during treatment – in fact on one occasion I could virtually see down to the bone – apparently the cancer cells had developed to the point where they might have got into my actual bone structure. It was to be a long time before I was declared to be completely free of malignant cancer.

Once I had managed to prove a point by actually walking out of the ward (mentioned earlier) using two sticks, I had to attend the hospital every few days for starters in order to have treatment that would eventually help the blood to flow freely down the veins in my leg to my right foot. When the dressings were eventually removed I realised that I had had a lot of my upper calf removed and there was an ugly looking scar and a piece out of my leg – a bit like a slice of meat. I also had to have a sort of foot to hip length canvas 'sock' on my leg. This could be blown up in such a way that the pressure forced the blood to go through the veins down from my body to the toes in my right foot. The pain was excruciating for a time and I must admit I dreaded it each time I went. But gradually the pain eased and I began to walk properly using only one stick. Then I got as far as walking without a stick and I knew that things were on the mend. I never let things get me down although it was hard work living on my own. Friends were very good, particularly Mary Nevill and Sheila Scatchard. They would do my shopping for me. Mary had her own life to lead as she was by this time divorced and her family and friends, several of whom I had met, were supportive and naturally wanted to help her with her own problems. I started going out for Sunday lunches at the Scatchards and I frequently went to the Moortown Rugby Club with them. I became a member for a time. I also went to the Adel Memorial Hall where I had already been a member for many years, starting in 1964, during my cricket playing days. My former School-Staffing Officer by the name of Barbara Wemyss called by once or twice and later invited me out for meals from time to time. With other friends who dropped by to see me I was rarely lonely. But I had of necessity to see Dr Lawson quite frequently and he was a great help with medication and the like. I kept on asking him when I could return to my job as Head at St Margaret's but there was no way that either Dr Lawson or Mr Browning would even consider it. It was silly of me really, but I wanted to get back into harness, as I loved working at the School. One day in a fit of frustration, after having asked Dr Lawson once again about when I could return, I politely said to him, "I might as well be retired as keep asking you". He immediately rang Mr Browning (he told me this afterwards) and told him what I had said. The next time I went to the hospital for my check up Mr Browning broached the subject of retirement. When I demurred he told me plainly that though my mind would be fine my body would not stand up to the stresses and demands of the job. He further suggested that if I returned it would undo all they were trying to do for me and the consequences would be very serious. He even intimated that I could be dead within three years. That was a nasty shock! I at last realised that I had been a bit of a guinea pig in terms of the research that had taken place in my case. They had taken lots of case notes which I was informed had been invaluable, but I was at risk and stress could be my downfall. I was shaken to the core, but in the end I had to accept that this was the case, and so for me the end of my career was in sight. I accepted the inevitable reluctantly, but I hope, gracefully. I got one small concession – I could return for the second half of the summer term in 1984 to clear up and make a normal exit. I would retire officially in August. I refused to be classed as disabled although apparently I could have been. I chose to retire normally - like most people. Actually it cost me money over the years, as I did not receive a full pension although I was given enhancement that took me to within 95 days of that. But at the time it was the way I wanted things and I have never regretted my decision. I came to realise that, although I appeared all right it was feared that if I were to be put under any stress the cancer would return and that would be that. Maybe today with all the research that has taken place in the world there might have been another path to be trodden. But the dangers were there and the troubles that have accrued, particularly in countries like Australia and New Zealand, due to the gap in the ozone layer that allows harmful radiation rays to penetrate the skin if there is over exposure, make me realise how lucky I have ultimately been. Melanomas are commonplace now in hot countries and research is still in progress. I was warned never to sunbathe, and always to keep my arms, legs, and head covered when out in the sun.

I suppose that what I saw at the time as a disaster for me in my life was actually the exact opposite and the subsequent freedom from work-related stresses was instrumental in my recovery although it was eight years before I got the all clear. I quickly learned to live with the uncertainty – not knowing how long there might be before the cancer reappeared. I had been warned this could happen, but that if I was still going strong after seven years of 'monitoring' by the specialist Mr Browning and his junior staff, the chances of a full recovery were considerably enhanced. I was advised to take life literally on a day-to-day basis and do whatever took my fancy. As Mr Browning once said, 'There are no rehearsals for living – life is for now'. That was wonderful advice! So, as I have already stated, I retired officially on August 31st 1984, ten days short of my 55th birthday.

CONTENTS

PART 2 September 1st 1984 to April 22nd 2000

SECOND TIME AROUND

PART 2
Autobiographical Memories of my Life
By George Christopher Turner

Second Time Around

Chapter 1 Starting retirement

On the morning of September 1st 1984 it took a while to sink in – I was no longer Headmaster of Horsforth St Margaret's School – in fact I was no longer a Headmaster. That was now in the past and I was technically on the Educational scrap heap! Now what?

My immediate thought was to get away from the area for a few days. In the first place I had never wanted to give up my job but illness had, in one sense, triumphed and it was really a question of coming to terms with life. Once the decision had reluctantly been made to retire I had been advised both by my Specialist, Mr Browning, and my Doctor, Dr Lawson, to go off somewhere and enjoy myself while I could. To quote Mr Browning, - "Go and fulfil whatever ambitions you have had while you were working, Chris – you'll love it!" Well, that one was easy!

I had always said that I wanted to visit my relatives and friends in the Antipodes. So now was my chance. The fact that walking properly was still a bit of a problem did not deter me in the slightest. I had already been to London, Ontario, in Canada for a second time to stay with my first cousin Gilbert's daughter Ann, and her husband Murray, for Christmas 1983 while virtually unable to walk at all. This had given me an insight into the help one could call upon from the Airlines – in this case British Airways, with whom I had arranged to fly. They had been absolutely fantastic. Daphne and Frank Sharman had met me at Kings Cross Station and I stayed with them overnight. They took me to Heath Row where I was transported in a wheel chair to the waiting area, going via the 'Duty Free' shop in order to purchase some presents to take with me for my relatives. When it was time to board the plane I was taken to the flight gate on a sort of electric 'train' – a long chassis mounted on rubber wheels with a row of eight seats facing outwards on either side. There were several other people in need of transport too. We were duly 'delivered' and I was taken to my seat that was an aisle seat in the centre of the plane – a Boeing 747. I had to change planes at Toronto and once again I was met and transported in a wheel chair right through the Airport to await my next flight to London, Ontario. Then things went slightly askew – someone had forgotten to arrange for me to be put on the next plane – one that only carried 20 passengers. In fact they wanted to lift me up to the cabin entrance in a forklift truck! As it was snowing hard I politely declined that offer and set off on my crutches to try and board via the gangway. I got to the bottom of the steps all right but once there I came a cropper. So two cabin-crew members virtually lifted me up into the plane and put me in the seat nearest the door, so all was well. They helped me down to the ground again at London airport where Ann and Murray were waiting for me – journey accomplished!

What a fantastic holiday that was! When I arrived Ann and Murray were kindness itself – nothing was too much trouble. First of all Ann took me round London and we visited the shopping centre, enabling me to buy presents for the family. The goods on offer seemed endless and, with Christmas in the air, everywhere was tastefully decorated for the festive season – shops, streets and the Malls. Their boys, Jamie and Mark, were both at school at that time. 12 year old Jamie was very much into sport, with baseball being his particular forte. Murray went along to help with the coaching out of school hours. Whenever there was a match I went to watch. It gave me an insight into the excellent facilities that were available at many schools in Canada – very impressive. Although he was only 7years old, Mark had a clear idea about what he wanted to do. He was more artistic and extremely interested in art, pictures and film productions. He spent a lot of his time studying photography and learning about the film industry.

The only thing lacking initially before Christmas was an abundance of snow. It was freezing and the roads were often icy. Apparently the temperature was too cold for snow. But because temperatures in winter were so much lower than we get in England the ice was truly firm and several inches deep. Thus the roads, although slippery, were, paradoxically, safer to drive on and the pavements were treated with salt and thus free of ice. There were literally mountains of road salt everywhere and everyone used it to good effect. It was still a problem for me as I initially had to use crutches to get about, but with every day I became stronger and could go for short walks near their house. Ironic really, as I was able to go out and about despite the bitter cold with temperatures often more than 20 degrees below zero, whereas locals found it virtually impossible to do so without dressing up in very warm clothing such as furs and the like – particularly where toes, fingertips and ears were concerned! This was because in summer temperatures are very high in Canada and as a result blood is thinner for people living in Ontario than it is for folk in England. But overnight, about five days before the festive Christmas holiday celebrations the temperature rose sufficiently and several feet of snow fell. We literally had to dig our way out. Neighbours appeared in the street and in no time people were getting together to help each other. Cups of tea appeared miraculously and I met several of the Neilsons' neighbours. There were parties too when the paths were cleared. The Christmas spirit had arrived - both out in the street and afterwards in beer mugs and wine glasses – overnight! The family celebrations were most enjoyable and Murray took me on two occasions to parties that he held on Fridays nights most weeks at his office. These were certainly different – solicitors, clients and ex-clients called in. As Murray was a Criminal Lawyer, and the youngest QC in the state of Ontario at the time, he was much in demand among what he termed as the less salubrious section of the population in London. I met all sorts of interesting people. One never knew if one was talking to one of Murray's colleagues from the law courts or to someone he had recently defended in the dock – almost everyone seemed to be wearing jeans! I thoroughly enjoyed the experience – it was what must have been almost a unique opportunity in one's life and it gave me some inkling into the attitudes of people who were in effect law-breakers. Having been so interested in criminology in my earlier days when I was at College – I once wrote a 10,000 word thesis about Crime and the Prison Service – I truly relished rubbing shoulders with a few of London's Canadian underworld at first hand. That was quite an experience! Murray was a 'dyed in the wool' fan of ice hockey. On every occasion that there was a match we went to watch. As it happened I was an essential part of these outings. Murray had severely injured his ankle and could not drive. I could drive, but not walk far, so I chauffeured him around on numerous occasions. I was also able to borrow Ann's car in order to visit her parents Vera (Viv to me) and Gilbert. Gil, who was over 14 years older than I, was my first cousin. He had been in the army since the age of 14 – put there in England in 1929 by his father Harry and his stepmother, who had been less than kind to him. They wanted him out of the way – a sad story that I had already learned about from my parents when I was in my teens. I met Gilbert for the first time when I was in my early twenties and we got on famously. My Mother and Father took a real interest in him too. I clearly remember the day that we first met when he visited our home at the Vicarage of the Parish of St Mary's Church, Far Cotton, Northampton. He brought his wife Viv and daughter Ann – then just 14 years old - to see us. He and I went out for a walk together and happened to meet Michael Robinson, the Curate who worked under my Father's auspices in the Parish. Casually I introduced Gil to him, saying, "Michael, this is my cousin Gilbert". I was amazed to see tears in Gil's eyes and afterwards, a bit embarrassed, I asked what was wrong. "That is the first time I have ever been referred to as a relative in the family", he replied. I have never forgotten that. It made me realise the importance of happy relationships in any family – something we so often just take for granted. I also recall Ann's excitement when she saw my motorbike, and inevitably at her request we went out for a ride!

While staying with the Neilson family I did two things of great significance. First, I made great strides towards walking properly again. Second, I gave up smoking. It was not until around the time of my cancer operation that medical proof had been found that smoking could cause serious damage to health. The first thing I noticed when I arrived at the Neilsons was a glass with wet cigarette ends in. There were pictures of affected lungs, and notices pinned up in various rooms too. One in particular on the fridge door caught my eye. It read, 'NO ONE EVER DIED FROM STOPPING SMOKING!' I asked Murray what that was about and he told me that he fully intended to stop smoking as he had become aware of the dangers. He further told me that he had consulted an expert who had given him all sorts of help and then actually charged him 175 Canadian dollars. That was worth £100 in our money. I resolved to give up immediately for free and never to smoke another cigarette again. What's more, I have never done so since!

I returned home towards the end of January 1984 after a wonderful holiday with my lovely relatives. Thanks to them I had made good progress towards recovery. When I was going through Toronto Airport on my way home I still had a packet with thirteen cigarettes in. I threw the packet in a bin. Before I got out of sight a 'down and out' tramp took the packet out of the bin, lit one, and put the rest in his pocket. He must have thought all his Christmases had come at once! As I've already said, I have never smoked a cigarette, cigar or pipe again and I even tried very hard to persuade others to give up. Mind you, it is often said that the true convert is usually the worst nuisance!

However, returning to my retirement, first things first – I wanted to be out of Leeds when children returned to school after the summer holidays on September 3rd 1984. I suggested to Jack Edmondson, a former Adel Cricket Club team-mate and subsequently a close friend, that we could fulfil a mutual ambition and go to Scarborough Cricket Festival.

One acquaintance of mine, whose child had attended St Margaret's School, was a top official at Wallace Arnold's Bus Company. I contacted him and he kindly arranged for us to stay at a boarding house situated very near the cricket ground at Scarborough. It was the one used by the Company for their drivers who stayed overnight during the Festival. It was quite luxurious so we were lucky. It also meant that I had only a short distance to go to get into the ground – on my two sticks. In fact people put themselves out to see that I was looked after, both at the digs and at the cricket ground. The weather was warm and quite sunny, and the three days of cricket that we saw was excellent, so really it was the perfect way to start early retirement!

O
n my return home I immediately set about the task of arranging my first trip to the Antipodes. My mindset was such that the fact that funds were rather limited became comparatively irrelevant – I was going to live life to the full! I noted that Garuda Airlines offered the cheapest flights to Australia and New Zealand. They are based in Jakarta, Indonesia. I wanted to see as much as possible while on the way and their flight to Australia made several stops en route. I finally made arrangements to set off from England in early November, having arranged to spend time with the Tysons in Melbourne before flying on to stay with my cousin Dorothy and her husband Ken at Linden-Tawa, near Wellington, in New Zealand. I was to be with them for Christmas. In the meantime I had continued to work very hard to learn to walk properly again so that I would be mobile enough to get around. It is surprising how quickly one improves, given the right motivation. I made a point of going for walks every day. I used to take Joss - a black Labrador belonging to Sheila Scatchard - with me whenever I could in order to ensure that both he and I got plenty of exercise. I spent much time throwing a ball for him, particularly around Golden Acre Park. There were plenty of seats in the park so if I needed a rest I could sit down and that was ideal. I also had physiotherapy sessions twice a week and further augmented this with the know-how I had learned about keeping fit from my days spent in the gymnasium at College. Over the years I had run several 'keep fit' classes. Now I used the exercises on my own path to recovery.

Chapter 2 My Great Adventure

The start of my 'great adventure' was low key. Philip drove me down to stay at Sunbury on Thames with my cousin Daphne Sharman and her husband Frank overnight. Early the next morning they drove me to nearby Heath Row Airport's Terminal 3 where my baggage was checked in. We said our goodbyes and I went to the 'Duty Free' area to purchase a few gifts to take with me.

I had booked a seat on the front row of the side aisle near the door of the massive Boeing 747 'Jumbo' jet so I had plenty of room to stretch my legs and walk about the plane. I had been given strict instructions to keep walking about every hour to avoid the problem of Deep Vein Thrombosis (DVT) – a blood clot which can form if one sits still too long after an operation without taking exercise. It was surprising how far it was just walking up one aisle of the plane and back down the opposite one! After quite a long flight, during which we were served with two meals, we stopped at Abu Dhabi for a couple of hours. The terminal building looked ordinary from the outside but was shaped like a massive green-coloured mushroom on the
inside – very picturesque. There were plenty of shops too – laden with tempting goods at reasonable prices. I enjoyed wandering around – everything seemed different somehow – the Arab clothing, the water fountains, and the general impression of opulence wherever one went. Even the toilets had gold door handles and the washbasins sported gold taps! Above all the whole place was spotless. There were no queues of frustrated travellers waiting to check in and get rid of their luggage – no hustle and bustle – and there was so much space. Seating in the air-conditioned waiting area was clean and comfortable and even the announcements could be clearly heard. For an airport it was idyllic.

We eventually boarded the Jumbo to continue the next leg of our journey. Looking out of the window of the plane one could see the runway stretching out into what appeared as a sandy plain – a sharp contrast to the magnificent terminal building we had just vacated. As we took off there was a heat haze hanging over the desert. Climbing away from the airport one could see tall buildings and the roads leading out of the city into the desert – like lengthy strips of dark ribbon lying across the endless sandy landscape.

As we climbed high into the sky it was fascinating to look out of the plane at the clouds. One got the illusion that it would be possible to walk on them – a bit like being at the North Pole!

Jakarta was the next port of call and it was dreadful – a complete contrast to Abu Dhabi. We left the plane and proceeded to a waiting lounge. As we had a scheduled wait of seven hours there was a lot of time to fill. I had hoped to have a sleep but it was far too humid. A new Airport was being constructed. The air-cooling system in the old building into which we were taken had broken down but was not being mended for obvious reasons, and the temperature was 110 degrees even with the windows open! It was too hot to go outside either. Eventually, after four hours, we managed to get a transfer to the next waiting area in preparation for the next section of our journey – to Singapore – and fortunately there the air-cooling system was in place. I ventured outside briefly, but even in the shade it was uncomfortable.

Eventually we took off again and landed in Singapore. A new Airport had just recently been completed and so everything was right up to date. I was able to have a cool shower there and felt human again – absolute bliss! The shops were well stocked and there was plenty on show to tempt travellers to spend their money. The eating areas were very clean and to me it seemed almost clinical. There were a few policemen with guns wandering around, but the worst thing I saw was a passenger who had thrown down a sweet paper being made to pick it up by a policeman. Apparently even the dropping of litter was considered a serious breach of the peace! It certainly seemed so as everywhere was so clinically clean, rather like being in dentist's waiting room – a vast difference from the untidy state of the Terminal Building at Heath Row! Our stopover lasted about three hours and was very pleasant too.

Next we flew to Bali. It was midnight by this time but it was still very hot. I stood at the top of the exit steps and the sweat was running down my face. It was quite possible to see round about – the airport itself was bathed in light and further afield one could make out what must have been thatch-roofed holiday huts leading to a beach nearby. The heat was much dryer than in Jakarta and as such not too unpleasant. Most of those joining our flight were Australians returning from holidays in Bali and its surrounding environs. Once everybody had settled in their seats the pilot warned us that there could well be some turbulence ahead on the final leg of the flight so seat belts should be kept fastened. We took off again and, in no time it seemed, we were flying round the edge of a storm. Lightning was flashing from one cloud to another – an incredible sight. The lightning looked pink and the inside of the cabin was lit up with a reddish tint for several seconds at a time. It was truly awesome and made one realise just how incredibly tiny and   insignificant we were! The plane shook and shuddered quite a bit, and on occasions we hit air pockets and fell through the air so to speak – like descending quickly in a lift. But as we had already been advised that it was necessary to keep our seatbelts on it wasn't too bad, although sometimes one's stomach felt as if it had been left behind! Eventually we bypassed the worst of the storm and the turbulence subsided. By this time dawn was breaking and breakfast was served. From a cabin window the sight of the jet engines driving us through the sky was very reassuring. Crossing the Australian coast, we flew over the deserts that make up much of the Northern Territory and Western Australia. This was another awe-inspiring sight. There was an occasional 'ribbon' of track or road to be seen, but otherwise it appeared uninhabited - apart from a very small cluster of buildings every now and again. These looked to be little more than pin pricks on a map – a truly amazing sight. However one could clearly see Ayers Rock - a huge mound standing out from the flat lands round about – and the town of Alice Springs, looking like a series of tiny white dots in a cluster with a narrow ribbon of road leading out from either side of the town.

It had taken some five hours to cross the Australian Continent. In the Airport lounge I had my first taste of Aussie beer, courtesy of a fellow Australian traveller who had joined us at Bali. Needless to say I returned the compliment. With a couple of hours to kill, we had 'downed' several more 'tinnies' and quite an impromptu party had taken place with other passengers joining us. There was a lot of leg-pulling so it was a great introduction to 'Ockers' for a 'Pom!' So the last leg of our journey to Melbourne was, to say the least, quite noisy!

With all the stopovers it had taken 38 hours from Heath Row to Melbourne. But it had been interesting, particularly as I had been able to see quite a lot at every place we had touched down. I must say that the various members of the aircrew with whom I came into contact were very helpful and nothing was too much trouble. The food was tasty too, with a comprehensive choice of dishes, considering the number of passengers to be served. Furthermore smoking was not permitted so the air in the cabin remained quite fresh. All in all it was an impressive journey made even better by the onboard entertainment – music of all kinds and comic shows too. There was a television screen at the front of the cabin for adverts and films to be shown. It also kept us informed as to where we were, how high we were flying, and how far we were from our destination – in fact there were so many relevant facts appertaining to the flight – temperature, speed, weather reports and places we were flying over that it was like a comprehensive geography lesson!

On arrival at Tullamarine Airport, after a delay getting through customs, I was met by Urs and Frank Tyson. The Airport is about 10 kilometres outside the city of Melbourne. Again, the facilities for parking are excellent and there was certainly plenty to see as we drove into the city.

On arrival at the Frank's house more celebrations followed – another party - and eventually I fell asleep in a chair half way through yet another glass of wine. Trouble was I poured the rest over my trousers! But it had been a great trip. I love flying anyway and I had met a lot of interesting travellers on the way. I slept for some thirteen hours and eventually managed to adjust my 'body clock' to fit in with the change of time zone. Needless to say there was plenty of 'catching up' to do! George Tribe rang up the next afternoon from his house in Rye, on the Mornington Peninsular, to welcome me and to ask if I would like to go over and stay with him and Bon. Having known George for over 30 years – in fact right from the time that he played for Northants where he had coached me as a youngster - I was delighted to accept.

Chapter 3 First experiences of Australia

In the next day or two Urs and Frank took me out and about to obtain my bearings in Kew itself and also see a few of the landmarks that enable me to get an idea of how to get about the city. I soon got the hang of using the excellent tram system in Melbourne and I spent several happy days wandering around the city, visiting places of interest and drinking delicious milkshakes! The shops were quite impressive and there was less hustle and bustle than we find at home. I guess that is because there is always enough room to spread out. I found my first visit to the Victoria market particularly fascinating as so many of the goods on display for sale were unobtainable back home. Much of it came from Africa, Japan and China, with clothing from Malaysia - a particular feature at this time. There were street hawkers too, with very persuasive methods of selling! I soon learned the art of bartering and got great pleasure from arguing about the prices of goods. The African sellers were particularly interesting to listen to. Their wares were usually laid out on the pavements and formed a colourful display of almost anything from belts, gloves and African-style shoes to bangles, beads and necklaces. There were also beautifully carved animals and birds. African art was different too, with pictures showing ways of life so different from ours. Of course on other stalls there were the inevitable Australian creatures in model form for sale, with soft toy koalas of all shapes and sizes intermingled with kangaroos and possums, together with other toys calculated to catch the eyes of children – and holiday makers from around the world.

Just down the road from the market was a massive motorcycle shop. There were bikes of every conceivable size and colour – and well known makes as diverse as cheap 50cc Hondas, so useful for getting round built up areas to very expensive Harley Davidsons, the pride of the long distance riders. These really were the last word in comfort. It allowed me to compare them with the various other long distance touring machines such as were being produced at that time by Japanese manufacturers such as Honda, Kawasaki and Suzuki.

There were theatres and museums as well as a large number of shops. I visited the newly built Melbourne Theatre with its top stretching upwards to a point, looking for all the world like a large net covered roof. The Melbourne Museum was next to the theatre and gave an insight into life as it had developed over 200 years. There was an Art Exhibition on the day I went showing work done by Aborigine artists. Many of the artefacts depicted showed how people had initially struggled to come to terms with a hostile environment. It was a fascinating place. I visited the Cathedral too, situated not far from the heart of the city. Eating places abounded and people sat outside in the warmth of the sunshine. It was a dry heat at that point and pleasant in the shade of the many tall buildings. The city of Melbourne certainly had a vibrant and exciting feel to it.

Inevitably sport of all kinds was in evidence. The Melbourne Cricket Ground (MCG) was, and still is, the major sporting venue. Interestingly enough it was still privately owned in 1984 and, so far as I am aware, still is. Australian Rules Football also loomed large and is played at the MCG. Needless to say I have watched both Cricket and Aussie Rules Football there on many occasions in the course of my visits to Melbourne over the years. The atmosphere in the ground is quite remarkable when there is a good crowd. It can hold over 90,000 spectators. This happens quite often, for the good citizens of the area are renowned as the keenest and most prolific watchers of top class sporting activities. The facilities are excellent and the rounded shape of the ground coupled with the high seating areas tends to throw the overall sounds across to the opposite side. I once visited the ground when there were just a few visitors having a guided tour. I was on the opposite side of the ground and could quite clearly hear what was being said on the far side! The MCG has a famous Sports Museum with memorabilia going back into the 1800s when the game was first played. Every corridor has pictures – most of them showing famous players – mainly Australian of course - or depicting scenes of a bygone age. They certainly love their sport and they like visitors to be very aware of that! I met no end of sportsmen during my visits and they loved nothing better than to have a go at us 'Poms' – all in fun of course. But they did NOT like being called 'Ockers' so I enjoyed rubbing it in whenever I could. It was a delightful atmosphere and one that I revelled in. they were kindness itself as a rule and like nothing better than to have someone answer them back in their own aggressive style! I very quickly learned never to accept the comments made without having something to say in reply. It seemed a bit strange at first but that is their way. In order to supplement the use of 'Ocker' I found an unusual word in an Australian dictionary. It was 'Noligoster' and was, to say the least, less than complimentary. I subsequently used the phrase and referred to whoever was taking the mickey as 'a noligostering Ocker'. This caused consternation as no one knew what it meant so when they asked I suggested that they looked it up in a dictionary. I reckon most of them could not even spell it. Anyhow it worked!

Traffic was not too bad either on this first trip but on each subsequent occasion that I returned to Melbourne and the Mornington Penninsula over the succeeding years this changed – so did the rush and bustle. Frank often asked me to drive and I needed no second bidding. It was good experience and Ursula was always happy to lend me her car. A lot of people were constantly emigrating to Australia from all parts of the world. In fact it was said even in 1984 that there were more Greek citizens in Melbourne than anywhere else - apart from in the Greek capital city of Athens. There were certainly a lot of them around.

Many areas in and around Melbourne have lengthy avenues of palm trees. They certainly enhance the views. The skyline was impressive too, even then. By now there will be lots more high buildings in the Skyscraper category of course. The cities in Australia are all growing quickly and numbers of inhabitants are increasing wherever one visits. The skyline at Sydney too was worth seeing. There are skyscrapers in every direction in the city. I saw what, for me, was an unforgettable sight as I flew into Tullamarine Airport. I noticed that it had grown larger and seemingly higher every time I visited the place during the next 17 years.

Inevitably my interest in seeing anything appertaining to cricket quickly surfaced. At this stage of his career Frank had temporarily forsaken the teaching profession. He had taught for several years at the Carey Baptist School, Melbourne, and then was appointed Head of the Victoria Cricket Association (VCA) – a post he held for 13 years. During that time he set up a Cricket Coaching Scheme, qualification for which was in three grades – termed in degrees of difficulty as Levels 1, 2 and 3. The majority of Cricket Clubs in the State of Victoria accepted this. In fact, soon after having spoken to George Tribe I found myself roped in by Frank to accompany George. He drove to Frank's house in Kew to pick me up, and we did an afternoon of cricket coaching at the Sorrento Cricket Club, on the Mornington Peninsula, about a two hour drive away. Afterwards I stayed on at Rye with George for a few days and again, there was plenty of catching up to do. I also met his partner Bon Carmody. She was a delightful person who enjoyed organising barbeques whenever she could find an excuse. Needless to say she had invited several friends round to meet me so that engendered another barbeque. George and I did the cooking outside (he was an expert fortunately!) and we had a ball – it was a great night. I met several new friends and in future visits I was often asked out to join them. These Aussies certainly knew how to enjoy themselves!

Frank returned to teaching at Ivanhoe Grammar School (IGS) when his contract with the VCA was completed. He also introduced his Coaching Scheme into the world of cricket in India. The main base used was Mumbai (Bombay) and he has visited that city, and others too of course, on a regular basis since his resignation from IGS, to ensure that the scheme remains fully operational. He has also been to Bangladesh to impart his cricketing expertise.

I used Frank Tyson's first Cricket Coaching Manual for many years when coaching youngsters and then continued with the updated version. Furthermore I 'preached the Gospel' about the manual as I felt it was the best available way forward. Sadly there was resistance to having it produced in this country. In my humble opinion a great chance was lost, in the world of English coaching of cricket in particular, to gain the use of his expertise. In addition to these jobs and projects Frank had become an expert cricket commentator for Australia's Television Sports Station, Channel 9. This Channel was on air under the auspices of the Australian millionaire, Kerry Packer. Packer revolutionised the idea of the 50 overs cricket match – we called it 'the Pyjama Game' - because the teams involved wore coloured outfits as opposed to white. It was played partially under floodlights. There was much razzmatazz – music being played when fours and sixes were hit and tunes played appertaining to batsmen when they were going into bat. The first game I saw was played at the Melbourne Cricket Ground. The MCG, which can hold up to around 90,000 people, was packed with enthusiastic spectators. There was a lot of opposition at the time although nowadays it is standard practice. Tony Greig, a South African who was permitted to play his cricket under the English flag, and had captained England at one time during his career when South Africa was banned from World Cricket, recruited leading players to take part - on Kerry Packer's behalf. But all his happened well after my 1984 visit.

Returning to December '84 – having spent a few days with George and his partner Bon at Rye I was driven back to Kew along the Mornington Peninsular coast road by George. It was the scenic route and it certainly lived up to its name. When I arrived back I found that a friend of the Tysons had come to stay. His name was Philip Thompson. He was a former West Indies Test Cricket Selector and well known in International Cricketing circles. He enjoyed following cricket tours being made by West Indies Test sides and they were touring Australia in the summer of 1984/5. We hit it off very well and he and I spent several days together going into the centre of Melbourne by tram, seeing the sights and generally thoroughly enjoying each other's company. There were several informal parties locally as well. One in particular comes to mind as it had a connection with Durham. Tom Cairns, Deputy Chairman of Shell Australia, and his wife had both been at The University – Tom at Hatfield College with Frank and his wife Edith at St Hild's College. It was most enjoyable and reminiscences came thick and fast. I also went with 13 year old Anna - Urs and Frank's younger daughter - to a concert by Roger Whittaker, at the Melbourne Theatre. It was excellent and showed up the acoustics in the building to good advantage.

At this time Frank was a commentator for Channel 9 and as such attended Test Matches. The next match was at the Oval, Adelaide, and the idea was for Urs, daughter Sarah, Philip Thompson and me to drive there for the match, due to start on December 7th. It was a special Test Match as it marked the Centennial Celebrations of the South Australian Cricket Association. Frank flew up a couple of days earlier as he had cricket business to attend to. He was making a cricket coaching video in conjunction with colleagues in Adelaide before starting his commentating sessions at the Oval.

We set off on the 500 mile drive on Dec 5th, motoring first as far as Ballarat. We went to visit Sovereign Hill, - a reproduction of the former gold-mining town - and the Gold Museum. Ballarat was the scene of the first ever gold rush in Australia – in 1851 – when upwards of 10,000 gold prospectors arrived to stake their claims. Inevitably there was fighting amongst the prospectors and several were killed. Sovereign Hill, opened in 1971, was fascinating. It faithfully recreated the lives and times of the period, with its shops as they would have been in the 1850s, the Stage Coach waiting outside the staging post, the Bakery, the Gold Mine workings, the Camp where the miners lived and the Prison – just a tiny wooden hut where criminals were locked in solitary confinement and left to sweat in the blazing sun. There was even a genuine rivulet where one could pan for gold. Rock breaking was shown. This was done with a heavy stone wheel that was pulled round in an endless circle by a horse. To add to the authenticity there were people dressed in the clothing of the 1850s – policemen and miners, shopkeepers and assistants who worked in the various stores, or in other occupations commensurate with the times. In the Gold Museum, built in 1972, there were a comprehensive variety of implements on show that had been use for mining. In complete contrast there were old cooking utensils of all kinds – in fact there was virtually everything that had been present when the Gold Rush had taken place. In pride of place were large nuggets of gold that had been mined. One, brought out in 1858, was called 'The Welcome Stranger', and was the second largest ever mined in Australia. That lot was worth over £200,000 in 1984. No chance to steal any though – the unbreakable glass casing was several inches thick and firmly fixed!

After an overnight stay in Ballarat with Joanna, Ursula's former partner in a dress shop business, we set off again. One bizarre feature of the territory through which we travelled was seeing the blackened trunks of the trees that had been burned during the forest fires of the previous season. It was quite a gruesome sight, but more interesting was seeing the green shoots of the new trees and bushes growing up among the burned out forestation. Every tree had pods inside nut-like kernels. These eventually burst open to let the seeds drop to the ground and start to grow. The incredible heat with temperatures reaching up to 1000 degrees causes this to happen. It is nature's way of rejuvenating the forests. Nature is certainly a wonderful thing!

Sarah and I shared the driving. After several hours during which we occasionally stopped at wayside pull offs for refreshments, Philip, who was sitting in the front passenger seat while I was driving, suddenly said in his fascinating West Indian tongue, "Man, is we nearly dere?" "Not yet", I replied, "there is still a long way to go". "Den how far's we come?" Sarah piped up from the back – "about 180 miles". Philip was silent for a second or two. Then he said, "Man, I'se been up an' down ma island 6 times already. It sure is a long way!" And with that he promptly went to sleep! In was ironic too that the roads on the Victorian side of the state border were quite rough – due no doubt to the havoc caused by the forest fires. The speed limit was 110 kilometres an hour – plenty fast enough on those roads. However, when we crossed into South Australia, away from where the fires had raged the roads were excellent, yet the speed limit dropped to a maximum of 100 kph and there were mobile police patrols there to enforce that limit!

Eventually we arrived and went to the International Hilton Hotel where Frank and the various others commentators were staying. The Australian players and officials were staying there as well. Frank had a room for his family on about the 8th floor as I recall. There were several others there too, including Philip, his son. Philip was an official photographer from a Melbourne firm and was taking pictures for the press. He and I went and found a couple of rooms at the 'Wellington'. It was a doss house – the equivalent of our downtown pub – and cost us just 10 dollars a night. The Tysons' room was 160 dollars a night! However we used the hotel anytime we wanted, except for sleeping, so that was fine. Tina Turner, the singer, (sadly no relation!) was doing a show there too although I did not go. George Tribe and Bon turned up on the third day of the Test and insisted on introducing me to various people in the cricket world. One such person was Richie Benaud whom I had already met - more of that later. During the conversation George told him of my operation to have a malignant melanoma removed. Immediately Richie pointed to three warts on his face – "like these?" he said. "Yes", I replied. "I must get rid of these then!" he commented. He did not refer to them again but I noticed a while later, when he was commentating on television, that they had been removed - a wise man! Much later that evening – around midnight - I was having a drink in the bar at the Hilton with Philip Tyson prior to our retiring to the 'Wellington' when two of the Australian Test players came into the bar and when we left they were still drinking. Not the best preparation for the next day's play I should have thought, as one of them, Rodney Hogg, was the Aussie's opening bowler!

So the first day of the Centennial Test dawned and after an excellent breakfast Philip Tyson and I set off for the ground. By 9am it was hot - already 37 degrees - and I had arranged to meet Philip Thompson at the Oval. This was to be a real celebration with well-known former cricketers being invited to the match. Foremost amongst the visitors were all the ex Captains of Teams that had toured Australia in past years. They were invited to represent their respective countries. Also there were others, like Philip Thompson, who had been instrumental in selecting players in the past. For me this was a unique opportunity to meet famous world-class cricketers of a bygone era.

I arrived at the ground, having met up with Philip Thompson, and we were walking towards the roped off area where the honoured guests were sitting when a lad of about 15 years old sidled up to me and tugged my blazer. He was severely disabled, suffered from spasticity, and found difficulty in controlling his muscles and thus his limbs. He had a slight speech impediment too. In his hand he held an autograph book. He said that he had tried to get some autographs from ex players that he had recognised but because of his disability he had been unable to do so. Philip Thompson stopped too and the lad, whose name I later found out was Ben, asked if I would get some signatures for him. I was very moved by his request and took his book, promising to meet him at the same spot after the day's play. Philip immediately took me with him and introduced me to several people that he knew, the first one being Gary Sobers. His name was the first on the page. Several others also signed when Philip explained what had happened, and I know that one or two went out of their way to speak to Ben himself. At the end of the day I returned the book to Ben. Each morning he waited for Philip and me near the entrance to the main stand and each day we got the autographs. They were on several pages and by the fourth day the job was completed – at least so I thought. On the last day he was there again. "We've got all the autographs, Ben", I said. "No mate", Ben replied. "I got Mr Thompson's but yours ain't there". "I quickly pointed out that I was not a celebrity and so obviously I had not even considered signing the book. "You are to me mate," he said, and indicated that I give him my autograph. I turned to a clean page but he insisted that I put mine with all the famous players. Very touched, and somewhat embarrassed, I did so. So somewhere then, in Australia, there is an autograph book with my name at the end of a page containing the names of those famous cricketers who had been to that match! The guests were paraded round the ground in a fabulous motorcade and there was a wonderful festive atmosphere about the whole thing. Australia's greatest batsman, Don Bradman, was there, together with some forty or so other all time greats. What an occasion that was!

Frank introduced me to Alan McGilvray, at that time the leading Australian Radio Commentator. We sat together for a meal on one occasion after the day's play was completed and found that we had a lot in common. We enjoyed each other's company and became friends. I also had the pleasure of meeting up with him again in England during an Australian tour and we spent an evening together after a day's play at Lords. Frank introduced me to many others too, and I spent a while in the Test Match TV Commentary Box in the company of Richie Benaud, Tony Greig, and Frank. It was a wonderful experience. It made me realise just how ordinary everyone is beneath his or her mantle of fame. They are all under constant pressure to get things right and it would seem that they are targets for the press whenever something controversial occurs. To see the array of TV screens available to the commentators was a lesson in itself. Every statistic – about the players and their records – was available at the touch of a button, and to see how professional these guys were beggared belief. I learned more about commentating on that day than I had ever done – before or since - and my admiration for them was profound.

There was a considerable amount of time spent socialising at this match. There were VIP tents where ex players and their families and friends were entertained with free drinks. Facilities for dinner were excellent too. I had been given a seat next to the roped off area in the viewing stand containing the guests so I was able to chat to Philip during the match. Seated near me on my other side were two young Australians who struck up an acquaintance with me – probably because they saw that I knew someone in the guest area. At lunch times each day they invited me to join them so we reserved a table and enjoyed excellent meals. They really wanted to meet someone well known – it was quite amusing actually. On the final day of the match Frank came across to the table and put his arms round their shoulders saying, "So you are the guys who have been looking after my friend are you? Thanks very much." The lads were speechless! As it so happened, a bit later on, Philip also came across and presented me with a tie from his club at Kingston, Jamaica as a keepsake to commemorate our time together. So the lads got their wish and met a couple of other well known ex cricketers who were with Philip – Gary Sobers (West Indies) and Bob Willis (England). I must say that I too thoroughly enjoyed meeting so many famous cricketers, past and present. It made one realise that they are no different from anyone else when it comes to conversing – they had just achieved greatness in the eyes of the public because of their outstanding abilities in the cricketing world. Northants was well represented – Freddie Brown, George Tribe, Frank Tyson, Bishan Bedi and a couple of others whose names escape me. They had a photo taken together – by Philip Tyson – and when I was last in the pavilion at Northampton some years ago it was displayed on the wall. There were so many memories for me connected with that match at the Oval, Adelaide, that it is one of the highest points out of all my visits to Australia.

Urs, Frank, Sarah and I returned to Melbourne on Dec 12th. Urs and Frank had an engagement to attend that evening. Also on Dec 13th they were due to go to a 'passing out parade' in the morning. As I was due to fly out to Wellington, New Zealand, that same morning they were unable to take me to the Airport. One of Bon's friends, a lady by the name of Ann, was contacted and as she was staying in Melbourne for a few days she agreed to see that I got to Tullamarine Airport in good time. She called at the Tysons' house to confirm the arrangement and at the same time invited me to out to supper at her Hotel. All went well and we had an enjoyable evening. However she had imbibed well so could not drive me back to the Tysons' house. Instead she lent me her car to get back 'home' but unfortunately I got lost and it took ages to find my way. I eventually arrived in the early hours of the morning having driven around the streets of Kew and the surrounding district for well over an hour and a half. Instead of a lengthy night's sleep I only managed four hours before I had to get up again in order to see Urs and Frank to thank them for their hospitality and say cheerio until my return to Melbourne from New Zealand. When I went back to the hotel where Ann was staying in the morning I found to my chagrin that the journey only took about 10 minutes! Still, I got my lift to the Airport so all was well. Having booked in we had time for a farewell drink before I went through to the waiting area reserved for passengers only.

Having boarded the plane that was to fly direct to Wellington I settled down to what I had hoped was to be a quiet flight where I could catch up on lost sleep. Not a bit of it – other passengers were leaning over me to get the signature of the chap next to me! We quickly swapped seats and after he had finished signing autographs he apologised for the disturbance. It turned out that he was the Coach for the New Zealand Tennis Team who had been playing in a tournament in Melbourne. Inevitably the conversation turned to sport and so it was a lively and enjoyable flight after all – the food supplied for us was good and – the drinks were free!

Chapter 4 Getting to know New Zealand

At the end of the three-hour flight from Melbourne the picturesque harbour at Wellington came into view. One could see a few ships at anchor in the bay, but the main feature that caught the eye was the hillside beyond the harbour. The houses built there made a beautiful sight with the multiplicity of colours – reds, greens, blues, browns and even a few yellow roofs - standing out in the bright sunshine. There were reflections on the windows from too. Our plane actually flew in directly over the harbour entrance and then banked sharply to the left. The runway appeared below us and I remember commenting that it looked quite short. My fellow passenger smiled and said, "It is, and look where it ends!" That really brought me up sharp – the runway actually went right out over the water. He then told me that normally the planes landed in towards the city, but if the wind was in a certain direction the plane landed the other way. On this occasion we would be pointing out towards the ocean when we stopped. The landing turned out to be hairy, although in my ignorance I was not really aware of the danger until we had come to rest. The sea was literally on either side of the plane and we were only a short distance from the end of the runway! There were vociferous comments from several passengers who regularly used this route – they were NOT amused. Whoever it was who uttered the words 'ignorance is bliss' on this occasion was certainly right! It was then that I recalled that Wellington is known as the windy city. The plane turned back towards the small terminal building and stopped nearby. Passengers disembarked and we trooped across to pass through customs in the main hall. As I came down the steps of the plane I felt a great sense of achievement. I had reached my goal! I had always had an ambition to visit both Australia and New Zealand and now I had arrived. Elated, I looked across at the crowd of people waiting to greet passengers. I saw the only three relatives that I had met in England – my cousin Dorothy Hamilton, her husband Ken, and Graeme, their son. I waved to them and was amazed to see several people waving back – the whole of Dorothy and Ken's family had turned out to welcome me – Graeme and his wife Janis, together with her children by a previous marriage, Bronwyn and Gareth, and Kris, who was also Graeme's daughter, and Judith, Dorothy and Ken's youngest daughter. The rest of the family were still at work. It was a truly magical moment that I have never forgotten. Ken detached himself from the party and came across to meet me after I had got through the customs check. His car was nearby and by the time we had got to it the rest of the family had got there too. They were all coming to Dorothy and Ken's house so we could all meet up for the first time. What a party that was! Inevitably at the time I could not remember all the names but it did not matter. My late father had been twice to New Zealand in the 70s, and it was a strange feeling to hear them talking about 'Uncle George', as they all called him, as if he was still alive. I guess that to them he was. It was indeed a truly memorable evening and quite emotional too as in my heart of hearts I had feared that I should not live long enough to fulfil my dream of seeing my father's side of the family. From childhood I had been brought up with aunts, uncles and cousins on my mother's side. I was the youngest of the lot by several years – apart from Daphne. She and I had much in common but the others were all much older and some were already grown up while I was still in my comparative infancy. Now, suddenly, on my father's side we were all pretty much of an age and I knew that this would be special. Ken and I hit it off from the word go. He was a great character. He loved to dominate in his family (Graeme told me all about that later) and he immediately went into this routine with me in his Kiwi accent, calling me 'boy' at one stage - in fun of course. I immediately replied, 'Yes, Bwana, is dat what you'se callin' me?' There was a howl of laughter and that was the first and last time he used it! He kept his family on their toes but every time he started to try to assert any authority where I was concerned I reverted to 'Bwana' and it was enough. We understood each other very well.

At that time Ken was an insurance agent and I used to go out with him to see customers. He was very highly thought of and his company invariably awarded him extra bonuses and a holiday every year for himself and Dorothy. Quite a few of his clients were Maoris – not known for saving anything, let alone money - but somehow he had persuaded them to invest. It gave me an early opportunity to meet several Maoris and I was able to get a glimpse of their culture and what made them tick. They were very happy go lucky folk who were not really too enamoured of the white people. They had a rather derogatory word for white folk, calling them 'Pakehas' (Europeans) in the same way that Africans talked about 'Blacks' and 'Coloured'. It was quite a shock to realise that there was a lot of mutual antipathy, although it was rather 'under cover' for the most part.

History tells us that towards the end of the 18th Century French, British and American ships came to catch whales around the coast of New Zealand. Then there were those who wanted to annex great areas of land when they had arrived in the country in the early 1800s and fighting had been fierce in some places. Many were killed and eventually it became necessary to come to some agreement to prevent unscrupulous land grabbers from destabilising the country. There were several white religious missionaries in New Zealand too. They were mainly British. Some Maori chiefs, backed by the missionaries, asked the British to stabilise the country. At the cessation of hostilities a formula for peaceful living was drawn up. Many of the Maoris were simple souls – lacking in education in the western style. They lived in tribes with chiefs who ruled them. Few, if any, could write to sign their names on a treaty. It was decided to call a meeting at a place in the north area of the North Island called Waitangi. Between 40 and 50 Maori chiefs and British leaders signed what became known as the Waitangi Treaty in 1840. The Chiefs simply made a mark on the treaty and their names were written in. All the others had to be visited by British representatives and it is said that many of those 450 Chiefs were persuaded to sign by being given gifts of blue beads! This treaty gave the Maoris the right to keep their lands and fishing rights. In return they were to recognise the sovereignty of Queen Victoria and they would have the same rights as the British settlers. The word Waitangi means 'weeping (or noisy) waters'. Thus the British managed to take control of the country, but resentment is still there all these years later.

I was invited to go to various functions, one of which was a meeting of Rotarians. Rotary is very strong in New Zealand. Everything went very well and the members greeted me effusively, making me initially feel most welcome. However unfortunately, as the evening wore on and some Rotarians got into their cups, a discussion started about the British who had turned their backs on trading with New Zealand and had joined what was then known as the European Common Market. There was what was termed a 'Butter Mountain' – this was the butter that had, in previous years, been exported to Britain. Now the British had refused to buy from New Zealand. Although I said very little, by the end of the evening some of the members had convinced themselves that I was personally responsible! However the next day all had returned to normal thank goodness. I have always felt that we let down New Zealand badly at that time when we suddenly ceased much of our trading with them in favour of the Common Market.

By now Christmas was almost upon us and another party was arranged at the Hamilton's house. I asked about Christmas trees and was taken to see what is known as the New Zealand Christmas tree. It is called the POHUTUKAWA – and with good reason. It has myriads of beautiful crimson flowers, whitefelted silvery leaves, and it flowers in December.

I went swimming every day too. Ken had a round pool and the idea was to set the water swirling round the pool one way and then swim against the way the water was going. It was hard work, and quite a job to even stay in one place. On Christmas Day the sun was shining and I went swimming before breakfast at 8.00am. I certainly remembered that! Then we had a Christmas party. The house abounded with Christmas decorations and everyone was in festive mood. I was very impressed by the fact that the children were not given expensive presents as a matter of principle – just sweets and small gifts. When I wanted to buy presents for everyone I was told that everybody contributed to a fund and presents were bought from that so I gave my share too. The family contributed to buy me a lovely book about New Zealand. It is still a much-valued book amongst my Antipodean memorabilia. But it still seemed strange to have been eating turkey and hot Christmas pudding inside when it was boiling hot outside!

The festivities continued off and on into the New Year with yet another party. There were other members of the family who had come from afar. My Aunt Dorothy, whom I had never seen before, came from Palmerston on the South Island to stay for all the festivities and it gave me the chance to really get to know her. Joan and her former daughter in law Janet joined the rest of the family. Christine and Ann, the other two Hamilton daughters, were there together with Ann's husband Craig, plus Aaron and Brent, their children.

Later on I stayed a day or two at Lower Hutt with Joan Comerford, another of my cousins and Dorothy's elder sister. That was fun and is mentioned later on in this diatribe. Ken also took me over the Rimatuka Pass towards Masterton on one occasion. The road up to the top of the pass was very twisting and steep and the view was truly superb. On another occasion we visited Paraparam or, as it was more commonly known, Paraparaumu (the Maori name). Here the sand on the beach is very dark – almost black I suppose. It is volcanic sand and can be found on the beaches up the coast. It is one of several village settlements, two others being named Paekakariki and Waikanae. Maori names have repetitive sounds and letters in many cases. Opposite is Kapiti Island – now a bird sanctuary, but formerly a Maori fortress where a famous Maori leader lived – Te Rauparaha. At one time he dominated much of the land in the northern, warmer areas of the North Island where a large number of Maoris lived. So many of the names of New Zealand's features – towns, villages, mountains and rivers – are, to my mind, beautiful sounding Maori words. Many of them reflect Maori beliefs and stories too and are well worth reading about.

Chapter 5 Touring the North Island

After the Christmas and New Year festivities were over and everyone returned to work I decided that I wished to travel around the North Island of New Zealand. Ken, who had an old Chrysler 'Valiant' Saloon car, kindly lent it to me to use while I was on holiday. We adapted the passenger front seat so that it folded out flat, for me to use as a bed. I was still recovering from the effects of the cancer and needed to have a sleep at times during the day. Walking far was also still difficult and took a lot out of me, although I was determined to continue to exercise every day in order to keep on the road back to fitness. So this was ideal. I could drive where the mood took me and sleep when I felt like it. I stored a small amount of food in the boot where it was reasonably cool and set off on January 3rd 1985. I had been warned before leaving home never to expose my body to the sun's rays, particularly when travelling in the Antipodes so I had plenty of sun cream – and long sleeved cotton shirts that I bought before leaving, plus a cap for good measure. My first stop was at Wanganui where I visited a Museum full of Maori memorabilia. It was quite unlike anything I had ever seen before - truly fascinating. Maori artwork is unique and examples of every kind abound. I found the war canoe to be the most fascinating reminder of the history of the country as it represents how warriors moved from place to place at high speed around the coasts. I also visited the Maori Church. The woodcarvings were very symbolic – and again, different. Nearby was the famous waterfall - 'Wanganui Falls' - with the rushing water cascading over the top and plunging deep down the rock face, throwing up beautiful white plumes of spray at the bottom. I spent the night in a wooden hut on an excellent motor camp site at Aramoho and met several New Zealand holiday makers who were travelling in the area, sharing experiences of all kinds over a few 'tinnies' before going to bed. Everybody I encountered showed such friendliness and made me so welcome.

The next part of my journey on January 4th provided unexpected drama. I set off in the morning, stopping off at Chateau Tongariro. This is in the picturesque

Tongariro National Park, with the volcanic mountains setting the scene as I drove through the area. For me Mount Ruapehu was of special significance, as its snow-covered peak seemed to dominate the surrounding countryside. I walked in the mountain woods and at one point looked down on Lake Taupo. It was in Taupo where I intended to stay as it was an interesting and colourful place, particularly along by the Lake. Before I got that far however I stopped off at Turangi and lazed in a thermal pool. It was so relaxing, sitting on a step in the warm water, that it was necessary for attendants to keep a watchful eye on swimmers or, I should say, people basking in the pool. One could easily have fallen asleep. The sun was hot, the sky was blue and there was no hint of what was about to happen. I eventually drove on to the outskirts of Taupo itself, intending to make my way down to the lakeside. Suddenly, as if by a miracle, the sky darkened – so quickly that I only just had time to drive into a nearby car park looking down towards the lake. In seconds Mount Ruapehu, which forms a magnificently high background across the far southern side of the Lake, disappeared and a storm raced across the lake towards Taupo itself. I shut the car windows and prayed! When the storm hit the car the rain was heavy that I could see absolutely nothing. It was as if a giant curtain had blotted everything out. The thunderclaps sounded like bombs being dropped – a sound I had not heard since my boyhood days on the Isle of Wight when the Second World War was at its height. The noise was deafening and the waters of the lake were spilling over into the car park – at least that is what it sounded like. I could hear it swishing round the lower bodywork of the 'Valiant' and water got in under the doors. Just as suddenly the thunder ceased, the waters receded and the sun came out. Then I noticed that at the edges of the roads there were deep concrete channels and the water drained away quite quickly. People came out on the streets nearby once more and life returned to normal. I went into the nearest milk parlour and ordered a large milkshake. They make the best milkshakes I have ever come across in New Zealand – succulently flavoured and with a large dollop of ice cream in – absolute bliss to taste! I got talking to a local who told me that this sort of storm did come from time to time, but that this one had been rather more special than usual – classic understatement! I returned to the car and lay down, intending to rest for a couple of hours. Actually I slept till the next afternoon, waking up 14 hours later! Luckily car parks were free in those days so nobody bothered me – and the car doors were not even locked. Quite a contrast from Britain I realised. I had a late breakfast – including another delectable milkshake. After that I went along the lakeside to watch the World Championship Speedboat Races. There was more excitement there too as the water was still quite rough. At one point the leading speedboat hit a wave, leapt into the air and turned turtle. The poor guy that was piloting it was badly injured and had to be hastily rescued by a safety speedboat that went out from the harbour. Sadly he had severely injured his back and was taken to hospital. His co-driver survived ok but was badly shaken. I was not surprised! The side of the speedboat was badly damaged and there was a huge piece out of the side near the pilot's seat. The steering wheel was twisted too. The winner had a boat named 'Scrubbers' and it boasted the most powerful engines in the Southern Hemisphere. It had been an exciting day, to say the least!

I drove out of Taupo on my way north towards Wairakie to see the Huka Falls which are a part of the Waikato River. This thermal area was billowing steam as I approached and, intrigued, I stopped to see the cause. It turned out to be a scheme that tapped the thermal resources in some way and produced electricity. Then I drove on until saw the incredibly powerful currents turning the waters of the river into white rapids. I parked the car and walked slowly along the riverside, eventually seeing where the river rushed over a sort of ledge and dropped down into a churning white pool of foam that spread rapidly outwards as the river widened. It was absolutely breathtaking.

By now its early evening and I was very tired. I saw a small clearing amongst the trees on the edge of what appeared to be a forest. I stopped the car, rolled over into the 'bed' and fell asleep. The next thing I remember was waking up as dawn broke. One minute all was silent – then the birds began to make their morning calls to each other and in no time it had all become a magnificent dawn chorus. I shall never forget the sheer poignancy of those sounds. I opened the car door and sat listening, utterly absorbed. At last I realised that this was what I really needed to help me on the road to recovery. I suppose it was a sort of existential experience – as if I was looking at life in a holistic dimension. Suddenly the world seemed a different place and I realised that I was appreciating the true joy of being alive and being able to commune with nature – even if only for a short while. But it really happened and it was a vivid part of my own personal experience. Maybe I appreciated that, although I was a very minute particle of the universe, as such my life was precious. I think it was at that moment that I determined in my own mind that I was going to beat the cancer and that being in New Zealand was part of the recovery cycle. It was indeed a uniquely surrealistic moment in my life.

I walked to the place where I had turned into what I now realised was a wood. There in front of me was a fence with a gate – firmly closed. A large notice hung over a fence pole that read 'The Lady Knox Geyser'
Opens at 10am.
Entry 1dollar.

I had some food and drink in the boot of the car so I wandered back and had a leisurely breakfast of sorts and sat reading for an hour. Then I wandered slowly across to the gate where a few other visitors were waiting. By now the sun was up and one felt the warmth of the day. Promptly at ten o'clock an athletic looking middle-aged man of about forty-five opened the gate. We all trooped in, paying our one-dollar fee at the gate. A few more people continued to appear, paying their dues and joining us. The group numbered about 20 in all and we waited expectantly. Our guide introduced himself as Bill. "Prisoners from the nearby jail worked here", he said, "breakin'up rocks. The weather got very hot during the day and the men would take off their shirts and put then in a pile over a small hole in the ground. Whenever they returned after workin' the shirts were strewn all over the place and arguments started as to who had thrown them about. Some men soon came to blows about it. Then one day one of the prisoners hung about when the others went to work and hid nearby to see who the culprit was. All of a sudden there was a mighty 'wooshin'' sound and the shirts rose into the air. The wind did the rest. Intrigued, the guard allowed the prisoners to watch what happened the next morning and the mystery was solved. Now watch". With the air of a magician about to pull a rabbit out of a hat the guide sprinkled something from a box into the hole over which the shirts had been thrown all those years ago. For a couple of minutes nothing happened. Then suddenly a fountain of steam shot up about 40 feet into the air – very spectacular! No one could ascertain why this had happened. The guide held up the box. Written on it was the magic word 'Persil'. Then he explained. "The prisoners washed their shirts each night on their return to the prison. The washin' powder that was used left a residue on the shirts. When they were put into a pile the powder element left formed a thin skin on the surface of the thermal water in the hole. Then, hey presto, when the pressure built up sufficiently under the surface the water broke through the skin and blew up into the air. Lady Knox, wife of the New Zealand Governor, saw this when visitin' the area and so the geyser was named in her honour. It is still known as Lady Knox's Geyser". That was certainly quite a story!

I continued on my journey through the beautiful countryside to Waiotapu Thermal Park, stopping off to see the famous mud pools and the Champagne Lake. Then I drove on to the Waimangu Scenic Reserve. I managed to walk a short way – to see Lake Rotomahana. Next, to soothe my aching muscles, I had a swim – if one can call it that because really it was more of a wallow – in the Polynesian Thermal Pool. It was certainly very relaxing and there was a notice warning people not to stay in the water too long as it was dangerous to fall asleep. Again I soon realised what that meant. I visited a local park before stopping off at the nearby 'Cosy Cottage Motor Camp' where I slept soundly in the car. The whole night cost me just a couple of dollars – less than a pound in our coinage. Everything was certainly very cheap in New Zealand.

On January 7th I drove on towards Rotorua where I had been invited to stay with John and Jill Marslin – friends of the Hamilton family. First I visited Rainbow Springs and Fairy Springs, with their picturesque rocks and thermal pools. I also looked round the Kiwi Museum and the Rotorua Art Gallery. Earlier I had seen an advertisement offering 50$ flights to the top of Mount Tarawera – a volcanic mountain that had erupted on a massive scale back in 1886. So massive was the eruption that it was apparently heard several hundreds of miles away in Christchurch on the South Island! It split the mountain in two and, sadly, buried the entire village of Wairoa near the base of the volcano. Some of the village ruins have been excavated and are open to the public, but unfortunately I was unable to walk down the many steps to see them.

On arrival at Rotorua Airport – really little more than a small 'terminal hut' on the edge of a large grassed field – I duly paid my fee and joined five other people who were waiting to be flown to the small landing area at the summit of Mount Tarawara. The plane we were to travel in was a Cessna. We squeezed in – there was not much room – and I was told to sit in the co-pilot's seat. I was lucky – I had a bit of space. We took off, flew across the blue and green lakes that feature in Maori beliefs and legend, and reached the mountaintop without incident. What I didn't know was that a message had been passed on to the airport staff by someone – I never did find out just who it was as the staff were sworn to secrecy before I had even arrived - that I was to be given a special treat, but more of that later.

Standing on the summit of that mountain seemed like being right on top of the world. The views were utterly magnificent with truly panoramic scenes laid out in all directions – wherever one looked. It was also incredibly quiet. Again, staring down into the massive crater stretching out directly below, one was very much aware of the insignificance of human beings when compared to the world around. I think that everybody in the party realised that this was a very special place and felt humbled by it all. I know I certainly felt that way. It seemed like a form of religious experience – something ethereal that was beyond our understanding. The pilot took a photo for each of us as we all had cameras. He was a guide as well.

Eventually we returned to the plane. I was very much aware that the 'runway' – if it could even be called that – was short..... very short! The pilot warned us quite casually that he would take off at the quickest rate possible, drop over the mountain's edge, and pick up more speed in a shallow dive in order to reach flying speed. Thankfully it worked – as usual of course – and we turned to fly back to the airfield. Suddenly the pilot grinned and, turning to the passengers who were sitting behind us, said "Folks the co-pilot is takin' over now". I was about to move, thinking there was someone else to fly the plane when he lifted his hands off the controls and said, "all yours, mate". I was thrilled and did not need a second invitation! I actually flew the plane right back to the airfield. The pilot told me to line it up for landing. I did this ok and was almost sorry when he took over to land. What a fantastic trip that was! Actually I had lost a red garnet ring somewhere on the mountain top but it did not matter. I had had possibly the most stimulating experience of my entire life. I was then presented with an official card stating that I had acted as co-pilot on that trip. It is one of my most treasured possessions. Finally I made my way to the Marslins' home - a lovely house overlooking Rotorua - and made myself known. They were most welcoming and I was treated to an excellent supper. Once again a few 'tinnies' were quaffed before retiring for the night.

I spent one more day in Rotorua, visiting the Agrodome where there were demonstrations – dogs at work rounding up sheep, sheep-shearing by an expert, and a sort of organised parade where various types of sheep were herded onto platforms. The clever thing about that was that the sheep had been trained to stand on platforms showing their specific breeds. That must have taken some doing. I also went to see actual kiwi birds in a darkened area – quite remarkable creatures. There were all types of exotic birds flying around too – very colourful. Add to that an afternoon in a Museum showing Maori culture at its best and it was a very full day. I also drove to the green and blue lakes, then on to Lake Tarawara – all very beautiful to behold. I reported the loss of my ring to the police in Rotorua. This gave proof that the loss had been reported - for insurance purposes.

On my return to the Marslins' house, there was a message awaiting me saying that Janet Comerford, the ex daughter in law of another of my cousins, Joan Comerford, had decided to have a few days holiday and would fly up to Whangerei to join me at some later stage of my trip. It turned out that she had been John Comerford's first wife. That was fine – the company would be welcome.

I left Rotorua on January 9th and motored to Plummer's Point, not far from Tauranga, to meet John, Joan's eldest son, and his second wife Chris, who were camping at a site near yet another thermal pool. We all went for a swim there. It was a lovely spot, seen on a warm and sunny day. John was one of New Zealand's leading experts in wine tasting and the evening was spent trying all the best wines – what an enjoyable experience that was. I certainly slept well in the car that night!

The next day dawned sunny and very clear. I went off on my own for the day, motoring up the coast to Waihi Beach. It was a very warm day so I decided to do some body surfing. I put my clothes near a beach chair, in a neat pile, about 70 yards from the water's edge and not too far from the road where I had parked the 'Valiant'. There was a four foot high wall at the side of the road between the car and the sand. I draped my towel round my shoulders to protect them from the sun even though I had also covered myself with sun blocker oil. This was standard practice wherever I went as I had been warned of the dire consequences of getting severely sunburnt. I hobbled slowly down to where the waves were pounding the shore. It was ideal for body surfing and for about 90 minutes I thoroughly enjoyed myself. It was certainly easier than walking. Then it happened. There was a loud booming sound and a small tidal wave came from seaward over the surf and swept up the beach, taking surfers and swimmers with it. We were unceremoniously dumped on the sand a long way up the beach. It was extremely painful, as it seemed as though we were being rubbed all over with sandpaper. It also caught out people who were sitting on beach chairs. They got absolutely soaked! Fortunately for me the people near where I had put my clothes were locals. They knew what the booming meant. They ran off the beach to the safety of the wall and they had managed to collect my clothes from the surging waters as they went. When I staggered back to the car I was very grateful to see two people hovering nearby with my pile of clothes. Fortunately I had a spare towel so was able to dry off, but I got traces of sunburn even in that short time as the sand had effectively removed all the cream I had put on. However, as I was wearing a pair of jeans that day and the salt from the seawater had soaked them, when they dried they were extremely stiff and difficult to put on again. That was quite a lesson to learn. That evening I returned to Plummer's Point as soon as I could in order to change into something more comfortable before spending another evening with Chris and John. Early the next morning it was obvious that the weather was changing rapidly. A warning that an extremely wet weather front was moving into the area was broadcast and all campers, including the Comerfords, hastily packed up tents and set off home – the site was low lying and the river could easily flood, depending on the severity of the storm. I was due to stay with Violet McGiven and her husband Irvine on their farm, a mile or two out of Matamata. Violet was the sister of John Scatchard, a friend from Leeds. In order to get to the farm I first had to drive back to Taurangi and then cross the Kaima Range – a hilly area. We said our goodbyes and set off. It was certainly a hairy journey. The road twisted and turned on itself. In effect it was like a mountain pass and I was grateful to reach Matamata before the weather deteriorated too much. But it was getting darker and more threatening by the minute. I found my way to the farm entrance at Waharoa and drove for about a mile on what was little more than a cart track. Just as I reached the farmhouse and went in through the front door the heavens duly opened. I did not even have time to get my overnight bag out of the car boot. Violet's family had driven to the farm to await my arrival and meet me – her daughter Sally Simpson, husband Brian and their two children, Rebecca and Laura. They decided to leave fairly soon after my arrival in order to get off the farm before the floods came and trapped them. In addition the electricity went off in the evening and so we sat chatting by candlelight. The storm continued for most of the night and by the time it had finished no vehicles could get in or out. This was the situation on the following day too. However on January 13th all was well again and Violet took me out to see the surrounding countryside. It is a picturesque area – very remote, with narrow roads and – fortunately – no traffic!

The next day I was given a real treat. The Simpson family took me on a 200 mile journey around the Coromandel Peninsular. Once again the scenery was superb. We even stopped off for a swim at one point – just to cool down!

I left on January 15th and drove up to Auckland to meet Kathleen Pointon, a cousin on my Mother's side of my family. She was staying with her friend from schooldays, Lou Tregidga. Lou's family owned the largest tomato growing complex in New Zealand at the time and Lou had a house nearby too. She and her husband had started the tomato growing business up originally. The next day Kath and I visited the Museum of Transport where there was even an old Lancaster bomber and a 'Vee One' flying bomb on show. Vee Ones were used by Germany to bomb London during the Second World War. It was a fascinating place that showed how transport and engineering had developed over the years. I also visited 'One Tree Hill' – a famous Auckland landmark and Eden Mount. Then we went to a barbeque put on by Mark and Margaret, Lou's oldest son and daughter in law. The following day Kath returned home to Raumati, not too far from Wellington, while I stayed on at Lou's place. In the evening Lou and her 6-year-old grand daughter Amy met me for a meal at the famous Waipuna Hotel in Auckland. Lou and I became good friends over the years and I stayed with her each time I visited New Zealand. Her family have always been very kind too and George and his first wife Lorraine have stayed with me in England. When Amy grew up she travelled to the United Kingdom twice. She worked in the hotel trade over here for a spell. She has stayed with me a couple of times and I have enjoyed showing her around the north of England. She loved the series of 'Pride and Prejudice' - with Colin Firth as Mr D'Arcy - as shown on NZ Television, so we went to Lyme Hall in Cheshire where some of the filming was done - courtesy of the National Trust. This was the highlight of her visit! She is now married and lives in New Zealand – a far cry from the 6 year old with whom I shared that meal.

The next day, January 18th, we went to Warkworth on the east coast, north of Auckland, to stay at a beach house owned by the family. George, another of Lou's sons, and his wife Lorraine were there. They had a large motorboat - owned by the family - and we went for a cruise to Kawai Island where Lord Grey, a former Governor General of New Zealand, had lived in a large mansion.

Then on the following day, came what, for me, was a real highlight. George took me fishing and let me pilot the boat. That was fantastic, but what was even more exciting was when we caught fish called kawai as we were returning home. In an hour I caught 13 and George caught several more – quite a haul. But the fish was not at all tasty. It was used mainly for shark bait. We had originally gone out to catch 'Snapper' – a truly succulent fish – but had had no luck. The next morning, before I left, we took George's two girls out so they could water ski behind his boat – again, it was great fun and they were very good at it!

My next stop was at the Museum at Matakoe. This was on Route 12, cutting across from the east side to the west coast. It is a fascinating place and shows just how the Kauri tree is utilised. Kauri is the hardiest tree known to man and cutting through Kauri wood demanded tremendous strength and patience of the prospectors in the early days before cutting machinery was invented. In addition to the wood there is a resin, or gum, that is collected from the trees and this can be used to fashion all sorts of shapes and mementoes. The wood is used for anything practical in terms of furniture and is guaranteed to last virtually for ever. I continued on my journey north and stopped for the night on a campsite at Kaitaia. Again, it was incredibly cheap and as I slept in the car overnight anyway there were no other expenses involved. It cost something around 3$ - under £ – and all the excellent facilities – toilet blocks, showers and a shop were available. It certainly helped me keep my holiday expenses down!

On January 21st I arranged a bus trip to the northern tip of New Zealand. This stopped first at yet another museum where there were all sorts and sizes of ancient household equipment, old vehicles of every kind, with and without engines - in fact if you named anything it was probably there! Then we continued up the single road to Cape Reinga. Our driver was a well-spoken and extremely polite Maori who entertained us by singing Maori songs to us on the way. He had a beautiful voice and the whole experience was quite moving. On arrival we were taken to the cliff edge. Below, and running out seawards was an ever moving line of wavelets running towards each other. It indicated where two great waters actually met – The Tasman Sea and the Pacific Ocean. It was an extraordinary sight, most particularly as the respective blues of the water seemed to differ slightly with the Tasman Sea looking darker – possibly just a trick of the light. The sky has always seemed a deeper blue in the Southern Hemisphere too. Maybe the ozone layer has something to do with this. Next came a barbeque on the beach. The idea was to go and enjoy a swim – a note worthy one as we were at the most northerly point of New Zealand – before sampling the delights of a Maori organised feast. Again, our driver cum host – a real jack-of-all-trades – sang to us. It was quite the most unusual trip I had ever experienced and it wasn't over yet. There were two buses at the point by this time and the passengers shared the 'barbie'. There was plenty of food and a fair number of 'tinnies' to wet our appetites – before, during and after!

An hour or so later we boarded our respective buses and the fun began again. First we drove along the centre of an actual riverbed – or, as it was known locally, the Te Paki Stream. The stream was only about three feet deep in the centre where we were driving – quite safe, but only if one knew what one was doing. Fortunately our driver did! The water near the banks of the stream was deeper – and of course the safety of the whole drive relied on knowing when the tides came in - and out. There were notices all over the place advising holidaying drivers not to take risks, but inevitably some people did. New Zealanders are great outdoor folk who like to take up challenges from time to time. That's fine if one assesses the dangers. However during our journey we saw one family who had got everything hopelessly wrong. They had been holidaying in a Campervan in the area and had decided to return to Kaitaia via a drive along the route known as '90 mile beach'. In order to get onto the beach it was essential to drive carefully along in the middle of a stream when the tide was going out. Sure enough there were large warning notices emblazoned with the magic words in large letters –

DRIVE ALONG THE <u>CENTRE</u> OF THE STREAM AND <u>DON'T STOP!</u>

These idiotic travellers had gone across to the left hand side of the river and had stopped by the bank. They had doubtless had lunch – and possibly a 'tinnie' or two. By the time they were ready for off the tide was racing in and they could not move. Apparently the more they tried to drive forward the deeper the wheels went into the sandy bed of the stream. A tractor came along to try to pull them out but by then it was too late, they had sunk in well and truly. As we passed by in the bus later in the afternoon – taking care not to stop anywhere - we could see the main part of the Campervan sinking slowly down into the water. I guess that at one point they had thought that they could get the vehicle unstuck. But it was too late as it had sunk right down into the soft sand. Sadly the vehicle had to be abandoned. It was certainly a very expensive mistake on the part of the owners!

We continued along the river until we drove out onto the beach. At no time could we stop as our bus would get bogged down in the sand – it was very exciting altogether. The so-called 90-mile beach was our 'road' and we drove for 60 miles at breakneck speed, racing the other bus. Actually we were told afterwards that buses always went in twos or threes in case anything went wrong. When I asked what they could do if one broke down the answer was short and to the point. 'Leave it!' said the driver. In fact in an emergency the other bus – if there were two, as in our case – cruised round very slowly while passengers alighted from the broken down vehicle and climbed aboard the other one as it kept moving - as slowly as possible. Apparently the buses all had some sort of buoyancy system that could be activated in an emergency so that the bus would not sink and could be retrieved at a later stage - apparently by boat! We were assured that this worked, but I was pleased that we didn't have to try it out!

We covered the 60 miles to our exit point from the beach in less than an hour – one of the most exciting drives of my life. There was a small rocky area where it was safe to stop. One could see where the beach continued south into the distance. Inevitably we had become friendly towards each other during the journey and on our return I took a couple of students - Marie and Todd - out for a most enjoyable meal at Mangonui, a small seaside town along the coast.

I started on my journey south, back towards Wellington – over 900 kilometres away. It was one of the few dull days that I encountered so I drove direct to Whangerei, saw the falls there, and went to straight to the campsite. I had a chance encounter with a traveller by the name of Paul. He thumbed a lift en route – he was hitch hiking around the North Island – and we quaffed a few beers at a local hostelry during the evening before returning to the campsite. He pitched a tent there overnight.

On January 23rd Janet Comerford flew in to Whangerei Airport. I met her and we drove to Pahia and went to see the Waitangi Treaty House. In there is the facsimile copy of a fascinating document, the Waitangi Treaty, signed with crosses by Maori leaders who attended a meeting with the white settlers. The Document offered the Maori tribes the protection of Queen Victoria in return for the Crown having the sole right to purchase their lands. In effect it allowed unlimited immigration to take place and the Maori found that they were being exploited by some ruthless traders. We went into the 'Marae' – the Maori Meeting House – and saw a Maori war canoe. There was also a Shipwreck Museum nearby that was worth a visit. We then crossed over by ferry to Russell and stayed at a famous old hotel, 'The Duke of Marlborough'. As I recall the food was excellent and there was entertainment and dancing during the evening.

The next day saw us take the 'Cream Cruise' in the Bay of Islands. We stopped off on one of the islands and I went for a swim before visiting the Cook Museum in NZ. This was particularly interesting as just prior to leaving England I had been to Whitby to visit the Cook Museum there. In the evening we walked up to Flagstaff Hill near the hotel to see the view of the bay.

On January 25th we set off for Auckland to stay with Janet's friends Sue and Trevor. They were delightful people and again we were able to have a swim in their garden pool to cool down after a hot day's travel.

The long drive back to Wellington was done the following day on what is known as the 'Desert' Road. This is in fact Route1 and goes through some of the more remote parts of New Zealand. Amongst other places it borders the Tongariro National Park and there are magnificent views of the various mountains that are such features of the North Island – Mount Tongariro, Mount Ngauruhoe and Mount Ruapehu. The journey from Auckland to Wellington is around 660 kilometres – over 400 miles.

Altogether it had been the most fantastic start to my holiday. Despite the limited amount of walking I was able to do when I started on January 3rd, by the time I had travelled all around the North Island I had managed to make great strides towards getting fitter and so I was able to get out and see the sights. Everybody that I called in to see on my travels were kindness itself and I resolved to make my home in Cookridge 'Open House' for visitors from the Southern Hemisphere when I returned home. I was in effect at the gateway to a new life – I was no longer hidebound by the restrictions of having to go to work so I could start planning the way that I wanted to live. Travel abroad to the Southern Hemisphere loomed large in my thinking and I even wanted to live in this part of the world for a spell – but more of that comes later on. I was still enjoying myself staying with my older cousin Joan Comerford in Lower Hutt. She took me to meet other members of my family and I even went to spend a day or two at a local school where I was invited to speak to classes about life in Britain. I was able to compare teaching methods and see how things were done 'down under'. One amusing thing happened in one class. A boy kept interrupting and wanting to know details of everything I talked about – so much so indeed that I had to shut him up as he was stopping the flow of stories and his classmates were not pleased with him. At the end of the lesson several of the class stayed behind to ask more questions – he was not one of them. I then went to visit Joan's younger son Peter and his wife Natalie who lived in the same place as the school I had visited. When the door opened who should be there but that very boy who had been such a nuisance. He was a third cousin of mine! I just smiled at him and whispered very quietly, "I'm back at school tomorrow. Better make sure you don't fool around". He didn't!

I was invited to join the staff during breaks and at dinnertimes. When most of them were present in the staffroom they started quizzing me about working conditions in England. But the burning question was not at all what I had expected. They just wanted to know what it was like to go on national strike. One NZ Teachers' Union had called for the first ever countrywide strike and the teachers were petrified that some would lose their jobs! I diplomatically forbore to mention that I had never 'gone on strike' as I have never believed that it is the right way to settle problems. Instead I passed on what I had always said to my own staff when questioned. "If you are a member of a Union they will expect your backing, always provided that a majority have voted in favour of strike action. On the other hand, if you do not approve of the action change to a Union that is not in favour of strike action, but make sure that you have some form of Union membership or insurance cover in case of need as you might want representation in any dispute that could arise in school or even in court". This advice caused much discussion but they still persisted by asking what many of us had questioned years before in England, "What effect has it on the children and parents?" I pointed out that teachers in NZ still had the respect of parents but that they might well forfeit that respect if repeated action took place. As to the consequences for the pupils, this had to be a matter of individual conscience and a decision like that was not easy. Afterwards they thanked me and I said that it had seemed just like a having a staff meeting at home! The one who gained most was the Head – he told me that it had revealed to him exactly how to approach the problem. Some things never change!

One quirk I had after my illness with cancer was to prove to myself that I could work again at something other than teaching. Through Janet Comerford, who worked as a secretary at the NZ Radio Station in Wellington, I applied for and got myself an interview early in February 1985 to see if I could do some work as a broadcaster – possibly as a newsreader or something similar. I was put in a soundproof studio and told to make a tape, reading various news items and articles, and improvising as someone introducing certain topical programmes. It took the best part of an hour. The upshot was that I was offered the opportunity - subject to my being permitted to stay in New Zealand for a year or two - to introduce Schools programmes! As I had not even disclosed that I had ever been a teacher, let alone a Headmaster, I thought that most amusing. I had high hopes of being able to get a work permit and take the job. But alas I came unstuck because, in order to remain in NZ I needed a place to live, or at least a genuine address other than where I was staying on holiday, in order to obtain a work permit. Initially I approached a property agent but before I could rent on a lengthy let I first had to satisfy the immigration laws. I went along to the Immigration Department. The moment they heard that my cancer had been a malignant melanoma they refused my request for a work permit or to stay – even for a year. I pleaded with the Officer involved but he was adamant on two counts – sadly both perfectly reasonable ones. First I might be a drain on their Medical Services if anything happened and I became ill again, and second, because there were 20,000 people out of work, I would be taking a job that could be done by one of those unemployed. In other words they did not want me – fair enough. I did suggest at one point that I was being offered the job because it was my voice that was required and that could not be replicated, but without success. So I failed. But at least I had proved to myself that I was employable so I had to be satisfied with that thought. Nevertheless I was disappointed.

During the first fortnight in February I spent time looking round Wellington. The main visits I made were to the Parliament Building - known as the 'Beehive' because of the design - the Maritime Museum, St Paul's old Cathedral and finally St Paul's new Cathedral. I also enjoyed some window shopping and walking in the Botanical Gardens. These were approached via a steep lift that went literally from the main street right up to the highest point overlooking the City of Wellington. One could walk down to the bottom again, or there were 'stations' where one could re enter the lift. My favourite restaurant was at street level – the milkshakes there were perfection! I did go to the cinema once to see the film 'Mutiny on the Bounty'. Much of the film had been shot in and around the New Zealand coast. There was one scary moment too. I went for a swim in the Wellington Harbour Bay – off a beach at Wainuiomata. A local policeman came down to the beach and shouted to me to get out of the water immediately as a shark had been sighted in the bay. I did not need a second bidding!

Chapter 6 Touring the South Island

When Graeme, Dorothy and Ken's son and my second cousin, had come over to work in England during the late 70s we had met several times when he stayed at the village of Warkton, near Kettering, with my father, and we formed a close family bond of friendship. Naturally we resumed this when I arrived in New Zealand. At the time Graeme was overseeing two garages in Johnsonville, just outside Wellington. I drove out to see him at one of the garages to renew our acquaintance. When I arrived I got the shock of my life! I heard one mechanic speak to a workmate and say, "Yes, that's him", and he came across to greet me with a broad grin on his face. "Do you remember me Sir? Martyn Vause". When I looked at the man I could see that it was indeed none other than a former pupil of mine! He had emigrated to NZ a year or two previously. He had been a 10 year old member of my class in 1964 when Holy Trinity C.E. School, Cookridge had first opened. Naturally I was absolutely delighted to see him and asked him how he was getting on. "Very well", he replied. "I have worked for Mr Hamilton ever since I first arrived in Wellington. Now I am looking for promotion – more responsibility – but I am unable to apply for the job here at the garage, as I have to have a written character reference. This is the way things are done over here". At that point Graeme came out of his office to greet me. Then he asked me about Martyn – did I remember him? I explained our connection and at the same time offered there and there to write him a character reference on the condition that he addressed me as 'Chris' and not 'Sir'. Martyn was absolutely delighted on both counts – so was Graeme! I duly produced a letter of commendation and Martyn got the promotion he wanted – and deserved. I think that of all the coincidences I have ever come across this was by far the most remarkable. To be able to help a former pupil in this way gave me more joy than almost anything I have ever had the pleasure of doing. And to think that Martyn had come to the other side of the world and finished up working for a member of my family! Inevitably Martyn invited me to his house to meet his wife and children. His wife had been a pupil at Abbey Grange C.E. Comprehensive School, Leeds at the same time as Martyn, who had moved on to Abbey Grange when he left Holy Trinity, and this was where they had met. I had a wonderful evening with them and it turned out to be one of several over the course of the 6 visits to NZ that I made between 1984 and 2001. Eventually he set up his own business in the motor trade, with Graeme's blessing, and to the best of my knowledge he is still doing very well. I always called in to see him at his garage at Porirua whenever I was in the area. In fact on one occasion I was invited to join him on a Sunday when he was taking part in a hill climbing trial in a jeep he had worked on. It was fantastic – in truth the climb was so steep that all the loose coins I had in my tracksuit pockets fell out! On another occasion we went to a party where the lads had an old motorcycle. I was in my element and was able to ride around the field where the party was being held. However as I got back to the party I swerved virtually out of control and I realised something was radically wrong. When I stopped and checked the front wheel the wheel nut had worked loose. I hate to think what would have happened if I tried to ride any further until it was tightened, but all was well and I set off again. The people at the party were great – all of them half my age or less – but they treated me as one of their own at the time. Whenever I happened to meet any of them on my travels locally they were always happy to spend time with me. It is a fact that young people in NZ never made age an issue. It was most refreshing and I hope that it is still the same today.

At the time, when I was away gadding around the North Island in the Chrysler 'Valiant' car that Ken had lent me, Graeme had decided to take a week's holiday so that he could join up with me. He arranged to take me on a whistle stop tour of the South Island in order that I could see the beautiful countryside - mountains, fiords, hills, plains, beaches, towns, settlements and holiday resorts. The idea was to go round the coast as far as time permitted. This in effect meant that when it was time for him to return home we could drive straight back to Picton at the tip of the South Island where he could board the ferry for Wellington. I, on the other hand, could wait there until Ken, Dorothy and Joan came across from Wellington on the ferry and we could set off again to go round the parts of the South Island that I had not seen with Graeme.

We set off on our journey from Linton at 6.30am on Saturday, February 16th 1985. It was a dull, overcast day with low cloud cover as we drove to the ferry port in Wellington, about 12 kms away. There were few formalities – just a quick check of our tickets to ensure we were booked in for the 8am car ferry - the SS Aramoana - to Picton and we joined the queue of cars waiting to board. We were soon driving into the bowels of the ship. We parked and went upstairs to enjoy a substantial breakfast. Fortunately the weather was calm. Sometimes the storms in the Cook Strait can make journeys very rough sailing. This was my first lesson – I had bacon, tomato, egg and fried bread while Graeme had 3 or 4 eggs with his meal of bacon, sausages, tomatoes, fried bread and anything else that was on offer. He followed this with several rounds of toast and jam or marmalade, plus at least two cups of tea or coffee. He certainly knew how to enjoy his food! I questioned him on this intake one day and he told me that while he had been in training with the New Zealand rowing team he had to keep his weight up at around 18 stones and it had become a habit. He had also had compulsory training for months in order to build up his over all strength and fitness so that when the Olympics came round he was at his peak. Very sadly things went seriously wrong a few weeks prior to the Games and he injured his back so badly, compressing several vertebrae in his spine, that he had to withdraw from rowing and give up the sport altogether. He had represented his country several times from the age of 19. I had initially met him at a rowing regatta near Nottingham when he rowed for New Zealand against a Russian crew in 1974.

We sailed across the Cook Strait and Marlborough Sounds into the Tory Channel and then into the lower part of Queen Charlotte Sound. The Islands were initially shrouded in low lying sea mist but as we approached the port of Picton the sun began to shine and the beauty of the surrounding landscape became clear. It was all very impressive, with the darkly shaded and inhospitable looking mountains towering in the background and the steep sides of the Sounds stretching right down into the waters.

After disembarking from the SS Aramoana we drove down Highway 1 as far as Blenheim before turning right to join Highway 6. Our journey took us through Nelson, Murchison, Reefton and Greymouth. The sky was a deep blue and the scenery was breathtaking, constantly changing as Graeme drove at breakneck speed through mountains and passes, crossing rivers and deep gulleys on long narrow bridges. There was virtually no traffic at all – a phenomenon that I had not really encountered anywhere else in the world when driving. At one point we covered around 40 kms before we saw another vehicle – a lorry that had failed to negotiate a sharp bend at the end of a bridge. We stopped briefly but there was no sign of the driver, or anyone else for that matter, so we continued on our way. Eventually we had a brief stop at Greymouth before continuing down the West Coast through Hokitika and Harihari, then turning away from the Highway and stopping off at the actual face of the Franz Joseph Glacier. What an incredible sight that was – ice and snow stretching as far as the eye could see. There were gentle rivulets of water dropping over the edges of the ice. A local guide told us that at night when the temperatures fell to zero and below the rivulets froze up. He also informed us that the actual face of glacier was gradually receding but that it would take thousands of years for it to disappear completely.....

The final leg of our journey that day took us past Mount Cook. Unfortunately the summit was shrouded in cloud. A local to whom we spoke assured us that this was quite normal – so much so that the summit was only very rarely seen, and then it would usually appear for just a short spell before disappearing into the mist and cloud once more. We motored on and found a campsite not far from the sea at Haast. We had travelled well over 700 kilometres that day. It was quite the longest journey through mountainous country that I have ever done in a car and it was completed in just over 10 hours driving with only three stops! For sheer exhilaration that had to be truly outstanding. We hired a log hut for the night before going out for an evening meal. We retired to bed on our return and as soon as my head touched the pillow I slept like a log for around 10 hours.

The next morning dawned sunny and warm. After breakfast at the site we set off again – only this time we motored towards the Haast Pass at a reasonable speed, taking in the exotic beauty of the scenery. I remember that at one point we were looking for a garage, as we were getting low on petrol. As there was so little traffic around and we appeared to be miles from anywhere I mused that if we ran out before finding a filling station we could face a long wait before anyone turned up. There were no telephones in the area that we could see, and mobile phones were not on the market then, so contacting the equivalent of our Automobile Association was not an obvious option! The first part of the journey was fairly flat. We ran alongside the Haast river and just as we reached the entrance to the Haast Pass, much to our relief, we passed through what I can only describe as a tiny hamlet with about three log houses and a local store with a single old fashioned petrol pump where the fuel was obtained by pulling a handle up and down. I have never been so grateful to see a place like that in my life! The owner came out and filled the car up, at the same time telling us that we were the first car he had seen that morning as "there ain't much traffic aroun' this neck of the woods. Motorists don't like comin' over the Pass as it's a bit rough". We didn't argue with him. However we found out just what he meant before too long. The road surface was not tarmac – just a well-flattened track, liberally covered with stones. Given the fact that there are mountains on either side it was quite a daunting prospect. I would imagine that it must have been positively off-putting when the clouds rolled in and darkened the place – a bit like Dante's lurid description of Hell! But we were lucky – the day was bright and sunny. Actually it probably wasn't as bad as it sounds and as Graeme was quite used to that sort of driving it did not matter, although one or two spots were a bit hairy where the road was steep and close to an overhang. I closed my eyes on more than one occasion and left it to Graeme to negotiate the ups and downs – and sharp corners. But he knew what he was doing and we got through the Pass without any serious incidents. I'm glad I wasn't driving! Many years later I went that way again and that time the road had been properly completed and the Pass was quite safe with all the sharp bends and the dangerous tracks eradicated. However I was so glad to have seen it before the work was done to make the Pass easy to travel through. There was something of the pioneer 'do it yourself' spirit very much in the air at that time.

At the end of the Pass is the head of Lake Wanaka and the road ran close to the shore. We stopped for a while on the shore of the Lake before motoring on to the township of Wanaka itself. The views of the lake were truly magnificent with the hills and mountains stretching away into the distance. We stayed with Bill, Dorothy's cousin, and his wife Jean, overnight. During the late afternoon Bill took us up a gravel track road along the Cattle Flats Gorge to see the Glacier on Mount Aspiring.

On Monday February 18th after a good breakfast we drove to Queenstown via Arrowtown. This old township was at the centre of a Gold mining area and this was reflected by names of shops. In particular I visited one local store called 'The Golden Nugget' with its wooden front reflecting the type of place prevalent in the main street.
On arrival in Queenstown we first went up by gondola to a high point overlooking the lake and its environs. By one of those coincidences that occasionally happen I got talking to a couple that came from Darlington in County Durham. We exchanged first names and sat together to have a bite to eat in the restaurant overlooking the Lake. Some years later I was attending a cricket dinner in Darlington one evening with a college friend, Dick Hansell. Incredibly, in his party were these same two people – they were friends of Dick's and they were throwing a party after the dinner for us. It turned out that they had mentioned to Dick that they had met a chap named Chris in Queenstown when they were on holiday. He realised who it was and as I went into the dinner he produced these two. What a meeting that was – and what a party afterwards! Sadly their names escape me after all this time.

We visited an old car museum where many of the real old vehicles had been preserved – an incredible collection. There was a house built entirely of bottles too – and it was in use. We also went on an old steamer – the TSS Earnshaw, built in 1912 and known locally as 'The Lady of the Lake' - that took us round part of Lake Wakatipu. It was all so picturesque when viewed from the centre of the lake.

During the night the weather changed and the rains came. It also turned bitterly cold. We had booked into a log cabin on a local campsite. When we arrived after supper in the town we found only four bare bunks with a mattress on each. There was no heating so it meant sleeping in our clothes – between two mattresses. It was uncomfortable to say the least! However in the morning we decided that, whatever the weather, we would see if the jet boat was running in the gorge of the Shotover River on the outskirts of Queenstown. When we arrived there were several others people keen to take the jet boat trip up the gorge. The only problem was the weather. The overnight rain had brought the water level up and the pilot of the boat was in two minds as to whether or not it was safe to take us out. In the end we went. It s the most incredible trip I had ever undertaken. The jet boat could travel in only a few inches of water due to its speed. The pilot was brilliant. He had to be as there was little room for error! We all finished up soaked but it did not matter. The adrenalin certainly flowed through my veins in abundance and the 'devil may care' attitude on board was reflected mainly through the skill of the pilot. He could turn the boat on a sixpence – and virtually did so. We went quite a way up stream to where another boat came from higher up the river. We then turned and tore through the water downstream, under overhangs and through incredibly narrow spaces between rocks. By the time it was all over I imagine that everyone on that boat had been given the most exciting few minutes of their lives! To illustrate the danger, two American tourists were killed a few weeks later. When the two boats already mentioned reached the same point on the river – one from downstream and the other from upstream – they crashed. After that boats were not allowed to enter the same areas at any point on the river. It was a salutary lesson. There were also people bunjay jumping from the bridge nearby. It certainly was some Outdoor Sporting Centre!

Our next port of call was Te Anau – the town at the southern end of Lake Te Anau. On the way we stopped off at Kingston to see the steam train that still ran there, known as 'The Kingston Flyer'. We drove along to Lake Manapouri where there was a massive hydroelectric project being carried out. Unfortunately we did not have time to visit the plant to see just what was being built. Back at Te Anau we went by boat to be taken round the glowworm caves – quite fascinating. It was incredible how much light the glow worms gave off. We stayed overnight at the local campsite.

By now it was Wednesday February 20th and time was beginning to catch up with us. Graeme had to be back at Picton on the Saturday to catch the ferry home and hand over the car to Ken, Dorothy and Joan. They were going to take me to parts of the Island I still hadn't seen. We drove to Dunedin, on the east side of the South Island, staying with family friends, Lou and Oliver Walrich. We met up briefly with Raelyn, my second cousin from Palmerston. First we drove around the city, then we all went out to supper at the Carnavon Restaurant – a railway coach! We were up until 3.30am and we quaffed a lot of whisky that night – too much!

On Thursday we motored to Palmerston. We stayed with my cousin Kathleen and her husband, Alan Clearwater and their son Kelvin. Their daughter Raelyn we had met at Dunedin. We also saw my Aunt Dorothy. This was the first time I had met her – quite a matriarch!

On Friday we drove to Christchurch, staying with Alan and Mary Marslin. We toured the city on a tram, visiting the Opera house, the Town Hall and the Cathedral. Then we drove out to the harbour at Littleton – where a ship had literally sailed into a crane instead of docking beside it – quite a bit of damage to both!

Saturday February 23rd. We left Christchurch early in the morning and drove at breakneck speed back to Picton, arriving just in time to see the ferry docking. Thus
Dorothy, Joan and Ken arrived and Graeme left to sail back to Wellington. What a wonderful holiday he had given me. I had seen so much – and for me there was still more to come.

With Ken driving at a considerably more sedate pace than Graeme had done, we set off and again drove to Nelson. From there we literally turned right and went over a high pass to Takaka, where we saw the local spring spurting high up out of the ground. Next we continued on to Collingwood. This was where Ken and Dorothy had spent their honeymoon years before. We went swimming from a small beach there before staying at a comfortable motel for the night.

The following day we retraced our steps to Nelson and had a look round before driving to Westport on the West Coast, driving along near the Buller River and passing through the Buller Gorge on the way to our destination. This is an extremely beautiful and remote area. Once again we found an excellent overnight Motel at Westport

From Westport we travelled down the west coast as far as Greymouth stopping a couple of times on the way. I was fascinated to see the Pancake Rocks at Punakaiki. These are a whole series of limestone pillars the centres of which are very hard. But the outer surfaces are softer and over a period of thousands of years rain and the sea have 'attacked' the joints in the beds of limestone. The softer parts have washed away, leaving the hard layers of rock sticking out. These resemble whole piles of pancakes – doubtless awaiting some form of syrup to complete them! There are several 'blowholes' too where the sea rushes through. It sounds like rolls of thunder and every now and then spouts of water – like geysers – erupt from the blowholes. The sense of power emanating from the blowholes is quite mind-boggling and shows how powerful water can be when compressed. We visited the Coalmine Museum at Greymouth too – well worth a visit.

After a good night's rest at Greymouth we drove across Arthur's Pass to Geraldine. Again, the scenery is mind blowing and the steep rocky sides of the Pass made it unforgettably awesome. Much of the road was still gravel surfaced and in places the road virtually turned back on itself in tight 'S' bends, making the driving both difficult and sometimes downright dangerous. Ken was extremely careful – he had to be as the heavy rains had rutted the road surfaces quite deeply. There were places to pull off to enjoy the view. At one viewpoint we saw a hilarious scene. An Indian tourist had stopped his car and had left it to sightsee, together with his wife and two children, despite notices warning drivers that there were Kea birds in the area and that they would jump up onto vehicles left standing unattended. Kea birds will eat absolutely anything and are considered highly intelligent creatures. They will often steal things that are being carried loose. On this occasion two Kea birds had flown on the bonnet of the car and were pulling away the rubber that holds the windscreen in place. Luckily the driver returned to his car and managed to shoo them away, but not before they had removed and flown off with most of the rubber! Apparently they can cause endless trouble if they get into houses. I'm not surprised after what we saw! Ken's comment was short and to the point. "Serve him right. He should read the notices". I forbore to point out that possibly the poor man did not read or speak English. Judging from the sounds coming from the rest of his family English was certainly not their first language! We stayed in a motel at Geraldine overnight.

By now it was Thursday February 28th and we drove to Lake Ruataniwha at Twizel to watch two of Dorothy's and Ken's daughters, Christine and Judith, compete in the double sculls race at the New Zealand Rowing Championship. They did well, and won their heat. There were other members of the family there too - June and Ernie – Dorothy's and Joan's cousin and spouse. We went to their house at Cromwell. Ernie had a garage full of motorcycles and go-carts – a real DIY man. Cromwell was soon to become part of a new reservoir.

The next day – March 1st – I was shown where the dam was being built as the major part of the Upper Waitaki River Power scheme. It had been worked on for 8 years and in 2 years more it would be completed. The water level in the river would then rise 40 metres. We then drove on round Alexandria and the surrounding area.

On March 2nd we reached Palmerston to stay with Kathleen and Alan for a few days. I had been there with Graeme a week before. I climbed up the steep grassy hill to the Puketapu Monument. I was taken out for rides around the coast to see the sights. We also spent a day in Dunedin for me to have a look round and then do some shopping. I bought several shirts, as prices were so cheap. One evening during our stay there was a family gathering with my Aunt at the head of the table looking every inch the true family Matriarch. It was very special as it was the only time I ever saw most of the immediate family together in one place.

On March 8th we went to see Mount Cook. It was a perfect day for it and I actually saw the summit. Mount Sefton was also clear for a while and the summit was briefly bathed in bright sunshine. Then the clouds drifted in again.

We returned to Lake Ruataniwha on the 9th to watch the girls in the semi final of their race. They came in 5th. The next day we drove back to Picton. It took 8 hours! We boarded the SS Arahuna this time and returned to Wellington and then home to Linden. Once again I had been given a most wonderful holiday.

My last port of call before returning briefly to Melbourne was to my cousin Kathleen at Raumati. She took me along to The Southward Museum. This was a privately owned museum that housed all kinds of memorabilia and famous vehicles, from Marlene Dietrich's Cadillac and Al Capone's bullet proof car with glass an inch thick, to racing boats, racing cars, veteran cars, aeroplanes, motorcycles of all ages, tricycles, bicycles and even carriages and carts that early settlers had used. It is without doubt the best museum of its type that I have ever visited. Every time I visited New Zealand over the past 25 years I have always spent a day at the Southward Museum. I even got to meet Mr Southward himself once.

The last few days prior to leaving New Zealand I spent walking around the city of Wellington. I had thoroughly enjoyed being able to get about, thanks to the generosity of my hosts, but it was time to leave. I did not wish to outstay my welcome – after all I was being invited back any time I wanted to make the journey and the thought of being able to return one day was of paramount importance as it gave me a target to aim at for the future. I fully intended to return, God willing!

Finally I somewhat reluctantly set off to return to Leeds, stopping off for a fortnight in Melbourne, to spend time with Ursula and Frank Tyson, Bon Carmody and George Tribe. While I was with them I went to watch some cricket at the Melbourne Cricket Ground and I did some more cricket coaching for Frank and the Victoria Cricket Association. I also attended a Fitness Centre for a week, doing exercises in water and generally improving my health as much as possible. I suppose I had achieved what I had thought was never going to be possible. I could walk well again and because I had not been under any stress I had recovered far better than I could ever have believed possible. It was time to go home and face whatever problems might come my way. I had spent almost all my money, initially feeling in my heart of hearts that I would not live to return home. But the miracle appeared to have happened and I am convinced to this day that the wonderful holiday I had been privileged to share with so many people in the Antipodes had sufficient influence on me both physically and mentally to give me the chance to survive the cancer that had plagued me. Freedom from stress was for me the key. Now was the time to resume a normal life – at least that is what I thought at the time!

My flight home with Garuda airlines proved to be slow but enjoyable. I landed in Bali for an hour, and then flew into Bangkok – an experience not to be missed. The airport was quite fascinating for me. It featured many oriental pictures and fiercesome creature-like statues that I could only assume were there to repel evil spirits or to engender some form of worship. The colours were bright with various shades of red being quite dazzling and contrasting strongly with other less outstanding backgrounds. I remember just wandering round the main building, looking at the brightly dressed shop assistants, airport staff and passengers waiting to fly out, and thinking just how much they stood out compared with the quieter dress styles worn by people from the west. From the windows of the waiting areas one could see the ornate temples and high buildings that were adjacent to the Airport and that stretched along the road with its heavy traffic – cars, buses, bicycles, and cycle taxis peddled by the driver, carrying people to venues around the city. I wished that I could just be taken round the local streets so that I could savour the atmosphere that seemed to emanate from the lively, bustling citizens of Bangkok. But alas the stopover was too short and we were not permitted to leave the airport building. But it was still an enjoyable and edifying experience.

The flight was punctuated by brief stops at a couple of other airports where Arab travellers disembarked en route. We landed at the Charles de Gaulle Airport as well, on the outskirts of Paris, and we had the thrill of watching 'Concorde' moving out to the runway in front of the 'Jumbo' I was in. As we were at an angle to the start of the runway we also saw it take off. What a superb looking aeroplane – and what a noise it made when it took off! That we could hear it distinctly, to say the least, was a complete under statement. It hurt one's eardrums. We followed it a minute later and in a short while we flew back to Heath Row. Having collected my cases and gone through Customs without difficulty Daphne and Frank picked me up and took me back to their house in Sunbury. I slept like a log!

Philip drove down the next day and took me back home to Leeds. I remember that once he had left me at my house and gone back home it suddenly hit me that I was alone again and for a day or two I felt lonely. I had shared my life with so many people during my vacation and I had stayed at so many different venues so there was always someone around. But the feeling certainly did not last long and friends called to see how I had fared on my travels once they knew I had returned safely. I must admit that at times I got so enthusiastic about what I had seen and done that it must have become a bit tedious for anyone listening. In fact Jack Edmondson and I were invited for lunch one Sunday at Sheila and John Scatchard's and I was then banned from mentioning anything about New Zealand or Australia. This was backed up by the threat of having no Yorkshire puddings put on my plate - and I loved my Yorkshire puddings! I had missed them more than anything else in the food line while I had been away so the 'bribe' worked!

My aim from the moment I returned home was to work to make sufficient money to return to the Southern Hemisphere once again. It was the best incentive I could have had!

Chapter 7 Starting again

Now came the moment of truth. It had taken most of the money I had in my bank to finance my trip to the Antipodes. I had already purchased Molly's half on the house after she had left and had set up a 12-year mortgage to cover the cost. The amount involved was £14,000 and I had to find the monthly payments amounting in total to around £360 each month – if I didn't my house would be at risk as that amount was combined with my own mortgage payments. In 1983 £360 was considered a lot of money and represented a large slice of my income. My yearly income as a Headmaster was just over £14,000 at that time and I was in the top 5% of wages being earned in the primary sector of Education. St Margaret's C.E. School was a large one, rated as Group 6. There were 460 children on role when I was first appointed and that controlled the salary scale for the duration of my Headship. What made things really difficult was that, due to my illness, I had been forced to retire in August 1984 on a pension of just over £6,000 and this was a problem. When I first came out of hospital after my two cancer operations I was automatically put 'on the dole' for three months and that brought in sufficient for my immediate needs when combined with my pension. Obviously I was not fit to do any work and I still had to make regular visits three times a week to Leeds General Infirmary in order to have further remedial treatment. Fortunately, although walking was still a bit of a problem I could perfectly well drive so getting there was not too difficult.

As well as a pension I received a lump sum of £19,000 from the Education Authority and my former next-door neighbour, Alan Rodger, who was well up in the financial world at Allied Dunbar, offered to help with investments for me. I immediately gave him £14,000 for this. In order for this money to start working to my advantage I had to agree not to withdraw any of it for the first year. This way he could invest it at a higher rate of interest. At the end of that year I would be able to withdraw £160 a month and this would enable me to help pay the mortgage. Furthermore, in 3 years he virtually doubled my investments so I was able to put a bit of money aside towards my next trip. Financially he was a real saviour for without the money he managed to make for me I should probably have had to consider moving. So it was up to me to find a way to add to the money that I had been paid while on the dole. I worked out that if I could raise about £10,000 in around three years I could survive all right. That became my ultimate goal and provided the incentive to prove myself once again. I needed to feel that I was going to give myself a great opportunity to see just what I could achieve. At the time it was purely personal but as I gained strength and got back to normal it became almost an obsession. I intended to prove to myself – and others - that life was still well worth living despite all that had happened.

Although details of our separation had already been settled by discussion to our mutual satisfaction prior to me being taken ill in September 1983, petitioning for divorce on the grounds of incompatability and the court granting it took until September 2nd 1985. Molly had found an apartment in 1982 but because of problems with the roof of the property she could not move in for 9 months. This meant that she needed to stay on during that period. It was an extremely sad time for both of us although it enabled us to sort out who was to have what. Molly moved out on April 7th 1983, when the repair work was completed on her flat. During that period I went away for a few days to stay with my friends Susan and Steve Taylor while Molly moved away. Coming home afterwards to what was to be from then on an empty house was hard but Philip was there to greet me on my return. I have never forgotten that wonderful gesture – it must have been very hard for him too. In fact the weekend following we went out together. He was learning to drive. We drove out to Sutton Bank on the Scarborough Road and stopped to have a look at the superb view and to watch the gliders taking off from the airfield at the top of the bank near the 'White Horse'. John and Sheila Scatchard were there with a large group of children. They stopped for a minute to chat and they invited me to call for a meal during the following week. A friendship developed with them. I had got to know Sheila professionally when she was Head Teacher of 'The Whartons' - a School in Otley. I was Chairman of the North West Leeds Head Teachers' Association during the 70s and we had meetings once or twice a term. She later spoke to me about making an application for a Middle School in Leeds and that was when I got to know something of her work. She got the Headship of Middlethorne Middle School.

However in the long run the important thing for me was that I had survived cancer for the time being and I decided there and then that I was going to start planning a new life here in the UK in order to make sufficient money to indulge my pleasure and return to the Southern Hemisphere again. Furthermore, provided that I was well enough, I did not intend to go back just once but whenever I could afford it. At one time I had even considered emigrating but this was a non starter as I would have been a possible drain on the health finances of either New Zealand or Australia so that was that! From now on the intention was to enjoy what life I thought I still had left and do as many of the practical things I had always secretly wanted to have a go at. I had nothing to lose at this stage!

I had always harboured an ambition to rebuild a car engine. I needed to find an old 'banger' really but it so happened that luck played its part once again in my life. Alan Willey, who had been on the staff at Horsforth St Margaret's School during my tenure as Headmaster – I appointed him as it happened – owned an old Fiat 138 hard top sports car. He was always having problems with it and had decided to change it for something better. The engine had been taken completely to pieces to find out what ailed it but it was going to cost quite a lot to put back together – hence the reason for his decision. It was to be scrapped as a cheaper alternative. Over the years we had become good friends. We shared a love of sports and, like I had once done at College, he had specialised in Physical Education. That was why I had appointed him in the first place. We always used to go swimming together on a Friday afterschool until I had to retire. In fact even on the Friday that I retired - in July 1984 after just six weeks back at School after my cancer operations – we went swimming as usual. I wanted to finish my career in Education doing something that I had made a habit of doing. I loved swimming and it was the best way that I could start to get fit again. Walking was a problem but swimming wasn't as the water took most of my weight and the buoyancy allowed me to exercise unencumbered.   One evening after returning from my first trip to the southern hemisphere we met up for a drink. The car was mentioned by Alan – I offered to buy it. The upshot was that I fetched it from the guy who should have rebuilt the engine and paid Alan £95 for the engine parts and the body shell. I managed to tow that back to my house. The engine parts were in a couple of boxes and I took those in the car too of course. The next problem was – where on earth do I start? Luck, in the shape of Joe

Adams, Sheila Scatchard's Dad, with whom I had struck up a friendship, came to my aid. He had been a driver. His career had been varied. He had driven for the brother of a member of the aristocracy for a time – I think it was for Lord Derby's brother - and had maintained the vehicles as well. He had been a long distance lorry driver, and he had also had to maintain vehicles when he worked for a Local Council Department. He had probably forgotten more about engines than I had ever learned! He was 78 years old but he still hankered after working with engines. Sadly his wife had died some years earlier. He offered to join me in the venture. He came across from his home in Armley whenever he could. It took about a year to rebuild the engine completely. He simply kept a close eye on what I was doing and put me right whenever things went wrong. They did - quite often!

The great day came when at last everything was ready, apart from filling the gearbox and the engine with oil. I went and bought the oil first thing that morning. Joe put it in and checked over everything. Then, with bated breath, I pressed the starter. The engine started at the second try and the shout of elation I gave must have been heard all over Cookridge! Immediately we got in and off we went for a short drive. But that was enough – the bodywork needed a bit of welding and then there had to be an MOT carried out before we had finished. We were both delighted! But unfortunately there was an unexpected downside.

So excited had I become that I had forgotten to check and make sure nothing had been left out, either on the ground or on the roof. Sadly, I had left my wallet on the top of the car after having fetched the oil, intending to put it in my pocket later. It came off as we went out of the drive of my house, along the street and round the first corner. I knew almost immediately – searching everywhere but without success. One of the local children found things that had been thrown down by whoever found it, but the wallet, my money and my two cards had gone. I immediately informed the National Westminster Bank and there should have been a stop put on both cards. But either their preventative system failed or someone was inefficient. Two days later I had a call from Nat. West. asking me if I had found one of the cards and had withdrawn any money from a wall cash machine. I hadn't, but the thief had - £50. He had used two machines so that was £100 taken. Two months later he had been on a spending spree in Newcastle to the tune of £850 on my second card. It cost me nothing in either case as I had reported it and was reimbursed, but it just showed that a so called system to prevent fraud just had not worked – typical, I'm afraid. I wrote a letter of complaint about the inefficiency of the system but got no reply – not really surprising I suppose as a newspaper report showed that several million pounds a year was fraudulently obtained through cards being lost or stolen.

That car, once it was passed as roadworthy, gave me much pleasure. It was also there for the use of any friends who came from abroad. George Tribe and Bon Carmody had it for an extended tour. Frank Tyson, and his son Philip, both used it at one time or another when they were over from Australia on holiday in England. My son Philip borrowed it on occasion and had fun with it too and even the occasional neighbour enjoyed using it. Michelle from next door borrowed it several times. It was a genuinely quick motor with good acceleration, reaching up to 100 miles an hour without too much difficulty, and it was fun to drive. I remember taking Jack Edmondson out in several times. On one occasion he encouraged me to see just what speed we could do. Jack enjoyed going fast! Eventually it ended life when Graeme, my second cousin Sarah's partner at that time, was involved in an accident on the M1. A lorry ploughed into the back of it while it was stationary at some roadworks just north of the London area. Fortunately Graeme was unhurt but the car was a complete write off. I eventually got £450 from the Insurance Company after a year of haggling. As I had spent about that much to get it going in the first place it had been a good investment, considering the pleasure I had enjoyed.

It is truly amazing what opportunities chance throws up during one's daily life. I first decided that I would go and look for a new car as my Triumph Accord was getting on in years. It had done 65,000 miles and was likely to start costing money to keep it going. I drove into a garage at the top end of New Road Side. It turned out to be a department of the main Horsforth Garage that was situated at the lower end of the same main road. The salesman gave his name as Phil Maskery and I was just in the process of stating that I wanted to see what cars were on sale when the telephone rang in the office. He answered it, at the same time inviting me in to sit down. Inevitably I got the general gist of the conversation – it was the boss of his firm enquiring as to whether someone could be found to take a car to Burnley for 8am the next morning - and would Phil see to it. The upshot was that I somewhat diffidently offered to help out. After all, I was not working for a living anymore. I could also see that this might well be used to my advantage. He was desperate – the car had to be delivered as soon as the garage at Burnley opened. What was worse was that another new car also had to be fetched from a garage at Birkenhead the next day. My offer solved his problem – and mine. He suggested that I could leave my car at his garage overnight and take the new Renault 5 home. He also worked out a timetable that would get me from Burnley to Liverpool and then on to Birkenhead the next day. He rang the garage there and told them I would arrive around two o'clock to pick up the car. Buying myself another car at that point was put on hold after that. I was no longer in the mood to discuss finance and as I was doing him a favour anyway I reckoned that I would be in a stronger bargaining position providing that I completed the work successfully.

Once I had parked the car in my drive overnight I proceeded to study train timetables in order to see if I could get the job done more quickly. I worked out that if I made three stops and changed trains at each station I could get from Burnley to Liverpool in a couple of hours or so. I also reckoned that if I got to Liverpool I could get across to Birkenhead, courtesy of the garage I was due to go to. So I did just that. I rang the Birkenhead garage in Mike Thorpe's name, as his representative, and in no time a car arrived to pick me up. As I was smartly dressed I must have given the impression that I was a senior member of the firm! I was given an executive lunch at the garage, courtesy of the Manager there. I then set off for Horsforth along the M62, arriving at just two o'clock. Phil was in the act of ringing the Birkenhead Garage to see if I had arrived there when I walked in. He was delighted! THEN we talked cars. I eventually bought a Renault 11 Saloon after being ferried down to the main garage by Phil. The boss, Mike Thorpe immediately asked if I would be prepared to deliver and fetch cars whenever I was needed. What a slice of luck! I accepted his offer but as I was on the dole once again I would not take cash payment for services rendered. Instead I settled for £10 of petrol per trip plus travel and eating expenses. This meant that I could run my car for virtually nothing. Mike was so pleased that I got my car on very generous terms as part of the deal as well. Better to be born lucky than rich I decided – and Phil Maskery and I became firm friends. I even got car servicing done at reduced rates so I had landed firmly on my feet!

The jobs came thick and fast. I was enjoying myself driving all around the country at somebody else's expense. I even took Jack Edmondson with me several times – and Joe Adams, Sheila Scatchard's Dad, came too. He and I once motored down to Kidwelly in South Wales and returned the same day – some 640 miles in all. I built up a backlog on the petrol front and so was able to fill up my own car whenever I felt like it. I worked with the Renault firm for a long time, fitting journeys in with other work that I started later. During the early days of my unofficial 'employment' I was asked to take a Renault 5 Diesel Turbo to a garage at Lanchester in County Durham. When I delivered the car I was to be driven across to Middlesbrough to fetch another Renault car back to Leeds. Two things of note happened that day. First I had to go to the garage where Phil Maskery worked, to fill up with diesel. The car stopped soon after I left the main garage – not even enough diesel to cover the half mile to the other garage where the fuel was kept! Filling an empty diesel car was difficult enough without this happening so I was a good half an hour adrift setting off and I could not afford to be late. But driving that turbo was dream and I made up the time by putting my foot down on the A1 – up to 100mph at more than one point. I was not stopped so all was well. I arrived at exactly 11.30am and after dealing with the delivery paperwork I was taken to Middlesbrough by car. I met up with my friend Dick Hansell, a guy who had been up at Durham at the same time as I was, for lunch. He was the senior manager at a Middlesbrough Insurance Company branch. Fortunately it was the same company that I used in Leeds – so every time there was a problem with my insurance I rang him. He always got it sorted out in quick time – a useful man to know!

After a good lunch he dropped me off at the garage where I was to pick up the car bound for Horsforth. I filled up with petrol and drove away WITHOUT PAYING. Nor had I remembered to fix the trade plates on the car so I was breaking the law in all directions! I realised what I had done and turned round as quickly as I could and returned to the garage, paid for the petrol and put the trade plates on just as a police car came into the forecourt. I was convinced by that time that he had followed me back to the garage. However I kept a straight face, drove casually out of the garage exit and stuck to the speed limit rigidly on the way home – third time might not have been so lucky!

Really I was incredibly fortunate. Sometimes I delivered vehicles to a food centre at Croydon, on the south side of London. In the summer months I left early - at 4.30am or thereabouts. I would stop off at Sunbury to see my cousin

Daphne and have breakfast. Sometimes I would deliver top range cars and I always dressed very smartly then. It worked wonders and I was invariably entertained to a good lunch by the management. On other occasions I would deliver refrigerator vans to Croydon. I dressed accordingly as if I was one of the staff – casual. Then when I arrived I would be treated to a wholesome meal in the staff kitchens before catching a train into the centre of London. I often spent the afternoon at a place of interest or went to the pictures before catching a long distance 'National' bus back to Leeds. That was a bit slow so after one extremely lengthy journey on the bus during very bad weather I opted to travel by train – more expensive – but I was not paying! I must say that I invariably looked forward to getting called in to drive a vehicle somewhere. On the trip to Kidwelly in South Wales, mentioned earlier, Joe Adams and I drove through the centre of that country – a beautiful drive – in a top of the range Renault 25. The job was to bring back a different coloured car – the one chosen by a lady customer. We came back much more quickly in the evening on motorways. What a great day out that was! I occasionally had to go to a port and pick up a car so that gave me a free half a day at the seaside. Sometimes I had to tow a new car somewhere – that was harder work. But as I had towed caravans around Europe while I was married that was no problem either. Sometimes I would return with cheques of up to £25,000 in payment for vehicles – lucky I was honest! The best thing about all that was that I was doing something I thoroughly enjoyed for free and was actually saving money at the same time. There was the occasional blip – like the day I took the latest model of the Renault 25 down to a garage in Hackney. The traffic was horrendous that day – the weather had been foul as I had driven down on the M1 and I had used up more petrol than usual queuing to get off the motorway and on towards my destination. Suddenly I heard a disembodied voice say, "This car needs filling with petrol". As I was on my own I could not believe what I had heard! Then I realised that it was a built in message. I duly pulled in and got one gallon of petrol. Soon after I got back into the traffic the message repeated itself – so much for being careful. Nobody had thought to tell me about the new innovation of the speaking vehicle computer!

As soon as I was well enough I came off the dole and did some work for cash. Initially I took a painting job on for my great friends Sue and Steve Taylor. Sue had been left a small farm by her Father and they decided to build a decent house on the land and move to the farm. I called in to see them one day during my travels and they told me they were looking for a painter to do the inside of the house. But the cheapest quote had been £3,500 and money was getting a bit tight. As I was about to go back on the dole for a second time I offered to do the job for £490 – the exact amount that I would have been paid on the dole. There was a bungalow near the new house and it was big enough for me to stay there with them until they could move. Naturally they were delighted. We had been great friends for many years. Thus they would gain and so would I. Furthermore I could get to the M1 easily so I could commute to Leeds and back if I had any work offered by the garage at any time. So I did the job and found that I had apparently got quite a talent for it. The builder that was in charge of the building of the house let me work in conjunction with his men and even offered me extra work if I wanted it, at another property. I did one or two other jobs for him and charged £5 an hour for my services so my finances were improving steadily. Then I got another idea, courtesy of the job I had done for the Taylors. Their acquaintances and friends called to see them and, luckily for me there were those who commented positively about the décor. My name must have been mentioned several times and suddenly I started to get offers of work. I decided that the best way to do the painting was when people were away so I offered to 'house sit' as well as decorate. Again, it was a good niche in the market. They were getting me for a fiver an hour and they were having their properties lived in. For that I required, in addition to accommodation, plenty of food and drink so that I was living absolutely free. Whatever I earned went into my savings fund and it was surprising how the financial situation improved. Added to that I had become Chairman of Governors at Ireland Wood Primary School near home so I sometimes had to return for meetings of the Governing Body and I was supplied with petrol by those employing me, as they wanted me back at their respective houses as soon as possible! So I was living two completely separate lives and I enjoying every minute. I did find that at times I needed to get away from the work so if I stayed for whatever length of time was required at a house, then came home and spent time with friends, both male and female. Of course I did not need to go away on holidays very often as I was away much of the time anyway. But I did go off to Scotland with Jack Edmondson now and again. I also had a couple of holidays a year with my former college room mate and pal Bryan Stubbs after he retired. His Geordie brand of humour had always appealed to me since the day we met and apparently I kept him equally amused. All these years later and we still go away for a few days whenever we can. He has been - and still is - a wonderful friend at this point in my life.

Time had passed quickly and I was in a position to think about changing my car again. I had always hankered after buying a Renault 11 turbo and one day Phil Maskery took me to look at one that had been brought into the garage. After a lot of talk and a chat with his boss, they agreed to let me have it at a knock down price. I was in my seventh heaven and, as I was still doing enough work locally delivering and fetching cars, petrol supplies were 'on tap' there for me. As soon as I got the car Jack and I went off for a holiday in it and I drove it a long way that time. We drove up to John o' Groats. We had hoped to take the ferry across to St Margaret's Hope but the weather was too rough. I remember that particularly as we stood and watched a storm out at sea heading towards the Shetlands and eventually putting it out of sight, although the rainbow that appeared was beautiful and very bright. However, sadly, it did not last long. We drove along the north coast and stayed at several good bed & breakfast houses during the trip – meeting some interesting people too. We travelled right round the coast of Scotland, covering over 3000 miles in about a week.

By now I had virtually achieved my aim. In three years I had comfortably reached my goal of £10,000. I had enjoyed myself and I was still going strong. I went out to France for six weeks to do some house painting and to mend some shutters - a common feature on windows in France. – I was also commissioned to oversee two French workmen putting in a large picture window at Daphne and Frank's beautiful converted barn near the seaside town of Portbail on the Cherburg peninsula. Portbail is just south of Cartaret where the ferry crosses to Jersey in the Channel Islands. It is about 30 miles from Cherburg. Their barn was a fantastic place with a large garden and a natural pool near the property's entrance. At the rear was a large patio, part shaded from the sun. Frank and Daphne came over during the last week to have a look at the work done and for us to enjoy a holiday together. John Scatchard rang me prior to my leaving Leeds to see if it would be possible for Sheila to have a few days holiday with us at the same time. She and John had been kind to me when I was ill and so now I was able to repay that kindness by arranging for her to stay at the barn during that week. I drove into Cherburg, through the early morning mist, to meet the boat and pick her up. We were able to see much of the area, even driving down to St Malo and also walking up through the steep and narrow streets of Mont St Michel to the monastery at the top. On our return to Leeds we brought back plenty of wine and beer as the supermarket in Cherburg was stocked with everything and we took full advantage of that!

September 10th 1989 was a real red letter day. I was invited by Daphne and Frank Sharman to go and stay with them at Sunbury for a few days, ostensively to go out for dinner to celebrate my 60th birthday. On arrival I upset the applecart a bit as I arrived earlier than intended just as a colourful banner was being hung up in the lounge-cum-dining room wishing me 'A Very Happy 60th Birthday', but the penny
still did not drop. Then people started arriving – firstly relatives that I had not seen for a good while, together with a host of friends including Eleanor Wells, who had known Daphne almost as long as she had known me. Most of the other friends lived nearby. In no time the party began, and how wonderful it was! The pleasure I got from seeing everybody was something really special and very moving. Daphne has always been very special to me family-wise – more like a sister than a cousin I suppose. She met most of my friends when we were in our teens. It was mainly the local family friends who were always so kind to me whenever I went to Sunbury. Frank and I had a genuine affinity in terms of cricket. He has been a leading light at the Sunbury Cricket Club – running junior teams, amongst other things, for many years and he has always helped me whenever I have needed it – particularly with the tours that I arranged for Ivanhoe Grammar School in later years.

I think that I was lulled into a false sense of security as time passed and I had had no return of my illness. I attended the hospital every few months to see that I was still in good shape. Then the blow fell – quite unexpectedly. At this point in my life I had survived for 7 more years to mid 1990 without trouble but I had been warned to report to hospital immediately if anything out of the ordinary occurred. I noticed that I was getting several small growths on my back because one day, after I had been swimming, an acquaintance whom I met regularly at Guiseley Baths mentioned, when we getting dressed in the changing room, that he had noticed I had what he thought was a rash on my back. Then it started to itch and that was enough. I went straight to see my local doctor at the Croft Surgery. He rang a colleague at the LGI and an appointment was made for the next day. I saw a young locum who took several spots from my back in order that a biopsy could be performed. He got in touch a fortnight later, by which time I was convinced that the cancer was back. I mentally prepared myself to see him and on arrival at the LGI I realised I might be in for a long wait as there were a lot of patients sitting in the waiting area. I had gone down to the Hospital on my motorcycle and left it round the corner from the main entrance at the rear of the Town Hall. Fortunately time was on my side for once and I was called in early. Most of the patients were at a separate clinic and were being seen by other consultants and doctors. By this time I was so het up that once I went in to see the locum I sat down and started immediately to comment that I had had seven wonderful years and that had all been special but that I had been half expecting something to happen eventually. Then he said quite casually, "The results of your biopsy are good. The cancerous spots are benign. I can also deal with any spots that need to be removed". I was only half listening. "I do beg your pardon – would you please repeat just what you've just said?" I queried. He did so and then asked me to take my shirt off so he could begin. Even then it had barely sunk in and I felt a bit punch drunk. I could not believe what I was hearing. By the time he had finished I was a bit sore but feeling absolutely exultant. I remember saying, "I was actually told by Mr Browning, the surgeon who did my cancer operations, that once I had suffered from a malignant cancer anything that returned would almost certainly also be malignant". Then he smiled and replied, "You are one of the very few fortunate people where this has not happened – I might almost say one in a million. Now go out and continue to enjoy life like you sound to have been doing already". And that was it. I thanked him, shook his hand, and walked out in a complete daze, trying to gather my thoughts together.

Outside the main entrance there was an ice cream van parked. It seems banal now, but I bought myself a cornet and just stood near that entrance thinking of the time when I had been a patient in the hospital in September and October 1983. Then it came to me what I must do. I got on my motorbike and drove out to Fewston, passing Swinstey Reservoir and the car parking area. I drove on up the hill to Fewston Parish Church of St Michael and St Lawrence, parked, went in and sat down to think and clear my mind. After a few minutes I knelt down, prayed for other people who were ill, and lastly thanked God for my own life. Then the emotion hit me. I was completely alone. I cried as I have never cried before, or since, for maybe half an hour. Then suddenly, almost as though someone turned off a tap, the tears dried up. I wrote a comment in the book of remembrance near the entrance giving thanks for my life. Then it was over. That experience must have been unique for me. I went back out into the sunshine, got on my bike and rode home. Now I could plan out my future again. Now I would start yet another period in my life.

Chapter 8 Working for fun

Prior to the experience mentioned at the end of Chapter 7 I heard from my long time friend, Frank Tyson. We had written to each other frequently over the years, ever since 1963, when he emigrated to Australia. Occasionally

Frank would ask me to carry out some family business for him. But the letter I received in March 1990 was certainly a bit different. He mentioned that he wanted to bring an Under 16 Cricket touring side to England in June 1991 and would I please try to fix up a fixture or two for him? Then we had a lengthy telephone call and the upshot was that I would arrange the entire English side of the tour – a programme of fixtures, transport, accommodation and extraneous visits to places of interest – for the period of a month. He offered to negotiate a fee of £1000, plus expenses, to be paid by the Ivanhoe Grammar School Tour Fund Raising Committee, for my services. I was still doing a few driving jobs and some house painting too, but this was coming to an end. So this suited my book very well. I had never attempted anything on this scale before outside of the 'umbrella' of the world of education.

Sorting out school trips and visits was just one of many jobs I had done while I was working as a Headmaster. Being responsible for organising timetables, sorting out a year long building project with all the attendant difficulties that entailed, together with the general day to day running of a large School would, I thought, stand me in good stead. What was more I was 12,000 miles away from the Ivanhoe Grammar School fundraisers. That was their problem! Being on my own would give me complete freedom to use my own initiative. I was fired with a determination to make a success of this venture - indeed it offered yet another superb new challenge. Once again I felt that I could do something truly worthwhile in my life that would benefit other people. I have always believed that sport is an international feature of all countries and that through mutual sporting links there will be a greater understanding on all sides of the spectrum. In a sense, maybe what happens off the field of play is of equal - if not even more – importance, as it engenders a mutual understanding of, and hopefully, respect for traditions and cultures of those with whom we come into contact. Over the years I have been fortunate to make several friends among cricketers from other parts of the globe and it has taught me a lot about how they and often their fellow countrymen tick.

I was advised that the 1991 Ivanhoe GS Under 16 Touring Party consisting of 18 boys and 3 staff members would arrive at Heathrow on Sunday June 23rd and leave again from Heathrow on Saturday July 20th. This would allow me plenty of time to ensure that arrangements were satisfactorily completed.

I relished the idea and at once started planning the basics. I decided that a maximum of 16 matches could be played in England and that it would be beneficial to see and experience as many areas of the country as was feasible in the time allowed. Furthermore I would arrange for visits of interest on rest days. I also resolved to visit every single venue personally in order to ensure that everything ran as smoothly as possible.

I asked for a float of £450 to cover expenses. I also intended to render a precise account of how the money was spent. Frank indicated a wish that the opposition chosen should be against good sides – even one or two representative League and County teams if possible - plus some Public School X1s.

First I got hold of an up to date book containing a list of Public Schools and their addresses from the local library. Included were named Staff at the respective Schools and I noted the names of those who were i/c cricket. Next I marked locations on a large map of England so that I could try to ensure that travelling distances between venues were not too far.

Transportation was to be done in two minibuses. I would drive one and lead the way to the various venues. A member of Staff would drive the other one. This gave us complete freedom to move the whole party around whenever and wherever we wished to go. Luggage would be strapped on the tops of the minibuses.

Logic suggested that the cricket tour should start at a Public School in the south of England, within easy reach of Heathrow. On the first night I arranged accommodation at a small hotel on the outskirts of Tonbridge in Kent. The first fixture was to be against Tonbridge School on Monday June 24th. The School kindly agreed to allow the boys to stay on overnight at the School with the boarders after the cricket match was finished so that the players could all meet together for the evening and get to know each other.

Having sorted out the start of the tour I next approached a number of Schools around the London area offering dates from June 26th to the 29th. In fact I was able to arrange a match every day so that, in theory, all the boys would be able to play some cricket during the first week.

The rest of the first half of the list eventually fell into place during the next few months. The Schools helped out where accommodation was concerned and either put the boys up or arranged suitable places for them to stay.

The fixtures were as follows:-

Mon.   June 24th   v Tonbridge School, Tonbridge, Kent

Wed.   June 26th   v King's College School, Wimbledon, London

Thurs.   June 27th   v Dulwich College, West Dulwich, London

Fri.   June 28th   v St Dunstan's College, Catford, London

Sat.   June 29th   v Alleyn's School, East Dulwich, London

Mon.   July 1st   v Wellingborough School, Wellingborough, Northants

Wed.   July 3rd   v Dame Allan's School, Newcastle

Thurs.   July 4th   v King's School, Tynemouth, Northumberland

The second half of the tour was, of necessity, arranged against representative sides. This was because the Public Schools broke up for the summer vacation in early July and many of their School Cricket XIs had various other commitments and most took part in cricket tournaments around the country.

In order to ensure that I could arrange four of the eight matches scheduled to be played against representative sides in Yorkshire I enlisted the help of Ralph Middlebrook who at that time was in charge at the Yorkshire Cricket School. He put me in touch with the coaches responsible for the selection and coaching of talented cricketers drawn from Schools in Yorkshire. These lads were the best cricketers in their respective schools and they were picked to represent their County Leagues.

The IGS tour party stayed at Carnegie College, Leeds while in Yorkshire.

The fixtures were scheduled to take place on the following dates:-

Fri. July 5th   v Northumberland Select XI
                     Played at Jesmond Cricket Ground, Newcastle

Mon. July 8th   v Leeds Schools Cricket Association Under 15s
                     Played at Menston Cricket Ground, West Yorks.

Wed. July 10th v Bradford League Cricket association Under 15s
                     Played at Pudsey St Lawrence, Leeds, West Yorks.

Thurs. July 11th v Yorkshire Cricket Association Under 16s
                     Played at Whitkirk Cricket Ground, Leeds, west Yorks.

Fri. July 12th   v Yorkshire Schools Cricket association Under 15s
                     Played at Batley Grammar School Cricket Ground, West Yorks.

I enlisted the welcome and invaluable help of Frank Sharman, Middlesex Colts Coach, for the final three matches that were scheduled to take place on the following dates:-

Mon. July 15th   v Surrey Colts Association Under 16s
                     Played at the Royal Grammar School Ground, Guilford, Surrey

Wed. July 17th   v Hertfordshire Colts Select XI
                     Played at St Albans School Cricket Ground, Hertfordshire

Thurs. July 18th v Middlesex Colts Association
                     Played at Sunbury Cricket Ground, Sunbury on Thames,
Surrey

Frank Sharman also made the arrangements for the tourists to stay at the Royal Holloway and Bedford New College during the final week of the tour prior to their return to Australia.

I hired two minibuses for the tour from Smiths Self Drive Company, Leeds.

With the fixture list virtually completed I could now turn my attention to making arrangements for visits to places of interest. I made these as varied as possible. In several cases the costs of taking the entire party to certain venues had to be considered, but the budget of £300 gave me considerable leeway when deciding which places would be of the greatest over all value. Combining historical background with up to date interests proved quite a challenge!

The following constituted the eventual list of arrangements made for visits:-

Tues. June 25th   Visit arranged to the Gray Nichols bat-making factory at Robertsbridge.

Sun.   June 30th   Visit arranged to Duxford Airfield, near Cambridge, then a drive through the City of Cambridge to see the University.

Tues. July 2nd   Visit arranged to Durham Castle and the Cathedral.

Sat.   July 6th   Visit arranged to see England v West Indies Test Match at the
Trent Bridge Cricket ground, Nottingham.

Sun. July 7th   Visits were arranged to the 'Tales of Robin Hood' Centre, the Brewhouse Museum, Nottingham Castle, the Nottingham Lace Centre, and the famous 'Trip to Jerusalem' hostelry where the Crusaders, led by King, Richard 1st - known as 'Richard the Lionheart', assembled prior to leaving for the Holy Land. The hostelry is part built in the Rock. We then visited the Sherwood Forest Centre.

Tues. July 9th   Trip arranged to the City of York to visit the Yorvik Centre and the National Railway Museum, followed by a walk along the Shambles, then through the City Centre and onto a section of the Wall.

Sat.   July 13th   Visit the Museum of Photography, Bradford, then sightseeing in
The Derbyshire Peak District en route to Denstone School in Staffordshire

Sun.   July 14th   Visit arranged to Stratford upon Avon en route to The Royal Holloway College at Egham, Surrey.

Tues.   July 16th   Morning visit arranged to Windsor Castle to see the Changing of

the Guard, St George's Chapel and the State Apartments. Afternoon:- Net Practice at Lords Cricket Ground.

Fri.   July 19th   Sightseeing and shopping in London.

This was the projected 1991 Ivanhoe Grammar School Cricket Tour Programme. However, due to the vagaries of our English climate things did not go to plan. One can arrange outdoor activities for many sports irrespective of weather conditions, but unfortunately cricket is not one of them.

Two members of Ivanhoe GS staff, in addition to Frank, accompanied the boys. David Waugh, a Deputy Principal of Ivanhoe, took nominal charge and was responsible for disciplinary matters while Graeme Renshaw, a Physical Education Specialist and Cricket Coach ensured that the boys maintained a fitness regime – mainly by example. He went out running every day and his cricket coaching skills were invaluable. Frank and Graeme did virtually all the coaching. I did some as well whenever time allowed and acted as team masseur when required. But my major job was to ensure that everything ran smoothly.

Before the tour commenced I had already visited every school that was hosting the tour party so I was able to effect introductions, check boarding arrangements and deal with anything that cropped up.

As it happened there was one crisis that could have had serious repercussions when the visit to the Robin Hood Exhibition took place. Two of the boys upset one of the young female ushers who was showing them around and after the tour party had left a letter of complaint was sent to my address. Luckily our next port of call was in Leeds and so I stayed at home overnight. The letter arrived early the following morning. It stated that, in effect, the complaint would be referred to the Nottingham Police Department unless immediate action was taken. Two members of staff had to drive to the Exhibition Centre in Nottingham to sort things out – not in any measure the sort of publicity needed for the tourists. Frank Tyson and David Waugh went to the Exhibition Centre and fortunately managed to pacify the staff involved there. This left Graeme Renshaw and myself to take the boys to York. In fact we were scheduled to visit the Yorvik Centre and the Railway Museum. In fact we also stopped in a small square and watched a travelling showman who provided free entertainment of a kind that the boys had not seen before – both sword swallowing and putting firebrands into his mouth! We also took them on a drive through the Yorkshire countryside and the consensus of opinion was that it was great to see what amounted to a different view around every corner – quite the opposite to Australia where forests and the outback tended to remain very similar for miles on end! The day out finished with a barbeque at a local Sports club, kindly arranged by John and Sheila Scatchard and Joe

213

Shelley. Then David Waugh and Frank Tyson returned, just in time to join in the festivities.

One of the more interesting aspects of the tour was advertising the fact that it was taking place. To this end I was assisted by Radio Leeds who gave me a broadcasting slot during one of the Sports Programmes appertaining to local events. The actual recording of the broadcast opened my eyes to the way these things are done! Peter Drury, who is now a well known Football Commentator, was 'learning his trade' with Radio Leeds, and he agreed to interview me at one of the Radio Station's studios. He commenced by asking me a couple of questions – to see if I could talk comprehensively about the tour I think. After a couple of minutes he said, "You don't need me to feed you questions. Just talk about the tour, leave an occasional gap when you take breath, and I will insert relevant questions that will tie the whole thing up afterwards". I did not need a second bidding..........

Several of my friends heard the completed broadcast but, sadly, I didn't. Having promised me the tape when it was finished with Peter Drury, much to my annoyance and his embarrassment, found that some stupid idiot (his words, not mine) had recorded over the top of the broadcast without his permission. I found out later that he had told the offender just what he thought of him – in no uncertain terms! However I was assured that it had been an excellent explanation of what was happening in the Yorkshire area. In fact as the tour progressed it was pleasing to see the number of cricketing enthusiasts who took time to come and watch the local matches.

There is no doubt that the locals got much pleasure from watching the enthusiasm and determination of the Australian boys. After all, they were just one School playing against what might be termed the cream of the age groups involved at county level. The future England International England Captain, Michael Vaughan, played for the Yorkshire Under 16 side at Whitkirk, Leeds. It was a great learning experience for all those involved in the Tour.

On his return to Ivanhoe Frank Tyson wrote an article about the tour. I have reproduced it exactly as he wrote it since it gives a very clear insight into the details of what actually happened:-

REPORT FROM THE COACH FRANK TYSON

Our great mistake ws probably unpacking our cricket bags at Tonbridge and taking out our bats and balls. Before that everything had gone like clockwork.

The touring party's jumbo jet left Tullamarine on June 20th, spot on time and arrived, as the French have it. "a l'heure" at Bangkok. There we spent a bare hour; just enough time to walk off the plane, upstairs then downstairs, to give the security guards practice at searching our baggage twice. Then it was up, up and away, over India, Afghanistan, Russia, the Baltic Sea, Denmark and, several excellent meals later, there we were in the immigration hall of London's Heathrow Airport at the ungodly hour of 6.00am.

Leaving the colonials in the "other nationalities" queue, Richard Haw and I used our Pommie passports to speed through the formalities and collect the baggage. Outside Terminal Four, stood our faithful tour organiser, Chris Turner, flanked by two minibuses – both parked illegally in accordance with some previously unlawful agreement with the local "grey ghosts". Up on the roof racks went our distinctive blue cricket bags, and within an hour of landing we were circling London on the M25 Orbital Motorway and heading for our first destination – the Kentich town of Tonbridge.

Our hotel was newly refurbished and comfortable – enough room outdoors to kick a footy and enough room insode to swing a cat. We arrived an hour early and took our Scottish host by surprise. Before the Sunday pm, the touring party was in the town centre, reconnoitring the market and making acquaintance of our favourite Scottish restaurateur, Mr McDonald. A good night's rest restored the players to their pristine form and at 10.00am we presented urselves at Tonbridge School ready for a net and our first match. Then we unwisely unpacked our cricket bats and took out the bats and balls!

Someone up there must have thought them to be the accoutrements of an aborigine rain-making ceremony. We had barely time to indulge in a short fielding practice and an even shorter batting and bowling stint when it started to rain – and rain - and rain - and rain. And that was the story of the team's visit to Tonbridge – Colin Cowdrey's former school – was participation in schoolmorning chapel, conducted in temporary premises because sadly, the college's noble church was terribly damaged by a spectacular fire last year.

So began a tour which saw the Ivanhoe side visit 16 school or club cricket grounds in a month. Notice that I said "visited 16 grounds" rater than "played 16 matches". In June 1991 there was a vast difference between going to an English cricket ground and playing a game of cricket. Jupiter Pluvius saw to that! In the team's first 10 days in England, in addition to the Tonbridge match, the games at Dulwich College and Dame Allan's School were completely ruined by rain; the matches against King's School Wimbledon and St. Dunstan's were left unfinished because of the Wimbledon week weather. At Dame Allan's School in Newcastle, it not only rained, but a thick sea-fret als limited visibility to about 20 metres! The finale to the St Dunstan's clash was a spectacular electrical thunderstorm, during which the pavilion was struck by lightning! An occurrence which even quietened Alex Pappos – if only for a frew minutes!

Deprived of valuable practice, the side managed a creditable draw against Alleyn's School, but subsequently went down to Wellingborough School and the Royal Grammar School Newcastle. Then began the difficult haul agaist representative U-16 and U-15 county sides, all of them assiduously preparing for the national Texaco 50-over tournament, and most of them with at least a couple of England players in their number. Brad Shadbolt scored ans immaculate century against the Northumberland U-16 XI on the Jesmond County Ground. Brad Joblin immediatey imitated him with an aggressive hundred against the Leeds Schools XI at Menston.

On Len Hutton's native ground of Pudsey St. Lawrence, Alex Severi bowled his heart out and Stuart Ward scored 87, only to see their team lose in the last over of the day to the Bradford League U-16's. At Whitkirk Ivanhoe faced a strong Yorkshire U-16, which contained four England representatives and a bowler who had won a 1000 pounds prize in the previous season as the best young player in the country. Andrew Cust's six-wicket return took the stuffing out of the Yorkshire batting and, in Ivanhoe's eyes at least, the home side were only saved from defeat by the timely arrival of the rain. At Batley, the tourist's batsmen gave a good account of themselves to record more than 200 before declaring. The smallness of the ground and local knowledge, however, were too much for the visitors who were unable to contain the U-15 Yorkshire batsmen.

In the final phase of the tour, Ivanhoe lost to strong Surrey, Hertforshire and Middlesex U-16 teams: losses which were softened by the increasing competitiveness of the touring side and the fact that they were sustained in the delightful surroundings of the magnificent Royal Guildford Grammar School, the Laurence Ground St. Albans and the Sunbury Cricket Club.

Rest days were few and far between. Even the journeys between fixtures were used to see as much of England as possible. On the day after the aborted Tonbridge fixture, we meandered through the drizzle down to Robertsbridge in Sussex and the Gray-Nicholls bat factory. Much money and willow changed hands. Our first stint in London ended witgh a Sunday morning drive through the West End and the City of London, before we turned our minibuses up the A11 towards Cambridge. A few miles short of Cambridge we made a detiur to inspect the Duxford Air Museum: a vast aerodrome which housed hundreds of planes of all sizes ranging from pre Second World War bi-planes to a full scale model of Concorde.

On to Cambridge and a leisurely drive through the city's streets produced the following commentary from a master:

> "There on your left is King's College Chapel and there is Trinity College. We are going along the Backs and past Fenner's and there on the right is "Parker's Piece" and near it several other college buildings".

Boys voice from the back:
"Yes but where's the University?"
Passing through Cambridge the minibuses traversed the fenlands close to the Isle of Ely, the fomer hide-out of Saxon outlaw, Hereward the Wake. This is not enough to keep members of the team awake however. It was a different story when we passed Caxton Gibbet. I explained:

> "In the olden days if a man stole a sheep, he was hanged on the gibbet, and while he was still alive, he waa disemboweled. His body was then cut into quarters and left to rot on the gibbet as a warning to others. The alternative to this punishment was transportation to Australia."

This time Brent Woodcock's voice from the back of the coach:

"I'd sooner go to Austalia, I think!"

On the party's way north from Wellingborough to Newcastle we passed through Durham and there visited Durham Castle and Cathedral. The Castle's baronial hall, the buttery and the keep evoked little interest, but the ghost of the black staircase and the mysterious sealed rooms beneath the keep were riveting stuff! In the Cathedral, the venerable Bede slept behind the eastern altar while Ivanhoe boys slept at the other end of the nave, awoken only by the clarion call to the refreshment bar in the cloisters!

On the sea front in Tynemouth stands the statue of Admiral Collingwood: a man who gave his name to some Melbourne suburb with an unsuccessful football club. Coincidentally, Tynemouth's local soccer team, Newcastle United, is known as the Magpies and play in black and white striped shirts. While in Newcasle we visited the Metro, reputedly one of the biggest shopping complexes in Europe. It is a long trip from Newacsle to Leeds especially when one detours to spend an interesting day at the England Vs West Indies Test at Trent Bridge and visit the Tales of Robin Hood Exhibition, Nottingham Castle, the Brewhouse Museum and the Trip to Jerusalem: the inn at which the Crusaders met before leaving for the Holy Land.

Our path from Nottingham to our next series of matches in Leeds led us through Ivanhoe country and to the Sherwood Forest Centre. A visit to the Great Oak, a mile inside the forest was a "must". Driver Chris went twice: once in the main party and once when he went back for his lost 'specs' – which were actually on the dashboard of the van!

The Leeds segment of the tour took us to nearby York on the free day. There we saw the famour Yorvik: the Viking museum. "But they are only models" complained one hard to please boy. Must be because no-one can get hold of a brand spanking new Viking nowadays! The capital city of the County of Broad Acres showed us the Shambles, the Minster and the Railway Museum and then it was back to Leeds via the beautiful Herrito country in the Yorkshire Dales.

The final major trek took us from Leeds south to London via Bradfordand Denstone. A scheduled two hour stop in Bradford to visit the National Museum of Photgraphy stretched to four hours as a result of careless shopping. Four hours in Bradford! At least it didn't raim – the only time it hasn't when I have been there! At Denstone the boys had a taste of life in an isolated public school – ten miles to the nearest town and only two exeats a term. Life in a dormitory can be pretty hard and one of the boys, missing his creature comforts, was heard to remark:

"I couldn't cut this for too long!"

Well at least there was Alton Towers nearby: one of the largest amusement parks in Europe. The following morning the party turned its steps into the grounds of what was once one of the noblest estates in England and enjoyed a morning on the rides and roundabouts.

Pur last thress games in London were interspersed with visits to Winsor Castle. It was interesting to see the changing of the guard – and disgusting to witness the French tourists throwing coins at the powerless sentries! The highlight of the trip for Mr/Colonel Waugh came with a visit to the Royal Tournament at Earl's Court. The boys were delighted with the show, Starlight Express – 20 tickets courtesy of Brian, a member of the Sunbury Cricket Club. Not mean these Poms – perhaps we can do something for Brian when he comes out for the World Cupin February? The last day was occupied with the madatory shopping in Oxford Street and at Harrods in Knightsbridge. One of the party was heard to remark that it was just like Northland! Funny – I haven't noticed all that many rich Arabs and rollers out Preston way!

Throughout the tour, the English hospitality was marvellous. After almost every game the hosts provided a meal, after which the obligatory presentation of ties, magazines and plaques took place. At Leeds, the locals even put on a good old Aussie 'barbie'! In Newcastle, Leeds and London, the team were accommodated in University Halls of Residence: Henderson Hall, Carnegie Polytechnic and the Royal Holloway and Bedford College. At Carnegie and the Royal Holloway, parties of French and Italien students were also contemporaneous guests and not one of the Ivanhoe party could speak French or Italian! Pity! I don't know who, what or how many, the staff were expecting at the Royal Holloway College when we arrived. It just seemed strange that the tables at which we ate, carried the names of some mythical person called 'Ivan Hoe'!

Initially slow to grasp the fundementals necessary for success on English pitches, towards the end of the visit, the Ivanhoe team found the necessary self discipline to bowl line and length and to school themselves to play straight and forward. They retuned a transformed and improved team and now containg the potential to win the AGS premiership in the next few years.

Let it be said that the boys and the School owe a tremendous debt to Mr Renshaw and Mr Waugh for the efficient and tactful way they managed the tour. While it was a tremendous experience for the accompanying members of staff, it is far from a holiday! A final word of thanks to the English tour orgabiser, driver, public-relations man and general factotum, Chris Turner of Leeds. His organisation was superb and there was not a hiccough throughout the tour. The minibuses were always at the right spotat the right time, the fixtures were spot on and there was not a night's accommodation or indeed a meal misplaced

Frank Tyson

Chapter 9 Preparing for my next trip

Now that the 1991 Ivanhoe Grammar School Cricket Tour was completed I turned my attention towards arranging a second trip 'Down Under'. This time I would widen my vistas and travel further. I had managed to recover most of the share losses that the 1987 monetary crisis had caused. These were on paper only as I did not need to take money from my shares at that time. Fortunately I was able to live on what I had earned during the mid eighties, once I had achieved my goal of the £10,000 needed to keep my house, as I continued working in order that I might pay off my mortgage earlier than the agreed 12 years. Thus I could save myself more capital. I was still able to run my car virtually for free where fuel was concerned. But that could not last much longer as Renault were changing their policy regarding the delivery of vehicles and this affected the way the garage got hold of the colours of vehicles that customers required. It meant that I would be needed less often. Actually just before I left to go on this trip the work ran out. Furthermore I had received £1000 for my work in organising the Ivanhoe GS Cricket Tour so there was some extra money in the coffers. I remember sitting talking to Philip and his close friend Nigel one day over a pint at a pub and they both encouraged me to go as soon as I could. That helped, but I made the final decision after attending the funeral of a close friend – John Cooke – who was the third member of the original Wednesday snooker group, formed in 1984 when three Head Teacher colleagues and I were all seriously ill and had to retire. I was now the only surviving member of the four so I felt that I wanted to take the opportunity to travel again while I was still fit and well.

Initially my ideas were simple. I contacted Austravel in early October 1991 – the travel agent I had used on my previous trip. They were most helpful and offered me the cheapest ticket that would take me to where I wanted to go and at the same time allow for 5 stopovers. This was a 'round the world' ticket, costing in the region of £700. The only stipulation was that I had to keep going forwards – I could not retrace my steps. On that basis I arranged my flights – Toronto, Canada - Los Angeles, America – Wellington, New Zealand – Melbourne, Australia - then back via Singapore – it was that easy. The only extra flight turned out to be the short flight from Toronto to London, Ontario and back again to Toronto. Ann, who travelled a lot by air, contacted her travel agent who sorted out an overnight stay at the Comfort Inn at Toronto for me when I returned there to continue my journey forward to America – for $49! So that was the basic plan. I was free to come and go as I wished. Then I decided on certain places that I definitely wanted to visit.

I planned to spend about a fortnight visiting my cousins and their families in London, Ontario, have a short break in Toronto, and then fly via Chicago to Los Angeles, California. There I would hire a car and drive out to the Quality Hotel, Anaheim. I intended to spend one day at Disneyland and the second day in Los Angeles, seeing round Universal Studios and visiting the famous Farmers' Market. There was a bus trip for that laid on from my hotel. Following that I would drive across the Mohave Desert to visit the Grand Canyon. The next leg of the journey would take me back across the Desert past the Edwards Airbase towards San Simeon and up the coast road –

known as 'The Big Sur' – via Monterey, to the outskirts of San Francisco. From there I would fly to Wellington, New Zealand, via Honolulu. All this would take around another 3 weeks. After a holiday in NZ I would fly on to Melbourne, Australia and continue my holiday there until I decided to return home. I had been offered several 'freebees' by grateful parents of the several of the boys who had been on the tour - if I wanted them. I reckoned that I would be away around 8 months. Apart from the places mentioned I decided to play everything else by ear and go wherever the whim took me. It was the opportunity I had always wanted – to be able to come and go exactly as I pleased. Age no longer mattered. I found that out on my trip in 1984/5 when I was travelling alone. People accepted you at face value so you were not in any measure stereotyped. They seemed to have no interest in the past, only in the present, and I had really appreciated that. In fact I had found it quite hard to settle when I first returned in 1984, but opening my house up to visitors from the Southern Hemisphere soon put that right. Now I could do all that again. I couldn't wait!

Chapter 10 Setting off round the world

1. Canada

On November 10th Philip took me to stay at Sunbury with Daphne and Frank. As a parting present they gave me a body belt in which I could carry my tickets, money and passport in safety. The next day they delivered me and my baggage Terminal 4 at Heath Row around 10.30am. There was the usual hustle and bustle – so many travellers coming and going – but I spent quite a while in the duty free area and bought a few presents to take with me – whisky for Murray and pens for Jamie and Mark. I had already bought Ann an eight inch high porcelain statue of a well-dressed Edwardian lady – something that I knew she would appreciate. The flight was called at 2pm and we took off on time, at 2.30pm. The flight took us over Iceland. This route was taken to avoid having to contend with high winds. We landed at Toronto Airport at 5.30pm, Canadian time, after an 8 hour flight, there being a difference of five hours between London and Toronto. But then came a delay and our flight to London, Ontario, eventually left at 10.45pm. On arrival at London it was found that most of the baggage had been left behind because too much fuel had been put into the plane and, rather than siphon the extra out, luggage had been left behind. This caused considerable irritation, but nothing could be done at the time and my baggage was delivered to the Neilson's house the following day. I had eventually gone to bed around 2am. It had been a long day!

On the first day of the holiday I went to see Gilbert (my cousin) and his wife Viv. On our return Jamie introduced me to a volley ball game played against a wall downstairs in the house. It was energetic – good training, but I felt stiff later on!

The next day Ann showed me round London after sorting out the previously mentioned hotel for me to stay at on my way back to catch my plane from

Toronto. The following day, after a further look round, I went to a party at Murray's office. As a successful criminal lawyer he had quite a different type of clientele! Everyone seemed to be dressed in jeans so it was impossible to tell who was whom as there were several lawyers and solicitors present as well as former clients. I found it absolutely fascinating, rubbing shoulders with both sides of the criminal spectrum!

Jamie was at Waterloo University. On November 15th Ann and Murray took me to watch him in action for Waterloo in a Volleyball match being played about an hour and a half's drive away against the University of Western Ontario. He played well although they lost.

On the 16th there was a pre-dance party at the house. We then all went off to the Law Society Dance and got back about 1.15am. They certainly lived life to the full! Fortunately though, the next day was less hectic. I went for a gentle walk across the nearby golf course in the morning. Then we went to see Anthony, Ann's brother and my second cousin, and his girlfriend Wendy whose Graduation Day it was. We finished up at the pictures in the evening and saw a thriller – 'Key Fear'.

On the 18th Jamie showed me round the University Campus. Later that day I met the Principal of Oakridge School and several of the staff. Then I went to stay with Viv and Gilbert. I had been invited to a meal with Ann & Eldon Walker. Ann was the niece of a former member of my staff at Kirkstall, Emily Slight. I again stayed overnight. Ann picked me up at dinnertime the following day and took me to see the oldest building in London – Eldon House. It was full of memorabilia from a bygone age. We visited the Art Gallery too.

On the 21st Mike Baxter, another cousin on Ann's side of the family, took me with him to Beaver Valley, passing through a number of small towns on the way. The weather was perfect and the scenery was equally enthralling. We stopped off at Meaford on the shore of Lake Huron to see the many yachts moored in the harbour. Then we saw a beautiful sunset on our way back. For the next couple of days I wrote letters to Philip and some of my friends back home – and on the quiet had a bit of a rest prior to setting off again on my travels. I had had a wonderful time, but the weather had turned and the winter snows came with a vengeance on November 24th. So it was time to move on. I made the necessary arrangements for my flight back to Toronto and went round the family to say my goodbyes.

On the 26th I travelled to the Airport courtesy of Ann and caught a plane at 4pm to Toronto. I sat next to one passenger, Peter Mount, with whom I conversed. He was a local businessman on his way home. On arrival at Toronto he kindly gave me a lift and dropped me off at the Comfort Inn. I immediately rang my friends Alan and Tricia Southard. They called for me in the evening and took me to a famous restaurant called 'Mother Tucketts'. Fortunately I had time to change into smart clothes before they arrived. I received a call in my room from the hotel management to say that my hosts had arrived. I found out later that they had a large financial interest in the hotel – no wonder I was well looked after! Mother Tucketts towered above many of the buildings in the city and was easily distinguishable, with the name shining out in bright green letters, as we drove through the city. The meal was superb and the company equally so. It was one of the major highlights of my visit to Canada. I got a taste of how the 'other half' lived! We returned about 10.15pm and after saying our goodbyes I went up to bed and fell quickly asleep.

The early morning call at 5.15am brought me to my senses with a rush. Breakfast had been laid on for me and then at 6am a courtesy car took me to the Airport. I have never been given such service like that anywhere else in the world. I am
convinced that it was the fact that I was a friend of the Southards. After all they virtually owned the place. Apparently Alan Southard was a millionaire – so the manager told me when I questioned him just before I left, but he had obviously had no particular wish for me to know as he probably felt that it might have spoiled our evening out I guess. I had no such inhibitions about that though!

2. America

When I arrived at the airport I had to fill in several official forms, for security I suppose, stating amongst other details, my business, the length of my stay, where I had been and who had been my host. By the time I had finished I felt almost like a criminal – as if I had no right to be let loose! However all was well and the plane left at 8am. My companion on the flight as far as Chicago was a young Canadian lady by the name of Jane Chopty. She lived in San Francisco with a young American but apparently things were going wrong between them and I became a somewhat reluctant confidant. However she insisted that I ring her and let her show me round San Francisco when I eventually arrived there. It was too good an opportunity to miss as by then I would be driving a hire car prior to flying on to New Zealand and so we could see a lot of the sights in half a day. But all that would be a good three weeks hence. She changed planes at Chicago and at the time that was that – I thought no more about it. With so many passengers alighting at Chicago it was nice to see that there was likely to be plenty of room for a change. I had a brief 'ride' around the airport – on a moving walkway. It was the perfect way to get around as it eventually returned to the point where I had first got on. As predicted there was plenty of room on the aircraft and one could move around easily. We flew out over snow-covered mountains in Colorado and got a few pictures. What is more, the pilot informed us that there was a following wind so we were going to arrive too early to land straight away at Los Angeles. This was a marvellous. The weather was perfect, bright and sunny, so he had managed to obtain permission to overfly the Grand Canyon at low altitude - something that very rarely happened. Better to be born lucky than rich! So we were all able to take photos galore. It was quite incredible, and extremely fortunate for me, although at the time I was unaware just how fortunate it would prove to be.

We duly flew into the airport at LA – through a brownish haze. Apparently this haze covers the place much of the time and the air was not good that day – in fact several people were wearing masks to combat the problem of air pollution. I presume they were asthmatics or had difficulty in breathing. My one aim was to get out of LA as soon as possible! With the help of a friendly member of the airport staff I was able to find the Alamo Car Hire firm easily. I upgraded the car that I had booked in Leeds when I realised just how far I was intending to drive. The Freeway was literally two sets of lights away so in no time I was heading out of the city towards Anaheim. I learned quickly what rush hours were like on the Freeway, but the number of lanes available to cope with heavy traffic made the driving bearable and once I had turned off the Freeway towards Anaheim the traffic was less dense. I found the Quality Inn easily enough around 8pm and parked up for the night. I thought that the worst of the day was over, but boy, how wrong I was!

On arrival at the Hotel I was shown my room and advised that if there was anything I wished to put in store for safe keeping there were facilities available. I spent a few minutes sprucing myself up after the journey then decided that an early night might be sensible as I had been warned that getting around Disneyland was quite exhausting – there was so much to see and I only had one day scheduled for my visit. Fortunately I had occasion to speak to the hotel receptionist on my way out to find the nearest café or pizza parlour, as I did not require a large evening meal at the hotel. I had had meals served on the plane and that had proved more than enough! During the conversation she pointed out that it was not wise to leave any valuables in my hotel room. Although security was tight things could still occasionally be stolen, particularly if guests forgot to lock the door properly. She asked if I had much money with me and advised me to put it all in a hotel safe - apart from any immediate requirements. I was carrying a substantial amount and had it

hidden in my body belt together with passport and tickets etc. so I used the safe facilities and thanked her for her help. I had taken only 3 dollars with me to cover the cost of a bite to eat and a coke. She pointed me in the right direction for the nearest eating venue, saying that the place was across the main road just beyond the traffic lights. I wandered up the road to view the many flashing signs – this part of Anaheim seemed awash with lights – and came towards the traffic lights. There was a dark area just short of the lights. As I approached the crossing a man stepped out of the dark area and spoke with an American twang - "I want money to catch a bus," he said quietly. I hesitated, thinking that he was a beggar down on his luck, and started to explain that I had none apart from three one dollar bills. Immediately he produced a knife from his pocket and held it threateningly towards me, repeating in a gruff American accent, "I want money, buddy, NOW!!!" I had not had time to feel afraid as it had all happened so quickly. I remember that he did have an old dark coat on and a scarf part covering his face. On his head was a dark woollen hat so there was no way that I could recognise him again – if there was ever to be a next time. Then I realised that he was shaking – he was frightened, possibly on drugs, and thus completely unpredictable. With me the adrenalin must have taken over. I pulled the dollar bills out of my top pocket and just waved them at him, at the same time shouting out "help!" at the top of my voice in the hope that there was someone nearby. As he tried to grab the money I let it go and just ran for my life in case he came after me to stab me. But he didn't. He just melted away into the darkness. As I no longer had any money I could not buy anything, but I stood in a lighted shop doorway for a couple of minutes and then the realisation of what had occurred suddenly hit me and I started to shake. The shopkeeper came out and I explained what had happened. He was sympathetic but obviously it was not the first time this had been done, judging from his attitude, and he told me to stay under the bright lights. I did not need a second warning and I hightailed it back to the hotel as quickly as I could. The receptionist was still on duty and called out, "That was a quick pizza, sir!" and laughed. Then I told her what had occurred. She immediately called a smartly dressed man from an inner office – the Manager I guessed, although he did not say so. I explained what had happened again. Both he and the receptionist were most attentive and concerned for my welfare. He immediately took me to the dining area and insisted that I have something to eat and drink – courtesy of the Hotel. But it was a sharp lesson that warned me to beware of danger. He told me of the high rates of crime that existed. He further mentioned that he thought that I had been fortunate and that I had taken the correct action – ie giving him the cash, then running and shouting out for help at the same time, while he was concentrating on taking hold of the money. When I asked him about crime in this part of Anaheim he admitted that there had been a spate of knifings in the area, some of which had been very serious. I told him of my impending visit to Disneyland. "There is a courtesy bus tomorrow morning so I advise that you use it. Walking around here on your own is not too safe here – especially at night." I certainly listened. I also booked a 52 dollar trip to Universal Studios and Farmers' Market for the following day. That was enough as I was leaving the morning after to head out towards the Grand Canyon where I had booked a flight with Grand Canyon Airlines. Confirmation of this by phone a day or two prior to arrival was required. At least, that was my immediate programme – so I assumed - but more of that later. After all the excitement and combined with jet lag from the flight I went straight to bed and slept dreamlessly through the night. I must certainly have been very tired!

The following morning the weather was sunny and warm. I found that I was none the worse for my previous night's experience. In fact it all seemed like a rather ugly dream. I was refreshed after a good night's sleep and I was hungry too. I had a large American style breakfast to set myself up for the day. However that meant that I missed the hotel courtesy bus so I walked to Disneyland, and crossed the massive car park near the main entrance. Once through one of the many turnstiles visitors entered another world – inhabited it seemed by many mythical characters from films made by the legendary Walt Disney. In the background was the Disney styled Ivory Castle - said to be based on Dunrobin Castle in Scotland - with its pointed turrets, towers, windows, lightly coloured walls, and high rounded gateways. On either side of the many walkways were reminders of classic tales like Alice in Wonderland, Peter Pan, Snow White and several other famous children's stories. Mickey Mouse, Minnie Mouse and Goofy, amongst other well known cartoon characters, paraded up and down and were happy to pose for pictures with their adoring public. Alice in Wonderland, Snow White and the Seven Dwarfs were there too, together with villains like Captain Hook and Long John Silver. It was a fantastic and entrancing scenario. I queued at various exhibits, took boat rides, train rides and even toured the whole site on a tractor drawn series of carriages when my feet would no longer carry me around. The shops too were quite different – bedecked with brilliantly coloured goods for sale. There were tables and counters, plus chairs and benches to rest on for the weary traveller. It was easy to get something to eat. There were lots of restaurants. I do not recall seeing any alcohol on sale so there was no trouble. Everyone was there to enjoy what was on offer. I spent eleven hours in Disneyland but made one mistake right at the end of the day. Having been on practically everything else I queued to go onto the Space Mountain, foolishly ignoring warning notices about the dramatic effects that were designed to give one the illusion of being in space. Having eventually got into a seat and being strapped in for my own safety I was completely unprepared for what happened next. We set off at express speed, being catapulted into 'space' – God only knows how the illusion was done. There tiny flashing lights in amongst space debris. Stars appeared at incredible speed – and disappeared again equally quickly, having threatened to engulf us all! People screamed - myself included I expect. In the end I just shut my eyes and prayed to reach the end of the ride in one piece without suffering a heart attack! It seemed to take for ever to get to the end and I felt groggy when I got out of my seat and staggered off. But no one even noticed, as almost everyone else was the same! That finished me. I felt sick and exhausted all of a sudden and I made my way to the exit. There were no courtesy buses to return us to the hotel so I waited until a party of people came out and I followed on close behind them. Luckily they went straight along to the very traffic lights where I had been accosted the previous evening so I knew where I was and got back safely into the Quality Inn. I made it to my room, collapsed on the bed and woke again in the early hours of the morning. I undressed, got into bed and went straight back to sleep. So far this trip of a lifetime had been extremely energetic!

Wisely I had arranged for an early morning call in order that I could have a leisurely breakfast before setting off for a tour round part of LA and on to Universal Studios and Farmers' Market. I showered and dressed, then had another large American breakfast down in the dining room. The minibus duly arrived. I happened to be the only Englishman on the bus and I proffered my ticket to the driver, wishing him a good morning. The driver, hearing me speak, immediately replied, and I realised that he too was English. He invited me to sit up front with him and explained that he was living in LA for a while. He was also a cricket buff and explained that around that area there were several cricket teams and a league or two. He offered me the chance to join him at a game later in the week but sadly I could not take up his offer as I was moving on the next day. He then proceeded to give us all an excellent summary of places as we passed them. We went to Hollywood and walked along Rodeo Drive. I recall seeing a well dressed man holding a large board advertising the fact that he was a vet looking for work – quite extraordinary I thought, but apparently he was well known and did work for film stars and other rich and famous people who lived in Hollywood. The driver took me into a jewellery store just to see what was on show. As we looked around we were offered a variety of free drinks by staff – hoping to get us to make purchases I suppose!

We stopped at one point to see the names of well-known people that were inlaid on star shapes into a concreted area. Famous film stars had their names there, together with handprints.

Universal Studios turned out to be quite extraordinary. There was just so much to see – mock ups of planes, a simulated earthquake, shows by stunt men. In one studio we saw how the filming of Superman was done. In fact a member of our group was cast as Superman. He put on the required clothes and I had visions of him being flown around the studio! Actually he never moved, apart from pointing his arms to simulate flight. There was just a blue background and it was all evolved from that with a wind fan blowing the cloak to make it stream out as if in the wind, and the cameraman did the rest. The result was quite remarkable, and we were treated to a clip of film showing our home grown Superman soaring through the sky to the rescue of a victim trapped by fire in an upper room of a large hotel. Having been royally entertained in that studio we moved on to see the mock up of the 'Memphis Belle' a plane apparently badly shot up while on a bombing raid. Again, we were shown how it was done – this time by stunt men who carried out all kinds of so-called 'daring deeds!'

While our party had been in the studios there had been a distinct change in the weather pattern. Gone was the bright blue sky – instead clouds had moved in. By this time I had joined a young Australian couple that were on their honeymoon and we were walking across an open area on our way to a music studio. All of a sudden there was a brilliant flash of forked lightning that lit up the place vividly and struck some object close to Universal Studios with a tremendous crash – maybe a tree or a building somewhere. A lengthy and extremely ear-splitting rumble of thunder followed this almost immediately. It was so loud that it brought to mind the times when, during the Second World War, as a youngster of 10, I had to spend many nights in an air raid shelter within the walls of Parkhurst Prison on the Isle of Wight. My father was one of two Prison Chaplains working there at that time - in 1940. Unsurprisingly, we youngsters who were in the shelter had been utterly terrified by the noise of bombs exploding near us. Thank God we did not receive a direct hit, otherwise I would not be here to write my story. In what seemed no more than an instant the temperature dropped dramatically and the wind rose to gale force. We struggled to get under cover and the Australian girl started to shiver and literally turn blue with the cold. Fortunately both her husband and I had light coats and she put those on. The next thing was to find somewhere warm so we went straight down into the music studio and stood beneath the floodlights. Then they were put off – for safety I suppose. Luckily there was a snack bar nearby for the musicians in the studio so we joined them, managed to get cups of tea, and she slowly recovered.

The storm was comparatively brief and incredibly within about 15 minutes the sun came out again and things were back to normal. Apparently this sort of weather is not unknown in and around Los Angeles, although thankfully it does not happen too often. Sadly, although we did not know at the time, on the freeway leading from the north side of the city the storm had swept across the desert and had whipped up a severe sandstorm that had blown across the freeway. There had been several accidents, several of them severe, and radio reports stated that dozens of motorists had been injured. Twelve had actually been killed. It was a major tragedy and the rescue services had been unable to go out to assist until the worst of the sandstorm had abated. They just were unable to see any distance. Absolute chaos ensued and in the evening the television news channels were showing the aftermath of the damage that had been caused. Roofs had blown off many buildings where the full force of the wind had struck and many shoppers were injured.

That was really the end of my visit to Universal Studios. We were transported back to our hotel, in places wending our way slowly through the crowded streets. After a meal with the honeymooners at the local MacDonalds I retired early to bed to rest up before setting out across the desert after breakfast the following morning, on my way to the Grand Canyon. I remember thinking that I wanted to leave the city as soon as I could – visiting Anaheim and Los Angeles had been quite an experience!

The next section of my journey should have taken me to the Grand Canyon National Park, with an overnight stay somewhere en route. The main item of local news of the morning was, unsurprisingly, the storm that had passed through parts of the city of Los Angeles and left a trail of destruction. There was a weather warning too stating that the storm was now slow moving but still quite active in the desert area. With that concern in mind I decided to stop overnight at a small town called Needles. The first part of the journey passed without incident and I thoroughly enjoyed the drive up to Barstow on Highway 15, with much of the scenery being different from anything I had expected or experienced anywhere before. I had expected to see a lot of sand everywhere but that was not the case. There was plenty of vegetation around once the city boundary was crossed and I found it all rather bizarre. I stopped off for lunch in what we would describe as a hamlet – three or four wooden houses and an excellent restaurant called Danny's somewhere along Hwy 40. The eye of the storm was north of this location, but as I proceeded on the wind got stronger and the car started to turn a sandy colour. Great tufts of tumbleweed blew across the surrounding desert to the road at times hitting the side of the car – rather like the scene from a cowboy film! By the time I arrived in Needles the wind was really strong and the storm appeared to be closer, but it bypassed the town and there was no problem. I drove down the main street and saw a sign advertising a cheap motel for 19 dollars. It was unoccupied so I booked in for the night. There was a 'takeaway' nearby so I bought a large hot pizza for my supper and retired to write some postcards before watching TV on what must have been the oldest set in America! It had more tape around the wires than I had ever seen before or since – but it worked. The shower room was actually built of stone and so was the floor in the shower. It was certainly cold on the feet! Still, it was ok for one night. I found out later that there were not many motels in the town anyway as people did not visit there too often. I wasn't surprised! The wind blew hard – the massive tufts of tumbleweed blew along the street and it was bitterly cold in the evening - not at all what I was expecting. Bed turned out to be the warmest place!

The next morning I arose early, had breakfast, and intended to set off again as soon as I could find a telephone and a post office. I had to ring the Grand Canyon Airlines Office first to confirm that I should be taking a flight that I had booked in the UK. It had all seemed so simple at the time, but with the weather problems I had encountered en route things had become more complicated and I was not yet even in the Grand Canyon National Park. Still, all I had to do was to ring – easy – or so I thought. It was still bitterly cold as I got into the car, as the sun had not yet risen. I drove slowly down the main street looking for the post office or for a local who would point me in the right direction. There was just one man out. He was working in his garden – to keep warm I suspect as he was warmly clad. He had a Stetson on and looked for all the world like a cowboy with his leather jacket – no guns though! I stopped and got out of the car to speak to him. He fitted my picture perfectly. "Howdee son, I'm Big John," he drawled and stuck out his hand - which I shook. "What can I do for ya?" I asked for directions to the post office and a telephone booth. Immediately he took me by the arm and led me towards his house. "You kin use ma telephone, I'll post yur cards and ma wife'll make ya a cup a coffee. Looks as though ya need one!" I did not need a second bidding – I was frozen. That cup of coffee went down very well! We introduced ourselves – Katie and John Hohstadt – and shook hands again. "Gee, you're a goddam limey? That's great. We don't see many of your guys here" – and with that he propelled me towards his somewhat antiquated telephone. Then the fun began.

December 1st – what a way to start the month! I rang the number of the Grand Canyon Airlines Office and a young lady with a high pitched voice answered. I asked her to confirm my flight through the Canyon, due in a couple of days. There was a brief silence, and then she said, "Sir, do you have a four wheel drive?" I answered in the negative. "Do you have any chains?" Again the answer was no. "Gee Sir, then you won't even git inta the National Park without a four wheel drive vehicle or a car with snow chains. We got five feet a snow up here and the roads in the park are snow covered. Normally we never git snow afor Christmas. It's come kinda early. Big lorries are gitin' through on the main highway, but that's all. I'll have to cancel yur bookin'. Just write down this number and present it to yur agent when you git home". She gave me the relevant cancellation number and ended the conversation with a real Americanism – "Have a good day." Not quite the right thing to say in this case!

The next on the list of events was to ring the number for Best Western – the Hotel chain that I was using in America – and cancel my three-day booking. This proved simple enough. So now I had to decide what to do next. I had five days to fill before I was due to drive across the desert to San Simeon. From there I intended to the drive along the 'Big Sur' – the coast road that runs north from LA through Monteray to San Francisco.

John and Katie both came in. "You got a problem?" I explained what had happened. Immediately Big John set the tone. "You can come with me inta the desert today. I take educational parties out from time to time just to show them what an interestin' place the desert is. I'm goin' to take a looksee at the places of interest and I guess you'll enjoy yourself. I git well paid by the education authorities and it boosts ma pension." What a great opportunity for me to see the place with an expert! He had a two seater open truck. By this time the sun was up and, paradoxically, it was getting really hot. Temperature changes in the desert are considerable – freezing at night and very warm in the daytime. I was learning quickly! He lent me an old brimmed hat to keep the sun off my head, then he asked me what my job had been. When I said I had been a Headmaster he looked perplexed. I explained and used the word 'Principal'. So that is what I became in his eyes. What was more remarkable – he too had been the Principal of the Primary School in Needles! With that sort of mutual background we were on the same wavelength and I had one of the most stimulating and exciting days of my holiday – and as it turned out there were several more to come.......

We set off along a tarmac road, travelling about a mile. Then, without warning, we turned off on to an unmade road, more of a dirt track, but the truck smoothed out the bumps quite effectively considering the rough terrain. First we visited the Indian village of Mohave. It was small and a bit rundown, but had a Community Building where the Red Indian locals held meetings and met up for social occasions. Unusually there were two species of Palm Tree there – one called feather palm and the other known as fan palm. There was also a ramshackle building - appropriately known as the 'Cry House' - where funeral services took place.

Our next port of call was at the old 'Ghost Town' of Oakman where we stopped for coffee. There was only one bumpy track road into the place. It looked like an old movie set such as was used in early cowboy films. Big John stopped outside a run down saloon and we went in. At one side was a long bar and a few fairly desperate looking characters who resided at Oakman. According to Big John it was the sort of place that the police visited only occasionally. Apparently there were quite a few criminal types living there. The police knew **who** they were of course, but more importantly they knew **where** they were. They could keep a check and that made things safer for other people! We sat at the bar and ordered coffee. John had simply warned me that if he decided it was necessary to leave I must follow him out of the place immediately. He neglected to tell me why. We had been in only a few minutes when a tall, fairly corpulent cowboy pushed open the swing doors, looked around, and came in. He came up to the bar and I was expecting him to order a drink in a deep bass voice. However his voice was almost falsetto. He ordered a whisky and sat near the door. Big John told me his name was Jake and frowned at me when I started to grin. A couple of minutes later another cowboy pushed open the swing doors, looked around and also came in. In contrast to the first man he was short and looked aggressive. He completely ignored Jake. John looked a bit strained but said nothing at that point. By this time I was convinced that these two characters were not for real and were only there to entertain visitors. That was a serious mistake! The little guy also ordered a whisky, but his voice was deep. He just said to the barman, "I want Whisky". The barman literally slid the whisky glass skilfully along the bar. Then the guy crossed the room, picked up a round topped table, took a baize cloth out of a drawer, spread it on the table, took out a pack of cards and sat down. Almost as if there had been some sort of signal the clientele of locals drank up and started to move out. John pulled my arm and as we went towards the saloon doors Jake went to the table and sat down opposite the little guy. No words were exchanged. The cards were dealt and that was it. By this time I was outside, very disappointed that I had not been able to stay and see more. Then John told me. These two were serious players and were known to carry guns. It was rumoured that both had shot people who got in their way, particularly when they were playing cards and nobody stood around when they got together. Apparently they hated each other! One final thing John showed me as we drove off. It was a notice near a gate. There was an old caravan on the other side of the gate. The notice, roughly painted in black letters, read, ***Anyone openin' this gate'll be shot ...*** We did not try that out either!

Our third desert stop was at the end of 'Gold' Road – an unmade track leading to an abandoned Gold Mine. Apparently there had been bloodshed there too some years before. We headed on down Silver Creek to Bullhead City and a place called Laughlin, the gambling town in Nevada, then on up to Grapevine Canyon where John showed me some Petroglyphs. These were rough pictures carved on rocks many years ago. Finally we drove alongside the Colorado River back to Needles – what a fantastic day! As well as the visits John had shown me several species of desert plants and for the first time I realised just how wrong my concept of a desert was. There was so much to see and to learn. I thanked John profusely, intending to go back to the Motel but neither Katie nor John would hear of it. Katie had already got a meal ready and had made up a bed for me. In fact they insisted that I spend the days I had spare with them.

Dec 2nd - The first shock of the next day came very early. There was a knock on my door at around 5.45am and John asked if I wanted any breakfast. What I did not realise until then was that many of the locals went out to the Overland Restaurant for their breakfasts and it was very much a social occasion. Big John lent me a warm jacket. I was introduced to so many folk during the meal – some in cowboy outfits or wearing warm clothing, including lumber jackets. When they took the jackets off they wore brightly coloured tops and lumberjack style shirts. They all had Stetsons as they entered and I was actually given one as a present. Everyone, it appeared, wore them as standard dress! Considering the early hour this place turned out to be the most welcoming town I have ever visited, before or since. Whenever I was out in the street I was greeted like an old friend – usually with the words "Howdee Partner," and almost invariably a conversation ensued – where to visit, what to see... and so on. They all knew Katie and John and really respected them. Many of them had been taught by John in former years and he was universally popular. I heard the comment - "Any friend of John's is welcome here" – several times, so I counted myself very fortunate! By 8am we were ready to go off on another sightseeing tour connected with John's work. We set off along Hwy 40, then turned onto Hwy 195 to Las Vegas, via a place imaginatively named Searchlight. We stopped for an hour in Las Vegas and entered one of the 'One armed bandit' gambling palaces. As we entered we walked past a gold plated Cadillac parked near the entrance. Inside we saw the owner – a lady who was apparently the wife of a Texan oil millionaire. All she did was to sit and play on a one armed bandit. I spoke to one of the men in charge who told me she came literally every day she was in Vegas and just played the machines – crazy! She was not alone either. Interestingly enough, everything in the place was free – food, drink, even a bedroom for the night. Apparently these places never closed. I played a dollar, won once, and then lost the winnings trying to increase my financial state. Once was enough!

Las Vegas was truly colourful and John drove me round the streets to see many famous buildings. Boxing appeared to be the major interest there. I expect that it still is. We had a bite to eat – all free of course – before setting off towards the Hoover Dam. We drove across the old Mohave trail (now a road) where in 1828 Red Indians pursued a famous pioneer named Jed Smith. They had raided the camp where he had been staying but on that occasion, because he was out prospecting, he escaped although most of the others at the camp were massacred. The Smith River was so named in his memory. The nearby mountains that we saw had names like Dead Mountains, Painted Mountains, Spirits Mountains and even McCulloch Mountain. We stopped in Excalibur - a famously named settlement by the river where one could see an old fashioned Paddle Steamer. As I recall it doubled as gambling den too. The Hoover Dam, built on the Colorado River, was originally known as the Boulder Dam until renamed in honour of President Hoover. He was instrumental in the construction. It was truly massive and is still one of the largest electric generating stations in the world. It stands on the border between the States of Nevada and Arizona. We made our way back to Needles via Boulder City and on the way Big John stopped off in the desert to check that the various plants that he was taking his clients out to see were still growing in profusion – they were! That evening I was introduced to Mexican food for the first time at the 'Real Vista' in the now familiar township of Needles – delicious!

Dec 3rd – Breakfast at 6.15am and the socialising with locals continued during the delicious repast of a large pancake covered with maple syrup. This seemed to be the regular breakfast meal at the Overland Restaurant. Afterwards we set off into the desert along a rough gravel road known as Route 66. Again I was shown yet more flora and fauna. There were so many varieties of cacti – he told me that some grew as high as 30 feet, but I did not see anything so large. There were also small prickly cacti – apparently quite succulent. By now I had got used to bouncing and bumping along corrals and dried up riverbeds. All the time we were fairly close to the Colorado River and before long we reached Lake Havasu City. The surrounding countryside is scenically superb with Mountains in the background. The main claim to fame of this city originated in London, England. London Bridge, mistaken by an American millionaire for Tower Bridge, was bought by him in 1968, taken down and transported to Havasu. It was rebuilt there and in 1971 was completed. The course of the Colorado River had actually been temporarily diverted at Lake Havasu in order that the Bridge could be built there. I remembered it well. I had actually stood in the centre of that Bridge at some point in the 1950s when it spanned the River Thames. I walked out once again to the centre of London Bridge. This time it spanned part way across the Colorado River to an island in the middle of the river. It was indeed an eerie feeling – like being back in England again. We had lunch at a nearby restaurant overlooking the bridge – quite an incredible feeling of nostalgia came over me for a time.

On our way back to Needles we passed the Parker Dam and Big John showed me the actual school where he had taught. Parker Dam is part of the reservoir where water is stored to serve people living in the Lower Colorado Basin area. So once again I had been given a wonderful day out – quite an emotional one too.

Dec 4th – There was a complete change of plan on this morning. I had not seen much of Needles itself so Big John and I decided to go for a 3 mile run. I was 62, John was 72 and very fit. To go out of the town boundary and run in the actual desert was another incredible experience. We stopped for a breather near the Colorado River, taking in the vastness of the flat land, with the mountains far away in the background. We ran back to town and stopped at the Senior Citizens' Club for coffee, at the same time meeting more of Big John's friends. Next we decided to take packed dinners out with us after we had showered and changed at John's house as we were driving out to Goff's Museum a few miles away. But we were completely unprepared for what we came upon on this particular trip!

We set off again along the main road towards the Museum. We had not gone far when we spotted what looked like a large shed on the road ahead – it was! As we got closer we realised that it was moving very gently along. Intrigued, we drove slowly past and were hailed by a man of indeterminate age. He had long hair and sported a straggly beard. He was walking beside two mules that were towing what we had termed a large garden shed. It had 4 small iron wheels. We stopped a few yards in front of him and got out of John's pick up. The man halted the mules and wandered towards us. Even Big John was almost – but not quite – lost for words. "Hallo," he managed. The man smiled and stuck out his hand. "Greetings, friends," he replied, and then proceeded to walk back towards his shed. "I was just about to rest here. There is a little grass and the animals can graze." "You mean these two mules?" I stuttered. Again the man spoke. "No. Wait till I open up". We noticed that there was some straw on the roof of the shed and what looked like corn sheaves as well. He pulled some of the straw off the roof and laid it on the sparsely grass covered area by the side of the road. Next he put down the sheaves. Then, like a magician about to perform a trick of some obscure kind, he opened the door of the shed, took out two blocks and put them in from of the rear wheels. Following out behind him came 2 burros, 3 goats and several chickens! The chickens went and picked at the corn sheaves while the man fetched animal feed from within the shed. Finally he spoke again. "I am walking three miles a day with this outfit. I hope to cover a thousand miles. I have decided to take time off and revert as near to nature as I can. I sleep with the animals in my caravan and I obtain food whenever I see a farm or pass through a settlement. I have money so that is no problem, and people are very kind. I have stayed on several farms during my journey and one family let me stop in their garden". By this time we had found our tongues again and in the course of conversation the guy told us that he was using desert roads because there wasn't too much traffic to contend with – in fact he said that there was virtually none and that it was nice to speak to someone again. It was refreshing to hear that he was not doing anything because of any religious motive – just that it was something he had always wanted to do. Eventually he loaded up his shed again, removed the blocks, bade us farewell and continued on his merry way. To my way of thinking he was one of the most contented people I have ever met – completely happy and enjoying his own company. Besides, if he spoke to his animals they did not answer back – what a guy!

We left the road soon afterwards and John put his vehicle into 4-wheel drive. We went through some of the most rugged country I have ever experienced – up the sides of gullies, down steep slopes and over rocky terrain. Eventually we reached a sort of rocky path, or passage. "We walk from here," said John, and off we went. He took me to a sort of cave or rocky overhang I suppose you could call it. There he showed some more petroglyphs (Red Indian drawings made on the rocks). Apparently these were the best-preserved drawings in the area. Goff's Museum boasted a lot of the old tools, machines and wagons that the pioneers had used. It came as a shock to realise that some of the stuff was only maybe 80 years old or less. I suppose pioneers going out into the desert would be looking for gold and would in effect take their goods and chattels with them – a bit like the man we had met with his animals and his home, I guess. By the time we got back I was ready just to stop bouncing up and down! But it was yet another wonderful day.

Dec 5th – My final day with John, and, yes, he had yet another surprise for me to take in. I had always assumed that an arid desert did not have grass. I had already learned from John about the various species of cacti and vegetation so I now knew that many plants and flowers could grow in some profusion. But this was different……

We set off across the desert once more. By now I was getting used to this mode of travel and 4 wheel driving became the norm in many rocky places. As usual he found the track he wanted and we drove about 5 miles. Then he pointed to a large house set out in what appeared to be in the middle of nowhere. I no longer expressed my surprise – I just accepted his word that it was where we were going to stop. But, funnily enough, he did not deviate from the track towards the property, but kept going virtually parallel with the direction I felt we ought to be travelling. My curiosity eventually got the better of me, "Why this way? Surely we should be turning right and going towards the house, not away from it." He grinned and pointed. "See that there, up front?" he said. There was a tall wooden bridge-like edifice with a large board on top. As we got closer I realised it was an entrance. The only thing was that he could have turned towards the house anywhere he chose as there was no fence to bar our way. But no, he drove up to it and I could see some roughly painted lettering on the board. **'Chrystal Star Ranch'** it read. We drove in under the sign and turned towards the house. He hooted as we stopped and out of the house came a short but sturdily built woman, "Howdee big John," she shouted as if he was miles away. "Howdee Molly," he replied, and gave her a big hug. "This 'ere's a limey friend o' mine from Leeds, England. Want ya to meet him." She advanced towards me with one arm outstretched. I went to shake her hand. But instead she delivered the most powerful slap on my back that all but sent me tumbling. "Howdee pardner," she yelled. "Welcome to ma Chrystal Star Ranch. You come to see what we're got?" Without waiting for a reply she set off - with us in hot pursuit. The house was on the top of a slight slope so it was impossible to see the land immediately behind it. "This way, son," she continued and went out through the back door. To say I was surprised would be to put things mildly. There, just outside the house, was a massive area of grass that would have done credit to many a park in Britain. It was fenced off in sections. A large herd of cattle was peacefully grazing in one section. There were sheep in another, horses in a third, goats in a fourth and poultry wandering everywhere in the yard and large garden near the house. And that was not all. There were unusual creatures too – llamas, a couple of camels and several other animals that would not normally be seen in that part of the world – I cannot remember them all. Naturally cats and dogs – particularly two sheep dogs – completed the picture. To me it appeared quite incredible – a zoo could not have done better. Later John told me that Molly's husband spent a lot of time travelling round the world buying livestock. But he added slyly, "I reckon he goes to git away from home. I couldn't live with that voice fur long never mind anythin' else!" He also told me that Molly always looked to see if visitors had come in under the ranch entrance. "If not, it is rumoured she won't let 'em in until they goes back and under the arch." Having met her I believed him! But for all that she was a kindly soul and happy to entertain us.

In the early afternoon we reached the foot of the Hualapai Mountains and drove up a short distance to the snowline. The views from up there were again magnificent and I counted myself so lucky to have had such a wonderful guide in John. Naturally I invited both Katie and John to stay with me in England but sadly it never happened.

We returned along the twisty route 66 to Needles for the last time and that evening I took them out for a slap up meal at a restaurant aptly named 'The Honey Bear'. It was excellent and rounded off five of the most exciting and informative days of my entire life. The hospitality had been wonderful, I met some fascinating people, and I had seen places and things that I had never even dreamed existed. At least it balanced out all the agro I had come across in Los Angeles and I saw very different life styles in both the city and the country. I never really felt entirely safe in LA. I was given several grim reminders of what can happen in crowded urban areas. By the same token I sampled the free and easy life away from the smoke – quite a contrast!

Dec 6th – I went for an early breakfast as usual to the Overlander Restaurant. If I am honest, I was genuinely sorry to be leaving such a friendly place. But it was necessary if I was to stick to my schedule. I had to cross the desert again and the day's forecast was for very warm weather. I left Katie and John about 8.30am and called at a local shop to purchase a crate of coca cola. I also had plenty of water with me to ensure that I did not suffer from dehydration. I drove back to Barstow and then on through Bakensfield and Paso Robles to San Simeon. There was very little traffic and I made excellent time crossing the Mohave Desert, driving the 430 miles in under 8 hours. I passed Edwards Air Base en route. It was where the US Air Force carried out high speed flying trials and it was the main flying test centre for many years. The temperature in the desert was very hot and I drank all the coke and most of the water I had brought with me. However it was pleasantly cool on the coast and the Silver Creek Motel where I stayed faced the sea. The countryside was beautiful too.

Dec 7th - The next morning the weather had changed and it was raining hard. I drove up the coast on Hwy 1 – known as the Big Sur. This is the scenic route and hugs the coast right up to Monteray. After a leisurely lunch I motored on towards San Francisco on Hwy 101. Unfortunately I turned off the road too soon and went into San Jose in error, but I soon managed to return to the 101 and drove to the Best Western Hotel in Millbrae. It was named as the IL RANCHO INN. This was my final destination as it was fairly close to the airport. I booked in for 3 nights. I then rang Jane Chopty, the girl I had sat next to on the flight from Toronto to Chicago and arranged to meet her the next day so that she could show me round San Francisco.

Dec 8th – I had an early breakfast and drove into San Francisco and managed to find Gough Street where Jane was living with her boy friend. We drove round much of the city during the morning and then went over the Golden Gate Bridge towards Sausalito – one of the most exclusive parts around the city. The houses were superb and must have cost a lot of money. The views from a high point near the Bridge were superb. Unfortunately it was very windy so there were no trips across to Alcatraz, the dreaded prison built on an island at the entrance to the Pacific Ocean. It is virtually escape proof. We drove to Fisherman's Wharf and Chinatown. I travelled on the Cable Car from the highest point of the journey down the steeply sloped California Street to the bottom and back up again. Jane had to get back around dinnertime so I returned to the IL Rancho Inn and wrote a thank you letter to Katie and John Hohstadt at Needles. I then went out for a meal in a local McDonalds and met an interesting guy who told me about the high rate of crime in the area. He also claimed to have a gun for protection. As he was in running kit I commented that he could not have it with him on this occasion, but he just smiled and picked up a bag with food he had just bought. He also had a gun in the bag. Wrong again!

Having spent half a day driving round San Francisco I decided to go on a sightseeing tour by bus. The hotel receptionist fixed up the trip for me with a very aptly named firm – Golden Tours. The tour certainly was excellent and I saw a quite different view of the city on the recognised tourist route – Twin Peaks, Victorian style houses, Cliff House and Presidio Park, a former military area that had served as an army base and was due to become part of the Golden Gate National Park. There were several other places of interest too. We also crossed the Golden Gate Bridge and this time I could take in the scenery more easily. We stopped back again off at Fisherman's Wharf for a break. Sitting next to me on the bus was an Austrian visitor – one Heinz Wacker - who spoke very good English. We walked round together and learned a lot about the sadder side of life in the city. It was salutary to see so many people – some either on drugs or drink we guessed - who were either beggars or down on their luck, just sitting around begging from visitors. I also saw how some Americans studiously ignored them when they asked for money and in some cases were openly rude to the beggar in question. We offered to buy a cup of tea and something to eat to one polite man who requested a handout and then asked him why he found it necessary to beg. The answer was simple. "The State of California don't operate no form of welfare for down an' outs", he told us. Apparently, because the climate is so inviting, all kinds of folk come to California. "They can sleep on the beaches at night cos that's free, and the State would go bust if they 'ad to give 'andouts to them as tried to claim it. California ain't no soft option no more." With that he thanked us politely and went off to try begging again. It was sad to see. It also served as a further warning that walking alone was not the wisest thing to do as muggings were common – particularly around Fisherman's Wharf.

The bus resumed the tour after an hour and a half. We drove through Chinatown and Nob Hill, where the rich lived, then finished the tour in the downtown shopping area in Westfield before heading back to the IL Rancho Inn. My final act was to walk along the shoreline at nearby Burlingame where I needed to go the next day to get to the Airport and return my hire car. I then had a bite to eat and went to bed – a hectic, tiring, but very enjoyable day.

Dec 10th My plane was not due out until 7.15pm so I drove up to a view point on the Heights of Burlingame. From there I could see the airport and the coastline. I then drove across the long bridge to Oakland and back before making my way once more to the IL Rancho Inn to collect my luggage. I took the car to the Alamo Depot at the Airport and made my way to the flight desk with ticket and luggage around 5pm. It was interesting to see the rush hour traffic wending its way very slowly past the Airport – I was glad I had avoided that! I had enjoyed much of what I had seen and done in the part of America I had visited but I got the distinct impression that there were pitfalls for the unwary traveller and I was surprised by the numbers of people who were out of work there. The police, particularly in Los Angeles, were numerous and, to me looked threatening, but I guess that was a necessary part of city life. It had all been a great experience and I had learned a lot from The Americans I had come across. Many were generous to a fault but seemed completely unaware of what was going on in other parts of the world. They did not want to know. Gun culture was very much a part of city life, but in contrast my experience of life while staying in Needles showed a complete contrast. It was all very different from home!

3. New Zealand

The flight from San Francisco took off on time. We flew to Honolulu Airport, Hawaii. It had been a bumpy flight as we were caught up on the fringes of a hurricane that actually hit Samoa and the serving of a meal on that leg of the journey was delayed for a while. Most passengers chose to leave the plane in order to stretch their legs for spell as we had been sitting for much of the flight with safety belts on. Even though it was just after midnight when we got there the atmosphere away from the air-conditioned area was hot and sticky so I did not go far. We flew on to Auckland where Lou Tregidga had come to meet up with me. There was a real bonus there. I was asked the reason for my visit to New Zealand. Without thinking I said I was en route to Wellington, and mentioned cricket as England were coming over for a cricket tour to NZ. Immediately Lou and I were taken to the VIP lounge and given breakfast, the hostess to whom I had spoken insisting that cricket followers should be given priority. Good for her - she apparently loved the game. We enjoyed that!

After a couple of enjoyable hours of chatting and arranging to meet up when I came up to Auckland, I flew on to Wellington where Ken Hamilton, my cousin's husband, met me at Wellington Airport and we drove to his house in Linden Tawa. It was a relief to arrive as I was ready for a bit of a rest after my experiences in America. It was lovely to see them again – during my previous visit in 1984/5 we had become close friends. Ken was now a successful insurance agent and he had a large clientele whom he visited regularly.

Ken gave his clients calendars at Christmastime and he liked me to go with him for company if I was around when he went out - and I could help too. But first I decided to see what sort of a deal I could make with car hire companies in Lower Hutt where Ken had his main office, and in Wellington. I tried Wellington first. I got quotes for a Toyota Corolla, a Mazda and a Ford Laser from Avis, Budget and the AA with unlimited mileage. I then went to Hertz in Lower Hutt, quoted the various prices and asked them to do better. I also went to Turner's Auction centre to see if it would be cheaper to buy a car there – but it wasn't so I shelved that idea. On our return to Linden there was a letter from Daphne telling me of the death of Eric (known to all as Tom) her brother and my cousin, in December. He had been a policeman for a spell before becoming a well-known crime reporter. He also wrote a number of books on the subject of criminology. 'Bernard Spilsbury: his Life and Cases' was probably one of his best-known books. I rang Kathleen Pointon, my cousin who lived at Raumati to tell her the sad news. I caught a train to Raumati the next day and stayed for a couple of nights. We rang Daphne at Sunbury to send our condolences and to arrange for a cheque to be given to Hammersmith Age Concern Department from us both.

Kath took me to the Southward Motor Museum the next day. What a superb collection of vehicles were on display! Without doubt it was the best Museum of its kind I had ever seen and we stayed there for several hours.

On my return the following morning I spent time sorting out my bank account in Wellington. The exchange rate was very good - $3.45 to £1- so I felt quite rich! I also obtained a cricket tour programme. I returned to Linden on the train and helped Ken further with his calendar deliveries. We went out again on the following day but disaster struck. The weather was foul – pouring with rain. Having parked the car just beyond a set of garden steps Ken went back to the house that was above the steps, through the garden wall. There was a brick slope above. I stayed in the car as he did not intend to stay. We were running late. After a while when he did not return I assumed he had changed his mind so I opened the car door to go up and join him. Instead, there he was, lying on the pavement in a terrible state. He had slipped on the path and had come tumbling down about 20 feet on his side. He said afterwards that he nearly managed to stop but unfortunately he missed the steps and fell over the wall – about 4 feet high and landed very hard. It turned out later that he damaged several ribs. We managed to get home and he went straight off to bed to try and sleep it off. Next day he said he was very sore but feeling better – not true..... he was in great pain round his rib cage...... not surprising! I went into Wellington and sat for an hour in Old St Paul's Church to think about Tom and pray for him. It was quite emotional. As a youngster I had always thought the world of him and would miss him. He had been very kind to me on several occasions when I had stayed at his place in Battersea. I rang Hertz about the car and they had brought the price down considerably. I decided to go into their office again after Christmas and see if I could bring the price down further and thus keep the car longer.

The Cricket Museum and Christmas

Dec 19th – I got on a train from Linden into Wellington. The bus stop was nearby and I had no difficulty in catching one through the city to the Basin Cricket Ground. I particularly wished to see the Cricket Museum that had been set up there a few years previously. I duly paid the entrance fee of two dollars, went in, and spoke to the curator, Terry Lee, who was on duty at the time. In no time the conversation led to how the Museum had been set up and by whom. Incredibly the man behind the whole project turned out to be a former dentist from Bradford by the name of Stan Cowman. His chief assistant was a New Zealander who went by the nickname of 'Wo' Wilson. He was in the office that day and again I soon got chatting to him. I decided that I would like to be associated with the work being done while I was in New Zealand so I arranged to meet Stan Cowman. I formed what was to be a friendship lasting until he died. I immediately became a Museum Curator and I spent many happy hours working at the Museum – cataloguing players from other lands including England. I remained a curator and every time I returned to Wellington over the years I always went and worked at the Museum whenever I could. I also sent articles from England now and again. Eventually the place became the official New Zealand Cricket Museum – a tribute to all the hard work that Stan and his loyal band of Curators had put in.

'Wo' Wilson was an interesting character. He told me of his service as a fighter pilot with the New Zealand Air Force in England during the Second World War. He was, in fact, a master of understatement. I gathered from him that he had been shot down at one point during a 'dogfight' (the word used by fighter pilots when engaging in battle against enemy planes). He flew both a Typhoon and a Tempest at various times and crash landed after a 'sortie' against a German Messerschmidt 109 fighter plane. One day he brought his logbook to the Museum for me to see. This was a book in which he had to record all the flights he had made during his war service. He had made a large number of flights and he had filled in the bare details of every flight undertaken. He had shot down several German aircraft. As usual there was a date in the first column, a description of his flight in the second, and once, under the heading of 'Comments', were the terse words 'Shot down '. Then there was a gap in the 'Dates' column until he recovered and went back to flying. He had been severely burned and was permanently scarred – what a character he was! We remained friends and kept in touch until he died. I had invited him to come to England to stay with me so that he could make a nostalgic visit to his old haunts once again but sadly he never managed it – a great pity.

Christmas duly arrived and the various families appeared for their Christmas lunch. My Aunt Dorothy had flown up from Palmerston on the South Island too, so it was a real family gathering. But Ken was still in pain and once everyone had gone home it was obvious that he would need treatment. We opened presents and I received an excellent cricket book called 'Rhythm and Swing' - about New Zealander Richard Hadley's cricket career. It is still a treasured possession.

After Christmas I spent several days at the Cricket Museum whenever I could find the time, classifying pictures and a variety of documents. I also enjoyed showing people around the various prize exhibits, one of which was unique and quite outstanding. It was a cricket ball, but with a difference. It had been made in a Japanese Prisoner of War Camp and was used in a series of cricket matches played on rough ground between the various cricket playing countries represented among the POWs – Australians, New Zealanders and British. A round stone was the core of the ball and it was covered very carefully with the string taken from POW parcels until it was the exact weight and size of a normal cricket ball. Bats were apparently made of wood cut from bed boards and the like, while stumps and bails were made from bushes and trees. The ball was brought back to NZ after the war and donated to the Museum when it was set up. It was considered to be of such value that it was securely locked in a thick glass case and as far as I know the case was never opened.

I also went once more to the Hertz office and eventually fixed a price that enabled me to have a car in all for 6 weeks instead of four – not all at once either, only when I required it. That was perfect! I purchased a sleeping bag and a few other items as I intended to sleep in the car like I had done on my previous trip in 1985.

Dec 31st – Stan Cowman, Head Curator of the Museum, introduced me to the various people who ran the Basin Cricket ground. They were John Gibson, Manager of the Wellington Team, Martin Crowe, a NZ Test player, Rodney Moore, General Manager of the Basin Ground, and David Gray, his Chief Assistant, jointly in charge of making arrangements for the forthcoming Test against England, in addition to their other duties. I also chatted to Simon Kellett of Yorkshire CCC, who was due to play for Wellington in a Shell Trophy match. Rodney Moore gave me a pass for the Test Match when it was to be played at the Basin too - quite a day! As I had already purchased tickets for the match I was able to give them away to Lindsay Cowie, another curator and friend from the Museum. The New Year was celebrated quietly with a few drinks during the evening.

I went to the Cricket Museum again on Jan 1st to meet Kevin Marshall – a Canterbury player who would be playing for Carlton in Yorkshire in the summer.

239

Jan 2nd – Graeme took me to the Wellington City Museum. There was an excellent display of Maori artefacts in one section, while the second section was devoted to James Cook, and the third to a study of Marine Life. We also drove up to Mount Victoria for the views of Wellington harbour and waterfront – superb.

1992: A North Island holiday trip

Jan 3rd – I fetched the hire car, a Nissan Sentra, from the Hertz Depot in Lower Hutt. It was a compact car and a pleasure to drive. I returned to Linden and prepared for my coming journey, starting early the next day.

Jan 4th – I left at 7am and breakfasted with Martyn and Andrea Vause at their house at Whitby. Martyn was a former pupil of mine at Holy Trinity School, Cookridge, Leeds, in 1965. I then drove on to Raumati. Kath was away but had offered to let me use her bungalow for a day or two. I bought some food at Crosslands Mall then drove to Waikenae and went for a swim. Next day I had breakfast again with Andrea and Martyn Vause. We then went to a barbeque on a farm with their friends, a lot of whom were English emigrants. It was a great day out. I rode a 250cc motorcycle round the farm while there and eventually got back to Raumati about 9.20pm

Jan 6th – I made another visit to the Southward Museum and stayed most of the day. I then went for another swim at Waikenae, before driving to Otaki to look round. I got back at 8pm.

Jan 7th – Drove via the Tkatawara Gorge to Upper Hutt and over the Rimatuka, up highway 2 through Masterton to Napier, arriving around 6pm. Before going to a campsite I went to find the McLean Cricket Ground. I spoke to a couple of friendly Maori people who invited me to sit with them at the match next day. I stayed at Kennedy Park Campsite and slept in the car overnight – very comfortable.

Jan 8th & 9th – I went to watch the cricket, and sat with the delightful couple I had met the evening before and met their friends. England had the better of things there and won the match. I spoke to Alan Lamb (Northants) and David Lawrence who were on the England tour. I had met Alan before at Northampton. He offered to get me some tickets for the game at New Plymouth.

That evening I was taken to the Returned Servicemen's Club (RSC) by a friendly guy named Colin Symonds, affectionately known to all as 'Squeak' – what a great

character! There I met a friend of his named Val Reynolds who offered me the use of his converted bus to stay in instead of sleeping in the car. At first I demurred and returned to Kennedy Park but on his way home he came into the Campsite, found my car and woke me up by knocking on the window. He insisted that I followed him to his bus. I did just that as he threatened to blow his horn and wake the nearby caravanners if I did not do as I was bid! Sure enough as I followed him, still only dressed in pyjamas, I just hoped I would not be stopped an arrested by police en route! I need not have worried – it was only a couple of streets away. It was a good move – the bed was very comfortable!

Jan 10th – I took a trip to Cape Kidnappers by tractor and trailer along the shoreline to see the thousands of Gannets that nested there. It was quite a climb – and an interesting experience. I visited the RSA again in the evening. It was a regular meeting place for the people I had got to know – they certainly liked their liquor!

Jan 11th – I played golf at Napier Golf Club with Brian Metcalfe the RSA secretary and took him out for a meal in Napier afterwards. He lent me a set of left hand clubs for my holiday stay. I could then return them to his sister who lived in Wellington if I could not get them back to Napier.

Jan 12th – Val showed me around Napier – a beautiful city. We had a barbeque in the evening and he invited the friends I had met while staying in this beautiful city - great.

Jan 13th - I left Napier and drove to Palmerston North. There I picked up Lindsay Cowie. We stayed at the Redwood Lodge Motel in Levin overnight after playing golf at the club there. The next day we drove to Otaki Golf Club and played golf once again - very enjoyable. We booked two more nights at the Motel and I was shown much of the lovely countryside. We also drove to an Army museum at Waiouru – interesting. We covered 430 kilometres that day. I dropped Lindsey off at his home and returned the car to Lower Hutt on the 16th after yet another game of golf at Levin and made my way back to my cousin's house at Linden by train. I had had a truly enjoyable 'holiday within a holiday' – so to speak.

England's International Cricket Tours
Before I left England I had been interested to hear about the England Women's Tour that was to be undertaken in New Zealand. Headingley was then used as the Headquarters of the England Ladies' International Cricket Team. I knew that match reports were sent to the England Secretary, John Featherstone at Headingley and, after a chat with him, I decided that I would make contact with the tourists when they came out to NZ and offer my services. The Team Captain, Helen Plimmer, was a PE teacher from Bradford. She had been told that I might get in touch with her at some point on the tour.

A triangular Tournament, starting on Jan 17th, had been arranged with Australia, England and New Zealand Ladies scheduled to take part so I went to watch. Unfortunately the first match between New Zealand and England was completely washed out. However I met the girls from Yorkshire – Helen Plimmer, Sue Metcalfe, Debbie Maybury and Jan Aspinall. The Team Coach turned out to be Ruth Prideaux, former wife of Roger Prideaux, whom I had met when he was playing for Northants and England some years before. Ruth was also a former England Ladies' International. She was a PE advisor from Yorkshire although I had not met her when I was a Head. I invited them to visit the Cricket Museum and 'Wo' and I gave the entire party a guided tour. It turned out that there was no one who was reporting the tournament for the England records so I offered to do the job. So I met the rest of the team as well as just those who hailed from Yorkshire. This delighted the management – one less thing for them to worry about!

The next day the weather had cleared up so I duly watched England play Australia. Australia won the match - 197 runs to England's total of 150. It was an enjoyable game. I wrote up notes about individual performances together with a match report, ready to be forwarded to Headingley. I also met Merrin Froggett, a former Test player who worked at Sandford School in Leeds and who had toured with Sue Hilliam, a former England tourist and the PE advisor to my School at Horsforth – a small world!

Again, on the third day of the tournament I saw Australian beat New Zealand fairly comfortably – NZ 130 runs, Australians 131 for 3wkts. So Australia had won the series. However on the extra day set aside in case of bad weather England beat NZ comfortably, scoring 168 for 9 and dismissing NZ for 126. I wrote the game up with comments on individual performances. During the day I met Mary Brito, the President of the New Zealand Ladies' International Federation, and her equivalent, Norma Izzard, the England Manager. I was invited to join them at a drinks party that had been laid on for both teams afterwards.

I spent the next afternoon and evening typing up the reports. When Ken came home he made the whole thing look very professional in the lay out of the comments and match data. He made 2 copies for me to send to John Featherstone, the secretary of the Women's Cricket Association at Headingley, and 2 copies to the Cricketer Magazine for possible publication.

The following day I posted the reports and went with Ken to Lower Hutt to collect the car again from Hertz. I then called at the house of another cousin, Joan Comerford, to say farewell to my Aunt who had been staying with her. In the evening I went to meet Paul Grayson of Yorkshire CCC who was playing cricket for Petone for the NZ summer.

England's International Men's Cricket Team had won the first Test v NZ by an innings and 4 runs – a good start to the tour after their win at Napier against Northern Districts – the game I watched while staying in Napier a fortnight earlier.

Their next game was to be played at Pukekura Park, New Plymouth. I set off around 10am and motored to New Plymouth, calling at cousin Kath's at Raumati, on the way. On arrival I went to the Auto Lodge, where the England Team were staying, to see Alan Lamb about the tickets. That turned out to be quite amusing. David Lawrence gave me directions to his room after I had dispelled suspicions to the group - also consisting of Graham Gooch and Micky Stewart, England's Captain and Team Manager respectively - that I was a reporter looking for a story! I went to his room and was about to knock when I heard him talking on the phone. I waited till he had finished, then knocked. It turned out that he was about to take a shower so when he opened the door he had no clothes on – apart from his cap! I think that he had half hoped that it might be one of the female staff so that he would 'put her off her stride' so to speak! He just laughed and said tickets would be at the ground for me the next morning. I then went to find digs and finished up at the Inverness Hostel for Backpackers. The next day I was introduced to an English lady who had just arrived, and was asked to show her to the Cricket Ground. She turned out to be Monica Reeve, mother of Dermot Reeve, one of the England cricketers. At the hostel were several permanent residents who really were people who were virtually living on the dole. Jobs were in short supply and, not to put too fine a point on it, they were strapped for cash. I managed to obtain several more tickets and I gave them to the Hostel manager, with instructions to pass them on to anyone there who wished to go to the match. I also requested that he did not tell them who the tickets had come from as I did not wish to cause embarrassment. The weather deteriorated for a time and during the break Monica and I went to Mount Egmont and up to Dawson Falls on a brief sight seeing tour. As the match was being broadcast locally, as soon as we heard that it was about to recommence we returned to the ground where I was introduced to Dermot Reeve and Roger Twose, another cricketer from Warwickshire who was spending the Antipodean summer playing local cricket. NZ Central Districts side scored a laboured 189 for 7. Alec Stewart and Graeme Hick opened the England innings and in just over two hours had scored over 200 runs between them – superb cricket to watch on the most beautiful ground I have ever visited – Pukekura Park. Hick scoring 100 in 69 balls and Stewart also scored 100 in quick time. Monica then introduced me to Indonesian food – certainly a bit different, but very enjoyable.

The next day the weather was again foul and the game was abandoned. My next match was scheduled in Napier on February 1st. The Ladies were playing a match there against a New Zealand under 23 XI. So I had 5 free days to enjoy.

Monica and I again went sight seeing for the next couple of days – first driving up Mount Egmont again (the Maori name is Mount Taranaki), this time to the Jackson lookout. The next day we visited the Glow-worm Cave at Waitomo – a fascinating place. But on our return we stopped at a Hotel for a bite to eat deep in Maori country and the atmosphere was, to say the least, hostile. We could not understand why. Normally Maori folk are so welcoming. There was a large group of Maori men in the lounge and they were not happy. Then, when we went outside we realised the problem. The police were there in some strength – they sent us quickly on our way. They were on a drugs raid and we had landed right in the middle of it. Apparently we were suspected of being police observers – hence the hostility! We drove on to Hamilton where Mrs Reeve was due to stay for a few days. I think one of her sons lived there. I continued to a town called Matamata – to stay with my friend John Scatchard's sister Violet, for a day or two.

The following morning we set off to see Mount Manganui before continuing along the coast to Ohope where I went for a swim. Across the water there was

White Island. There had been a volcanic eruption there a few days previously and we could see clouds of smoke and steam up above the Island – quite a sight. A helicopter had been there at the time and was unable to take off due to the ash clogging up the motor – not funny. But fortunately no one was hurt. We then drove back via Rotorua past the Blue Lake and the Green Lake, objects of Maori superstitions. Our journeyings continued for the next couple of days – to Karako Park, a large thermal area where there was a large Cave and the surrounding scenery was very impressive, quite awe inspiring in fact.

Jan 31st - I left Matamata, after having had a lovely break, to drive on to Napier to meet up with the friends I had made back in 1985, in the evening at the Returned Servicemen's Club. I drove through breathtaking scenery - Mount Manganui, Te Puke, Whakatane, Opotiki and through the Waioeka Gorge to Gisbourne. This was forbidding, with the Waioeka River in full flow near the roadside and Mountains towering above. The road was narrow and contained many twists and turns with sharp bends for good measure! I was once again reminded that New Zealand's outback was still very much in the process of being pioneered for future generations of travellers and one could easily come across unexpected hazards – floods, rock falls and road blockages. It made one realise how insignificant we are when compared to the might of virtually untamed and unexplored country. At home in Britain there are usually many ways to reach destinations. In New Zealand there is often only one road and it was usually nothing more than a track with a rough surface and no tarmac. One gets used to it but it is quite off-putting for starters! By the time I arrived in Napier I was ready for a reunion party. I went straight to the RSA where I still had honorary membership and was amazed when I walked in to see how many friends were awaiting my arrival. The beers were lined up on the table and food was laid on too. I made deep inroads into both! There was also a dance taking place. At the end of the evening, when I got back to Val's bus – he still owned it – I slept like a log. It had been quite a night and the hospitality had been fantastic!

Feb 1st – I arrived at McLean Park, the Napier cricket ground, and met up with the Management teams. In the afternoon I was introduced to Murray McKearney, the millionaire patron of the Napier Club. He kindly invited me to join him and his wife the next day at the match – to share their picnic.

One English lady by the name of Wendy Watson scored an excellent 153 runs and England scored 241 for 6. NZ replied with 28 for 1 at close of play. I wrote up my report at the ground before joining friends at the RSA for the evening. I had a most enjoyable time at the ground the next day – an excellent picnic shared with Norma and Murray McKearney - delightful people. New Zealand scored 248 for 7 declared. England then finished on 99 for 1 with Helen Plimmer 51 not out. I then returned to Val & Ina Reynolds house after play ended. Their daughter Sharon cooked a Chinese meal for us all – excellent fare!

The next morning I went to McLean Park at 10am to meet up with Tim Cockle of the Hawkes Bay Cricket Association. He makes arrangements for players wishing to play a season in NZ. I made a request for Mark Whitehead of Adel

Cricket Club for the summer of 1992/3. The vacancy would be at Napier, Tim's Club. I sorted out the details regarding digs that were always arranged for young players.

This was the last day of the Ladies' match. England declared at 238 for 9. NZ lost 8 wickets in their 2nd innings so the match was drawn. There was an informal gathering afterwards with speeches being made. Arrangements had been made for a barbeque in the evening for us all at Bruce Rolls' house. It started at 7.30pm. After eats and drinks it got lively and several girls ended up in the swimming pool. I managed to make a hurried retreat while they were deciding I should be next! But it was a great night and everyone went away after having been very well looked after by Meegan, the President of the local Cricket Association who had been responsible for the outstanding organisation.

Val had just started up a car washing business. I worked out all his GST costs (our equivalent is VAT). Next I went out for the day with 'Squeak' who took me up into the Te Raki Mountains on an unmetalled road through Rissington and Puketitiri. We drove back and down to Waimarama beach and went for a swim. But time was pressing so we put the car through its paces and covered the 48 kilometres in 31 minutes. It certainly was a good little car. Finally I visited the Dolphinarium before calling at the RSA to say goodbye to all my friends from Napier. I returned the left-handed set of golf clubs to Brian Metcalfe too. They had proved invaluable.

Feb 5th – I set off after breakfast, at 9.45am, to drive to Wellington in time for the third Men's International Test Match between NZ and England. I picked up a hitchhiker named Chris Rooke. He was travelling round the world the opposite way from me. He ran a Chinese Medicine Clinic in London – a very interesting person. We stopped off at Masterton for a swim. Afterwards, as we crossed the Rimutaka Mountain, the rains came in force. Five minutes after we had passed Upper Hutt the road became impassable and was closed. I dropped the hitch hiker at the YMCA at Wellington, took my luggage back to Linden and then returned the car to Lower Hutt.

I attended all five days of the Test Match and worked in the Cricket Museum most of the time. The cricket was interesting and it ended in a draw. One unfortunate feature though – the England fast bowler David Lawrence was running up to bowl on the last day when there was a loud crack and he screamed in pain. He had somehow cracked his kneecap. It was a dreadful business and he was carried off in absolute agony, helped by Ian Botham and Team Manager Micky Stewart. A reporter foolishly tried to take a picture of Lawrence in his agony and Ian Botham unceremoniously pushed him out of the way. This caused a stir in the papers but he was fully justified in taking the action he did. It served the reporter right!

Feb 6th - I took Aaron, my second cousin Ann's nine year old son, to the first day of the Test Match. I met a number of people that day – Stephen Green, the Head Curator from the Cricket Museum at Lords, Ted Dexter, former Captain of England, and Monica Reeve. I also met Kath and Jeff Creswell from the club I belonged to in Leeds and the place where I had played cricket for ten years – the Memorial Hall in Adel, and they brought a message of greeting from my golfing partner, Bruce Poll.

On the 2nd day I met Paul Grayson of Yorkshire CCC. I arranged to go and watch him and Simon Kellett playing for their respective teams, Petone and Upper Hutt, at the Petone ground on Feb 22nd. We also arranged to go out for a meal at a well known fish restaurant nearby afterwards.

On the 3rd day I sat with Jeff Cresswell and Ken Dagnall who had refereed the Football Match at Wembley against Germany in 1966 when England won the World Cup. I spent half an hour talking to Bob Bennett, the England Cricket Tour Manager, while we were watching the cricket from the Main Stand. I also met and sat with the Mayor of Wellington.

On the 4th day I worked in the Museum for much of the day - apart from attending a dinner with Ken Dagnall at the invitation of David Gray – NZ Manager of the Basin Ground for the Test Match.

On the 5th day I again worked in the Museum. Alan Lamb scored an attractive 142 runs for England. That was the end of the match. Although I had enjoyed the whole game I felt that the greatest pleasure was gained from the number of interesting people I met during the five days. I also had the satisfaction of being able to watch from various parts of the ground and thus enjoy the atmosphere.

Feb 11th – Once again I fetched the car from Lower Hutt, picked up my luggage from Linden and drove up to New Plymouth via my cousin Kath's at Raumati. I went straight to the haunt of backpackers, Inverness House, arriving at 5pm. I received a warm welcome from Bob, the manager. In the evening he took me to play bowls with him at the Smart Road Bowling Club where he introduced me to other members. Again I was made very welcome. I played a couple of games but found that the type of grass that was used for the greens was lightning fast and initially I had difficulty in even keeping the woods out of the ditch at the opposite end! At the close of proceedings I was given a honorary membership and a badge as a memento of my visit. We returned to Inverness House and I met up with some of those people who were virtually permanent residents. Again, they gave me a warm welcome.

Feb 12th – The Test Match between NZ Ladies and the England Ladies commenced at 10.30am at Pukekura Park, but it was very short lived. England lost their first wicket in the opening over – Helen Plimmer. Then the rains came. One spectator, Gilbert Knight, who was staying with friends from England at the Fitzroy Motor Camp, joined me and I drove with him up to Dawson Falls. Later we returned to Fitzroy for supper at the Pizza Hut. I then took him back to the Motor Camp and met his friends Pat and Steve, for coffee before returning to Inverness House.

On the second day it was extremely warm. England amassed a total of 231 for 7 with Carol Hodges scoring 96 and Wendy Watson 70. After the day's play was completed Gilbert and I drove up Mount Egmont (Mt Taranaki in Maori) to Lawson's View Point. It was cloudy near the summit. We returned via the coast road and stopped at the Egmont Lighthouse – interesting. I had supper at the Pizza Hut again.

Day 3 was a cricket disaster. It rained all day. That was most frustrating for me as I had been officially invited to join the New Zealand commentator for the rest of the Test Match and work with him. It was the nearest I came to broadcasting in New Zealand. So Gilbert and I went to Waitomo Glow-worm Caves – my second visit. We then travelled back about 50 kilometres along an unmetalled coast road. That was a truly genuine driving experience - potholes, cattle on the track – the lot
– and a road full of sharp corners, hills and steep gradients. We never saw anyone apart from the occasional farmer driving his sheep – I was not surprised. But it was fun – and it wasn't my car! The countryside was very green and looked beautiful. We had travelled over 400 kms!

On day 4 the match was called off altogether so I never got to commentate – a real shame. However we stayed in the pavilion and watched NZ v England play in a One Day International (ODI) Match on TV. In the evening we attended a Maori 'Hangi' where the food is wrapped up in large leaves or, in this case, cloths, buried in the ground on red hot stones and left to cook. It was the most succulent food I have ever tasted! Then we were entertained by a group of Maori singers – superb entertainment. Sadly it was the end of the tour so we said our goodbyes and went back to our respective digs.

Feb 16th – I drove back to Raumati to stay with Kath for a few days. We chatted a lot and went swimming each day. It suited me as I had done a lot of travelling and needed a rest. However during the night of Feb 19th there was an earthquake nearby and this upset Kath considerably. The house shook and things fell to the floor. We sat up for quite a time until everything settled down – not a nice experience. At lunchtime I went off to the Southward Car Museum again as there was an Austin car rally on. It was fascinating, especially as my first car, bought in 1953, had been a 1932 Austin 7. I met several of the owners and enjoyed chatting about the respective vehicles.

Feb 20th – I returned to Linden to leave my luggage then went to the Cricket Museum. I wrote a note in the messages book there to say goodbye as I should not have time to call there again on this trip. I then drove to Porirua to see Martyn Vause. The next day I sorted out clothing that I did not need. I had still got the warm clothing that I had needed in Canada and America due to the cold weather. I sent it home. I also sent a Maori walking stick that I had purchased at the Waitomo Cave shop earlier in the holiday.

The Cricket World Cup competition was due to start on the 22nd. I watched the opening ceremony from Eden Park, Auckland on television. Then NZ beat Australia in the first match by 248 runs to 210. Next I drove to Petone to watch the local cricket side, captained by Paul Grayson, play Upper Hutt, captained by Simon Kellett. The result was a draw. Afterwards we went to the Harbour Inn, a famous local fish restaurant.

Feb 23rd – I went to Whitby to see Andrea and Martyn Vause and they had arranged to take me to Whiteman Valley watch a 4 wheel drive competition. Martyn had a go with me as passenger – very exciting! It was incredibly steep and I recall that all the loose change in my pockets fell out and finished up on the floor of the vehicle. That was a great day.

Feb 24th - I went to Raumati to show Kath some photos and to say goodbye. We drove along the coast road but the high winds and rain made driving dangerous.

· Feb 25th - With the World Cup in full swing I watched NZ beat Sri Lanka on TV. The match was played at Hamilton. In the late afternoon I returned the car to the Hertz depot at Lower Hutt. In all I had covered over 8,500 Kilometres – around 5,400 miles - without the slightest problem with the car. Ken gave me a lift home from Lower Hutt. He had been there at his office all day. That evening I took them out for a meal, at the Plaza International, as a 'thank you' for letting me use their home as a base during my stay in NZ.

Feb 26th – South Africa beat Australia. I watched it on TV. The next morning I flew to Auckland to be met by Lou Tregidga, Kath's old school friend. We went back to her house and I collected a ticket for the match at Eden Park on the following day. That proved to be a great day out with NZ beating South Africa. The crowd were very partisan – quite intimidating.

During my time watching the Ladies playing in NZ I got to know Barbara and Dennis, the mother and father of Emily Drumm, a New Zealand player. They invited me to supper on Sunday March 1st in Auckland. This was a delightful evening.

On March 2nd we went to Warkworth to see George and Lorraine Tregidga, Lou's son and daughter in law. I drove Lou's car. They had a beach house at nearby Scandrett and George took me out all day deep sea fishing. What an experience! The boat had replaced the one they had had when I was in NZ in 1985. It was a massive 225 horsepower engine and I got to drive it – just my cup of tea! I reached 70 kilometres per hour but could not go faster as it was quite choppy off shore. I caught 7 beautiful snapper fish and we had one for supper. It tasted delicious! It was one of the main highlights of my holiday in New Zealand. The next day George took me round to see the sights, but it was cloudy and overcast. Lou and I returned to her house in the evening. The next morning I confirmed my flight for Thursday to Melbourne.

On March 4th I was taken to see how the Tregidga Tomato business was run. It is the largest business of its kind in the Southern Hemisphere. It was amazing to see the new machines that sort out and pack tomatoes automatically. I then went to see how Philip, another of Lou's sons ran his lettuce growing business. On the last evening we visited Valentines for a meal. The Smorgasbord was excellent!

Summing up - this visit to New Zealand turned out to be far better than I could have dreamed of. Dorothy and Ken were most kind and generous to let me travel back and forth, using their home as a base. Working at the Basin in the Cricket Museum was most interesting. The cricket as a whole was excellent. I saw so much of the game I love – Test Matches on beautiful grounds – with Pukekura Park being an absolute gem and the pick of the bunch. It is 'stepped up' on three sides with seats at a low level and places to sit on each level of the steps up. It is not that big as a ground but the surrounding areas are parklands, awash with foliage of every kind. There are lakes, walks and play areas abounding too. Places on the North Island were enhanced at Christmas by the beautiful red coloured Pohutukawa trees, also known as the New Zealand Christmas trees. In fact the flora and fauna of the country is outstanding. Driving around the country was marvellous after the crowded roads of Britain – so little traffic! I met so many interesting people during my travels. I suppose the biggest compliment was – I did not wish to leave!

4. Australia

March 5th – Having arrived at the airport in good time there was the almost inevitable delay – the computer booking in passengers was apparently malfunctioning and so I left Auckland an hour and a half late – at 11.35am – and I arrived 3 hours later after an uneventful flight, to be met by Urs and Frank Tyson at Tullamarine Airport outside Melbourne. We went to their house at Kew. The weather was hot and humid – in sharp contrast to NZ. My friends George Tribe and Bon Carmody came in the early evening and we had a few drinks, and went out for a meal at an Italian Restaurant – delicious!

March 6th - I took Frank to Tullamarine Airport. He was flying to Sydney where he was helping to raise funds with a cricket promotion for the Australian Olympic Athletes. Afterwards I drove to Ivanhoe Grammar School and met up with Graeme Renshaw and David Waugh, who had been on the 1991 IGS Cricket Tour. I also saw several of the boys too. I then met several other teachers and parents and got a truly royal reception. I finished up having supper with Rona and John Gowans whom I had already met when they joined the tour as parents on holiday. It was a delightful day and quite nostalgic.

It was back to Tullamarine again the next morning to pick Frank up. We had lunch and then drove to Ballarat where Joanne, Ursula's erstwhile business partner, lived. We all went to the house of two friends – Margaret and Adrian – for drinks. I was to return there after supper to sleep. I did just that after supper at Joanne's. However, when I returned there was more excitement than anyone bargained for. I heard a buzzing sound in the kitchen. Adrian, on investigation, had to beat a hasty retreat as a wasp or two threatened to cause chaos when he opened the kitchen toilet door. Adrian also heard the buzzing. It appeared to come from behind a panelled wall. We watched for a while – then we saw a wasp or two disappearing through a hole in the wall. We blocked it up immediately after Adrian had squirted some lethal wasp killing powder through the hole. We eventually went to bed after midnight. In the morning he removed the panel and there they were – thousands of wasps. Fortunately for us they were now all dead – but it was quite an experience!

March 8th - After breakfast I returned to Joanne's. Her daughter Gabby had been in an accident the previous evening but was ok. Gabby asked me to take her to where it had happened. I was deputed to go as I guess everyone else was too annoyed with her. I did not enquire why – I just guessed. She was one very lucky girl! After lunch we went to Daylesford. It was a former convent that had been turned into a sort of market – lovely building. We continued sightseeing and returned to Ballarat by a different route. I drove as usual. After supper I went back to Adrian's place – minus wasps!

March 9th – We went to watch England play Sri Lanka in the Cricket World Cup. England won, but the best thing about the day was the lovely way the Sri Lankans endeared themselves to the crowd. They were delightfully happy people. They wore brightly coloured clothing and they sang and talked to everyone. At the end the crowd clapped them as they left. Pity that does not happen in our world more often! While walking amongst the dense the crowd at dinnertime I heard a distinctive voice that I recognised. It was that of an Australian by the name of Brian Robertson. I had first met him at Headingley when the Australians were on tour in England. I called his name out and worked my way towards him and we eventually caught up with each other – a remarkable coincidence. We had a chat and arranged to meet up in Melbourne. After having an enjoyable barbeque at Margaret and Adrian's place I drove us the two hour journey back to Kew. The roads were good – several dual carriageways, and wide with it.

March 10th – I drove out to stay with Bon and George at Rye. There was a candlelight barbeque supper laid on. Bon invited several friends and I was able to meet yet more people! Connie, a radio broadcaster, invited me to take part in one of her phone in broadcasts at the Community Radio Station 3RPP (Radio Port Philip).

March 11th – Drove up to Arthur's seat. The weather was cooler thank goodness and the humidity had gone. We picked up Bon's friend Maureen from Rosebud where she had a florist's shop and we went for lunch at the Pioneer Car Museum Restaurant. I was shown various other interesting views before we returned to Rye, dropping Maureen off en route at Rosebud. George and I watched Australia versus Pakistan on TV.

March 12th – I first returned to the Tysons at Kew, then went to the Melbourne Cricket Ground (MCG) to visit the Cricket Museum there. Next we watched England play South Africa. England managed to win – much against the odds in my opinion – when rain intervened at the crucial moment. The rule which was invoked meant that, due to the intervention of the weather, the England players were declared winners on run rate. It was in my opinion a travesty – one ludicrous rule that had not been properly thought through.

March 13th - Frank and I went for a swim during the afternoon. In the evening Ursula, Frank and I went out to a business dinner with John Reid, former Captain of the NZ cricket team in the 50s, and a South African friend, Doug Catto. A proposition was put forward concerning the sale of a newly marketed form of grease, the idea being to promote the improved product in Australia. Frank was not keen.

March 4th – We drove to the Tysons' beach house at Fairhaven on the Coast Road from Geelong towards Adelaide. It was a lovely place, 5 minutes from the sea. It was originally burned down in the bush fire in 1984 and had been rebuilt.

During the next two days we went walking along the beach, swimming, and sight seeing locally. We also watched one or two Cricket World Cup matches on TV. I was taken for a ride through the very picturesque Otway Ranges where off road the undergrowth is very thick. I also saw the Anglesey Golf Course, famous for the kangaroos that graze there and ignore the golfers as they play through! We returned to Melbourne on March 17th after a ride along the Coast Road to Apollo
Bay, a well used and attractive holiday centre.

I wrote to Philip to let him know my new flight date. I then went to the MCG to watch the final of the Cricket World Cup. George Tribe was going to join me and had left a complimentary ticket at the ground for me. But where was it? I tried several venues outside the main stadium and eventually found a ticket in the name of C. Turner. I assumed it was for me so took it and entered the ground to wait for George. After a few minutes of waiting – rather on tenterhooks as George was not the most reliable chap on the planet – he appeared, waving a ticket! So now we had two. I hastily went back to where I had picked up the first one – obviously in error – and hopefully the customer who had ordered it actually got it! Fortunately I never had to wait to find out. Frank and Ursula had been invited to a reception and as I had taken the car to the ground I was expecting to pick them up afterwards. At least that was the plan – more of that later. The match was a good one. Pakistan won by 22 runs. George and I had a fabulous view. We went right to the top of the Grandstand and literally looked down onto the ground from a great height. All around was pitch black and so it was an absolutely fantastic scene.

After the match George went home. I waited outside the main stand for the Tysons but they never showed. Apparently Frank had drunk a 'bevy' or two too many and got into an argument – with Neil Harvey I think Urs said, but I could not be sure. It did not matter. She had set off home in a taxi as she was annoyed with him. He had followed on – also by taxi. When she arrived she got Anna to come back quickly to the ground with her to find the car. They knew whereabouts I intended to park but did not know the exact spot. Eventually they discovered it and managed to leave a note for me. They got away from the ground before the 90,000 spectators came out at around 10.30. I waited until around midnight, thinking they had been delayed, then returned to the car, which was by that time standing almost alone in the car park. I saw the note and drove back to Kew – not easy at night as I was not sure of the way. Eventually I followed the tram tracks. When I went up to bed Frank was fast asleep – on my bed! So I had to use a spare bed and that was the only way I was going to get any sleep! Nevertheless it had been a wonderful day and was really the main reason that I had for being in Melbourne. It was the major highlight of my holiday.

The following day, after going again to the 'Winning Edge' gym, I went to Ivanhoe GS again. I spent a while seeing people at the School then joined in at a barbeque – again at the Gowans' home. I met several parents of boys who had been on the 1991 tour as well as the boys themselves. It was a great night out!

On March 27th I caught a train to Frankston after a workout at the 'Winning Edge'. George met me and we went to the Red Hill Show Ground to help Connie Jacinskas set up the drinks tent ready for the Red Hill Show the next day. We were up with the lark in the morning and I drove Bon, George and Betty, Bon's friend, to the Red Hill Show Ground. Preparations were soon completed and by lunch time the show was well under way. There was so much to see during the breaks from serving beer in the tent – Shire horses, horse jumping and a variety of sideshows too. In fact there was so much on show it was difficult to see everything.

During the day there were several of us serving drinks and towards the end of the day all the officials turned up to 'wet their whistles' and things got hectic. But it was great fun and after it was all over Connie, Betty, Maureen, Bon, George and I all went to the 'Gazebo' restaurant for a meal – we deserved it! There was some entertainment too but it was not good and we left. As we had a mountain road to traverse to get Connie home I agreed to drive her and as Maureen had a Nissan Patrol – a 4 wheel drive shooting brake - we used that and drove on to George's place afterwards. The following evening there was yet another barbeque at Bon's and I met still more of her friends. One was a real character by the name of Annette Proposch – rough of voice but with a heart of gold – a true Aussie. I had always had a secret idea of what a genuine Aussie female was like – she was it!

On March 30th I went to the 3RPP studio to do a ten-minute interview with Connie. The broadcast started at 2pm and I met the other interviewee at about 1.45. It was Miles Sharpe who had featured in 'Z Cars' and 'Boys in the Bush' - amongst other shows. He was a great character. I suggested that after his interview he stay in the studio as I intended to take the mickey out of Connie – in fun of course – because for two days she had continually introduced me to dozens of folk - even including one or two film stars and politicians – as "Chris Turner, a former cricket player and now commentator from England. But don't mention cricket to him as England just lost in the World Cup Final". She also encouraged them to listen to her radio programme the next day as I was to be there as a guest. Naturally most of the comments had been ribald and there were more than a few mickey takes – in good fun, I might add. But after two days I got fed up with this and as I was to be on her programme there would be a chance. Aussie humour being different from ours I guessed that something simple that took the mickey at their own cricket team might catch a raw spot or two!

At 2pm Miles Sharpe and I were introduced and he was interviewed about his work. Connie was an excellent interviewer so I knew I had to get in quickly before she had a chance to start my ten-minute session. When he finished Miles stayed in his seat instead of leaving the studio. I already had a microphone – one that I could switch on myself – perfect! No one in the studio apart from Connie knew me, of course, and certainly they were not aware that I had used microphones regularly all my life - ever since the age of 10 when in the choir at Magdalen College, Oxford. As Connie started I surreptitiously switched on the mike. As soon as she trotted out the bit about 'being a cricketer but that I did not talk about that as England lost in the World Cup Final' etcetera, I interrupted. She attempted to stop me by waving her arm in my direction but I continued, "Connie, I have a question for you." The producer started to react too, waving his arms languidly at first, then more violently, but to no avail. Like a true professional she recognised that we could not both natter at once. "Yes, what is your question?" she said between her teeth, rather peeved that I had spoiled her introduction. "What is the difference between the Australian Cricket Team and a teabag?" I asked. "I don't know, mate. What is the difference?" and she repeated what I had just asked. By this time Miles' English sense of humour must have been in tune with mine and he guessed there would be a punch line to follow. He grinned like a Cheshire Cat. "The teabag stays in the Cup longer," I retorted with a deadpan face. No one apart from Miles Sharpe even blinked for what seemed like an age – actually about 5 seconds I would guess. After all nine times out of ten no one really listens to anyone else in a studio broadcast, a fact I've realised over the years. But on this occasion one of the technicians, who was holding a sound mike behind me, did and he suddenly guffawed. Then the rest followed in the studio as they realised what had been said. Connie, who was standing up next to me, waved frantically at the guy responsible for putting on records – it was a show that played requests too. She introduced the next record and immediately switched off her mike while the record was playing. She cuffed me around the ear – not hard – and hissed, "You f*****g pommie b*****d. You did that on purpose!" Then she laughed out loud and asked me to stay on for the rest of the broadcast. I think she thought she might get her own back, and if not it would enjoyable anyway. Perhaps she felt it would add to the content of the programme – a brave woman! Thinking it would not be a long time I agreed. It turned out to be a three-hour programme! It was great fun. The phones rang red-hot and I spent a lot of time chatting to folk. There was also a chance to tell stories that appertained to practically anything. I was amazed at the number of British ex-patriots who rang up. I was in my element and told several stories, one of which I will mention as an example. I told of the time as a young man I had gone to a football match at Filbert Street, Leicester. A burly looking centre forward by the name of Hines was playing that day. He had an experienced inside left next to him by the name of Arthur Rowley. He had played at the highest level and was still good, although a veteran who tended not to run too fast or for too long. Time and again he passed the ball just in front of Hines, who kept shooting – and missing. Eventually the crowd shouted at Hines at one point – "Shoot, Hines!" and they groaned when he missed yet again. However a wag standing next to me shouted out in a lull, "Don't just shoot Hines. Shoot the b****y lot!" Within seconds the phone rang. I answered and a voice shouted excitedly, "I was standing next to him at that match too!" He was – he even gave me the year and the eventual score! Ever after, whenever I went in to do a broadcast, he would ring up to have a chat about home. I guess he was quite nostalgic, but I never actually met him so I don't really know. He did say his name was Horace – Horry to the Aussies who have this awful penchant for shortening names, and mine was no exception. Connie had me reading everything she could lay her hands on – dedications, lists of names, addresses, stories, even some poetry and something I had never heard of before – Cheerios. These turned out to be record requests as it happened. We also linked up with a sponsor of the radio station from Melbourne who was a lecturer in economics. He was carrying out research on how to make the best use of land so farmers around the world could maximise their profits and benefit their respective countries at the same time. I even got caught up in that, and asked about the UK. "Trouble with you Poms," he said, "is that your country is so small – you do not have that much to develop". There appeared to be no immediate answer to that apart from pointing out that we are considerably more than one country – England, Ireland, Scotland and Wales - but not to him!

When the broadcast was over Connie decided that I had earned a drink at the local hostelry – but the producer of her show waylaid us before we could leave the building. We went along to his office. "That was the best show we've put out for years!" he said. "Can you come back next week?" I was delighted. I had had fun and working with Connie was a real pleasure. Fortunately she felt the same way. The upshot, in the end, was that I was invited back to do a series of shows with her. A car would be sent to Melbourne for me each week and I could stay around and holiday in the area whenever I liked. This suited me fine as it meant that I should be working as well as sight seeing and I would have places to stay.

My first 'hostess' from 3RPP was Bon's and Connie's friend, Maureen Hodge. She duly arrived after lunch and took me out to the Rye 'Back' beach, which is a picturesque spot. However when I wanted to swim there she pointed out that it was highly dangerous – rip tides and constantly changing beach depth patterns as a result made it unsafe – so that was a non starter. Instead we drove along the coastline before going to her home where I was to stay for a couple of nights. I met her daughter and future son in law there and we sat up chatting till late. I borrowed the Nissan on the second day after dropping Maureen and her daughter off at her shop in Rosebud and I drove to Cape Schenk National Park and walked along several bays in the Bridgewater Bay area. It was interesting as the bush - very thick foliage - extended right to the cliff edge and paths had been cut through it for access. The attraction was a place on the cliff where swimmers could jump down into a deep-water pool. I did not fancy that at all! I was driven to George's house in the evening after I had picked up Maureen and her daughter from work at their florists.

The next day Bon and George took me across to Queenscliffe on a ferry. It was real Victoriana, with balconies and Victorian style buildings – a delightful place. On the way back the boat was 'joined' by several dolphins. They were incredible to watch and they entertained the passengers with their effortless water gymnastics. In the evening we went for a meal at the residence of

Annette Proposch. It was certainly a place with a difference – large L shaped rooms and a balcony set out for barbeques and parties - typically Australian! It was an excellent evening with plenty of badinage in the form of Aussie humour – not always easy to comprehend at first but one soon got used to it. Much of it was mickey taking – particularly when directed at poms in general, but that is par for the course in Australia. Providing you give as good as you get they love it although I found out on the quiet that they are not the best at taking jokes directed at themselves. However - apart from the intended butt of the joke - the rest reacted with much amusement. Talk about hitting a man when he is down - I just loved that!

I returned to the Tysons the next day and found people having a look around their house. It was due to be sold the following morning. It was all intriguing, with an auctioneer doing his best to sell out the property in the open air at the front of the house. Normally the auctioneer brings a 'stooge' bidder to try and up the price. As it happened the person who should have been there was taken ill at the last and there was a bit if a hiatus – who could he get? Frank promptly offered me! I was briefly coached and was given the reserve price above which I must not go, in the hope that it would be topped. As there were quite a few people having a look round in the morning I affected to be a stranger too, also taking a look – quite hilarious really as Anna, Frank's younger daughter, kept sidling up to me and making rude remarks! The auction began and my first bid was upped and so it went on – very slow. In the end my bid was not upped so technically I had purchased Frank's house! It was then withdrawn from sale. In the evening I went out for a delightful meal with the Renshaws. Graeme Renshaw had been on the 1991 IGS Cricket Tour to England as fitness coach.

April 5th – Urs, Frank and I drove to Adelaide via Ballarat to stay with a cousin of Frank's, Marion and her husband Harold – a long journey. Frank and I shared the driving. We stayed for 5 days, during which time we made one trip into the wine growing area of the Barossa Valley. We visited several vineyards. But guess who was driving – me! Urs and Frank had copious wine tastings whenever we stopped, but, alas, I had to keep down to the bare minimum commensurate with safety. The Aussie police are not impressed with anyone over the limit. However I made several purchases. Frank and I also went to the Adelaide Oval – the Cricket Ground - meeting Peter Philpott, a former Australian test bowler, for a business lunch. I took several photos of the Bradman stand – from the actual pitch, no less. That was the nearest I ever got to standing on a Test Match wicket. I photographed the Cricket School nets at the Centre of Excellence, where young Australian cricket hopefuls are put through their paces. We also had a look round Adelaide – one of my favourite cities. One eating-house had a brilliantly conceived name where Thailand food was served – 'THAI ME KANGAROO DOWN' – good food it was too! We returned to Melbourne and then Kew on the 10th – some 775 kilometres – a long drive, but very little traffic.

April 11th – Another broadcast to be done at 3RPP Studio. My 'driver' Maureen fetched me in the afternoon as she could leave her flower shop for her daughter to run. She was to become a partner in the business. I was taken to the National Golf Club on the Mornington Peninsular for a slap up meal. This broadcasting lark was becoming fun and I enjoyed being so well entertained. Apparently the waiters and other staff listened to the broadcasts by Connie every week so, because I had become part of it all, I was an instant mini celebrity wherever I went. Mind you, When I asked why so many people listened I was told that it was such a rural area that it was the only radio station they could get. That put it all into perspective! Afterwards I went for a swim at the Nepean Country Club – again all laid on by the broadcasting people.

The next day, April 13th, I drove to the studio around 11am in time to go through what we were going to do in 3 hour programme that started at 1pm. I discovered the name of the studio – the Moorooduc Cool Store Studio – not the sort of name that trips easily off the tongue! Afterwards I was entertained at a drinks party nearby that evening – very enjoyable. I had taken tapes of this particular broadcast as a memento. Apparently the show had again been well received. We also did another show later in the week and this time we went to another barbeque with Connie's friends. When we arrived an extraordinary thing happened – a lady got up, came round and hugged me and burst into tears! I was somewhat embarrassed as to the best of my knowledge I had never met her. She then told me that I had introduced a song called 'Tears' by Ken Dodd. She was right, and I had waxed lyrical about it at the time as it had had a considerable significance in my own life at one stage. It was also of importance to her too and that was what had triggered her emotions off. Fortunately her husband was highly amused. Now him I had already met and so that was the connection. I was later invited to share a meal with them at some future date. So it just shows – notoriety can quickly become a two edged sword! The rest of the party had been amused spectators and I inevitably got my leg pulled – Aussie fashion!

As I was enjoying my trip so much I decided to lengthen my stay in Oz so I had to drive to the British Airways Office in Melbourne. Maureen, who by now had taken over all driving duties for me from the studio – it was voluntary work apart, I presume, for expenses – drove with me to where George Tribe was staying with his son in Melbourne and dropped me off there. This done George and I drove to the office and I arranged to fly home to England in the Aussie winter – on June 18th. As events turned out it was very fortunate that I had made that arrangement as I was taken seriously ill at the end of May and ended up in hospital – more of that later. My next long trip was to be with Bon and George. Bon had a luxury apartment at Currumbin, about 20kms south of Surfers Paradise. We were to set off on Easter Sunday, April 19th, and make for Sydney where we would spend the first week of this holiday at an apartment belonging to Janet, George's daughter, and her husband Brian. Maureen and I had become good friends by now and she took me to see the sights around the Mornington Peninsular and up into the Dandenongs. As it happened she belonged to a scheme that enabled her to stay for a week at a holiday resort once a year. She had arranged to stay at Caloundra, which is north of Brisbane, in mid May and I was invited to join her for another week's holiday, starting on May 17th.

April 15th – I drove across to Kew to see Urs and Frank before they jetted off to India and Sri Lanka where Frank had cricket commitments. He had introduced his coaching scheme to both countries and as an essential adjunct he had to lecture and train those who were competent to carry out the coaching techniques - a system essential to the success of the venture. They would be away until June 7th.

On April 17th Maureen took me to the Dandenong Ranges. I found the area fascinating. We passed through several small settlements – Emerald, Kallista, Orlinda and Sassafras. The Shirebrook Forest abounded with tall eucalyptus trees with the bark literally hanging off the trunks in long paper strips. We found an English style tearoom-cum-pub called the 'Pig and Whistle' at Sassafras where we had a so called 'Devon' tea. We visited the Dandenong Observatory and looked at the wonderful view of Melbourne in the distance before returning via Montmorency – an enjoyable day out.

April 18th – I went to the Sorrento Yacht Club for a food and wine tasting and met Bon's family before returning to pack ready for the start of our journey up to Sydney and then Currumbin.

April 19th - Easter Sunday. We set off for Sydney at 7.30am. George drove the first 200 kms to Sale. We went on to Narooma via Merimbula on the east coast road and stayed in a motel overnight. Again, the scenery was superb. We left after breakfast – around 9.30am - and drove to Bateman's Bay via Moruya and Bateman's Creek, then on to a place named Mollymook for lunch with Max, a friend of George's. He was the spitting image of the old film star Wilfred Hyde White – he even spoke like him – uncanny! The beaches and the surf looked beautiful in the sunshine. We duly drove on to Sydney and eventually managed to find Jan's apartment. It was ideal for a holiday base. There was just so much to see in and around Sydney and we went out everyday to visit somewhere different. The Sydney Harbour Bridge dominates much of the city and watching people walking up the bridge superstructure was tiring in itself! As it was holiday time there was less traffic than usual so it was easy to get around. Watson Bay, Rose Bay, the Yacht Club area with its myriad of beautiful yachts – all this was breathtaking. We
went to Bondi and walked along the front by the beach. It was not quite what I had been led to believe but it was certain a large area and there were surfers out off the beach, riding the waves. Parking near Circular Quay proved a problem so we continued on past the Darling Harbour Complex and into the Centennial Park Complex. That was enough for one day. Bon and I went for a drink and a bite to eat at the Lord Dudley hostelry - known as the 'Four in Hand'.

On day 2 George and I walked to the 'Victor Trumper' Park. We went on into the city, to the Victoria Mall. It had been beautifully resurrected for Sydney's Bicentenary Celebrations. Circular Quay was next and we went on a boat called the Sundowner around Sydney Harbour. It was a breath-taking cruise and the views were stunning. We then ate at a café in a part of Sydney known as the Rocks an area close to Circular Bay.

Day 3 – We drove along Oxford Street to Balmain, Birch Grove, Lane Cove and Hunters Hill before crossing the Paramatta River. We went to Longnose Point, Birch Grove, where we had a breakfast picnic overlooking the Walsh Bay Dock area. We motored on to Newport and had lunch at the Newport Arms Hotel on Pitwater. Palm Beach was next, then Pacific Ocean surf beaches, followed by Whale Beach, and finally Manly before driving over Sydney Harbour Bridge and home – another truly wonderful day.

Day 4 – We went down to Double Bay for a walk, along the coastal road and back to the shopping centre. In the afternoon George showed me the Sydney Rugby League and Cricket Grounds. He and I stopped at the Lord Dudley in the hope of seeing Alan McGilvray the cricket commentator. I had met Alan on previous occasions both in Adelaide and at Lords. Unfortunately as it happened he was away on holiday. We had supper there and retired about 9.15pm in order to get a good night's sleep before driving on up to the Palm Beach Apartment Building, Currumbin, just south of Surfers Paradise. In the morning Sydney was bathed in sunshine so I was lucky enough to see the city in all its glory as we left to drive up the coast road. I drove 900kms that day! It was 'Anzac Day' so traffic was light. Again, the scenery was superb – in places a lot of the road was border-lined by trees as we were in effect driving through forestation, but I enjoyed it. Bon's apartment on the eighth floor was lovely while Palm Beach and the coast towards Surfers Paradise certainly enhanced the view. There was a swimming pool below on site so George and I made that our first priority. We swam there first thing every day. Bon went off to see friends so George and I drove up into the Mountains – to Mount Couzal – and walked through part of the bush. There was a cascade too, the water dropping down into a stream beneath. We came back via Burley Heads and watched people surfing for an hour.

April 29th – We had a morning swim and after breakfast we walked along the beach. Bon's car needed a new tyre and another one changed for the spare so I set off to find my friend Rod Lightfoot who had a Tyre & Exhaust Centre in Ourimbah Road, Tweed Heads. Before emigrating he had run an identical business at Guiseley near Leeds. In fact I had two tyres put on and wheels balanced. After all I should be using it quite a lot. I noticed that the silencer was a bit noisy too. We went to 'Sizzlers' for an evening repast – very good value and cheap! In the evening Rod took me to the Jupiter Casino near Surfers Paradise – what a place!

April 30th – I had a swim at 8am and after breakfast went with George to Rod's work place at Noosa to have a new back box for the silencer. On the way back we stopped off at a 'pokey' club for a drink and sat chatting for an hour or two. That was a relief as I wanted to recharge my batteries and I have always needed a quiet day now and then.

May 1st – After a morning swim and breakfast we went to the Royal Pines Golf Club at Ashmore. A Japanese group ran it and the rest of the families were catered for when someone was playing golf - a swimming pool, one arm bandits – the lot. It could be an expensive day out for the unwary. We went on to the Marina Mirage Hotel and Shopping Complex at Surfers Paradise before driving back to Palm Beach on the coast road.

May 2nd – First we had a swim and then had a lazy morning sitting on the balcony watching beach guards having a practice at rescuing surfers who might be in trouble. George and I went to watch a Rugby League match being played by boys at the Currumbin Tugun Club. We went back for another swim as it was a very hot day and afterwards settled down to quaff wine during the evening while sitting out on the balcony – bliss!

May 3rd – Bon had a dinnertime barbeque and her various friends came - plus Rod. He and I left about 3pm to watch a football match at his club. We then went to his house for a pizza. When I got back the girls were still celebrating and were well away. They left about 10.30pm – a very boozy day for them!

May 4th – After a swim George had a meeting to go to in Surfers Paradise so Bon and I went to the newly opened 'Film World' run by Warner Brothers. It was quite interesting although, as I had already been to Universal Studios in Los Angeles, I found it a bit tame.

May 5th – After George and I had our morning swim we all drove to Sanctuary Cove. On the way we visited Sovereign Point where the cheapest houses cost a million dollars! Lovely houses, but on reclaimed swamp land. After lunch at the Cove we visited Nan Rogers, one of Bon's friends. I booked my bus ticket to and from Brisbane Airport for Thursday May 7th when we returned to Palm Beach.

May 8th - After a swim I went to Tweed Heads to see Rod, then bought presents for Bon and George as a thank you for having me to stay with them. I packed ready for my impending trip to Cairns.

May 7th – I caught the bus to Brisbane Airport at 9.40am arriving at 11.30am. The plane for Cairns left at 1.30pm. My travelling companion turned out to be an International Netball Referee – a most interesting conversationalist. On landing at Cairns I took a taxi and found a place called the Adobe Motel. It had a swimming pool. I shared my table with a fascinating guy called John who told me so much of how he lived up north. It was incredible to hear his stories – seeing crocodiles and even sharks up rivers - being trapped in floods for several days – the stories were endless and we sat for well over 2 hours. For once I hardly said a word. I did not need to! He should have written a book. Perhaps he has by now. After supper I fixed up three trips. Each day a bus fetched travellers from every Motel as required and took them to trip assembly points – a great system.

Day 1 - Trip 1 – Atherton Tablelands and Kuranda. I was picked up at 7.45am and taken to the station. It was raining heavily. A steam engine pulled the train up to Kuranda through fabulous countryside up past Stoney Creek and the Barron Falls. The tour allowed two and a half hours at Kuranda – a town lived in and run entirely by Aborigine people. They made a living selling to tourists and they had some good stuff - most of it hand made. I bought a belt. Their wares were mainly made of wood or leather and there was clothing of all types too. We left around 12.30pm and had a scenic tour of the Tablelands, going via Mareeba, Tolga, Kairi and others I cannot now recall. I remember seeing a massive anthill – about 6ft high – incredible! We pulled in at a road side stall to buy some exotic tropical fruits. We saw Tinaroo Dam and the Giant Fig Tree in the rain forest. We stopped for an hour at Lake Barrine before coming down a steep and winding road to Cairns. That was quite scary in the very heavy rain and even the driver seemed pleased to have got down in one piece! It was an excellent trip.

Day 2 - Trip 2 was local. It was a tour of Cairns and its environs. We visited the Botannical Gardens and the Flying Doctor Base. This was most instructive - it certainly was an impressive set up. People could be in touch by radio for virtually twenty-four hours a day and there were always doctors on call for emergencies. We went on to the 'Wild World' of large crocodiles, kangaroos and birds etc. We visited an Opal Mine and Palm Cove. Again it was all very interesting and times exciting, especially when the crocodile keepers, armed only with brooms, approached the crocs, moved them around and fed them. They were long, vicious brutes with massively wide jaws. Seeing them when they were eating food convinced me that anyone of those we saw could easily bite legs and arms off – no thank you! When I returned to the Adobe Motel I watched the English Cup Final between Liverpool and Sunderland as it was being played – it seemed so unreal to be watching it on the opposite side of the world.

Day 3. I decided to have a day walking around Cairns. I walked across a park towards the beach. As I did so I noticed several Aborigine families arriving with around 20 children in tow. They also had crates of 'tinnies' - bought from the local store I presume. As soon as they were settled they opened the first crate of beer and started to imbibe. I walked to the esplanade and sat down to read. Earlier, before the heat of the day, there had been a triathlon race. I met two locals, Mark and his wife Desley, who were seated nearby and who told me about it. They proved to be most friendly and pleasant. They were interested in hearing about my trip and I suppose that the Adobe Motel must have been mentioned at some point. Later on I walked to the pier Market Place and watched the boats. I also walked around the streets of central Cairns. It was not a large area. About 5pm I walked back across the Park. The Aborigine children were still playing happily but their parents were, without exception, hopelessly drunk and incapable. It was so sad to see. It was always said that Aborigines could not take the white man's liquor. Now I had experienced it for myself. I booked another trip for the next day – to Fitzroy Island and Moore Reef - when I got back to the Motel.

May 5th – Trip 3 - Even before I had left home I had planned that this would be a red-letter day in my round the world journey. Swimming with fish had always been a dream of mine ever since I had been swimming off the shore at the port of Tarbert at the northern end of the Mull of Kintyre in Scotland, collecting large scallop shells to use as fish course 'plates'. I had been diving down about 10 feet to pick up the big shells when a lorry came and dumped some used shells in the water nearby. Suddenly the sea was alive with fish of all sizes swimming frenetically towards the discarded scallop shells and I was in effect pushed out of the way – none to gently either! But it was really the thrill of a lifetime.

A courtesy bus picked me up at 7.55am from the Adobe Motel and took me to the harbour where I embarked on a small, but powerful, pleasure motor launch. Our first stop was at Fitzroy Island. We went on a conducted walk in the rain forest and also saw the beautiful beaches of almost white sand. After just over a couple of hours on Fitzroy Island we embarked again for Moore reef. On arrival at midday we went snorkelling. I have never seen such a wonderful variety of coloured tropical fish, and to be able to swim amongst them was the most wonderful experience. It was as if you became a part of the shoal. There was even a small shark. We had been warned that there were a few small ones about but that they were quite harmless, and fortunately that turned out to be correct! The idea was that everyone could have a swim and that at three different times a glass bottomed boat would take passengers to see the multi-coloured coral that constituted a small part of the Barrier Reef. However, so enthusiastic was I that I stayed in the water for nearly two hours instead of one. Luckily as I surfaced at one point I saw the boat preparing to leave on the final trip. I had no time to dry off or get dressed so I just got over the side into the boat. And what a wonderful sight – the coral was beautiful and absolutely breath taking. We eventually returned to Cairns around 5.45pm. I went back to the Adobe Motel and had a swim there – to wash off the salt from the sea water really as I had got pretty hot on the open boat and was afraid that I might have got a touch of sunburn and that would turn sore. I was ok fortunately and none the worse from being in the sun. No sooner had I returned to my room than the phone rang. Incredibly it was a call from Mark inviting me to join him and his wife Desley at a barbeque at their house the   following evening. I would be picked up too. So altogether I had realised my dream and had experienced a truly fantastic day into the bargain.

May 6th – I went for a walk in the morning and then decided to take a boat trip round the swamplands on the SS Louisa. It was interesting to see the mudslides where the crocodiles slid in and out of the water. I returned in good time for the barbeque. They had a lovely house in Cairns and they entertained me extremely well. It was a great experience to spend an evening with two such interesting people. I actually had some turtle meat – very tasty! I got back well after midnight and went for a swim in the dimly lit pool before going to bed. I just loved the life style I was having the chance to enjoy!

May 13th – Unfortunately this was my last day so I decided to catch a Catamaran up to Port Douglas – a fair way north along the coast - and return by bus to Cairns. On arrival I wandered round Port Douglas. It was only a small town so that did not take long. Next I wandered down to the beach intending to have a swim. There I saw what looked like a metal fence, in the shape of a very large oblong, going from
the edge of the beach out into the sea. It turned out to be a fully enclosed area. There was a large notice warning people not to swim outside the fence as sharks often visited that part of the coast. I was informed by a beach

lifeguard that unfortunately there had been some shark attacks on people who ignored the notice – he did not just use the word 'people' either – his language was considerably more flowery. I decided not to swim at all in the end as there was no one else in the sea. It was not too inviting!

Suddenly the weather changed and in less time than it took me to get off the beach and into a café where it would be dry dark clouds came over very quickly and the tropical rains came with a real vengeance! In no time I was soaked and the atmosphere had turned noticeably fresher. A lady who was standing in a shop doorway beckoned me in. Fortunately it was still pleasantly warm and I soon dried off using my swimming towel. It was as good as a swim really! The tropical rainstorm passed over after a couple of hours – the streets that had flooded briefly returned to normal as the water drained quickly away and life started up again with people appearing as if from nowhere. There were several people literally steaming as they dried off. I caught a bus back along the coast road and returned to Cairns. In fact, as I had had to get to the bus station while it was still drizzling I had got wet again and it took a while to dry off in the bus. The draught through the open windows felt cold indeed but there was no harm done. I packed ready to go back to Currumbin on the morrow.

May 14th – I woke early and went for a 6am swim on this lovely morning. I sat around the pool after breakfast chatting to the manageress and the owners John and Gwen O'Brian. They had made me very welcome – in fact the whole experience was special and I was sorry to leave. The only problem I had was coping with the heat around the middle of the day – boy, it was HOT!

A taxi ran me to the Airport and I flew out at 1.30pm. On the way back to Brisbane, with the sun being so bright, everything below us was crystal clear and I could see the Barrier Reef easily – massive and very impressive. For once luck was with me when we landed at 3.20pm. My luggage was out of the plane first so I managed to catch the 3.30 bus – just. It was a two and a half hour journey back to Palm Beach, Currumbin. As I was hot and sticky I went for yet another swim in the pool at 6.30pm. Wow – what a way to live!

May 15th – George and I swam before breakfast. I then took Bon's car to Tweed Heads to Rod's place to have the silencer tightened up. I also felt the car pulling to the left. There was a slow puncture so that was mended too. I returned to Palm Beach in time to go to Surfers Paradise with Bon so she could do some shopping. The shops were full of people – not my scene - so I retired to enjoy my favourite drink – a vanilla milkshake.

May 16th – George and I swam before breakfast. There were some surfer races along the beach. I watched from the balcony – walking along the sand had been hard work when I had gone along once before. The birds – parakeets with exotic red and blue plumage - were flying around and at one point George had no less than five on his arm' including one on his head – quite a sight. I met up with Rod at lunchtime. We called in at K Mart and I bought some vouchers for Bon and George to purchase a present or two each. We watched some football in the afternoon at Madgereeba where Rod's

Club played their matches. They won both so he was pleased. I went back to his house for the evening. It had actually been quite cool and wet for once.

May 17th – We went for a swim. Maureen Hodge arrived to take me to stay with her at a holiday condominium at Caloundra. It was pouring with rain so it was a good day to travel. The lengthy journey was slow and after doing some shopping on arrival at the local market we called it a day and watched a bit of TV. There is no doubt, when the tropical rains come driving is no pleasure and walking is virtually impossible.

May 18th – It was still raining so we went to a small place called Mooloolaba to visit 'Underwater World' This place was absolutely superb. The building housed the start of a glass tunnel that went out into the sea and to a coral reef. Again, every conceivable variety of fish seemed to be there in the water, including even a large manta ray and several sharks. It was quite eerie to be only the thickness of the glass away from these creatures – it was as if you could virtually touch the fish and other water reptiles that were present. I had never seen anything like it before anywhere in the world – it was incredible. It eventually stopped raining so we went for a swim to finish off the day.

May 19th – I had a yen to do some 4-wheel driving. Maureen was happy to let me drive her Nissan 4 wheel drive vehicle – so we drove to Mapleton and continued through onto the Mapleton Forest Drive route. Prior to entering the forest we had to see a Forest Ranger as there could be considerable danger in what we intended to attempt. After being briefed by the Ranger we set off along a well used route. We then decided to re route ourselves and we picked a little used narrow forestry track and literally drove to the top of a mountain using 4-wheel drive. It was great fun but quite tricky in places – I was in my element and just loved it! Eventually the track petered out and we drove back 8 kilometres to the proper route. The scenery was beautiful. We then ate at a place called the 'Big Pineapple' for a pineapple delight and an ice cream – decadent but tasty! We were absolutely exhausted by the time we got back. I went to bed early and slept like the dead! Driving where we did was a fantastic experience and one that I doubt I shall ever get the opportunity to repeat.

May 20th – Very wet again today so we visited the Air Museum for a couple of hours after doing some shopping. We also drove along to Golden Beach and then along the esplanade. Later we watched a State of Origin Rugby League match on TV – rough and tough! Then I watched England v Pakistan until 3.30am. England won.

May 21st - The weather was still lousy – apparently unseasonal too. Just did some shopping after I had stayed in bed to make up for my late night.

May 22nd – Sunshine at last – so we drove to Buderim to visit the local market and had a swim in the pool there too. We drove on to Forest Glen Park to see the deer, wallabies and kangaroos. There were also some Koalas. We returned to Caloundra, then went out to Maroochydore for a meal with two of

Maureen's old friends, Annette and Colin. I again stayed up to watch another England v Pakistan cricket match.

May 23rd – At first, as a lovely sunny and warm day was in prospect we drove to the 'Glasshouse' Mountains. On the way we diverted and went through an area that was being flattened and continued for a couple of miles on an unsurfaced track before we reached an area of swamp land – impossible to drive through. We returned to a lookout point to see the mountains all around us – Mt Beerwah, Mt Ngungum, Mt Coonowrin, Mt Coochin, Mt Tibragargan, Mt Tibberowuccum and Mt Beerburrum. On we went to Maleny, saw the mountains again and drove across to the coast. We continued on unsurfaced roads and even saw a lyrebird and a goanna. Another great trip that again was certainly very different!

May 24th – Drove to Noosa Head via Mooloolaba and Maroochydore, stopping for an hour at Coolum to watch the surfers At Noosa we had a swim – the water was exceptionally warm and the sun was hot. We returned via Sunshine Beach.

May 25th – We set off to go to Mapleton Falls - passing through Kenilworth via Belli. We diverted to go over the Obi Obi Bridge. It was an all-wooden affair. As we approached a car drove onto the wooden bridge - which was really little more than two shored up wooden planks - stopped, and the driver got out. We waited but he had decided that he just wanted to chat to someone. It turned out that he had not seen a soul for three weeks as his homestead was some 50 kilometres from his nearest neighbour! Eventually we continued up a narrow twisting unsurfaced road that at times was little wider than our vehicle. It was good fun but quite hairy at times. We got to Mapleton Falls and then walked in the rain forest. It was virtually dark in there. The trees and foliage let very little light through. Afterwards we went to an excellent craft shop at Montville and we saw a glassblower at work.

May 26th – A quiet day, just driving to Maroochydore to watch the pelicans – an unusual sight – before going for a swim at Buderim. The sea was warm and the day was sunny.

May 27th – I went for a swim in the Pacific Ocean but only stayed in for ten minutes and was then told that sharks also like those waters just off the coast. I got out quickly! We went for a short ride round and then took the Nissan back to clean it up before setting off back to Maureen's home at Bittern. It had been a most enjoyable holiday and having had a 4-wheel drive handy so that we could go to places off the beaten track was a bonus.

May 28th – We set off from Caloundra and called in at Tweed Heads to Rod's place to have the tracking checked. We had lunch in Tweed Heads and continued down the Pacific Highway to Kempsey. On arrival we booked in at a Motel. I was not feeling well. I turned out to have contracted gastro enteritis and was extremely sick throughout the night. By the morning I was exhausted.

May 29th I asked for a doctor to come to see me. He gave me the necessary treatment – tablets etc. This cost $40. I remained in bed all day. Apparently it was described by the doctor as possibly being Bangkok flu. Late in the day there was a complication. My right leg, where I had had the operations to get rid of the malignant melanoma in 1983, became inflamed and I could not sleep.

May 30th – I felt well enough to travel but I could not drive at all. Maureen drove to Bowral and we went to the Cricket Museum but were too late due to my illness – fair enough. It was 4.15pm. We found a motel and I went straight to bed again. I was given some supper. I then slept for 11 hours, only waking up once. I was very fortunate to have Maureen to keep an eye on me.

May31
st – Maureen drove me to the Bowral Hospital. My intention was to request antibiotics as I did not wish to stay in hospital. However Dr Ann Sutherland put me in my place well and truly. She insisted that I stay in bed for four days at least as I needed immediate treatment – otherwise the consequences could be fatal. After that I did not argue! Maureen kindly agreed to stay in Bowral until I was well enough to travel. Any form of transport other than being taken in her vehicle would have been prohibitively expensive. The duty nurses, male and female, were marvellous and did absolutely everything they could. It turned out that I had Cellulitis –a nasty form of septicaemia - and was very ill. I had penicillin injections and antibiotics to start treatment. A patient who was in the bed opposite was named Stuart McDonald. He was a great joker. We became friends then and have been ever since.

June 1st & 2nd – I had to remain in bed for a start and rest my leg. Stuart had an operation for varicose veins. He was a mining surveyor and walked upwards of 10 kilometres a day – underground. Next to him was Sam Airey, a dairy farmer – another really great guy. I started to feel better on the second day. Poor old Sam had to go home as his operation was cancelled. He had a tooth abscess. Considering how ill I had been I must say that still I enjoyed my time in the hospital. The nurses were fine and Stuart, despite his own problem, was kindness itself. There was plenty of good-humoured banter and that helped a lot. On the afternoon after I was admitted Stuart and I were taken into a lounge where there was a television set. We sat and chatted for a spell then Maureen came and joined us. That evening we watched the Motorcycle Grand Prix, followed by the Monaco Grand Prix. We had been permitted to have a few tinnies and were in festive mood by 2am. We decided to have a wheelchair race of our own back to the ward. All went well till we collided as we passed the female ward. We eventually got back to bed amid much spluttered laughter. The next afternoon, as we were being taken to the lounge again, a woman shouted from her ward as Stuart and I went by, "Were you the two jokers who wus muckin' about in the night up and down the corridor?" We apologised profusely for having woken her up. "No mate", she said, "It's about b....y time some b.....r livened this f.....g ward up!" There was no answer to that! I spent the morning sitting with my leg up on a chair chatting to Sam about dairy farming – butterfat content etc. as I knew something about that – then he had to go home. We had two visitors before we went to the lounge – a Nun and a Roman Catholic Priest. The Nun was delightful but I was convinced after I had talked to the Priest that he had once had links with the IRA!

June 3rd – I was permitted to travel provided I went straight to bed on my return and then went to see a doctor. This made for something of a quandary for me as Urs and Frank were not back from India until June 8th. However Maureen offered to let me stay on until I could return to Kew and the Tysons. She would be at work of course, but I had to stay in bed and rest.

We set off from the Hospital – Maureen had to do all the driving now - and went to the Bradman Museum at the Bowral Cricket Ground. It was on this ground that Don Bradman played most of his cricket as a boy and then as a young man. I went in my official capacity as a Yorkshire CCC representative. The curator showed us round. I bought some mementoes of the visit. We then drove on to Canberra and visited the Parliament Building before pressing on to Bombala in a mountainous region. It was bitterly cold there overnight and cars were covered in frost – just like being at home! On arrival I went straight to bed to rest my leg.

June 4th – The ice was really thick on the windows of the Nissan and took a lot of clearing. We left Bombala around 9.30am and drove back on the Stryzelski Way to Cann River, then along Prince's Way to Norwell. Next we passed through Kurramburra and finally we reached Bittern. After a bite of supper I went straight to bed to take the weight off my leg – annoying but absolutely necessary. I was extremely grateful to Maureen Hodge for driving me all the way back from Bowral – an ambulance would have cost an absolute fortune! The leg was still red and rather sore but it was getting better gradually.

June 5th & 6th - remained in bed most of the time. The drugs I had been given were very strong and had a sleepy and 'far away' effect on me – so I slept a lot and that helped. I was supposed to have gone to the Tyson's Beach House for a last break but illness prevented me and I had to stay at Bittern. I got up on the second afternoon but promptly fell asleep in the chair.

June 7th – I was still feeling a bit groggy so stayed in bed till dinnertime. Connie rang to confirm that I could still do another broadcast with her. I said that was ok. I spoke to Frank who rang about fetching his son Philip and daughter in law Liz from Tullamarine Airport at 5pm on June 8th.

June 8th – I felt better and got up about 11.00am. Maureen took me back to Kew after work and stayed for supper with Tysons. Anna, Liz and Philip were there too.

June 9th - I went to see Frank's doctor – Dr Campbell. He put me on another course of tablets for a further period and arranged for me to see him on 17th. He would then decide if I was fit to fly home. I had to keep in touch with Pickfords of Horsforth, my Insurers, re payment to be sent to Bowral Hospital for the treatment I received. I went to Ivanhoe Grammar School at midday to meet Frank English. First of all I was taken to the dining hall to have lunch. I also spent time in the staffroom chatting to various teachers, including David Waugh and Graeme Renshaw. Later on we went round the School and met various other members of staff and several of the boys who had been on the cricket tour in 1991. I called at John Gowans' place too.

June 10th – I went with Frank to the Carey Baptist School where Frank still coached cricket. It was the first School at which he taught on his arrival in Australia. We met up with Mick, a friend of Frank's who was still on the staff, and had a drink at the local hostelry. Several other members of staff also joined us at various stages of the lunch hour. I rested up in the afternoon as my leg was still a bit swollen and sore.

June 11th – Went to Carey again for Frank to arrange his next coaching session. We then went the Victoria Cricket Association Office. I purchased some gifts – a few ties. I also got a copy of Frank's new Coaching Manual. Then we picked up Ursula and all went across to see Keith and Vicki Burnham. Keith had been president of the first cricket club Frank had played for when he moved to Australia in 1963. We had a delicious meal with them and a very enjoyable evening too.

June 12th – Frank dropped me off at IGS and I had most enjoyable lunch with Charles Sligo, Headmaster of the School. I found him a fascinating character. I arrived at 12.30pm – we were still in discussion at 3.45pm! We touched on a variety of interesting aspects of education, including the philosophy behind what was being attempted at IGS. He was a visionary where future plans and ideas were concerned. I went across to see John Gowans at his house for a couple of hours and then he took me to Rossi's Italian Restaurant. On arrival I suddenly realised that he had organised something special in my honour. The boys who had been on the tour were there and so were many of their parents. Ursula and Frank were also present. They had kept the secret well! I made a short speech to thank everybody for honouring me in this way – it was very touching and I really appreciated it very much. I was able to meet parents personally, and to be thanked for what I had arranged for their boys on tour was very moving for me. I suppose it was the first time in my life that so many people had turned up to show appreciation for what I had done. It certainly made it all even more worthwhile!

June 13th – David Waugh picked me up at 11am - in his Rolls Royce. This was his particular joy – he said he had always wanted to own one! We went to the MCG where we had a leisurely lunch, then we watched an Aussies rules match – Geelong beating North Melbourne by 192 to 109. In the evening Urs, Frank and I went to have a meal with Judith and Frank English. It was, as the Aussies say, a beaut!

June 14th – I got some packing done as time was running out and I had a lot to do. I had a commitment to do another broadcast on June 15th on the Mornington Peninsula at 3RPP and I had been invited out to have a meal with John and Chris Hodge, Maureen's family at Brighton. She arrived to take me out to stay at Bittern overnight so that we could go out for the meal. I could also get to the studio easily the next day. Unfortunately though, I had done too much rushing around and my leg had swollen up again and was very sore.

June 15th – I stayed in bed during the morning and by the time Maureen had been to work and then come to fetch me and deliver me at the Studio things had improved again, thank goodness. I was concerned that Dr Campbell might refuse me permission to fly home when I went to see him. The afternoon programme went very well and was recorded for me. We all went for a farewell drink afterwards and I was invited to return whenever I could to do another programme or two. I resolved to do so there and then. I was then taken back to Bittern and after a light meal I went to bed. The medication I had been taking made me very sleepy but it had the right effect and the subsequent rest helped to get rid of both the swelling and the soreness.

During the time I was doing the broadcasts I decided to write some short poems to thank everyone who had been so kind to me while I had been with the production team at Radio Port Philip – 3RPP. This I read out during the last broadcast. It was fitting as most of them were in another room listening to the radio and had no idea that it was coming!

SHARING LIFE

A stranger came by.
You expected nothing,
Just offering him the greatest gift of all –
FRIENDSHIP.
It was freely given,
And joyfully accepted.
You let me share your company,
You gave me a glimpse of your world.

Paths have crossed,
Tiny facets of our lives have touched,
And we are taught, if we are wise,
By new experiences.
Good friendships bring joy.
Happiness is the nectar of life.
So I move on refreshed,
And a better person for having been here.

The people I have met
In many walks of life,
Each one with hopes and fears
So often shared with friends,
Enriching life's journeying
From the earliest years, till now.
As for the future, there is more to learn
And memories to cherish.

June 16th – Maureen came home from work to return me to the Tyson residence for the last time after broadcasting. I had thoroughly enjoyed the experience at the Studio and I had met some lovely people. Their philosophy was simple – offer entertainment and a means to communicate with other people via the radio station. Sometimes there were emergencies – people being taken ill – and really the 3RPP was a lifeline. They had instant access to the various essential services and apparently there were people who listened to the broadcasts at these service areas. The station covered an area about 300 kms in every direction. Because of the location – the Mornington Peninsular – it was the only radio link in the area. To have been able to link up with all these people was an education in itself. Phone in broadcasts were genuinely important and, at the same time, popular. Prior to the broadcast I had discovered that Connie herself was unwell too and to cheer her up I wrote poem for her – in Yorkshire dialect. I called at her house to give her a copy and she asked me to read it. I did so, and a glazed look came over her face. When I had finished she said, "Chris, I didn't understand a single word!" The fact of the matter was that I had read it to her in broad Yorkshire dialect! I then had to explain what it all meant – just shows you we don't always understand everything we hear. Here is what I wrote for her:-

TRUE VALUES IN LIFE

The greatest riches tha' can find
Lie not in gilts or gold
They're made of less material stuff
Which can't be bought or sold.
For friendship is eternal –
It never asks for owt –
In Yorkshire, as t'locals say,
"Tha' do'ont get owt fo' nowt!

So brass tha's got a plenty
If friendships be sincere.
Then brace thissen an' chuckle
When t'lads gi' thee a cheer,
And give us all some pleasure –
I beg just one more boon:
Make 'aste an' use that treasure –
Keep faith – an' GET WELL SOON!

We returned to Kew and then we all went out for a final 'Cheerio' meal – Liz and Philip Tyson, Maureen, Caroline - who was a friend of the family - Ursula, Frank, and myself. It was an excellent meal, but, as I vaguely recall, the service left something to be desired. Still, we can't always have everything in this world! We returned to Kew for coffee and port. The party broke up around midnight after a most enjoyable evening.

I had written a poem for Maureen to thank her for the many kindnesses she had shown to me during my stay in the area around Rye, Sorrento and Dromana. She lived some distance away at Buderim. Much of my time there had of course been spent with my friends Bon Carmody and George Tribe and we had arranged an extended holiday together on the Gold Coast where Bon had an apartment. We had driven up to Curumbin from Rye in George's old car – a journey of over 900 miles, and George and I had shared the driving. We had also stopped off at a motel on the way up to Sydney for one night. We spent a week of our holiday in the city itself. Maureen had later driven the entire journey up to Bon's place alone with only one overnight stop at a motel en route – quite a drive. She had then picked me up and driven on to Caloundra. I was particularly grateful to her when I was taken so ill on the journey back to Melbourne as she had stayed for four nights at Bowral while I was in hospital there and had driven me back the rest of the way.

Earlier, as a voluntary transport driver for the Radio Station, she had fetched me from Melbourne on several occasions when I was taking part in broadcasts at 3RPP, seen to it that I had somewhere to stay, and then driven me back to the Tysons' house in Kew over two hours drive away. It was inevitable that we should became close friends during my visits to the Mornington Peninsula Radio Station. This is what I wrote - in blank verse:-

THE REALITY OF FRIENDSHIP

I was a stranger passing this way.
We met.
We became friends – close friends.
We shared intimate moments.
There was tenderness.
There was laughter.
There was joy.

Then came sickness.
Now came a moment of truth.
There was still kindness – and consideration.
There was still tenderness.
Fun and laughter, they were still there – and concern.
Then there was care, and more fun, and laughter –
And - finally – joy again.

Now I am better - in health,
And as a person.
You are as you are;
I, too, am as I am.
Our paths have crossed.
Our lives have touched.
It's beautiful – a time to cherish.

In the game of life such moments are fleeting.
When loneliness intrudes –

When you feel sad –
Read – and touch. Recall a happy memory or two.
You made them – and shared some –
And no one can take them away.

June 17th – I saw Dr Campbell at 9.30 and was given the all clear to fly home. He warned of a possible small thrombosis at the back of my leg and also said that it was likely that my leg might swell up with the travel. He gave me specific letters to be delivered to my doctor immediately on my return. He warned me that there would be a risk, but provided I took care I should be all right. I rang BA, confirmed my flight and requested a seat that would allow me to keep my leg raised as much as possible. I was requested to go early to the Airport so that suitable arrangements could be made.

June18th – Ursula and Frank took me to Tullamarine Airport for 10.15am. My flight was due out at 1.30pm. I reported to the desk, put my luggage through customs, and was allocated an excellent seat on the front row of the upper deck of the Boeing 747 Jumbo Jet. I had been upgraded and so had extra room too. I said farewell to the Tysons and sat in the waiting lounge until it was time to board. I was helped to my seat and the cabin crew looked after me very well. I had interesting travelling companions – a biochemist travelling via the UK to Lausanne and a retired Hospital Matron who made sure that my leg was ok – a bonus, that! There was also a traveller who had a fund of amusing stories to relate. It was the ideal situation for me. There were also four films shown and plenty of food to eat. I eventually arrived at Heath Row around 6am on June 19th. My cousin Daphne and her husband Frank picked me up and took me back to their house in Sunbury. I was then able to rest up for the entire day – just watching cricket from Lords. Pakistan was playing England. Frank went to the match but was back early as it rained – surprise, surprise! I went to bed at 8.30pm. My son Philip rang to say he would come down, stay overnight, and we would return to Leeds the following day – Sunday. It was wonderful to see him again. We returned safely to Leeds. That was the end of what had been the most fantastic eight months of my life. I had travelled a very long way in each country that I had visited. I had met no end of people. I understood so much more about life than when I had originally left home – the innate kindnesses that were shown to me, particularly when things went wrong in America. Cricket had given me so much pleasure and I had been able to repay that in some measure whenever I could. Becoming involved with the Cricket Museum at the Basin, Wellington – taking an interest in the International Cricketing sides on tour in New Zealand – the Returned Servicemen's Club in Napier – really the list is endless. The incredible help given to me when I travelled around New Zealand – the deep sea fishing, the chance to sail and even to fly a Cessna for half an hour, and the good natured friendliness that accompanied all these activities. Australia had offered me the chance to broadcast, to travel, to have short vacations within my main holiday and to generally enjoy every minute. Again, the cricket connections – the ex Australian players from Northants like George Tribe – people whom I had met when they were at the top of their sporting achievements, players, cricket commentators, spectators, reporters – it had all happened for me. My dream of going to the Barrier Reef, driving in the outback, walking in rainforests and the bush – I had actually had the chance to do all these things. Perhaps the most important thing of all was what I proved to myself. I set off, having just the bare bones of the journey I intended to make around the world. Each time something occurred out of the ordinary I was able to cope – even when I became ill there were people who helped me and looked after me. I certainly learned a lot about the way some folk lived. It took all sorts to make up that fantastic world I had travelled in!

Chapter 11 Improving fortunes

During the course of my trip I had made arrangements for my house to be let for six months. The actual tenancy was not taken up until I had been away for a while and was part of the reason I was happy to extend the length of time I was away from home in NZ and Oz. In fact on my return the tenants – Mrs Crowther and her young son - had not left my house as the tenancy still had two days to run, so I stayed with Philip at his house, 24, Springfield Gardens, Horsforth, for a couple of days. I did go over and meet Mrs Crowther on the day that they were due to move as the Estate Agent who had sorted out the lease was also present to check the inventory plus the gas and electricity used, as this was her responsibility. However her young son, who had made some friends amongst the local children, did not want to leave when the time came – not surprising really. When his mother wanted him to set off he struggled with her and kicked out, as little children sometimes do to register their dislike of what is happening. Unfortunately his foot caught me - right on the nerve ends where I had previously had my cancer operation. That really hurt! However fortunately there was no lasting damage. Poor Mrs Crowther was highly embarrassed! On the whole the house had been looked after fairly well although I found a few things that had been broken discreetly hidden at the back of a cupboard. It could have been a lot worse.

The next two days were spent in having services reconnected and post redirected back to my address. It took weeks for the Post Office to put that right. Then I had the arduous job of putting together various bills showing the costs that had accrued while I was in hospital in Bowral, plus writing to the Insurance Company to explain exactly what had occurred. The car needed re-licensing and the cheque that had originally been sent from the DVLA in November 1991 to cover the amount refunded on my motor tax disc was out of date and had to be returned for another to be issued. My motorbike also needed taxing and both vehicles needed MOTs. The television needed another licence too. I then had AA membership to sort out again, plus obtaining a refund for the Grand Canyon Airline ticket that I was unable to use due to the inclement weather. My former secretary Joyce Williamson was retiring from St Margaret's School and Sue Hilliam, the PE advisor, was retiring too so there were two parties to attend in the near future. So one way or another there was a lot to do!

But the saddest thing of all was to hear that Dick Hansell's wife Jean had died on June 26th at Darlington. The funeral was to be on June 30th and neither of my vehicles were due to be relicensed until July 1st. Urs and Frank rang from

Australia to ask me to represent them at Jean's funeral. I was going anyway and I managed to arrange for Brian Saunt and his wife to pick me up on their way to Darlington. Fred Andrews, a neighbour, kindly drove me to the meeting point at Boston Spa on the A1. It was a very sad affair for us all as she was a very popular and kindly person. But it was a blessing too as she had suffered a lot of pain with cancer despite all the drugs she was given. I met friends at the wake afterwards that I had not seen since I left Durham. Brian Saunt kindly brought me back afterwards on his way home.

Before leaving Northampton I had done a variety of jobs outside teaching, in my spare time. I had worked in a National Children's Home for quite a while in order to supplement my income. I had been on the Parish Church Council at St Matthews, Northampton, and for a while had responsibility for keeping accounts of the income engendered by a voluntary envelope payment scheme. This idea ensured that the PCC knew approximately how much money was available for charities, building renovations and a variety of other things connected with the running of the Church. When I moved to Leeds I was happy to continue to do voluntary work and also to supplement my income for a time by working for the Milk Marketing Board, courtesy of my father in law Willie Holroyd. He was Chief Milk Recorder for Yorkshire at the time. My work took me to several farms in the area. I personally took butterfat samples from a few dairy herds. This meant getting up and arriving between five and six o'clock in the morning for the first milking, then returning after work for the evening milking. In other cases I collected samples taken by dairy herdsmen themselves after I had finished work and these I delivered to the MMB Office in Harrogate. All this extra curricular activity caused much amusement among the staff at the school where I worked, Holy Trinity CE, as I used to come into school wearing my farming clothes on the occasions when I had been out in the early morning. I kept a change of clothing in the men's cloakroom and effected a quick transformation to normality, ready to teach. What is more, I was never late. However one morning I got too close behind a cow with fairly disastrous results and on that occasion when I went into school there were plenty of remarks, particularly from the two other men on the staff when they entered the men's cloakroom – so I got my revenge! I thoroughly enjoyed going out to farms in the summer but winter trips were often cold and considerably less inviting. Still, we always had endless large cups of tea to hand in the cow byres – it served two purposes – warming hands in order to write down the butterfat milk yields on the relevant sheets, and then as a drink – resourceful people are farmers! I did that extra job for two years, until I became a Deputy Head at Whinmoor CE Primary School in September 1966. After that there was no time to go to farms in the early mornings as I had to travel 10 miles to and from work every day.

Molly and I did some book reviews and readings for a magazine produced for blind people – that was interesting and worthwhile. I have kept that up ever since and have regularly read a variety of articles for the 'Magazine for the Blind' sent out every month to a large number of blind listeners. I have also helped out occasionally with the reading of current sporting articles for a weekly programme distributed to those who enjoy hearing the details of, and comments about, a number of sporting activities – racing, football, rugby, cricket, tennis etc.

As my philosophy in life has always been not to buy anything I could not pay for at the time I had seldom been in debt, apart from having a mortgage to pay every month and this was simply part of the monthly budget. However when I was left on my own in 1983 I needed either to sell the house in Cookridge or purchase the half that was in Molly's name. I decided on the latter so my mortgage shot up from a pittance to a considerable amount and, as I have already written, I found various ways to supplement my income. My target had been to pay the extra off in 12 years. I improved on that considerably. My shares had by now recovered from the losses sustained in 1987 and I found that by cashing some shares in I could pay off a lump sum - £4346 – to clear the debt. By today's figures that does not sound much but it was a considerable amount then – well over half of my Teacher's Pension for a year. That I did on July 17th 1992 – a red letter day in my financial life. Later, when I had fully recovered from the illness – Cellulitis - that had struck me down in Australia, I continued with the work ethic but did so more or less on my own terms – occasionally delivering cars or helping people out when needed. I recall driving up to Glasgow and Edinburgh to deliver carpet samples – quite an undertaking as time was of the essence on that occasion. On another occasion I went in a convoy, delivering a car to a firm in Glasgow. There were ten cars in all. We stopped for lunch on the way. After we had all arrived safely and delivered our vehicles we were transported back to Leeds in a 12 seater bus. One trip I particularly enjoyed was being asked by Randerson's of Horsforth to go to Nottingham to pick up a brand new Peugeot 405 model that had just come on the market. I was driven there by an employee of the firm, we had lunch, and then I had the pleasure of the drive back. What a car that was!

During the latter part of the year Philip returned home to live for a while. Sadly his marriage was on the rocks and he and Rachel split up after less than two years. I'm sure this must have been a time of great turmoil for them both, but they were not happy together so it was a right and sensible decision. Paradoxically for me it was great to have my son home again and I thoroughly enjoyed his company during the period that he needed a place to live. He had financial outgoings too so being at home helped a bit. At one point during the course of our time together he actually helped me – one could almost say, in return. Had we not chatted a lot I suppose he might never have had the opportunity of saying what he did. One day in particular we had been discussing the breakdown of my marriage to his mother Molly in 1983 and I made comment that I did not like the thought of any criticism of her. I guess that actually I had 'carried a torch' for her for the nine years since we had split up. I had actually loved her very much and although I had not said much about it I could not put her entirely out of my mind even after all this time. It was, in truth, foolish, and in my heart I knew that. But Philip put it into words that clarified the situation as it really was and it must have been a hard thing for him to do. He pointed out that she was happy with Clive so she did not need anything from me. Thus it would be sensible for me to 'get a life' and go and enjoy myself with no regrets about the past. There was more discussion too, and it set me thinking hard. My dear son had given me good, sound advice and the least I could do was to listen. I did, and on his return from work the following day I met him literally at the front door, put my arm around his shoulders, and thanked him for what he had said. He was relieved too when I said that it was exactly what I had needed and he was the one person that was close enough to me to be able to get through the emotional barrier that I had put up between myself and other people. It was as if my mind had cleared and I had finally accepted what had probably been there all the time. I have never forgotten it and while I live I never shall. As well as emotion there was pride – pride that we shared a mutual trust as equals and yet still as father and son. He had contributed greatly to an important turning point in my life and he had met someone else too – Mandy Richardson as she was then. It was delightfully obvious that they were happy to be together and I saw the change that came over him – it was as if a cloud of despondency had lifted and he was content once more. It was not long before they decided to live together in a newly completed ground floor apartment at Lakeside Gardens in Rawdon. At some point afterwards I met her parents Margaret and John Richardson, and we got on extremely well. They are lovely people and have always been good friends to me.

With Philip now settled my general aim was to continue to supplement my income in order that I could return once more to the Southern Hemisphere in 1994. I had made a lot of friends out there and I thoroughly appreciated the laid back way of life that existed for most people I met. They worked hard – and played hard, particularly in the world of sport. I strongly subscribed to that ethic – I always had during my lifetime but it was by no means universal in the UK. As I mentioned earlier I had spent a lot of time working for blind people on a voluntary basis. This was confined mainly to the reading of articles for a monthly talking magazine that was sent out to blind people. I had also gone out to see anyone who needed help – writing letters, reading material received in the post, being taken to appointments such as banks, doctors or dentists etc. – that sort of thing. I could do this on a regular basis if required and I was approached by the Association for the Blind. I should receive a small fee, courtesy of the Association, to cover any expenses that might be involved. So for a fixed period I used to help a teacher by the name of Philip Lucas with literally anything he required. Philip had lost his sight around the end of his teenage years so he had clear memories of so much that he had acquired before the onset of blindness. This made things difficult for him in many ways. He had been independent as a youngster in his schooldays and had taken part in sport – particularly cricket. Suddenly he found that he had to learn a whole new way of life. Obviously this must have been very hard to take – having to rely on other people and his guide dog. He coped well on the whole but he found difficulties that had not existed before. He had become a Salvation Army Captain and had worked abroad – there was always someone to attend to his needs and he was perfectly capable of doing missionary work. He married the lady with whom he was working and who looked after him. When they returned to this country his wife had two ailing parents living in Worcester. She went to look after them in their declining years, and Philip got a job in the teaching profession that brought him to Leeds for a time. He was something of an author, specialising in short stories and articles, and he needed someone to assist him when he was doing his writing. I was ideal for this sort of work – it enabled him to write more quickly because I could see at a glance if he had made any mistakes while producing his work on his computer. I could also offer advice and pass on ideas. Some of his writings were about cricket and, again, as a former cricketer I could discuss ideas with him. In addition I was able to help him with his school marking. This meant that he could more comfortably teach sighted children as well as those whose sight was impaired. I used to mark the work and then tell him just what was required in order to correct the work done by his sighted pupils. I also read his correspondence out to him. Eventually he moved to Worcester to live with his wife again and I was available to help someone else.

Next I was asked to offer my services to a man by the name of Martin Milligan, a person for whom I came to have the greatest respect. He was a tutor in political philosophy at Leeds University, an interesting and stimulating man to talk to. His blindness had affected him from very early days so he was completely at ease with everything appertaining to normal life. In fact the contrast between Philip Lucas and Martin could not have been greater. Although the work was basically along more or less the same lines – reading any correspondence that arrived at Martin's house and occasionally checking what he had written - that is where the similarity ended. I arranged to go to his house just once a week. In effect I finished up being there three or four times a week – he was such an interesting man to work with. He was writing a book in tandem with a sighted lady colleague who lived in Scotland. They had had similar views on politics and those in themselves gave great food for thought. Martin had taken his degree at St Andrews' University and I guess that is where they became acquainted. He was initially a member of the Communist Party and studied their philosophies in much detail. However, after he had been to Russia to experience what the life was like for himself he changed his views radically and eventually turned towards the Labour Party after studying the political ideologies of both Liberals and Conservatives. But it did not end there. His work took him into the realms of politics abroad and he had a fundamental background that covered various other political beliefs in detail – particularly those in the American Continent. He felt that the political thinking in the United States was still basically very insular, just as it had been before the Japanese bombed Pearl Harbour. That had brought America into the Second World War. He felt that their politicians still showed a marked lack of understanding when it came to world politics. He considered that was very dangerous in many respects and he always feared that one day they would stack up problems for Europe, and possibly the rest of the World, based on ignorance of the over all political Global spectrum that was constantly changing. He further believed that Britain was laying herself open to future problems by giving away our sovereignty – yet he was by no means a supporter of the Royal Family and their attendant privileges. I learned more about politics from helping him with the book he was writing than I had ever done before or, indeed, since. Sadly he died before the book was completed and I never heard whether or not his Scottish co-writer completed it – I hope she did. He was a humanist too and we had many a fireside discussion about that. One thing I never quite understood. One day he asked me to hand him his filing box. The cards were all in Braille and they were colour coded. As there was a word at the top of each card in Braille identifying just which one he required I thought nothing more about this. Then one day I asked him about colours. He said that each colour had a slightly different texture and, incredibly, simply by touching a colour he could tell me what it was! I think that it was at that point that I fully understood just how sensitive the senses that he had actually were. When Martin died his humanist style funeral was certainly different. People were invited to stand up and speak about him and it was then that I realised just how well he was loved and respected – a truly modest but great man.

During the summer I went to visit my former college friend Bryan Stubbs up at Heighington, near Newton Aycliffe for a few days. At one point we decided to visit the Bishop's Palace at Bishop Auckland to see some art that was on show there amongst other exhibits. While studying the pictures I chanced to speak to a New Zealander and his wife, Murray and Margaret Olds, who were touring Britain in a Campervan. I have always had 'open house' for people, particularly from the Southern Hemisphere, and the result was that I invited them to come and stay for a few days when they were in my neck of the woods. They were going to York so it was decided that they should come across from there. They did just that about a week later and I took them round much of Yorkshire. It was a great holiday break for them and they invited me to stay with them when I was next in New Zealand.

Chapter 12 A second IGS Cricket Tour

In mid 1993 I was once more asked to consider organising another Cricket Tour for Ivanhoe Grammar School in 1995. The tour would be led by Frank English, Deputy Head of IGS. I had enjoyed doing the 1991 tour, but it had started off simply as a favour for Frank Tyson – this one should be easier as I now had the contacts. I also had a computer. Writing letters and saving everything should make things much more comprehensive, and this time it would be done on a proper business footing. Frank Tyson had left IGS some time before. With the experience I had gained in 1990 I decided that my fee should properly reflect the actual amount of work required to organise the tour - £1,500 plus a £500 float to cover all expenses up front. Last time I had found that there was sometimes a delay of several weeks when I made the necessary claims after paying out of my own pocket – this time I decided to work to a budget and send details of how the money was being spent. This was accepted so I determined to plan ahead. I could then address a meeting of IGS parents who had youngsters eligible age-wise to take part in the tour, while I was making another visit to the Southern Hemisphere in 1994.

On the 1991 tour our travels took us from Tonbridge in Kent up north to Newcastle and thence back down to Sunbury on Thames. This time I thought it would be a good idea to play some matches in Wales, and then make our way up north as far as Yorkshire. I followed that by working out an itinerary that would bring us down the centre of England and on to Dulwich College before heading back towards the Royal Holloway College where I could get accommodation for the last two nights of the tour. The last match would again be played at Sunbury on Thames Cricket Ground. I received a request from

IGS that as many matches as possible should be played against other Schools rather than representative sides. This gave me a firm foundation upon which to build. First I studied a map of England and Wales and worked out an approximate route. I then obtained a list of Public Schools and picked out ones that were within reasonable distance of the route. I decided to contact all of those that I had picked out, knowing that it was normal for most schools to prepare their fixture lists well in advance. By allowing nearly two years before the onset of the projected tour I reckoned that I would be in with the chance of obtaining fixtures more or less within the time span I required. At least, that was my original plan.

While I was staying at Sunbury with my cousin Daphne in June '93 I had a piece of luck. I visited Dulwich College to see a friend, Rick Wilson, who had been the Master in charge of cricket at Dulwich College when Ivanhoe GS had played there in 1991. In the course of conversation I mentioned that IGS were hoping to tour again in the summer of 1995 and I mentioned the idea I had regarding playing a few fixtures in Wales. It was then that he told me that Dulwich College had a Field Centre at Glentawe in the Upper Swansea Valley in Wales and he offered to arrange for IGS to use it for 5 nights if I wanted him to. I accepted gratefully and immediately picked out schools within a reasonable distance of the Centre – Llandovery College, Monmouth School and Christ College, Brecon. Each establishment was willing to arrange a fixture. There was also the Big Pit Museum at Blaenavon that would be an interesting place to take the boys to on one of the non-match days.

I made contact with Bristol Grammar School on my return home. They offered to arrange a match and also to try and fix a date that would fit in with my projected itinerary. I intended to drive to Bristol on the day the tourists landed at Heath Row so the Cricket Master, Rick Sellers, further suggested that I might be able to find accommodation at the Camden Hotel in Bristol on the first night, prior to staying with boys from the School for the following two nights. He also generously offered the tour party the use of the School cricket nets on the first day in order that they could get some practice and start to get used to English conditions. Sorting out the dates eventually turned out fine so the first section of the trip could be quickly pencilled in. From there onwards the tour more or less fell into place so that by February 13th '94 I knew most of the Schools and Colleges that we should be going to play matches against. Time was important as I was due to fly off to New Zealand and Australia on February 14th '94 and would be attending a meeting of IGS parents and boys involved in the tour while I was in Melbourne. I could make arrangements for visits on non-cricketing days when I returned home on May 14th. Furthermore I could also do a pre-tour journey, going to all Schools involved and sorting out details of the routes between the respective establishments.

In my quest to keep fit, despite advancing years, I went swimming as often as I could. I belonged to a Swimming Club that was organised by my friend Tony Oates, a golfing associate of long standing and a member of the Adel Memorial Hall complex. I had been a member of that same establishment since 1964, having played cricket for the Adel Cricket Club for 12 years before an ongoing back injury signalled the end of my playing career in September

1976. I also belonged to the Bowls Section at the Club. On November 29th '93 I went along to the Holt Park swimming pool as usual, meeting up with other club swimmers. It was a very cold evening and it had been raining when we arrived. When we left a couple of hours later the rain had turned to snow and the roads were covered to a depth of about three inches. I set off for home, driving very slowly, turned left off the Otley Old Road and almost immediately right into Moseley Wood Drive. Under the snow the rain had frozen and conditions were such that vehicle control went virtually by the board. I got almost to the bottom end of the street and slid into a parked car before hitting a lamp post on the opposite side of the street and coming to rest on the pavement. It all seemed to happen in slow motion, but the car door was damaged and, as it later turned out, the two front engine mountings were knocked out of alignment when I hit the lamp post. I could still drive the car but it was necessary to have the damage mended as soon as possible. As usual there was a waiting list at the BMW garage where my Insurers insisted that the work was done. Eventually the car was taken in on February 9th '04 after being assessed a couple of days previously. I was given a courtesy car while the work was being completed. It was ready for collection on February 12th. I took it straight home and garaged it up on blocks for the duration of my trip to the Southern Hemisphere. I thought that was the end of the matter but I was wrong. There was a potentially very serious problem when I returned in May – more about that later.

Chapter 13 1994 - My third Southern Hemisphere trip

On Sunday Feb 13th Mandy and Philip drove me down to Sunbury and we stayed with Daphne and Frank overnight. It was snowing the next morning so we decided to leave for Gatwick Airport earlier than planned – just as well as traffic was at a standstill from time to time. We had just arrived when, to add to the chaos, there was a bomb scare lasting an hour and a half so Mandy and Philip were unable to set off home again! The plane was delayed too and we left around 3.45pm. But on this occasion the weather did passengers a good turn as we had to fly to Los Angeles over Greenland. The views were fantastic – fiords, mountains, ice flows – the lot! We then flew over Hudson Bay and across Canada where the snow lay deep everywhere. We even saw Salt Lake partly frozen over – a rare sight we were informed. We landed at Los Angeles after a ten and a half hour flight and only stayed for a couple of hours for refuelling before heading off in the dark to Auckland. We had now made up the time lost at Gatwick and were back on schedule. Despite the darkness it was difficult to sleep as people were constantly moving about in the 'Jumbo'. But there were films and we were well fed. Things went all right until we ran into strong winds as we were approaching Auckland Airport. Apparently the pilot had chosen to carry out the actual landing himself (or herself) and we were made aware of this when we were told to put on our seat belts. I noticed that the crew also put seat belts on in good time and as I was sitting on the row nearest to an exit in the centre section of the plane I was directly opposite a couple of the stewardesses. It was the older one who informed me that a manual landing was being carried out. The plane was swaying about and the wings appeared to be vibrating. The stewardess who had spoken to me was obviously aware that there was an additional element of danger and she commented that the actual landing was leaving much to be desired (her words were considerably stronger than that). At that point we touched down heavily and appeared to 'crab' sideways towards the edge of the runway. It certainly was a hairy moment as the engines went into reverse thrust in order to eventually stop the plane. We slowed right down and started to taxi towards our landing bay. I could see through a cabin window that the grassy line of the runway was very close indeed – our wingtip was actually over the edge and the stewardess was not at all impressed. I think she may have even been someone of senior rank as she obviously annoyed and I suspect that she probably gave the pilot a real telling off later! It reminded me of just how dangerous take offs and landings can be. It was easily the bumpiest and most frightening landing I had ever made and I was just grateful to be down still in one piece. There were several extremely shaken passengers who made their way into the main building.

New Zealand

Once I had cleared customs I got my luggage and found Lou Tregidga waiting for me. It was 6.30am so we went back to her house in Favona Road. I began to flag around midday so I had a couple of hours sleep while Lou went out to a lunch party. On her return I dressed up smartly and in the early evening we went to a dinner in a reception room at Eden Park – the Auckland Cricket Ground. The event was a dinner for the Rotarians and Lou's son Mark was in charge. He was Chairman in 1994. The speeches were excellent – and short! Lou introduced me to several people, chief of whom was a gentleman named Lionel. He was 93 years old and an absolutely delightful guest. Considering that I had travelled across the world and had only arrived that morning I managed well, but I was certainly tired by the end of the evening. On our return to Lou's place I fell into bed and slept like a log.

On Feb 17th we went to see David Tregidga, another son, and his wife Melanie. They took us to the Harbour to see the yachts that were taking part in the Whitbread 'Round the World' race. What a fantastic sight it was to see all the sleek high-masted ships being made ready for the next leg of the race. There was a truly festival atmosphere during that late afternoon and evening, and we were royally entertained in a special tent connected with the firm that David worked for.

The following day I had to deal with a change of plan for my return home in May. Philip had rung to say he could not meet me on May 8th and suggested that I extend my trip to May 13th and fly home then. I rang Air New Zealand in the morning to get the flight tickets changed. Once that was done we set off to drive to Warkworth where the family had a beach house and a new sea going motor cruiser. We were due to stay a couple of nights. The next day I got up at 6am and went for a run along the beach before breakfast. George Tregidga again took me out deep sea fishing and let me take over. I really loved that. It is something that has always appealed to me. We fished for 'Snapper' for about 5 hours. We caught plenty of fish but the only problem was that several were too small to keep and were thrown back. Nevertheless we returned with a good catch. We had a delicious meal that evening!

After breakfast the following day Lou and Lorraine, George's wife, returned home while George and I washed the boat. We then watched the start of the Whitbread Race. We had intended to go out to sea and watch them but the weather was too rough off our coast so we saw it all on TV. It was a beautiful sight – quite incredible. The big racers were surrounded by pleasure craft full of well wishers. We then drove back to Auckland.

My last day with Lou was spent at the family's massive tomato growing factory. I also bought some tomatoes for my cousin Kathleen Clearwater. I was due to fly to Dunedin that afternoon to stay with her and her husband Alan at Palmerston for a few days. In the afternoon, prior to my flight, I sorted out the paperwork required by Air New Zealand in order that my May 13th flight could be ratified. The flight proved uneventful although one could see the extent of the floods in parts of the South Island. Alan met me and we drove to Palmerston, arriving at 9.15pm. There was a lot of catching up to do!

In order to keep fit I was doing a lot of walking each morning and Palmerston was no exception. This walk turned out to have a bonus as well as the expending of energy. There was a monument on the top of a hill known as 'Puketapu' – a Maori word - overlooking Palmerston and I toiled up to the top. The views were magnificent, and well worth the effort.

By the time I had walked down again I noticed a number of motorcycles in the main street. I approached them and found that it was a club formed for anybody who owned a Triumph motorbike. I had had two Triumph machines myself so I stayed and chatted with several of the owners and one of them even let me ride his bike! After lunch we drove to fetch Kathleen's mother (also my Aunt Dorothy of course) from the home where she had moved to in order to be looked after and we took her to shop in Dunedin. I bought some clothes - shirts etc. Everything was so cheap! It was Aunt Dorothy from whom I managed to obtain a photograph of George Sewell, the first driver of the Stirling Single no.1 railway engine starting in 1870. That original engine is still housed in York Railway Museum.

Over the next couple of days Kathleen took me sightseeing. There were two things in particular that intrigued me:- 1. Macrae's Gold Mine, an incredible place where there is a17 kilometre seam and where much of the wealth of New Zealand comes from. 2. The Moeraki Boulders. These are massive spherically shaped boulders that are around 4 feet across and weigh several tons each. They are up to 60 million years old, originally formed on the seabed from lime salts around a small central stone and gradually appeared on the beach due to coastal erosion that has taken place over many thousands of years. It is also likely that some have been washed up on the shore over a very long period of time......

I flew back to Wellington on Feb 25th and Ken picked me up. I sorted out a hire car from a firm by the unusual name of 'Rent a Dent'. I wanted it for ten days from March 4th. Again it was cheap by our standards in England – around £170. We then drove up to Victoria Mount above Wellington –

fabulous view! I spent the following day working as a Curator at the Cricket Museum at the Basin – Wellington's Cricket Ground at that time. As it happened there were lots of visitors and it showed how popular the place had become.

On Feb 27th I called to see my cousin Kathleen at Raumati. She had become a 'guinea pig' for a completely new way of dealing with malignant melanomas – the very thing I had had in 1983. She had also had operations to remove these nasty growths. It seemed to have worked wonders and she was better than I had ever seen her. In fact the treatment was successful and she lived for several more years. It is apparently now one of the standard chemotherapy treatments offered to patients. It isolates the melanoma and a form of direct injection is used.

I spent the next few days meeting friends – Stan Cowman, Lindsey Cowie and David Parsons, all of whom worked at the Cricket Museum. I also walked round Wellington, visiting the 'Beehive' – that is the appropriately named Parliament Building. The railways in the country are excellent – at least they certainly were in 1994 – so getting around was easy and cheap.

I caught a train to Carterton to see my second cousin Ann and her husband Craig. This time I travelled through the long Rimatuka tunnel. The surrounding bush was incredibly thick and bordered the railway line as we approached the tunnel entrance. They took me to a Paua Shell factory where the shells were being cleaned and shaped. Unfortunately it rained heavily on the way back so I could not see any of the countryside on my return journey. I took Dorothy and Ken out for a 'Chinese' at Porirua in the evening. I then spent the next day preparing for my trip.

On March 4th I collected my hire car, a 2 year old Mazda 828, and drove to Raumati to have lunch with my cousin Kath. Afterwards I continued on my way to Napier, stopping off first at the Southward Museum. Inevitably I went straight to the RSA upon arrival in Napier where a warm welcome awaited me from my friends – Val, 'Squeak' (Colin Simmons), Brian Metcalfe the club secretary, and several others. We certainly downed a few 'tinnies' during the evening! I then retired to sleep in Val's bus.

The following morning Squeak called round and we spent the day watching local cricket at Nelson Park with two friends of his – Wendy and Robin. Ina and Val arranged to have a barbeque the next evening after Val and I had been on a sight seeing trip around the environs of Napier in my car. Several friends dropped by – more tinnies were quaffed! Amongst them were two Maori friends, Anna and Tony. I had originally met them on a previous visit in 1992. They invited me to spend the next evening with them and we visited the Shakespeare Inn – yet more tinnies! I needed a few, having spent 3 hours helping Val with his new business – a carwash – it was hard work!

I took Squeak out the next day in the car. First of all we called to see Wendy and Robin – they had invited me for a meal in the evening. He then took me to his old haunts about 20kms up the coast, before we turned off at the 'Devil's

Elbow' and drove on unmetalled roads up into the hills and travelled to Tatoio where we stopped off and went into a most unusual place run by a genuine old timer. It was a sort of museum. It certainly had everything that had been used by his ancestors.

There were a couple of old cars, one dating back to the very early 1900s. The other was probably bought new in about 1920 – and he still drove that one! There was a large coin collection too. The rest of the stuff was of the household variety, pictures, washing tubs, old fashioned scales and weights and a hundred and one other bits of what he described at the time as memorabilia. He had a fund of interesting stories too – mainly reminiscences of bygone days – enough to make one's hair curl. He even brought out some old guns that he told us had been used to by his grandparents and parents to defend themselves and the children against would be thieves and rustlers – no love lost there! We eventually got away and travelled back on more unmetalled roads, finally getting back to Napier in time to watch a large Japanese cargo ship dock. We must have covered about 120kms – most of it on unmetalled roads. I was glad that the car I had was not my own – only hired!

I spent a lovely evening with Wendy and Robin. On the last day but one of my stay in Napier I spent much of the time sorting out bills and other things to do with the financial side of Val's new carwash business. In the evening I took Val, his wife Ina, daughter Sharon and son Dwayne out for a meal at the 'Golden Crown' – after a final visit to the RSA.

On my final day at Napier I played golf with Brian Metcalfe with a set of left handed clubs borrowed from a member of the Napier Club and at the '19th hole' I renewed acquaintance with people I had met a couple of years previously. One guy said, "Thought I hadn't seen you around for a few weeks" – it had been two years!

I must say that the friends I made in Napier were wonderful to me. They were also the most prolific drinkers I ever came across anywhere and that included Australia!

The next day I drove to Matamata via Taupo, where I stopped to walk once again along the shore of Lake Taupo – a truly lovely spot. At Matamata I stayed with Violet McGiven, John Scatchard's sister. She was now a widow and had moved from the farm into a pleasant bungalow in the town.

In the morning following my arrival we walked round Matamata. It is only a small town so it did not take long. In the afternoon Violet took me for a ride in her new car – a Ford Laser Ghia – through Peria, Matai, Buckland, Karapiro, across the dam and on to Horahora before returning to Matamata. We then went out for a meal at the Hot Springs Hotel at Okoroire. We had a lovely day.

Next morning we decided to visit Rotorua, joining her daughter Sally, her two children, Laura and Rebecca, and husband Brian for a picnic but as soon as they arrived things fell apart. Violet collapsed, fainted and seemed to suffer mild convulsions. An ambulance was called and Violet went to the Hospital with Sally and Brian and I took the children for a walk. Eventually we returned to Sally's house and it was decided that we had better stay overnight with them at Putaruru. Then the children became ill so it was a bit of a shambles. The following morning Brian succumbed to the bug – whatever it was. Fortunately Violet was better and I took her to her home before continuing my journey to the Travellers International Motor Inn, near Auckland Airport.

I had to return the car to the 'Rent a Dent' Office. It had served me well. Murray Olds and his wife Margaret met me around dinnertime. We drove across Auckland to Mount Eden and the over all views of Auckland were superb. It is a lovely city. We then drove along Queen's Street, the main street in Auckland and visited the Oriental Market – a truly fascinating place and very cosmopolitan. Back we went, over Auckland Bridge, to their house in Torbay, dropping off my case before going on to Brown's Bay.

We got up early next morning. It was raining so we decided to go to Parakei, quite a long drive away, where there is a natural hot spring swimming pool. It was very energy sapping, so I moved on to the normal pool – it felt positively icy by comparison! It was certainly a 'different' day!

I knew that there was some treat in store for me today but had no idea what had been planned. As a child I had lived on the Isle of Wight and had learned the rudiments of sailing and at some stage it had been mentioned in conversation when Margaret and Murray stayed at my house in the summer of 1993. We drove to the port at Auckland and I was introduced to a friend of theirs – Bruce Brown. He took me down to a quay near the Auckland Bridge and invited Murray and me aboard his yacht.

We set off and chugged through the moored boats around. As soon as we were clear of them he stopped the engine and turned to me. "It's all yours for the next few hours mate', he said, grinning. "Let's hoist the sails". It was as if all my Christmases had come at once!

I literally sailed this 28 foot yacht for 90 minutes across to a volcanic Island by the name of Rangitoto and managed to sail close to a wharf there without difficulty. Murray and I then disembarked and hiked up to the top of the Island to see the superb views. New Zealanders certainly love their views! That was a 50 minute climb. We then set off down the opposite side and 75 minutes later we came upon the yacht once more. Bruce had sailed it round to the other side of the Island to pick us up. Again, I sailed the yacht back to his mooring buoy in Auckland Harbour. What a fantastic day that was. Bruce was certainly a great guy. It was certainly a red letter day for me! I had always had a secret ambition to sail in Auckland Harbour ever since my first visit in 1985.

The heat hit us the following morning and it became very humid so we stayed indoors. However as the evening came the atmosphere freshened and we decided to go to the pictures to see a film called 'Shadowlands'. It was the story about

CS Lewis, a famous writer in later years. The film was initially set at Magdalen College, Oxford, where he was a student and the opening scene showed the choristers walking into the College Chapel for evensong. It was an emotional moment for me as I had been a chorister at Magdalen from 1939 to 43 and had done that same walk for 4 years virtually every day that we were singing there. CS Lewis had been at the College as a student after the First World War ended in 1918. He later became a lecturer in English at Magdalen College in 1926 and stayed for 29 years so he was there during my time in the choir.

March 18th Another special day – I had heard of Kelly Tarleton. He was an explorer, a photographer, an inventor, an expert in marine archaeology, an experienced diver and, for good measure, a salvage expert. He had spent much of his life diving to examine shipwrecks. He had always wanted to share his experiences, particularly those of marine life in the Southern Ocean, with others. To this end he, together with the help of his wife Rosemary, built an aquarium, named after him – Kelly Tarleton's Underwater World. It was a place that I had always wanted to visit and this was the day.

We arrived at opening time – around 10am – and the place was not yet heaving with visitors. Inside was an exact replica of the cabin where Captain Scott and his explorers had lived for around three years, from 1910 to 1913, during their expedition to the South Pole. They actually arrived at the South Pole on January 12th 1912. A Norwegian expedition, led by Roald Amundsen had got there just a month earlier. Scott's expedition was second. In order for visitors to experience the freezing temperatures and see the many King and Gentoo penguins that inhabited the South Pole area there was a room where the temperatures were replicated, with snow and ice to add to the scene. I went in, suitably attired in clothing similar to that worn by the explorers. It was bitterly cold! There were penguins in a nearby enclosure too in what for them was the normal temperature. They obviously loved it! Feeding time was fascinating to watch – in fact there were so many interesting sights to take in that I promised myself that I would return one day.

So much for the Antarctic experience on land – there was a lot more to enjoy in the sea. There was a superbly constructed underwater tunnel through which one could see an infinite variety of Marine life. Fish were swimming literally only a few inches (or, in modern parlance, centimetres) above one's head – it was as if the creatures could virtually be touched. There were four different species of shark, a giant octopus, several eels, one of which, a Moray Eel, was very large. There was also a stingray - and giant turtles - plus a variety other large sea creatures. In fact there were so many different types that I cannot even begin to remember them all. But I do recall seeing literally myriads of fish of so many different kinds and stunning colours that the mental pictures have remained etched in my brain to this day. There were many crustaceans and small sea creatures in separate tanks too – sea horses being, for me, the most intriguing. They seemed to have an air tantamount to arrogance about the way they hung motionless in the water – truly remarkable to see.

We were there for much of the day. Afterwards we visited Devonport Village. Margaret and I went by ferry while Murray drove the car round and met us there. This was a lovely old (by New Zealand standards) place with plenty of character and tradition. The houses were mainly of 19th Century origin – genuine Victoriana - and were in a good state of preservation. There are three volcanic mountains too where Maori people have lived for over 600 years. The soil was ideal for growing a form of sweet potato called kumara, much loved by the Maori – it probably still is. We finished the day at Denny's where I treated my hosts to a delicious meal – and one of the main ingredients was – kumara! Without doubt Kelly Tarleton's was the most interesting place of its kind that I saw during my travels in New Zealand.

On my penultimate day with Margaret and Murray I was taken for a two hour ride to Matakohe. Here was another place of genuine interest – the Kauri Wood Museum. The Kauri tree is reputed to have the hardest and most enduring wood in the world. The wood is known to have survived being in swamps for up to 300,000 years! On a later trip that I took, intrigued by what I had learned about the Kauri tree, I went up to the northern part of the North Island – to Awanui and Kaitaia – to see trees taken from the swamps being dried out and used for making a variety of things – bowls, animals, all sorts of saleable objects. I even watched articles being carved and fashioned, ready to be sold. I even bought a bowl which is reputedly between 30,000 and 50,000 years old. But that is another story.

Australia

Today, March 20th, I got up at 4.45am and Margaret and Murray Olds took me to Auckland's International Airport in Mangere in plenty of time to prepare for my flight to Tullamarine Airport just outside Melbourne, Australia. The plane was an hour late leaving – at 9am instead of 8am – arriving at Tullamarine Airport at 11am. Urs and Frank were there to greet me. Immediately they whisked me off to a street party in Melbourne. This was interesting in that part of the street was lined with chairs and shaded tables, most of which were filled with people enjoying a bevy or two in the lovely weather. We also quaffed a drink or two - together with Ursula's friend Joanne, who appeared with her daughter. The party was destined to continue at the Tysons' house when the ladies had done a bit of shopping. Frank and I returned to Kew to supplement the supply of drinks. There was a liquor store around the corner – how fortunate! Frank cooked 'Scouse' on the barbeque in the evening. I do not recall just what ingredients were used apart from the obligatory sausages, but it was delicious! Bon and George Tribe rang to fix up for me to stay with them on March 24th.

March 21st – Today I went with Frank to a cricket coaching session at Carey Baptist School. We then joined Mick Boyd at a local hostelry. Mick had worked with Frank when he was on the staff at Carey. I also proof read an article Frank had written about George Tribe and his career in cricket. Next day I went to Ivanhoe Grammar School to discuss details regarding the forthcoming Cricket Tour in 1995. I also saw some of the boys who were on the '91 tour. They were now the backbone of the School team. I then returned with Frank English to his house. He lent me an old banger for my weekend drive to Rye. During the next couple of days I sorted out problems with the car that Ursula ran, went to more cricket practices at Carey, and had another jar or two with Mick Boyd. He can certainly down his pints at a rate!

March 23rd – Ursula and Frank went off to Canberra to stay with Sarah, their older daughter who was due to give birth sometime in the next week or two. In addition they were hoping to sell their house at Kew at some point and prospective buyers were going to be brought by the Estate Agent to have a look round. I was staying in the house off and on and the idea was for me to keep it looking neat and tidy. This was ideal from their point of view as it meant that I was there to keep an eye on the place and deal with post and messages. I had the use of Ursula's car too so I could get around easily.

March 24th – I drove down to Rye and went with Bon and George to a 'Probus' dinner at Sorrento – it was very tasty! I also met more friends of theirs. The next day was a busy one as we were getting the VIP tent ready for the 1994 Red Hill Show. Connie was in charge as usual and I joined a host of friends who were setting out tables and chairs and generally making the tent an attractive venue for VIPs.

March 26th The Show started quite early – before the sun got too hot. Again, there were a variety of side shows and the official judges were kept busy deciding who had won prizes in the cattle sections. Horses featured too – dressage, jumping – the lot. There was a beauty contest that was overseen by Maureen Hodge, the lady who had been instrumental in fetching me for broadcasts on my previous trip in 1992, and her friend Ian Packham. The VIP tent was packed for most of the day and, together with another guy, Fred someone or other, I served literally hundred of drinks by the glassful as instructed. This in itself was nothing special, but one amusing story comes to mind. One of the attractions at the show had been a log chopping contest by muscular lumberjacks who normally worked in the forests. Drinks were being given by the glass – until a group of them came into the tent. One of them came up and ordered six – that was all he said – so I started to pour glasses of beer. "No mate", said this joker, glaring hard at me, "I meant six b****y bottles". I did not argue! It was another successful Red Hill Show, and afterwards Connie got a party of us together. About a dozen of us went to Arthur's Restaurant at Arthur's Seat. From there we all went on to Keith Jefferson's place – he was a local bigwig and a close friend of Connie's – and left about 2am. What a great day - and night – that was! Needless to say, the next day was a very quiet one while we all recovered! Connie told me in secret that she had been awarded the Order of Australia Medal in the Queen's Birthday Honours List - the highest honour that can be given in Australia. I decided to write a poem in recognition of what she had achieved and give it to her before I left to return home.

I stayed on at George's place for another day. He took me out to see Blairgowrie and then we went to Sorrento Beach. This was near to where Harold Holt, Prime Minister of Australia in 1967, was tragically drowned on

December 17th 1967 while swimming. His body was never recovered. The next day I returned to the Tysons' house in Kew to ensure that everything was ok and to sort out Frank's mail and messages. I rang him that evening to say that all was well and I gave him the relevant messages. There was a message for me from Alex Ransom, a friend of Frank's, inviting me to see round Caulfield School the following morning. He was the Master in charge of PE and Sport. I thoroughly enjoyed the visit and later in the day I joined John Gowans to attend a concert at Melbourne Grammar School. His son Andrew was a flautist and was taking part. The Music Society of Victoria was giving the concert and pupils from the School were members of the orchestra. It was one of the best concerts I had ever attended.

I was informed by the Estate Agent the following morning that there were people due to visit the next day around lunchtime. He wanted the place to be empty so that he could take the prospective buyers round so I went out for lunch with Maureen Hodge at Edith Vale. I returned in the afternoon and the visitors had been and gone. I was invited to a couple of Aussie Rules Footie Games – one at the MCG on Monday April 4th with Brian Robertson and Saturday April 9th with Graeme Renshaw at Waverley Park.

April 1st – Went out to lunch with John Gowans. We went on a tour of Melbourne and he showed me the various outstanding features of the city – Theatre, Museum, Art Gallery, Victoria Market, Flinders Station and Richmond Cricket Ground. We drove across to Williamstown where there were yachts and other craft in abundance. The view of the city from there was quite outstanding too. From there we drove to the then newly completed South Bank Complex down by the River Yarra and walked right along the wide parade that catered for the many visitors who could enjoy that area. The temperature was a pleasant 20 degrees – a welcome change from the humid conditions that had prevailed for several days previously. In the evening Rona and John had arranged a barbeque and I met several of their friends. It was a most convivial evening! I returned home around 10pm. The following day was fairly quiet until the evening. I joined the Gowans at their home once again and stayed overnight.

April 3rd – John took me for a day out. We left at 7.30am to drive to Portsea via Hastings and Sorrento for starters. We continued into Gyppsland and made our way to Cowes. The place was heaving! Next we visited Philip Island. There were penguins there but, alas, they only appeared at night. San Reno and Dalston came next, then Wonthaggi where John's father had worked as a miner as a young man. We visited the mine, walking in down a steep slope into the bowels of the earth. It took us about an hour to see everything – there was a pit pony still working there as from time to time coal was brought out from the pit. Finally we drove back to John's house, arriving around 6pm – quite a day out! I returned to the Tyson residence at Kew once again and the great news was from the Tysons in Canberra – Sara had given birth to a baby boy – James Miles. That day had been wonderful - a real highlight of my stay in Australia.

April 4th – Caught a tram to MCG and joined up with Brian Robertson around 12.20pm. We watched Collingwood versus Carlton. Collingwood won by 100 points to 66 – a runaway victory. We then went on to the Collingwood Club to meet Wendy, Brian's wife. There were a variety of gambling machines there – not really my scene. I had my sunglasses stolen – pity – they were an expensive pair. Ah well, C'est la vie! I returned to Kew in the evening. The following morning I gave the house a good clean as more people were due to see round with a view to possible purchase. I drove across to spend the evening with Wendy and Brian, returning to Kew around 10pm.

April 6th – Got up at 5.45am and took a couple of photos showing dawn breaking – it was a truly beautiful sight. But the saying 'Red in the morning, Shepherds' warning', rang true and the weather changed. It became colder and started raining. I drove to the join the Gowans at their house. We then drove to Fairhaven on the Coast Road to Adelaide. They had a house there. Their two sons, David and Andrew had already arrived. It was quite a long drive and there was plenty to see. The beach was only a couple of minutes away and in the morning we went for a walk along the sands to a lighthouse – a long walk. Next I was taken for a long ride along the coast to Apollo Bay and back through the Otway Ranges on a really rough un-metalled road. John's vehicle was a four wheel drive – we needed it! But the views were superb and the occasional wallaby made an appearance at the side of the track.

April 8th – before leaving Fairhaven we checked out the holiday home that belonged to the Tysons. As we drove back we passed the nearby Golf Course. That was a bit different. There were a score or more Kangaroos literally on the opening hole of the course. It was fascinating to see people 'playing through' – the 'roos' did not move far, they just ignored the players. It was certainly an unusual hazard! John took me on a driven tour of Geelong Grammar School and the playing fields – a large complex. Geelong itself was quite a big town. I returned to Kew in the evening. That Saturday morning I went to Ivanhoe Grammar School to meet up with a few friends before heading off to Waverley Park with Graeme Renshaw to see Essendon versus St Kilda in an Aussie Rules Footie Match – an exciting game with plenty of vocal support in evidence. It appeared an extremely energetic way to spend an afternoon as the players did a lot of running on a very large pitch! I enjoyed the experience and the rules were very simple. There were only a few to follow so it was easy to understand.

On Sunday the weather seemed good. I made contact by phone with two friends of Eleanor Wells whom I had met a year or two before at her Mother's house in Markyate, a few miles north of London. Their names were Mary and Neville Thurgood. He was a sort of one man travelling comedian who went out to small Australian rural communities and put on shows for them. They invited me to call at their newly rebuilt house at Mount Macedon. It had previously been burned down in a massive forest fire. I drove out to their place about 100 kms north of Melbourne and spent an enjoyable afternoon with them before heading back to the city. As I passed Tullamarine Airport the sky darkened quite suddenly and by the time I entered the outskirts of Melbourne it was raining cats and dogs! I had to drive through the city to get to Kew – hard enough in the daytime when I could see, but at night it was very difficult. Needless to say I got lost. The rain was causing flooding on several of the roads leading into Melbourne. I picked out Swanston Street in the centre of the city and drove part way along before preparing to turn left towards some tram tracks that I hoped would lead me to Kew. As I did so the car in front of me seemed to lurch to one side. Fortunately I managed to avoid it. The car had gone down into a concrete type ditch that had collapsed but there was no way that anyone would get out of their vehicles as the rain made it difficult to even pick out the pavements. I had never experienced rain like it before or since. The water was up to the car axles and actually leaking in under the passenger door. I was just praying that the car would not stop! After what must have been at least an hour driving slowly round, looking for the right road containing the tram tracks, the rain became less fierce and the flood water drained quickly away. I found a landmark and thankfully returned to Kew without further incident. But I do not recommend getting lost in teeming rain in a large and virtually strange city – not an experience to have too often! I slept well that night, but was awakened early by the sound of loud thunder and more heavy rain. Naturally I stayed in the house and the Estate Agent called in. He first thanked me for keeping the house clean and tidy and then told me that it had been sold to a couple from Gisborne – so, no more visitors would be coming. The weather eventually cleared up, but it showed just how bad it could be. When the rain stopped there was, for me, quite a strange phenomenon. It was as if a warm mist had descended over the place. It soon cleared as the sun quickly dried off the pavements and roads. It became quite warm again that evening.

April 12th – During the morning I received a telephone call from a senior representative of the Australian Cricket Board, no less. He asked if I would be prepared to arrange a cricket tour for an all Aborigine team on my return to the UK, providing that the money could be found to sponsor them. Apparently I had been recommended after news of the tour I had already successfully organised filtered back to the Board from a source unconnected with anyone directly involved in the tour in England. I was also currently organising a second tour for June 1995 – the representative knew that as well. I felt honoured and was delighted to accept provisionally. I was told I should be well paid for my work – always useful! However, the tour was first postponed and then eventually cancelled due to lack of funding – very disappointing from my point of view as it would have been another 'first' for me, and the possibilities of organising future tours for the ACB would have been something very special indeed. Frank would have loved that too as it would have drawn us even closer together as I would have wanted him to become involved in the business side of things in Australia once I had returned home. We have both always believed in promoting the underdog, so to speak, and here was a possible chance of a break through for Aborigine cricket and cricketers. How I would have loved to organise that – in fact we both would! I got the distinct impression that when it came to International sides in any sport in Australia the Aborigines did not feature very highly, although they must have had some good players. History is full of unlikely happenings and ironically it was a side made up of Aborigine cricketers who made the first ever tour of England in the 19th Century. The following report gave details of the tour in an English newspaper:-

In 1868, a team consisting of Aboriginal cricketers became the first Australian team to tour England. The team was captained by Charles Lawrence, a member of Stephenson's England touring team to Australia in 1861. He had remained in Australia afterwards, and mainly recruited players from the Harrow and Edenhope areas of the Wimmera region in Western Victoria. The Touring Party included outstanding cricketers such as Johnny Mullagh. The team played 47 matches, winning 14, drawing 19 and losing 14. In addition to cricket, the players demonstrated athletic prowess before, after, and during games, including throwing boomerangs and spears! The heavy workload and inclement weather took its toll with an Aborigine by the name of King Cole contracting a fatal case of tuberculosis during the tour.

April 13th Maureen was visiting her daughter in Melbourne and called in for lunch at the Tysons. I then went shopping in Kew and met up for an evening 'nosh' at an Indian restaurant, 'The Nawab' with Wendy and Brian Robertson. They liked Indian food too. I then called at the Tysons' next door neighbours – the Sorrels – for a few drinks. The next day I drove via Rosebud to stay with Bon and George. I called in at Maureen's shop to buy flowers for Bon. The following morning Bon turned out to be poorly after having a flu jab so George and I went for a drive. At Sorrento George showed me the tram depot that overlooked the pier before driving on to Portsea and Bay Beach for a walk. Finally we watched surfers at Portsea Ocean Beach before returning to George's home. Next day dawned bright and warm so we all went to the Boneo Road Market. Much of the stuff being sold was home made, and it was very good. In fact I bought several presents to either give to friends in Oz or to bring home. We had lunch at a well patronised restaurant by the exotic name of 'Poffs'. The food was excellent and the view was good too. It was next door to the Red Hill Show Ground. Up to that point the weather had been fine but during the following morning the rains came – again they were very heavy and roads briefly flooded, then cleared again just as quickly. I returned to Kew via Nepean Way, along the coast road. An invitation to a meal, on Wednesday April 20th, awaited me – from the Sorrels next door. As time was beginning to run out I caught a tram into Melbourne the next day and did some serious shopping – for presents to bring back to the UK.

I arranged to address a meeting, giving details of the projected 1995 Cricket Tour, at Ivanhoe Grammar School on May 3rd. This allowed me plenty of time to get up to Thirlmere to see Ann and Stuart McDonald – Stuart was the guy I met while in Bowral Hospital on my previous visit to Oz. Fortunately for me the Gowans were due in Sydney on Saturday April 23rd and their route took them right past Thirlmere so they offered me a lift with them. Rona and I set off to Tullamarine Airport to pick up John who had been away on business. Again, the Airport was on our way so after picking him up around 10pm (his plane was late!) we drove straight up to Wangaratta, arriving at 12.45am. After coffee we retired to bed. I had already arranged to meet Frank in Canberra on April 26th at Sara's house at the end of my holiday with Ann and Stuart, in order that we could all return to Melbourne together.

The next day John drove like the wind up to Thirlmere to drop me off. It was a long way! We only stopped briefly for a breather, arriving in Thirlmere around 4.15pm. It had been quite a drive, but Australians are used to driving long distances. The roads were excellent and the traffic was light. The only problem I saw was watching people driving close to vehicles in front of them – tailgating it is called. It means that the vehicle behind gets pulled along in the wake of the vehicle in front and that improves petrol consumption no end. But it also causes accidents! Lorries seemed to be the worst offenders and they are certainly very big in Oz.

Day 1 of my holiday with Ann and Stuart was a trip to Sydney. I had never been to many parts of the city and so I was given a guided tour there before going up to the 'Rocks' area. Next we went through the newly opened tunnel under the Harbour, turned round and crossed over the Sydney Harbour Bridge and along the waterfront. We took in the Opera House, crossed on the ferry to Manly and walked around the market there. The journey back was done on the Jet Catamaran. Once back to the car we drove the 120kms to Thirlmere in time to enjoy a barbeque with neighbours and friends. Inevitably the drink flowed and Stuart and I finally retired to bed at 4am! What a truly marvellous day (and night) that was!

April 25th was Anzac Day. We eventually surfaced and drove to Picton to see the gambling that went on. By tradition this sort of gambling was only permitted on this particular day of the year. The official game was called 'Two up'. Three coins were tossed up and the winners were those who had bet on the two that were the same. Large bets were placed and as the drink flowed the bets got larger. As always the 'Banker' won. He collected the losing bets, and there were plenty! We left before the fighting started. The beer being drunk was a special brew called 'Bock' – of German origin, and very potent! Later that afternoon we drove round the area to see the local sights.

On April 26th Stuart fetched his Dad and we drove to Canberra. We went round the Canberra War Museum. This was really very moving and gave one the impression of just how many Australians had died during World War Two. We drove on towards Chisholm, where Sara's house was. Urs and Frank were staying there of course. I said my goodbyes to Stuart and his Dad after we had all had a 'cuppa' and they left to drive back to Thirlmere.

The next morning was bright and warm so Frank and I went for a swim. He then took me on a tour of Canberra showing me the old Parliament buildings. We also visited the New Parliament and were able to walk round as Parliament was not in session. That evening we dined out and really enjoyed ourselves.

After rising at 7.30am Frank and I went for a leisurely swim at the Tuggerah Sports Complex. We said goodbye at midday and drove, via Coomera and Bombala, over the Australian Alps – over 3000 feet high - before stopping at the Golden Beach 'Flag' Motel at Lakes Entrance. This was the way that I had been driven back from Bowral two years previously by Maureen Hodge after my illness, so I was familiar with the road.

The last leg of the journey took us back to Melbourne through Gyppsland – a lush and green area at this time of the year - good land for cattle grazing. On arrival I found an invitation for me to go to Ivanhoe GS to see their rendition of 'Hello Dolly'- it was excellent. Frank English again lent me an old car to drive out to George Tribe's place at Rye. I had been invited to a dinner dance by Connie Jacinskas and her husband. I borrowed Frank's dinner suit – a perfect fit fortunately – and drove to Rye, changed into the borrowed 'penguin' suit, and then met up with some of the party at Keith Jefferson's house. The dance was at the Nepean Club. George did not go so I took Bon. On arrival I was announced as the guest of Bill Goodrum, the Shire President – a real honour! There were 12 in our party – all friends that I had made over the times when I had been staying on the Mornington Peninsular. They had got together to make my evening very special. I really appreciated that. It turned out to be one more of the highlights of my trip. I was due to do another broadcast with Connie the next day. Once again the broadcast went really well and Connie was delighted. We went onto yet another barbeque and before she left Connie gave me a set of tablemats as a memento of my visit and as a 'thank you' for all the broadcasts we had done together during my visits. It was very touching.

I returned to Kew on May 2nd and had lunch at Sorrento with Maureen. We watched pelicans being fed on the beach – most unusual! Before I left I called at Connie's house to give her a copy of the poem I had written in honour of the award she had been given. She was delighted and asked me to read it for her. I think she was concerned that I might have written it in the Yorkshire dialect like I had done once before!

Fred – the bearded wonder – was in overall charge of broadcasting. Connie – seated in the car – was head of programming and was the senior broadcaster. I became a temporary broadcaster whenever I was in the area during my visits to Australia. John owned the car. He was a veteran car enthusiast and occasional broadcaster. I must say that for me Connie had been special. It was by sheer chance that we had first met at a barbeque at Bon and George's place and that had led to so much that I had enjoyed. The broadcasts were fun and fortunately they were generally well received, judging from the comments made. When I looked into all the things that she had done for the community in which she and her husband lived I realised just what a remarkable career she had had. She used to make collections for various charities – cancer in particular – and she was often seen on the streets in Dromana with a collecting bucket. She raised over 200,000 dollars towards the building of the Jean Turner Nursing Home at Rosebud. Her connections with the family of the former Prime Minister of Australia, Sir Robert Menzies, were remarkable. She had nursed his son Ian through a terminal illness and had then stayed on to look after Sir Robert during his last days. She herself was very ill with cancer when she went to the ceremony, accompanied by her grandson Joseph who had come over from France for a holiday, and her friend Maureen Hodge, having been in hospital until a day or two before she travelled to Government House in Melbourne. I wrote this:

In Honour of Connie

Great strength of purpose is a wonderful thing
For an outgoing person like you
Who freely works hard in the service of man
In a way that's both honest and true.
For many accept – when there's work to be done –
That, as always, some one will be there
To take up the challenge – whatever it is –
And thus show the world that they care.

It's not always easy to find such a one
Upon whom we can truly rely,
In this day and age it is often the rage
To say "Right mate", then let things slide by.
For standards have fallen in many respects
And 'Religion' is 'making a buck'.
Coining money seems best, to hell with the rest,
Just too bad for the guy out of luck.

But Connie, my friend, you are staunch to the end
And 'FAIR DINKUM', I guess you would add,
Yourself you don't spare and in all things you share
True emotions – both happy and sad.
But greatest of all is the HONOUR bestowed
For a life that's been tested and tried,
AN AUSTRALIAN TRUE – yes Connie, that's you –
You can claim both with CREDIT and PRIDE.
Your country is proud of the work that you've done
And honours you – just as it should –
You've fought a hard fight and the battle is won
To share things in your life that are good.
For those who are grateful for what you've achieved
This short tribute will happily serve.
"WE'RE PROUD OF THE HONOUR THAT YOU HAVE RECEIVED,
IT'S NO MORE THAN YOU TRULY DESERVE!

The poem was later published in the Southern Peninsula Gazette on June 21st 1994 under my name, to commemorate her visit to Canberra where she received her reward from Governor Richard McGarvie.

I then returned to Kew and spent the evening preparing notes ready for the Cricket Tour Meeting at IGS at 8pm the next evening.

Frank and I got up early in order to play some golf in the morning. We then went to a cricket match – India versus an Australian XI - at Melbourne Grammar School, and I spent an enjoyable hour chatting to Doctor Rao, the

Indian Consul, and Sunil Gavaskar, a famous Indian cricketer. I then left to go to IGS for the meeting with parents and lads who would be considered for the tour party. It went extremely well and I enjoyed 'getting back into harness' so to speak.

I only had 3 more days left so it was time to visit friends to say goodbye until the next visit. On May 4th I went for a meal with Frank English and his family and to discuss further details about the 1995 tour. Mind you, I got caught up in the rush hour traffic and got lost, but it worked out all right in the end and I arrived more or less on time. I had left Kew early just in case that happened – just as well!

On May 5th I had lunch out and walked along the bank of the Yarra River. It was a beautiful day. I really felt nostalgic as I have always enjoyed staying in Melbourne. By the time I returned to Australia Urs and Frank would have moved up to yet another area called Sorrento - near Surfers Paradise - and so I would no longer have a base in Kew. Once again, unbeknown to me, the 1991 Tour party had laid on an evening at 'Rizzi's Restaurant' for my benefit. John and Rona Gowans had conned me into thinking that we were just going there for a private meal and Urs and Frank had kept the secret yet again. It was really touching to see them there, together with so many of the lads, most of whom had now left school. Several parents came too and I was asked to speak after John had started things off. I must admit that I had a lump in my throat at the start. It was all so unexpected, but the loyalty of all those people was something to treasure and I felt highly honoured to be considered as a part of them all. In fact several lads later joined various Cricket Clubs in England for a season and I always made a point of going to meet them at the clubs where they were playing. Of course it worked both ways as I was approached by several clubs to give an assessment of their capabilities before they accepted them. One or two even came over for work experience and I was entertained at Dulwich College by one lad – Vaughan English - who had been on the 1991 tour. One just never knows just what influences youngsters, but there is no doubt that the 1991 tour to England had immeasurably broadened their horizons.

On my final day in Australia I returned the car that Frank English had lent me, only to find when I arrived at his house that the passenger door had been damaged, presumably in a car park. However fortunately it was not serious. I went to IGS to see Charles Sligo, the Headmaster and spent an enjoyable hour in his company. I also sought out David Waugh and Graeme Renshaw at lunchtime to say farewell.

That evening Frank had a meeting so Urs and I sampled food at a local Thai Restaurant – very enjoyable! That was it. I finished packing and went to bed early as I had to be off to Auckland in the morning. I was having a few more days there before returning home.

Frank was leaving at the same time. He was flying to Mumbai (Bombay) for three weeks – paving the way for Indian cricket enthusiasts to become qualified Cricket Coaches. He had introduced the Indian equivalent of his 3 levels Coaching System, based on the one he had set up in Victoria when he was in charge at the Victoria Cricket Association (VCA).

May 7th – We set off to Tullamarine airport after a late breakfast. We said our goodbyes there after having a leisurely lunch. My plane left on time and after a three and a half hour flight I arrived at Auckland Airport. Lou Tregidga was there to meet me. We had a bite to eat during the evening and Lou wanted to know all about my time in Australia so it was after midnight before we retired. Murray rang and we arranged to meet on Wednesday May 11th.

May 8th – Lou took me to meet her 4th son, John and his wife Evelyn at Paeroa. I drove for Lou as usual. Fortunately she was only too happy to let me do so. We spent a pleasant day with them before returning to Lou's house in Mangere. Soon after we got back my cousin Dorothy rang to tell me that her mother – my Aunt – had died on April 15th - while I was in Australia. The news put a bit of a damper on the evening but it could not be helped – one of those things. After all she was 96 years old when she died.

May 9th – We had a 'stay at home' day as I had various letters to write and some washing to do. I was tired too as I had been on the move almost non-stop for quite a while. At 5pm we visited Lorraine and George, who only lived at the top end of the long drive. That was relaxing too.

May 10th – Lou wanted to visit Kelly Tarleton's Underwater World and Antarctica after I had waxed so lyrical about it all. We drove across to Kelly Tarleton's and saw much of what I had mentioned. Unfortunately though, the Antarctica Exhibition - done in mock snow cats - had gone wrong so she missed that bit. It was still an enjoyable trip and after a late lunch we returned to her home in Mangere after doing some shopping in nearby Otahuhu.

May 11th - The next morning I met up with Margaret and Murray Olds and they took me to the Victoria Market. It was ideal as I wanted small gifts to take home and some larger ones to give to both Lou and the Olds. We had lunch at Murray's house at Torbay before he took me back to Mangere. About 6pm Lou and I went off to a birthday party. One of her grandchildren was 18. We had a delicious Indian meal cooked by Marilyn, her daughter in law. It was a delightful evening and a lovely way to complete my last day prior to flying home.

May 12th - My plane was not due out of Auckland until 10pm so I had time to pack. After a lazy day we went for tea with Lorraine and George. Lou and George were going off to a concert so Lorraine took me to the Airport around 8pm. In the end the plane left an hour late. There was an uneventful eleven hour journey to Los Angeles.

May 13th - After a two hour stopover at LA we flew to Frankfurt – not the nicest of waiting lounges there though. After further annoying delays I arrived back at Gatwick at 5pm. Daphne and Frank met me and took me back to their house in Sunbury. The trip had taken 30 hours in all, but Air New Zealand had given excellent in flight service. After an enjoyable evening meal I first fell asleep in a chair, then retired early to bed. I was very tired and in need of a really good night's rest!

May 14th - Mandy and Philip fetched me from Sunbury - a quick turn round as we wanted to get back to see the Cup Final. We did just that, then I took them for a meal at the White Hart in Poole before retiring to bed around 10pm – tired, but glad to be home safe and in one piece.

Chapter 14 Picking up the threads again

After so much travelling it was lovely not to have to rush off anywhere and I had the opportunity to unpack at leisure. I sat down quietly when everything was put away and considered just what I would be doing next. I contacted the Hospital Broadcasting Service to let them know I had returned and was ready to be included in the cricket commentating schedule whenever they required my services. In fact it worked out well. I was not on any original list of course as I had been abroad when it was made out, so I became a sort of 'roving' commentator who could be called upon when required. In fact I found that I was actually commentating more often than most people as I would turn up at matches and promptly become part of the team for that day. It suited me to be able to choose my days at Headingley – I had plenty of office work to complete finalising the fixture list for the coming 1995 Ivanhoe Grammar School Under 15 Cricket Tour of England. In addition there were a lot of non-cricketing arrangements to make. As well as playing cricket I felt that it was important that the tourists should be able to experience at least a part of life in Britain and to this end I had carte blanche as far as the Ivanhoe Management Team was concerned.

I eventually arranged the following programme of visits for June/July 1995:-

Monday June 12th - The first part of the tour was due to take place in Wales, with a match to be played at Bristol Grammar School. Isambard Kingdom Brunel's famous ship, the SS Great Britain, would be on public show in the dock area, not far from the Camden Hotel, Bristol, where the boys would be staying for the first night of their tour. They were also to be billeted with parents of boys in the Bristol Grammar School XI for the second night and so they would probably get an opportunity to see the great ship. It was, by coincidence, the ship that transported the first ever English Cricket Touring Party to Australia in 1861.

Wednesday June 14th - The party were to be billeted at the Dulwich College Field Centre at Glyntawe in Powys, for four nights. There were three matches to be played on successive days – at Llandovery College, Christ College, Brecon and Monmouth School - leaving two days free. I made arrangements for a visit to be made to the 'Big Pit' Mine at Blaenavon, Gwent, on Saturday June 17th. On the 18th the party would go into the Dan-yr-Ogof Caves en route to Ellesmere College in Shropshire. The College had a house for the boarders and the tourists were scheduled to stay there overnight – in the sick bay.

June 19th - After playing a match against Ellesmere College the party would move on that evening to Wrekin College, Shropshire, to play against a combined Shropshire XI the following afternoon. In the morning arrangements were to be made by the School for a visit to the Ironbridge Gorge and Blist's Museum. Immediately after the match we were scheduled to move on for two nights to Shrewsbury School, Shropshire. Accommodation was to be laid on in School boarding houses and there was a fixture to be played on Wednesday June 21st.

The next visit was to be made to the Museum of Photography in Bradford. Accommodation was offered at Woodhouse Grove School in Apperley Bridge, Bradford, for two nights. A match was to be played there on Friday June 23rd.

June 24th – On the way to Denstone College in Staffordshire the party would stop off at nearby Alton Towers for the day. A match was due to be played at Denstone on Sunday June 25th. Two nights would be spent at the College.

Monday June 26th – We would drive to Nottingham - stopping at Sherwood Forest Visitors' Centre on the way - and visit the 'Tales of Robin Hood' Exhibition. I had also arranged a guided tour of the famous Trent Bridge Cricket Ground in the late afternoon. We would subsequently stay at the nearby Milford Hotel.

Tuesday June 27th – There would be fixture at Oakham School, Rutland. Oakham Castle could be visited the following morning before driving on to Wellingborough School in Northamptonshire. We should be staying for two nights at the Euro Hotel, and playing against Wellingborough School on Thursday June 29th.

Friday June 30th – On our way to the next cricketing venue we would tour the city of Cambridge before visiting nearby Duxford Aerodrome. Afterwards we should proceed to Alleyn's School, Dulwich, to stay for two nights. A match had been arranged for Saturday July 1st.

On the Sunday July 2nd the party could go sightseeing in the City of London before returning to King's College School, Wimbledon, where they would be given accommodation for two nights. A match was to be played there on the following day.

On Tuesday July 4th the team were scheduled to play St Dunstan's College, Dulwich, and the School had offered accommodation for two nights. The next day, July 5th, the party would again go into the City of London to shop and for more sightseeing.

On July 6th there was to be a match against Dulwich College, and on July 7th the final game to be arranged would be against Middlesex Colts Under 15 side, at Sunbury on Thames in Surrey. The party would stay at the Royal Holloway College at Egham, Surrey, for their last two nights.

Their final visit would be to Windsor Castle on July 8th. The boys would be flying back home to Australia the following day, July 9th.

In addition to the problems of arranging the over all programme for Ivanhoe I became involved in trying to sort out a post for Frank Tyson at a School in the UK. He had taught for a year at Denstone School in 1988/9, but initially they did not use his expertise as effectively as they could have done. Traditional teaching dies hard and his updated ideas probably fell on deaf ears. I felt that the advice he received - from another source on that first occasion - concerning where to teach was of very limited value. This time, after some discussion, he asked me to sort out something worthwhile for him. He knew I had the connections required and so it was up to me. The ideal situation would be for him to be able to take up a teaching post for a period of around six months in order for him to put his stamp on both the sporting and academic sides of a School. It would also be useful if the job was based near my home as he also wanted to do some speaking engagements. I had organised some for him while he was at Denstone – I could do equally well – better in fact, if he was close enough for me not to have to travel long distances to pick him up, as on most occasions I drove him to the various venues.

Initially I had approached Woodhouse Grove School, and found that there was a vacant position for the right candidate on the sporting side of the curriculum. I had certain connections with Woodhouse Grove, mainly as a result of my friendship with Stan Dawson and his wife Kath. Stan was an important member of the Hospital Broadcasting Service, both as a commentator and an organiser. Kath was Deputy Head of Woodhouse Grove School. As such she was able to utilise her position to put forward Frank Tyson's name to the Headmaster, David Welsh, and at the same time give me the opportunity to recommend him – something I was delighted to do. The outcome was that he was offered a teaching post, to start in January 1995, for two terms. This was ideal. It meant that he could use his expertise as a cricket coach more or less straight away, before the start of the cricket season, and help Ian Frost, the resident teacher in charge of sport, to put together an in depth coaching scheme which, hopefully, would be of considerable benefit to the School for years to come. On the academic side Frank gained his degree at Durham in English Literature with French as a subsidiary subject. He also speaks excellent French. This would be of considerable value to the School too.

Frank's book on Coaching, first published in 1985, was aptly named 'The Cricket Coaching Manual'. It was a comprehensive update of an earlier coaching manual, also written by him, entitled 'Complete Cricket Coaching', and first published in 1976. These works were quickly adopted by the Victorian Cricket Association of Australia, and together with his ability to organise competent coaches to implement his ideas, formed the platform upon which he built up the comprehensive cricket skills that have been imparted to generations of Australian schoolboys ever since. I actually took part in a few coaching sessions when I was staying in Australia so I could better understand for myself the tremendous impact his ideas were having at both School and Club level. His first book I used to supplement the knowledge

I had obtained when coaching youngsters – it became a sort of cricketing 'bible'. There were lessons to be given on virtually every aspect of the game, and his expert analysis of possible errors as well as of correct movements when playing strokes as a batsman opened the eyes of many a coach. His equally superb analysis of just how bowlers could release the ball in such a way as to obtain the right results when bowling, without injuring themselves in the process, are just as effective. I must say that I felt that the English Cricket Board missed a trick after they failed to give him any backing when he tried to find a sympathetic publisher in Britain for his work, and I spoke about that on more than one occasion at after dinner speeches. But I realised that there were others in Britain who put forward their own excellent ideas. Fair enough, but although I have read several books on the subject I have never found one that analysed movements so clearly or explained so precisely how bowling, batting, fielding and catching should be done. Intrinsically woven in with all this is a scientific form of analysis of the reasons behind individual performances coupled with the most important basic necessity – motivation. In this case Australia's gain was England's loss.

There was also the question of sorting out venues where he would make after dinner speeches. In fact he had already been busy on that himself and so by the time he was due to arrive there was a list of Cricket Clubs and Societies that would claim his attention – and supplement his income afterwards. And there was more – Yorkshire County Cricket Club was happy to have him do some coaching at the Cricket School during his time at Woodhouse Grove. Altogether he would be working hard and it would be financially rewarding. Not to be outdone, Northants CCC got on the bandwagon and arrangements were in hand for a spell of consultative coaching during a holiday period. In fact in the end he made more from the so called 'extras' than from his teaching salary! A bungalow near the School became vacant and so Urs and Frank had a place to live. I became involved prior to their arrival and so the bungalow was ready in time for them to take up residence – well, almost ready. They arrived in Leeds on January 21st and spent just a couple of days with me prior to moving in. In fact I drove Frank to start work at the School on the morning of Monday Jan 23rd and Ursula and I then moved their luggage into the bungalow before going off to do the shopping – quite a start!

Chapter 15 Holidays in Britain with friends

Despite the commitments on my return from Australia in May '94 I managed to take a most enjoyable holiday with Jack Edmondson. He was good company and loved the chance to see places normally out of his reach as he did not drive. Over the years we have shared several journeys – once getting up as far as John o'Groats. That trip was certainly not without incident! I recall that we arrived in Wick and decided to stop for a bite to eat and a look round. We duly returned to the car – I owned a Renault 11 turbo at the time – went to drive away, and found we had a flat tyre. These tyres were brand new, having been fitted less than a week before. This all happened on a Saturday afternoon, and normally garages close early. We managed to get to a local tyre fitting garage around 3pm. The moment I asked for my tyre to be mended the mechanic removed it and looked for the air leak. He found it right on the rim of the tyre – the one place where tyres cannot be vulcanised – so I had to purchase another tyre. The mechanic was very apologetic and told us that he had been faced with the same problem – a pin pushed in right on the rim – from several other motorists, all of them English. No sooner had he fitted a new tyre and we had left the garage I realised that the other front tyre was going down slowly too. This could have had extremely serious consequences had we been driving at any speed over about 25mph. So we returned to the garage around 5pm, just as they were about to close. Again the mechanic examined the tyre and this time we could see the problem. The pin had even been left in, which was why the tyre was only deflating slowly. This time the mechanic did not hesitate. He recommended that we report to the police what had happened. We did so and were informed that a gang of youngsters were deliberately targeting holidaymakers by sticking pins into tyres. The police knew what had happened but as there were only two policemen in Wick altogether they were unable to catch anyone. So that cost me £120 for two more new tyres – an expensive place to stop! Eventually reinforcements were apparently called in and the police apprehended two lads of about 15 years old, catching them at work in the car park. When taken to court they admitted to the police what they had done and excused their conduct by saying they hated b****y Sassenachs! I expect they were fined, but it was the motorists who had really paid out. No, the English were apparently not popular! Needless to say we cancelled our rooms at a Bed and Breakfast house despite the protestations of the people who owned the place and we moved on elsewhere as quickly as possible!

The next day we set off again and were driving along a lonely country road. We saw a garage on our left but did not need to stop. Coming the other way was another car – no problem – until without warning the lady driving suddenly pulled straight across the road in front of us to enter the garage forecourt. I literally stood on the brakes and managed to stop sideways across the road. A lady of middle years got out of the other car, came back towards us – and burst into tears. "I live doon the road aboot a mile", she sobbed. "I ha' been comin en heer for uver forty yeers and I ha' niver seen anither car afore". "Well, you have now", I retorted. Then the driver's companion got out the other side of the car. She must have been ninety if she was a day. So we beat a hasty retreat in case she had a heart attack – but it was certainly close. Even Jack got upset about that one! Still, we did get to John o'Groats – and it poured!

We could see across the water to the Orkneys but the ferry was not running as it was too rough. Then a storm swept across the nearest land over the channel and the view was completely blotted out. What a desolate place that was! We drove along the coast road through Thurso and on to Dounreay – near the Nuclear Plant. By now the rain was flooding the road and so we found a B & B and our luck changed. The landlady was absolutely delightful and made us so welcome. When her husband came home they insisted that we join them. He worked at the Dounreay Nuclear Plant and he explained just how everything worked – I wished afterwards that he hadn't as it sounded distinctly dodgy. Some years later, when I was there again with Bryan Stubbs, I stopped to see if the lady still did B & Bs. She did not. Sadly her husband

301

had died of cancer and there was a suspicion that the nuclear fallout had affected him. I have no idea how true that was, but I do remember that the press and TV reported that there had been a lot of trouble at the Nuclear Plant at one time.

Jack and I continued right along the north coast of Scotland to Durness where we stayed in a white cottage on the cliff. The wind was so strong that it was difficult to keep one's balance, let alone walk far! I remember how impressive the Highland Mountains and Hills seemed – almost evil when the dark clouds scudded across the sky and blotted out the sun. There was comparatively little vegetation and the rocks stood out in bold relief, particularly as the evening sun cast ever longer shadows across this barren land. The noise of the waves crashing against the lower reaches of the cliffs added to the general maelstrom and the over all turbulence is something I have never experienced anywhere else in Britain. But I well recall a violent storm when I was travelling down the west coast of New Zealand's South Island. There was lightning and thunder too, to add to the deafening noise – not the best place to get caught in!

The next day we drove down the west coast, through Laxford Bridge, Kylestrome, and Ledmore, to Ullapool. This proved to be quite interesting as the fishing fleet were moored in the harbour. After a night there we worked our way along the coast to Gairloch, calling in at Inverewe Gardens –a National Trust property of considerable beauty. Because of the location of the Gardens there were areas that were so well screened by nature that both tropical vegetation and Palm trees could be viewed in abundance. There was also a Japanese Garden with exotic plants and bushes, more reminiscent of Far Eastern climes. Then we drove along the coast road to Cove. There was a deserted gun emplacement still standing – just one of several that had been there during the Second World War. This was because convoys used to gather in Loch Ewe prior to sailing to Russia. On our return to the main road at Poolewe, home of a religious sect called the 'Wee Frees', we stopped by the beach at Naast and walked out to the waterline where some researchers were taking samples of what we had assumed was sand. Actually it wasn't sand at all, but myriads of minute pinkish coloured shells. When we asked why there was such interest in the beach itself we were informed that there was a salmon farm likely to be set up there as conditions were ideal. To the best of my knowledge the salmon farm is still there. We stayed overnight at Gairloch, in a room overlooking Strath Bay.

Continuing our journey the next day we passed along the edge of Loch Maree to Kinlochewe, through Glen Docherty and on to Achnasheen, along the shore of Loch Carron, past Strome ferry, and turned right onto the A87 along to the Kyle of Lochalsh. Nowadays there is a bridge – prior to that there was only a regular ferry crossing to Kyleakin on the Isle of Skye. We spent a day driving round Skye, stopping off at the capital, Portree for an hour. We drove up the east coast to Duntulm, where we stayed overnight. In the morning we drove down the west coast, taking in the magnificent Cuillins with the peaks of the mountains standing out in dark relief against a bright, clear blue sky. That was special! Finally we motored on to Armadale where we caught the ferry across to Mallaig on the mainland.

The journey from Mallaig, past the white sands of Morar, the sandy shores and beach rock pools of Arisaig, plus the superb scenery to Glenfinnan - where Bonnie Prince Charlie raised his standard in 1745 when he tried to regain the throne - must rank as one of the most picturesque parts of 'Bonnie Scotland'. Indeed the railway journey from Fort William to Mallaig is featured as one of the most scenic and beautiful in the entire United Kingdom and possibly in the rest of Europe too. It is something truly special and should be a 'must' for any visitors to that part of Scotland. We stopped overnight at Fort William.

Fort William had painful memories for Jack. On one occasion we had motored out to the base of the mountain of Ben Nevis, along Glen Nevis. There was a car park at the far end, literally below one of the starting places for visitors who wanted to climb up towards the top. For less ambitious visitors like us there was a rocky path actually going downwards towards the river – called the 'Water of Nevis' - and we set off for a stroll. Jack, being Jack, missed his footing and fell, scraping his arm. He yelled blue murder! I got him back to the car park. There was a streamlet running off the mountain down to the river so I stuck his arm in the water to clean his wound. Hospital was the next port of call to give him an anti-tetanus injection. He just did not wish to go, convinced that he was half dead and would have to stay. I was not impressed – I sat him in the car and just drove straight there. His attitude changed when we arrived – nurses were practically queuing up to inject him before letting him go! We got a cup of tea and a biscuit too – generous folk at that hospital! I think we have had more laughs over that incident than anything else that happened to us. In fact he is the only man I know who actually fell UNDER Ben Nevis!

The Visitors Centre at Glencoe came next. The story of the massacre of the MacDonalds by the Campbells in 1692 is legend of course, and there is still bad feeling that shows its head occasionally. 38 members of the Clan MacDonald were murdered by Campbells, who had initially accepted their hospitality. This was because the MacDonalds, through their Clan leader, Alistair Mclain, had not offered their pledge of loyalty to William of Orange and his wife Mary, the Monarchs of England, in the time set out to do so. This was due to the inclement weather encountered by Mclain who had left it to the last minute to sign the pledge and got stuck in the snow. A further 40 souls died of exposure on the snow covered hills around Glencoe. This story was re-enacted and recorded on film for visitors to see. We then drove up Glencoe and on to Arrochar. From there we returned via Jedburgh to Leeds.

Jack and I had several holidays in Scotland – going up to places like Inverness, across the Cairngorms, and to several of the places already mentioned. We also visited the Mull of Kintyre, driving up through Glasgow, past Loch Lomond, along to Inverary and Lochgilphead. We went up to Oban too, via Balachullish. The fantastic scenery that Scotland offers surpasses anywhere else in the UK in my opinion, and makes for easy driving as the volume of traffic has always seemed less, and there are so many side roads that one can take. Often they are just single track with passing places at frequent intervals.

On another trip we decided to visit Wales. During the war Jack, who served in the RAF, did his basic training in Aberystwyth. He had never been back in over 50 years and so we decided that we would make our way there while touring the country. We set off across country early in the morning – we did not use motorways unless absolutely necessary – passing through Huddersfield, Holmfirth, Stalybridge, Wilmslow and Knutsford, eventually arriving at Chester in time for lunch at the oldest pub in the city. From there we bypassed Wrexham on the A483 and turned right onto the A5 to Llangollen, a picturesque part of the country, before heading southwest towards Dolgellau and Machynlleth, stopping overnight at a B & B on the way. The next day we arrived in Aberystwyth and Jack took great delight in showing me round. We wandered along the waterfront where, in the days when he had been training, he had done his square bashing, marching up and down repeatedly with a rifle on his shoulder. We went to what had been his favourite café and while we were there he engaged an old gentleman in conversation. This chap had lived there all his life so Jack quizzed him about various streets and buildings. The upshot was that we went to his old billet, the Brynawell Hotel. This was along the front too. In his courting days, he told me, Mary, his future wife, used to come from Leeds to stay with friends nearby, and he could see her when he was off duty, which wasn't very often! We stayed in Aberystwyth overnight. I think that of all the places we visited that was the one Jack enjoyed most!

The following day we drove northwards up the West Coast, finishing up at Beddgelert in Gwynedd, where we stayed overnight. There is a story attached to the place – maybe a 13th Century myth – or maybe not. Gelert was the name of a hunting dog that was the favourite of Prince Llewelyn. One day the Prince and his wife went out hunting, leaving their infant son with a nurse and a servant to look after him. Unfortunately they also went out - for a walk - leaving the baby unprotected. The Prince noticed that his favourite dog Gelert was not in the pack. When Llewelyn and his wife returned the dog ran out of the house to his master, wagging his tail. He was covered in blood. When Prince Llewelyn and his wife
approached the cradle it was overturned, the swaddling clothes were blood covered and of the baby there was no sign. In a fit of rage Llewelyn ran the dog through with his sword and killed him. Then they heard the babe crying. He was unharmed, with the body of a dead wolf beside him. Overcome with remorse, Prince Llewelyn, who realised that the dog had managed to kill the wolf and save his baby son, buried the dog in a meadow nearby. The name 'Beddgelert' actually means 'The Grave of Gelert', and that is how the village got its name.

From Beddgelert we went up north to Llanberis, past Mount Snowdon, up to Caernarfon, and then to Llandudno on the Welsh Coast where we found a B & B. We drove up the Great Orme that evening to savour the magnificent view. The next day we drove along the north coast road past two Holiday Camps at

Rhyl and Prestatin before cutting inland onto the A55. The road took us round Chester again and this time we stayed on the motorway until we got back to Leeds. It was a great holiday, although some of the signposts in Wales fooled us. Most showed both Welsh and English names, but out in the country this was not always the case – only Welsh! Much of the holiday while in Wales was completed on narrow back roads whenever possible, and some even went across field tracks. Jack had 14 gates to open at one time or another – he got fed up with that! Even so he admitted that it had been a most enjoyable holiday!

As well as having holidays with Jack I also went away a couple of times a year, if family circumstances allowed, with my former College room mate, Bryan Stubbs. Our friendship began in September 1950 and has lasted ever since. His dry Geordie wit appealed to me from the day we met and still does. We have toured in Scotland frequently, covering much the same sorts of areas as I did with Jack. We also occasionally headed south too, spending one memorable holiday in Norfolk. Bryan enjoys getting off the main roads and we managed to find no end of 'off the beaten track' roads – quite often taking us along out of the way parts of the Scottish coast. We joined the National Trust of Scotland so we sometimes planned our vacations around National Trust properties. In fact that was how I first found Blair Castle at Blair Atholl. We had been staying in Pitlochry, having been to the superb Theatre there. Pitlochry is just off the A9. We more or less 'followed our noses' on a minor road until we stopped at the Pass of Killicrankie where there had been a battle in 1689. The Scots, led by John Graham, Viscount of Dundee, fought against Government troops who were under the command of General Hugh Mackay. The Scots, although outnumbered by two to one, ambushed Mackay's soldiers in the pass of Killicrankie and routed his army. One soldier, trooper, Donald MacBean, is reputed to have leaped across an 18 foot gap over the river to escape from the claymores being wielded by the Highlanders – a truly remarkable feat! Viscount Dundee, who lived at Blair Castle, was killed in the attle. He is buried in the Castle grounds. Intrigued by this story, Bryan and I motored on and found the Castle at Blair Atholl. It is well worth making a visit there. On that particular trip we motored on to Inverness and along the east coast to Dunrobin Castle. This is the Castle upon which Walt Disney is reputed to have based Disneyland. On that occasion we continued across the Highlands before turning south again to Fort William where we stayed overnight. We then motored through Glencoe and eventually returned to Bryan's house at Heighington in County Durham – a long drive that day. We have visited most areas of Scotland over the years and, despite the myth that it is always raining there we have enjoyed good weather most of the time. It is a wonderful country.

Finalising the IGS Tour arrangements
I enjoyed Christmas 1994 and the New Year, but now the pressure to put the finishing touches to the Ivanhoe Grammar School 1995 Cricket Tour, due to take place in June, began to rear its ugly head. In addition to finalising the arrangements that I had been in the process of making in 1994 there was the vexed question of ensuring that the route was correctly planned. The biggest problem about that is when matches are being played around the London

area. To this end I found that the AA Route planners were helpful to a point. I contacted them and they supplied me with the two copies of the various relevant routes from one school to the next. These routes are very detailed, with precise directions and mileages, but in practice there is no substitute for actually trying them out and making one's own notes. It also meant that I could meet all the teachers involved at their respective schools. It was an interesting challenge. I could not travel right round the route in one go – it was too far. Instead I arranged to visit separate sections of the country, making something of a holiday of it as well. The Schools were so helpful and almost invariably offered me a bed for the night. I accepted most offers with great alacrity as it turned out that they entertained me too and many a pint was downed during the course of a visit! But the main thing was that I established a rapport with everybody involved. Apparently the Schools were delighted that someone actually
came to see them rather than just wrote letters. They felt it was so much easier to confirm arrangements. I was even mistaken for an Australian in two or three cases until I put them right.

As it happened this was just as well as things did not always go too smoothly when the touring party wanted to play matches with different rules from those usually followed. Fortunately these were matters over which I had neither responsibility nor control. We had come across similar problems on the 1991 tour and on one occasion there was quite a rumpus. Wellingborough School had got hold of two experienced Umpires, neither of whom had any connection with the School. An arrangement had been made between the two teachers in charge of their respective teams to allow 12 players to be involved in the game. As only eleven could be on the field at any time it was decided that one boy who bowled might not necessarily bat, and vice versa. Unfortunately no one remembered to tell the Umpires. IGS batted first and one lad by the name of Vaughan English made a good score. When Wellingborough School batted he did not appear on the field. Another lad took his place and came on to bowl. After a while one of the Umpires spotted that this had happened, consulted his colleague, suspended play, and initially refused to continue umpiring. They were convinced that the Australian side were cheating and all mayhem was let loose when the players came off. Fortunately an early tea was taken as it was about time anyway, but the Umpires needed a lot of persuading that everything was above board and the Wellingborough teacher in charge was somewhat embarrassed – so was Graeme Renshaw, the IGS teacher. It was my first real experience of the seriousness with which Umpires can take matters in School matters – I was glad not to be involved on that occasion as I knew both teachers well. There were one or two other minor incidents but none sufficient to rock the boat.

Travelling round to all the schools took time. Really it was a question of being able to spend time with the masters involved, but it made things much easier from the moment the tour started. I made arrangements with each school to make contact with them before we actually arrived in order to ensure that whatever accommodation being offered was in place on arrival. I also ensured that we arrived within the time span arranged, so I timed journeys between schools as accurately as possible. This worked well most of the time, but one was not always able to avoid rush hours and driving in the London area always turned out to be something of a lottery.

I was in touch with Frank English, the IGS Tour leader, whenever necessary and sent him a complete run down of arrangements, together with the over all projected plan of events. Below is the cost analysis for the 1995 Ivanhoe Grammar School Junior Cricket Tour:-

ACCOMMODATION

All schools who have boarding facilities – no cost.

Camden Hotel, Bristol	
B & B for 1 night @ £20 per head and an evening meal + VAT	£380.00
Milford Hotel, Nottingham	
B & B for 1 night @ £20 per head and an evening meal + VAT	£380.00
Euro-Hotel, Wellingborough, Northants	
B @ B only for 2 nights at £15 per head + VAT	£540.00
Royal Holloway College, Egham, Surrey	
B & B only for 2 nights @ £18.21 per head + VAT	£692.07
SUM TOTAL FOR ALL ACCOMMODATION	£1992.07

CATERING
Estimated costs based on numbers of meals required:-

Lunches – packed if available – at £3 per head	£627.00
Lunches purchased at cafes & restaurants – at £5 per head £190.00	
Breakfasts – external catering at Dulwich Field Centre	£285.00
Evening meals - £6 per Head	£228.00
SUM TOTAL for food required other than in accommodation	£1330.00

TRANSPORT

12 seater minibus with lap belts, towbar and roof rack	£838.95
Crash Damage Waiver	£255.00
VAT @ 17.5%	£191.44
15 seater minibus with lap belts, towbar and roof rack	£946.28
Crash Damage Waiver	£255.00
VAT @ 17.5%	£210.22
Trailer with cover: 8ft by 5ft by 6ft	£250.00

VAT @ 17.5%	£43.75
Total	<u>293.75</u>
SUM TOTAL	<u>£2990.64</u>

FUEL

Based on the known mileage of the routes being taken - at 16 mpg.

1120 miles per vehicle @16mpg – 70 galls per vehicle at £3 per gall.
£210.00

	£210.00
Extraneous journeys estimated at 320 miles per month	£60.00
	£60.00
SUM TOTAL	£540.00

VISITS

The Big Pit, Blaenavon £57.75

Dan-yr-Ogof Caves, Glyntawe £41.25

Ironbridge Gorge and Blist's Museum £8.55

National Museum of Photography & Film show £44.46

Alton Towers £85.50

Sherwood Forest Visitors' Centre free

'Tales of Robin Hood' 43.50

Nottingham Castle & Brewhouse Museum £9.50

Oakham Castle and Rutland County Museum free

Duxford Aerodrome £38.00

Windsor Castle £92.00

SUM TOTAL	£420.00

SUMMARY OF COSTS

ACCOMMODATION	£1992.07
CATERING	£1330.00
TRANSPORT	£2990.64
FUEL	£540.00
VISITS	£420.00

OVER ALL ESTIMATED SUM TOTAL   **£7273.22**

The original estimated cost only covered the section of the tour that was scheduled to take place in England. I gave a figure of up to £10,000 to the School and that was to include my fee of £1500. Extraneous expenses covering correspondence and postage, travel, telephone calls etc. were contained within a budget of £600. The actual amount totalled £9373.22, well within the estimated amount.

The boys, and the masters who accompanied them, were able to make a deal with the Airline transporting them from Australia to England and back again. From what I was told, the fact that they were travelling as a large group was a great help as it enabled the relevant Airline to offer cheaper rates.

Schedule of the Ivanhoe Grammar School U-15 England Cricket Tour 1995.

Dates	Venues	Accommodation
Sun June 11th	Tour Party arrives	Camden Hotel Bristol
Mon 12th	Nets – Bristol Grammar School	Bristol GS
Tues 13th	v Bristol Grammar School	Glyntawe
Wed 14th	v Llandovery College	Glyntawe
Thurs 15th	v Christ's College Brecon	Glyntawe
Fri 16th	v Monmouth School	Glyntawe
Sat 17th	Visit: The Big Pit Blaenavon	Glyntawe
Sun 18th	Visit: Dan-yr-Ogof Caves.	Ellesmere
Mon 19th	v Ellesmere College	Wrekin
Tues 20th	v Wrekin/Shropshire XI	Shrewsbury
	Visit Ironbridge Gorge am	
Wed 21st	v Shrewsbury School	
	Shrewsbury	
Thurs 22nd	Visit: Mus of Photography on to Leeds	Woodhse Gr
Fri 23rd	v Woodhouse Grove School	Woodhse Gr
Sat 24th	Visit: Alton Towers on to Denstone	Denstone
Sun 25th	v Denstone School	Denstone
Mon 26th	Visit: Nottingham – Tales of Robin Hood	Milford Hotel
Tues 27th	v Oakham School	Oakham
Wed 28th	Visit: Oakham Castle on to Wellingboro'	Euro Hotel
Thurs 29th	v Wellinborough School	Euro Hotel
Fri 30th	Visit: Duxford Aerodrome on to Alleyn's	Alleyn's
Sat July 1st	v Alleyn's School	Alleyn's
Sun 2nd	Visit: City of London sightseeing	King's CS
Mon 3rd	v King's College School, Wimbledon	King's CS
Tues 4th	v St Dunstan's College	St Dunstan's
Wed 5th	Visit: London – shopping & sightseeing	Dulwich
Thurs 6th	v Dulwich College	Dulwich
Fri 7th	v Middlesex County Colts U-15	Holloway
Sat 8th	Visit: Windsor Castle	Holloway
Sun 9th	Tour Party leave	

During this 1995 Cricket Tour, as opposed to the 1991 IGS Cricket Group's experiences, the weather was much kinder and all matches achieved a result. By the end the boys were physically tired – 16 matches arranged and all completed in a month – quite a busy timetable. I must admit that the Staff – myself included – had begun to feel the effects of constant travelling and were ready for a break too!

The aftermath of the tour

This is a fairly lengthy précis of the report on the tour, written by Frank English on his return to Ivanhoe…...

We arrived at Heathrow to be greeted by Chris Turner, sporting his new touring cap in case we did not recognise him, and set off at a whirlwind pace to avoid the dreaded Heathrow Parking Police. For the next month the pace did not diminish one jot! Bristol Grammar School welcomed us with open arms, setting the exemplar for the seemingly endless hospitality we received throughout the country. Our expectations of a vigorous game were not actually realised here. Maybe we expected just too much from the All England Under 15 Rugby Finalists!

After some general sightseeing around Bristol, and an attractive city it was, we moved on to Wales, and the Dulwich Field Centre. Llandovery College is perhaps the most famous Rugby School in the whole country. The list of Welsh International players is legendary. Cricket is not very 'big' in Wales. It was here that Marcus Toovey's tour virtually ended. While trying to hit a massive six his kneecap became dislocated. What made it worse was that he insisted on staying on the field and repeated the exact shot on the very next ball. The result…… hospital…… crutches…… plaster…… agony…… frustration, and finally many visits to the famous Orthopaedic Hospital at Oswestry before eventually returning home.

Perhaps our closest game eventuated next at Christ College, Brecon. It was the occasion when it was the turn of the batsmen to bowl and the bowlers to bat up the order. We had a very lucky win, running out a batsman who took a silly single in the last over and so leaving us with a win by 4 runs. Mr Kempen captured some good footage throughout the tour, and particularly at this match.

Monmouth another city built around a Castle to protect the Welsh from the dreaded English – added more vistas to our ever expanding horizons. The Ivanhoe innings closed at 8/284. The Monmouth team was all out for 145. However we were continually brought into the 20th century by the presence of jet fighters screaming overhead!

Our visits to the mines and caves of Wales was another eye-opener. The mines took us back into the last century, and the exploitation of children. We certainly were an unusual bunch in our helmets and miners gear when we emerged from our tour below. The thought of not seeing daylight for six or seven months of the year would be a bit much to expect in any era, and was enough to make us happy to be 20th Century tourists.

On Monday June 19th we left the lilting language of the Welsh behind, and ventured into the beautiful countryside close to Chester. The school at Ellesmere, with its vaster open spaces (including a golf course) appeared from nowhere and was not what we would have expected so far away from the town. The staff were entertained by the Headmaster, and in turn, the Cricket staff. It was here at the match that we learned that not all Englishmen accept losing with grace!

On moving on to Wrekin we found that the hospitality stakes continued to materialise in a major way in our lives. We were met by members of the School first eleven, who insisted on carrying our bags to the rooms of the building that had been allotted to us. It seemed that just about all schools were Co-Ed. The Wrekin school team were boosted by five County under age players to set us a challenge. Mr and Mrs Sligo came up on the train for the day to visit us and saw a fine display of cricket - IGS 9/218 and Wrekin 10/190.

Although situated not far from Wales Shrewsbury School epitomised the typecast English 'upper class' boarding establishment. The only difficulty with that myth was that no one told the students that they had been put in a mould. It was such a big school we had to drive everywhere! Matthew Logan (137) and Michael Padbury (138) put on 278 for the first wicket and the team scored 5/305. Shrewsbury were dismissed for 233.

Before arriving at Woodhouse Grove School the next day, we visited the National Museum of Photography in Bradford on our way to Leeds. Judging by the fact that no one complained, it must have been a reasonable experience. The match was won easily with scores of 2/134 – 10/133.

Apart from long queues at Alton Towers and the fact that Marcus Toovey was to fly out from Heathrow in the evening, the other happening that focussed a few minds was Andrew Fox taking the keys to the trailer to the fun park 100 miles away. Some two and a half hours and a new set of keys later the baggage trailer was hitched and finally delivered to Denstone, then Mr Turner and I took Marcus to London, where he was put in a wheelchair and given rapid exit through customs and on to the plane to Australia via Hong Kong. We won again 10/175 – 10/145.

And so on to Nottingham, scene of much of the heritage of names we have at Ivanhoe. From the old Oak in the forest to the walls of the Castle, we covered it! We held ancient swords and battleaxes, shields and daggers, and were generally glad to be living in the 20th Century. Mr Turner had arranged a visit to Trent Bridge Cricket Ground, where we were all presented with a tie and had a guided tour through the hallowed Members Rooms. We were also treated to two hours of the most entertaining cricket that anyone could wish to see when Nottingham took on the Kent bowlers, and won the match in the last few overs. Nottingham Forest Soccer Ground was next – overall, it was a great day!

Oakham, a school we had heard so much about from Mr Turner, turned out to be everything he said it was, and more. Whichever way we looked at it, this school, of all we visited, seemed much like our own in spirit and attitude. Scores were 6/107 and 10/104. Indeed, the staff were treated royally by their corresponding numbers, one of whom owned two Whisky Distilleries and lived in a house that was built in 1647. Some boys bought boots at the market, which has run weekly for almost 700 years. We entered the Castle and really were in a place of history.....right down to the horseshoe tax which has to be paid by Royalty to this day. Our visit to Burley house will be something to remember, even apart from the local press photo. To see the only Taiwanese deer in the World, and more so to be able to feed them, was special. To see the wealth of the original "House", now being renovated, was something extraordinary. Then to top it off, we saw the "Triangular Lodge" and then the bones in the crypt of the oldest Church in the area at Rothwell......What a day!
(After the tour was over I was asked to write an article for publication in the local press in Rutland – see below. Because of the danger that publicising the existence of the Taiwanese deer might attract unwanted attention that specific section was omitted)

A visit to Burley House

I first saw Burley House during the Second World War. Here at Burley on the Hill, one of Rutland's many picturesque villages, it was then being used as a hospital dedicated to looking after wounded servicemen who had fought so bravely in the defence of freedom. The circumstance of my first glimpse was a trifle bizarre - as a pupil at Oakham School I had to run the "Burley triangle" from time to time and on one occasion I decided to go a bit further than normal in order to vary the routine (and probably have a rest - running was not my favourite pastime!). I continued along the road which borders the estate and there was the House in all its glory. I was so taken with what I saw that day that I vowed that one day I would visit its hallowed portals if ever the opportunity arose. Little did I realise that it would be just over half a century before this chance eventually occurred......
Oakham School nurtured in me a love for cricket which has remained undimmed with the passing years. When the time came to hang up my boots I continued to take an interest in helping young cricketers from any part of the world in whatever ways I could. Suffice it to say that my latest venture was to organise a cricket tour for a party of boys and staff from Ivanhoe Grammar School, Melbourne. Oakham School was on the itinerary - we had a 'rest' day after the match so where better to visit than Burley House, former home of George Finch, Earl of Winchilsea and Nottingham In 1787, when he was 35 years old, he founded the Marylebone Cricket Club and, in 1790, hosted the first 'international' match between an All England team and Hampshire. This match was played on the grassland outside the present iron gates on the North Front. For the record, Hampshire won by 7 wickets.

312

Our guide for the visit was none other than the present Head gardener, Ray Hill. A veritable mine of information, he first took us into the Front Hall to quench our thirst - it was very warm day - and to explain just what was being done in the way of renovation. Burley House is being restored to it former magnificence and for those lucky enough to be able to live there it will indeed be a delight. The builders were kind enough to allow us to mount the Grand Stairs, alas still covered with cardboard to protect the English red oak steps from damage during the renovations. The scene which greets the eye through the windows is indeed positively breathtaking. The magnificent trees which border the field beyond the South Front with its Great Terrace and stone balustrade are much enhanced by the herd of deer which roam freely around the estate and, when necessary, take shelter from the vagaries of our English climate. One deer in particular delighted the boys when it literally joined the party and greatly enjoyed the attention lavished upon it. Beyond the trees is a lake and to enhance the background still further the comparatively new vista of Rutland Water completes one of the most memorable views I have ever witnessed.

After lunch - eaten in the shade of the North Front of the House where the eye is held by the Great Courtyard with its long colonnades emphasizing the Italian style influence which is greatly in evidence throughout the property - we visited the impressive 13th Century Parish Church with its Norman style arches. Our guide showed us recumbent statues and also various other features of historical interest, including the font which is around 500 years old, before allowing the energetic ones to climb up the narrow stone steps to the belfry to see the workings of the clock.

A short walk through the trees and back to the house completed a truly wonderful visit for all of us in the party. Our Australian friends will have taken back many enjoyable and lasting memories of their successful cricket tour. However, I guarantee that none will be more deeply ingrained in their memories than the day they visited Burley House with its history plus its ancestral connection with the M.C.C. and cricket in general.

Published in July 1995

The boys on the last tour still talk with interest of Wellingborough School, and the wonderful way they had been treated. We were not disappointed. Due to circumstances beyond the School's control we had to book at a local small boarding Hotel. The Indian Ancestry of the owner ensured that, no matter where we were, we could always smell the curry. But the English breakfasts were always good, and everyone enjoyed having a television in their room. The girls came in vast numbers to watch the match, so there was some outstanding fielding at times! We won the match 9/127 against 84 all out. Yet again we had the 'professional' Cricket Coach shaking his head and wondering what had gone wrong, but not really listening to the obvious answers he was given.

On our journey to London we stopped off at Duxford Air Museum after driving through Cambridge to see some of the University Colleges. We were *entertained by flying displays from Spitfires and Mustangs, and being able to see and walk through Concorde was an experience not easily forgotten.*

The match at Alleyn's did not live up to expectations. Nor did the pitch, although the spinners were not complaining! We had expected the London Schools to all be somewhat more experienced. The School put on plenty of food for us though and gave us accommodation at the Diana Boarding House/Hotel, so they were top class in the hospitality stakes. As the match finished early, we decided to try out the subway system and experience London on a Saturday night. We spent much of the next day being genuine tourists. The open top double-decker bus was a great way to see the city and certainly gave an amazing perspective of historical London, and whetted the appetite for the shopping expedition to come.

Monday 3rd July saw us venture to Kings College, Wimbledon's sports ground. We again played 'English rules' and decided that we would have to go for runs and hope to get them all out. Unfortunately they did not try to get the runs, and played not to lose the match. So much for what they thought was an 'honourable' draw – about 150 behind for the same number of overs. We made 4/303, KCS did not lose all their wickets and finished around 4/181 runs behind – a draw...... They could not fathom our disappointment.

The St Dunstan's sports ground was a long way from their School, but situated in a very nice suburb. Lunch was excellent, as was afternoon tea. The inevitable bar was open for spectators during the match. St Dunstan's were 123 all out. We scored 125 for the loss of 1 wicket.

The next day – Shopping! Shopping! Shopping! It seemed there is no end to it in London, whether it be Lilywhites, Harrods, Liberty - Carnaby or Oxford Street. There seems to be no end to the traps for unwary buyers.

Dulwich College, that bastion of London and English Society, was to be our highlight match of the tour. We had heard of their 3 year unbeaten record in England. This was a match we really wanted to win. We scored 231 for 8 and dismissed Dulwich for 06. The post match despondency of the Dulwich boys though soon gave way to their duty as hosts, and they had everyone home for a shower and change before coming back to take part in out 'End of Tour' Dinner in their magnificent Pavilion. It was a great celebration. The evening concluded for the team around 10.30pm, and they ostensively went home to bed, for we had one more match to play the next day. Somehow the Dulwich boys thought otherwise, and they were determined to have their billets celebrate the end of their school year with them! Many almost saw the sunrise, which made it difficult to see the ball later in the morning. Middlesex Colts won at Sunbury - Colts 167 - IGS 123 all out.

Our stay at the University of London, Egham Campus, for our last couple of nights was something some of our party will remember for a long while. 300 Italian girls make a lot of noise!

Saturday 8th July saw most members miss breakfast. It was either 7.45am or miss out. We went to Windsor Castle which as well worth visiting. At night we went to the 'Rocky Horror Show' – an experience never to be forgotten!

Up bright and early – our last day in England! Almost everyone went to breakfast. What a rush it was to pack and move out of Royal Holloway College! There was a presentation to Mr Turner, as it was the last day we would see him in England, and he had done so much for us on the tour. Heathrow! Always a rush! Bags to be stored. Parking Police to be avoided. Vans to be cleared. Goodbyes to Mr Turner. Boy were those bags heavy! Off to Lords! Both Dulwich College and Shrewsbury School had something to do with our visit on the last day in England. Off we went. Tradition! Tradition! Yes it was interesting. Not what we would have expected after knowing the MCG, but special - the home of so many Australian victories. Next stop Hong Kong! At last…..our journey home.

Our thanks to all who made the tour possible. To the parents of the team for the help and forbearance. To the staff for their assistance, guidance and advice. To all those mentioned in our tour booklet. To Mr Turner for his planning skills and careful driving, and to all who in anyway helped us to make this such a wonderful experience. Thank you!

FW English
Assistant Headmaster
27th July 1995

I have no doubt that the results obtained by the tourists must have delighted everyone at the School, but the fact that they won their matches, while pleasing at the time, meant that they had probably not gained as much benefit from their cricketing experiences as their predecessors in 1991. But they were a very good side and went on to win their Premiership League in the 1996/7 season – I saw the final match, having flown in from New Zealand where I had been on holiday. Hopefully, their determination to do well rubbed off on some of the English teams that they beat. In my opinion, based on what I have seen while on holiday in Australia, the standard of schoolboy cricket is better and there is a much more positive attitude towards winning. Games are usually settled by one side making a higher run total so the draw does not feature large in the Australian mentality. I am inclined to that approach, it has a greater expectation and a more positive thought process as there is no place to hide. Rightly or wrongly they certainly do not like to lose!

Chapter 16 Finally achieving an ambition

Although approaching my 65 birthday I still had one ambition unrealised. Many years before, in the summer of 1952, I was due to go on a Cricket Tour with Bede College. Unfortunately I was unable to go due to the illness of my father – in fact I left college early in order to help out at home in my father's new Parish at Rothwell, Northants, where he was the newly appointed Vicar. He had several speaking commitments amongst other things and he needed me to fulfil them for him while he was in the Prince of Wales Hospital in

Tottenham having a gastric ulcer removed. In the event it took several months for him to recover as well so that had to be covered, one way or another. Ever since then I had always hoped to be able to tour abroad, but there appeared to be little chance of that happening. Furthermore two unfortunate problems cropped up immediately after the IGS Tour had ended. I had again contracted Cellulitis right after the end of the tour. But now I carried the tablets necessary to combat the problem before it took too great a hold on my leg and I was able to complete the business of returning the transport to the correct places before resting up for a spell. That led to another problem. It was sunny and warm on July 11th '95. I intended to rest up in the shade outside the back door of my house on a long beach chair. Alas, just as I was getting myself outside I tripped on the back step and fell. Shortly afterwards, on Tuesday August 15th, I was commentating at a match at Headingley – the Nat West semi-final. I went into the dining room at the tea interval for a light snack. I sat on a tubular chair. Unfortunately it was broken and must have been put out in error. I sustained a severe injury to my back and this involved an Insurance Claim – eventually settled in the sum of £5000. This took a year to settle, by which time I had bought a car with an automatic gearbox as I could not drive easily any other way. I had also spent a considerable amount of money having treatment for my back. For a spell I could only stand or lie down. Sitting was not even an option. The sum just about covered my expenses.

One autumn evening I received a call from Colin Kleiser, the Master in charge of cricket at Christ College, Brecon, asking me if he could come and stay for a couple of days. That was fine and he duly arrived in November '95. For some reason he always favoured eating fish and chips and he asked to go to Harry Ramsden's! We did so and suddenly he said he wanted to take a cricket tour to Australia and would I help? He wanted someone with a basic knowledge of conditions out there – fine. Then he dropped a further bombshell – would I be prepared to go out with the school to Australia on tour? As I was already thinking about going out to Melbourne again anyway I needed no second bidding! His final surprise came when he admitted that he had watched me coaching the Australian lads during their tour and would I come to the College at Brecon and do some coaching please? Back trouble or no back trouble I was definitely happy to take part. What a chance that was to finish my connection with cricket tours in style! I immediately doubled the treatment I was having in an attempt to recover more quickly. I do not know if that did actually help much, but the motivation certainly did!

We commenced cricket training in April '96. I drove to the College at Brecon and was given a room to use each time I went. The resident Cricket Coach, Bill Higginson, who formerly played for Middlesex, was welcoming and things went well. I spent about a week each month with the boys, practising in the nets. Bill was usually present and we tried to motivate the boys. Cricket is not too important in Welsh establishments. It comes a poor second to rugby. Still, we managed to inculcate some enthusiasm. A couple of the staff, when they saw the way the wind was blowing, wanted to change their minds and join the touring party but Colin decided otherwise. After all there were fares to consider and really they just wanted to come for the ride. Fortunately by then I was accepted in the staffroom – certainly by the English contingent. I was also doing quite a bit of commentating at Headingley as well so it was a busy summer, but I thoroughly enjoyed my days at Headingley. We had been joined, if memory serves me right, by Jack Wainwright, who was involved with Rugby League too as a professional commentator. In his younger days he had played in the Bradford Cricket League for Undercliffe with considerable success. But the highlight of the summer holiday came in August. Mandy and Philip had decided to 'tie the knot' and get married. They also wanted to go to America for their holiday so they arranged to be married on the shore of Lake Tahoe, California. It was a wonderful, romantic idea, and I am sure that it meant so much – it was just for the two of them, and rightly so. They had a wonderful honeymoon, judging from the video they showed me, and their happiness was obvious. They had a reception for us all on their return home.

Some of the Welsh teachers at Christ College were a bit awkward for a time and lapsed into their native welsh tongue whenever I was present but that was easy to ignore as I did not understand a word! It was interesting though, to see that there was some antipathy towards the English – common enough, I was laughingly told. It soon faded out and things were fine. There was little of that amongst the boys although paradoxically the tour Captain, Rhodri Jones, spoke English only as a second language and told me he did not like the English. However I apparently was an exception and we got on extremely well – fortunately! The most popular lad was a Sri Lankan, Kaveenga Dias – an absolute charmer and a good bowler too.

There is no doubt that the boys had made progress during the summer term and their enthusiasm showed. When I was around it was normal for them to spend extra time in the evenings with me, being coached on aspects of fielding – an obvious weakness that was difficult to eradicate. Bowling and batting skills were not too bad and again had improved considerably during the summer. They were playing school matches most weeks and they even entertained an MCC side on one occasion. I thoroughly enjoyed my time at the College although driving down from Leeds was initially fraught with difficulty once again due to the severe back problem and I had to stop every half hour on the journey just to ease the pain. Eventually it got so bad that I was forced to seek further medical help and over a period of about 8 weeks I had two epidural injections in my spine, the second one in mid November, just to enable me to travel.

Coaching at the College continued apace from September and the rapport that I built up with the boys was good. However the really deep enthusiasm and determination to do well whatever the odds was not there in several of the boys and I could foresee that some of them might well become disheartened. It was all a question of motivation and I felt that I was ploughing a lone furrow at times. Having done two tours with Australian sides I knew that more was needed and I did run a couple of seminars with the lads to try and motivate them. But it was frustrating. They certainly showed what could be done on the rugby field so I tried to get this to spill over into their cricketing psyche and for a few it worked. On my last visit before leaving for Australia I suggested to Bill that the idea I had put forward several times - at least half an hour should be set aside before every match to practice catching, throwing, and fielding –

should become a 'must'. Unfortunately I was not there at the final briefing when it was once again mentioned. If I had been the boys would not have been asked by anybody – they would have been told, and in no uncertain terms!

I left on November 28th for Melbourne and stayed with Elaine and Peter Kempen until the tour began. I had the job of checking to see that everything was in place in Australia, ready for the tour. It was. The Christ College tourists arrived around 8.30am at Ivanhoe Grammar School ready to be billeted.

Some weeks prior to the boys leaving I produced some useful written data about conditions they would come across in Australia for them to digest as a visual follow up to what I had already discussed with them. It was as follows:-

PITCHES

Wickets are faster than those at home. They are very hard compared with wickets in the UK and the ball comes through much more quickly. Sometimes there is a 'matting' of grass, which tends to kill the pace.

BOWLING

Pace bowlers will find that the seam on a cricket ball is considerably reduced after several overs of sustained fast bowling due to the hard wickets and the shine soon fades. The seams sometimes tend to 'string'. The ball comes through the air more quickly due to the rarer atmosphere. Also there is the problem of HIGH BOUNCE, making it difficult for the FAST bowler to claim LBWs.

The high bounce is the direct result of the extremely hard surface engendered by the clay-based wickets. A good length for these wickets is obtained by pitching between 18" and two feet shorter than in the UK (but no more than that as Aussie batsmen are often good 'pullers' of the short ball) – hence the higher bounce.

Most Australian slow bowlers are wrist spinners. They can thus get some movement off the pitch. Orthodox finger spin is rarer than in the UK as the ball does not turn much once the seam is flattened. It is important to give the ball more air, particularly for the finger spinner. The alternative, as in the UK, is to push the ball through more quickly and fairly flat. It is essential to KEEP THE BALL WELL UP to the batsman. NEVER BOWL SHORT. Line and length has got to be a 'MUST'.

BATTING

In Australia many batsmen tend to move the back foot in towards the stumps as the initial movement. It is the norm for many players as there is little chance of an LBW being given because the ball bounces so high UNLESS

THE BALL IS PITCHED RIGHT UP, in which case a different shot would be played anyway.

The forward DEFENSIVE shot which we use in the UK is played less often in Australia. If it is used the foot must be RIGHT UP TO THE PITCH OF THE BALL with the bat angled downwards. As the ball comes through more quickly Australians tend to play through the ball using the forward drive, making it a deliberate scoring stroke. IT IS IMPORTANT TO REMEMBER THAT THE BALL TRAVELS FASTER THROUGH THE AIR and arrives more quickly than at home. That is why many Aussie batsmen tend to move back initially to give them a fraction more time to 'see' the ball.

FIELDING

The ball tends to travel FARTHER and FASTER because the atmosphere is clearer and there is less humidity.

Health hints
FLUID INTAKE and SKIN PROTECTION

A HIGH LIQUID INTAKE IS ESSENTIAL as dehydration can be a problem.

IMPORTANT - 1/ NEVER GULP DOWN liquid – ALWAYS sip SLOWLY however thirsty you feel.

2/ ALWAYS APPLY the strongest possible recommended SUNSCREEN to ALL exposed parts of the body – lips, face and arms in particular – to prevent exposure to Ultra Violet Rays.

Failure to do so is dangerous. Always wear a hat or cap. UV rays penetrate through cloud.

As I expected, the tour became a huge learning curve for the boys. Of the nine matches played they won only once – at Scotch College, Adelaide. Australians play a simple basic form of cricket – a team wins or loses. There are no draws – no playing to ensure that the team does not lose in the event of the opposition scoring a lot of runs. In my opinion this is the diet on which school teams should be fed. Look for the winning habit rather than trying to make sure a team does not lose. We are, of course, talking of young players. As they reach maturity in the game of cricket then the introduction of other rules is permissible and sensible. At Test Match and County level the draw becomes an important issue as points are involved and this has a bearing on end of season results. Test Match Series are decided upon by the number of matches won and the draw is necessary in order to try to ensure that when the next game is played the opposition has not managed to gain advantage by winning and being ahead in the series. It is still a level playing field – both teams can still gain an advantage at the end of the game providing one side can dismiss the other for a lower score. I am inclined to the view that in order to produce players of the future there has to be a certain input that produces a positive attitude and it needs to start at an early age. – it certainly does in Australian schools.

Tour games were played at the following venues:-

<u>The Melbourne Stage</u>

Geelong College – 2 matches
1. Geelong 145 for 4   Christ College 94 for 9   Lost
2. Geelong 153   Christ College 88   Lost

Ivanhoe Grammar School – 2 matches
1. IGS 113   Christ College 63   Lost
2. Christ College 195   IGS 198 for 5

Camberwell Grammar – 1 match
Christ College 136   Camberwell Grammar 137 for 3   Lost

<u>The Adelaide Stage</u>

Prince Alfred College -1 match
Prince Alfred College 204 for 5   Christ College 48   Lost

Scotch College – 1 match
Christ College 217 for 4   Scotch College 192 for 2   Won

Immanuel College – 1 match
Immanuel College 199 for 7   Christ College 152 for 9   Lost

Westminster School
Westminster School 158 for 7 Christ College 124   Lost

The report written about the tour mentioned many aspects of the tour – not least the wonderful reception given to us all at every school we played. Billets were fine and the Australian parents involved looked after the boys very well. It is interesting to note Colin's opening comments:-

For the first ever undertaking by Christ College cricketers – and it was also, in fact, the first time a school from Wales had dared to go on tour with its own boys, as opposed to an amalgam of players – one ought, with a degree of indulgence, to count it as a successful venture that should rebound to the reputation of our School. The initial choice of Australia was intended to be a stern test of our cricketing worth. That it certainly was, for we managed only one win with eight matches lost, as drawn games are impossible under the 'overs' playing conditions that operated throughout our tour. No hanging on, no crawling away when manifestly outplayed in Australia, as often happens here in the UK, for the side that scores most runs wins. Simple. Simple and positive. Nothing negative is allowed to interfere with that principle, so when an Australian boy crosses the 'line of white fever' (the boundary) there is only one aim in his mind – WIN. The dedication of coaches and players to that end was a real eye-opener to Bill Higginson and myself, whereas Chris Turner, our Australian expert, had warned us what to expect from tough opponents.

Colin Kleiser - Master I/C Cricket 1996.

The rest of the report pointed out the strengths and weaknesses. In my book there were too many players -18 – on tour for the number of matches arranged, and to ensure that everyone had a fair crack of the whip in terms of games played the strongest team was never picked and Colin mentioned this almost as a mitigating factor. My personal feeling was that it would not have made too much difference.

The Tour effectively ended for me at Adelaide. On the social side of the trip I was extremely fortunate to be billeted with the Westminster School Cricket Coach, Phil Stewart. We got on extremely well and formed a friendship that is still strong. We have had holidays at each other's places of residence in later years and by a happy coincidence Phil has been across to Britain on two or three occasions. Westminster School looked after the tourists extremely well. In fact we were in billets connected with the School for the whole of the Adelaide Section of the tour.

Phil was also the Cricket Coach for the South Australian Ladies' Cricket Team. We finished the actual playing part of the tour a couple of days before the boys were due to return home to the UK. The Westminster School staff took them out and showed them round the area so they were well catered for. In fact one of the masters involved with the organisation of the 'domestic' side of the tour, David Jarman, had previously taught at Christ College, Brecon so links with the Welsh School was already very strong. In turn, I had a link with Ivanhoe Grammar School as I had run two tours for them and had been to the School several times. It is always a problem to finance School Tours to other countries as sometimes the major outlay has to be made for places to stay. In this case however the Schools in Australia were most generous with their help in this respect and the resultant cost to each boy was considerably less than it might have been. In addition to this I did not need to be included in the School finances initially as I was intending to go out to the Southern Hemisphere again anyway.

As a matter of interest, Colin Kleiser had organised a concert in aid of funds for the trip about six weeks or so before we were due to set off. He is a pianist of good repute and all the boys who were coming on tour were involved as well. At Colin's request I managed to unearth the words for a famous Australian song, 'Waltzing Matilda'. This is the most widely known 'bush ballad'. Matilda is actually a bag that was slung over a bushman's back, where he carried anything he owned. Bushmen normally always went everywhere on foot. The boys learned the words (or, rather, had copies of the words on sheets of paper) and sang the song with great gusto. I did a song called 'Laura' – quite a haunting song for a start. Colin then proceeded to 'pep it up' in no uncertain terms! Still it went down all right and we made a few bob for the tour funds. Unfortunately I don't think Colin publicised it very well as afterwards a lot of children said that they would have come – and staff too.

Christ College paid for my two internal flights – from Melbourne to Adelaide and back again. Internal flights in Australia were very cheap so that did not greatly add to the burden of payment. I financed all my trips to the School prior to the tour as well. I was given food and lodging during my stays – sleeping in the sick bay on each visit. I made a bit of a holiday of it all as well, and I was able to travel round the beautiful countryside when I wasn't with the boys in the indoor nets. I was also taken out to various local hostelries once I had got to know a few people. The Welsh certainly like their beer!

At this point I must say that it was interesting to see just how the School was run. The pupils as a whole seemed to have a lot of freedom. Of course the majority of them probably lived locally anyway but there were boarders too. Several were the sons of men serving abroad in the forces. This rang a bell. When I was away at School, both at Magdalen and Oakham, this applied, particularly as there was a war on and soldiers were in the fighting line. There were several who had come to live in England for one reason or another. One lad in particular, Daveenga Dias, who was Sri Lankan, set a very good example. Whatever he did he worked extremely hard and he was keen to try out ideas. What is more he was always asking questions – one felt that he really wanted to learn about the best way for him to use what talents he had – and he had plenty!

The Headmaster was welcoming whenever I met him during my stays at the School. He had only recently been appointed and one got the distinct impression that he was keen to introduce his own brand of enthusiasm for success to his pupils. After the tour was over I wrote to him at some length as to my thoughts on the whole trip. His letter in reply to mine was as now follows:-

DP Jones (MA(Cantab)   Christ College
Headmaster   Brecon
                                                       Powys
                                                       LD3 8AG

Chris Turner Esq
c/o 5 Merton Street

Ivanhoe
VICTORIA 3079
Australia
Dear Chris

Thank you very much indeed for your letter which I received this morning detailing the boys' exploits during the cricket tour in Australia. It was very kind of you indeed to take the trouble to write so exhaustively. I found your letter fascinating readingand, as must often be the case, I found myself linking the boys achievements with their character at school. I am sure that the boys will have learnt much, even if they might not realise that they were learning it at the time and with luck it should lay foundatons for a good cricket season at the end of our year. Certaily we look forward to entertaining some of our opponents back here at Christ College in due course. I was also grateful to receive your advice on the weaknesses in the tour's itinerary so that if we ever embark on a similar venture again, we shall know some of the pitfalls to avoid.

Thank you for commenting on the socialside of the Tour and it is very good to read that you assessed the boys as being very good ambassadors for their school. I dare not ask if you, Colin and Bill had a good time, but judging from the grin which has played around Colin's lips since he came back, I'm sure you all had a wonderful management Tour as well. I hope you will forgive mw if I quote one or two of your words to the school when I speak to them in Assembly tomorrow morning.

Thabnk you very much indeed for all your contributions in helping to make what was evidently a very successful Tour

Very best regards

Yours sincerely

Phillip Jones

I duly left the tour party at Adelaide Airport and, while they were homeward bound, I flew back to Melbourne to stay with Frank English for a few days over Christmas. They took me with them to an informal Christmas Eve Carol Service. It was held outside in the sunshine – a lovely experience. There were no end of people there and it was a truly festive occasion. In fact I had never been to a more informal gathering. I spent Christmas Day with the Tysons. They had sold their house and had moved to Sorrento, near Surfers Paradise, but they were staying in Melbourne over Christmas with Anna. We went for dinner to the parents of Anna's then boyfriend – now husband – Mr and Mrs Powers, Ironically it was a poor day weather-wise but faired up in the evening and after I had returned to my temporary 'base' with Frank English I retired early to get ready for the morning's festivities on Boxing Day. This was an early morning pre - Test Match breakfast at a large Hotel nearby. Frank English and I went together, had an excellent breakfast, and then listened to a couple of former Australian cricketers reminiscing about their days playing for

Australia. After that we went across to the Melbourne Cricket Ground and spent an enjoyable day watching Australia playing against the South Africans on the opening day of the Boxing Day Test. I also watched on succeeding days. Australia won the match by an innings and 196 runs, Greg Blewitt scoring 214 runs for Australia and Steve Waugh also scoring a century. The South Africans were bowled out cheaply twice.

With New Year coming up celebrations would be taking place everywhere and fireworks seem to dominate the scene in most places, particularly in the major cities. One thing, Aussies certainly know how to celebrate! The inevitable series of barbeques invariably take place. This year we went next door to join the Sorrel family and, as appears to be the custom, guests provide plenty to imbibe while the hosts provide the repast. It seemed strange to see out the old year and toast in the new in such a warm climate. The Melbourne skyline was lit up with such a massive fireworks display – set off close to the banks of the Yarra River - that it must have been seen all over the city. The following morning we cleared the swimming pool in Frank's garden and spent a pleasant day sitting around and taking a dip from time to time. I went in more than anyone else – just to keep cool!

My next port of call was to the Gowans. They too had a family barbeque that evening and their pool was also very much in use. John took me out for a ride around the area and showed me more of the scenic views that seem to be such a feature of Victoria. I then motored down to see Bon and George Tribe at Rye for a couple of days before returning to the Tysons in Kew. Bon mentioned that Connie, the lady with whom I had done several broadcasts with the 3RPP Radio station on previous trips, was not well. I watched some local cricket for a change and thoroughly enjoyed myself. The enthusiasm that is part of the game certainly gives a clue as to the way in which budding young Australian cricketers are brought up. Winning is everything, no matter what sport is being played, and sides really hate to lose. Of course they normally only play at weekends and games can last for two weekends at a time. In cricket there is very much a feeling of 'Let me get at the opposition bowlers and knock hell out of them' from the batsmen, while the bowlers take exactly the opposite view – particularly the fast bowlers. The pitches are not all that perfect either so the ball flies around quite a lot!

On January 10th I flew from Tullamarine Airport to Wellington after John Gowans had given me a lift to set me on my way. This time I had arranged to hire a car in New Zealand from a firm called 'Rent-a-dent'. I had got to know the proprietors on my previous trip. One of their reps met me at the Airport and took me to fetch the car – a two year old Mazda. As it turned out, initially I had planned beforehand that Ken would be fetching me and I would have to go back to the garage near the airport two days later. Instead, after a couple of phone calls, I arranged to visit the garage and pre pay the hire charge when I landed. The owners kindly let me have the car a couple of days early – for free. That would not happen at home! I drove out to Dorothy and Ken at Linden. Needless to say there was a lot of catching up to do. On this trip I had come to New Zealand to watch the three Test Matches being played, at various venues, between NZ and England and in between times I could catch up with my friends if I had transport. First I went to the Basin – the cricket ground at Wellington - to work in the Cricket Museum for the day and to watch a local match in the Shell trophy Series between Wellington and Otago. When I entered the Long Room at the ground during the lunch break I was hailed by name. Of all people, there was my friend Ralph Middlebrook, Director, and Head Cricket Coach at the Headingley Cricket School! His son, who had come out to play cricket for the season in NZ, was at the match and Ralph had come to spend time with him. So we had a long chat and agreed to meet up at the first Test in Auckland. That was fortunate as Ralph had tickets for every day of that match. He had a spare one for the first day too, and agreed to leave it at the Oval Cricket Ground, Auckland, with a gateman nearest the main entrance to the ground, for me to use. He could only go to the first day of the Test match himself as he had to fly home from Auckland the following day – Jan 25th. He offered me the other tickets for the rest of that first Test Match – yes please! More of that story comes later. We had a few beers together during the day and I showed him round the Cricket Museum where I was working as a curator.

By now Martyn Vause, my ex-pupil from Holy Trinity School, Cookridge, who had worked for my second cousin Graeme for a while, had set up on his own in business in Porirua, the next town along the road from Linden. On January 12th after doing some local shopping for more films for my camera, I found Martyn's Tyre Garage and spent a pleasant morning chatting to him. He had certainly done well for himself and had plenty of trade. It was great to see how well he had got on in his career – a far cry from 1964 at Holy Trinity CE Primary School!

The next day I set off on my journeying again, going for a couple of nights to see Kathleen at Raumati, along the coast. It was a gorgeous day so we went down to the beach for a swim. There were several of her acquaintances there too. The sand is actually very dark. The first time I saw it I thought it was just dirty – very wrong thinking! It is actually the residue from the volcanic influences of hundreds of years previously. Opposite Raumati Beach is the Island of Kapiti. It is a primarily a bird sanctuary and in the waters can sometimes be seen dolphins, whales and seals. I saw dolphins there once, and on another occasion, a couple of seals basking in the sun just off the coast. I had always secretly hoped that the dolphins would come in close to the beach, as they sometimes did, but it never happened while I was there. I would have loved to have swum with dolphins! Few people lived on the island and ferry trips could be taken to explore the place, although I never actually went. Birdwatchers were always there in abundance and I was told that all kinds of bird species were there. We swam again the next morning, visited the Southward Car Museum in the afternoon, and I met a couple of Kath's friends in the evening – a busy day.

Napier was next on my list for visiting – on Jan 15th. Once again I stayed with Ina and Val. I first went straight to the RSA Club to meet up with Val and everybody else I knew. It is really quite remarkable to note that most of the people I had ever met in Napier had some connection with that place. Of course, the meals were excellent, particularly the one we had that evening, and the staff and members were very welcoming, so I suppose that accounted for the popularity of the place – and it was so cheap. At least it was as far as I was concerned as the monetary exchange rate was quite heavily in my favour - Sterling £1 = 3.45 NZ$. With everything so cheap for me it was possible to afford virtually anything I required. Funnily enough I always bought two pairs of trainers at a certain shop in Napier every time I went on my journeying there because they had two velcro straps in place of the laces, and were so comfortable. Incredible as it may seem, they cost me only the equivalent of just $18 - £4 a pair! There was a particular firm in New Zealand too – the 'Warehouse' – where one could buy virtually anything – including the kitchen sink! They had stores throughout the country and if any of the goods a customer required were not available at that particular store they could be obtained from another store quite easily by post or extra deliveries. But one had to wait a few days. I went one better and arranged my journeys so I could drive to wherever my requirements were housed, picking things up en route. The firm even arranged for things I wanted to be stored to await my arrival – talk about good business sense! I had only time to stay for 4 days in Napier on this occasion and I had some cricket business to do while I was there for a young man who played his cricket at Adel. But it was all great fun and I shall never forget the warmth of welcome I always received. For me it is the friendliest country I have ever visited and Napier was the tops for friendly faces, but then I was not living there permanently. From people who had emigrated to NZ I heard conflicting reports. The pay was poor and there was resentment as jobs were scarce – fair enough, it is not my homeland. Some years previously I had tried to get permission to stay on for a year in order to do some radio work for the NZ Broadcasting Service. The offer of a job was conditional on my being allowed to stay in NZ. No luck – the authorities would not sanction it on medical grounds. I was sad, but I understood. I think the problem lay in the fact that once a family emigrated from the UK the money earned was insufficient for disillusioned emigrants to return home. I was approached on several occasions by people who wanted to return to the UK. They enquired about the cost of living 'back home', as they put it. Unfortunately the news I gave them of the continual rise in the cost of living in the UK did not give any cause for optimism. I always felt it was a case of 'look before you leap'. I never encouraged anybody to emigrate to NZ, although it is a beautiful country.

On Jan `19th I motored to Matamata to visit Violet McGiven, John Scatchard's sister for a couple of days. The last time I had called there her family were all taken ill, but this time there was no such problem and Violet took me to see her daughter Sally and husband Brian. Brian was a teacher at a local school in those days. He was trying for promotion and when we called we had a long chat about it all. The problems are the same the world over – it is often not what you know, rather which political party you have leanings towards and thus are inclined to vote for. In the UK that problem had been more or less nailed down, but NZ were still light years behind us in these matters and Brian was, for my money, a victim. I suggested that he kept his feelings to himself, but alas it was too late for that – C'est la vie!

I motored on to Auckland on Jan 21st and drove out to Torbay to stay with Margaret and Murray Olds. Sadly, by this time, Margaret was displaying more severe signs of Alzheimer's disease and life was difficult for both of them. Murray was adamant that Margaret should stay with him at home, but their children all felt that Margaret might be better served in a home that specialised in looking after Alzheimer patients. But Murray would not hear of it. He felt that he could cope and naturally he wanted to do so. But the writing was on the wall. Eventually it had to happen. Still that was in the future at that point. The following day we went to see Lesley, their daughter, and their son in law Mark. I had always got on very well with Mark, who held a high profile job in the City. He invited me to join him and his friends for the Sunday of the Test Match. I had met several of them on previous visits and they always made me very welcome. His firm hired a 'box' for the day – that is, a private area for use only for invited guests. Having spent time with him previously at cricket matches I was only too happy to accept. Food and drink were laid on for guests and as I had been with him before I knew what to expect! We still send the occasional e-mail to each other all these years later – he is a great supporter of the Kiwis, both for cricket and rugby.

I set off early on Jan 24th in order to ensure that I either met Ralph or got the ticket he would have left with the gateman for me. When I arrived there was no Ralph visible and apparently no ticket either – at least the gateman denied that one had been left. As I was smartly dressed in blazer and was wearing an England Cricket Tie I insisted that I be let in so that I could go to the ticket office. I assumed that the ticket would be there. It wasn't, so I asked the official cricket announcer to page Ralph Middlebrook. He did just that and Ralph came hot foot to the Office, thinking that there had been some message for him from home. He was very relieved when he saw that it was only me! Yes, he had left the ticket at the gate as arranged, but the gateman had decided to hang on to it! Fortunately we tracked him down, sitting in a shed just outside the ground, so all was well. It was a 'genuine error' apparently. Just after Ralph had left the ticket with him he had been redirected elsewhere – that was his story. It was probably a pack of lies but as we had got the ticket we left him to be dealt with by the guys in the ticket office. Much more amusing was the fact that, just as the announcement asking 'Mr Ralph Middlebrook to report to the Cricket Office at the entrance to the ground' was put out on the tannoy, the TV broadcast to England began. It was the first announcement everyone watching at the Cricket School at Headingley heard – and everywhere else too, I presume, heard it as well! Ralph got his leg pulled no end on his return to work, and so did I some weeks later when I eventually returned home and called in at the Cricket School. They were all convinced that we had done it on purpose. In fact protestations were useless so we left it all to their imagination. It was even mentioned to me by one or two of my acquaintances at home – most notably by Joe Shelley, a close friend of mine. As I said to him when he mentioned it – "At least you knew that he was there". I then told him that it was me who was looking for him!

My day with Mark was fabulous. The 'box' was high up in the grandstand and the view was superb. The cricket was exciting, the food and drink was plentiful, and the conversation was, to say the least, stimulating, especially on that day New Zealand had the upper hand for a time. Fortunately for me it did not stay that way!

Having travelled with 'Gulliver's Travel Company' while in Oz I was aware that they were bringing parties out to New Zealand for the Test Series as well. I knew several of those who would be travelling so on the fourth day I went looking for them. Each party always has a cricketing celebrity to look after them and this one had the former England Umpire Dickie Bird in attendance. I'm sure they enjoyed that initially, but he rather lost favour when he 'forgot' where his pockets were and expected free booze at all times. They had got wise to him by the time I caught up with them and the first thing I was requested NOT to do was to offer Dickie a drink. Monica Reeve, Dermot Reeve's mother, was there as was Geof Cresswell, a fellow member of the Adel Memorial Hall Association, Leeds. This was the club where I played cricket from 1965 to 76. The travelling party had decided that it was about time Dickie forked out some cash and bought a round of drinks! I never saw it but I expect he had to in the end – that group had travelled together on previous trips before and knew the ropes! But it was all good humoured and we had a lot of fun together as I joined them for the last two days of the match. The result was a draw, but that did not matter. We had a good time.

During the following week Murray and Margaret took me out to the usual haunts in and around Auckland – the Victoria Market and Kelly Tarleton's. I went off to the Transport Museum, a day's job to go right round. I went into the city to walk down Queen's Street. There were so many places of interest down by the docks as well – several ships and a 'round the world' yacht were on show. We also went swimming at a pool where the water was natural warm, coming up from a hot spring. The standard pool nearby, by contrast, felt freezing!

On Feb 6th I flew to Wellington and went straight to the Basin to watch the second Test Match. My family, Dorothy and Ken, were away but I stayed instead with Stan Cowman and his wife at Upper Hutt until the match was over. England won by an innings and 68 runs. As I recall, the former Australian cricketers who played in the first post war match in 1946 were invited to be present at this match. I showed Neil Harvey round the Cricket Museum. We had met on previous occasions, at Headingley and in Australia when I was with Frank Tyson, at the MCG. Ted Dexter, former Captain of England, was also there. I also enjoyed the pleasure of sitting in the stand with the friends I'd seen at Eden Park, Auckland in the first Test.

On Feb 11th I flew to Christchurch, staying at a local Hotel overnight. The next day I took the Trans Alpine train across the country from Christchurch to Greymouth and back – a truly fabulous trip through mountainous country. The train stopped half way across to enable passengers to see the sights. I had been across by car before but the train passed through different areas from time to time, where the rail link had been cut though the mountainous region.

In the evening I was picked up by Murray's sister and her husband, Margaret and Colin Norton and I spent two days with them at Amberley. They took me across to stay with Pam and Ron Panckhurst, Margaret Olds' brother and sister in law, during the Test Match at Lancaster Park Ground, Christchurch, and the One Day International that took place a couple of days later. England won the Test Match by 4 wickets after an exciting last day where the game was in the balance. Atherton scored a century and Cork helped England to victory by 4 wickets. Daniel Vettori, then a schoolboy, played his first game for New Zealand. After the One Day International was over I drove to Palmerston to see my cousin Kathleen and Alan for a couple of days. We went sight seeing and had a look at the Moeraki Boulders. These are very large spherical boulders, anything between a metre and two metres in diameter, that have been worn smooth by the action of the waves and are made of mudstone with pieces of local bedrock embedded in them. They lie on the Koekohe beach on the Otago coast.

Time was running out now so I caught a plane to Auckland, having been taken by Kathleen to the local Airport at Dunedin. Lou Tregidga met me and I spent three days with her, visiting her family and generally enjoying ourselves.

Then the wheels started to come off a bit. I was due to catch a plane to Melbourne and was taken to Auckland Airport at 5.30am. The plane was due to leave at 7.30am but the computers had gone down so there was complete chaos. We eventually got away very late and I arrived at Tullamarine Airport around midday. As there had also been several other flights arriving at the same time it was impossible to find Frank English, who had come to pick me up and take me to see the final competitive cricket match to be played by Ivanhoe Grammar School. If they won they would win the Premiership for the first time for over 30 years. These were the lads that I had arranged the tour for over here in England in 1995 so I wanted to be there to enjoy their triumph if they won. I managed to fight my way to the reception desk and they put out an emergency call for Frank. As it happened he was only about 20 yards away, but there was such a general melee that he could not find me either! We soon caught up, and drove at breakneck speed to the ground where they were playing. All the parents were there and were delighted to see me as apparently the boys had decided that I was a sort of good luck charm! Anyway, whether or not that helped I don't know but they did win and the celebrations went on for quite a while. I was delighted to have been able to get there in time despite the panic. It was probably the highlight of my trip as I had always secretly harboured the idea that they could be a Championship side – and they were. Now I could withdraw from the 'International' scene of schoolboy cricket with honour – a dream had been realised and I had been part of it! Whatever one might hear to the contrary elsewhere, for my part the Australians I had been fortunate enough to encounter anywhere in the world have been good value. There is no doubt that for me cricket opened up avenues in travel, international organisation and valued friendships, quite apart from the tremendous satisfaction that I experienced. I had given back a lot to the sport that I have always loved and what is more it had been appreciated in full. If I never achieve anything else during what time I have left I reached the pinnacle of my ambitions in that direction at least in 1997. I found similar joys in New Zealand too. The help I was able to offer to what is now recognised as the New Zealand Cricket Museum at the Basin Cricket

Ground, Wellington has been another plus in my life. In truth I suppose the fact that I was forced to retire early through serious illness opened up a complete new career and a genuine second chance to contribute something in the hard world of sport – a world I have come to understand. There is no magic spell to weave – it came from hard work and determination never to give up, whatever the problem. Having travelled alone – really there were only two choices for me. Either I sat back and let things slide – not even an option really – or I faced my problems and was fortunate enough to succeed. Much of those early decisions stemmed from two factors – firstly I did not know how long I was likely to keep cancer at bay and so secondly there was no time for rehearsals! A chance remark by the man who operated upon me, Mr Browning, set the pattern really. When I returned after six months in New Zealand and Australia in 1984 and 85 he said something akin to this, "I am delighted to see you Chris – surprised, but delighted. Your holiday abroad has probably helped to save your life as no one could get to you so there have been no worries. Now go out and enjoy your luck". So far I have done just that!

During the course of my visits to Australia I had always quite fancied staying in the outback. Ivanhoe Grammar School cottoned on to this and I was invited to go with a party of children as a guest teacher to what was then known as Charnwood. This was the Outdoor Education Centre situated in the bush where youngsters got the chance to literally rub shoulders with the great outdoors. I spent five days with the group and took a small part in the everyday activities. I also had the opportunity to go out with people who actually lived around the site – not teachers as we know them at School, but as men and women who learned how to survive out in the bush. It was fascinating – there are things that we were shown that the youngsters could not wait to try out – bush walking and bush craft, canoeing, navigation techniques and a host of other things too. The children slept in tents and were responsible for seeing that everything was properly laid out and organised so that everyone benefited. There were various types of animals to be seen, koalas, kangaroos, possums – you name it - even anteaters. I was taken out at night and, with the aid of powerful torches, shown the wild life than abounds after dark. One night a storm was brewing. We watched the koalas perched at the tops of gum trees eating the leaves as if they were going out of fashion. In fact koalas need those leaves to keep them calm. It acts like a drug I suppose, and they can get very nasty if they are deprived of the leaves. Little did I know I would get personal experience of that! A storm broke just after midnight with lightning flashing and thunder rumbling. I was sleeping on my own in a hut on the edge of the camp. After a while I heard footsteps and the pattering of feet. I presumed that children in the nearby tents were in trouble and had come under the cover that was over the platform of my hut, like a wooden roof to keep off the sun. The noise continued. I had been advised by Mr McDonald, who was I charge of the camp, not to go out alone at night or open up the door of my hut. "The children have to learn to fend for themselves", were his words. Eventually the storm passed – maybe only after about ten minutes or so, and the noise outside abated. When I got up in the morning the deck outside my door had dozens of tiny footprints on it. On enquiring I found out that it was not children there at all – it was the koalas that had come down from the trees for shelter and apparently they can be pretty nasty to say the least! I did not say a lot, but I was very pleased I had not gone out after all!

One trip I was taken on was to Benalla, the home town of Ned Kelly, the infamous bushranger who led a gang of criminals in the area and beyond...... I had become friendly with one of the bushrangers and he offered to take me there. I had mislaid my watch at the time and he had a friend who would lend me a cheap one while I was at the camp. My main reason was to visit the memorial put up to honour a very brave man by the name of 'Weary' Dunlop. His full name was Ernest Edward Dunlop, a surgeon who was captured by the Japanese in Bandung, Java. He was in Changi Prisoner of War camp in Singapore for a spell and he devoted his time tending the sick. His heroism became a byword and he restored morale amongst the Australian troops during those terrible days and was revered by them. He saved countless lives. He was decorated and became known as Sir 'Weary' Dunlop.

On my return to Kew I was invited to the school when the boys who had won the Premiership were duly acknowledged by the then new Headmaster, Rod Fraser. I also visited and stayed with Bon and George, and other friends who lived in the Mornington Peninsular area, being invited to several parties and barbeques.

On March 10th I flew to Sydney where I was met by Ann and Stuart McDonald. They drove me back to Thirlmere, their home, after we had had a look around the fabulous Darling Harbour area of Sydney. We went out somewhere almost every day and they showed me so much of that part of the country, particularly up in the Blue Mountains. But the highlight of this trip was special. A friend of Stuart's had found an unusual way of making a lot of money – he had become a dollar millionaire by the simple expedient of taking chickens around the state and selling them. I never understood how he had done it and neither did Stuart! However he had bought himself an ocean going boat that he kept at the mouth of a river just north of Sydney – Hawksbury River, I think. He invited Stuart and I out for the day to have a picnic on board. Stuart had told him of my interest in boats and this guy was fantastic. He simply took me onto the top deck, started up the boat – and then disappeared down below, leaving me with Stuart who left it to me to steer. I was in my seventh heaven – especially as there were no other boats nearby, so I could not cause danger to anyone else. The owner came back up with food but I was too excited to eat much, and besides I was busy! I had four hours of sheer delight, actually sailing straight out to sea for an hour and a half before turning along the coast and eventually heading back to the bay. I was even permitted to berth it. Luckily I did all right and nothing went wrong. He was a lovely guy but as mad as a hatter, judging from some of his exploits! I think he probably sailed very close to the wind as far as the law was concerned. I did hear later that his business got into difficulties but I think that was because of rivals rather than dishonest dealings. Mind you, there were a lot of things that I came across with various friends because money was the God, and anything went if it made a few bucks – at least that is what Australians said. Ironically I actually found that they conformed to rules and regulations far better than back in the

UK. But one never voiced that opinion as they liked to think that they were a defiant nation. They were and probably still are, but only if they feel threatened. It was a strange anomaly really, but every country is different. They thought that English people were all very reserved – we probably are outwardly but that is often where it stops!

My final port of call before returning home was with Urs and Frank Tyson at their new home in Sorrento. I flew to Brisbane and they picked me up at the Airport.
We visited Liz and Philip, their son and daughter in law. I was always made very welcome at their home too as I had known Urs and Frank's children for many years and it was lovely to see them again. We then drove to Sorrento, about an hour from Brisbane. Everywhere looked white, fresh and modern. The sun shone and the climate seemed perfect. No wonder they had moved! Frank loves the sun anyway so he was really happy with the move. I fell in love with the bungalow – it was spacious and there was a swimming pool in the garden. What more could a man want? Frank was in the process of negotiating a ten year deal with a Health Club in the area. Again it offered everything and I was even given free honorary membership - while I was staying in the area - as part of Frank's contract. The fact that he was obviously well known certainly appeared to be a useful asset for him. We went there every day - Frank to 'pump' iron and me for a swim. In those days I could still swim a mile when I felt like it. I did so three or four times. It was excellent for the fitness levels. There were lots of other activities going on too – a great place.

One day we went up into the hills behind Surfers Paradise. It was quite an experience and made one realise just how many people live near the coast and how few live away. There were clubs of various kinds dotted along the edge of the beaches and I must say that it all appealed to me tremendously. Money seemed in abundance and the eating places reflected the variety of immigrants from so many nations. Ursula took great delight in taking me off to the various restaurants so that I could sample the many different types of food on offer. There were shopping centres everywhere, neatly laid out. There were new estates springing up and people were falling over each other to buy. It was all incredibly lively and new. I met several of Frank's new friends in the cricket world and went to the club where Ralph Middlebrook's son was going to play. In fact the lad finished up living with the Tysons for a spell as there were certain financial difficulties that needed sorting out. So I had over a fortnight of sheer delight staying in Sorrento. As I always finished up driving Frank around too I was able to learn my way about quite quickly. Somehow, every time I stayed with them the car Urs owned needed some small thing putting right. This time it was a leak at the front of the roof. So I was useful as well, as a guest who both drove and mended things!

But sadly all good things come to an end, and on April 2nd I set off from Brisbane Airport for Bangkok and on to Heath Row. Bangkok was boiling hot – Heath Row was the exact opposite. One incident sticks out in my mind. I had bought a few presents back with me, including three cigarette lighters. When I declared what I was carrying a customs officer at Brisbane queried these so I got them out of my bag. "Sorry mate, you can't take three lighters," he said. "Why not?" I questioned. "Only one is allowed," he replied firmly. "Okay, you keep the other two", was my response. "No thanks mate", he explained. "I've already got 299 of the damn things in my garage. A Pom came through the other day and he had bought his 300 workforce a lighter each!" Apparently someone on a Japanese Airline had caused a serious fire some time before on board a plane so the Customs Authority limited the number to be taken home to one. Daft really, when it only needs one lighter to be lit to cause a problem – funny lot they are! In fairness to them, the customs officers thought it was a daft bit of legislation too. They thought that the simplest answer was to confiscate them all. I caught a plane to Manchester and Philip was waiting there to meet me – another trip done – now back to normality – at least that is what I thought.

Chapter 17 Accidents, Medical and Physical problems

For some time, although I had been gadding about around the Southern Hemisphere I had been concerned that I had a problem with, of all things, my navel. I had been getting some sort of swelling that at one time I could control by pushing the protrusion back into place – an umbilical hernia. However I realised that it was getting worse as it kept popping out and refused to stay back. Any pressure and it simply popped out again. I went to see a specialist who recommended an immediate operation as there was a danger that there could be more serious consequences if it was not dealt with as soon as possible. To cut a long story short, I was taken in to the Nuffield Hospital in Horsforth and an operation was carried out to effect a repair. Anyhow, whatever was done – it worked. I had to be careful not to put any strain upon the front stomach muscles around the area of the operation for an extended period. It was about that time that I started to experience some pain in my left hip. As I had always suffered from back trouble, ever since I had sustained two chipped vertebrae in my lumbar region after a rugby accident in 1952, I initially put it down to that, but it continued to be a bit of a nuisance. My doctor gave me pain killers and that seemed to solve the worst of the problem for the time being. During the summer of 1997 I continued with my cricket commentating and I also continued with the work I had been doing for years – reading articles to be put on tapes for a magazine sent out to blind people.

I continued to ride my Honda motorcycle although I was reluctantly beginning to realise that it would not be too long before the pain I was experiencing in my right leg would curb the amount of riding I could do. I still got a lot of pleasure from being able to go off into the countryside – I simply stopped a few more times en route. But the writing was on the wall. What is more Jack Edmondson was more reluctant to go out with me as often as he used to. He had been having problems with his back but he steadfastly refused to have any treatment – a fact that was eventually to have serious consequences. His daughters tried their best to get him to see a specialist but he continued to refuse until one day, in a weak moment the combined efforts of Sheila and John Scatchard, two of his daughters and I persuaded him to give in and he went. He had a treatment or two and then said, "I wish I had done this years ago". I think we all felt as if we could shake him as we had tried and tried to get him to listen! But sadly it was really too late for him – the degeneration had gone too far. Gradually he deteriorated in health and he stopped going out or coming on holiday. That was 10 years ago and he has not been far since, if memory serves me right. Over time he has become chair bound and has relied on the National Health Service to sort him out – a task that has been beyond anybody really as he left things so late – a great shame. Now he has to have someone to call in every day to help him dress and undress. He is in such pain that even getting his meals is an effort for him. To think that when I first knew him he was a fine cricketer, even in his forties, truly grieves me for we have had a good friendship over the years. He is lucky to have three such helpful daughters – without them he would have been in worse trouble.

But life had to go on and in 1998 found that I was beginning to find that my back was again becoming more painful. I was lucky – I had been helped several years ago by a lady, Mrs Betty Moody, who was at the top of her profession. She had lost her husband when he was still young – I had her son Robert Moody, in my class at Holy Trinity School in 1965/6 at the time. Naturally one always tries to be kind and helpful when these things happen to other people and I was able to help Robert to try to understand. Some years later when I had become a Headmaster I was off school because my back had yet again seized up and I could not walk for a time. Eventually, each time it happened, the Doctor would give me permission to go off and try to walk again after about three weeks. I always went to Golden Acre Park as there were plenty of seats around the place if I needed to rest. I was in the Park on one occasion and she saw me. She immediately insisted that I go to her house and she would give me treatment. She was in charge of the Physiotherapy Department at the LGI at the time. She did a wonderful job and refused to take payment, except in kind – bottles of wine etc. She also insisted that I go to see her each time I felt the problem coming on. In effect she changed my life and I shall always be grateful to her. She married again – a younger man in the same profession – and changed her name to Wordsworth. She actually came up with the solution to the worst of the problem. On one occasion, when she was giving me some pain relieving treatment near the base of my spine – in the lumbar region – she suddenly asked me to tell her when I felt a sharp increase in the pain I was experiencing. She then proceeded to press each vertebral she was three quarters of the way up to the top of my spine. Suddenly I felt what I would imagine be an electrical shock – so violent that I gasped out loud. Immediately she said, "We have found it – referred pain is the crux of the problem," and she started massaging around that vertebra and every now and again pressing it firmly. For starters it still hurt, but gradually the pain eased and I was able to stand up straight for the first time in months. It was such a remarkable transformation that I could hardly believe it was happening! She then explained that a Neurological Surgeon in New Zealand by the name of Maitland had studied this problem in detail and realised that the source of many spinal problems were well away from the areas where pain was felt. From then on, whenever I had cause to ask her to deal with my attendant back pain that was where she did the massage – the Maitland Treatment. It worked every time and the over all improvement was quite remarkable. I still suffered but she held the key to making things much better and I shall be for ever grateful to her. Eventually I had an operation on my back, but not until years later when there was further spinal deterioration.

Although I was helped by the treatment I received, as the year went on I found that, despite the award of £5000, which had helped me in my quest to get the sort of medical help I required, the pain in my right hip was giving some cause for concern. I was now having regular physiotherapy treatment with Paul Wordsworth, Betty's husband, and this continued throughout much of the year. It limited the time that I was able to go away, but I was fortunate that friends from the Southern Hemisphere appeared from time to time in Leeds and spent holidays with me. I had always been very much aware just how expensive things would appear to people from overseas. That is why I have always had 'Open House' for my friends. It has enabled them to stay in England and at the same time has cut the cost of living for them.

Elaine and Peter Kempen also came over from Melbourne for a few days in May and I was able to show them around Yorkshire. Ironically, the week before they came I had decided to purchase a car with an automatic gearbox and I picked it up the day before they arrived. It was a Red coloured Renault Laguna. I took them to Whitby. We arrived in the car park near Whitby Abbey – and the silencer fell off! I called out the AA who sent a man to make a temporary replacement – he managed to replace the silencer and we got back to Leeds without further incident. Horsforth Garage, where I had bought the car, replaced the silencer so all was well. I had been working at the Garage from time to time so luckily they looked after me properly. We were then able to do several other trips around the County. It was a most enjoyable time.

Less happy was the fact that Murray brought Margaret over from Auckland for a summer holiday in June/July and this proved very traumatic for her. She was no longer able to cope with normal life. In order to enable them to go away in their Campervan which I kept stored each winter on a farm nearby, it was necessary for them to go somewhere for short periods so that Margaret could cope with the travel when they went off for a longer trip to Wales and then down south. Fortunately Murray had friends in various parts of the country so he was able to keep visits to campsites down to a reasonable minimum. When things got too difficult for them they would return to my house for a few days before going off elsewhere. I was aware that Margaret's doctor had given permission for her to travel. Personally I think he made a bad judgement. I suspect that Murray more or less persuaded him to agree, but that is only conjecture. In fairness he did his best and managed to contain the worst excesses. The trouble was that she would do things like order food at a restaurant and then refuse to eat it. She would then become very tearful, convinced that Murray was ill treating her – total fiction of course, but embarrassing for him and anyone with them at the time. The final straw came on the way home when, after getting back as far as Brisbane where Murray's sister lived, he decided to take her to Darwin. She was in such a state by then that he had to turn straight round and return to Darwin and thence home to Auckland. He later told me that Margaret had suddenly got out of her seat at one point during the flight on the way home, gone to the plane door and attempted to open it. The problem was – the plane was flying at 39,000 feet! Fortunately the safety catches on the 'Jumbo' held and she was dissuaded from further efforts in that direction! Apparently one of the cabin crew sat with her for the rest of the flight and looked after her very well. The air hostess in question was kindness itself. But that was the end of any more attempts to travel far. It was extremely sad. When I first met her I was most impressed. She was a kind and friendly soul but the illness caused much unhappiness for her – and Murray too. Eventually he was persuaded to let her spend the latter months of her life in a special home where she was well looked after until she died in 2001.

Ursula and Frank had come back for the summer term. Frank had another contract with Woodhouse Grove School for the summer. I had arranged several speaking engagements for Frank once again so we spent a lot of time together, particularly when I drove him to the places involved – mainly cricket clubs of course. IGS were over for yet another cricket tour but they did not come up North so we could not catch up with them. But it was lovely to have the Tysons both so close and we were able to enjoy visits out and about during holidays and weekends.

I was still commentating regularly at Headingley so it was a very busy summer. I had built up a good commentating relationship with Jack Wainwright over the past year or two and we had become friends too. We did several lunchtime broadcasts together, with Jack talking about local cricket in Yorkshire and me expounding the merits of cricket in the Southern Hemisphere. Some of the other commentators quite enjoyed listening as well. It was an interesting period from my point of view as we could both speak from personal experience. On one or two occasions during the season he had brought his wife Margaret along to sit in the commentary box for the day and we had spent a pleasant time chatting together when my commentating duties permitted. In those days guests were welcome and sometimes we would entertain blind people who wanted to listen to our commentaries. Nowadays, due to the advances in modern technology our commentaries can be picked up at any point in the ground and blind people do attend matches, picking any atmosphere there may from within the crowd itself, particularly during the shorter and currently better attended versions of cricket – 50/50 and 2020 matches.

I had continued with the reading of articles for the magazine that was put together for blind people to listen to. I completed my readings in late August and once again Hilary Finnigan had found me some interesting pieces to work on. Hilary has, over the years, spent a lot of her time sorting out the readings for all of those taking part.

Having finished my readings for 1998 I spent a week away in Scotland with Bryan Stubbs at the end of September. I also visited friends in Northamptonshire and my cousins Daphne and Mollie respectively in Sunbury on Thames and Westerham in early December for a spell. It had been a busy year and I decided to return once more to the Southern Hemisphere in the not too distant future. Really, as always, it was a question of finance. My shares had continued to produce funds and so by now I was in a better position to decide just when it would be convenient to travel. I had loved the style of living on the other side of the globe every time I had travelled there and I had made lots of friends. In other circumstances I could easily have settled in either New Zealand or Australia. Mind you, my money has always gone much farther too as the cost of living out there was so much lower than in the UK.

At Christmas for some years there has been an enjoyable 'get together' of readers and others connected with the production of the Reading Magazine for the Blind. Like me Jack Wainwright was one of the readers. I attended the party at the Centre for the Blind at their Shire Oak premises at Headingley on Friday December 3rd. Margaret and Jack both attended the party as well and inevitably Jack and I spent much of the evening chatting together about sport. Jack was very much into Rugby League as a professional commentator at matches, particularly at Keighley, where he was heavily involved. Margaret helped to entertain visitors from the opposition at Keighley up in the board room too. At the end of the evening we all went our separate ways, Jack having mentioned that he would be attending a match as usual, although on this occasion he was not due to commentate. I mentioned that I was driving down to Sunbury on the Sunday.

I was listening to the local news on Saturday and to my horror I heard that Jack had collapsed and died while at a match. I could not believe it – I had spent the previous evening with him and his wife Margaret. He had seemed rather tired but not excessively so. I immediately rang Stan Dawson to make sure that it was our Jack Wainwright. Stan sadly confirmed that it was. I wrote to Margaret to express my deepest sympathy. Jack was well known and much admired in the world of local sport and he knew so many sportsmen personally. I know that as a sign of respect a minute's silence took place at Keighley Rugby League Ground. I certain missed his expertise and all round knowledge when the cricket commentary season started at Headingley in 1999.

Christmas was lovely – I spent it with Mandy's family at Baldersby, near Thirsk, in the company of Margaret and John, Margaret's Dad Michael, and her brother Michael, Mandy and Philip. I spent a lot of time chatting to Michael senior. He told me about his early life in Ireland in his gentle Irish brogue – fascinating to listen to in every sense. On Boxing Day the men went off to Ripon for a convivial pint or two while a lovely dinner was made ready for our return. The atmosphere over Christmas was really special and everybody was always made to feel welcome.

Inevitably, once I had made my mind up I started to make plans. I think that has always been half the fun. Each time I have travelled there had always been an underlying theme of some kind to spur me on – something that gave me a reason, or, if you prefer, an excuse to find out more about how people live in other parts of the world. But the organisation of my trip would come later in the year. In the meantime I continued to help out with readings etc. for the Magazine for the Blind and I made myself available for any blind people who wanted someone to aid them in whatever they were doing. From memory, I think I was also still helping Martin Milligan with the work he was doing towards his publication, but after all this time I cannot be sure of the dates. In any event, as I mentioned earlier in this book, I was fascinated by the research that he had done into the direction that political thinking was taking both Great Britain and the rest of the World. It was a sad loss to the University when he died with his writings still incomplete.

A visit to Durham University

Then another surprise came my way. Ursula and Frank were coming over to England yet again, only this time school teaching was not on the agenda. The University of Durham wanted to honour Frank for all that he had done in his lifetime, particularly in the world of cricket. They had invited him to attend certain events at the University on June 10th and 11th. He had contacted me immediately to ask me to accompany him – an honour in itself. Naturally I was delighted to agree.

I received an invitation from Dr. Peter Slee, Director of Corporate Communications at the University, to attend the Palatinate Dinner on June 10th as a guest and to join the 1953 Reunion Dinner on June 11th. A room had been booked for me at the Royal County Hotel in Old Elvet, Durham for the two nights in question and the University would settle the bill. The only stipulation was that we had to buy our own drinks!

We first went straight to the Royal County Hotel in old Elvet, Durham to change and get ready for the evening's festivities. This meant that, for once, I could have a drink or two as I could leave my car in the hotel car park. A taxi was sent to pick us up and we were duly taken to the drinks reception at Hallgarth Manor. Peter Slee was on hand to greet us and to introduce us to Jonathan Edwards and his delightful wife Alison. We also met the various dignitaries with whom we should be sitting during the Dinner as we were on the top table. Ursula and I then went out on to the lawn to enjoy the sunshine. Fortunately it was a pleasantly warm evening. We were quickly joined by Alison and then a student, who had been detailed to look after our needs and ensure we were served with drinks. I was also introduced to Sir Kenneth Calman, Vice Chancellor of the University, next to whom I was sitting at dinner. He was a charming companion, and when I mentioned that I had been several times to Australia he told me that he had spent 10 years in Hospitals out there studying the dangers of melanomas. I explained that I had been operated on in 1983 for the removal of a malignant melanoma. He spoke at some length of his work, telling me that Australia, who had had to deal with the problem for years, were way ahead in their treatments. His job had been to learn all he could from them and pass on his knowledge to English cancer surgeons – a fascinating man. He did tell me that I had been fortunate to have been operated on successfully as in the 80s little was known of the condition in this country at that time and there were many pitfalls to the two operations I had. We got on extremely well. At one point a raffle was held and – wonder of wonders – I won it! I was told that my prize was not ready for collection yet. I waited with bated breathe, thinking that perhaps I had won a holiday or something of value at least. All the prizes were handed out. Then came mine

– it was a copy of the evening's event signed by Frank! I was probably one of the few people in the room for whom this was no prize at all. However I had to accept it with good grace and when it was all over Kenneth Calman asked if he might have the prize as a donation to the University. So somewhere is, or at least was, Frank's signature on a programme equivalent to the blue one shown a couple of pages back, put into a picture frame, and underneath was a caption to the effect that Chris Turner had donated it to the University. I must admit I would much rather have had a bottle of whisky as my prize! The irony was that Frank had already set aside a programme for me with his personal comments on it – the one reproduced in this book!

For the record Jonathan and Frank were the first ex-Durham graduates ever to have presented the Palatinates – rather like school colours – to students from outside the confines of the University. It was a real break with tradition and an honour for them as well. We then retired to the Hotel for more drinks and retired to bed around 2am – quite a night!

After a leisurely breakfast the next morning we had a look round our old haunts while Ursula did a bit of shopping, before having a lunchtime snack in the Hotel. Then Frank and I made our way down to the Racecourse Cricket Ground to watch the University 1st XI playing against Scotland. Four other ex players from the early 50s had also been invited to meet up at the Cricket Pavilion for afternoon tea before we all attended a Reunion Dinner in St Cuthbert's Society Senior Common Room, South Bailey, Durham. A taxi was laid on to take us to St Cuthbert's. The Northern Echo sent along a reporter and a photographer. A comprehensive article appeared in the paper on June 15th together with a photograph or two. Graeme Fowler, formerly opening bat for Lancashire and at this time University Cricket Coach and former Durham student, was also there. He presented us all with Durham University cricket ties. When I had originally attended Bede College in 1950 there had been controversy about students who took Teaching Certificates – the University did not recognise the students as members of the University at that time so I was not able to play in University matches. This was a real bone of contention. However when the obligatory Bachelor of Education Degree was introduced at Durham for all teachers apparently it was an automatic award if we claimed it. I had never bothered, but of course all Bede College students were immediately recognised and accepted as members of the University retrospectively. I mentioned this and was informed of what had been agreed. So I accepted the tie with pleasure.

The names of those present at the dinner are shown on the 1953 Reunion sheet printed a couple of pages back. The evening proved to be quite unique for me. I did not know everyone who attended as I was not at Durham in 1953. I had not seen John and Pat Dale for a long time. John and I played together in the Northants County League for Vallence Cricket Club, a team based in Northampton, back in the early 60s. The last time I had met Tom and Edith Cain had been in Melbourne, when they entertained Urs, Frank and I at a sort of unofficial Reunion of Durham ex-students. Tom was the 'second in command' of the fuel firm 'Shell Australia' – a high profile and very demanding job by all accounts. Don Harrison I had not met since I left Durham in 1952 and the same applied to Warren Bradley. Warren was a fine cricketer, but was probably better remembered as the only footballer to win both amateur and professional caps in the same season He played briefly for Bolton reserves for starters, then joined Bishop Auckland. They won the Amateur Cup Final three times – in 1955, '56 and '57. He then joined Manchester United after the Munich Air disaster decimated their team in 1958, accepting professional terms as a part time player. He was a teacher and was able to combine the two. Footballers only earned low wages in those days – around £20 a week – in those days. He scored 21 goals in 63 games. He even played against Real Madrid in the days of Di Stefano, Santa Maria, and Puskas. He had certainly earned his reputation. By this time he had just retired, having finished up as a Schools Inspector. I had not previously met David and Cynthia Day. Sam Stoker proved a fascinating host. I sat with him over dinner and he regaled me with several highly amusing stories of his time at Durham, both as a student and later as a lecturer and resident professor. It was certainly one of those occasions which stands out in my memory. I also recall that, having vacated my room at the Hotel the following morning after an extremely hearty breakfast, I unwittingly managed to take my room 'key' – a plastic card – back with me to Leeds. I was able to return it a few weeks later when Bryan Stubbs and I paid a visit to Durham – they had not even missed it!

With time being of the essence there was a lot to be fitted in before Urs and Frank returned to Australia on August 8th. There were friends in other parts of the country – particularly in the Northampton area – together with a players' reunion at the Wantage Road Ground. This is the home of Northamptonshire County Cricket. We drove to Northampton and stayed with Pauline and Lewis McGibbon. I stayed for one night while the Tysons stayed longer. I went off to see Susan and Steve Taylor, my lifelong friends, for a spell before returning to Leeds. After a week or so I motored halfway down the M1 and met up with Lewis, who had transported Urs and Frank up to transfer to my car. We then returned to Leeds.

Lewis and Frank had opened the bowling for Northants on several occasions back in the 50s. I recall going to fetch Frank from the Northants Pavilion after the reunion and meeting up with several of the cricketers that I had known and played with in the late 40s, when I had been trying to make a name for myself with the Northants Club. The fact that I failed to reach the level required for inclusion as a professional cricketer hurt at the time, but the friendships I had made then ultimately turned out to be of much greater significance in the long run. People like George Tribe, a Test player for Australia in 1946, who became important to me as a close friend in later years. Brian Reynolds, the Northants wicket keeper, with whom I played golf, and Jack Manning who I met again in Adelaide in 1984, and Vince Broderick, a player who turned out with me for Rothwell Cricket Club were but four. I lived at Rothwell at the time and became a playing member there for several years. There were several more too whose names are on the list of former 'capped' players – players who were award their county caps in recognition of the successful careers they had at Northants.

On our return to Leeds there were still several places to go to. We spent a day at Middleton in Lancashire, where Frank was born. We visited both the Schools he had attended, Boarshaw Primary and Queen Elizabeth's Grammar School, at the personal invitations of the respective Headmasters. We also went to see the memorial plaque to his brother who had died not too long before. We drove to Blackpool to see a couple of his relatives too.

Our next port of call was Scotland. We drove up to the Isle of Skye, stopping off at Furnace, near Inverary, at a 'bed and breakfast' house run by friends of mine, Ann and Jim Middleton. They made us very welcome. We travelled up the coast road through Oban and Ballachulish, stopping off for the night in Fort William. From there we travelled up to Skye, crossing the new bridge that had been built to join the Isle to the mainland. Lodgings were found at Portree, capital of Skye, down by the docks. Places to stay were at a premium, and I remember trying to get into the tiny room the Tysons had booked. It was so small that it was virtually impossible for them to do anything but roll into bed at the end of the evening. Ursula was not amused! I was in a penthouse at the top of the building and that was little better. The next morning we drove across the Isle to Dunvegan before turning south and driving through Bracadale and Glen Drynoch to Sligachan. We saw the true majesty of the Cuillin Hills. This was what we had come for so after that we headed to Armadale and caught the ferry to Mallaig. The drive from Mallaig to Fort William is one of the most beautiful in Scotland. Again we stopped in Fort William overnight, going along Glen Nevis to the bottom of the mountain before retiring. The following morning we drove up through Glen Coe to Crianlarich, along the west side of Loch Lomond and eventually got back to Leeds – a long drive. It had been a lovely holiday and we had seen so much. We had been to Scotland on two or three occasions previously. I recall with much amusement the time we went to the Theatre at Pitlochry. As luck would have it the play was about the washerwomen who worked at a Glasgow communal wash-house. The script was very authentic so much of the language was in colloquial Scottish brogue. Ursula face gradually assumed a fixed stare during the performance, and afterwards she complained that she had not understood a word! I have been many times to that theatre and I have sometimes found plays in 'braw' Scottish dialect very difficult to comprehend. Poor Ursula had no chance!

After a couple of days rest Dick Hansell drove them down to Northampton and stayed overnight. I received a phone call from Dick after he returned home. It had apparently not been too happy an experience for him when they all went out for dinner. First Lewis made a decision that he and Dick would split the cost of the evening equally. Dick did not have a drink but the booze cost plenty on top of the bill. He then had to drive Lewis's car back as Lewis had had a skinful. Apparently there had been an argument while driving home. To put it politely, Dick had decided that he would not return there again to fetch the Tysons after their holiday so, amid a few well chosen epithets from Dick, I was 'elected!' That would be my job. Pauline and Lewis took them to a villa they owned in Portugal for a week. I gathered, on their return, that it had been a boozy do and the wine had flowed freely. I fetched them back from Northampton so they could collect their belongings. Next day I drove them to the Service station on the M42 at Tamworth where Daphne and Frank Sharman picked them up and took them on to their home in Sunbury for a couple of days before seeing them off from Heathrow. So back they went to Australia, ready to enjoy the summer months at their home in Sorrento, near Surfers Paradise.

My life was still full and I was going out regularly with Philip and his friend Nigel to watch Leeds United play football. We had season tickets and as I had been a supporter since 1964 it was something that Philip had more or less grown up with. We went together in the early days and saw Leeds United in their heyday as a team under the tutelage of the then Manager, Don Revie. They developed into a fine team although the reputation of being rough and tough came – and stuck. In the days of Billy Bremner, Jack Charlton, Johnny Giles, Norman Hunter et al, the team became renowned around the world – but unfortunately not always for all the right reasons. At top level they became unpopular. Part of that was jealousy because of their prowess and success, the rest was because they gave no quarter and gained a fearsome reputation amongst other top clubs both at home and abroad. They gained an insular mentality, particularly amongst many supporters. It was in effect 'us against the rest'. They won the League and the FA Cup too in addition to other successes over the years until ambition overcame sense and the club got into deep financial straits. The club was demoted twice and has only just got its head back above water. But again that was, in terms of this book, still for the future. I decide to have another trip 'down under' in the New Year of 2000 AD. Thus I should spend three months abroad at the start of the 21st Century – another adventure. Once again I put together a rough plan of where I was going. By now the necessity to plan too far ahead had become unnecessary. I was experienced in terms of travel. Furthermore when anything went awry I knew that I could cope perfectly well. I had had several instances of that happening during my travels, both at Airports and elsewhere. There is no denying that being on one's own in a crisis can be a two edged sword. At least one needs only to think of oneself. On the other hand, no one owes you a living and you sink or swim by yourself. I must say that on several occasions, when I have sought local advice – such as when a car breaks down in the middle of nowhere – people do try to help. Being in America on my 'round the world' trip was perhaps the perfect example when I was stranded in Needles. For me adaptability had to be the key when I only had myself to think about. I felt that nothing would change my life again – but I was quite wrong. All I had done in the planning stage was to confirm my dates of arrival in New Zealand and Australia respectively – the rest was more or less left to chance. I had several bases – the Olds in Auckland, Val Reynolds in Napier, my cousin Kathleen Pointon at Raumati, Graeme Hamilton near Wellington, Pam and Ron Panckhurst near Christchurch and my cousin Kathleen Clearwater and her husband Alan at Palmerston, and that covered New Zealand. Sadly Dorothy and Ken Hamilton were not well. They had moved from Linden, near Wellington, to a home in a Retirement Village near Raumati where there was plenty of good medical care available. Dorothy had had a stroke and Ken was suffering from emphysema – difficulty in breathing properly. In Australia there were the Gowans and the Kempens in Melbourne, Phil Stewart in Adelaide, Stuart and Ann McDonald near Sydney and the

Tysons in Sorrento, near Surfers Paradise. I sorted out dates of actual arrival so that I could be picked up at the various airports too. But sometimes these arrangements are in the lap of the Gods – more of that later.

Chapter 17 Shared Happiness – a second chance

There was still plenty to do before I went off on this trip. In November there was the Annual dinner for the Hospital Broadcasting Service members at Sandmoor Golf Club. While I was there I decided that I wanted to have a word with my golfing friend John Herbert. While I was chatting to him after the meal and prior to leaving, Margaret Wainwright came across. She knew John well too and we all enjoyed a pleasant conversation together. I found out later that Margaret had actually asked Stan Dawson if I was at the dinner. I can't imagine why, but obviously he must have said yes!

I was not leaving for the Southern Hemisphere until shortly after the turn of the century – a memorable event in itself. Prior to that was Christmas of course, and I was looking forward to celebrating that at Baldersby with Margaret and John Richardson, who had again kindly included me in their family Christmas. Naturally Philip and Mandy would be there together with her Grandfather Michael.

With Christmas coming up there was another party arranged at Shire Oak for readers in early December. I chanced to attend a Committee Meeting of the 'Reading for the Blind Association' although I was not actually a member of the Committee. Margaret Wainwright's name was mentioned and it was decided to invite her to the 'do'. Hilary Finnigan, the articles' editor, offered to fetch her from her home in Rawdon. That would have been a lengthy round trip for her, and as I lived in Cookridge and already knew her I agreed to save Hilary a long journey. I said I would ring her and offer her a lift. This I did, she accepted, and we went off to the party. I then drove her back to her house in Rawdon at the end of the proceedings. There was a show on television being hosted by Michael Parkinson and as it happened we had both expressed a desire to see it. The upshot was that Margaret invited me in for coffee and we watched it together. I had been on my own for a long time and had settled into a pleasant and happy bachelor lifestyle. Nevertheless I suppose I realised that I had genuinely thoroughly enjoyed her company - something I was almost reluctant to admit to myself. Before I left I did make the suggestion that if she felt like going to the theatre or out for a meal at some stage in the near future I should be happy to join her. I went home that evening and decided to wait and see if anything came of my offer. Eventually I could not stand the suspense any longer and I rang to invite her out for a meal. It was the most sensible thing I could have done! We had a delightful meal at the Bracken Fox Pub on Wetherby Road and found that we had much in common. It was inevitable I suppose – we were mutually very attracted and suddenly all the plans I had made for the next few months seemed infinitely less satisfying – in fact I even felt reluctant to go. We talked it over and decided that maybe it would be a good thing if I went ahead as planned as it would help us to see if we both felt the same way on my return. Suddenly age did not seem to matter any more and I sensed a happiness within me that I guess I had not realised I could feel again. We kept our feelings pretty much to ourselves until around Christmas. After all I was going to stay with Mandy's parents, the Richardsons, at Baldersby for Christmas with Mandy and Philip and the rest of Mandy's family. I had been before and it had been really special so I was in for a good time. Actually I did tell them that I had met Margaret again and they were delighted. Of course Philip and Nigel had already guessed there was something different about me as we had been for a drink after a match at Leeds United just before Christmas. They were very pleased for me – they even bought me an extra drink each!

By now we were spending a lot of time together and I had told my friends about Margaret. We went to Ann Bell's for a traditional New Year party and my long time friends – most dating back to when my family first moved into Cookridge from Northampton in 1964 - were agog to meet her. We had all met up together virtually every year to celebrate the coming of the New Year.

 Altogether this New Year was, to say the least, somewhat different! We spent much of our time together over the New Year and Margaret met some more of my friends. By the same token, I met some of her friends too at Yeadon, and also a couple with whom she worked, Paula Priestner and Ann English. Ann was going through a bad time right then and I was able to be around when she required someone to help. Margaret was still working full time as a 'front of house' receptionist at Whittakers.

As the time for me to set off again for the Southern Hemisphere drew ever nearer we decided to have a quiet few days away first. I was due to go to stay at a hotel near Manchester Airport on Sunday January 23rd. Philip was taking me there so that I could stay overnight and get to the airport reasonably early on the Monday. We went to stay at a guest house in Kettlewell on the previous Thursday, returning home on the Saturday. We had a lovely time and the weather behaved itself too. We visited Grassington and had a good look round the place as well as enjoying a drive in the virtually deserted countryside. A gentleman by the name of Paul Philips was staying at the guest house with his mother. We got on well with them and Paul has visited us a time or two since. It seemed no time before we returned home and I still had some packing to do in addition to making sure that I had got things like tickets, passport and all the other things essential for a good trip.

We decided to keep in constant touch by phone and share the cost on my return – that turned out to be quite an expensive telephone bill! Philip took me to the Hotel on Sunday evening and we had dinner together before he left – very enjoyable. But it was a lonely evening once he had gone so – guess what - I rang Margaret in Rawdon and we chatted to while away the time!

Chapter 18 My fourth visit to NZ & OZ

The following morning I was up with the lark and was given an early breakfast before being driven to the Airport for around 8am. The flight was on time, leaving at 10.30am for Heath Row. The onward flights were uneventful. We stopped over at Los Angeles Airport – an awful place to get any food or drink. Of all the airports I have visited LA was, at that time, by far the worst. However I arrived at Auckland International Airport at 5.50am, having had a reasonable night's sleep during the flight, to be met by Murray and Margaret Olds.

My first concern was to stay with them – really to give Murray some moral support. His wife Margaret, who had been diagnosed with Alzheimer's disease some time before her last trip to the UK, was getting progressively worse and really should have been having outside help. She was also suffering with toothache. Murray, by his own standards, was doing what he felt was right for her to the very best of his ability. His family were by this time rather concerned for both of them. Apart from the difficulty of remembering anything or anybody, including me, there was the ever present danger that she would slip out of the house and wander off. Murray also had to cope with everything at home and at times the frustrations were obvious. Sometimes she could not work out who I was or why I was in the house – and the same applied to Murray. We spent what time we could out walking – mainly on the beach at Torbay. I also went off for a run each morning and evening, partly to keep myself fit and partly to get out on my own.

On my arrival I had become very much more aware of a 'shadow' that was affecting my sight somewhat. It was really a broken series of dark spots that were ever present – even when I closed my eyes. The light in New Zealand was much brighter than at home so the problem became something of a concern. I went to an optometrist in Torbay for a consultation. She immediately put my mind at rest by asking me what at the time I thought of as a peculiar question. She asked me if the dark area was spiderlike. It was not – just a series of random spots that seemed to move whenever I turned to look at anything. She then talked about the difference in the clarity of the light in the Southern Hemisphere and suggested that I purchase some darker sunglasses with a tolerance of UV30. She stated that this would diffuse the bright light – and once I had found the right sunglasses in a shop in Torbay it did, so there was no further cause for alarm. I did not need any treatment. Apparently the eye problem solves itself as it is some sort of rather dusty substance that becomes sticky. It eventually washes away, but takes a long time to do so. She was right about that – it certainly took a very long time!

Margaret Olds' family were very kind and caring. Daughter Lesley entertained her mother whenever she could. The family had a small swimming pool and we all enjoyed that with her. Then there would be a barbeque outside or a meal indoors, depending on the weather. David, another son, played the piano and he and I sang a few songs for her too. This seemed to strike a chord and she sometimes had brief lucid spells when she chatted quite normally to David. But then, sadly, that only happened occasionally as David was at work most of the time. One day we went to watch her grandson Scott climbing at an indoor club where climbers were roped for safety. He was only 5, but he was absolutely fearless and the people who ran the indoor climbing school predicted a great future for him if he continued in similar vein.

Meanwhile I was having daily calls to and from Margaret in Yeadon. The calls were a source of pleasure and relief for me. I stayed for nine days before setting off on my travels on February 2nd – something I was looking forward to – and how! Murray had an old car that he lent me so that I could travel around the North Island. My first port of call was to my dear friend Lou Tregidga with whom I had stayed on previous trips. Inevitably there was a lot to talk about – we certainly did that! We visited various members of her family during my stay and attended one party at her eldest son Mark's house. He was entertaining a party of Chilean Rotarians. It was quite fascinating hear just what life was like for them in Chile when compared to the experiences they were having on their trip. They were delightful people – very happy-go-lucky. Mark was president of the Auckland Rotarians at that time. We went to a barbeque at her daughter Ann's house and spent another afternoon at a barbeque with second son George and his new girlfriend Carol. It seemed to be an enjoyable nonstop round of eating and drinking   at barbeques! In fact the last one was at her son Philip's property. He made a living growing lettuce – a change from the tomato growing business favoured by most of the rest of the family. Another brother, David, was present too, with his family. Amy, the oldest of Philip's children, was there – so grown up. I had first met her when she was six years old. I think she was Lou's favourite grandchild really although she never said so of course. Amy had stayed with me when she had first come to England.

On February 8th I drove to Matamata to stay with Violet (John Scatchard's sister). Again, we visited her family – Sally, Brian, Rebecca and Laura. The last time I had been with them during a previous trip they were all taken ill and I had left them in various stages of recovery. Things were happier this time and we stayed for supper. The next day I went into an Interflora shop in Matamata and had a red rose sent to Margaret for Valentine's Day.

I drove on to Napier expecting to stay with Ina and Val in the bus, but unfortunately they had been called away as his mother had died. I then briefly set off for Raumati, but on the outskirts of the city turned back as I particularly wanted to meet up with my friends again at the RSA. Lucky I did as it happened for when I arrived everything had been arranged for my stay with another guy. I shared a lovely meal with those friends and I stayed with 'Squeak' (Colin Simmonds) and his partner. They really were a most loyal set of people. The next day I wandered round Napier, then drove along the coast with Squeak. I stopped off to look again, photograph, and marvel at the beautiful tree-lined streets of Napier with their palm trees in Kennedy Road, and Norfolk Pines in Te Awa Avenue very much in evidence. A few beers in Squeak's garden followed by a tasty meal cooked for us by his partner Anita finished off the day. Once again I had enjoyed the company of several very generous people – they liked their booze too!

Next morning, Saturday February 12th, I drove from Napier to Kath's house in Raumati. That evening Kath and I walked on the beach for over an hour. It was truly a 'balmy' night with the temperature pleasantly cool after the heat of the day. Margaret rang, just as she did most days. Those calls were most welcome as it kept me in close touch with her and with things back home. On Sunday we went swimming from the beach, meeting up with some of Kath's friends again. Later we were in contemplative mood and talked until late into the night. She had had several operations for the removal of melanomas from her right leg and the medical people had decided to use her as a guinea pig for a new approach to chemotherapy. Treatment was given as a form of injection at the top of her leg, thus avoiding the onset of dizziness and sickness that so often followed previous chemotherapy treatments. It appeared to be working and in fact she did have an extended period at the end of her life – around three years. The next morning we got up early, before the heat of the sun really broke through. We walked along the beach and Kath showed me where she had done the lovely painting she gave me of the beautiful island of Kapiti, a mile or two across the water. Later that day I went to see my cousin Dorothy and her husband Ken. Sadly both were struggling – in fact Dorothy was chair-bound. She had no sense of balance and was suffering with ulcers. She was having a course of antibiotics, but they did not seem to be helping at that stage. Ken was having difficulty breathing – possibly the fact that he smoked a lot was catching up with him and he was developing emphysema. It was extremely sad to see these two lovely people in such dire straits. Over the years, whenever I had stayed in New Zealand, we had enjoyed some great times together and they had been so kind to me – as indeed had all the family. Typically they insisted that I stay for a bite to eat and we reminisced about the good times we had shared together. Afterwards I drove to the Southward Museum and spent an hour wandering in the grounds on my own, deep in thought. I must admit that I was upset to see my friends in such a sad state, but that's life and eventually I accepted it. Then I entered the Motor Museum and once again had a good look round at the exhibits - one of my favourite places.

My next port of call was Graeme's house in Upper Hutt. I then motored on to the Basin Cricket Ground in Wellington to see Stan Cowman and do some work at the Cricket Museum. I took Stan and his wife out for an early evening meal before returning to Graeme's place. We sat up chatting until well after midnight. Actually the car was playing up a bit so Graeme arranged for the brakes to be sorted out the next day – the brake fluid needed replacing. While that was going on I went with Stan to watch a cricket match at the new Sports Ground in Wellington. New Zealand was supposed to be playing Australia but the weather let us down. It rained virtually non stop and the match never really got started. I met several friends at the ground though, so it was still enjoyable. Then Stan dropped me off at Graeme's place again on his way home. I got the car back the following morning. It had needed over $300 worth of work to put it right! But that was necessary as I was due to drive back up to Auckland during the next couple of days. In fact I stopped off at a farm belonging to Violet's son and daughter in law for the night. My main memory of their farm was what I saw in the early hours, just as the sun came up. The sunrise was absolutely beautiful and the hills opposite the farm were bathed in a purple hue – absolutely breathtaking. I then drove on to Auckland, calling in briefly to see Violet at Matamata on the way.

On arrival at Torbay, after a hair-raising drive through Auckland on the motorway during the rush hour I went with Margaret and Murray for a meal at their daughter Lesley's house. Husband Mark came home later and arranged to pick me up and take me to the One Day International match – New Zealand versus Australia. Australia won easily enough and I was royally entertained by Mark and his workmates from KMPG. The firm forked out for everyone. It was one of the highlights of the whole trip for me. On Sunday February 20th we swam in the pool at Lesley's house, then watched the America's Cup race. The yachts made a wonderful spectacle. Murray drove me across to Lou's house the following morning. She had prepared a lovely meal for me to share and afterwards we passed the evening catching up on things. She is a very interesting person to talk to. She told me how she and her husband had started the tomato growing business. They lived in a tent for quite a while until they could afford a house. She cooked over a hole in the ground for all that time – what a character! My son Philip kept in touch by e-mail and I was able to utilise a computer in the firm's office at the tomato growing business premises. In fact I was fortunate to be able to have the use of a computer at several places where I stayed – quite a novelty at the time. I took Lou and her grand daughter Amy out for a meal on the 22nd at an aptly name restaurant – Valentines! That was my last night on the North Island of New Zealand. Margaret and I had been in touch virtually every day of this trip and it made such a difference. I was enjoying myself, but I was also very much looking forward to returning home so that we could get together again.

On 23rd Lou dropped me off at Auckland Airport at midday. I flew to Christchurch Airport where I was met by Ron Panckhurst, brother of Margaret Olds. He took me to his home at West Melton, just outside Christchurch. It was lovely to catch up with Ron and his wife Pam. Having stayed with them on a previous trip we certainly had a lot to catch up on and a few beers were not to be refused either! I met a couple of other friends of theirs too who had dropped in for a chinwag – mainly about cricket. This was a great start to my stay.

Early the next morning I went out for a walk, stopping off at a farm nearby where 'trotting' horses were regularly exercised. This proved fascinating as the horses moved very differently from ordinary racehorses. The owners of the farm trained the horses specifically for the trotting races, where the horses do not just run flat out. These horses have a frame on two wheels behind them when they compete and a 'jockey' sits on the frame to control the way that the horses move. In races trotting is permitted – but not galloping. In fact I got up early every morning of my stay just to watch the horses in training. There were seven horses harnessed and held in a straight line under a rigid sort of pole. They followed a vehicle at a fixed speed – all trotting, virtually in step. It was spectacular to watch! Later in the day the horses were trained individually round the large oval track. The training track replicated a real one so the horses were familiar with the over all concept of the races they were required to take part in. I did go and watch a race or two at one point – quite an education! After breakfast I went by bus into Christchurch, known as the Garden City, to have a look round. It is a fabulous place, particularly around the centre. Trams literally ran all day on a fixed track around a route in the central area, and passengers could get on and off wherever they wished. This proved most useful as there was much to see. On the first part of my tram ride I went right round so that I could see just what I would find most interesting. I bought a ticket that allowed me to spend 4 hours utilising the tram to move around. It was a real dream day, the like of which I had not experienced before. In all I was in the city for about 6 hours and part of the pleasure was to walk along the bank of the river Avon beneath the trees that provide shade from the sun. It was 32 degrees that day and felt HOT! Pam worked at Hagley Community College so I went to meet her there and was shown around – quite a picturesque establishment where students engendered a vibrant and friendly atmosphere – maybe too good to do overly much work! There is a large park outside the College where sports are played. Pam gave me a lift back after work. Their home was a fascinating place. Pam was very much into gardening, while Ron had branched out and was literally an inventor-cum-model builder who designed all sorts of equipment for use in colleges and elsewhere. While I was there he was in the process of making a sort of hovercraft platform where a person could literally be conveyed around in any direction in safety. Students would be able to study the mechanics of such a model in depth – fascinating. I was used as a sort of guinea pig, on the principle that if I could move around on it anybody could. On that occasion I 'passed the test' so Ron reckoned that anyone could safely use it! At the end of the day we sat outside in the evening sun and enjoyed a companionable drink or two. Pam had a computer so I arranged to send a few e-mails the next day – if only it had been that simple!

February 25th – I got up early again and went out to watch the horses trotting round the track nearby – doing their training in preparation for racing at the weekend. After a leisurely breakfast I opened up the computer. There were messages awaiting my attention. The first one came from Phil Maskery letting me know that he was now working in South Africa. Mike Thorpe, who owned the garage in Horsforth where I had fetched and delivered cars, also had business interests in South Africa and had asked Mike to work for him out there. It was connected in some way with documenting and supplying spare parts for second hand helicopters – another of Mike Thorpe's business interests. Mike Rhodes sent the second, letting me know how things were at home. He was living in my house at the time and keeping an eye on things. But the most important one was from Philip and Mandy. It contained happy news and sad news too. The wonderful news was that Mandy was pregnant – the thought of at last becoming a Grandfather was truly thrilling and I was over the moon. But this joy was tempered a little by the fact that Mandy's Grandfather Michael had succumbed to cancer and had died. Naturally Margaret and John Richardson, Mandy's parents, were very upset. I was sad too, for Michael and I had got on extremely well during the time I had known him. I loved to hear him talk of his early days in Southern Ireland – working with horses was one of his favourite topics. One got the impression that life was lived at a slow, sensible pace when he was a boy – no rushing hither and thither in a mad rush to make money. He was truly a product of Eire and spoke slowly, with a lilting, gentle Irish accent, as if weighing up every word. As the Irish would say of a man like him, "He was a lovely fella". We had shared many a social whisky together so it was only fitting that I would 'lift a glass' and toast his memory at the appropriate moment. I did just that as I shall mention again, but first I sent a brief e-mail to Margaret and John expressing my sadness and my sympathy.....

The next day proved a bit different. We walked along to Edendale where some of the richer people around Christchurch lived. The houses and gardens were lovely and we visited one of them where friends of my hosts lived. It even had mock pillars inside - very unusual! On our return we had a tinny or two, watched the boat race and then watched Australia beat New Zealand in a one day match. That evening Pam and Ron had arranged a party and I met several of their friends. New Zealanders love to sing and I had to 'sing for my supper'! Fortunately I was able to make a reasonable offering on the music front as I had a tape of some songs that I had recorded back in England for Margaret and I sang them 'live' so to speak. This went down well and inevitably Ron and Pam demanded to meet Margaret! As, unknown to her, I had already decided to fix up a holiday next year for both of us in the Southern Hemisphere, this was the perfect opportunity to use Christchurch as our main base and travel around both South and North Islands. So that was all tentatively arranged. Murray had already lent me his old car before and was quite happy to do so again if we came, as a sort of pay back. I had looked after his Campervan in England for quite a while. Murray's car was parked up at the farm so we could fly into Christchurch, do a trip around the South Island and then catch the ferry from Picton across the Cook Strait to the Capital City of Wellington. On a good day it was a fantastic voyage. Mind you, it could be rough too. I found that out the first time that Graeme and I crossed from Wellington to Picton in 1984! Lou had also broached the subject of meeting Margaret when I had stayed with her and all the Hamilton family in Wellington and Raumati had indicated that they would like to meet her too. So that was NZ sorted! As I had travelled almost the entire length and breadth of both Islands during my previous visits I felt that I knew my way about easily enough. I had made so many friends there too so there was always someone to see when I had visited before. I made a note of the addresses that I should need in order to get some background re costs and ferries. There are excellent Information Centres for visitors in most places of any size as well.

My last three days where very busy. On Sunday February 27th Ron and Pam took me to see the new Arthur's Pass Bridge – quite a remarkable feat of engineering that got rid of a genuine danger spot where many a motorist had come to grief. One sometimes forgot that in terms of through roads and passes the South Island of New Zealand was still in the comparatively early stages of development. The future lies in tourism as it is probably the most beautiful and interesting countryside that I have ever visited. The South Island is like great swathes of Europe all put into one vast area – hills, valleys and mountains, rivers, fiords, lakes and waterways, desert lands, plains, highlands and lowlands – you name it and it is there. Much of it is just like Scotland – apart from the heather. Perhaps one day even that will be brought in, but I hope not. It would deprive the Island of its unique heritage. We stopped for lunch in the pass, then retraced our steps to Castle Hill Village – an unusual living area to say the least. There were some remarkable houses there, quite different in design from anything I had seen before or have come across since. Then we passed through Otira Gorge with its waterfalls and springs and finally through Porter's Pass – a journey of about 300 kilometres – a brilliant day.

On the next day Colin and Margaret came over from Amberley for lunch. It was great to see them again – lovely people. In the evening Ron invited me to go with him to listen to the 'Barber Shop' evening. Ron sang in that. I did better than listen as well – I also joined in. Quite an experience that was! When we returned home I offered up a prayer for Michael, Mandy's late Irish Grandfather before downing a few whiskeys – deliberately spelt with an 'e' because that is the Irish way – in his honour. He was a fine man.

On my final day, February 29th I went into Christchurch once more – visiting the Antartica Exhibition and then going round the Mall again by tram. I also saw a beautifully laid out cottage that belonged to Ron and Pam's friends, Michelle and Doug, whom I had met previously at a party. Some dwellings I had visited in New Zealand were quite unlike any places I had seen before – this was one of them. That evening I took Pam, Ron and Jenna, their daughter, out for a slap up meal – a grand way to complete my time with them. I also sent Margaret a 'dialect' poem for fun -

For a Lovely Yorkshire Lass

Since time we've bin a'courtin'
I've allus fancied thee
As one who is reet sportin'
An' just t' lass for me.
So dun't be feelin' mardy,
Jus' 'cos I've gone away
Or time'll 'ang fair tardy –
Accountin' ev'ry day.
Jus' see it as a partin'
As wun't be ower long,
Then if tha's truly 'laikin'
Put on another song.
It may not be perfection,
But then – tha's got a choice
To make thine own selection
An' listen to a voice.
Like lad as sings on CD
Down at t' Albert 'all,
Or Frankie's 'Swingin' Lovers'
For friends who come t' call.
But when tha's finished swoonin' –
Oh aye, that's all jus' fine,
Then listen to some croonin' –
Jus' see t' voice is MINE!
Pin back them lovely lug'oles'
An' listen to 'BLUE MOON',
Imagine that I'm with thee –
Surrender to t' tune –

An' jus' remember this luv,
Tha'll niver be alone,
'Cos thanks to modern science,
There's allus telephone –
An' words I'll pray thou'll treasure
From conversation's 'cup',
For they'll then gi' thee pleasure
An' mek tha's toes curl up!
Because I say them often
Tha' can believe they're true,
I want to mek thee realise
I mean them – I LOVE YOU!
So when tha's feelin' knackered
An' climbin' stairs t' bed,
Just look at that KOALA –
Then get it in yer 'ead
I really WANT to be there,
To 'old thee through t' night
An' show thee what these words mean
With hands that feel so right.
See lass, jus' tha' remember
I miss thee so – indeed
I want my arms around thee
Protecting one I NEED.
I want to mek thee 'appy,
To banish pain and strife.
Let's CHERISH one another,
An' share what's good in life.
No thoughts of bein' lonely,
Let's try jus' to mek sure
It's what us both can fettle
We aren't ALONE NO MORE!
We need t' LOVE each other –
To strive wi' might an' main
To share each other's laughter,
Emotions, tears and pain –
To ease the stress an' tension
In ways we both decide –
Too intimate to mention,
But will not be denied.
An' just in case tha's doubtin –
(If so I think tha's mad!)
The future truly beckons
Yet includes what we've 'ad.
Thus – let's BOTH clasp the nettle
And take each other's 'and.
Let's tread life's path together
In step – Ee, t' will be grand!
An' when it comes to livin'
The courtin' need not stop.

We're both a tad romantic
An' like a bit o' slop.
THEE - FLUFFY TOYS and FLOWERS -
ME – MOTORBIKES and CARS –
Together we can SHARE these –
An' then – there's pubs an' bars
And all t' lovely workmates
An' lots of my friends too.
But I'm a LUCKY FELLA
'Cos my best friend is YOU!!!!

On, March 1st Ron saw me off at Christchurch Airport, I then had a real piece of luck. I flew into Tullamarine Airport outside Melbourne, expecting to be met by Rona and John Gowans as we had planned – or so I thought. They were not there so I settled down on a seat near the exit to the car park, thinking that I would spot them when they arrived. Eventually I rang their home – no reply. Just as I was about to try and get to their place by bus and tram an truly incredible thing happened – one of their sons, Andrew, wandered into the Airport - and walked straight past me. Thinking he had come to fetch me I wandered across in order to make contact. As I did so who should appear through the passenger exit but Rona and John! They had been in Christchurch, New Zealand, as well, at the same time as I had. They too had been on holiday and had no idea that I had arrived! Naturally I still assumed that they were looking out for me. I was completely wrong – not that it mattered, but they were expecting me a day later. If Andrew had not happened to come to meet his Mum and Dad I would never have seen them at all. Still, it was a bonus for John as he would not now have to drive out to the Airport to fetch me the next day. I remember that in the evening it was still thirty three degrees. It had been a very warm day – up around forty degrees – that's hot by any standards! Rona and John were living near the centre of Melbourne, near the famous Lygon Street. There are more restaurants to the square inch in that street than anywhere else I have been to - apart from Rudesheim in Germany. I would imagine that one could get virtually any kind of food at some place in Lygon Street. Italians were there in numbers and when an Italian car - a Ferrari - won a Grand Prix in Melbourne Lygon Street was shut – literally. There were parties that went on for two or three days! It still is a great place to go out for a meal – whatever your nationality. Unfortunately Rona's dad was ill and her mother had broken a bone in her foot too so Rona disappeared off to Bendigo to look after them for a few days. It was a pity, as we were all due to go to Fairhaven, their place by the sea, for a day or two. John and I went anyway the next afternoon, via Geelong. But I went into the centre of Melbourne in the morning and walked the length of Swanson Street and Little Collins Street – quite a step! I must say that the souvenir shops were there in abundance so buying presents to bring home would be no problem. The temperatures were too hot for me outside so I was glad when we left. It was raining by the time we arrived in Fairhaven, thank goodness – it cooled things down a bit comparatively – still twenty one degrees! It was too hot to sleep in comfort though.

Next morning we got up early and went for a walk along the beach at 7am. It was cool and very pleasant. We drove to Lorne for breakfast and on along to Wye – a beautiful area to see all round there. We were back by 10am before the heat of the day. It was lovely just to sit around in the shade and downing a few glasses of wine and a tinny or two during the day – to keep us cool – of course!

Sadly all good things come to an end and we had enjoyed a lovely weekend. We got up early again and went for two walks along the beach before leaving to return to Melbourne. On our return I went off to the nearby Victoria Market and bought Margaret a fluffy toy koala and a kangaroo, amongst other things. Then there was a gentle reminder of home in the evening – we watched the film 'Brassed Off' – quite nostalgic. Today turned out to be different. I was invited to go to Ivanhoe Grammar School for the afternoon. Unbeknown to me a barbeque had been laid on in my honour and several of the 1991 England Cricket Tour Party managed to appear too. I have never ceased to be amazed at the loyalty of those boys and staff. Every time that I have visited Melbourne they have always got together to meet me. This time I was presented with a staff shirt to wear at Aussie rules matches and there was a lovely cake with 1991 on it! John and Rona, together with Graeme Renshaw had arranged it and to see so many of the lads again was a real tonic. I shall never forget them. The 1995 tour party were also well represented, together with several parents whom I had previously met. It was a great party – quite emotional too.

By now I had got the walking bug although I was having some trouble with my right hip. I walked around the centre of Melbourne and through a park located at the end of Lygon Street near the Gowans' place. There it was cool and a fountain was spraying water out. Several people just stood in the spray to cool down! While I was staying so near the centre of Melbourne I was able to have a good look round and I spent a couple of days doing just that. It was an enjoyable way to pass some of my time visiting various places of interest. I felt that the place had so much to offer. It was a vibrant city – there was always something taking place, particularly in the sporting world. Most of the buildings were, by my standards at any rate, modern. But there were areas where the accent was upon Victoriana – particularly the architecture of many of the public buildings. The people were friendly and happy to direct me to places – I needed to ask passers by the way quite often. By now the likes of Swanson, Flinders, La Trobe, Myers, Collins and several more Streets were no longer just names – I walked along them, sometimes going into shops and looking for presents to bring back home and at other times just window gazing. There were pavement cafes too where I delighted in indulging in my favourite drink – a milkshake with ice cream in – truly delicious and thirst quenching.

But best of all for me was the Victoria Market. There was so much on offer on the stalls and street artists painted a variety of colourful pictures, sitting or standing at their easels. I should have loved to have purchased a picture or two but sadly there was no way I could have got them into my luggage. Aborigine traders laid their wares out on the pavements – mainly leather goods such as belts and thongs. There were also all kinds of creatures carved from wood and other materials – birds, animals, fish, and even ceremonial weapons, ranging from spears and shields made of animal skin on bamboo frames to letter openers in the form of knives of wood. There were carved shells, beads, necklaces and even wooden buttons, all beautifully shaped, patterned and painted, to show them off to the best advantage and to attract would be customers. They were happy outgoing people, mixing freely with many others from Africa and the Southern Hemisphere in general, all of whom had wares to sell. The interesting thing was that everything on sale seemed to reflect the various themes and countries from whence the people came. One can read of the many different cultures in books – I was actually physically sharing in them and lapping up the chances to speak to people from so many different parts of the world. There was no particular pressure to make purchases – more the desire to converse and to show off things, many of which they had probably made themselves. In New Zealand I had bought various things made of Kauri wood when I was up in the north of the North Island – reputedly the hardest and most durable in the world. I engaged in conversation with several Maoris who were working at the market and they were delighted to be able explain just how they fashioned things from such hard wood. That led on to place names. As I had visited most of the areas in the North of NZ from which they came they were happy to tell me more about their particular towns and settlements, and how the industry of producing goods for sale was organised. There were no factories – goods were simply produced at their homes and taken to outlet stores to be passed on to those who specialised in making sales at home and abroad. The beauty of the system lay in the fact that literally anyone could make or carve something and deliver it to be sold so no one needed to be out of work. If it was any good it was purchased at any one of the outlet stores – the equivalent of what is termed the 'middle man' in Europe and sold on wherever there was a lucrative market. Some of these men and women made a good living by travelling to markets around the world. I think that I probably learned more about the happier side of human nature at the Victoria Market than anywhere else on my travels.

On March 8th I went to stay with Wendy and Brian Robertson. I had previously met and entertained Brian on a couple of occasions at my home in Leeds when the Australian International cricketers were on tour, and I had spent time with them both in the bar at the MCG during previous visits. They took me to watch Australian Rules 'Footie' at the Melbourne Cricket Ground – an anomaly in terms actually as the Ground is used by the Australian Football League and various other sporting activities as well. Cricket pitches are literally laid in the centre of the Ground in the summer, lifted at the onset of winter, then replaced the following summer. The grass only takes about 3 weeks before it is ready to use. Richmond beat Melbourne 93-91 in an exciting match. The basic rules of the game are as follows:- The primary aim of the Australian Rules Football Game is to score goals by kicking the ball between the middle two posts of the opposing goal. There are 4 posts in all. 6 points are awarded for kicking through the middle two posts and only 1 point through the side posts. The winner is the team who has the higher total score at the end of the fourth quarter. If the score is tied then a draw is declared. Players may use any part of their body to advance the ball. The primary methods are kicking, handballing and running with the ball. There are restrictions on how the ball can be handled, for example players running with the ball must intermittently bounce or touch it on the ground, throwing the ball is not allowed and players must immediately dispose of the ball if they are caught holding it. There is no offside rule and players can roam the field freely. It is an extremely physical game!

On the next day they took me with them to the Crown Casino. Wendy and I walked along the recently developed waterfront and visited the Art Gallery to see some brilliant satirical art by Spooner, an Australian artist, while Brian went into the Casino to gamble. We joined him later and had a bite to eat there before returning to their home. One of their daughters, Claire, called that evening.

The following day I took the Robertsons out to lunch and their two children, Elizabeth and Claire, joined us together with a cousin named James and two other friends. It was enjoyable, the youngsters being very friendly. For some reason Brian seemed to resent this and was distinctly boorish despite the fact that I was entertaining him and his family to lunch. He was rude and uncouth, showing his dislike of 'poms' – the only time I have ever come across it in such an outrageous fashion. I completely ignored him and said nothing. The youngsters felt he had made himself look foolish and they showed it. Afterwards they politely apologised to me for his rudeness. As I was returning to stay with the Kempens after lunch anyway it was of no consequence. I mentioned it later to the Kempens. One of their sons, Kristian or Drew - I cannot remember which one now - knew him of old – he was an umpire locally and was apparently well known for both his lack of manners and his bad language. Ah well, it takes all sorts......!

Peter took me to watch a University cricket match the next day and I was able to meet several people responsible for the team and for the league itself. I was delighted as they were some of the people who had been responsible for young players from England being able to spend an Australian summer season playing cricket for teams in Victoria – some as professionals I think. That evening I had the pleasure of entertaining the whole Kempen family at a well known Chinese Restaurant. It was most enjoyable.

The following morning I got up early and went for a walk before the real heat of the day came. The Temperature reached 37 degrees – too hot for me – I stayed in the coolest room in the house which, fortunately, was the lounge. But at 9pm the weather changed and it rained. What bliss that brought – everything cooled down!

In heat where better to go than to a swimming pool? I did just that next morning although the temperature was reasonable – a mere 21 degrees. Peter took me there in his new Mercedes, but there was something of a shock awaiting me. Lying on a stretcher was the body of a dead man. Just what had happened I did not know, but it was still an eerie feeling. I went inside the pool building determined to concentrate on my swimming. In fact I swam some 70 lengths that day – well over a mile. By the time I had finished, got dried and dressed again all was well and the stretcher had disappeared.

Next I went up to the shops on Doncaster Road and had a haircut – not that there was much on top – only around the sides! I had always wanted to visit the wineries in the area so Elaine sorted that out for the morrow. The drive to the Wineries – the first was called 'Domaine Chandon' - along the Maroondah Highway was picturesque to say the least. Seeing literally what seemed like hundreds of rows of vines stretching into the distance made one realise the vast amount of work that must be done to harvest all the grapes. It was a fascinating visit, seeing the fomentations in large vats, and rounded off with a glass of Chardonay. Next we went to Yering Station and to De Bortoli's for an excellent lunch. We saw kangaroos, a dead wombat, and live echidnas. These are egg laying burrowing mammals with spikes on their bodies, rather like hedgehogs. Finally we stopped at Sugarloaf Reservoir on our way back to see the view - a wonderful day!

On this occasion during my trip I had not seen Anna, Urs and Frank's younger daughter. She had got married by now and I wanted to give her a wedding present, even though it would be a bit after the happy event. I rang and arranged to have lunch with her. It was another hot day, but once I got to into Melbourne I was able to pass through several buildings that were connected by a series of wide walkways, all in the shade, before midday. This took me to the Myer shopping centre where I bought a glass flower vase that I had seen there on a previous visit. Anna was delighted with her present and we had a most enjoyable lunch, but as she was still working she had to be back at work by 1.30pm.

Afterwards I walked along Bourke Street before returning to the Kempens. The following afternoon John Gowans picked me up and drove me out to stay with George Tribe at Rye. I was looking forward to spending a few days with him. Bon had gone up to her apartment in Currumbin on the Gold Coast.

On arrival at George's house in Rye I found him ready to go out to lunch. We joined a friend of George's, Ken Hands, and went to the RSL (Returned Servicemen's League) for an excellent lunch. This meal I particularly recall – the main course was SHARK! As it turned out it was absolutely delicious and every time I have had the opportunity to eat shark meat since I have done so – a real delicacy. We then returned home to quaff wine and chat, retiring to our respective beds after midnight.

Off we went again in the morning after a run before breakfast. George was certainly fit! A friend by the name of Annette Proposch joined us for coffee and then lunch at the Dromana Winery – part of the Dromana Estate Vineyard. The surroundings were delightful and it was all quite hilarious. Annette was a typical 'dyed in the wool' Aussie with a sense of humour to match. She could certainly tell a story or two!

We had an early morning run each day at Rye, before driving to see places on the coast. There we walked as well, usually along either cliffs or beaches. George even took me to Mornington Peninsula's Cheviot Beach near Portsea and showed me where, in 1967, Harold Holt, the Prime Minister of Australia, drowned while swimming in the surf. He was an experienced diver who ignored pleas from friends not to enter the water as it was a rough sea. His body was never discovered.

By now it was March 22nd. I returned to Rona & John's place where there was a barbeque arranged. Rona's former boss Alan and his wife, Philippa were the principal guests- another enjoyable evening!

The next day I spent the morning sorting out a credit card that I had brought with me from New Zealand. I had had a bank account there and had been assured by my friend Murray, a former bank manager, that I could use the card in Australia – but no, it just did not work. Fortunately I had a card from home that gave me what I needed but it was a shock to realise that these things could go wrong so easily. I took the family out for a meal to a restaurant on Lygon Street – Saneros – quite a place. The food was excellent and so was the wine. Restaurants are common on Lygon Street so competition is fierce. That is all to the good for the punter!

Next day I flew to Adelaide where I was met by Phil Stewart. I had stayed with him during the Christ College, Brecon Cricket Tour in 1996 and we had kept in touch.

He gave me a guided tour of the city of Adelaide in easy stages, starting that evening at Windy Ridge. It certainly was windy – and cold too, but I got a great view of the city with its myriad of streetlights and brightly coloured buildings – shops, hotels, nightclubs – the lot. It was magnificent! After a good night's rest we drove out to Glen Elg first and spent a day there. The next outing was to the Barossa Valley to see the Wineries. We visited 'Penfolds Winery', passing Jacob's Creek after which a famous Penfold Wine is named. Naturally I tasted samples and I bought a bottle but Phil did not drink. I had no such inhibitions! I was also able to see around the city of Adelaide. It was a very clean, thriving place. I mentioned that I hoped to bring Margaret with me next time and Phil immediately offered to lend me his place if we came – a great gesture and much appreciated.

From Adelaide I flew to Sydney and was met by Ann and Stuart McDonald. We had first met when I was taken ill and finished up in Bowral Hospital on a previous trip. He was a patient there at the same time. After visiting Ann's Mother we drove back to their home at Thirlmere. After a good night's sleep I was ready for the next outing. This was a trip back to Sydney. I had asked to go to Paddy's Market – a large area – but it was shut! This was real blow as it had been a place of great interest on a previous visit. Next we visited the site of the coming Olympic Games. What a fantastic set up that was! It took us ages to walk around and we were able to see inside the Swimming pool as it was not only completed but was being used too. That was enough for me. We returned to Thirlmere and I opted to swim in their garden pool. There was slight problem – 3 red-back spiders! They are very poisonous so Stuart removed them. I did go in but there was just that uncomfortable feeling that there might be another red-back lurking unseen at the bottom of the pool. Fortunately I was quite wrong. Red-backs can kill and they are quite large.

Not a creature to get too close too! We sat up pretty late chatting. Stuart was indeed very interesting company. I had told them both about Margaret during the day and they had immediately insisted that I bring her with me next time. They offered to entertain us too – fantastic!

This day was unforgettable. Stuart took me to the Nan Tien Buddhist Temple at Woollongong. Nan Tien literally means 'Paradise of the South'. The Temple itself is very ornate and I was very impressed by the serenity that seemed to permeate the whole place. It was all so tranquil and the emotions that it engendered in me throughout my visit were, to say the least, strong and very heartfelt. It was as if the whole atmosphere that the stillness and virtual silence engendered offered a theme of complete peace and contentment. I can now understand why followers of Buddha appeared so happy and smiling. Wherever we walked it was the same. Incredibly Ann, one of the guides to whom I spoke, came from Goathland in Yorkshire. She had been in Australia for 23 years. We went up to the first floor of the Pagoda. The ashes of former Buddhists are kept there in boxes, clearly labelled so the relatives may find them and pay their respects. Even when we left the feeling of contentment remained for a time – until we returned to the heavy traffic and busy roads! We went on to have a meal with Larissa and Shane, Ann and Stuart's daughter and her husband whose parents were there too. It was a special day altogether.

We drove to Bowral the next day to see Stuart's Dad, Alan. He had suffered a couple of strokes but had recovered well. We then went on to the Bradman Museum, situated at the Bowral Cricket Ground. Sir Don Bradman had played much of his early cricket there before moving on to the International scene....

Today turned out to be another special one for me. I had already met Ian, a friend of Stuart's, and he had arranged to take us to Hawksbury River, north of Sydney, where he owned a modern seagoing Cruiser by the unusual name of 'Hair Razor!' Stuart drove. Neither Ian's wife Diana nor Ann could come as they were busy. Ian was a dollar millionaire who had made his money transporting chickens to various places in Australia. Just how that worked I never quite discovered but it certainly did for him! We went out from the river mooring towards the open sea and I had the incredible luxury of being left in charge on the top deck to take the boat seawards as quickly as I wished – and it certainly was quick! We eventually anchored off Pitcairn point for dinner before cruising for another couple of hours. I was in my element. I have always loved the sea and it had been my intention to try and serve in the navy during my 2 year National Service period after the end of the Second World War. Sadly I could not as I had heart trouble that had been with me since I was born and I was rejected for the forces. Eventually we returned to the moorings. I had had a fantastic time! One thing that particularly impressed me - Ian was a kind and generous sort of a person who wanted to share his good fortune with others – a marked difference to a lot of people who only wanted to accumulate wealth and to hell with anyone else! But what I do remember was Ian driving back to Thirlmere – it was truly hair-raising as he was in one heck of a hurry – I shut my eyes at times! Maybe that is why he named his boat 'Hair Razor' in the first place!

That signalled the end of a truly enjoyable holiday cameo – we did so much in a short space of time. Ann and Stuart took me to the Airport at Sydney – named the Kingsford Smith Airport after the famous Australian pioneer aviator Sir Charles Kingsford Smith. He flew the first ever airmail flight from New Zealand to Australian and England. Amongst my souvenirs is a letter written by my Aunt Dorothy and Uncle Norman Bell from Balclutha, New Zealand. It was carried to my Grandfather in Peterborough on that first flight – something historically special!

On the final leg of this trip I flew to Coolangatta Airport where I was met by Ursula and Frank Tyson. We returned to their lovely home in Sorrento and went for a swim to cool down! They have a kidney shaped pool in their garden – just right for cooling off in and for swimming a few strokes too. Whenever I have stayed with them I have put the pool to good use – morning noon and night. The garden surrounds are high enough to keep out anything greater than a gentle breeze under normal circumstances although after a cool night an early morning dip can be quite a wake up call! Frank also belonged to a local Health club. There was a large pool there. The rules of the place allowed for friends of members to take part in any of the Club's activities. They were very generous to me and gave me temporary membership for the duration of my stay in Sorrento. These guys in the Southern Hemisphere countries of Australia and New Zealand are all so much more laid back than our people at home. It is a way of life with most of them and one gets the impression that they really want you to enjoy the facilities that their countries offer rather than to screw folk for every penny they can get!

This last part of my trip, staying at Sorrento with the Tysons, is really meant to be a bit of rest before I fly home. Invariably whenever I have stayed with them I have become a sort of instant handyman – particularly where cars are concerned.

The roof of Ursula's Rover car was leaking so after breakfast I started work to mend it. That meant getting rid of rust with a wire brush, filling holes with body-filer and allowing it to harden, sandpapering off to get the affected area smooth, then spraying on undercoat. Once all that was done it then needed spraying with at least two coats of body paint to try and ensure a decent paint match. There was something else - a squeak somewhere. A touch of WD40 sorted that out – that stuff is a miracle cure! The whole job took nearly a week and by the time it was completed it looked as good as new. What was amusing was that the next door neighbour, Beryl, got me to clean and re-spray a few rust spots on her husband Ray's car. Sorrento was experiencing hot temperatures too, so much of the time I spent indoors near a cooling fan! We also went out for the occasional lunch at the Broadbeach Surf Club. The dining area was open to the elements and a cooling breeze from off the sea blew through the building. We also had a barbeque or two – both at the Tysons and at a neighbour's house. The evenings were lovely after the heat of the day. But incredibly, one day it actually rained. I ran outside and cooled off in the rain!

By April 10th I had finished all the chores that I had been doing on cars and a few other items and I went with Ursula to see my friend Rod Lightfoot who had a tyre and silencer business in Tweed Heads. She needed the odd new tyre and the wheels needed balancing. I also arranged to go for a meal at Dawn and Rod's house on April 19th. Urs and I then had lunch at the Palm Beach Surf Club. The next day we drove to Sanctuary Cove – quite a place! Houses in that area cost big bucks – around a million at a time! It was a popular place with restaurants and shops galore.

Now I started to look out for presents to bring home. Urs took me to a large market near Sorrento that seemed to have everything! But there was sting in the tail. I decided to change the oil, filter and plugs on the Rover for her next day. That evening I took Urs and Frank out for a meal at a restaurant, aptly named 'Champagne', in Broad Beach.

The next morning we went the Health Club for a swim – I swam a long way that morning. I remember that I weighed myself before I had my swim, and decided that I needed to cut down on my food and drink intake and do more exercise. I had put on several unwanted pounds and they could not all have come from the previous night's meal – big though it was! Then, after we had eaten breakfast, I got cracking on the car. It proved really hard and took it out of me because it was such a hot day, so I spent the rest of the day either sitting in the shade or retiring indoors to try and keep cool under one of the fans. We were due for a fairly energetic time the next day as we were off the Brisbane.

This trip proved of particular interest. We drove up the new M1 Highway – two tolls to pay - to Brisbane to stay with Philip and Liz Tyson. Frank and I decided to take his older grand child Lewis on a trip up river. We travelled on a catamaran up to the Business Park in the city. That was most enjoyable - a great journey, and Lewis just loved it! We had a bite of lunch before walking along through the city centre to the railway station to catch a train back. We had actually gone to have a look at their house. It had literally been 'lifted' onto stilts and so they have a complete new ground floor. Australians are nothing if not innovative! It serves another purpose as well in case of flooding, although if one is lifted because of the danger of water getting into an existing property it cannot be used as another permanent living space – but it certainly solves a problem!

During the course of this holiday I had written several letters to Margaret and we had been in almost daily touch by phone. Whenever I have had the time I have written a poem or two as well to send to her. One gift was a St Christopher medallion. He is of course known as the Patron Saint of Travellers so I wrote a few humorous verses to go with it.

MY PLEA TO SAINT CHRISTOPHER

This gift serves as a token
For one I hold most dear.
No word needs to be spoken,

Its message is quite clear,
"Protect this lovely lady" –
She drives quite fast you see.
She's really rather special –
That's just 'twixt you and me.

Lift her upon your shoulders
And carry her with care,
But watch the blessed traffic
ST CHRISTOPHER, BEWARE!
When YOU first crossed the river
There were no boats in sight.
The rocks were good protection,
They kept you safe each night.

But now, with traffic islands
And multi-coloured lights,
It's easy to be side-tracked
And suffer nasty frights.
So look for hidden dangers
When driving down each road.
Don't even talk to strangers –
Mug up the HIGHWAY CODE!

Just use your special talents
To keep the cars in line,
And if someone encroaches,
Shout "Bugger off, it's mine!
I booked this space especially,
So sod off back again.
There's two in this 'ere motor
YOU need the SINGLES lane.

You'll upset Mr Prescott,
The motorists' 'Bete noir'.
He'll wag his little finger
And stop you where you are.
Then all the other drivers
Behind you in the line
Will swear like ruddy troopers
While police hand you a fine.

Now you just curb your language,
No real need to swear.
Just point me out and tell 'em
A SAINT is sitting there!
I know they cannot see me,
That's no cause for alarm.
I'M watching ALL the traffic
And saving her from harm".

So when YOU think of rushing
Remember to recall –
You clout another vehicle –
You'll end up LAST of all.
Again, the police will stop you –
More fines, despite your talk,
A BAN upon your LICENCE,
And then – YOU'LL HAVE TO WALK!

The reference to Mr Prescott is engendered by the fact that at the time he was Minister of Transport and had just introduced the idea of speeding up traffic flow by having separate 1 only and 2+ lines – a line for single drivers on their own and the other for cars with more than one person in, including the driver.

On April 17th we went once more to the Health Centre and I swam fifty lengths – the equivalent of a mile. Later, after breakfast, Ursula and I went shopping again. I was buying a special present for Margaret, and I wanted to buy something for Ursula as a thank you present – so there was plenty to do. Furthermore yet another barbeque was to take place in the evening. This time it was to entertain three of Frank's former pupils who had been at Woodhouse Grove School during his time on the staff. They were introduced to me as Nick, Steve and Gwyn – delightful young men who I think were on working holidays. I did not catch all of what they were saying and thought this strange at the time. The following morning I found that I had lost all hearing in my right ear. I did wonder if swimming had caused the problem, but to be on the safe side I went to see a local doctor. He recommended Oil of sulphur to loosen any possible wax in the inner ear and also prescribed some anti biotic tablets to prevent infection. It could have had a bearing on my flight home – changes of air pressure during the journey. This could have had serious consequences, but fortunately things cleared up completely in a couple of days. Apparently I had got a minor ear infection.

On April 19th we met Rod and Dawn for a meal at the Broad Beach Surf Club. Urs and Frank had met Rod before during a previous holiday that I had spent with them in Sorrento. It was very busy there that evening, but we enjoyed the general atmosphere and as the evening progressed the temperature dropped outside and it was pleasantly cool when we left. As usual the meal was extremely good too. On my final day I went with Frank to a Probus meeting to listen to Alex Bell, a former Mayor of the Gold Coast area. Afterwards I went one more time to the Shopping Centre to purchase some coasters with Aborigine designs on them. I found Aborigine paintings and drawings quite fascinating – so different from standard Western art. But unfortunately we saw a serious road accident as well. I was driving at the time and it brought home to me the possible dangers that can affect holidays. Having seen badly injured people being taken out of the vehicles I decided that it was time to go home!

Anticipation

A telephone rings by my bed
And your dulcet-toned voice speaks.
Suddenly, in Winter, it is Spring.
I listen, breathless, to the words.
My heartbeat starts to quicken –
And, in a flash, Spring turns to Summer.

This is the romance of our souls,
Indefinable, but real –
Like a bright star in the galaxy –
A Planet of reflected light.
We sense it and know it's there.
It is ours and it sparkles for us.

Although for now we are apart
We are no longer alone.
I think about you throughout the day –
I dream about you in the night.
Your face shines through the ether.
Thus we are together in spirit.

One day you'll curl up in my arms –
No more need for distant dreams -
Precious moments which are ours alone.
And while you are in relaxed sleep
I may steal a gentle kiss.
Thus my contentment will be complete.

Good night, Princess; Sleep well my love.
Perchance you may dream of me
And share – in secret – what we both feel.
Sweet dreams are those where no one comes -
Except by invitation.
So I shall always be there for you.

I have not mentioned much about my contacts with Margaret while away – just brief comments that we spoke to each other most days - but I wanted to finish my recollections of this extended holiday trip by writing down another of the poems that I had written earlier in my trip. It encapsulates just how much I was missing her and it gives a fitting end to what had been in effect the precursor of a further holiday in New Zealand and Australia, but this time together. There were others of a more personal nature and I wrote several letters as well.

To complete this journey there was only the flight from Brisbane.

April 21st was another beautiful day as we headed to Brisbane Airport, having left Sorrento at 9.30am. Frank had business to see to in Brisbane around noon and then they were going to spend a few days holiday with Liz and Philip, helping them to get the latest part of their 'lifted' house properly painted and furnished. We arrived at the airport at 10.50am – it was boiling hot once more and the forecast was that when the weather finally broke the rains would arrive in abundance. Having already sampled some of that I was glad to be getting on my way before that happened! The stopover was at Singapore Airport. I looked forward to that as there were excellent facilities to have a refreshing shower there. I took full advantage of that facility and then had a gentle wander around the shopping area before settling down at a restaurant for a coffee. There had been excellent meals served on the plane – a 'Jumbo' or Boeing 747 – so food was out on this occasion! The flight itself had been quite uneventful – just long. It was between eleven and twelve hours if memory serves me correctly. The in flight entertainment was also good – better than I had ever experienced before as this was one of the newest planes.

The second section of the journey to Heath Row was uneventful too. It was a night flight and for once I was able to sleep throughout much of the flight. Breakfast was served sometime before we arrived at Heath Row. At this point my 'body clock' was still working on Southern Hemisphere time, but apart from feeling sleepy again after being transported across the Airport from one terminal to another I coped perfectly well. The last leg of the journey was from Heath Row to Manchester where Philip was waiting to pick me up. After going through the usual passport formalities and waiting to pick up my cases everything went smoothly. We drove back to Leeds via the M62 and it was lovely to get home again. I was most grateful to Philip – he had made the final leg of the journey so easy and comfortable. I phoned Margaret and in no time it seemed she came in the front door. My happiness was complete and I knew immediately that I had found exactly what I had been seeking – we were together again after what had seemed a very long separation.

The date was April 22nd - now we could truly start to enjoy life together......

16726953R00195

Made in the USA
Charleston, SC
07 January 2013